501

MUST-KNOW SPEECHES

501

MUST-KNOW SPEECHES

Bounty
Books

Publisher: Polly Manguel

Project Editor: Emma Beare

Contributing Editor: Cathy Lowne

Designer: Ron Callow/Design 23

Production Manager: Neil Randles

This paperback edition first published in Great Britain in 2009
by Bounty Books, a division of Octopus Publishing Group Limited
Endeavour House, 189 Shaftesbury Avenue, London WC2H 8JY
www.octopusbooks.co.uk

Reprinted 2010

An Hachette UK Company
www.hachette.co.uk

A CIP catalogue record is available from the British Library

ISBN: 978-0-753717-72-1

Printed and bound in Hong Kong

Note: Because they reflect the era in which they were given and the views of the people giving them,
some of the speeches in this book may contain sexist or racist terms. The publishers apologise
for any offence caused.

Contents

Introduction

What makes a speech memorable? Is it the language used, the character of the speaker or his or her way with words, the ideas the speech contains, when and where it is delivered, the effect on people nearby or its message to history as a whole? The answer is that it can be any or all of these. From Socrates to Benjamin Franklin, from Saint Francis of Assisi to Joseph Stalin and from John Winthrop to John F. Kennedy, people have used speeches to inspire, elicit sympathy, threaten, start wars or revolutions, announce innovations, make peace, set the course for a way of life of a whole people, provoke thought or laughter and reaffirm belief. They can be patriotic, filled with love, chilling or overflowing with hatred. They can move nations, as did President Reagan's speech after the *Challenger* disaster, or revolt the world, like the vitriolic videos made by terrorists.

Of course, it is not just political leaders who use language to inspire: a few words at the right time and place can make the difference between victory and loss, or at least undignified loss and heroic failure, such as Lt Col William B. Travers' line in the dirt at the Alamo. Judges, too, can express their decisions in ways that affect people for generations to come. A prisoner may make a speech to plead for his or her life or, knowing that the result is inevitable, use his or her final public words to make a point, as did Socrates and John Brown. In many situations it can take many speeches, by many people, over many years to bring about change, however inspirational any one speaker is: the anti-slavery issue, women's suffrage and civil rights movements achieved their successes through a gradual groundswell that eventually changed majority public opinion.

Some of the speeches in this book were made to just a few people, some remarks to just one other person. Some are in the form of later, written versions as only anecdotal evidence of the original verbal version survives. Some were first recorded in writing only decades or even centuries after the death of the original speaker, for instance those from the Ancient History section and quotations from the *Bible*. It is only over the past 150 to 200, and particularly the past 70, years we have had access to verbatim originals – since the advent of the mass media – and in that time the art of speech-making has evolved enormously. From impassioned speeches that lasted for hours and relied on persuasive arguments and demolition of the opinions of an opponent in the pre-mass-media era through newspaper reports, radio broadcasts and then TV addresses to today's sound bites, the way people communicate has changed forever, and this includes politicians. Even in recent years our leaders have used the media differently: 20 years ago, a broadcast would be timed to make the prime-time news, but with 24-hour news the message can be repeated over and over. Today, news can spread round the world in fractions of a second, be downloaded to a cell phone or other PDA, endlessly replayed on the web and shared, linked or bookmarked.

In eleven chapters – Ancient History; Love; War & Revolution; Religion; Science & Medicine; Patriotism; Philosophy; Humanity/Liberty/Tyranny; Sport; Politics & International Affairs; and Miscellaneous, *501 Must-Know Speeches* contains a selection of speeches, extracts from interviews, off-the-cuff remarks, retorts, exchanges and announcements from across the world, as well as one or two from less obvious sources, and from a wealth of political opinions and ideologies, belief systems, scientific standpoints and moral outlooks. Each is accompanied by a short background explanation to put it into context with details of when and where it was given, together with a snippet of information about the speaker. Some contain ideas that are easy for all to agree with, others not so easy, and some will be repellent to almost everyone, but are included for completeness. Hopefully, all will provoke thought.

7

ANCIENT
HISTORY

Pericles c. 495–429 BC

NATIONALITY:
Athenian
WHEN:
Winter 431–430 BC
WHERE:
Athens' Kerameikos, northwest of
the Acropolis
YOU SHOULD KNOW:
The speech appears in Thucydides'
History of the Peloponnesian War.

In the winter of 431/430 BC, Athens' de facto leader, Pericles, delivered the traditional eulogy to those Athenians who had died in battle during the preceding 12 months. Athens had long been the most powerful of the Greek city-states, but rival Sparta was now in the ascendant and its army at Athens' gates. Although more than a quarter of the population would be dead within one year, and Pericles himself within two, the siege was not broken by the Athenians' surrender for another 26 years. The speech – known as the funeral oration of Pericles – is partly in praise of the dead, and of Athens' greatness, but is also an exhortation to the living to live up to the standards of the dead and continue the fight.

Most of those who have spoken here before me have commended the lawgiver who added this oration to our other funeral customs; it seemed to them a worthy thing that such an honour should be given at their burial to the dead who have fallen on the field of battle. But I should have preferred that, when men's deeds have been brave, they should be honoured in deed only, and with such an honour as this public funeral, which you are now witnessing . . .

I will speak first of our ancestors, for it is right and seemly that now, when we are lamenting the dead, a tribute should be paid to their memory. There has never been a time when they did not inhabit this land, which by their valour they have handed down from generation to generation, and we have received from them a free state. But if they were worthy of praise, still more were our fathers, who added to their inheritance, and after many a struggle transmitted to us their sons this great empire . . .

Our form of government does not enter into rivalry with the institutions of others. We do not copy our neighbours, but are an example to them. It is true that we are called a democracy, for the administration is in the hands of the many and not of the few. But while the law secures equal justice to all alike in their private disputes . . . and when a citizen is in any way distinguished, he is preferred to the public service, not as a matter of privilege, but as the reward of merit . . .

I have dwelt upon the greatness of Athens because I want to show you that we are contending for a higher prize than those who enjoy none of these privileges, and to establish by manifest proof the merit of these men whom I am now commemorating. Their loftiest praise has been already spoken. For in magnifying the city I have magnified them, and men like them whose virtues made her glorious. And of how few Hellenes can it be said as of them, that their deeds when weighed in the balance have been found equal to their fame! Methinks that a death such as theirs gives the true measure of a man's worth; it may be the first revelation of his virtues, but is at any rate their final seal. For even those who come short in other ways may justly plead the valour with which they have fought for their country; they have blotted out the evil with the good, and have benefited the state more by their public services than they have injured her by their private actions. None of these men were enervated by wealth or hesitated to resign the pleasures of life; none of them put off the evil day in the hope, natural to poverty, that a man, though poor, may one day become rich. But, deeming that the punishment of their enemies was sweeter than any of these things, and that they could fall in no nobler cause, they determined at the hazard of their lives to be honourably avenged, and to leave the rest. They resigned to hope their unknown chance of happiness; but in the face of death they resolved to rely upon themselves alone. And when the moment came they were minded to resist and suffer, rather than to fly and save their lives; they ran away from the word of dishonour, but on the battlefield their feet stood fast, and in an instant, at the height of their fortune, they passed away from the scene, not of their fear, but of their glory.

Such was the end of these men; they were worthy of Athens, and the living need not desire to have a more heroic spirit, although they may pray for a less fatal issue. The value of such a spirit is not to be expressed . . . I would have you . . . fix your eyes upon the greatness of Athens, until you become filled with the love of her; and when you are impressed by the spectacle of her glory, reflect that this empire has been acquired by men who knew their duty and had the courage to do it, who in the hour of conflict had the fear of dishonour always present to them, and who, if ever they failed in an enterprise, would not allow their virtues to be lost to their country, but freely gave their lives to her as the fairest offering which they could present at her feast. The sacrifice which they collectively made was individually repaid to them; for they received again each one for himself a praise which grows not old, and the noblest of all sepulchres . . . that in which their glory survives, and is proclaimed always and on every fitting occasion both in word and deed. For the whole earth is the sepulchre of famous men; not only are they commemorated by columns and inscriptions in their own country, but in foreign lands there dwells also an unwritten memorial of them, graven not on stone but in the hearts of men. Make them your examples and, esteeming courage to be freedom and freedom to be happiness, do not weigh too nicely the perils of war . . .

Portrait bust of Thucydides

Wherefore I do not now commiserate with the parents of the dead who stand here; I would rather comfort them. You know that your life has been passed amid manifold vicissitudes; and that they may be deemed fortunate who have gained most honour, whether an honourable death like theirs, or an honourable sorrow like yours, and whose days have been so ordered that the term of their happiness is likewise the term of their life. I know how hard it is to make you feel this, when the good fortune of others will too often remind you of the gladness which once lightened your hearts. And sorrow is felt at the want of those blessings, not which a man never knew, but which were a part of his life before they were taken from him. Some of you are of an age at which they may hope to have other children, and they ought to bear their sorrow better; not only will the children who may hereafter be born make them forget their own lost ones, but the city will be doubly a gainer. She will not be left desolate, and she will be safer. For a man's counsel cannot have equal weight or worth, when he alone has no children to risk in the general danger. To those of you who have passed their prime, I say: 'Congratulate yourselves that you have been happy during the greater part of your days; remember that your life of sorrow will not last long, and be comforted by the glory of those who are gone.

For the love of honour alone is ever young, and not riches, as some say, but honour is the delight of men when they are old and useless.

To you who are the sons and brothers of the departed, I see that the struggle to emulate them will be an arduous one. For all men praise the dead, and, however pre-eminent your virtue may be, hardly will you be thought, I do not say to equal, but even to approach them. The living have their rivals and detractors, but when a man is out of the way, the honour and good-will which he receives is unalloyed. And, if I am to speak of womanly virtues to those of you who will henceforth be widows, let me sum them up in one short admonition: To a woman not to show more weakness than is natural to her sex is a great glory, and not to be talked about for good or for evil among men.

I have paid the required tribute, in obedience to the law, making use of such fitting words as I had. The tribute of deeds has been paid in part; for the dead have been honourably interred, and it remains only that their children should be maintained at the public charge until they are grown up: this is the solid prize with which, as with a garland, Athens crowns her sons living and dead, after a struggle like theirs. For where the rewards of virtue are greatest, there the noblest citizens are enlisted in the service of the state. And now, when you have duly lamented, every one his own dead, you may depart.

Pharoah Merenptah
born c. 1273 BC, reigned 1213–1203 BC

NATIONALITY:
Egyptian
WHEN:
Year 5 of Merenptah's reign
WHERE:
Merenptah's mortuary temple in ancient Thebes
YOU SHOULD KNOW:
This stele contains the first known reference to Israel outside the Bible.

Merenptah, the thirteenth son of Ramesses II, succeeded to his father's throne at the age of 60. Relatively little is known about his nine-year reign, except from inscriptions at his mortuary temple concerning his military campaigns against the Libyans and the rebellious 'Asiatics' of various nations. This first reference to the people of Israel makes it clear that at this stage they did not have a settled home: while Ashkelon, Gezer and Yanoam have the hieroglyphs indicating a foreign city-state and people, Israel is indicated as a foreign people only. The 125-inch black granite stele was found by the British archaeologist Flinders Petrie in 1896 and it is now in the Egyptian Museum in Cairo.

The princes are prostrate, saying 'Shalom'!
Not one is raising his head among the Nine Bows.
Now that Libya [Tehenu] has come to ruin,
Hatti is pacified.
The Canaan has been plundered into every sort of woe;
Ashkelon has been overcome;
Gezer has been captured;
Yanoam is made nonexistent;
Israel is laid waste and his seed is not;
Hurru is become a widow because of Egypt.

Gaius Julius Caesar 100–44 BC

The Rubicon once served as the dividing line between Italy proper and the province of Cisalpine Gaul, which was governed in 49 BC by the brilliant soldier, politician and proconsul, Julius Caesar. It was strictly forbidden for a Roman to cross the Rubicon with legions of soldiers at his back – a measure introduced by the Senate to protect Rome and its republican status – and to do so was an act bound to provoke civil war, which it did. Within a little over 18 months, Caesar had defeated his rivals to become the absolute ruler of the Roman Empire.

NATIONALITY:
Roman
WHEN:
January 10, 49 BC
WHERE:
The Rubicon stream in
northeastern Italy
YOU SHOULD KNOW:
The crossing is thought to have
occurred at the site of the modern-
day town of Savignano sul Rubicone,
a few miles northwest of Rimini.

‘Alea iata est’ – ‘The die is cast’.

*Julius Caesar crossing the
Rubicon on horseback.*

Mark Antony/Marcus Antonius 83–30 BC

NATIONALITY:
Roman
WHEN:
March 20, 44 BC
WHERE:
The Forum, Rome, Italy
YOU SHOULD KNOW:
This version of Antony's speech at Caesar's funeral was written by William Shakespeare some time around AD 1600. He based his play, *Julius Caesar,* on Plutarch's (AD 46–120) Life of Brutus and Life of Caesar.

Five days after the assassination of Caesar by a group of senators who feared that he would seek to have himself declared emperor, his funeral took place. The conspirators had been given an amnesty, but in his eulogy Mark Antony demolishes the assertions of Brutus (Marcus Junius Brutus, 85–42 BC) about Caesar's ambitions and, although he abides by an agreement not to accuse them directly of being traitors, his sarcastic description of them as 'honourable', combined with the revelation that Caesar had left most of his property to the people, turned the crowd against the assassins. Ironically, the conspirators' actions led ultimately to the Republic's transformation into the Roman Empire in 27 BC when Caesar's heir Octavian (Gaius Julius Caesar Octavianus, 63–14 BC) was granted the title Augustus.

Friends, Romans, countrymen, lend me your ears;
I come to bury Caesar, not to praise him.
The evil that men do lives after them;
The good is oft interred with their bones:
So let it be with Caesar. The noble Brutus
Hath told you Caesar was ambitious:
If it were so, it was a grievous fault;
And grievously hath Caesar answer'd it.
Here, under leave of Brutus and the rest, –
For Brutus is an honourable man;
So are they all, all honourable men, –
Come I to speak in Caesar's funeral.
He was my friend, faithful and just to me:
But Brutus says he was ambitious;
And Brutus is an honourable man.
He hath brought many captives home to Rome,
Whose ransoms did the general coffers fill:
Did this in Caesar seem ambitious?
When that the poor have cried, Caesar hath wept:
Ambition should be made of sterner stuff:
Yet Brutus says he was ambitious;
And Brutus is an honourable man.
You all did see that on the Lupercal
I thrice presented him a kingly crown,
Which he did thrice refuse: was this ambition?
Yet Brutus says he was ambitious;

And, sure, he is an honourable man.
I speak not to disprove what Brutus spoke,
But here I am to speak what I do know.
You all did love him once, – not without cause:
What cause withholds you, then, to mourn for him? –
O judgment, thou art fled to brutish beasts,
And men have lost their reason! – Bear with me;
My heart is in the coffin there with Caesar,
And I must pause till it come back to me.
(interruptions from citizens, agreeing)
But yesterday the word of Caesar might
Have stood against the world: now lies he there,
And none so poor to do him reverence.
O masters, if I were disposed to stir
Your hearts and minds to mutiny and rage,
I should do Brutus wrong and Cassius wrong,
Who, you all know, are honourable men:
I will not do them wrong; I rather choose
To wrong the dead, to wrong myself, and you,
Than I will wrong such honourable men.
But here's a parchment with the seal of Caesar, –
I found it in his closet, – 'tis his will:
Let but the commons hear this testament, –
Which, pardon me, I do not mean to read, –
And they would go and kiss dead Caesar's wounds,
And dip their napkins in his sacred blood;

A bust of Mark Antony

Yea, beg a hair of him for memory,
And, dying, mention it within their wills,
Bequeathing it as a rich legacy
Unto their issue.'
(*further interruptions from citizens, calling for him to read the will*)
Have patience, gentle friends, I must not read it;
It is not meet you know how Caesar loved you.
You are not wood, you are not stones, but men;
And, being men, hearing the will of Caesar,
It will inflame you, it will make you mad.
'Tis good you know not that you are his heirs;
For if you should, O, what would come of it!
(*interruptions*)
Will you be patient? will you stay awhile?
I have o'ershot myself to tell you of it:
I fear I wrong the honourable men
Whose daggers have stabb'd Caesar; I do fear it.
(*interruptions from citizens calling the conspirators murderers*)
You will compel me, then, to read the will?
Then make a ring about the corpse of Caesar,
And let me show you him that made the will.
Shall I descend? and will you give me leave?
(*citizens agree and give him room to stand*)
Nay, press not so upon me; stand far' off.
If you have tears, prepare to shed them now.
You all do know this mantle: I remember
The first time ever Caesar put it on;
'Twas on a Summer's evening, in his tent,
That day he overcame the Nervii.
Look, in this place ran Cassius' dagger through:
See what a rent the envious Casca made:
Through this the well-beloved Brutus stabb'd;
And as he pluck'd his cursed steel away,
Mark how the blood of Caesar follow'd it, –
As rushing out of doors, to be resolved
If Brutus so unkindly knock'd, or no;
For Brutus, as you know, was Caesar's angel:
Judge, O you gods, how dearly Caesar loved him!
This was the most unkindest cut of all;
For when the noble Caesar saw him stab,
Ingratitude, more strong than traitors' arms,
Quite vanquish'd him: then burst his mighty heart;
And, in his mantle muffling up his face,
Even at the base of Pompey's statua,
Which all the while ran blood, great Caesar fell.

O, what a fall was there, my countrymen!
Then I, and you, and all of us fell down,
Whilst bloody treason flourish'd over us.
O, now you weep; and, I perceive, you feel
The dint of pity: these are gracious drops.
Kind souls, what, weep you when you but behold
Our Caesar's vesture wounded? Look you here,
Here is himself, marr'd, as you see, with traitors.
(*citizens call for revenge and make to leave*)
Stay, countrymen.
(*interruptions*)
Good friends, sweet friends, let me not stir you up
To such a sudden flood of mutiny.
They that have done this deed are honourable:
What private griefs they have, alas, I know not,
That made them do it; they're wise and honourable,
And will, no doubt, with reasons answer you.
I come not, friends, to steal away your hearts:
I am no orator, as Brutus is;
But, as you know me all, a plain blunt man,
That love my friend; and that they know full well
That gave me public leave to speak of him:
For I have neither wit, nor words, nor worth,
Action, nor utterance, nor the power of speech,
To stir men's blood: I only speak right on;
I tell you that which you yourselves do know;
Show you sweet Caesar's wounds, poor dumb mouths,
And bid them speak for me: but were I Brutus,
And Brutus Antony, there were an Antony
Would ruffle up your spirits, and put a tongue

15

In every wound of Caesar, that should move
The stones of Rome to rise and mutiny.
(*citizens call for mutiny and threaten to burn
the house of Brutus*)
Yet hear me, countrymen; yet hear me speak.
Why, friends, you go to do you know not what.
Wherein hath Caesar thus deserved your loves?
Alas, you know not; I must tell you then:
You have forgot the will I told you of.
Here is the will, and under Caesar's seal.
To every Roman citizen he gives,
To every several man, seventy-five drachmas.
(*citizens praise Caesar*)
Hear me with patience.
Moreover, he hath left you all his walks,
His private arbours, and new-planted orchards,

On this side Tiber: he hath left them to you,
And to your heirs forever; common pleasures,
To walk abroad, and recreate yourselves.
Here was a Caesar! when comes such another?
(*citizens take the body to be cremated,
theatening to set fire to the conspirators' houses
with brands from the pyre*)
Now let it work. Mischief, thou art afoot,
Take thou what course thou wilt! 🟥

NATIONALITY:
Chalcedonian/Athenian
WHEN:
380 BC
WHERE:
Piraeus
YOU SHOULD KNOW:
Thrasymachus was a member of the
Sophist school of philosophy.

Thrasymachus
459–400 BC (Plato c. 428–348 BC)

Among Plato's most important works is The Republic, *which was
written in c. 380 BC. It is one of his Socratic dialogues –
fictionalized accounts of discussions between Greek
philosophers – although it is probable that the ideas mentioned
reflect those of the protagonists. In a discussion
on the nature of justice, and on whether the
just man is happier than the unjust man, he
has the Chalcedonian philosopher
Thrasymachus say that justice is not about
right or wrong, but is in the interest of those in
power. In the dialogue, Sophocles proves this
definition wrong. The modern equivalent could
be said to be 'Might is right'.*

🟥 I proclaim that justice is nothing else than the
interest of the stronger. 🟥

Detail from painting of Plato and Aristotle

Socrates c. 469–399 BC

Although Socrates was tried on a charge of corrupting his pupils by encouraging them to think for themselves, it was in reality a political trial. Within his lifetime, Athens had gone from the height of its powers to humiliating defeat by Sparta and its allies and the city's rulers may have resented his attempts to call them to a sense of justice and halt what he saw as the moral decline of the day. He may have also questioned whether Athenian democracy was in fact the best form of rule. During this speech – known as the Apology of Socrates – he almost seems to be goading his judges into passing the death sentence by praising Sparta in comparison to Athens.

NATIONALITY:
Athenian
WHEN:
399 BC
WHERE:
Athens
YOU SHOULD KNOW:
Very little of Socrates' own work is known and most of the information we have about his life and philosophy comes from Plato, Aristotle, Xenophon and Aristophanes.

'I know not, O Athenians! how far you have been influenced by my accusers for my part, in listening to them I almost forgot myself, so plausible were their arguments however, so to speak, they have said nothing true. But of the many falsehoods which they uttered I wondered at one of them especially, that in which they said that you ought to be on your guard lest you should be deceived by me, as being eloquent in speech. For that they are not ashamed of being forthwith convicted by me in fact, when I shall show that I am not by any means eloquent, this seemed to me the most shameless thing in them, unless indeed they call him eloquent who speaks the truth. For, if they mean this, then I would allow that I am an orator, but not after their fashion for they, as I affirm, have said nothing true, but from me you shall hear the whole truth. Not indeed, Athenians, arguments highly wrought, as theirs were, with choice phrases and expressions, nor adorned, but you shall hear a speech uttered without premeditation in such words as first present themselves. For I am confident that what I say will be just, and let none of you expect otherwise, for surely it would not become my time of life to come before you like a youth with a got up speech . . .

Let us, then, repeat from the beginning what the accusation is from which the calumny against me has arisen, and relying on which Melitus has preferred this indictment against me. Well. What, then, do they who charge me say in their charge? For it is necessary to read their deposition as of public accusers. 'Socrates acts wickedly, and is criminally curious in searching into things under the earth, and in the heavens, and in making the worse appear the better cause, and in teaching these same things to others.' Such is the accusation: for such things you have yourselves seen in the comedy of Aristophanes, one Socrates there carried about, saying that he walks in the air, and acting many other buffooneries, of which I understand nothing whatever. Nor do I say this as disparaging such a science, if there be any one skilled in such things, only let me not be prosecuted by Melitus on a charge of this kind; but I say it, O Athenians! because I have nothing to do with such matters. And I call upon most of you as witnesses of this, and require you to inform and tell each other, as many of you as have ever heard me conversing; and there are many such among you. Therefore tell each other, if any one of you has ever heard me conversing little or much on such subjects. And from this you will know that other things also, which the multitude assert of me, are of a similar nature . . .

With respect, then, to the charges which my first accusers have alleged against me, let this be a sufficient apology to you. To Melitus, that good and patriotic man, as he says, and to my later accusers, I will next endeavour to give an answer; and here, again, as there are different accusers, let us take up their deposition. It is pretty much as follows: 'Socrates,' it says, 'acts unjustly in corrupting the youth, and in not believing in those gods in whom the city believes, but in other strange divinities.' Such is the accusation; let us examine each particular of it. It says that I act unjustly in corrupting the youth. But I, O Athenians! say that Melitus acts unjustly, because he jests on serious subjects, rashly putting men upon trial, under pretence of being zealous and solicitous about things in which he never at any time took any concern . . .

That I am not guilty, then, O Athenians! according to the indictment of Melitus, appears to me not to require a lengthened defence; but what I have said is sufficient. And as to what I said at the beginning, that there is a great enmity toward me among the multitude, be assured it is true. And this it is which will condemn me, if I am condemned, not Melitus, nor Anytus [his accusers], but the calumny and envy of the multitude, which have already condemned many others, and those good men, and will, I think, condemn others also; for there is no danger that it will stop with me . . .

Be well assured, then, if you put me to death, being such a man as I say I am, you will not injure me more than yourselves. For neither will Melitus nor Anytus harm me; nor have they the power; for I do not think that it is possible for a better man to be injured by a worse. He may perhaps have me condemned to death, or banished, or deprived of civil rights; and he or others may perhaps consider these as mighty evils; I, however, do not consider them so, but that it is much more so to do what he is now doing, to endeavour to put a man to death unjustly.

Now, therefore, O Athenians! I am far from making a defence on my behalf, as anyone might think, but I do so on your own behalf, lest by condemning me you should offend at all with respect to the gift of the deity to you. For, if you should put me to death, you will not easily find such another, though it may be ridiculous to say so, altogether attached by the deity to this city as to a powerful and generous horse, somewhat sluggish from his size, and requiring to be roused by a gadfly; so the deity appears to have united me, being such a person as I am, to the city, that I may rouse you, and persuade and reprove every one of you, nor ever cease besetting you throughout the whole day . . .

[He is declared guilty by a majority of voices.]

That I should not be grieved, O Athenians! at what has happened – namely, that you have condemned me – as well many other circumstances concur in bringing to pass; and, moreover this, that what has happened has not happened contrary to my expectation; but I much rather wonder at the number of votes on either side. For I did not expect that I should be condemned by so small a number, but by a large majority; but now, as it seems, if only three more votes had changed sides, I should have been acquitted. So far as Melitus is concerned, as it appears to me, I have been already acquitted; and not only have I been acquitted, but it is clear to everyone that had not Anytus and Lycon come forward to accuse me, he would have been fined a thousand drachmas, for not having obtained a fifth part of the votes . . .

[The judges pass sentence, and condemn Socrates to death]

In the next place, I desire to predict to you who have condemned me, what will be your fate; for I am now in that condition in which men most frequently prophesy – namely, when they are about to die. I say, then, to you, O Athenians! who have condemned me to death, that immediately after my death a punishment will overtake you, far more severe, by Jupiter! than that which you have inflicted on me. For you have done this, thinking you should be freed from the necessity of giving an account of your lives. The very contrary, however, as I affirm, will happen to you. Your accusers will be more numerous, whom I have now restrained, though you did not perceive it; and they will be more severe, inasmuch as they are younger, and you will be more indignant. For if you think that by putting men to death you will restrain anyone from upbraiding you because you do not live well, you are much mistaken; for this method of escape is neither possible nor honourable; but that other is most honourable and most easy, not to put a check upon others, but for a man to take heed to himself how he may be most perfect. Having predicted thus much to those of you who have condemned me, I take my leave of you . . .

You, therefore, O my judges! ought to entertain good hopes with respect to death, and to meditate on this one truth, that to a good man nothing is evil, neither while living nor when dead, nor are his concerns neglected by the gods. And what has befallen me is not the effect of chance; but this is clear to me, that now to die, and be freed from my cares is better for me. On this account the warning in no way turned me aside; and I bear no resentment toward those who condemned me, or against my accusers, although they did not condemn and accuse me with this intention, but thinking to injure me: in this they deserve to be blamed . . .

But it is now time to depart – for me to die, for you to live. But which of us is going to a better state is unknown to everyone but God.

King Pyrrhus of Epirus 319–272 BC

By the early 3rd century BC Rome had expanded her territory to a large part of the Italian peninsula but then, after a minor skirmish in 281 BC with Tarentum – one of the Greek colonies in southern Italy – first came into conflict with the Greeks, led by Pyrrhus. The Greeks and their allies won a series of battles at Heraclea (280 BC), Asculum (279 BC) and Beneventum (275 BC), but with such great losses that the Greeks were eventually forced to admit that they could no longer protect their overseas colonies in the region and the term Pyrrhic victory came to mean a victory not worth the cost.

NATIONALITY:
Greek
WHEN:
279 BC
WHERE:
Asculum (now Ascoli Satriano),
Apulia, Italy
YOU SHOULD KNOW:
From the 8th century BC much of southern Italy was settled by Greek colonists, and this area was known as Magna Graecia (Greater Greece).

If we are victorious in one more
battle with the Romans,
we shall be utterly ruined.

Pyrrhus

Hammurabi, King of Babylon

reigned c. 1792–1750 BC

NATIONALITY:
Babylonian
WHEN:
c. 760 BC
WHERE:
Ancient Babylonia
YOU SHOULD KNOW:
The code is the source of the maxim 'An eye for an eye, a tooth for a tooth'.

Hammurabi was the sixth king of the Amorite dynasty, who expanded a small city-state to a large empire during his long reign. Although fragments had been known about for many years, the stele containing a long prologue describing the king's achievements and 282 provisions – The Code of Hammurabi – was discovered in 1901 in the Elamite city of Susa. The 2.2 m (7 ft 5 in) black diorite stele is now in the Louvre in Paris. The laws are chiefly about family life, property and trade but provide a great deal of detail about life in ancient Babylonia.

'If a man, in a case pending judgement, has uttered threats against the witnesses, or has not justified the word that he has spoken, if that case be a capital suit, that man shall be put to death.

If he has offered corn or money to the witnesses, he shall himself bear the sentence of that case.

If a man has stolen the goods of temple or palace, that man shall be killed, and he who has received the stolen thing from his hand shall be put to death.

If a man has stolen ox or sheep or ass, or pig, or ship, whether from the temple or the palace, he shall pay thirtyfold.

If he be a poor man, he shall render tenfold.

If the thief has nought to pay, he shall be put to death.

If a man has stolen the son of a freeman, he shall be put to death.

If a man has captured either a manservant or a maidservant, a fugitive, in the open country and has driven him back to his master, the owner of the slave shall pay him two shekels of silver.

If either a governor or a magistrate has taken to himself the men of the levy, or has accepted and sent on the king's errand a hired substitute, that governor or magistrate shall be put to death.

A votary, merchant, or foreign sojourner may sell his field, his garden, or his house; the buyer shall carry on the business of the field, garden, or house which he has bought.

If a man has taken a field to cultivate and has not caused the corn to grow in the field, and has not done the entrusted work on the field, one shall put him to account and he shall give corn like its neighbour.

If he has not cultivated the field and has left it to itself, he shall give corn like its neighbour to the owner of the field, and the field he left he shall break up with hoes and shall harrow it and return to the owner of the field.

If a man has given his field for produce to a cultivator, and has received the produce of his field, and afterwards a thunderstorm has ravaged the field or carried away the produce, the loss is the cultivator's.

If a man has neglected to strengthen his bank of the canal, has not strengthened his bank, a breach has opened out itself in his bank, and the waters have carried away the meadow, the man in whose bank the breach has been opened shall render back the corn which he has caused to be lost.

If a man without the consent of the owner of the orchard has cut down a tree in a man's orchard, he shall pay half a mina of silver.

If an agent has taken money from a merchant and his merchant has disputed with him, that merchant shall put the agent to account before God and witnesses concerning the money taken, and the agent shall give to the merchant the money as much as he has taken threefold.

If a wine merchant has collected a riotous assembly in her house and has not seized those rioters and driven them to the palace, that wine merchant shall be put to death.

If a votary, a lady, who is not living in the convent, has opened a wine shop or has entered a wine shop for drink, that woman one shall burn her. If the wife of a man has been caught in lying with another male, one shall bind them and throw them into the waters.

If the owner of the wife would save his wife or the king would save his servant (he may).

If a man has forced the wife of a man who has not known the male and is dwelling in the house of her father, and has lain in her bosom and one has caught him, that man shall be killed, the woman herself shall go free.

If the wife of a man her husband has accused her, and she has not been caught in lying with another male, she shall swear by God and shall return to her house.

If a man has put away his bride who has not borne him children, he shall give her money as much as her dowry, and shall pay her the marriage portion which she brought from her father's house, and shall put her away.

If a woman hates her husband and has said 'Thou shalt not possess me', one shall enquire into her past what is her lack, and if she has been economical and has no vice, and her husband has gone out and greatly belittled her, that woman has no blame, she shall take her marriage portion and go off to her father's house.

If she has not been economical, a goer about, has wasted her house, has belittled her husband, that woman one shall throw her into the waters.

If a man's wife on account of another male has caused her husband to be killed, that woman upon a stake one shall set her.

If a man has married a wife and she has borne him children, and that woman has gone to her fate, her father shall have no claim on her marriage portion, her marriage portion is her children's forsooth.

If a man has married a wife, and she has not granted him children, that woman has gone to her fate, if his father-in-law has returned him the dowry that that man brought to the house of his father-in-law, her husband shall have no claim on the marriage portion of that woman, her marriage portion belongs to the house of her father forsooth.

If a man has set his face to cut off his son, has said to the judge 'I will cut off my son,' the judge shall enquire into his reasons, and if the son has not committed a heavy crime which cuts off from sonship, the father shall not cut off his son from sonship.

If he has committed against his father a heavy crime which cuts off from sonship, for the first time the judge shall bring back his face; if he has committed a heavy crime for the second time, the father shall cut off his son from sonship.

If a son of a palace warder, or of a vowed woman, has known his father's house, and has hated the father that brought him up or the mother that brought him up, and has gone off to the house of his father, one shall tear out his eye.

If a man has caused the loss of a gentleman's eye, his eye one shall cause to be lost.

If he has shattered a gentleman's limb, one shall shatter his limb.

If a man has made the tooth of a man that is his equal to fall out, one shall make his tooth fall out.

If a man has struck a gentleman's daughter and caused her to drop what is in her womb, he shall pay ten shekels of silver for what was in her womb.

If that woman has died, one shall put to death his daughter.

If the daughter of a poor man through his blows he has caused to drop that which is in her womb, he shall pay five shekels of silver.

If that woman has died, he shall pay half a mina of silver.

If he has struck a gentleman's maidservant and caused her to drop that which is in her womb, he shall pay two shekels of silver.

If that maidservant has died, he shall pay one-third of a mina of silver.

If a man has hired an ox and through neglect or by blows has caused it to die, ox for ox to the owner of the ox he shall render.

If a man has hired an ox, and God has struck it and it has died, the man who has hired the ox shall swear before God and shall go free.

If a shepherd to whom cows and sheep have been given him to breed, has falsified and changed their price, or has sold them, one shall put him to account, and he shall render cows and sheep to their owner tenfold what he has stolen.

If in a sheepfold a stroke of God has taken place or a lion has killed, the shepherd shall purge himself before God, and the accident to the fold the owner of the fold shall face it.

If a shepherd has been careless and in a sheepfold caused a loss to take place, the shepherd shall make good the fault of the loss which he has caused to be in the fold and shall pay cows or sheep and shall give to their owner.

If a man has bought a manservant or a maidservant and has a complaint, his seller shall answer the complaint.

If they are natives of another land the buyer shall tell out before God the money he paid, and the owner of the manservant or the maidservant shall give to the merchant the money he paid, and shall recover his manservant or his maidservant. 🟥

The Delphic Oracle

NATIONALITY:
Greek
WHEN:
c.547 BC
WHERE:
Delphi, on the slopes of
Mt Parnassos, Greece
YOU SHOULD KNOW:
Croesus' great wealth is the origin of
the phrase 'As rich as Croesus'.

In ancient Greece, people consulted oracles to help them make important decisions. At Delphi, where an oracle was in operation for hundreds of years, the oracles were delivered by a priestess known as the Pythia, from a cave above a deep fissure that may have been filled with trance-inducing gases expelled from the geological fault below. Answers from the Pythia were notoriously ambiguous, none more so than that given to Croesus of Lydia (born 595 BC, reigned c. 560–547 BC), who consulted various oracles as to whether he should pursue his military campaign against the Persians. He took her answer to mean that the Persian empire would fall, but instead lost his own.

If Croesus attacks the Persians, he will destroy a great empire. 🟥

Pheidippides 530–490 BC

In the summer of 490 BC, only two major Greek city-states, Athens and Sparta, were not under the control of Persia. When the Persian navy appeared off Marathon, the Athenian army went to meet them, sending their best herald, Pheidippides (also known as Philippides), to Sparta to ask for help. He apparently managed the 150-plus miles over rough terrain in two days. However, when he reached Sparta, he discovered that the citizens were in the middle of a religious festival and could not join leave for another six days, so he returned to Marathon to let the Athenian generals know. Somehow, the Athenians won a convincing victory and Pheidippides was sent the 25 miles to the city to break the news. As he delivered his message, he died.

NATIONALITY:
Athenian
WHEN:
Summer of 490 BC
WHERE:
Sparta and Athens
YOU SHOULD KNOW:
The length of the modern marathon –
26 miles, 385 yards – was fixed in
1921 and is the distance that was
first used in the London Summer
Olympics in 1908.

❝ Rejoice, we have won. ❞

Socrates c. 469–399 BC

After his death sentence, Socrates is imprisoned. His wealthy friend Crito appears early one morning to tell him that he is due to be executed the following day. Socrates refuses Crito's offer to pay to help him to escape on moral grounds and the pair argue about the nature of justice and injustice. Finally, the man who is to give Socrates the drink containing Hemlock appears. After asking the man for instructions, Socrates drains the cup. Soon, the poison starts to take effect and his legs become numb. His final request – that Crito make the traditional thanks offering to the god Asclepius for being cured of an illness – shows that Socrates thought that the right cure for life is death.

NATIONALITY:
Athenian
WHEN:
399 BC
WHERE:
Athens
YOU SHOULD KNOW:
This part of the story of Socrates'
last few hours appears in Plato's
The Crito.

❝ Crito, we owe a cock to Asclepius. Do pay it. Don't forget. ❞

Tobacco card illustration of Plato

Gold Roman Aereus showing Caesar Augustus

Gaius Julius Caesar

100–44 BC

NATIONALITY:
Roman
WHEN:
61 BC
WHERE:
Rome
YOU SHOULD KNOW:
The Vestal Virgins attended the sacred fire of the goddess Vesta, which if it went out foretold disaster for Rome.

Julius Caesar became Pontifex Maximus, chief priest of Rome's state religion in 63 BC and the following year, his wife Pompeia hosted one of the most important religious festivals of the Roman year, Bona Dea ('Great Goddess'). This was strictly a women-only event, involving the sacred rites of the Vestal Virgins. However, a young patrician called Publius Clodius Pulcher disguised himself as a woman and attended the rites. He was caught and prosecuted for sacrilege. The suspicion was that he was either planning to seduce Pompeia or was already having an affair with her. Even though Clodius was acquitted, Caesar divorced Pompeia. The idea that relatives and spouses of leaders must be above suspicion still holds true today.

I considered that my wife ought not even to be under suspicion.

Anonymous

NATIONALITY:
various
WHEN:
AD 52
WHERE:
Rome
YOU SHOULD KNOW:
If the Emperor wanted to spare a wounded gladiator's life, he would give a thumb's-down, not a thumb's-up.

In the ancient Roman Empire, public entertainments often took the form of contests between trained combatants called gladiators, between animals, between gladiators and animals, or even on occasions in the form of huge mock naval battles called naumachia. Whereas gladiators were highly trained professionals and did not always fight to the death, participants in the naumachia were usually prisoners of war who were condemned to death, and it is from the Emperor Claudius' naumachia of AD 52 that the only record of this phrase – or at least something very close to it – exists, although the gladiators may have said something similar. The lives of the victors in the naumachia were, traditionally, spared.

Ave, Caesar, morituri te salutant (Hail, Caesar, those who are about to die salute you).

Lucretia died 509 BC

NATIONALITY:
Roman
WHEN:
509 BC

For the first two-and-a-half centuries of its existence, Rome was ruled by kings. The last of these was the despotic Lucius Tarquinius Superbus (Tarquin the Proud). His son, Sextus

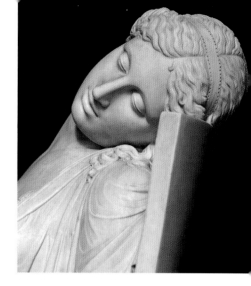

Detail of the head of Lucretia

Tarquinius raped Lucretia, the wife of Lucius Tarquinius Collatinus, and she subsequently committed suicide in front of her husband and brother, Lucius Junius Brutus. They led a revolt against the king and became the first consuls of the Roman Empire. Lucretia became renowned as the archetype of female virtue for the Romans and later the Christians. Brutus is thought to be the direct ancestor of the Marcus Junius Brutus who took part in the assassination of Julius Caesar in 44 BC.

❝ ... what can be right with a woman who has lost her honour? The traces of another man are on your bed, Collatinus. But the body only has been violated, the mind is guiltless; death shall be my witness. But give me your right hands, and your honour, that the adulterer shall not come off unpunished. It is Sextus Tarquin, who, an enemy in the guise of a guest, has borne away hence a triumph fatal to me, and to himself, if you are men . . . It is for you to see what is due to him. As for me, though I acquit myself of guilt, from punishment I do not discharge myself; nor shall any woman survive her dishonour pleading the example of Lucretia. ❞

WHERE:
Collatia, Rome
YOU SHOULD KNOW:
This version of the story comes from Book I of Livy's *History of Rome* (Titus Livius, 59 BC–AD 17).

Horace (Quintus Horatius Flaccus) 65–8 BC

Horace was the most famous lyric poet during the reign of Augustus. The best known line from the second poem of the third book of his odes contained the line 'Dulce et decorum est pro patria mori', which means 'It is sweet and glorious to die for one's country' – an idea that is still commonly promoted and held today. Augustus, at this time, was fearful that what he saw as the moral decadence of the young, especially of the noble classes, would lead to the downfall of the Roman Empire, and he actively promoted such virtues as marriage and military service and this ode reflects that. It is ironic that earlier in his life Horace had deserted the army in Greece.

NATIONALITY:
Roman
WHEN:
before 23 BC
WHERE:
Rome
YOU SHOULD KNOW:
In 1917, the British war poet Wilfred Owen called the famous line in his poem of the same name – a cry against the brutality of war – 'The Old Lie'.

❝ AGAINST THE DEGENERACY OF THE ROMAN YOUTH.
Let the robust youth learn patiently to endure pinching want in the active exercise of arms; and as an expert horseman, dreadful for his spear, let him harass the fierce Parthians; and let him lead a life exposed to the open air, and familiar with dangers. Him, the consort and marriageable virgin-daughter of some warring tyrant, viewing from the hostile walls, may sigh – Alas! let not the affianced prince, inexperienced as he is in arms, provoke by a touch this terrible lion, whom bloody rage hurries through the midst of slaughter. It is sweet and glorious to die for one's country; death even pursues the man that flies from him; nor does he spare the trembling knees of

Bust of Horace

effeminate youth, nor the coward back. Virtue, unknowing of base repulse, shines with immaculate honours; nor does she assume nor lay aside the ensigns of her dignity, at the veering of the popular air. Virtue, throwing open Heaven to those who deserve not to die, directs her progress through paths of difficulty, and spurns with a rapid wing grovelling cowards and the slippery earth. There is likewise a sure reward for faithful silence. I will prohibit that man, who shall divulge the sacred rites of mysterious Ceres, from being under the same roof with me, or from setting sail with me in the same fragile bark: for Jupiter, when slighted, often joins a good man in the same fate with a bad one. Seldom hath punishment, though lame of foot, failed to overtake the wicked. 🟥

Demosthenes 384–322 BC

NATIONALITY:
Athenian
WHEN:
330 BC
WHERE:
Athens
YOU SHOULD KNOW:
This speech is also known as On the Crown.

In 330 BC, another Athenian orator, Ctesiphon, proposed that Demosthenes be given a crown for his tireless promotion of war against the forces of Philip II of Macedonia and his son Alexander. Although Athens had lost, Demosthenes remained more popular than the pro-Macedonians who were in power. Among these was Aeschines – a long-term enemy of Demosthenes – who decided to prosecute Ctesiphon on grounds of legal irregularies in what was a thinly disguised attack on Demosthenes, whom he had previously accused of bribery and improper conduct. The following extracts from towards the end of the lengthy speech Demosthenes made in defence of Ctesiphon are a masterpiece of rhetoric.

It was my lot, Aeschines, when a boy, to frequent the schools suited to my station, and to have wherewithal to avoid doing anything mean through want. When I emerged from boyhood, I did as was consistent with my origin: filled the office of Choregus [a leader of a chorus], furnished galleys, contributed to the revenue, and was wanting in no acts of munificence, public or private, but ready to aid both my country and my friends. When I entered into public life, I deemed it proper to choose the course which led to my being repeatedly crowned both by this country and the other Greek states, so that not even you, my enemies, will now venture to pronounce the part I took other than honourable. Such then were my fortunes . . .

But you, venerable man, who look down upon others, see what kind of fortunes were yours compared with mine! Brought up from your boyhood in abject poverty, you both were helper in your father's school, and you ground the ink, sponged the forms, and swept the room, doing the work of a household slave, not of a freeborn youth. When grown up, you recited your mother's books as she performed her mysteries, and you helped in her other trickeries. At night, dressed like a bacchanal, and draining the goblet, and purifying the initiated, and rubbing them with clay and with bran, rising from the lustration [purification ritual], you ordered them to cry, 'I've fled the evil; I've found the good'; bragging that none ever roared so loud before; and truly I believe it; for

Demosthenes, a master of rhetoric

do not doubt that he who now speaks out so lustily, did not then howl most splendidly . . .

Draw then the parallel between your life and mine, Aeschines, quietly and not acrimoniously; and demand of this audience which of the two each of them had rather choose for his own. You were an usher – I a scholar; you were an initiator – I was initiated; you danced at the games – I presided over them; you were a clerk of the Assembly, I a member; you, a third-rate actor, I a spectator; you were constantly breaking down – I always hissing you; your measures were all in the enemy's favour – mine always in the country's; and, in a word, now on this day the question as to me is whether or not I shall be crowned, while nothing whatever is alleged against my integrity; while it is your lot to appear already as a calumniator, and the choice of evils before you is that of still continuing your trade, or being put to silence by failing to obtain a fifth of the votes . . .

In what circumstances then ought a statesman and an orator to be vehement? When the State is in jeopardy upon the ruin of affairs – when the people are in conflict with the enemy – then it is that the strenuous and patriotic citizen appears. But when Aeschines cannot pretend to have any ground whatever for even charging me with any offence in public life, or, I will add, in private, either in the name of the country or his own – for him to come forward with a vamped up [fabricated] attack on my crowning and my honours, and to waste so many words upon this subject, is the working of personal spite and envy, and a little mind, and shows no good man.

To me, indeed, Aeschines, it appears from these speeches of yours, as if you had instituted this impeachment through a desire of making a display of vociferation, not of punishing anyone's misconduct. For it is not the speech of the orator, Aeschines, that avails, nor yet the compass of his voice, but his feeling in unison with the community and bearing enmity or affection towards them whom his country loves or hates. He that thus possesses his soul speaks ever with right feeling. But he that bows to those from whom the country has danger to apprehend, does not anchor in the same roadstead [mooring] with the people; accordingly he does not look for safety from the same quarter. But mark me, I do: for I have always made common cause with the people, nor have I ever taken any course for my peculiar and individual interest. Can you say as much? Then how? – You, who, instantly after the battle, went on the embassy to Philip, the cause of all that in these times befell your country; and that after refusing the office at all former periods, as everyone knows? – But who deceives the country? Is it not he that says one thing and thinks another? And who is he upon whom at every assembly solemn execration is proclaimed? Is it not such a man as this? What worse charge can anyone bring against an orator than that his words and his sentiments do not tally? Yet you have been discovered to be such a man; and you still lift your voice and dare to look this assembly in the face! . . .

What alliance ever accrued to the country of your making? Or what succours, or goodwill, or glory of your gaining? Or what embassy, or what other public functions, whereby the state acquired honour? What domestic affair, or concern of the Greek states, or of strangers, over which you presided, was ever set right through you? What galleys, what armaments, what arsenals, what repairs of the walls, what cavalry? In what one of all these particulars have you ever proved useful? What benefit has ever accrued to either rich or poor from your fortunes? None. – 'But, hark!' says someone. 'If nothing of all this was done, at least there existed good dispositions and public spirit.' Where? When? you most wicked of men? – Your contributing nothing was not owing to your poverty but to your taking special care nothing you did should ever counteract the schemes of those to whom all your policy was subservient. In what, then, are you bold, and when are you munificent? When anything is to be urged against your countrymen, then are you most copious of speech – most profuse of money – most rich in memory – a first-rate actor – the Theocrines [a paid informer whom Demosthenes had spoken against] of the stage! . . .

Two qualities, men of Athens, every citizen of ordinary worth ought to possess (I shall be able in general terms to speak of myself in the least invidious manner): he should both maintain in office the purpose of a firm mind and the course suited to his country's pre-eminence, and on all occasions and in all his actions the spirit of patriotism. This belongs to our nature; victory and might are under the dominion of another power. These dispositions you will find to have been absolutely inherent in me. For observe: neither when my head was demanded, nor when they dragged me before the Amphyctions, nor when they threatened, nor when they promised, nor when they let loose on me these wretches like wild beasts, did I ever abate in any particular my affection for you. This straightforward and honest path of policy, from the very first, I chose; the honour, the power, the glory of my country to promote – these to augment – in these to have my being. Never was I seen going about the streets elated and exulting when the enemy was victorious, stretching out my hand, and congratulating such as I thought would tell it elsewhere, but hearing with alarm any success of our own armies, moaning and bent to the earth like these impious men, who rail at this country as if they could do so without also stigmatizing themselves; and who, turning their eyes abroad, and seeing the prosperity of the enemy in the calamities of Greece, rejoice in them, and maintain that we should labour to make them last for ever!

Let not, oh gracious God, let not such conduct receive any manner of sanction from thee! Rather plant even in these men a better spirit and better feelings! But if they are wholly incurable, then pursue themselves, yea, themselves by themselves, to utter and untimely perdition by land and by sea; and to us who are spared vouchsafe to grant the speediest rescue from our impending alarms, and an unshaken security! "

NATIONALITY:
Macedonian
WHEN:
348 BC
WHERE:
Olynthus, northeastern Greece
YOU SHOULD KNOW:
Philip was the father of
Alexander the Great.

Philip II of Macedonia 382–336 BC

Plutarch (Lucius Mestrius Plutarchus, c. AD 46–120) was a Greek historian and among his works is the Opera Moralia, in the third volume of which is a collection of sayings of Greek and Roman kings and commanders (regum et imperatorum apophthegmata). One of his stories is about when the Macedonians conquered their former ally Olynthia after Philip II bribed two leading citizens – Lasthenes and Euthycrates – to surrender it. Philip's soldiers taunted the two men as traitors, so they complained to Philip, who retorted with the statement below, meaning that his soldiers were too rough and stupid to tell anything but the truth. Interestingly, when Desiderius Erasmus first translated this from the Greek in the sixteenth century, he misread skaphe (trough) for skapheion (spade).

‘ Macedonians hath not the with to call a spade by any other name than a spade. "

Plutarch, historian and author of Opera Moralia

Gaius Octavianus Augustus
born 63 BC, reigned 27 BC–AD 14

The Res Gestae Divi Augusti (The Deeds of the Divine Augustus) is his statement of what he had done for the city of Rome as a member of the second triumvirate after Caesar's death but especially during his 45 years as sole ruler. The way in which his accomplishments are described is a masterpiece of early political spin. He glosses over events that might reflect badly on him and never fails to mention the accomplishments of his chosen heir Tiberius. What cannot be argued with is that he had brought stability and wealth to Rome, and that he had indeed made the city more beautiful.

NATIONALITY:
Roman
WHEN:
before AD 14
WHERE:
outside the mausoleum of
Augustus, Rome
YOU SHOULD KNOW:
Although Augustus did not,
technically, hold the title of Emperor,
he was in practice an absolute ruler,
with right of veto over the senate,
complete control of the army and a
large proportion of the empire's vast
wealth at his disposal.

'I found Rome a city of brick and left it a city of marble.

At the age of 19, on my own initiative and at my own expense, I raised an army by means of which I restored liberty to the republic, which had been oppressed by the tyranny of a faction. For which service the senate, with complimentary resolutions, enrolled me in its order, in the consulship of Gaius Pansa and Aulus Hirtius, giving me at the same time consular precedence in voting; it also gave me the imperium. As propraetor it ordered me, along with the consuls, 'to see that the republic suffered no harm'. In the same year, moreover, as both consuls had fallen in war, the people elected me consul and a triumvir for settling the constitution.

Those who slew my father I drove into exile, punishing their deed by due process of law, and afterwards when they waged war upon the republic I twice defeated them in battle.

Wars, both civil and foreign, I undertook throughout the world, on sea and land, and when victorious I spared all citizens who sued for pardon. The foreign nations which could with safety be pardoned I preferred to save rather than to destroy. The number of Roman citizens who bound themselves to me by military oath was about 500,000. Of these I settled in colonies or sent back into their own towns, after their term of service, something more than 300,000 and to all I assigned lands, or gave money as a reward for military service. I captured 600 ships, over and above those which were smaller than triremes.

Twice I triumphed with an ovation, thrice I celebrated curule triumphs, and was saluted as imperator 21 times. Although the Senate decreed me additional triumphs I set them aside. When I had performed the vows which I had undertaken in each war I deposited upon the Capitol the laurels which adorned my fasces. For successful operations on land and sea, conducted either by myself or by my lieutenants under my auspices, the senate on 55 occasions decreed that thanks should be rendered to the immortal gods. The days on which such thanks were rendered by decree of the senate numbered 890. In my triumphs there

ABDIC

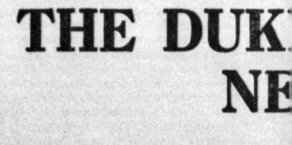

THE DUK
NE

KING EDWARD'S
THE THRON
FOR M

BY HIS

T HE KING'S MESSAGE TO P
WAS READ BY THE SP
HOUSE OF COMMONS TH
THE SPEAKER ALSO AN
OF THE DUKE OF YORK.

CATION

OF YORK THE
W KING

ESSAGE :—"I RENOUNCE
FOR MYSELF AND
DESCENDANTS."

LOVE

RE BROTHERS

FROM PLANE
TO No. 10

NAMENT, ANNOUNCING HIS ABDICATION,
ER (CAPT. FITZROY) IN A CROWDED
FTERNOON.

NCED THE ACCESSION TO THE THRONE

Mrs. Simpson's Lawyer
Returns

THERE was unusual activity
to-day at the Villa Lou Viel
Cannes where Mrs. Simpso

Martin Luther King, Jr

1929–1968

NATIONALITY:
American
WHEN:
July 23, 1956
WHERE:
American Baptist Assembly and
American Home Mission Agencies
Conference, Green Lake, Wisconsin
YOU SHOULD KNOW:
In 1964 Dr King became the youngest
recipient of the Nobel Peace Prize.

*King and his followers kneel in
prayer prior to going to jail in
Selma, Alabama.*

*In the highly racially segregated southern USA of the 1950s, there
was an increasing realization that violent protests by African-
Americans were counterproductive. A young Baptist minister in
Birmingham, Alabama, King had encountered the idea of non-
violent resistance to an evil regime in Henry David Thoreau's
'Essay on Civil Disobedience' while at college and had later been
introduced to the theories of Gandhi. His merging of these ideas
with that of Christian love was key in the spread of the Civil
Rights movement. This is part of a much longer speech that King
gave in answer to the question 'How will the oppressed peoples of
the world wage their struggle against the forces of injustice?'*

At the center of non-violence stands the principle of love.
    Another basic factor in the method of non-violent resistance is
that this method does not seek merely to avoid external physical
violence, but it seeks to avoid internal violence of spirit. And at the
center of the method of non-violence stands the principle of love.
Love is always the regulating ideal in the technique, in the method
of non-violence. This is the point at which the non-violent resister
follows the love and Savior Jesus Christ, for it is this love ethic that
stands at the center of the Christian faith. And this stands as the
regulating ideal for any move or for any struggle to change
conditions of society.

Charles, Prince of Wales

born 1948

NATIONALITY:
British
WHEN:
February 24, 1981
WHERE:
in the grounds of Buckingham
Palace, London
YOU SHOULD KNOW:
On July 29 1981 Charles and Diana
had a fairytale wedding in St Paul's
Cathedral, but within a few years the
marriage was collapsing into an
acrimonious mess, with each using
friends to brief against the other and
both of them committing adultery.

*After months of speculation in the media and the hounding of
the 19-year-old girl by the press, their engagement was
announced and the Prince of Wales and Lady Diana Spencer
gave a press conference. Asked by one journalist whether they
were in love, Diana replied, 'Of course', while Charles' response
was that he was, too, but added:*

Whatever love means.

Diana spoke candidly on 'Panorama'.

Diana, Princess of Wales

1961–1997

In November 1995, British journalist Martin Bashir interviewed the Princess of Wales for the BBC programme 'Panorama'. It was the first time that any member of the royal family had talked – in public at least – so candidly about their private lives and exposed just how badly, and how early, the marriage had begun to break down. Responses to Bashir's carefully crafted questions portray Diana as a victim whose uncaring husband was jealous of her popularity, a family that gave her no support or advice and labelled her as mentally unstable and friends who betrayed her at every turn. The following answer was to Bashir's question about whether Camilla Parker-Bowles was a factor in the breakdown of the marriage. It led to public vilification of Camilla that lasts to this day.

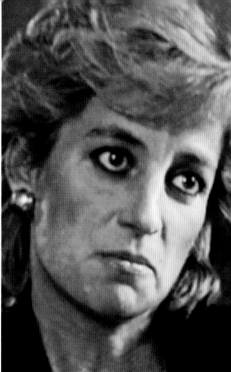

Well, there were three of us in this marriage, so it was a bit crowded.

NATIONALITY:
British
WHEN:
November 1995
WHERE:
On BBC television
YOU SHOULD KNOW:
Martin Bashir is the journalist whose 2003 interview with Michael Jackson probably contributed to the star being accused of child molestation.

Engagement picture of Charles and Diana

Former White house Intern, Monica Lewinsky hugs President Clinton.

NATIONALITY:
American
WHEN:
August 17, 1988
WHERE:
The White House, Washington D.C.
YOU SHOULD KNOW:
President Clinton was the first Democrat to be re-elected since Franklin D. Roosevelt and only the second president to be impeached.

President William Jefferson Clinton born 1946

Persistent claims of inappropriate behaviour – first with Paula Jones and then Monica Lewinsky – dogged President Clinton through the first half of his second term, although he had consistently denied any wrong-doing. However, when evidence did emerge, he was forced to testify before the grand jury that he had lied in his sworn deposition in January. The independent counsel he mentions is Kenneth Starr, who had also spent years ferreting out details of the Clintons' business dealings over what came to be known as Whitewatergate. Although much of the detail that appeared in the press was manufactured or exaggerated, President Clinton's presidency was weakened and the nature of the scandals may have contributed to the Republican victory of November 2000.

This afternoon in this room, from this chair, I testified before the Office of Independent Counsel and the grand jury.

I answered their questions truthfully, including questions about my private life, questions no American citizen would ever want to answer.

Still, I must take complete responsibility for all my actions, both public and private. And that is why I am speaking to you tonight.

As you know, in a deposition in January, I was asked questions about my relationship with Monica Lewinsky. While my answers were legally accurate, I did not volunteer information.

Indeed, I did have a relationship with Ms Lewinsky that was not appropriate. In fact, it was wrong. It constituted a critical lapse in judgment and a personal failure on my part for which I am solely and completely responsible.

But I told the grand jury today and I say to you now that at no time did I ask anyone to lie, to hide or destroy evidence or to take any other unlawful action.

I know that my public comments and my silence about this matter gave a false impression. I misled people, including even my wife. I deeply regret that.

I can only tell you I was motivated by many factors. First, by a desire to protect myself from the embarrassment of my own conduct.

I was also very concerned about protecting my family. The fact that these questions were being asked in a politically inspired lawsuit, which has since been dismissed, was a consideration, too.

In addition, I had real and serious concerns about an independent counsel investigation that began with private business dealings 20 years ago; dealings, I might add, about which an independent federal agency found no evidence of any wrongdoing by me or my wife over two years ago.

The independent counsel investigation moved on to my staff and friends, then into my private life. And now the investigation itself is under investigation.

This has gone on too long, cost too much and hurt too many innocent people.

Now, this matter is between me, the two people I love most – my wife and our daughter – and our God. I must put it right, and I am prepared to do whatever it takes to do so.

Nothing is more important to me personally. But it is private, and I intend to reclaim my family life for my family. It's nobody's business but ours.

Even presidents have private lives. It is time to stop the pursuit of personal destruction and the prying into private lives and get on with our national life.

Our country has been distracted by this matter for too long, and I take my responsibility for my part in all of this. That is all I can do.

Now it is time – in fact, it is past time – to move on.

We have important work to do – real opportunities to seize, real problems to solve, real security matters to face.

And so tonight, I ask you to turn away from the spectacle of the past seven months, to repair the fabric of our national discourse, and to return our attention to all the challenges and all the promise of the next American century.

Thank you for watching. And good night. 🙿

Pierre Elliot Trudeau 1919–2000

Until the young Justice Minister Trudeau's Criminal Law Amendment Act 1968–69 was passed laws in Canada against homosexuality had been draconian, attitudes harsh and homosexuality almost invisible. Despite his having been brought up a Roman Catholic, he believed that religion and politics should be kept separate and his legislation also relaxed divorce laws and included the legalization of abortion, contraception and lotteries. Although he was unpopular with the conservative members of the Liberal Party, the public, especially younger people, found him inspirational and he was elected leader of the party in April 1968, becoming – at the age of 48 – Prime Minister two weeks later.

🙿 There's no place for the state in the bedrooms of the nation. What's done in private between adults doesn't concern the Criminal Code. 🙿

NATIONALITY:
Canadian
WHEN:
December 21, 1967
WHERE:
At a press conference after introducing legislation in the Canadian House of Commons

YOU SHOULD KNOW:
The phrase first appears – in nearly identical form – in an editorial by Martin O'Malley in the *Globe and Mail* newspaper.

A demonstrator shows his support for Trudeau.

John Wesley 1703–1791

NATIONALITY:
British
WHEN:
July 9, 1782
WHERE:
Birmingham, England
YOU SHOULD KNOW:
Wesley was still travelling and
preaching well into his late 80s.

*Originally an Anglican minister, John Wesley became
disillusioned with corruption within the established church,
where it seemed that who a minister knew was far more
important to his career than any ability he might have, and
landowners could give the living in the local parish church to
their own friends and relations. His long, hectoring sermons
led to his banishment from churches, so he preached in fields,
to as many as 30,000 people, and eventually founded the
Arminian branch of the Methodist church. This sermon is on
the subject of God's love for Fallen Man.*

How exceeding common, and how bitter, is the outcry against our
first parent for the mischief which he not only brought upon
himself, but entailed upon his latest posterity! It was by his wilful
rebellion against God that 'sin entered into the world'. 'By one
man's disobedience', as the Apostle observes, the many, hoi polloi,
as many as were then in the loins of their forefather, 'were made',
or constituted, 'sinners':

'For all this we may thank Adam', has echoed down from
generation to generation . . . Nay it were well if the charge rested
here: But it is certain it does not. It cannot be denied that it
frequently glances from Adam to his Creator. Have not thousands
even of those that are called Christians, taken the liberty to call his
mercy, if not his justice also, into question on this very account?
Some, indeed, have done this a little more modestly, in an oblique
and indirect manner; but others have thrown aside the mask, and
asked, 'Did not God foresee that Adam would abuse his liberty?
And did he not know the baneful consequences which this must
naturally have on all his posterity? And why, then, did he permit
that disobedience? Was it not easy for the Almighty to have
prevented it?' – He certainly did foresee the whole. This cannot be
denied: For 'known unto God are all his works from the beginning
of the world'; rather, from all eternity, as the words *ap aivnos*
properly signify. And it was undoubtedly in his power to prevent it;
for he hath all power both in Heaven and Earth. But it was known
to him, at the same time, that it was best, upon the whole, not to
prevent it. He knew that 'not as the transgression, so is the free
gift'; that the evil resulting from the former was not as the good
resulting from the latter, – not worthy to be compared with it. He
saw that to permit the fall of the first man was far best for
mankind in general; that abundantly more good than evil would
accrue to the posterity of Adam by his fall; that if 'sin abounded'
thereby over all the Earth, yet grace 'would much more abound';
yea, and that to every individual of the human race, unless it was
his own choice . . .

. . . mankind in general have gained, by the fall of Adam, a capacity of attaining more holiness and happiness on Earth than it would have been possible for them to attain if Adam had not fallen. For if Adam had not fallen, Christ had not died. Nothing can be more clear than this; nothing more undeniable. The more thoroughly we consider the point the more deeply shall we be convinced of it. Unless all the partakers of human nature had received that deadly wound in Adam, it would not have been needful for the Son of God to take our nature upon him. Do you not see that this was the very ground of his coming into the world? 'By one man sin entered into the world, and death by sin: And thus death passed upon all', through him in whom all men sinned. Was it not to remedy this very thing that 'the Word was made flesh', that 'as in Adam all died, so in Christ all' might 'be made alive'? Unless, then, many had been made sinners by the disobedience of one, by the obedience of one many would not have been made righteous: So there would have been no room for that amazing display of the Son of God's love to mankind: There would have been no occasion for his being 'obedient unto death, even the death of the cross'. It could not then have been said, to the astonishment of all the hosts of Heaven 'God so loved the world', yea, the ungodly world, which had no thought or desire of returning to him, 'that he gave his Son' out of his bosom, his only-begotten Son, 'to the end that whosoever believeth on him should not perish, but have everlasting life.' . . .

. . . What is the necessary consequence of this? It is this: There could then have been no such thing as faith in God thus loving the world, giving his only Son for us men, and for our salvation. There could have been no such thing as faith in the Son of God, as 'loving us and giving himself for us'. There could have been no faith in the Spirit of God, as renewing the image of God in our hearts, as raising us from the death of sin unto the life of righteousness. Indeed the whole privilege of justification by faith could have had no existence; there could have been no redemption in the blood of Christ; neither could Christ have been 'made of God unto us', either 'wisdom, righteousness, sanctification' or 'redemption' . . .

. . . what unspeakable advantage we derive from the fall of our first parent with regard to faith; – Faith both in God the Father, who spared not his own Son, his only Son, but 'wounded him for our transgressions' and 'bruised him for our iniquities': and in God the Son, who poured out his soul for us transgressors, and washed us in his own blood. We see what advantage we derive therefrom with regard to the love of God; both of God the Father and God the Son. The chief ground of this love, as long as we remain in the body, is plainly declared by the Apostle: 'We love Him, because He first loved us'. But the greatest instance of his love had never been given, if Adam had not fallen.

And as our faith both in God the Father and the Son receives an unspeakable increase, if not its very being. from this grand event, as does also our love both of the Father and the Son; so does the love of our neighbour also, our benevolence to all mankind, which cannot but increase in the same proportion with our faith and love of God. For who does not apprehend the force of that inference drawn by the loving Apostle: 'Beloved, if God so loved us, we ought also to love one another'? If God SO loved us, – observe, the stress of the argument lies on this very point: SO loved us, as to deliver up his only Son to die a cursed death for our salvation. Beloved, what manner of love is this wherewith God hath loved us; so as to give his only Son, in glory equal with the Father, in Majesty co-eternal? What manner of love is this wherewith the only-begotten Son of God hath loved us so as to empty himself, as far as possible, of his eternal Godhead; as to divest himself of that glory which he had with the Father before the world began; as to take upon him the form of a servant, being found in fashion as a man; and then, to humble himself still further, 'being obedient unto death, even the death of the cross!' If God SO loved us, how ought we to love one another! But this motive to brotherly love had been totally wanting if Adam had not fallen. Consequently, we could not then have loved one another in so high a degree as we may now. Nor could there have been that height and depth in the command of our blessed Lord, 'As I have loved you, So love one another'.

Jawaharlal Nehru 1889–1964

Mohandas Karamchand Gandhi (1869–1948), also known as 'Mahatma' (Great Soul), the inspirational leader and civil rights activist, who had helped to bring India through the struggles of Independence and the horrors of Partition had been murdered on January 30, 1948 by a radical Hindu who believed that too much had been conceded to Pakistan. It was the sixth attack on his life, coming only ten days after a previous aborted attempt. Independent India's first Prime Minister, Nehru, spoke the eulogy, an extract of which is below, at his friend and mentor's cremation the following day.

NATIONALITY:
Indian
WHEN:
January 31, 1948
WHERE:
At Ghandi's funeral, near New Delhi, India.
YOU SHOULD KNOW:
Both Indira Gandhi, Nehru's daughter, and his grandson, Rajiv Gandhi, also served as Prime Minister. They were both assassinated.

He has gone, and all over India there is a feeling of having been left desolate and forlorn. All of us sense that feeling, and I do not know when we shall be able to get rid of it. And yet together with that feeling there is also a feeling of proud thankfulness that it has been given to us of this generation to be associated with this mighty person. In ages to come, centuries and maybe millennia after us, people will think of this generation when this man of God trod on Earth, and will think of us who, however small, could also follow his path and tread the holy ground where his feet had been.

Let us be worthy of him.

Saint Bernard of Clairvaux
1090–1153

Engraving of Bernard of Clairvaux

NATIONALITY:
French
WHEN:
c.1150
WHERE:
In a sermon
YOU SHOULD KNOW:
Despite the dog connection, this is not the Saint Bernard after whom the dog breed is named.

A Cistercian abbot, and very conservative, Saint Bernard of Clairvaux was one of the leading theologians of the 12th century. For a period he was more influential than the popes of the day. Under his leadership, Cistercian monasticism – with its emphasis on poverty, abstinence and prayer – spread far and wide across northwestern Europe. He was instrumental in suppressing the Cathar and Waldensian heresies, in sorting out the unholy mess of the schism of 1130–1138 when there were two rival popes, in promoting the cult of the Virgin Mary and in encouraging the Second Crusade to the Holy Land. His most important work was De Diligendo Deo (On the Love of God), but the line below – meaning that to be with me you must put up with the things about me that you don't like – has passed into more common knowledge.

Qui me amat, amat et canem meum. (Love me, love my dog.)

Virgil Publius Vergilius Maro, 70–19 BC

Virgil is widely regarded as one of the best Roman poets of the era after the death of Julius Caesar. The first of his major works, the Eclogues (or Bucolicae) were written to be performed on the stage. They contain a heady mixture of eroticism and Virgil's own political vision and are chiefly set in the countryside and feature shepherds. The tenth Eclogue is the passionate last oration of the poet Gaius Cornelius Gallus in Arcadia. He envisages his friend dying of love in a beautiful landscape, and thus started the pastoral tradition in Western arts and literature.

NATIONALITY:
Roman
WHEN:
c.37 BC
WHERE:
On the stage in Rome
YOU SHOULD KNOW:
The image of a golden age heralded by the birth of a boy in the fourth Eclogue was taken by people at the time to refer to Octavian (Augustus) and by later Christian writers to Christ.

ECLOGUE X – GALLUS
This now, the very latest of my toils,
Vouchsafe me, Arethusa! needs must I
Sing a brief song to Gallus- brief, but yet
Such as Lycoris' self may fitly read.
Who would not sing for Gallus? So, when thou
Beneath Sicanian billows glidest on,
May Doris blend no bitter wave with thine,
Begin! The love of Gallus be our theme,
And the shrewd pangs he suffered, while, hard by,
The flat-nosed she-goats browse the tender brush.
We sing not to deaf ears; no word of ours
But the woods echo it. What groves or lawns
Held you, ye Dryad-maidens, when for love-
Love all unworthy of a loss so dear-
Gallus lay dying? for neither did the slopes
Of Pindus or Parnassus stay you then,
No, nor Aonian Aganippe. Him
Even the laurels and the tamarisks wept;
For him, outstretched beneath a lonely rock,
Wept pine-clad Maenalus, and the flinty crags
Of cold Lycaeus. The sheep too stood around-
Of us they feel no shame, poet divine;
Nor of the flock be thou ashamed: even fair
Adonis by the rivers fed his sheep-
Came shepherd too, and swine-herd footing slow,
And, from the winter-acorns dripping-wet
Menalcas. All with one accord exclaim:
"From whence this love of thine?" Apollo came;
"Gallus, art mad?" he cried, "thy bosom's care
Another love is following."Therewithal
Silvanus came, with rural honours crowned;
The flowering fennels and tall lilies shook
Before him. Yea, and our own eyes beheld
Pan, god of Arcady, with blood-red juice
Of the elder-berry, and with vermilion, dyed.
"Wilt ever make an end?" quoth he, "behold
Love recks not aught of it: his heart no more
With tears is sated than with streams the grass,
Bees with the cytisus, or goats with leaves."
"Yet will ye sing, Arcadians, of my woes
Upon your mountains," sadly he replied-
"Arcadians, that alone have skill to sing.
O then how softly would my ashes rest,
If of my love, one day, your flutes should tell!
And would that I, of your own fellowship,
Or dresser of the ripening grape had been,
Or guardian of the flock! for surely then,
Let Phyllis, or Amyntas, or who else,
Bewitch me- what if swart Amyntas be?
Dark is the violet, dark the hyacinth-
Among the willows, 'neath the limber vine,
Reclining would my love have lain with me,
Phyllis plucked garlands, or Amyntas sung.
Here are cool springs, soft mead and grove, Lycoris;
Here might our lives with time have worn away.
But me mad love of the stern war-god holds
Armed amid weapons and opposing foes.
Whilst thou- Ah! might I but believe it not!-
Alone without me, and from home afar,
Look'st upon Alpine snows and frozen Rhine.
Ah! may the frost not hurt thee, may the sharp
And jagged ice not wound thy tender feet!
I will depart, re-tune the songs I framed
In verse Chalcidian to the oaten reed
Of the Sicilian swain. Resolved am I
In the woods, rather, with wild beasts to couch,
And bear my doom, and character my love
Upon the tender tree-trunks: they will grow,
And you, my love, grow with them. And meanwhile

I with the Nymphs will haunt Mount Maenalus,
Or hunt the keen wild boar. No frost so cold
But I will hem with hounds thy forest-glades,
Parthenius. Even now, methinks, I range
O'er rocks, through echoing groves, and joy to launch
Cydonian arrows from a Parthian bow.-
As if my madness could find healing thus,
Or that god soften at a mortal's grief!
Now neither Hamadryads, no, nor songs
Delight me more: ye woods, away with you!
No pangs of ours can change him; not though we
In the mid-frost should drink of Hebrus' stream,
And in wet winters face Sithonian snows,
Or, when the bark of the tall elm-tree bole
Of drought is dying, should, under Cancer's Sign,

In Aethiopian deserts drive our flocks.
Love conquers all things; yield we too to love!"

These songs, Pierian Maids, shall it suffice
Your poet to have sung, the while he sat,
And of slim mallow wove a basket fine:
To Gallus ye will magnify their worth,
Gallus, for whom my love grows hour by hour,
As the green alder shoots in early Spring.
Come, let us rise: the shade is wont to be
Baneful to singers; baneful is the shade
Cast by the juniper, crops sicken too
In shade. Now homeward, having fed your fill-
Eve's star is rising-go, my she-goats, go.

Jesus Christ c. 7–4 BC–AD 26–36

NATIONALITY:
Galilean
WHEN:
c. AD 36
WHERE:
Jerusalem
YOU SHOULD KNOW:
The four Gospels differ in the details they contain: this appears only in John, chapter 15.

Among the tumultuous events of the last week of Jesus' life related in the Gospels and Corinthians, the Last Supper stands out. His actions had provoked the religious leaders and they decided to have him put to death, saying he was a danger to public order and their own authority. However, they sought to make the Roman governor Pontius Pilate responsible for the decision. Jesus was aware of his looming fate, and predicted both Judas' betrayal and Peter's denial.

9 As the Father hath loved me, so have I loved you: continue ye in my love.
10 If ye keep my commandments, ye shall abide in my love; even as I have kept my Father's commandments, and abide in his love.
11 These things have I spoken unto you, that my joy might remain in you, and that your joy might be full.
12 This is my commandment, That ye love one another; as I have loved you.
13 Greater love hath no man than this, that a man lay down his life for his friends.
14 Ye are my friends, if ye do whatsoever I command you.
15 Henceforth I call you not servants; for the servant knoweth not what his lord doeth: but I have called you friends; for all things that I have heard of my Father I have made known unto you.
16 Ye have not chosen me, but I have chosen you, and ordained you, that ye should go and bring forth fruit, and that your fruit should remain: that whatsoever ye shall ask of the Father in my name, he may give it you.
17 These things I command you, that ye love one another.

Painting of Jesus Christ

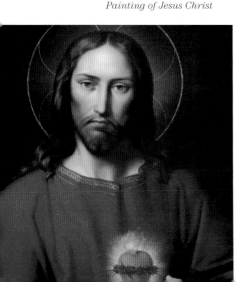

George Graham Vest 1830–1904

George Graham Vest was one of the leading orators of his time and served for 24 years as Senator for Missouri (1879–1903), but he is best remembered for a speech he made in court while acting as prosecuting counsel in a case against a man accused of killing a foxhound called Old Drum that had strayed onto his property. Whether he would have won the case if he had simply summed up his evidence is not known, but this emotional appeal about the loyalty, friendship and unselfishness of man's best friend certainly worked on the jurors' minds and they found the defendant guilty.

NATIONALITY:
American
WHEN:
September 23, 1870
WHERE:
Old Johnson County Courthouse,
Warrensburg, Missouri
YOU SHOULD KNOW:
During the Civil War Vest served as a Democrat Representative in the Confederate Congress, then in the Confederate Senate.

'GENTLEMEN OF THE JURY: The best friend a man has in this world may turn against him and become his enemy. His son or daughter that he has reared with loving care may prove ungrateful. Those who are nearest and dearest to us, those whom we trust with our happiness and our good name, may become traitors to their faith. The money that a man has, he may lose. It flies away from him, perhaps when he needs it the most. A man's reputation may be sacrificed in a moment of ill-considered action. The people who are prone to fall on their knees to do us honor when success is with us may be the first to throw the stone of malice when failure settles its cloud upon our heads. The one absolutely unselfish friend that a man can have in this selfish world, the one that never deserts him and the one that never proves ungrateful or treacherous is his dog. GENTLEMAN OF THE JURY: A man's dog stands by him in prosperity and in poverty, in health and in sickness. He will sleep on the cold ground, where the wintry winds blow and the snow drives fiercely, if only he may be near his master's side. He will kiss the hand that has no food to offer, he will lick the wounds and sores that come in encounters with the roughness of the world. He guards the sleep of his pauper master as if he were a prince. When all other friends desert, he remains. When riches take wings and reputation falls to pieces, he is as constant in his love as the Sun in its journey through the heavens.

If fortune drives the master forth an outcast in the world, friendless and homeless, the faithful dog asks no higher privilege than that of accompanying him to guard against danger, to fight against his enemies, and when the last scene of all comes, and death takes the master in its embrace and his body is laid away in the cold ground, no matter if all other friends pursue their way, there by his graveside will the noble dog be found, his head between his paws, his eyes sad but open in alert watchfulness, faithful and true even to death. '

Elizabeth I

born 1533, reigned 1558–1603

NATIONALITY:
English
WHEN:
November 30 1601
WHERE:
The Council Chamber,
Whitehall, London

At the age of 68, Elizabeth made what was to be her last speech to members of her parliament. Despite increased prosperity and stability in the country, she was in dire financial straits because Parliament voted on how much money the monarchy received. Shortly before, she had been forced to give up several lucrative monopolies that she had been in the habit of using to reward her favourites and this speech is not simply a summation of what she had done for the English people and her love for them, but a furious tirade against public accusations of corruption.

‘Mr Speaker, We have heard your declaration and perceive your care of our estate. I do assure you there is no prince that loves his subjects better, or whose love can countervail our love. There is no jewel, be it of never so rich a price, which I set before this jewel: I mean your love. For I do esteem it more than any treasure or riches; for that we know how to prize, but love and thanks I count invaluable. And, though God hath raised me high, yet this I count the glory of my Crown, that I have reigned with your loves.

Of myself I must say this: I never was any greedy, scraping grasper, nor a strait fast-holding Prince, nor yet a waster. My heart was never set on any worldly goods. What you bestow on me, I will not hoard it up, but receive it to bestow on you again. Therefore render unto them I beseech you Mr Speaker, such thanks as you imagine my heart yieldeth, but my tongue cannot express . . . For had I not received a knowledge from you, I might have fallen into the lapse of an error, only for lack of true information.

Since I was Queen, yet did I never put my pen to any grant, but that upon pretext and semblance made unto me, it was both good and beneficial to the subject in general though a private profit to some of my ancient servants, who had deserved well at my hands. But the contrary being found by experience, I am exceedingly beholden to such subjects as would move the same at first. And I am not so simple to suppose but that there be some of the Lower House whom these grievances never touched. I think they spake out of zeal to their countries and not out of spleen or malevolent affection as being parties grieved. That my grants should be grievous to my people and oppressions to be privileged under colour of our patents, our kingly dignity shall not suffer it. Yea, when I heard it, I could give no rest unto my thoughts until I had reformed it. Shall they, think you, escape unpunished that have oppressed you, and have been respectless of their duty and regardless our honour? No, I assure you, Mr Speaker, were it not more for conscience’ sake than for any glory or increase of love that I desire, these errors, troubles, vexations and oppressions done by these varlets and lewd persons not worthy of the name of subjects should not escape without condign punishment. But I perceive they dealt with me like physicians who, ministering a drug, make it more acceptable by giving it a good aromatical savour, or when they give pills do gild them all over.

I have ever used to set the Last Judgement Day before mine eyes and so to rule as I shall be judged to answer before a higher judge, and now if my kingly bounties have been abused and my grants turned to the hurt of my people contrary to my will and meaning, and if any in authority under me have neglected or perverted what I have committed to them, I hope God will not lay their culps and offenses in my charge. I know the title of a King is a glorious title, but assure yourself that the shining glory of princely authority hath not so dazzled the eyes of our understanding, but that we well know and remember that we also are to yield an account of our actions before the great judge. To be a king and wear a crown is a thing more glorious to them that see it than it is pleasant to them that bear it. For myself I was never so much enticed with the glorious name of a King or royal authority of a Queen as delighted that God hath made me his instrument to maintain his truth and glory and to defend his kingdom as I said from peril, dishonour, tyranny and oppression . . .

'For I, oh Lord, what am I, whom practices and perils past should not fear? Or what can I do? That I should speak for any glory, God forbid.' And turning to the Speaker and her councillors she said, 'And I pray to you Mr Comptroller, Mr Secretary and you of my Council, that before these gentlemen go into their countries, you bring them all to kiss my hand.' "

Saint Paul

Saul of Tarsus died c. AD 67

Saint Paul was one of the most active of the early Christian missionaries, travelling widely around the Mediterranean to spread the word. He is thought to have lived in Corinth in Greece in the early 50s AD because there is a reference to the proconsul Gallio, who is known to have been in Corinth around then. Paul seems to have argued with other followers of Christ over issues such as whether Gentiles could be admitted into the faith and whether they should be circumcised and follow the Jewish dietary laws – mandatory for Jewish members of the early church. Some of his teachings do not sit easily with those in the Gospels, but his influence on Christian theology is profound.

NATIONALITY:
Hellenistic Jew
WHEN:
Possibly some time after AD 51–53
WHERE:
In the first letter to the Corinthians

Love is patient and kind. Love knows neither envy nor jealousy. Love is not forwards and self-assertive, nor boastful and conceited.

She does not behave unbecomingly, nor seek to aggrandize herself, nor blaze out in passionate anger, nor brood over wrongs.

She finds no pleasure in injustice done to others, but joyfully sides with the truth.

She knows how to be silent. She is full of trust, full of hope, full of patient endurance. "

WAR &
REVOLUTION

Woodrow Wilson 1856–1924

NATIONALITY:
American
WHEN:
1918
WHERE:
Washington, DC, USA
YOU SHOULD KNOW:
The ideas in this speech formed the basis for the peace settlement and the negotiations for the Versailles Treaty and the League of Nations.

With the increased numbers of troops and firepower granted by American participation, the tide of World War I turned in 1917. On January 8, just over ten months before the armistice, President Wilson set out in a speech – from which the long preamble and closing remarks are omitted here – to a joint session of Congress the terms for the surrender of the Central Powers. It is known as the Fourteen Points for Peace, or just Fourteen Points. The points include practicalities such as which territories should be returned to their previous nations and aspirational ideas for the formation of new countries out of the Austro-Hungarian and Ottoman Empires, freedom of the seas for all, open trade and peaceable relations between all countries. The negotiations for the Versailles Treaty compromised on many of these because other leaders saw them as unachieveable. Because of this, Senate did not ratify the treaty and the US did not join the League of Nations.

I. Open covenants of peace, openly arrived at, after which there shall be no private international understandings of any kind but diplomacy shall proceed always frankly and in the public view.

II. Absolute freedom of navigation upon the seas, outside territorial waters, alike in peace and in war, except as the seas may be closed in whole or in part by international action for the enforcement of international covenants.

III. The removal, so far as possible, of all economic barriers and the establishment of an equality of trade conditions among all the nations consenting to the peace and associating themselves for its maintenance.

IV. Adequate guarantees given and taken that national armaments will be reduced to the lowest point consistent with domestic safety.

V. A free, open-minded, and absolutely impartial adjustment of all colonial claims, based upon a strict observance of the principle that in determining all such questions of sovereignty the interests of the populations concerned must have equal weight with the equitable claims of the government whose title is to be determined.

VI. The evacuation of all Russian territory and such a settlement of all questions affecting Russia as will secure the best and freest cooperation of the other nations of the world in obtaining for her an unhampered and unembarrassed opportunity for the independent determination of her own political development and national policy and assure her of a sincere welcome into the society of free nations under institutions of her own choosing; and, more than a welcome, assistance also of every kind that she may need and may herself desire. The treatment accorded Russia by her sister nations in the months to come will be the acid test of their good will, of their

comprehension of her needs as distinguished from their own interests, and of their intelligent and unselfish sympathy.

VII. Belgium, the whole world will agree, must be evacuated and restored, without any attempt to limit the sovereignty which she enjoys in common with all other free nations. No other single act will serve as this will serve to restore confidence among the nations in the laws which they have themselves set and determined for the government of their relations with one another. Without this healing act the whole structure and validity of international law is forever impaired.

VIII. All French territory should be freed and the invaded portions restored, and the wrong done to France by Prussia in 1871 in the matter of Alsace-Lorraine, which has unsettled the peace of the world for nearly fifty years, should be righted, in order that peace may once more be made secure in the interest of all.

IX. A readjustment of the frontiers of Italy should be effected along clearly recognizable lines of nationality.

X. The peoples of Austria-Hungary, whose place among the nations we wish to see safeguarded and assured, should be accorded the freest opportunity of autonomous development.

XI. Rumania, Serbia, and Montenegro should be evacuated; occupied territories restored; Serbia accorded free and secure access to the sea; and the relations of the several Balkan states to one another determined by friendly counsel along historically established lines of allegiance and nationality; and international guarantees of the political and economic independence and territorial integrity of the several Balkan states should be entered into.

XII. The Turkish portions of the present Ottoman Empire should be assured a secure sovereignty, but the other nationalities which are now under Turkish rule should be assured an undoubted security of life and an absolutely unmolested opportunity of autonomous development, and the Dardanelles should be permanently opened as a free passage to the ships and commerce of all nations under international guarantees.

XIII. An independent Polish state should be erected which should include the territories inhabited by indisputably Polish populations, which should be assured a free and secure access to the sea, and whose political and economic independence and territorial integrity should be guaranteed by international covenant.

XIV. A general association of nations must be formed under specific covenants for the purpose of affording mutual guarantees of political independence and territorial integrity to great and small states alike.

In regard to these essential rectifications of wrong and assertions of right we feel ourselves to be intimate partners of all the governments and peoples associated together against the Imperialists. We cannot be separated in interest or divided in purpose. We stand together until the end.

Adolf Hitler 1889–1945

NATIONALITY:
Austrian/German
WHEN:
1938
WHERE:
Berlin, Germany
YOU SHOULD KNOW:
Eduard Benes was President of
Czechoslovakia.

The Sudetenland was the German name for the areas of Czechoslovakia where a majority of the population were ethnic Germans. In March 1938, Germany had annexed Austria and was now threatening the same for the Sudetenland, on the grounds that the ethnic Germans were being oppressed by the Czechoslovak authorities, but in reality as a preliminary to taking over the whole country. In an attempt to prevent a wider war, the Western powers urged the Czechoslovak government to agree to the annexation. In Hitler's rant of September 26 during the negotiations for the Munich Agreement, which was signed on September 30, he claimed that he had no more territorial issues in Europe, but he took the rest of Czechoslovakia in the spring of 1939 and then the western area of Poland later in the year before turning his attention to his western neighbours.

'And now before us stands the last problem that must be solved and will be solved. It is the last territorial claim which I have to make in Europe, but it is the claim from which I will not recede and which, God willing, I will make good.

The history of the problem is as follows: in 1918 under the watchword 'The Right of the Peoples to Self-determination' Central Europe was torn in pieces and was newly formed by certain crazy so-called 'statesmen'. Without regard for the origin of the peoples, without regard for either their wish as nations or for economic necessities Central Europe at that time was broken up into atoms and new so-called States were arbitrarily formed. To this procedure Czechoslovakia owes its existence. This Czech state began with a single lie and the father of this lie was named Benes. This Mr Benes at that time appeared in Versailles and he first of all gave the assurance that there was a Czechoslovak nation. He was forced to invent this lie in order to give to the slender number of his own fellow-countrymen a somewhat greater range and thus a fuller justification . . .

So in the end through Mr Benes these Czechs annexed Slovakia. Since this state did not seem fitted to live, out of hand three-and-a-half million Germans were taken in violation of their right to self-determination and their wish for self-determination. Since even that did not suffice, over a million Magyars had to be added, then some Carpathian Russians, and at last several hundred thousand Poles.

That is this state which then later proceeded to call itself Czechoslovakia – in violation of the right of the peoples to self-determination, in violation of the clear wish and will of the nations to which this violence had been done . . .

I have only a few statements still to make: I am grateful to Mr Chamberlain for all his efforts. I have assured him that the German

Hitler declares his intention to march into Sudetenland.

people desires nothing else than peace, but I have also told him that I cannot go back behind the limits set to our patience. I have further assured him, and I repeat it here, that when this problem is solved there is for Germany no further territorial problem in Europe. And I have further assured him that at the moment when Czechoslovakia solves her problems, that means when the Czechs have come to terms with their other minorities, and that peaceably and not through oppression, then I have no further interest in the Czech state. And that is guaranteed to him! We want no Czechs!

But in the same way I desire to state before the German people that with regard to the problem of the Sudeten Germans my patience is now at an end! I have made Mr Benes an offer which is nothing but the carrying into effect of what he himself has promised. The decision now lies in his hands: Peace or War! . . .

Now I go before my people as its first soldier and behind me – that the world should know – there marches a people and a different people from that of 1918! . . .

And we wish now to make our will as strong as it was in the time of our fight, the time when I, as a simple unknown soldier, went forth to conquer a Reich and never doubted of success and final victory . . .

In this hour we all wish to form a common will and that will must be stronger than every hardship and every danger.

And if this will is stronger than hardship and danger then one day it will break down hardship and danger.

We are determined!

Now let Mr Benes make his choice! 🟥

Neville Chamberlain 1869–1940

In a radio broadcast on September 27, 1938, at the height of the crisis surrounding Germany's intention to annexe the Sudetenland, British Prime Minister Neville Chamberlain gave an update on negotiations. While he sympathized with the Czechoslovak government's attitude to the idea of giving up their defensive border, he was going to sacrifice that country's sovereignty to appease Hitler and (as he still hoped) prevent a wider war. It was a useless hope as Hitler intended to occupy the Sudetenland in any case, and for every concession Chamberlain wrenched out the Czechoslovak government, Hitler imposed new ones.

NATIONALITY:
British
WHEN:
1938
WHERE:
London, England
YOU SHOULD KNOW:
Chamberlain's father and half-brother had also been Members of Parliament.

Tomorrow Parliament is going to meet, and I shall be making a full statement of the events which have led up to the present anxious and critical situation.

An earlier statement would not have been possible when I was flying backwards and forwards across Europe, and the position was changing from hour to hour. But today there is a lull for a brief time, and I want to say a few words to you, men and women of Britain and the Empire, and perhaps to others as well.

First of all I must say something to those who have written to my wife or myself in these last weeks to tell us of their gratitude for my efforts and to assure us of their prayers for my success. Most of these letters have come from women – mothers or sisters of our own countrymen. But there are countless others besides – from France, from Belgium, from Italy, and even from Germany, and it has been heartbreaking to read the growing anxiety they reveal and their intense relief when they thought, too soon, that the danger of war was past.

If I felt my responsibility heavy before, to read such letters has made it seem almost overwhelming. How horrible, fantastic, incredible it is that we should be digging trenches and trying on gas-masks here because of a quarrel in a far-away country between people of whom we know nothing. It seems still more impossible that a quarrel which has already been settled in principle should be the subject of war.

I can well understand the reasons why the Czech Government have felt unable to accept the terms which have been put before them in the German memorandum. Yet I believe after my talks with Herr Hitler that, if only time were allowed, it ought to be possible for the arrangements for transferring the territory that the Czech Government has agreed to give to Germany to be settled by agreement under conditions which would assure fair treatment to the population concerned.

You know already that I have done all that one man can do to compose this quarrel. After my visits to Germany I have realised vividly how Herr Hitler feels that he must champion other Germans, and his indignation that grievances have not been met before this. He told me privately, and last night he repeated publicly, that after this Sudeten German question is settled, that is the end of Germany's territorial claims in Europe.

After my first visit to Berchtesgaden I did get the assent of the Czech Government to proposals which gave the substance of what Herr Hitler wanted and I was taken completely by surprise when I got back to Germany and found that he insisted that the territory should be handed over to him immediately, and immediately occupied by German troops without previous arrangements for safeguarding the people within the territory who were not Germans, or did not want to join the German Reich.

I must say that I find this attitude unreasonable. If it arises out of any doubts that Herr Hitler feels about the intentions of the Czech Government to carry out their promises and hand over the territory, I have offered on part of the British Government to guarantee their words, and I am sure the value of our promise will not be underrated anywhere.

I shall not give up the hope of a peaceful solution, or abandon my efforts for peace, as long as any chance for peace remains. I would not hesitate to pay even a third visit to Germany if I thought it would do any good. But at this moment I see nothing further that I can usefully do in the way of mediation.

Meanwhile there are certain things we can and shall do at home. Volunteers are still wanted for air raid precautions, for fire brigade and police services, and for the Territorial units. I know that all of you, men and women alike, are ready to play your part in the defence of the country, and I ask you all to offer your services, if you have not already done so, to the local authorities, who will tell you if you are wanted and in what capacity.

Do not be alarmed if you hear of men being called up to man the anti-aircraft defences or ships. These are only precautionary measures such as a Government must take in times like this. But they do not necessarily mean that we have determined on war or that war is imminent.

However much we may sympathise with a small nation confronted by a big and powerful neighbour, we cannot in all circumstances undertake to involve the whole British Empire in war simply on her account. If we have to fight it must be on larger issues than that. I am myself a man of peace to the depths of my soul. Armed conflict between nations is a nightmare to me; but if I were convinced that any nation had made up its mind to dominate the world by fear of its force, I should feel that it must be resisted. Under such a domination life for people who believe in liberty would not be worth living; but war is a fearful thing, and we must be very clear, before we embark on it, that it is really the great issues that are at stake, and that the call to risk everything in their defence, when all the consequences are weighed, is irresistible.

For the present I ask you to wait as calmly as you can the events of the next few days. As long as war has not begun, there is always hope that it may be prevented, and you know that I am going to work for peace to the last moment. Good night. 🔸

Josiah Mwangi Kariuki 1929–1975

Josiah Kariuki became politicized at an early age after hearing a speech by socialist leader Jomo Kenyatta denouncing British policy in the area. Imprisoned for seven years for his part in the Mau Mau uprising, after independence in 1963 he became Kenyatta's private secretary and held a number of government posts. This version of the oath was repeated seven times and people taking it had to bite into a slaughtered goat. The British spread rumours about much wilder rituals including bestiality, rape and human sacrifice. The uprising cost the lives of 32 Europeans and many thousands of Kenyans.

NATIONALITY:
Kenyan
WHEN:
1950s
WHERE:
Kenya
YOU SHOULD KNOW:
There were several versions of the 'Mau Mau' oath.

I speak the truth and vow before God
And before this movment,
The movement of Unity,
The Unity which is put to the test
The Unity that is mocked with the name of 'Mau Mau',
That I shall go forward to fight for the land,
The lands of Kirinyaga that we cultivated,
The lands which were taken by the Europeans.
And if I fail to do this
May this oath kill me,
May this seven kill me,
May this goat kill me. 🔸

Neville Chamberlain 1869–1940

NATIONALITY:
British
WHEN:
1938
WHERE:
Heston Aerodrome, England
YOU SHOULD KNOW:
In Czechoslovakia the Munich Agreement was called the Munich Dictate.

On September 30, 1938 the leaders of Germany, France, the United Kingdom and Italy met to finalize the details of the handover of the Sudetenland. The Czechoslovak government was not invited to send a representative. The Czechoslovaks had hoped that France – with whom they had alliances – would defend them. If France had declared war on Germany then, the UK's alliance with the former would have guaranteed British participation in hostilities; also, the Soviet Union had expressed a willingness to co-operate if required. Because Hitler had overstated German military power, France felt in no position to intervene militarily and Italian leader Mussolini, who knew the true state of Germany's forces, persuaded Hitler to sign the agreement in order to buy time for both countries to build up more armaments. Thus Mr Chamberlain came back from Munich with another agreement that the Germans had no intention of keeping.

Chamberlain declares 'Peace in our time' after returning from signing the Munich Agreement.

' My good friends, for the second time in our history a British Prime Minister has returned from Germany bringing peace with honour. I believe it is peace for our time. '

Neville Chamberlain 1869–1940

Despite Hitler's assurances of the previous year, Germany continued its expansionist activities in 1939 and on September 1 invaded Poland, which it had agreed under the terms of the Molotov-Ribbentrop Pact to divide with the Soviet Union. France declared war on Poland and the United Kingdom followed suit on September 3, but neither country did anything concrete to assist their allies. The Soviet invasion of the east of the country began in the middle of the month. Parliament immediately passed the National Service (Armed Forces) Act, enacting the conscription of all male residents of the UK aged between eighteen and forty-one. Chamberlain hung on as Prime Minister until May 1940 but resigned in the wake of the German invasion of the Netherlands, Belgium and France.

NATIONALITY:
British
WHEN:
1939
WHERE:
London, England
YOU SHOULD KNOW:
When it had become obvious that the invasion of Poland by Germany was inevitable, three Polish destroyers that would otherwise have been sunk by the German navy were moved to Edinburgh and fought alongside the Royal Navy.

Newspapers spread the word.

I am speaking to you from the cabinet room of 10 Downing St. This morning the British Ambassador in Berlin handed the German Government a final note stating that, unless we heard from them by 11 o'clock that they were prepared at once to withdraw their troops from Poland, a state of war would exist between us. I have to tell you now that no such undertaking has been received, and that consequently this country is at war with Germany.

You can imagine what a bitter blow it is to me that all my long struggle to win peace has failed. Yet I cannot believe that there is anything more, or anything different, that I could have done, and that would have been more successful. Up to the very last it would have been quite possible to have arranged a peaceful and honourable settlement between Germany and Poland. But Hitler would not have it; he had evidently made up his mind to attack Poland whatever happened. And although he now says he put forward reasonable proposals which were rejected by the Poles, that is not a true statement. The proposals were never shown to the Poles, nor to us. And though they were announced in the German broadcast on Thursday night, Hitler did not wait to hear comments on them but ordered his troops to cross the Polish frontier the next morning.

His action shows convincingly that there is no chance of expecting that this man will ever give up his practice of using force to gain his will. He can only be stopped by force, and we and France are today in fulfillment of our obligations going to the aid of Poland who is so bravely resisting this wicked and unprovoked attack upon her people. We have a clear conscience, we have done all that any country could do to establish peace, but a situation in which no word given by Germany's ruler could be trusted, and no people or country could feel itself safe, had become intolerable. And now that we have resolved to finish it, I know that you will all play your parts with calmness and courage.

David Farragut 1801–1870

NATIONALITY:
American
WHEN:
1864
WHERE:
Mobile Bay, Alabama, USA
YOU SHOULD KNOW:
Farragut joined the Navy at the age of nine and commanded his first ship – a prize taken by USS *Essex* in the War of 1812 – aged twelve.

Farragut's record in the Civil War was mixed, but one of his greatest tactical triumphs was at Mobile Bay on August 5, 1864, when he guessed that the mines laid in the bay – which were known as torpedoes at the time – would have been in the water so long that many of them would have failed. From his perch in the rigging of the USS Hartford, *he saw that other ships in his fleet were moving backwards. When the reply to his query of why they were not going forwards was 'Torpedoes', he simply ordered them to continue their attack. It was a decisive victory and led to the capture of the Confederacy's last major port on the Gulf of Mexico, cutting off more supplies and increasing the Union stranglehold on the south.*

Admiral David Glasgow Farragut

Damn the torpedoes! Four bells. Captain Drayton, go ahead! Jouett, full speed!

Osama bin Laden born 1957

In February 1998, the militant group al-Qaeda released a fatwa against America and Americans, citing the continuing US military presence in Saudi Arabia after the First Gulf War – to them holy land that no non-Muslim should set foot on – and American foreign policy towards Israel as justification for, and a call to carry out, attacks on them. The group had already carried out attacks on American civilian targets, notably the first on the World Trade Center in 1993, and many against American military personnel. In August, US embassies in Tanzania and Kenya were attacked, resulting in the deaths of some 300 people and injuries to more than 4,000, most of whom were locals, and in 2000 the USS Cole *was bombed, giving the movement confidence for the devastating attacks in America the following year.*

NATIONALITY:
Stateless
WHEN:
1998
WHERE:
Somewhere in Afghanistan
YOU SHOULD KNOW:
A fatwa is a religious opinion, issued by an Islamic scholar. To Sunni Muslims they are non-binding, but they may be binding to Shia Muslims, depending on the scholar's status.

> For more than seven years the US has been occupying the lands of Islam in the holiest of places, the Arabian peninsula, plundering its riches, dictating to its rulers, humiliating its peple, terrorizing its neighbours, and turning its bases in the peninsula into a spearhead through which to fight the neighbouring Muslim peoples. The ruling to kill the Americans and their allies—civilian or military—is an individual duty for every Muslim who can do it in any country in which it is possible to do it.

Oliver Cromwell 1599–1658

After the deposition and death of Charles I in January 1649, the Irish Catholic population and the Scots began violent revolts against British rule and murdered large numbers of Protestants. Cromwell led an army to Ireland to defeat the rebellion, but the cruelty of his actions in suppressing it, by which the populations of entire towns were slaughtered, led to centuries of resentment. Because it was a Catholic rebellion he appears to have seen it in terms of a holy war. The following year, he undertook a similar operation against the rebelling Scots who had proclaimed the son of the old King, monarch. Because they were predominantly Presbyterians, he was less blood-thirsty than in Ireland.

NATIONALITY:
British
WHEN:
1649
WHERE:
Ireland
YOU SHOULD KNOW:
In 1661, on the twenty-second anniversary of the execution of Charles I, Cromwell's body was disinterred from its vault at Westminster Abbey and ritually executed.

> Put your trust in God, my boys, and keep your powder dry.

Charles I is beheaded.

Charles I born 1600, reigned 1625–1649

The English Civil War lasted on and off from 1642 to 1649. It was about both politics and religion, with a strong-minded Parliament battling with a royalist faction led by a king who believed he was divinely appointed and answerable only to God. The king and the Archbishop of Canterbury were seen to be trying to bring the Church of England closer to Roman Catholicism, which was outlawed at the time. Puritans and other non-conformists were persecuted, even to the point of torture. The king had also been raising taxes illegally – only Parliament had the power to do so – and there were fears that he was trying to create an absolute monarchy. In 1647, the king had escaped from the siege of Oxford to the Scots army, who handed him over to the Parliamentarian army. After a show trial in which we was found guilty of treason, he was executed on January 30, 1649. He said the words below from the scaffold just before his execution.

NATIONALITY:
British
WHEN:
1649
WHERE:
London, England
YOU SHOULD KNOW:
Charles I was the second king of England to be declared a saint. The other was Saint Edward the Confessor.

'I must tell you that the liberty and freedom consists in having of Government, those laws by which their life and their goods may be most their own. It is not for having share in Government, Sir, that is nothing pertaining to them. A subject and a sovereign are clean different things. If I would have given way to an arbitrary way, for to have all laws changed according to the Power of the Sword, I needed not to have come here, and therefore I tell you . . . that I am the martyr of the people . . .

I go from a corruptible to an incorruptible Crown, where no disturbance can be, no disturbance in the world. '

Winston Churchill 1874–1965

NATIONALITY:
British
WHEN:
1940
WHERE:
London, England
YOU SHOULD KNOW:
Churchill spent most of the 1930s isolated from power, until he was made First Lord of the Admiralty on September 3, 1939 – the day Great Britain declared war on Germany.

During the 'phoney' war after the invasion of Poland, Winston Churchill had urged for a British forces' occupation of strategic sites in Norway and Sweden, but did not get the backing of Prime Minister Chamberlain or the rest of the cabinet. After the start of the German invasion of Norway in April 1940, it became obvious that very few people apart from some Conservative MPs had faith in Chamberlain's ability to lead the country through the inevitable war and he resigned. Churchill's first speech to the House of Commons as Prime Minister, given three days after his appointment on May 13, is the first of the memorable war-time speeches in which he stirred the public into supporting the war. He concluded:

' . . . I would say to the House, as I said to those who have joined this government: 'I have nothing to offer but blood, toil, tears and sweat.'

We have before us an ordeal of the most grievous kind. We have before us many, many long months of struggle and of suffering. You ask, what is our policy? I can say: It is to wage war, by sea, land and air, with all our might and with all the strength that God can give us; to wage war against a monstrous tyranny, never surpassed in the dark, lamentable catalogue of human crime. That is our policy. You ask, what is our aim? I can answer in one word: It is victory, victory at all costs, victory in spite of all terror, victory, however long and hard the road may be; for without victory, there is no survival. Let that be realised; no survival for the British Empire, no survival for all that the British Empire has stood for, no survival for the urge and impulse of the ages, that mankind will move forward towards its goal. But I take up my task with buoyancy and hope. I feel sure that our cause will not be suffered to fail among men. At this time I feel entitled to claim the aid of all, and I say, 'come then, let us go forward together with our united strength. '

Suleyman the Magnificent

born c. 1495, reigned 1520–1566

NATIONALITY:
Ottoman Turkish
WHEN:
1526
WHERE:
Mohacs, Hungary

During the reign of Suleyman the Magnificent, the Ottoman Empire expanded greatly until at its height it covered land from west of Algiers to Persia and almost all of the Balkan Peninsula. At the Battle of Mohács in 1526, the superior numbers and tactics of the invaders defeated the Hungarian defenders in under two hours. They combined infantry and cavalry with ambush and counter-attack in a devastating fashion that old-fashioned medieval methods could not hope to beat. In the battle the 20-year-old Hungarian king fell off his horse face-down into a ditch. His gold armour was so heavy that he could not move and he was found the following day. This undignified death moved Suleyman to say the words below.

' I came indeed in arms against him; but it was not my wish that he should be thus cut off while he scarcely tasted the sweets of life and royalty. '

Ottoman emperor Suleyman the Magnificent

British soldiers fighting at Dunkirk.

Winston Churchill 1874–1965

NATIONALITY:
British
WHEN:
1940
WHERE:
London, England
YOU SHOULD KNOW:
More than 30,000 men died during the evacuation.

The lightning-swift advance of German forces across northern France in May and the surrender of Belgium cut off most of the Allied troops, leaving them pinned against the English Channel. Between May 26 and June 4, 1940 more than 338,000 British, French and Canadian soldiers were evacuated from the area around Dunkirk in a flotilla of every type of vessel that could be found, with the Navy protecting them from the U-boats of the German Navy and the Royal Air Force protecting them from the Luftwaffe. On the last day of the rescue, Winston Churchill addressed the House of Commons, trying both to instil a sense of danger in the British public and to obtain assistance from the American government. He ended the long speech detailing the course of the operation and the losses of men and material with a stirring call to arms.

Even though large tracts of Europe and many old and famous States have fallen or may fall into the grip of the Gestapo and all the odious apparatus of Nazi rule, we shall not flag or fail. We shall go on to the end, we shall fight in France, we shall fight on the seas and oceans, we shall fight with growing confidence and growing strength in the air, we shall defend our Island, whatever the cost may be, we shall fight on the beaches, we shall fight on the landing grounds, we shall fight in the fields and in the streets, we shall fight in the hills; we shall never surrender, and even if, which I do not for a moment believe, this Island or a large part of it were subjugated and starving, then our Empire beyond the seas, armed and guarded by the British Fleet, would carry on the struggle, until, in God's good time, the New World, with all its power and might, steps forth to the rescue and the liberation of the old. "

Hiram W. Johnson 1866–1945

A staunch isolationist, Senator Johnson was vehemently against the proposed entry of the US into World War I, and in a speech to the US Senate in early 1917 argued that one problem was that the beginning of the war had been surrounded in so much propaganda it was difficult to tell which side was at fault and therefore which side the US should join, if at all. The use of propaganda surrounding warfare continues to this day, and its effect on public opinion is all the more pronounced because modern media and information technology allow it to be disseminated so quickly.

NATIONALITY:
American
WHEN:
1917
WHERE:
Washington, DC, USA
YOU SHOULD KNOW:
Hiram Johnson represented California for 35 years, first as governor, then senator.

" The first casualty when war comes, is truth. "

Sir Charles Dilke 1843–1911

Sir Charles Dilke was under-Secretary to the British Foreign Office when the decision to invade Egypt in order to protect the Suez Canal was launched in July 1882. An insurrection, begun under the leadership of an army officer called Ahmed Urabi, led to the deployment of the British and French fleets to Alexandria in May 1882, but in the end the British acted alone and the rebellion was ended at the Battle of Tel el-Kebir on September 13 by an army under the control of Sir Garnet Wolseley. The occupation, which was intended to be only temporary, lasted until 1956.

NATIONALITY:
British
WHEN:
1882
WHERE:
London, England
YOU SHOULD KNOW:
He lost his role in government in 1885 after a scandal in which he was accused of committing adultery with Virginia Crawford, the daughter of his mistress.

" As regards the Suez Canal, England has a double interest; it has a predominant commercial interest, because 82 per cent of the trade passing through the Canal is British trade, and it has a predominant political interest caused by the fact that the Canal is the principal highway to India, Ceylon, the Straits and British Burmah . . . China, where we have vast interests to our Colonial Empire in Australia and New Zealand. "

Nazi soldiers salvaging belongings left by Russians retreating to Leningrad.

Joseph Stalin 1879–1953

On June 22, 1941 German troops crossed western borders of the poorly defended Soviet Union, with which it had signed a non-aggression pact two years earlier when the two countries divided up Poland between themselves. On July 3, Stalin made a broadcast (extracts below), calling on citizens to fight the German troops by any means, send all useful material, including grain, to the east where it could be protected and used in the war effort, to destroy anything that might prove of use to the Germans and to denounce any third columnists whose words or actions were detrimental to the war effort.

❛ Comrades! Citizens! Brothers and sisters! Men of our army and navy! I am addressing you, my friends.

The perfidious military attack on our fatherland, begun on June 22 by Hitler's Germany, is continuing . . .

Above all, it is essential that our people, the Soviet people, should understand the full immensity of the danger that threatens our country and abandon all complacency, all heedlessness, all those moods of peaceful, constructive work . . . there must be no room in our ranks for whimperers and cowards, for panicmongers and deserters, our people must know no fear in the fight and must selflessly join our patriotic war of liberation, our war against the Fascist enslavers . . .

The people of the Soviet Union must rise against the enemy and defend their rights and their land. The Red Army, Red Navy and all

NATIONALITY:
Georgian
WHEN:
1941
WHERE:
Moscow, Russia
YOU SHOULD KNOW:
More than 23,000,000 Soviet citizens – military and civilians – died during World War II, amounting to 13.71 per cent of the population. Only Poland lost a greater proportion of its population, 16.70 per cent – 5,600,000 people.

citizens of the Soviet Union must defend every inch of Soviet soil, must fight to the last drop of blood for our towns and villages.

We must wage a ruthless fight against all disorganizers of the rear, deserters, panicmongers, rumourmongers, exterminate spies, diversionists, enemy parachutists . . .

We must reckon with all this and not fall victim to provocation. All who by their panicmongering and cowardice hinder the work of defence, no matter who they are, must be immediately hauled before a military tribunal . . .

Collective farmers must drive off all their cattle and turn over their grain to the state authorities for transportation to the rear. All valuable property including non-ferrous metals, grain and fuel which cannot be withdrawn must without fail be destroyed.

In areas occupied by the enemy, guerrilla units, mounted and on foot, must be formed; diversionist groups must be organized to combat enemy troops, to foment guerrilla warfare everywhere, to blow up bridges, roads, damage telephone and telegraph lines, and to set fire to forests, stores and transports . . .

Forward to our victory!

Muhammad Ali born 1942

Early in 1966, as more troops were needed to fight in Vietnam, the regulations concerning exemption from the draft were revised and one of the people caught in the wider net was World Heavyweight Champion boxer Muhammad Ali, who was by now also a prominent member of the Nation of Islam movement, with controversial opinions. After he received notification of his revised status, he publicly stated that as far as he was concerned war not ordered by Allah or the Prophet was against the teachings of the Koran and that he was not trying to dodge the draft but a conscientious objector. When he attended his induction in April, he refused to step forward when his name was called. Within hours he had lost his world title, boxing commissions started to revoke his boxing licences, he became vilified in the mainstream media and two months later he was convicted of draft dodging.

NATIONALITY:
American
WHEN:
1966
WHERE:
Miami, Florida, USA
YOU SHOULD KNOW:
The Supreme Court overturned his conviction in 1971, ruling that insufficient note had been taken of his conscientious objection.

Keep asking me, no matter how long,
On the war in Vietnam, I'll still sing this song:
I ain't got no quarrel with no Viet Cong.

Ali, interviewed by the press after his indictment.

AL-Jazeera Exclusive

خاص بالجزيرة

Osama Bin Laden appeared on Al-Jazeera television praising the attacks of September 11.

Osama bin Laden born 1957

In an interview in October 2001 on the Al-Jazeera Arabic television network conducted a few days after American operations in Afghanistan began, Osama bin Laden admitted inciting acts of violence against the West, but not any responsibility, and said that if America had proof it should show it. He used what he described as the West's oppression of Muslims in Palestine, and the deaths of millions in Iraq during the First Gulf War as justification for retaliatory attacks on Westerners and predicted the fall of the West. In response to a question from the interviewer about whether he regarded the actions of the 9/11 hijackers as terrorism, he described such actions as self-defence, defence of the Palestinians and the liberation of holy sites and possessesions and added:

NATIONALITY:
Stateless
WHEN:
2001
WHERE:
Somewhere in Afghanistan
YOU SHOULD KNOW:
The interview was shown on CNN in January 2002.

If inciting people to do that is terrorism, and if killing those who kill our sons is terrorism, then let history be witness that we are terrorists.

Laurence Binyon 1869–1943

This poem was written by Laurence Binyon at the outbreak of World War I when the toll of casualties was a shock to everyone. It is widely used at Remembrance Day services in many Commonwealth countries and at Anzac Day commemorations in Australia and New Zealand. The last line of the fourth verse – the citation – is repeated. Binyon worked in the British Museum in London and was too old to be drafted for active service, but volunteered for work as a medical orderly with an ambulance unit on the Western Front in 1916. He is commemorated on a slab in Westminster Abbey's Poets Corner, along with other war poets such as Wilfred Owen.

NATIONALITY:
British
WHEN:
1914
WHERE:
London, England
YOU SHOULD KNOW:
Anzac Day is on April 25, and commemorates the first landing of Australian and New Zealand troops in the disastrous Gallipoli campaign of 1915.

FOR THE FALLEN

With proud thanksgiving, a mother for her children,
England mourns for her dead across the sea.
Flesh of her flesh they were, spirit of her spirit,
Fallen in the cause of the free.

Solemn the drums thrill; Death august and royal
Sings sorrow up into immortal spheres,
There is music in the midst of desolation
And a glory that shines upon our tears.

They went with songs to the battle, they were young,
Straight of limb, true of eye, steady and aglow.
They were staunch to the end against odds uncounted;
They fell with their faces to the foe.

They shall grow not old, as we that are left grow old:
Age shall not weary them, nor the years condemn.
At the going down of the Sun and in the morning
We will remember them. We will remember them.

They mingle not with their laughing comrades again;
They sit no more at familiar tables of home;
They have no lot in our labour of the day-time;
They sleep beyond England's foam.

But where our desires are and our hopes profound,
Felt as a well-spring that is hidden from sight,
To the innermost heart of their own land they are known
As the stars are known to the Night.

As the stars that shall be bright when we are dust,
Moving in marches upon the heavenly plain;
As the stars that are starry in the time of our darkness,
To the end, to the end, they remain.

*Poppies in the Garden
of Remembrance at
Westminster Abbey*

Dwight D. Eisenhower 1890–1969

NATIONALITY:
American
WHEN:
1953
WHERE:
Washington, DC, USA
YOU SHOULD KNOW:
Eisenhower's war-time headquarters in London was at 20 Grosvenor Square.

In one of his first major speeches after his inauguration – known as the 'chance for peace' speech – President Eisenhower spoke to the American Society of Newspaper Editors on April 16, 1953. As Supreme Allied Commander in Europe during World War II and a veteran of World War I, he had seen enough war to last a lifetime and pledged to use the nation's wealth for better projects. Within weeks he had signed the armistice that ended the Korean War and by the end of the year he had outlined his proposals for a body concerned with nuclear cooperation and monitoring, which was set up in 1957 as the 'Atoms for Peace' organization – now the International Atomic Energy Agency.

' . . . In this spring of 1953 the free world weighs one question above all others: the chances for a just peace for all peoples. To weigh this chance is to summon instantly to mind another recent moment of great decision. It came with that yet more hopeful spring of 1945, bright with the promise of victory and of freedom. The hopes of all just men in that moment, too, was a just and lasting peace . . .

This common purpose lasted an instant and perished. The nations of the world divided to follow two distinct roads . . .

The way chosen by the United States was plainly marked by a few clear precepts, which govern its conduct in world affairs . . .

This way was faithful to the spirit that inspired the United Nations: to prohibit strife, to relieve tensions, to banish fears. This way was to control and to reduce armaments. This way was to allow all nations to devote their energies and resources to the great and good tasks of healing the war's wounds, of clothing and feeding and housing the needy, of perfecting a just political life, of enjoying the fruits of their own toil.

The Soviet government held a vastly different vision of the future. In the world of its design, security was to be found, not in mutual trust and mutual aid but in force: huge armies, subversion, rule of neighbor nations. The goal was power superiority at all cost. Security was to be sought by denying it to all others . . .

The amassing of Soviet power alerted free nations to a new danger of aggression. It compelled them in self-defense to spend unprecedented money and energy for armaments. It forced them to develop weapons of war now capable of inflicting instant and terrible punishment upon any aggressor.

It instilled in the free nations . . . the unshakable conviction that, as long as there persists a threat to freedom, they must, at any cost, remain armed, strong, and ready for the risk of war.

It inspired them – and let none doubt this – to attain a unity of purpose and will beyond the power of propaganda or pressure to break, now or ever . . .

The free nations, most solemnly and repeatedly, have assured the Soviet Union that their firm association has never had any aggressive purpose whatsoever. Soviet leaders, however, have seemed to persuade themselves, or tried to persuade their people, otherwise.

And so it has come to pass that the Soviet Union itself has shared and suffered the very fears it has fostered in the rest of the world . . .

What can the world, or any nation in it, hope for if no turning is found on this dread road?

The worst to be feared and the best to be expected can be simply stated.

The worst is atomic war.

The best would be this: a life of perpetual fear and tension; a burden of arms draining the wealth and the labor of all peoples; a wasting of strength that defies the American system or the Soviet system or any system to achieve true abundance and happiness for the peoples of this Earth . . .

This is one of those times in the affairs of nations when the gravest choices must be made, if there is to be a turning toward a just and lasting peace.

It is a moment that calls upon the governments of the world to speak their intentions with simplicity and with honesty.

It calls upon them to answer the question that stirs the hearts of all sane men: is there no other way the world may live? . . .

The free world knows, out of the bitter wisdom of experience, that vigilance and sacrifice are the price of liberty . . .

So the new Soviet leadership now has a precious opportunity to awaken, with the rest of the world, to the point of peril reached and to help turn the tide of history.

Will it do this?

We do not yet know. Recent statements and gestures of Soviet leaders give some evidence that they may recognize this critical moment . . .

As progress in all these areas strengthens world trust, we could proceed concurrently with the next great work – the reduction of the burden of armaments now weighing upon the world. To this end we would welcome and enter into the most solemn agreements . . .

The peace we seek, founded upon decent trust and cooperative effort among nations, can be fortified, not by weapons of war but by wheat and by cotton, by milk and by wool, by meat and timber and rice. These are words that translate into every language on Earth. These are the needs that challenge this world in arms . . .

We are prepared to reaffirm, with the most concrete evidence, our readiness to help build a world in which all peoples can be productive and prosperous . . .

I know of only one question upon which progress waits. It is this: What is the Soviet Union ready to do? . . .

. . . where then is the concrete evidence of the Soviet Union's concern for peace?

There is, before all peoples, a precarious chance to turn the black tide of events.

If we fail to strive to seize this chance, the judgment of future ages will be harsh and just.

If we strive but fail and the world remains armed against itself, it at least would need be divided no longer in its clear knowledge of who has condemned humankind to this fate.

The purpose of the United States, in stating these proposals, is simple. These proposals spring, without ulterior motive or political passion, from our calm conviction that the hunger for peace is in the hearts of all people – those of Russia and of China no less than of our own country.

They conform to our firm faith that God created man to enjoy, not destroy, the fruits of the Earth and of their own toil.

They aspire to this: the lifting, from the backs and from the hearts of men, of their burden of arms and of fears, so that they may find before them a golden age of freedom and of peace.

Mao Zedong 1893–1976

NATIONALITY:
Chinese
WHERE:
Hunan, China
WHEN:
1927
YOU SHOULD KNOW:
Mao Zedong learned about Communism while working as an assistant librarian at Beijing University.

In 1927 Mao Zedong (Mao Tse-tung), co-founder of the Communist Party of China, conducted an investigation into the possibilities of stirring up a revolution among the peasants of Hunan Province. Previous attempts had been made in cities, but because the urban population made up only a small fraction of the total, these had foundered. He concluded that the rural population was ripe for revolt and later in the year led the unsuccessful Autumn Harvest Uprising in Changsha, Hunan, before retreating to Jiangxi province, where he helped to set up the small Soviet Republic of China in the Jinggang Mountains. Any people who dissented from his policies of land, military or party reform were swiftly, and brutally, eliminated.

' . . . In a very short time, in China's central, southern and northern provinces, several hundred million peasants will rise like a mighty storm, like a hurricane, a force so swift and violent that no power, however great, will be able to hold it back. They will smash all the trammels that bind them and rush forward along the road to liberation. They will sweep all the imperialists, warlords, corrupt officials, local tyrants and evil gentry into their graves. Every revolutionary party and every revolutionary comrade will be put to the test, to be accepted or rejected as they decide. There are three alternatives. To march at their head and lead them? To trail behind them, gesticulating and criticizing? Or to stand in their way and oppose them? Every Chinese is free to choose, but events will force you to make the choice quickly. '

Mao Zedong 1893–1976

NATIONALITY:
Chinese
WHEN:
1949
WHERE:
Beijing, China

On June 30, 1949 Chairman Mao gave an address to celebrate the Communist Party of China's twenty-eighth anniversary, which is known as his 'lean to one side' speech. Although they had similar ideologies, China and the Soviet Union shared a mutual distrust, and in this speech Mao sought to reassure the Soviet government that China was not abandoning its Communist ways. It was also a warning to the American administration and to dissidents within the country that China remained firmly anti-imperialist, in part because of Chinese experiences at the hands of the West during the nineteenth century. The Soviet government remained unconvinced of his goodwill and sincerity and relations remained frosty during the following decades.

‘ . . . You are leaning to one side. Exactly. The 40 years' experience of Sun Yat-sen and the 28 years' experience of the Communist Party have taught us to lean to one side, and we are firmly convinced that in order to win victory and consolidate it we must lean to one side. In the light of the experiences accumulated in these 40 years and these 28 years, all Chinese without exception must lean either to the side of imperialism or to the side of socialism. Sitting on the fence will not do, nor is there a third road. We oppose the Chiang Kai-shek reactionaries who lean to the side of imperialism, and we also oppose the illusions about a third road . . . ’

Robert Nivelle 1857–1924

General Nivelle of Verdun

In the early stages of World War I, Colonel Robert Nivelle had been so successful in artillery action against the Germans that he was promoted to general and was designated to lead the French Second Army at the Battle of Verdun. His tactics were successful, but costly in terms of his own soldiers' lives. The phrase quoted is the termination of his order of the day for June 23, 1916. Over the ensuing months the French did re-take some ground, and in December he was made commander-in-chief of the French armies. Although a brilliant tactician at a local level, his inflexibility and arrogance did not make him suited to command the whole army. After the Nivelle Offensive of 1917, which cost the lives of 187,000 of his soldiers, he was removed from his command and subsequently sent to Africa.

‘ Ils ne passeront pas! (They shall not pass!) ’

NATIONALITY:
French
WHEN:
1916
WHERE:
Verdun, France
YOU SHOULD KNOW:
Nivelle's phrase was used on propaganda posters in the same way as Uncle Sam's 'I want you for U.S. Army' and Kitchener's 'Your country needs you'.

Donald Rumsfeld born 1932

NATIONALITY:
American
WHEN:
2003
WHERE:
Washington, DC, USA
YOU SHOULD KNOW:
The Baghdad Museum, from which 15,000 artefacts were looted under the eyes of coalition forces and whose doors were concreted up for several years to prevent further losses, re-opened in February 2009, two days after Abu Ghraib prison re-opened as Baghdad Central prison.

Within a day or so of the invasion of Iraq in the spring of 2003, journalists embedded with troops were sending back reports of widespread rejoicing, but mixed with scenes of violence, looting and destruction. On April 11, Defense Secretary Donald Rumsfeld and Chairman of the Joint Chiefs of Staff Richard B. Myers gave an upbeat news briefing. During the question-and-answer session after the briefing, several journalists asked about the negative coverage in some sections of the press. After saying that most of the looting was occurring at buildings that were symbols of the regime and joking 'Let's go get that newspaper' about one that had been particularly critical, Secretary Rumsfeld replied to the question, '...what plan was there to restore law and order?' with the comments below, which was widely reported around the world as an uncaring-sounding 'stuff happens'.

Rumsfeld: Well, let's just take a city. Take the port city, Umm Qasr – what the plan was. Well, the British went in, they built a pipeline bringing water in from Kuwait; they cleared the mine of ports; they brought ships in with food; they've been providing security. In fact, they've done such a lousy job, that the city has gone from 15,000 to 40,000. Now think of that. Why would people vote with their feet and go into this place that's so bad? The reason they're going in is because there's food, there's water, there's medicine and there's jobs. That's why. The British have done a fantastic job. They've done an excellent job.

And, does that mean you couldn't go in there and take a television camera or get a still photographer and take a picture of something that was imperfect, untidy? I could do that in any city in America. Think what's happened in our cities when we've had riots, and problems, and looting. Stuff happens! But in terms of what's going on in that country, it is a fundamental misunderstanding to see those images over and over and over again of some boy walking out with a vase and say, 'Oh, my goodness, you didn't have a plan.' That's nonsense. They know what they're doing, and they're doing a terrific job. And it's untidy, and freedom's untidy, and free people are free to make mistakes and commit crimes and do bad things. They're also free to live their lives and do wonderful things, and that's what's going to happen here.

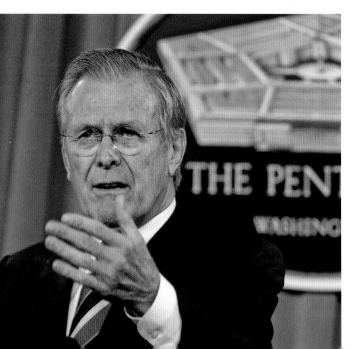

Donald Rumsfeld responding to press questions over his handling of the war in Iraq.

Vladimir Ilyich Lenin 1870–1924

After the crushing of the 1905 Russian Revolution, Lenin went into exile in Europe and by the time of the February Revolution of 1917, when the Tsar was toppled, was in neutral Switzerland, developing his version of Marxism and calling for World War I to change from a war between imperial powers to a class war. The provisional government's continuation of fighting in World War I led to disillusionment among the people, which Lenin and his fellow Bolsheviks exploited, leading to first the July Days unrest, then the October Revolution, which saw the Bolsheviks take power and Lenin become the first Chairman of the Council of People's Commissars. Within weeks he issued the Decree on Peace, calling for cease-fire negotiations (extracts).

Lenin adressing a meeting.

The workers' and peasants' government, created by the Revolution of October 24–25 and basing itself on the Soviet of Workers', Soldiers' and Peasants' Deputies, calls upon all the belligerent peoples and their government to start immediate negotiations for a just, democratic peace . . .

The governments and the bourgeoisie will make every effort to unite their forces and drown the workers' and peasants' revolution in blood. But the three years of war have been a good lesson to the masses – the Soviet movement in other countries and the mutiny in the German navy, which was crushed by the officer cadets of Wilhelm the hangman . . .

The workers' movement will triumph and will pave the way to peace and socialism.

NATIONALITY:
Russian
WHEN:
1917
WHERE:
Moscow, Russia
YOU SHOULD KNOW::
Russia left World War I on March 3, 1918, under the terms of the Treaty of Brest-Litovsk.

William T. Sherman 1820–1891

After the capture and near-destruction of Atlanta, General Sherman deployed his forces to protect his supply lines and set up a major stores depot at Allatoona some miles to the north of the city in a site protected by a man-made pass. Early in October, he realized that Confederate General Hood had targeted the depot and sent General Corse to take extra troops to defend the garrison. On October 5, the Confederate troops attacked, but after more than three hours of fierce fighting were forced to withdraw because they knew that reinforcements would soon be arriving from nearby Kennesaw Mountain as Sherman had signalled to that effect.

NATIONALITY:
American
WHEN:
1864
WHERE:
Kenneshaw Mountain, Georgia, USA
YOU SHOULD KNOW:
The exact wording of the signal is debated. Other versions are 'Hold the fort, we are coming.' and 'Hold the fort, help is coming.'.

Hold the fort, for I am coming.

A smiling Ho Chi Minh

Ho Chi Minh 1890–1969

During World War II, Vietnam had been occupied by the Japanese and after their defeat the Viet Minh – together with other revolutionary and nationalist groups such as the Constitutional Party and the Party for Independence – were determined not to allow the former colonial power, France, to reassert control. After the August Revolution of 1945, Emperor Bao Dai abdicated, Ho Chi Minh declared independence and the Viet Minh emerged from the ensuing bloodbath as the most powerful party. The statement below indicates the guerrilla tactics that his forces would use over the next eight years against the French and again against the American army between 1965 and 1975.

NATIONALITY:
Vietnamese
WHEN:
1946
WHERE:
Hanoi, Vietnam
YOU SHOULD KNOW:
The French government was forced to give up Vietnam after the Battle of Dien Bien Phu in 1954.

'If the tiger ever stands still, the elephant will crush him with his mighty tusks. But the tiger will not stand still. He will leap upon the back of the elephant, tearing huge chunks from his side, and then he will leap back into the dark jungle. And slowly the elephant will bleed to death. Such will be the war in Indochina.'

Ehud Olmert born 1945

NATIONALITY:
Israeli
WHEN:
2006
WHERE:
Jerusalem
YOU SHOULD KNOW:
The two captured soldiers' bodies were returned in 2008.

On July 12, 2006, Hezbollah launched rocket strikes into Israel and attacked two Israeli armoured cars near the border, killing three soldiers, wounding three and capturing two (five more were killed and three more wounded soon after). At a press conference with the Japanese Prime Minister Koizumi, the Israeli Prime Minister Olmert blamed the Lebanese government. Within hours, Israel launched strikes into southern Lebanon. Over the next three-and-a-half weeks, Israeli efforts to obliterate Hezbollah resulted in more than 115,000 shells being fired and the destruction of an estimated 400 miles of road, 15,000 homes (and 130,000 damaged), 350 schools, Beirut Airport, two hospitals, electricity, water and sewage plants and more than 20 fuel stations, resulting in more than 1,200 deaths. Hezbollah launched daily rocket strikes into Israel, killing about 160 people.

'. . . I want to make it clear: This morning's events were not a terrorist attack, but the action of a sovereign state that attacked Israel for no reason and without provocation. The Lebanese government, of which Hezbollah is a member, is trying to undermine regional stability. Lebanon is responsible and Lebanon will bear the consequences of its actions . . .'

Donald Rumsfeld born 1932

In a Q&A session at a NATO summit in June 2002, a journalist posed a question about terrorism and weapons of mass destruction (WMD) and what Secretary Rumsfeld meant when he said the situation was worse than generally understood. The reply hints that the intelligence community were digging into old data for clues as to whether Iraq retained – or was working on – WMD capability. This hunt resulted in such documents as the September dossier – the UK government list of (false) claims about such things as Iraqi attempts to buy uranium from Niger.

NATIONALITY:
American
WHEN:
2002
WHERE:
NATO HQ, Brussels, Belgium
YOU SHOULD KNOW:
As well as serving as Secretary of Defense twice, Donald Rumsfeld has also been White House Chief of Staff, US Ambassador to NATO and a member of the House of Representatives.

Sure. All of us in this business read intelligence information. And we read it daily and we think about it and it becomes, in our minds, essentially what exists. And that's wrong. It is not what exists.

I say that because I have had experiences where I have gone back and done a great deal of work and analysis on intelligence information and looked at important countries, target countries, looked at important subject matters with respect to those target countries and asked, probed deeper and deeper and kept probing until I found out what it is we knew, and when we learned it, and when it actually had existed. And I found that, not to my surprise, but I think anytime you look at it that way what you find is that there are very important pieces of intelligence information that countries, that spend a lot of money, and a lot of time with a lot of wonderful people trying to learn more about what's going in the world, did not know some significant event for two years after it happened, for four years after it happened, for six years after it happened, in some cases 11 and 12 and 13 years after it happened.

Now what is the message there? The message is that there are no 'knowns'. There are thing we know that we know. There are known unknowns. That is to say there are things that we now know we don't know. But there are also unknown unknowns. There are things we don't know we don't know. So when we do the best we can and we pull all this information together, and we then say well that's basically what we see as the situation, that is really only the known knowns and the known unknowns. And each year, we discover a few more of those unknown unknowns.

It sounds like a riddle. It isn't a riddle. It is a very serious, important matter.

There's another way to phrase that and that is that the absence of evidence is not evidence of absence. It is basically saying the same thing in a different way. Simply because you do not have evidence that something exists does not mean that you have evidence that it doesn't exist. And yet almost always, when we make our threat assessments, when we look at the world, we end up basing it on the first two pieces of that puzzle, rather than all three.

A painting of the Duke of Wellington on the eve of Waterloo

Arthur Wellesley, Duke of Wellington 1769–1852

Wellington described his soldiers on several occasions as the scum of the Earth, notably after the battle of Vitoria in 1813 when they had followed the battle with a night of looting and destruction. Here he is saying it in a conversation recorded by Philip Stanhope. The system of recruitment for the British army was haphazard, as the wealthy could buy rank while the majority of the lower ranks joined to 'take the king's shilling', with little regard to whether or not they were suited to military life. Parties of recruiters travelled across the country: a favourite method when recruits were needed was to get potential soldiers drunk so they either signed up recklessly or passed out and could be fooled the following morning into thinking they had joined.

NATIONALITY:
Anglo-Irish
WHEN:
1831
WHERE:
London, England
YOU SHOULD KNOW:
He is also reported to have said in Spain in 1809 that he didn't know what effect his inexperienced new recruits would have on the enemy but they frightened him.

A French army is composed very differently from ours. The conscription calls out a share of every class – no matter whether your son or my son – all must march; but our friends – I may say it in this room – are the very scum of the Earth. People talk of their enlisting from their fine military feeling – all stuff – no such thing. Some of our men enlist from having got bastard children – some for minor offences – many more for drink; but you can hardly conceive such a set brought together, and it really is wonderful that we should have made them the fine fellows they are.

Hamas

NATIONALITY:
Palestinian
WHEN:
1988
WHERE:
Gaza, Palestine
YOU SHOULD KNOW:
Hamas is an acronym for Harakat al Muqawama al Islamiyya – 'Islamic Resistance Movement'; also means 'zeal'.

Below is the introductory statement of the Hamas Charter or Covenant, which was formulated in August 1988, the year after the first Intifada in the occupied territories. Its 36 articles lay out the reasons for the militant group's foundation and its principles and objectives, including that it is an Islamic movement; that Palestine is an Islamic land, consecrated to be so for ever; that no one has the right to give up any of that land; that Israel should be destroyed; that all Muslims have the right and duty to destroy their enemies in Jihad; and that international peace conferences are only a means of setting infidels on Islamic land.

Allah is its target, the Prophet is its model, the Koran its constitution: Jihad is its path and death for the sake of Allah is the loftiest of its wishes.

Young supporters of Hamas march in Gaza City.

In The Name Of The Most Merciful Allah

Ye are the best nation that hath been raised up unto mankind: ye command that which is just, and ye forbid that which is unjust, and ye believe in Allah. And if they who have received the scriptures had believed, it had surely been the better for them: there are believers among them, but the greater part of them are transgressors. They shall not hurt you, unless with a slight hurt; and if they fight against you, they shall turn their backs to you, and they shall not be helped. They are smitten with vileness wheresoever they are found; unless they obtain security by entering into a treaty with Allah, and a treaty with men; and they draw on themselves indignation from Allah, and they are afflicted with poverty. This they suffer, because they disbelieved the signs of Allah, and slew the prophets unjustly; this, because they were rebellious, and transgressed. (Al-Imran, verses 109–111).

Israel will exist and will continue to exist until Islam will obliterate it, just as it obliterated others before it (The Martyr, Imam Hassan al-Banna, of blessed memory).

The Islamic world is on fire. Each of us should pour some water, no matter how little, to extinguish whatever one can without waiting for the others. (Sheikh Amjad al-Zahawi, of blessed memory).

Thomas 'Stonewall' Jackson

1824–1863

At the Battle of Chancellorsville, generals Lee and Jackson scored a notable success against the General Hooker's Army of the Potomac. At dusk, the assault ceased and Jackson made his way back to his HQ. A Confederate North Carolina regiment challenged the general with the traditional 'Who goes there?' but before anyone had a chance to respond fired on them, hitting the general and killing several staff members and horses. The injuries and the botched evacuation led to the amputation of one of his arms. He contracted pneumonia and died on May 10. Even in his final delerium, he was thinking of his forces, before finally finding peace.

It is the Lord's Day; my wish is fulfilled. I have always desired to die on Sunday . . .

Order A.P. Hill to prepare for action! Pass the infantry to the front rapidly! Tell Major Hawks . . . Let us cross over the river, and rest under the shade of the trees.

NATIONALITY:
American
WHEN:
1863
WHERE:
Guinea Station, Virginia, USA
YOU SHOULD KNOW:
Although General Jackson is buried at Lexington, Virginia, his amputated arm is buried in Orange County, near the field hospital where it was removed.

Emperor Hirohito

1901-1989, reigned 1926–89

NATIONALITY:
Japanese
WHEN:
1945
WHERE:
Tokyo, Japan
YOU SHOULD KNOW:
There were at least two attempts to destroy the recording before it was broadcast and it was eventually smuggled out of the imperial palace to the radio station in a laundry basket.

After the bombing of Hiroshima and Nagasaki, the Japanese government was forced to advise the Emperor that surrender to the Allies was the only option and on August 13 or 14 the Emperor recorded the Gyokuon-hoso, the Jewel Voice broadcast, in which he read out the Rescript on the Termination of War, accepting the terms of the Potsdam Declaration of July 26: unconditional surrender. Japanese refusal to agree to the declaration had been the final reason for President Truman's decision to use atomic weapons on Japanese civilians. The formal language used and scratchy quality of the broadcast confused many of the population.

To our good and loyal subjects: After pondering deeply the general trends of the world and the actual conditions obtaining in our empire today, we have decided to effect a settlement of the present situation by resorting to an extraordinary measure.

We have ordered our Government to communicate to the Governments of the United States, Great Britain, China and the Soviet Union that our empire accepts the provisions of their joint declaration.

To strive for the common prosperity and happiness of all nations as well as the security and well-being of our subjects is the solemn obligation which has been handed down by our imperial ancestors and which we lay close to the heart.

Indeed, we declared war on America and Britain out of our sincere desire to insure Japan's self-preservation and the stabilization of East Asia, it being far from our thought either to infringe upon the sovereignty of other nations or to embark upon territorial aggrandizement.

But now the war has lasted for nearly four years. Despite the best that has been done by everyone – the gallant fighting of our military and naval forces, the diligence and assiduity of out servants of the State and the devoted service of our 100,000,000 people – the war situation has developed not necessarily to Japan's advantage, while the general trends of the world have all turned against her interest.

Moreover, the enemy has begun to employ a new and most cruel bomb, the power of which to do damage is, indeed, incalculable, taking the toll of many innocent lives. Should we continue to fight, it would not only result in an ultimate collapse and obliteration of the Japanese nation, but also it would lead to the total extinction of human civilization.

Such being the case, how are we to save the millions of our subjects, nor to atone ourselves before the hallowed spirits of our imperial ancestors? This is the reason why we have ordered the acceptance of the provisions of the joint declaration of the powers.

The mushroom cloud towering over Nagasaki after the second nuclear bomb.

We cannot but express the deepest sense of regret to our allied nations of East Asia, who have consistently cooperated with the Empire toward the emancipation of East Asia.

The thought of those officers and men as well as others who have fallen in the fields of battle, those who died at their posts of duty, or those who met death [otherwise] and all their bereaved families, pains our heart night and day.

The welfare of the wounded and the war sufferers and of those who lost their homes and livelihood is the object of our profound solicitude. The hardships and sufferings to which our nation is to be subjected hereafter will be certainly great.

We are keenly aware of the inmost feelings of all of you, our subjects. However, it is according to the dictates of time and fate that we have resolved to pave the way for a grand peace for all the generations to come by enduring the [unavoidable] and suffering what is unsufferable. Having been able to save and maintain the structure of the Imperial State, we are always with you, our good and loyal subjects, relying upon your sincerity and integrity.

Beware most strictly of any outbursts of emotion that may engender needless complications, of any fraternal contention and strife that may create confusion, lead you astray and cause you to lose the confidence of the world.

Let the entire nation continue as one family from generation to generation, ever firm in its faith of the imperishableness of its divine land, and mindful of its heavy burden of responsibilities, and the long road before it. Unite your total strength to be devoted to the construction for the future. Cultivate the ways of rectitude, nobility of spirit, and work with resolution so that you may enhance the innate glory of the Imperial State and keep pace with the progress of the world. 🟥

Rheinhard Heydrich 1904–1942

Heydrich chaired a conference in the Wannsee suburb of Berlin on January 20, 1942 to discuss the 'final solution to the Jewish problem'. The attendees included SS leaders from Germany and areas under German control to the east. Adolf Eichmann had drawn up a list of the remaining numbers of Jews in Europe and Heydrich detailed how many had already been removed through migration or other methods. The meeting was convened primarily so that Heydrich could inform the other participants of a decision already made by the German high command so that they could start drawing up plans for its implementation.

NATIONALITY:
German
WHEN:
1942
WHERE:
Berlin, Germany
YOU SHOULD KNOW:
This is not actually a verbatim transcription as the only records of the meeting were watered down by Eichmann. The discussion about what the final solution – the murder of millions of Jewish, Romany, homosexual and other 'degenerate' people – was far more explicit.

Under proper guidance, in the course of the final solution the Jews are to be allocated for appropriate labour in the East. Able-bodied Jews, separated according to sex, will be taken in large work columns to these areas for work on roads, in the course of which action doubtless a large portion will be eliminated by natural causes. The possible final remnant will, since it will undoubtedly consist of the most resistant portion, have to be treated accordingly, because it is the product of natural selection and would, if released, act as the seed of a new Jewish revival. 🟥

De Gaulle broadcasting to the French people from London.

Charles de Gaulle 1890–1970

In the wake of the German invasion of France in May and early June 1940, Colonel, later General, de Gaulle was one of the few commanders to achieve any tactical success against Hitler's army. On June 6 he was put in charge of liaison with Britain and when Marshal Pétain made it obvious that he would seek an armistice, he and several of his fellow officers escaped with a large amount of gold and set up a government in exile in London. From here he led the Free French Forces until 1943, for the remainder of the war. The day after his arrival in London, June 18, he made a radio broadcast and issued a statement urging his countrymen to continue to resist, both in the north, which was under German control, and in the south, where Marshal Pétain had set up a puppet government in Vichy.

La France a perdu une bataille! Mais la France n'a pas perdu la guerre! (France has lost a battle, but France has not lost the war!)

NATIONALITY:
French
WHEN:
1940
WHERE:
London, England
YOU SHOULD KNOW:
He was sentenced to death on August 2, 1940 by the Vichy regime for treason.

Helmuth Weidling 1891–1955

The following order was broadcast to the people of Berlin by loudspeaker on May 2, 1945, two days after the death of Adolf Hitler. On the previous day, Joseph Goebbels, his successor as Chancellor, had refused to surrender the city unconditionally. After Hitler's suicide, Helmuth Weidling, the general who had been given the command of the last defence of Berlin, went to meet General Vasily Chuikov, commander of the Soviet 8th Guards Army, in order to prevent further deaths. Capitulation had begun the previous day because Berlin's defenders were rapidly running out of ammunition.

On April 30, 1945, the Führer committed suicide, and thus abandoned those who had sworn loyalty to him. According to the Führer's order, you German soldiers would have had to go on fighting for Berlin despite the fact that our ammunition has run out and despite the general situation which makes our further resistance meaningless. I order the immediate cessation of resistance. WEIDLING, General of Artillery, former District Commandant in the defence of Berlin.

NATIONALITY:
German
WHEN:
1945
WHERE:
Berlin, Germany
YOU SHOULD KNOW:
Weidling was taken back to the Soviet Union as a prisoner of war and did not return to Germany alive.

Crazy Horse c. 1840–1877

One of the most successful native American warriors, Crazy Horse led his fighters in some of the most famous battles of the 1860s and 1870s against the settlers' troops, as well as fights with other tribes in the 1850s and 1860s. His conflicts included the battles of Red Buttes and Platte Bridge Station, the Fetterman Massacre, the Wagon Box fight, and the battles of Little Bighorn and Wolf Mountain. He is said to have used the traditional Sioux battle cry (below) to spur on his warriors and put the fear of God into his enemies on many occasions. He died at Camp Robinson, Nebraska, after surrendering in May 1877 at the conclusion of the Great Sioux War.

❝ Ho'ka hey (Today is a good day to die). ❞

NATIONALITY:
Oglala Lakota
WHEN:
Various times
WHERE:
Various battles
YOU SHOULD KNOW:
The literal translation of his name from Lakota is 'His-Horse-is-Crazy'.

Chief Crazy Horse fought bravely against General Custer at Little Bighorn.

Vladimir Peniakoff 1897–1951

Vladimir Peniakoff was a Belgian of Russian extraction who fought with the French in World War I and the British in North Africa, Italy and Austria during World War II. Because Major Peniakoff had lived in Cairo for years before the war, and had learned how to navigate in the desert, he was seen as an ideal man to lead a small commando unit. In 1942 he was put in charge of a group of 195 soldiers who operated behind enemy lines, spreading 'alarm and despondency' among the opposing forces by blowing up fuel lines and tanks and destroying aircraft. Although the official title of the unit was the No 1 Long Range Demolition Squadron, which operated under the British 8th Army, it was known to its members as 'Popski's Private Army' or the PPA.

NATIONALITY:
Belgian
WHEN:
1942
WHERE:
Cairo, Egypt
YOU SHOULD KNOW:
The phrase comes from the Army Act of 1897, which states that the penalty for any person subject to military law found spreading alarm and despondency is penal servitude.

❝ Spread alarm and despondency. ❞

81

Hussein firing a pistol in celebration at the end of the First Gulf War.

Saddam Hussein

1937–2006

At the beginning of Operation Desert Storm, the phase of the First Gulf War that involved the aerial bombardment of Iraq's military capability, Saddam Hussein was at his most ebullient. In the end, it was not a great showdown. Within days, the Iraqi air force had been rendered useless, air defences and communications capability had been destroyed and civilian infrastructure had been damaged. The Iraqis did manage to bring down a surprising number of coalition planes and they fired missiles at Israel, hoping that Israel would react. That would have prompted friendly Arab nations to join Iraq. Coalition ground troops entered Iraq on February 24, and two days later Iraqi forces began to retreat into Iraq, setting fire to the Kuwaiti oil fields as they went. They were pursued over the border, but the coalition forces turned round after President Bush declared a ceasefire on April 6.

NATIONALITY:
Iraqi
WHEN:
1991
WHERE:
Baghdad, Iraq
YOU SHOULD KNOW:
Many of the human-rights abuses that Iraqi troops were said to have committed in Kuwait that were used to justify the invasion were later found to be faked.

The great duel, the mother of all battles has begun. The dawn of victory nears as this great showdown begins.

Woodrow Wilson 1856–1924

NATIONALITY:
American
WHEN:
1917
WHERE:
Washington, DC, USA
YOU SHOULD KNOW:
His presidential library is in his
birthplace, Staunton, Virginia.

*Wilson was the
28th President of the USA.*

On January 22, 1917 President Wilson addressed the Senate saying that he had had communications with representatives from both sides in Europe. He outlined the need for 'peace without victory' where no party would feel overly aggrieved, all countries would be equal in rights and people would not be forced to swap from one power to another. The ideas in this speech would emerge in a more concrete form in the Fourteen Points of Peace speech the following year. The idea of not inflicting a humiliating defeat on Germany did not appeal to the French, and the subsequent punitive reparations and restrictions on armaments that were imposed caused resentment among Germans and the growth of groups such as the Nazis.

On the eighteenth of December last I addressed an identic note to the governments of the nations now at war requesting them to state, more definitely than they had yet been stated by either group of belligerents, the terms upon which they would deem it possible to make peace. I spoke on behalf of humanity and of the rights of all neutral nations like our own, many of whose most vital interests the war puts in constant jeopardy. The Central Powers united in a reply which stated merely that they were ready to meet their antagonists in conference to discuss terms of peace. The Entente Powers have replied much more definitely and have stated, in general terms, indeed, but with sufficient definiteness to imply details, the arrangements, guarantees, and acts of reparation which they deem to be the indispensable conditions of a satisfactory settlement. We are that much nearer a definite discussion of the peace which shall end the present war. We are that much nearer the discussion of the international concert which must thereafter hold the world at peace. In every discussion of the peace that must end this war it is taken for granted that that peace must be followed by some definite concert of power which will make it virtually impossible that any such catastrophe should ever overwhelm us again. Every lover of mankind, every sane and thoughtful man must take that for granted.

I have sought this opportunity to address you because I thought that I owed it to you, as the council associated with me in the final determination of our international obligations, to disclose to you without reserve the thought and purpose that have been taking form in my mind in regard to the duty of our Government in the days to come when it will be necessary to lay afresh and upon a new plan the foundations of peace among the nations.

It is inconceivable that the people of the United States should play no part in that great enterprise. To take part in such a service will be the opportunity for which they have sought to prepare themselves by the very principles and purposes of their polity and

Crazy Horse c. 1840–1877

One of the most successful native American warriors, Crazy Horse led his fighters in some of the most famous battles of the 1860s and 1870s against the settlers' troops, as well as fights with other tribes in the 1850s and 1860s. His conflicts included the battles of Red Buttes and Platte Bridge Station, the Fetterman Massacre, the Wagon Box fight, and the battles of Little Bighorn and Wolf Mountain. He is said to have used the traditional Sioux battle cry (below) to spur on his warriors and put the fear of God into his enemies on many occasions. He died at Camp Robinson, Nebraska, after surrendering in May 1877 at the conclusion of the Great Sioux War.

> Ho'ka hey (Today is a good day to die).

NATIONALITY:
Oglala Lakota
WHEN:
Various times
WHERE:
Various battles
YOU SHOULD KNOW:
The literal translation of his name from Lakota is 'His-Horse-is-Crazy'.

Chief Crazy Horse fought bravely against General Custer at Little Bighorn.

Vladimir Peniakoff 1897–1951

Vladimir Peniakoff was a Belgian of Russian extraction who fought with the French in World War I and the British in North Africa, Italy and Austria during World War II. Because Major Peniakoff had lived in Cairo for years before the war, and had learned how to navigate in the desert, he was seen as an ideal man to lead a small commando unit. In 1942 he was put in charge of a group of 195 soldiers who operated behind enemy lines, spreading 'alarm and despondency' among the opposing forces by blowing up fuel lines and tanks and destroying aircraft. Although the official title of the unit was the No 1 Long Range Demolition Squadron, which operated under the British 8th Army, it was known to its members as 'Popski's Private Army' or the PPA.

NATIONALITY:
Belgian
WHEN:
1942
WHERE:
Cairo, Egypt
YOU SHOULD KNOW:
The phrase comes from the Army Act of 1897, which states that the penalty for any person subject to military law found spreading alarm and despondency is penal servitude.

> Spread alarm and despondency.

George W. Bush born 1946

The day after the anniversary of 9/11, President Bush addressed the UN General Assembly about his government's intentions with regard to Iraq. He detailed the 16 UN resolutions concerned with illegal weapons, sanctions-busting, prisoners of war and human rights issues that he claimed Saddam was breaking and getting away with because of UN appeasement. He also stated his belief that Iraq had weapons of mass destruction and that it posed a risk to American allies in the region. The message that the US would take action, with UN backing or not, angered many.

NATIONALITY:
American
WHEN:
2002
WHERE:
New York, USA
YOU SHOULD KNOW:
While the accusations of human-rights abuses and sanctions-busting were justified, that of possessing an illegal weapons programme was not, and that of sponsoring international terrorism remains unproven.

Mr Secretary General, Mr. President, distinguished delegates, and ladies and gentlemen: We meet one year and one day after a terrorist attack brought grief to my country, and brought grief to many citizens of our world. Yesterday, we remembered the innocent lives taken that terrible morning. Today, we turn to the urgent duty of protecting other lives, without illusion and without fear . . .

Above all, our principles and our security are challenged today by outlaw groups and regimes that accept no law of morality and have no limit to their violent ambitions. In the attacks on America a year ago, we saw the destructive intentions of our enemies. This threat hides within many nations, including my own . . . And our greatest fear is that terrorists will find a shortcut to their mad ambitions when an outlaw regime supplies them with the technologies to kill on a massive scale.

In one place – in one regime – we find all these dangers, in their most lethal and aggressive forms, exactly the kind of aggressive threat the United Nations was born to confront.

Twelve years ago, Iraq invaded Kuwait without provocation. And the regime's forces were poised to continue their march to seize other countries and their resources. Had Saddam Hussein been appeased instead of stopped, he would have endangered the peace and stability of the world. Yet this aggression was stopped – by the might of coalition forces and the will of the United Nations.

To suspend hostilities, to spare himself, Iraq's dictator accepted a series of commitments. The terms were clear, to him and to all. And he agreed to prove he is complying with every one of those obligations.

He has proven instead only his contempt for the United Nations, and for all his pledges. By breaking every pledge – by his deceptions, and by his cruelties – Saddam Hussein has made the case against himself . . .

If the Iraqi regime wishes peace, it will immediately and unconditionally forswear, disclose, and remove or destroy all weapons of mass destruction, long-range missiles, and all related material.

If the Iraqi regime wishes peace, it will immediately end all support for terrorism and act to suppress it, as all states are required to do by UN Security Council resolutions.

If the Iraqi regime wishes peace, it will cease persecution of its civilian population, including Shi'a, Sunnis, Kurds, Turkomans, and others, again as required by Security Council resolutions.

If the Iraqi regime wishes peace, it will release or account for all Gulf War personnel whose fate is still unknown. It will return the remains of any who are deceased, return stolen property, accept liability for losses resulting from the invasion of Kuwait, and fully cooperate with international efforts to resolve these issues, as required by Security Council resolutions.

If the Iraqi regime wishes peace, it will immediately end all illicit trade outside the oil-for-food program. It will accept UN administration of funds from that program, to ensure that the money is used fairly and promptly for the benefit of the Iraqi people.

If all these steps are taken, it will signal a new openness and accountability in Iraq. And it could open the prospect of the United Nations helping to build a government that represents all Iraqis –

a government based on respect for human rights, economic liberty, and internationally supervised elections . . .

My nation will work with the UN Security Council to meet our common challenge. If Iraq's regime defies us again, the world must move deliberately, decisively to hold Iraq to account. We will work with the UN Security Council for the necessary resolutions. But the purposes of the United States should not be doubted. The Security Council resolutions will be enforced – the just demands of peace and security will be met – or action will be unavoidable. And a regime that has lost its legitimacy will also lose its power . . .

Neither of these outcomes is certain. Both have been set before us. We must choose between a world of fear and a world of progress. We cannot stand by and do nothing while dangers gather. We must stand up for our security, and for the permanent rights and the hopes of mankind. By heritage and by choice, the United States of America will make that stand. And, delegates to the United Nations, you have the power to make that stand, as well.

President Bush addressing the United Nations.

Kofi Annan born 1938

*In an interview with BBC reporter Owen Bennett-Jones at the UN
Headquarters on September 16, 2004, UN Secretary-General Kofi
Annan was directly asked about whether he thought that the US
was becoming a unilateral superpower. Mr Annan replied that he
thought that there had been painful lessons for all over the previous
year and that everyone was concluding that working through the
UN was the better option, adding that he hoped that there was no
other operation like that in Iraq, done without UN approval and
broader international support. When pressed on whether he
thought that Resolution 1441 did give legal authority for the war,
he replied as below, adding to further questions that the war was
not in conformity with the UN Charter and that in his opinion
was illegal.*

Well, I'm one of those who believe that there should have been a second
resolution because the Security Council indicated that if Iraq did not
comply there will be consequences. But then it was up to the Security
Council to approve or determine what those consequences should be.

NATIONALITY:
Ghanian
WHEN:
2004
WHERE:
New York, USA
YOU SHOULD KNOW:
The Secretary-General's opinion was
strongly refuted by the US, UK and
Australian administrations, and as the
interview was conducted only six
weeks before the US Presidential
elections, he was accused in some
quarters of political interference in
domestic issues.

Martin Niemöller 1892–1984

*In 1946, Martin Niemöller, a Lutheran pastor and concentration
camp survivor spoke widely about the need to avoid political
apathy in the face of political oppression, even if one is not
threatened oneself. There are several variations of this poem that
encompass other groups including socialists, Jehovah's
Witnesses, schools, the press and the church. He had founded the
anti-Nazi Bekennende Kirche (Confessing Church) in 1934, and
in 1937 was sent to Sachsenhausen concentration camp. In 1941
he was moved to Dachau, where he remained for the rest of the
war. He believed that the people of Germany had a collective
responsibility for the horrors of the Nazi era, which he expressed
in his most famous poem.*

In Germany, they came first for the Communists, And I didn't speak
up because I wasn't a Communist;
And then they came for the trade unionists, And I didn't speak up
because I wasn't a trade unionist;
And then they came for the Jews, And I didn't speak up because I
wasn't a Jew;
And then . . . they came for me . . . And by that time there was no one
left to speak up.

NATIONALITY:
German
WHEN:
c. 1946
WHERE:
Germany
YOU SHOULD KNOW:
This was Martin Niemöller's
preferred version of the poem.

87

Central Committee of the Communist Party of China

NATIONALITY:
Chinese
WHERE:
Beijing, China
WHEN:
1966
YOU SHOULD KNOW:
The chief ideological hates of the Cultural Revolution were the Four Olds: Old Customs, Old Culture, Old Habits and Old Ideas.

The Cultural Revolution was Mao's attempt to regain control of the mechanisms of power in China, which he had lost during the Great Leap Forward, a disastrous attempt at land and industrial reform of the preceding years. The Cultural Revolution was a 16-point ten-year plan but in the end lasted only three years before Mao declared it over, although some observers argue that it finished only in 1976 with the fall of the Gang of Four: Mao's last wife Jiang Qing, Zhang Chunqiao, Yao Wenyuan and Wang Hongwen. The student Red Guards – under the direction of the Central Committee – created total anarchy, destroying anything that did not conform to the cultural ideas of Mao, killing thousands, destroying churches, temples, monasteries and mosques, torturing people or ritually humilating them and forcing intellectuals and other 'counter-revolutionaries' to undertake public self-criticism.

' . . . Although the bourgeoisie has been overthrown, it is still trying to use the old ideas, culture, customs, and habits of the exploiting classes to corrupt the masses, capture their minds, and endeavour to stage a comeback. The proletariat . . . must meet head-on every challenge of the bourgeoisie in the ideological field and use the new ideas, culture, customs, and habits of the proletariat to change the mental outlook of the whole of society . . . our objective is to struggle against and crush those persons in authority who are taking the capitalist road, to criticize and repudiate the reactionary bourgeois academic 'authorities' and the ideology of the bourgeoisie and all other exploiting classes and to transform education, literature and art, and all other parts of the superstructure that do not correspond to the socialist economic base, so as to facilitate the consolidation and development of the socialist system . . . '

A mass demonstration during the Cultural Revolution of the late 1960s.

William T. Sherman

1820–1891

The signing of the treaty with the Sioux.

When General Sherman's troops captured Atlanta in early September 1864, after a four-month siege, he ordered the population to leave and destroyed every public building, apart from churches and hospitals. Thousands of homes were also burned down. His purpose in this destruction was to prevent the once-prosperous hub city continuing its role in the supply of provisions and munitions to the Confederate Army. Two months later, his army set off for Savannah on the coast, another major supply point. During the march he operated a scorched earth policy, ordering his men to kill livestock, burn crops, consume all supplies and destroy civilian infrastructure such as the railways. They made the 300-mile march in a month, and took Savannah within a few days. The remarks below were addressed to President Grant in a letter and to the mayor of Atlanta.

NATIONALITY:
American
WHEN:
1864
WHERE:
Atlanta, Georgia, USA
YOU SHOULD KNOW:
About 10,000 slaves joined Sherman's army.

'Until we can repopulate Georgia, it is useless for us to occupy it; but the utter destruction of its roads, houses and people will cripple their military resources. I can make this march, and make Georgia howl.'

Pierre Bosquet 1810–1861

Pierre Bosquet was one of France's most successful generals since the time of Napoleon and men under his command were instrumental in the conduct of the Crimean War of 1853–1856, during which the British and French armies (and later Sardinia-Piedmont) joined with the forces of the Ottoman Empire to prevent Russian expansionism in southeastern Europe. He made the comment below at the Battle of Balaklava on October 25, 1854 while observing the disastrous Charge of the Light Brigade in which, because of muddled orders, an unsupported charge of 600 British cavalrymen was directed straight towards a gun battery, leading to the deaths of about half of them.

NATIONALITY:
French
WHEN:
1854
WHERE:
Balaklava, Russia
YOU SHOULD KNOW:
The Charge of the Light Brigade was the subject of a poem of 1855 by Alfred, Lord Tennyson, highlighting both the courageous and tragic aspects of warfare.

'C'est manifique, mais ce n'est pas la guerre: c'est de la folie. (It's magnificent, but it is not war: it is madness.)'

89

Adolf Hitler 1889–1945

NATIONALITY:
Austrian/German
WHEN:
1940
WHERE:
Berlin, Germany
YOU SHOULD KNOW:
The projected invasion of Britain was
called Operation Sealion.

In May and June 1940, Hitler invaded and successively conquered Belgium, the Netherlands and northern France, with Paris falling on June 14. A puppet government was installed in Vichy in the south. On July 19, 1940 Hitler gave a speech at the Reichstag in which he appeared to offer peace to the UK, although the Luftwaffe had already started bombing airfields to destroy the Royal Air Force and make the projected invasion easier. This peace proposal was rejected, so Hitler ordered the air-drop of copies of the speech on the night of August 1–2 to persuade the British people not to support their government's stance.

I have summoned you to this meeting in the midst of our tremendous struggle for the freedom and the future of the German nation. I have done so, firstly, because I considered it imperative to give our people an insight into the events, unique in history, that lie behind us, secondly, because I wished to express my gratitude to our magnificent soldiers, and thirdly, with the intention of appealing, once more and for the last time, to common sense in general . . .

If we compare the causes which prompted this historic struggle with the magnitude and the far-reaching effects of military events, we are forced to the conclusion that its general course and the sacrifices it has entailed are out of proportion to the alleged reasons for its outbreak – unless they were nothing but a pretext for underlying intentions . . .

This revision [of the Treaty of Versailles] was absolutely essential. The conditions imposed at Versailles were intolerable, not only because of their humiliating discrimination and because the disarmament which they ensured deprived the German nation of all its rights, but far more so because of the consequent destruction of the material existence of one of the great civilised nations in the world, and the proposed annihilation of its future, the utterly senseless accumulation of immense tracts of territory under the domination of a number of states, the theft of all the irreparable foundations of life and indispensable vital necessities from a conquered nation. While this dictate was being drawn up, men of insight even among our foes were uttering warnings about the terrible consequences which the ruthless application of its insane conditions would entail – a proof that even among them the conviction predominated that such a dictate could not possibly be held up in days to come. Their objections and protests were silenced by the assurance that the statutes of the newly created League of Nations provided for a revision of these conditions; in fact, the League was supposed to be the competent authority. The hope of revision was thus at no time regarded as presumptuous, but as something natural. Unfortunately, the Geneva institution, as those responsible for Versailles had intended, never looked upon itself as a body competent to undertake any sensible revision, but from the very outset as nothing more than the guarantor of the ruthless enforcement and maintenance of the conditions imposed at Versailles.

All attempts made by democratic Germany to obtain equality for the German people by a revision of the Treaty proved unavailing . . .

It is always in the interests of a conqueror to represent stipulations that are to his advantage as sacrosanct, while the instinct of self-preservation in the vanquished leads him to reacquire the common human rights that he has lost. For him, the dictate of an overbearing conqueror had all the less legal force, since he had never been honourably conquered. Owing to a rare misfortune, the German Empire, between 1914 and 1918, lacked good leadership. To this, and to the as yet unenlightened faith and trust placed by the German people in the words of democratic statesmen, our downfall was due.

Hence the Franco-British claim that the Dictate of Versailles was a sort of international, or even a supreme, code of laws, appeared to be nothing more than a piece of insolent arrogance to every honest German, the assumption, however, that British or French statesmen should actually claim to be the guardians of justice, and even of human culture, as mere effrontery. A piece of effrontery that is thrown into a sufficiently glaring light by their own extremely negligible achievements in this direction. For seldom have any countries in the world been ruled with a lesser degree of wisdom, morality and culture than those which are at the moment exposed to the ragings of certain democratic statesmen.

The programme of the National Socialist Movement, besides freeing the Reich from the innermost fetters of a small substratum of Jewish-capitalist and pluto-democratic profiteers, proclaimed to the world our resolution to shake off the shackles of the Versailles Dictate.

Hermann Goering 1893–1946

NATIONALITY:
German
WHEN:
1941
WHERE:
Berlin, Germany
YOU SHOULD KNOW:
After the war, Goering was tried at Nuremberg and sentenced to death. He committed suicide by poison the night before his intended execution.

Six months before the Wannsee Conference in which Rheinhard Heydrich outlined to a group of senior bureaucrats the measures they were to take towards the extermination of the Jewish race, Reichsmarschall Göring issued written and verbal orders to Heydrich to implement the plan. The written orders do not mention what the 'complete solution' was but Eichman would have been in no doubt what was meant. Millions of Jews and other people had already been killed but this was the first order for the total destruction of the race. In the spring of 1942, the mass-extermination programme began, with people being rounded up and deported to the death camps in eastern Germany and Poland from all over Europe.

I hereby charge you with making all necessary organizational, functional and material preparations for a complete solution of the Jewish question in the German sphere of influence in Europe.

Hermann Goering, who became Hitler's deputy in 1939.

Karl Marx 1818–1883

NATIONALITY:
German
WHEN:
1848
WHERE:
London, England
YOU SHOULD KNOW:
The first edition of the Manifesto was published in German, and although it was listed as being the work of both Marx and Friedrich Engels, the latter said that it was almost all Marx's work.

The preamble, below, to The Communist Manifesto is a general statement of intent (this version is from the 1888 English edition) of the newly formed Communist Party. It compares Communism to a spectre in order to point out that leaders are decrying the movement without understanding it. The manifesto itself is divided into sections: Bourgeois and Prolitarians; Prolitarians and Communists; Socialist and Communist Literature; and Position of the Communists in Relation to the Various Existing Opposition Parties. The second part contained the 'ten planks', which included the abolition of property and giving of rents of land to public purposes; heavy progressive income tax; abolition of rights of inheritance; confiscation of the property of emigrants and rebels; centralization of credit in the hands of the state; centralization of communication and transport in the hands of the State; extension of public ownership of factories and farms; equal liability to work and the establishment of industrial and agricultural armies; and free education for all children and abolition of child labour in favour of a combination of education and industrial production.

*Karl Marx, the founder
of Communism*

‘ A spectre is haunting Europe – the spectre of Communism. All the Powers of old Europe have entered into a holy alliance to exorcise this spectre: Pope and Czar, Metternich and Guizot, French Radicals and German police-spies.

Where is the party in opposition that has not been decried as Communistic by its opponents in power? Where is the Opposition that has not hurled back the branding reproach of Communism, against the more advanced opposition parties, as well as against its reactionary adversaries?

Two things result from this fact.

I. Communism is already acknowledged by all European Powers to be itself a Power.

II. It is high time that Communists should openly, in the face of the whole world, publish their views, their aims, their tendencies, and meet this nursery tale of the Spectre of Communism with a Manifesto of the party itself. ’

Richard Dimbleby

1913–1965

On April 15, 1945 the 11th Armoured Division of the British Army reached the concentration camp on the outskirts of the small northwest German town of Bergen. They were accompanied by BBC journalist Richard Dimbleby, whose 12-minute radio broadcast on the Home Service on April 19 began to reveal to the public the horrors of what had happened to millions of people from across Europe. The survivors were washed, deloused and moved to the former tank camp next door before former guards were forced to bury the dead in large pits and the entire camp was torched. Because the inmates were so near to dying of starvation when the camp was liberated, and because typhus was rife, more than 13,000 more died during the next couple of months.

THIS IS THE SITE OF
THE INFAMOUS BELSEN CONCENTRATION CAMP
Liberated by the British on 15 April 1945.

10,000 UNBURIED DEAD WERE FOUND HERE.
ANOTHER 13,000 HAVE SINCE DIED.
ALL OF THEM VICTIMS OF THE
GERMAN NEW ORDER IN EUROPE,
AND AN EXAMPLE OF NAZI KULTUR.

British soldiers in front of a commemorative sign outside Belsen Concentration Camp.

> ... In the shade of some trees lay a great collection of bodies. I walked about them trying to count, there were perhaps 150 of them flung down on each other, all naked, all so thin that their yellow skin glistened like stretched rubber on their bones. Some of the poor starved creatures whose bodies were there looked so utterly unreal and inhuman that I could have imagined that they had never lived at all ...
>
> This day at Belsen was the most horrible of my life.

NATIONALITY:
British
WHEN:
1945
WHERE:
Bergen-Belsen Concentration Camp, Germany
YOU SHOULD KNOW:
The food rations the British army had with them were too rich for the starving inmates' stomachs, so they were fed on Bengal Famine Mixture, a sugar-and-rice-based mix flavoured with paprika.

Macarthur 'returns' to the Philippines.

Douglas MacArthur

1880–1964

Having left the Philippines with a small group of his command and his wife and son on March 11, 1942, General MacArthur travelled to Melbourne to organize the defence of those parts of the Pacific that the Japanese had not already overrun. At this time, there was a distinct possibility that they had Australia in their sights. The Allied fightback in the Pacific began in August with the invasion of Guadalcanal and proceeded on an almost island-by-island basis, with most of the major battles being at sea. After the war, General MacArthur became the Supreme Commander of the Allied Powers in Japan, and was de facto interim leader of the country for the next few years, during which time its reconstruction was organized and its new constitution set up.

NATIONALITY:
American
WHEN:
1942
WHERE:
Adelaide, Australia
YOU SHOULD KNOW:
The battle for Corregidor, the small island that guarded the entrance to Manila Bay, was the defeat that marked the fall of the Philippines on May 6, 1942.

' The President of the United States ordered me to break through the Japanese lines and proceed from Corregidor to Australia for the purpose, as I understand it, of organizing the American offensive against Japan, a primary object of which is the relief of the Philippines. I came through and I shall return. '

Douglas MacArthur 1880–1964

In 1949, General MacArthur handed control of Japan to the new government but remained in the east until 1951, when President Truman dismissed him from his command after he had publicly queried the administration's policy of limiting the Korean War in order to avoid a wider conflict with China and the involvement of the Soviet Union, which by now possessed nuclear weapons. The general gave a farewell address to Congress, during which he stated his belief that criticism of him among people who did not understand warfare or the threat that communist China posed had distorted his position and led to his being labelled a warmonger, whereas in fact as a soldier with more than 50 years' experience, he loathed war and felt it a useless way to end international disputes. He ended his address:

Douglas MacArthur making his farewell speech to Congress.

I am closing my 52 years of military service. When I joined the army, even before the turn of the century, it was the fulfillment of all my boyish hopes and dreams.

The world has turned over many times since I took the oath on the plain at West Point, and the hopes and dreams have long since vanished, but I still remember the refrain of one of the most popular barracks ballads of that day which proclaimed most proudly that old soldiers never die; they just fade away.

And like the old soldier of that ballad, I now close my military career and just fade away, an old soldier who tried to do his duty as God gave him the light to see that duty. Goodbye.

NATIONALITY:
American
WHEN:
1951
WHERE:
Washington, DC, USA

YOU SHOULD KNOW:
The more commonly used version of this is 'Old soldiers never die – they just fade away.'.

Jiang Qing 1914–1991

A former actress, Jiang Qing married Mao Zedong in 1938 and became one of the most formidable politicians in China. In 1966 she was appointed deputy director of the Central Cultural Revolutions Group, which directed the pogroms against intellectuals. She also produced operas and ballets on revolutionary themes which were designed to replace more traditional forms. One of her great fears was the spread of cultural influences from the West, so these were routinely denounced as bourgeois, un-Chinese and decadent. After Mao's death in 1976, she fell from power spectacularly. At her trial in 1980–1981, she was completely unrepentant and claimed that everything she had done was in order to defend Mao and on his orders. She was sentenced to death but that was commuted to life imprisonment. She died in 1991.

NATIONALITY:
Chinese
WHEN:
1966
WHERE:
Beijing, China
YOU SHOULD KNOW:
Jiang Qing was one of the members of the Gang of Four who led the Cultural Revolution and tried to seize power after Mao's death.

Imperialism is moribund, capitalism parasitic and rotten. Modern revisionism is a product of imperialist policies and a variant of capitalism. They cannot produce any works that are good . . . On the other hand, there are some things . . . such as rock-and-roll, jazz, striptease, impressionism, symbolism, abstractionism, Fruvis, modernism . . . there is decadence and obscenity to poison and corrupt the people.

Jiang Qing is greeting the French President, Georges Pompidou.

Pope Pius XII (Eugenio Pacelli) 1876–1958

NATIONALITY:
Italian
WHEN:
1942
WHERE:
Vatican City, Italy
YOU SHOULD KNOW:
At his trial at Nuremberg, von Ribbentrop attested that the Pope continually issued private protests to Hitler about the Holocaust.

Before and during World War II, Pope Pius XII was severely criticized for not explicitly condemning the persecution of the Jewish people by Nazi Germany. He condemned the mass deportation of people on many occasions, but his refusal to mention the Jewish people by name led his opponents to claim that he was an anti-Semite and political leaders to warn that the Vatican would lose its image as an institution of moral prestige. He did once explain privately that he could not single out one people because he had to remain politically neutral. He also declined to condemn Nazi policies against Catholic priests, which had started after he criticized the German government. Below is an extract from his Christmas message of 1942.

‘ Mankind owes that vow to the countless dead who lie buried on the field of battle . . . Mankind owes that vow to the innumerable sorrowing host of mothers, widows and orphans . . . Mankind owes that vow to those numberless exiles . . . Mankind owes that vow to the hundreds of thousands of persons who, without any fault on their part, sometimes only because of their nationality or race, have been consigned to death or to a slow decline. Mankind owes that vow to the many thousands of non-combatants, women, children, sick and aged, from whom aerial warfare . . . has . . . taken life, goods, health, home, charitable refuge, or house of prayer. ’

Napoleon Bonaparte 1769–1821

NATIONALITY:
French
WHEN:
1812
WHERE:
Paris, France
YOU SHOULD KNOW:
The retreat was made more difficult because he had destroyed most of the crops on the way to Russia, and had to use the same route back.

Napoleon's 1812 attack on Russia, culminating in the Battle of Borodino on September 7, marked both the greatest extent of Napoleon's empire and the beginning of its downfall. Rather than surrender the city, the Russians had evacuated it and set fire to it and the Tsar did not surrender. About a month later, with unrest at home and the prospect of a harsh Russian winter, Napoleon turned for home, leaving the army to follow. Fewer than 40,000 of the 450,000 personnel he had set out with made it out of Russia because of continued Russian military action, the winter weather and the murder of stragglers by vengeful peasants. At the Beresina river alone, he lost 35,000 men. In December, before his full losses were apparent, he made the following remark to the Polish Ambassador, Abbé de Pradt.

‘ Du sublime au ridicule il n'y a qu'un pas. (From the sublime to the ridiculous there is but one step.) ’

Anthony C. McAuliffe 1898–1975

During the German Ardennes offensive in the winter of 1944–1945, General Heinrich Freiherr von Lüttwitz laid siege to the garrison in the town of Bastogne, a vital target for the Germans as it was the meeting-point of seven strategically important roads. His demand to the commander of the garrison that he surrender received a one-word reply from McAuliffe. The 101st Airborne Division, of which McAuliffe was in temporary command in the absence of General Maxwell Taylor, managed to hold off the German forces until the arrival of elements from the 4th Armored Division. He was given his own division to command soon after and rose to become Commander in Chief of the US Army in Europe in 1955.

'Nuts! '

NATIONALITY:
American
WHEN:
1944
WHERE:
Bastogne, Belgium
YOU SHOULD KNOW:
The Ardennes offensive is commonly known as the Battle of the Bulge.

General McAuliffe

Ferdinand Foch 1851–1929

Ferdinand Foch, who later became Marshal of France and Supreme Commander of the Allied Forces, was in charge of the French 9th Army during the first Battle of the Marne, when his soldiers succeeded in halting the German advance towards Paris. His tactics were later criticized as being a major cause of the heavy losses during that battle and those of Ypres, the Somme and the Artois offensive and he was removed from his command at the end of 1916. He was recalled a few months later and during 1918 was responsible for the manner in which the last year of the war was conducted. He accepted the German surrender but was a bitter opponent of the Versailles Treaty as he believed that its terms would lead to another war within 20 years.

NATIONALITY:
French
WHEN:
1914
WHERE:
The first Battle of the Marne, France
YOU SHOULD KNOW:
Some historians think he said this during the second Battle of the Marne in 1918.

'My centre gives way, my right retreats; situation excellent. Impossible to manoeuvre. I shall attack! '

L. Paul Bremer III born 1941

NATIONALITY:
American
WHEN:
2003
WHERE:
Baghdad, Iraq
YOU SHOULD KNOW:
Saddam Hussein was tried in 2005 and 2006 on separate charges, found guilty on November 5, 2006 of human rights abuses, and hanged on December 30.

Paul Bremer was Director of Reconstruction and Humanitarian Assistance in post-war Iraq from May 2003 to June 2004. He led the civilian administration that oversaw the setting up of a new constitution and the rebuilding of Iraq's infrastructure as well as dealing with the immediate need for food, water and medical aid. He left on June 28, 2004, the day the Iraqi Interim Government took over limited sovreignty of the country. During his period in charge he authorized the de-Baathification of government posts – that is the removal of anyone who belonged to Saddam Hussein's party from their jobs – as well as the disbandment of the Iraqi army. Both actions led to widespread discontent among the suddenly jobless and are believed by many to have fuelled the insurgency that has persisted ever since.

Bremer at a news conference in Baghdad

'Ladies and gentlemen, we got him.

Saddam Hussein was captured Saturday 13 December at about 2030 local, in a cellar in the town of al-Dawr which is about 15 kilometres south of Tikrit.

Before Dr Pachachi, who is the acting president of the governing council, and Lieutenant General Sanchez [the top US military commander in Iraq] speak, I want to say a few words to the people of Iraq.

This is a great day in Iraq's history.

For decades, hundreds of thousands of you suffered at the hands of this cruel man.

For decades, Saddam Hussein divided you citizens against each other.

For decades, he threatened an attack on your neighbours.

Those days are over forever.

Now it is time to look to the future, to your future of hope, to a future of reconciliation.

Now is the time for all Iraqis to build a prosperous, democratic Iraq, at peace with itself and with its neighbours.

Iraq's future, your future, has never been more full of hope.

The tyrant is a prisoner.

The economy is moving forward. You have before you the prospect of a sovereign government in a few months.

With the arrest of Saddam Hussein, there is a new opportunity for the members of the former regime to end their bitter opposition.

Let them now come forward in a spirit of reconciliation and hope, lay down their arms, and join you, their fellow citizens, in the task of building the new Iraq.

Now is the time for all Iraqis – Arabs and Kurds, Sunnis, Shia, Christian and Turkmen – to build a prosperous, democratic Iraq, at peace with itself and with its neighbours. '

Woodrow Wilson 1856–1924

While there was carnage on land for the whole of World War I, at sea the Allies had kept the German fleet more or less confined to harbour. However, all shipping was vulnerable to attack by German submarines, especially the large convoys bringing supplies from across the Atlantic. Under pressure from the American government, Germany had stopped attacking neutral shipping, but resumed in February 1917. This, combined with an approach to Mexico to ask if it would attack America, guaranteed that America would join the Allies. On April 2, President Wilson asked Congress to approve his decision to go to war, which they did two days later.

NATIONALITY:
American
WHEN:
1917
WHERE:
Washington, DC, USA
YOU SHOULD KNOW:
President Wilson is buried in the Washington National Cathedral.

'. . . On the third of February last I officially laid before you the extraordinary announcement of the Imperial German Government that on and after the first day of Feburary it was its purpose to put aside all restraints of law or of humanity and use its submarines to sink every vessel that sought to approach either the ports of Great Britain and Ireland or the western coasts of Europe or any of the ports controlled by the enemies of Germany with the Mediterranean. That had seemed to be the object of the German submarine warfare earlier in the war, but since April of last year the Imperial Government had somewhat restrained the commanders of its undersea craft in conformity with its promise then given to us that passenger boats should not be sunk and that due warning would be given to all other vessels which its submarines might seek to destroy, when no resistance was offered or escape attempted, and care taken that their crews were given at least a fair chance to save their lives in their open boats. The precautions taken were meagre and haphazard enough, as was proved in distressing instance after instance in the progress of the cruel and unmanly business, but a certain degree of restraint was observed. The new policy has swept every restriction aside. Vessels of every kind, whatever their flag, their character, their cargo, their destination, their errand, have been ruthlessly sent to the bottom without warning and without thought of help or mercy for those on board . . .

. . . It is a war against all nations. American ships have been sunk, American lives taken, in ways which it has stirred us very deeply to learn of, but the ships and people of other neutral and friendly nations have been sunk and overwhelmed in the waters in the same way. There has been no discrimination. The challenge is to all mankind. Each nation must decide for itself how it will meet it. The choice we make for ourselves must be made with a moderation of counsel and a temperateness of judgment befitting our character and our motives as a nation. We must put excited feeling away. Our motive will not be revenge or the victorious assertion of the physical

Wilson addresses Congress in 1917, proposing a war against Germany.

might of the nation, but only the vindication of right, of human right, of which we are only a single champion.

With a profound sense of the solemn and even tragical character of the step I am taking and of the very grave responsibilities which it involves, but in unhesitating obedience to what I deem my constitutional duty, I advise that the Congress declare the recent course of the Imperial German Government to be in fact nothing less than war against the government and people of the United States; that it formally accept the status of belligerent which has thus been thrust upon it; and that it take immediate steps not only to put the country in a more thorough state of defense but also to exert all its power and employ all its resources to bring the Government of the German Empire to terms and end the war . . .

It is a distressing and oppressive duty, Gentlemen of Congress, which I have performed in thus addressing you. There are, it may be, many months of fiery trial and sacrifice ahead of us. It is a fearful thing to lead this great and peaceful people into war, into the most terrible and disastrous of all wars, civilization itself seeming to be in the balance. But the right is more precious than peace, and we shall fight for the things which we have always carried nearest our hearts – for democracy, for the right of those who submit to authority to have a voice in their own governments, for the rights and liberties of small nations, for a universal dominion of right by such a concert of free peoples as shall bring peace and safety to all nations and make the world itself at last free. To such a task we can dedicate our lives and our fortunes, everything that we are and everything that we have, with the pride of those who know that the day has come when America is privileged to spend her blood and her might for the principles that gave her birth and happiness and the peace which she has treasured. God helping her, she can do no other. "

Jawaharlal Nehru 1889–1964

NATIONALITY:
Indian
WHEN:
1947
WHERE:
Delhi, India
YOU SHOULD KNOW:
The following day, the Constituent Assembly became the Indian Parliament.

On the eve of independence from Britain, Nehru spoke to the Constituent Assembly of India about his hopes for the future. An unforeseen consequence of the partition of India and Pakistan when they both became independent was the rioting and massacres that accompanied the exchange of populations to and from mainly Hindu India and predominantly Islamic Pakistan. Estimates of the number of deaths vary from 200,000 to 1,000,000. This occurred partly because the administrations of the new nations were ill prepared to deal with large population movements but chiefly because the process of partition was muddled and the borders had not been fully set.

Long years ago we made a tryst with destiny, and now the time comes when we shall redeem our pledge, not wholly or in full measure, but very substantially. At the stroke of the midnight hour, when the world sleeps, India will awake to life and freedom. A moment comes, which comes but rarely in history, when we step out from the old to the new, when an age ends, and when the soul of a nation long suppressed finds utterance. It is fitting that at this solemn moment, we take the pledge of dedication to the service of India and her people and to the still larger cause of humanity . . .

It is a fateful moment for us in India, for all Asia and for the world. A new star rises, the star of freedom in the East, a new hope comes into being, a vision long cherished materializes. May the star never set and that hope never be betrayed!

We rejoice in that freedom, even though clouds surround us, and many of our people are sorrow-stricken and difficult problems encompass us. But freedom brings responsibilities and burdens and we have to face them in the spirit of a free and disciplined people . . .

Our next thoughts must be of the unknown volunteers and soldiers of freedom who, without praise or reward, have served India even unto death . . .

. . . And to India, our much-loved motherland, the ancient, the eternal and the ever-new, we pay our reverent homage and we bind ourselves afresh to her service. 🟥

Gerhart Riegner 1911–2001

On August 8, 1942, the Swiss representative of the World Jewish Congress sent a telegram via American and British diplomatic channels to Rabbi Stephen Wise, the head of the organization. Because the diplomats didn't believe it and regarded its contents as hysterical scare-mongering, even though mass deportations had been going on for several years and evidence was emerging that deportees were being killed, it was not forwarded by the British Foreign Office for some time and the US State Department more or less ignored it. What action they would have been able to take to prevent the programme being carried out is still debated.

NATIONALITY:
Swiss
WHEN:
1942
WHERE:
Geneva, Switzerland
YOU SHOULD KNOW:
In 1983 German industrialist Eduard Schulte was revealed as the source of Riegner's information.

The motto above the gates reads 'Work Makes One Free'.

❛ Received alarming report about plan being discussed and considered in Führer headquarters to exterminate at one fell swoop all Jews in German-controlled countries comprising three and a half to four million after deportation and concentration in the east thus solving Jewish question once and for all stop campaign planned for autumn methods being discussed including hydrocyanic acid stop 🟥

Harold Ickes 1874–1952

NATIONALITY:
American
WHEN:
1941
WHERE:
New York,USA
YOU SHOULD KNOW:
The attack on Pearl Harbor that led
to the US administration's decision to
go to war came a little under six
months later.

As with World War I, America held off from direct military involvement at the beginning of World War II, although massive food aid was being given to the Allies. Because of anti-communist fears, pro-fascist propaganda and the tenets of the Monroe doctrine many Americans felt it would be wrong to intervene. Secretary of the Interior Harold Ickes, in this speech of May 18, 1941, issued a call to the American people to remember the ideals with which their country had been founded and a bleak warning of what would happen if they buried their collective head in the sand.

Harold Ickes at work

‘What has happened to our vaunted idealism? Why have some of us been behaving like scared chickens? Where is the million-throated, democratic voice of America?

For years it has been dinned into us that we are a weak nation; that we are an inefficient people; that we are simple-minded. For years we have been told that we are beaten, decayed, and that no part of the world belongs to us any longer.

Some amongst us have fallen for this carefully pickled tripe. Some amongst us have fallen for this calculated poison. Some amongst us have begun to preach that the 'wave of the future' has passed over us and left us a wet, dead fish . . . many of us are listening to them and some of us almost believe them.

I say that it is time for the great American people to raise its voice and cry out in mighty triumph what it is to be an American . . .

What constitutes an American? . . . An American is one who loves justice and believes in the dignity of man. An American is one who will fight for his freedom and that of his neighbor. An American is one who will sacrifice property, ease and security in order that he and his children may retain the rights of free men. An American is one in whose heart is engraved the immortal second sentence of the Declaration of Independence . . .

If we are to retain our own freedom, we must do everything within our power to aid Britain. We must also do everything to restore to the conquered peoples their freedom. This means the Germans too . . .

. . . the British are not fighting for themselves alone. They are fighting to preserve freedom for mankind. For the moment, the battleground is the British Isles. But they are fighting our war; they are the first soldiers in trenches that are also our front-line trenches . . .

. . . liberty never dies . . . Genghis Khans come and go . . . Attilas come and go. The Hitlers flash and sputter out. But freedom endures . . .

. . . We will help brave England drive back the hordes from Hell who besiege her and then we will join for the destruction of savage and blood-thirsty dictators everywhere. But we must be firm and decisive. We must know our will and make it felt. And we must hurry. ’

George Aiken

1892–1984

*By the autumn of 1966, the war in
Vietnam was becoming increasingly
unpopular, because of its cost in
terms of money and lives in what
seemed to many to be a conflict about
a people they knew little about and
cared even less. In a speech to the
Senate on October 19 Vermont
Senator George Aiken proposed the
simple solution below. If such a
declaration were made, he argued,
de-escalation could start immediately. This is more or less what
happened in 1963, as he pointed out, but in the meantime
millions more people had died and the North Vietnamese
conquered the South anyway.*

Vermont Senator George Aitkin
listens to a testimony.

> The United States could well declare unilaterally that this stage of
> the Vietnam War is over – that we have 'won' in the sense that our
> Armed Forces are in control of most of the field and no potential
> enemy is in a position to establish its authority over South Vietnam.

NATIONALITY:
American
WHEN:
1966
WHERE:
Washington, DC, USA
YOU SHOULD KNOW:
The basic idea in this speech is
sometimes known as the Aiken solution.

Gaspard de Coligny 1519–1572

*Admiral Gaspard de Coligny was the first victim of the St
Bartholomew's Day Massacre. Two days earlier, on August 22,
1572, he had been shot and wounded in the street. As the
leading military tactician on the Protestant Huguenot side, he
was an important target for the Catholic Duke of Guise, with
whom he had been enemies for years. When the attackers broke
into the house where he was staying, he ordered his men to
escape rather than defend him, saying that he was prepared to
die. When the murderers found him in his room, he was leaning
against the wall as he could not stand. One of them, Besme,
asked him whether he was the admiral. He responded as below,
before he was stabbed repeatedly then thrown out of the window
to the courtyard below, where his head was cut off. His courage
in the face of death gained him admirers the world over.*

NATIONALITY:
French
WHERE:
Paris, France
WHEN:
1572
YOU SHOULD KNOW:
Coligny was a leading founder of
Fort Caroline, an early French colony
in Florida.

> I am. Young man, you ought to consider my age and my infirmity.
> But you will not make my life shorter.

Franklin D. Roosevelt 1882–1945

NATIONALITY:
American
WHEN:
1936
WHERE:
Chautauqua, New York, USA
YOU SHOULD KNOW:
Despite his anti-war leanings, President Roosevelt realized that war was inevitable and started both a domestic military build-up and negotiations with the French for the sale of ammunitions and aircraft.

President Roosevelt delivering his 'I hate war' speech.

During the Presidential election campaign of 1936, President Roosevelt toured widely, and in August returned to one of his favourite stomping grounds, Chautauqua. In a speech that defined his foreign policy for most of his second term, the need for peaceful relations with other countries, including his 'good-neighbor' policy with regard to the countries to the south, and neutrality for countries farther away. The 'weapons' he describes as having been given to him by Congress are the first Neutrality Acts, which enabled him to embargo the sales of armaments to 'belligerent' nations and in some cases travel to them.

As many of you who are here tonight know, I formed the excellent habit of coming to Chautauqua more than 20 years ago. After my inauguration in 1933, I promised Mr Bestor that during the next four years I would come to Chautauqua again; it is in fulfillment of this that I am with you tonight.

A few days ago I was asked what the subject of this talk would be, and I replied that for two good reasons I wanted to discuss the subject of peace. First, because it is eminently appropriate in Chautauqua; and, secondly, because in the hurly-burly of domestic politics it is important that our people should not overlook problems and issues which, though they lie beyond our borders, may, and probably will, have a vital influence on the United States of the future.

I say this to you not as a confirmed pessimist but as one who still hopes that envy, hatred, and malice among nations have reached their peak and will be succeeded by a new tide of peace and good will. I say this as one who has participated in many of the decisions of peace and war before, during, and after the World War; one who has traveled much, and one who has spent a goodly portion of every 24 hours in the study of foreign relations.

Long before I returned to Washington as President of the United States I had made up my mind that, pending what might be called a more opportune moment on other continents, the United States could best serve the cause of a peaceful humanity by setting an example. That was why on March 4, 1933, I made the following declaration.

'In the field of world policy I would dedicate this nation to the policy of the good neighbor – the neighbor who resolutely respects himself and, because he does so, respects the rights of others – the neighbor who respects his obligations and respects the sanctity of his agreements in and with a world of neighbors.'

This declaration represents my purpose; but it represents more than a purpose, for it stands for a practice . . . the whole world now knows that the United States cherishes no predatory ambitions. We are strong; but less powerful nations know that they need not fear our strength. We seek no conquest: we stand for peace.

In the whole of the western hemisphere our good-neighbor policy has produced results that are especially heartening.

The noblest monument to peace and to neighborly economic and social friendship in all the world is not a monument in bronze or stone, but the boundary which unites the United States and Canada – 3,000 miles of friendship with no barbed wire, no gun or soldier, and no passport on the whole frontier.

Mutual trust made that frontier. To extend the same sort of mutual trust throughout the Americas was our aim.

The American republics to the south of us have been ready always to cooperate with the United States on a basis of equality and mutual respect, but before we inaugurated the good-neighbor policy there was among them resentment and fear because certain administrations in Washington had slighted their national pride and their sovereign rights . . .

Peace, like charity, begins at home; that is why we have begun at home. But peace in the western world is not all that we seek.

It is our hope that knowledge of the practical application of the good-neighbor policy in this hemisphere will be borne home to our neighbors across the seas . . .

For ourselves we are on good terms with them – terms in most cases of straightforward friendship, of peaceful understanding.

But, of necessity, we are deeply concerned about tendencies of recent years among many of the nations of other continents. It is a bitter experience to us when the spirit of agreements to which we are a party is not lived up to. It is an even more bitter experience for the whole company of nations to witness not only the spirit but the letter of international agreements violated with impunity and without regard to the simple principles of honor. Permanent friendships between nations as between men can be sustained only by scrupulous respect for the pledged word . . .

We are not isolationists except insofar as we seek to isolate ourselves completely from war. Yet we must remember that so long as war exists on Earth there will be some danger that even the nation which most ardently desires peace may be drawn into war . . .

I wish I could keep war from all nations, but that is beyond my power. I can at least make certain that no act of the United States helps to produce or to promote war. I can at least make clear that the conscience of America revolts against war and that any nation which provokes war forfeits the sympathy of the people of the United States . . .

In one field, that of economic barriers, the American policy may be, I hope, of some assistance in discouraging the economic source of war and therefore a contribution toward the peace of the world. The trade agreements which we are making are not only finding outlets for the products of American fields and American factories but are also pointing the way to the elimination of embargoes, quotas, and other devices which place such pressure on nations not possessing great natural resources that to them the price of peace seems less terrible than the price of war.

The Congress of the United States has given me certain authority to provide safeguards of American neutrality in case of war.

The President of the United States who, under our Constitution, is vested with primary authority to conduct our international relations, thus has been given new weapons with which to maintain our neutrality.

Nevertheless – and I speak from a long experience – the effective maintenance of American neutrality depends today, as in the past, on the wisdom and determination of whoever at the moment occupy the offices of President and Secretary of State . . .

We seek to dominate no other nation. We ask no territorial expansion. We oppose imperialism. We desire reduction in world armaments.

We believe in democracy; we believe in freedom; we believe in peace. We offer to every nation of the world the handclasp of good neighbor. Let those who wish our friendship look us in eye and take our hand.

Mitsuo Fuchida 1902–1976

NATIONALITY:
Japanese
WHEN:
1941
WHERE:
Pearl Harbor, Oahu, Hawaii
YOU SHOULD KNOW:
After several very near escapes during the war, including being the only member of a group who went to Hiroshima the day after the bombing not to suffer radiation sickness, he became a Christian.

Just after sunrise on the morning of December 7, 1941 Mitsuo Fuchida led the first of two waves of aircraft on the attack on Pearl Harbor. Although the aircraft had been spotted by US radar, the officer in charge of the radar installation thought they were US bombers arriving from California and ignored them. At 7.40 am Fuchida lit a green flare to signal the final manoeuvres before the attack, and at 7.49 his radio operator broadcast the code 'To, to, to', meaning 'charge'. Four minutes later, he sent the signal below back to the fleet flagship Akagi, *the code indicating that the attack had been a complete surprise. The second wave of the attack came as the first aircraft made their way back to their carriers.*

❛ Tora! Tora! Tora! ❜

Napoleon Bonaparte 1769–1821

NATIONALITY:
French
WHEN:
1815
WHERE:
Laffrey, France
YOU SHOULD KNOW:
The period between Napoleon's escape from Elba and the Battle of Waterloo is known as the Hundred Days and the path he took from the coast to Grenoble is still known as the Route Napoleon.

On February 26, 1815 Napoleon and the members of his guard who had accompanied him into exile escaped from Elba and landed on the French coast at Golfe-Juan on March 1. Avoiding areas he knew were not loyal him, he and his men headed for Grenoble. The French government sent the 5th Regiment to arrest him on March 7, but he walked towards them and greeted them with the two sentences below. As one, the men of the regiment changed sides. The following day, the 7th Regiment followed suit. By March 20, he was back in Paris and in command of the army, if not the country. He lost it for the last time three months later at the Battle of Waterloo.

❛ Soldats du 5e, je suis votre empereur. Reconnaissez-moi. S'il est parmi vous un soldat qui veuille tuer son empereur, me voilà.
(Soldiers of the 5th, I am your emperor. Know me. If there is among you a soldier who wants to kill his emperor, here I am.) ❜

Napoleon is welcomed back from Elba.

Admiral Yamamoto

Isoroku Yamamoto 1884–1943

After the attacks on Pearl Harbor and other allied sites in December 1941, the Commander-in-Chief of the Combined Fleet, Admiral Isoroku Yamamoto, made the comment below in an interview for the daily newspaper Asahi Shimbun. *Even before the attack, he had realised that he would have to destroy the US Pacific Fleet completely in order for the pre-emptive strike to work. Because that aim was not achieved – and because of the issue of the timing of the attack – he knew that he had succeeded in doing just what he did not want. He knew, too, that the American military had a far greater capacity than Japan's to re-arm and redeploy ships and aircraft and had earlier said that he would be able to win victory after victory for the first few months but if war carried on longer than that, he could not predict the outcome.*

' A military man can scarcely pride himself on having 'smitten a sleeping enemy'; it is more a matter of shame, simply, for the one smitten. I would rather you made your appraisal after seeing what the enemy does, since it is certain that, angered and outraged, he will soon launch a determined counterattack. '

NATIONALITY:
Japanese
WHEN:
1942
WHERE:
Osaka, Japan
YOU SHOULD KNOW:
The quote attributed to the admiral in the film Tora! Tora! Tora! – 'I fear all we have done is to awaken a sleeping giant and fill him with a terrible resolve', does not appear to have been spoken by him.

Osama bin Laden born 1957

In an interview in Time *magazine towards the end of 1998, Osama bin Laden responded to a question from the interviewer about whether Al Qaeda was trying to acquire chemical and nuclear weapons. As ever, he gave an ambiguous answer, but it became apparent after he had been driven from his network of caves in Afghanistan that he had been pursuing a biological-weapons programme. Documents were found in the caves and in other Al Qaeda houses with designs for nuclear, biological and chemical weapons and there have been numerous reports over recent years of attempts to procure the materials needed to make them.*

' Acquiring weapons for the defence of Muslims is a religious duty. If I have indeed acquired these weapons, then I thank God for enabling me to do so. And if I seek to acquire these weapons, I am carrying out a duty. It would be a sin for Muslims not to try to possess the weapons that would prevent the infidels from inflicting harm on Muslims. '

NATIONALITY:
stateless
WHEN:
1998
WHERE:
Somewhere in Afghanistan
YOU SHOULD KNOW:
Al Qaeda's chemical weapons expert, Abu Khabab al-Masri, died in a US rocket strike in the summer of 2008.

Franklin D. Roosevelt 1882–1945

NATIONALITY:
American
WHEN:
1941
WHERE:
Washington, DC, USA
YOU SHOULD KNOW:
The attack was meant to come after the Japanese declaration that negotiations were at an end, but this took so long to transcribe at the Japanese embassy that the attack was already under way.

The day after Japan attacked the US Pacific Fleet's headquarters at Pearl Harbor, on Oahu, and several other targets across the Pacific, President Roosevelt addressed a Joint Session of Congress to ask them to declare war against Japan. The Japanese aim had been to destroy America's ability to deploy aircraft around the Pacific Ocean, but the aircraft carriers were out on manoeuvres and so escaped the attack. However, 300 aircraft and 18 ships were destroyed or damaged severely, 2,402 people were killed and 1,282 wounded. The Japanese had intended to prevent the Americans entering the war in the Pacific but instead precipitated it.

Yesterday, December 7, 1941 – a date which will live in infamy – the United States of America was suddenly and deliberately attacked by naval and air forces of the Empire of Japan.

The United States was at peace with that nation and, at the solicitation of Japan, was still in conversation with its government and its Emperor looking toward the maintenance of peace in the Pacific.

Indeed, one hour after Japanese air squadrons had commenced bombing in the American island of Oahu, the Japanese Ambassador to the United States and his colleague delivered to our Secretary of State a formal reply to a recent American message. And, while this reply stated that it seemed useless to continue the existing diplomatic negotiations, it contained no threat or hint of war or of armed attack . . .

The attack yesterday on the Hawaiian Islands has caused severe damage to American naval and military forces. I regret to tell you that very many American lives have been lost . . .

Yesterday the Japanese Government also launched an attack against Malaya.

Last night Japanese forces attacked Hong Kong.

Last night Japanese forces attacked Guam.

Last night Japanese forces attacked the Philippine Islands.

Last night the Japanese attacked Wake Island.

And this morning the Japanese attacked Midway Island . . .

I believe that I interpret the will of the Congress and of the people when I assert that we will not only defend ourselves to the uttermost but will make it very certain that this form of treachery shall never again endanger us.

Hostilities exist. There is no blinking at the fact that our people, our territory and our interests are in grave danger.

With confidence in our armed forces, with the unbounding determination of our people, we will gain the inevitable triumph. So help us God.

I ask that the Congress declare that since the unprovoked and dastardly attack by Japan on Sunday, December 7, 1941, a state of war has existed between the United States and the Japanese Empire.

Roosevelt signs the declaration of war against Japan, the day after Japan bombed Pearl Harbor.

Douglas Haig

1861–1928

During the major German assaults on the Western Front in the spring and early summer of 1918, they regained much of the ground that the Allies had spent the previous two years attaining at a cost of millions of lives. At the time of the German operation Georgette in Flanders, Field Marshal Haig issued the order that included the lines below. The urgency for the German attack was because their leadership knew that American forces were building up and would soon be too strong for them, although in reality it was a last desperate attempt. By the summer gains had slowed and when the last offensive – an attempt to cross the strategic River Marne in early July – was repulsed by American resistance, it signalled the end of German gains.

With our backs to the wall, and believing in the justice of our cause, each one of us must fight on to the end.

NATIONALITY:
British
WHEN:
1918
WHERE:
The Western Front
YOU SHOULD KNOW:
After the attempt to cross the Marne petered out, the Allies counter-attacked and within little more than four months, fighting was over.

Carl von Clausewitz 1780–1831

Carl von Clausewitz was a brilliant military thinker, who is largely remembered for his treatise Vom Kriege *(On War), which was published by his widow from 1832 onwards. It is a philosophical examination of warfare in the light of his experiences in the Napoleonic and French Revolutionary Wars, including the way that the nature of warfare had changed in the former with the coming together of large armies from countries across Europe to defeat a common enemy. He saw the military legacy of the Napoleonic Wars as being absolute warfare, but with military aims secondary to political ones.*

Kind-hearted people might of course think there was some ingenious way to disarm or defeat the enemy without too much bloodshed, and might imagine this is the true goal of the art of war. Pleasant as it sounds, it is a fallacy that must be exposed: war is such a dangerous business that the mistakes which come from kindness are the very worst.

NATIONALITY:
Prussian
WHEN:
c.1830
WHERE:
Potsdam, Brandenburg, Germany
YOU SHOULD KNOW:
Prussia was a Germanic state originally covering parts of what is now northern Poland, Lithuania and the Russian area that lies between them on the Baltic coast. At times, its lands covered much of what is now northern Germany and parts of the Netherlands.

Joseph Stalin 1879–1953

NATIONALITY:
Russian
WHEN:
1941
WHERE:
Moscow, Russia
YOU SHOULD KNOW:
Operation Barbarossa was named after the German Holy Roman Emperor Frederick II Barbarossa, who led the forces of the Third Crusade.

In June 1941, Germany broke the non-aggression pact of 1939 and invaded the Soviet Union in the attack code-named Operation Barbarossa. Stalin was taken by surprise because although he knew that German troops were massing on the eastern borders, he had not expected an attack until after Hitler's planned conquest of the UK. On July 2, in a radio broadcast to the nation, the opening of which is below, he denounced the Germans and urged the people to devote all their efforts to the defeat of the enemy.

Soviet leader Joseph Stalin

Comrades! Citizens!

The perfidious military attack by Hitler's Germany on our motherland, begun on June 22, is continuing. In spite of the heroic resistance of the Red Army and although the enemy's finest divisions and finest air units have already been shattered and have met their doom on the battlefield, the enemy continues to push forward, hurling fresh forces into the fray . . .

. . . History shows that there are no invincible armies and that there never have been. Napoleon's army was considered invincible, but it was beaten successively by the troops of Russia, England and Germany. Kaiser Wilhelm's German army in the period of the first imperialist war was also considered an invincible army, but it was defeated several times by Russian and Anglo-French troops, and was finally routed by the Anglo-French troops. The same must be said of Hitler's German fascist army today. This army has not yet met with serious resistance on the continent of Europe. Only on our territory has it met with serious resistance. And if as a result of this the finest divisions of the German fascist army have been defeated by our Red Army, it shows that Hitler's fascist army can also be and will be defeated as were the armies of Napoleon and Wilhelm.

Lyndon B. Johnson 1908–1973

NATIONALITY:
American
WHEN:
1964
WHERE:
Washington, DC, USA
YOU SHOULD KNOW:
In the first incident on August 2 the USS *Maddox* had been in North Vietnamese territorial waters. The report of a second incident on August 4 was later found to be an error.

In response to the Gulf of Tonkin incidents of August 2 and 4, 1964 in which US naval vessels had reportedly been attacked in international waters, President Johnson made a broadcast to the nation. He repeated his promise of there being 'no wider war' and within days Congress had passed the Southeast Asia Resolution, Public Law 88-408, which gave him the power to use military force anywhere in southeast Asia and intervene in countries threatened by communist forces, without having to wait for a formal declaration of war by Congress.

The Hueys landing under sniper fire near Bong Son.

' My fellow Americans: As President and Commander in Chief, it is my duty to the American people to report that renewed hostile actions against United States ships on the high seas in the Gulf of Tonkin have today required me to order the military forces of the United States to take action in reply.

The initial attack on the destroyer Maddox, on August 2, was repeated today by a number of hostile vessels attacking two US destroyers with torpedoes. The destroyers and supporting aircraft acted at once on the orders I gave after the initial act of aggression. We believe at least two of the attacking boats were sunk. There were no US losses . . .

In the larger sense this new act of aggression, aimed directly at our own forces, again brings home to all of us in the United States the importance of the struggle for peace and security in southeast Asia. Aggression by terror against the peaceful villagers of South Vietnam has now been joined by open aggression on the high seas against the United States of America . . .

It is a solemn responsibility to have to order even limited military action by forces whose overall strength is as vast and as awesome as those of the United States of America, but it is my considered conviction, shared throughout your Government, that firmness in the right is indispensable today for peace; that firmness will always be measured. Its mission is peace. '

Georges Clemenceau 1841–1929

Georges Clemenceau, a former Prime Minister of France, was not alone after the first few months of World War I in criticizing the way the French were conducting the war, with strategic as well as military decisions being made by the army's General Staff, particularly the Commander in Chief Joseph Joffre. Parliamentary sittings had been abandoned at the beginning of the war and a succession of short-lived squabbling governments seemed impotent to impose their will on the army, if they had one, until Clemenceau returned as Prime Minister in 1917. He set about arresting third columnists, began inspiring the troops and consulting the generals. Although his decisions were not always sound, the French and their allies managed to hold off the Germans until the Americans had sufficient resources to join in.

' War is too serious a business to entrust to military men. '

NATIONALITY:
French
WHEN:
c. 1915–1916
WHERE:
Paris, France
YOU SHOULD KNOW:
This is sometimes quoted as 'War is too serious to be left to the generals.'

Clemenceau was known as the 'Tiger of France'.

Harry S. Truman 1884–1972

NATIONALITY:
American
WHEN:
1945
WHERE:
USS *Augusta*
YOU SHOULD KNOW:
President Truman was on his way back to the US from the Potsdam Conference when he made this speech.

When Vice President Harry S. Truman became President in April 1945, on the death of President Roosevelt, he did not know about the Manhattan Project to develop atomic and nuclear weapons. After the Axis powers had been defeated in Europe in June he turned his attention to the Far East, where war was continuing. Negotiations with the Japanese had been underway, but they did not accede to the Allies' demand for an unconditional surrender. President Truman then had the choice of a quick strike or months of costly fighting. He chose the former and on August 6 the Enola Gay *dropped an atomic bomb on the city of Hiroshima.*

Sixteen hours ago an American airplane dropped one bomb on Hiroshima, an important Japanese army base. That bomb had more power than 20,000 tons of TNT. It had more than 2000 times the blast power of the British 'Grand Slam', which is the largest bomb ever yet used in the history of warfare.

The Japanese began the war from the air at Pearl Harbor. They have been repaid manyfold. And the end is not yet. With this bomb we have now added a new and revolutionary increase in destruction to supplement the growing power of our armed forces. In their present form these bombs are now in production, and even more powerful forms are in development.

It is an atomic bomb. It is a harnessing of the basic power of the universe. The force from which the Sun draws its power has been loosed against those who brought war to the Far East.

Before 1939, it was the accepted belief of scientists that it was theoretically possible to release atomic energy. But no one knew any practical method of doing it. By 1942, however, we knew that the Germans were working feverishly to find a way to add atomic energy to the other engines of war with which they hoped to enslave the world. But they failed. We may be grateful to Providence that the Germans got the V-1s and V-2s late and in limited quantities and even more grateful that they did not get the atomic bomb at all.

Hiroshima was flattened, apart from the 'A-bomb dome'.

Churchill reviewing the defences.

Winston Churchill 1874–1965

Two weeks after the evacuation of British troops from Dunkirk on June 18, 1940 there were still about 50,000 members of the British Expeditionary Force fighting in France alongside the French Army. However, defeat in the 'Battle of France' was by now almost inevitable and troops were being pulled back. The French would have to seek terms for surrender a week later and with France in German hands, the British Isles would be under direct threat. Churchill outlined to the House of Commons why and how he was convinced that the army, navy and air force would be able to repel invasion and concluded:

'What General Weygand called the Battle of France is over. I expect that the Battle of Britain is about to begin. Upon this battle depends the survival of Christian civilization. Upon it depends our own British life, and the long continuity of our institutions and our Empire. The whole fury and might of the enemy must very soon be turned on us. Hitler knows that he will have to break us in this Island or lose the war. If we can stand up to him, all Europe may be free and the life of the world may move forward into broad, sunlit uplands. But if we fail, then the whole world, including the United States, including all that we have known and cared for, will sink into the abyss of a new Dark Age made more sinister, and perhaps more protracted, by the lights of perverted science. Let us therefore brace ourselves to our duties, and so bear ourselves that, if the British Empire and its Commonwealth last for a thousand years, men will still say, 'This was their finest hour.'.'

NATIONALITY:
British
WHEN:
1940
WHERE:
London, England
YOU SHOULD KNOW:
The only parts of Great Britain successfully occupied by German forces were the Channel Isles.

Wilhelm II

1859–1941, reigned 1888–1918

One of the chief aims of Kaiser Wilhelm II, Emperor of Germany and King of Prussia, was the foundation and expansion of a powerful battlefleet with which to protect the interests of Germany and foster his imperial ambitions. Despite never achieving the latter, his vast navy and the armaments he built up were useful in World War I. He sought to avoid an all-out war, but once it was inevitable became an enthusiastic supporter of his forces.

NATIONALITY:
German
WHEN:
1901
WHERE:
Hamburg, Germany
YOU SHOULD KNOW:
He was a grandson of Queen Victoria.

'We have fought for our place in the Sun and won it. Our future is on the water.'

A Nazi rally at Nuremburg

Anonymous

A variety of sources are claimed for this widely used phrase, including a Hitler Youth Movement marching song, the slogan of the National Socialist press – 'Today Germany belongs to us – tomorrow the whole world' – or even Hitler's autobiography Mein Kampf (My Struggle), where it appears as: 'If the German people . . . had possessed tribal unity like other nations, the German Reich today would be the master of the entire world.'. It was widely believed that he had used the better-known version in at least one speech before 1939. But if he did, no proof has as yet been found.

Today Germany, tomorrow the world!

NATIONALITY: German **WHEN:** Early 1930s **WHERE:** Germany	**YOU SHOULD KNOW:** Adolf Hitler wrote *Mein Kampf* while serving five years in jail for high treason for having been one of the leaders in an attempted *coup d'etat* in 1923.

Tony Blair born 1953

On March 18, 2003 the House of Commons debated the imminent invasion of Iraq. During the debate Prime Minister Blair gave an impassioned speech in which he reiterated his belief that the invasion was justified because Saddam Hussein was in breach of various UN resolutions, including 1441, and that it was only through force that his threat could be neutralized. During the short time that the International Atomic Energy Agency weapons inspectors had spent searching for evidence of weapons of mass destruction programmes they found nothing concrete. But faulty intelligence coupled with a disbelief that Saddam would comply unless forced led to a dismissal of the claim that he had no programme and had dismantled the weapons several years earlier.

. . . We are now seriously asked to accept that in the last few years, contrary to all history, contrary to all intelligence, he decided unilaterally to destroy the weapons. Such a claim is palpably absurd . . . Iraq continues to deny it has any WMD, though no serious intelligence service anywhere in the world believes them . . .

The way head was so clear. It was for the UN to pass a second Resolution setting out benchmarks for compliance; with an

Blair addressing the nation.

ultimatum that if they were ignored, action would follow.

But, of course, in a sense, any fair observer does not really dispute that Iraq is in breach and that 1441 implies action in such circumstances . . .

I have never put our justification for action as regime change. We have to act within the terms set out in Resolution 1441. That is our legal base . . . *"*

NATIONALITY:
British
WHEN:
2003
WHERE:
London, England
YOU SHOULD KNOW:
Although some people accuse Mr Blair of war crimes, he has been awarded the Congressional Gold Medal, the Presidential Medal of Freedom and the David Dan Prize.

Albert Einstein 1879–1955

NATIONALITY:
German/Swiss/American
WHEN:
1946
WHERE:
Princeton, New Jersey, USA
YOU SHOULD KNOW:
Confirmation that Einstein's Theory of General Relativity was correct came when simultaneous observations of stars in the field of the eclipsed Sun in 1919 appeared to change position as the Sun passed them, proving that large objects such as the Sun can bend light.

Before the dropping of the atom bomb on Hiroshima, Einstein had predicted that such devices would have horrendous effects. He is reported to have been so distraught that his work had contributed to such a terrible force for destruction that he expressed a wish to have been a watchmaker (or a plumber, or any of various other artisan professions). In an address at a symposium in Princeton the following year – The Social Task of the Scientist in the Atomic Era – he discussed his vision of a paradoxical future in a world where war must be prevented, but in order to do so, everyone must prepare for war.

' The position in which we are now is a very strange one which in general political life never happened. Namely, the thing that I refer to is this: To have security against atomic bombs and against the other biological weapons, we have to prevent war, for if we cannot prevent war every nation will use every means that is at their disposal; and in spite of all promises they make, they will do it. At the same time, so long as war is not prevented, all the governments of the nations have to prepare for war, and if you have to prepare for war, then you are in a state where you cannot abolish war.

This is really the cornerstone of our situation. Now, I believe what we should try to bring about is the general conviction that the first thing you have to abolish is war at all costs, and every other point of view must be of secondary importance. *"*

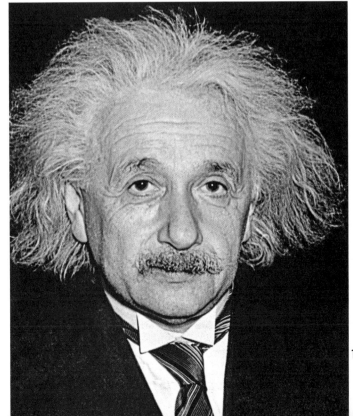

Nobel Prize winner Albert Einstein

George W. Bush born 1946

NATIONALITY:
American
WHEN:
2003
WHERE:
On the deck of USS *Abraham Lincoln*
YOU SHOULD KNOW:
Towards the end of his second term, President Bush conceded that on reflection the speech – and the declaration on the banner – were premature.

Standing on the deck of USS Abraham Lincoln, *in front of a banner proclaiming 'Mission Accomplished' President Bush addressed a crowd of military personnel. He started by saying that the major combat operations in Iraq were over and that work would now be directed towards reconstruction and the setting up of a new democratic government. He also repeated warnings that any terrorist who sought to harm America or its allies would bear the consequences. His assessment that operations in Iraq were by no means over and that insurgency would be a continuing problem have proved only too right, but the assertion that Saddam Hussein's regime was supporting Al Qaeda has since been discounted by most authorities.*

'. . . my fellow Americans, major combat operations in Iraq have ended. In the battle of Iraq, the United States and our allies have prevailed.

And now our coalition is engaged in securing and reconstructing that country.

In this battle, we have fought for the cause of liberty and for the peace of the world. Our nation and our coalition are proud of this accomplishment, yet it is you, the members of the United States military, who achieved it. Your courage, your willingness to face danger for your country and for each other made this day possible.

Because of you our nation is more secure. Because of you the tyrant has fallen and Iraq is free . . .

This nation thanks all of the members of our coalition who joined in a noble cause. We thank the armed forces of the United Kingdom, Australia and Poland who shared in the hardships of war. We thank all of the citizens of Iraq who welcomed our troops and joined in the liberation of their own country.

And tonight, I have a special word for Secretary Rumsfeld, for General Franks and for all the men and women who wear the uniform of the United States: America is grateful for a job well done.

With new tactics and precision weapons, we can achieve military objectives without directing violence against civilians.

No device of man can remove the tragedy from war, yet it is a great advance when the guilty have far more to fear from war than the innocent.

In the images of celebrating Iraqis we have also seen the ageless appeal of human freedom. Decades of lies and intimidation could not make the Iraqi people love their oppressors or desire their own enslavement.

Men and women in every culture need liberty like they need food and water and air. Everywhere that freedom arrives, humanity rejoices and everywhere that freedom stirs, let tyrants fear.

We have difficult work to do in Iraq. We're bringing order to parts of that country that remain dangerous. We're pursuing and finding leaders of the old regime who will be held to account for their crimes. We've begun the search for hidden chemical and biological weapons, and already know of hundreds of sites that will be investigated . . .

The transition from dictatorship to democracy will take time, but it is worth every effort. Our coalition will stay until our work is done and then we will leave and we will leave behind a free Iraq.

The battle of Iraq is one victory in a war on terror that began on September the 11th, 2001 and still goes on . . .

The liberation of Iraq is a crucial advance in the campaign against terror. We have removed an ally of al-Qaeda and cut off a source of terrorist funding . . .

And wherever you go, you carry a message of hope, a message that is ancient and ever new. In the words of the prophet Isaiah, 'To the captives, come out; and to those in darkness, be free.'.

Thank you for serving our country and our cause.

May God bless you all. And may God continue to bless America.

Slobodan Milosevic 1941–2006

On June 28, 1989 Serb President Milosovic gave a speech at the monument to the battle of Kosovo. Since 1974, Kosovo had been an autonomous region within Yugoslavia populated mainly by ethnic Albanians, but to the Serbs it remained their spiritual homeland. Demands for greater Kosovan autonomy and discrimination against Serbs and Montenegrins there led Milosovic to institute a repressive constitution. His speech at the heart of Kosovo three months after the suppression of riots was a reassertion of Serbian control and a forewarning, as Yugoslavia fell apart in the worst violence in Europe since the end of World War II.

By the force of social circumstances this great 600th anniversary of the Battle of Kosovo is taking place in a year in which Serbia, after many years, after many decades, has regained its state, national, and spiritual integrity. Therefore, it is not difficult for us to answer today the old question: how are we going to face Milos? Through the play of history and life, it seems as if Serbia has, precisely in this year, in 1989, regained its state and its dignity and thus has celebrated an event of the distant past which has a great historical and symbolic significance . . .

The lack of unity and betrayal in Kosovo will continue to follow the Serbian people like an evil fate through the whole of its history. Even in the last war, this lack of unity and betrayal led the Serbian people and Serbia into agony, the consequences of which in the historical and moral sense exceeded fascist aggression . . .

Let the memory of Kosovo heroism live forever!

Long live Serbia!

Long live Yugoslavia!

Long live peace and brotherhood among peoples!

NATIONALITY:
Yugoslav/Serbian
WHEN:
1989
WHERE:
Gazimestan monument near
Pristina, then in Yugoslavia
YOU SHOULD KNOW:
The Milos he refers to is Milos
Obilic, the legendary hero of the
Battle of Kosovo.

RELIGION

God

WHEN:
During the 40 years the Israelites
were in the wilderness
WHERE:
Mount Sinai, Egypt
YOU SHOULD KNOW:
Mount Sinai is 2285 m (7497 ft) high.

During the 40 years the Israelites wandered in the wilderness after they left Egypt, God spoke to Moses at the peak of Mount Sinai. He gave him the Ten Commandments on two stone tablets, instructions on the design of a container to house them, as well as many other laws. This text is taken from Exodus XX: 1–17 of the King James' version of the Bible, but put into the order more commonly used today. The container – tabernacle – in which the two tablets were to be put is the Ark of the Covenant, named after the covenant of faith between God and the Israelites.

And GOD spake all these words, saying,

I am the LORD thy God, which have brought thee out of the land of Egypt, out of the house of bondage.

1. Thou shalt have no other gods before me.

2. Thou shalt not make unto thee any graven image, or any likeness of any thing that is in Heaven above, or that is in the Earth beneath, or that is in the water under the Earth:

Thou shalt not bow down thyself to them, nor serve them: for I the LORD thy God am a jealous God, visiting the iniquity of the father upon the children unto the third and fourth generation of them that hate me;

And shewing mercy unto thousands of them that love me, and keep my commandments.

3. Thou shalt not take the name of the LORD thy God in vain; for the LORD will not hold him guiltless that taketh his name in vain.

4. Remember the sabbath day, to keep it holy.

Six days shalt thou labour, and do all thy work:

But the seventh day is the sabbath of the LORD thy God: in it thou shalt not do any work, thou, nor thy son, nor thy daughter, thy manservant, nor thy maidservant, nor thy stranger that is within thy gates: for in six days the LORD made Heaven and Earth, the sea, and all that in them is, and rested the seventh day: wherefore the LORD blessed the sabbath day, and hallowed it.

5. Honour thy father and thy mother: that thy days may be long upon the land which the LORD thy God giveth thee.

6. Thou shalt not kill.

7. Thou shalt not commit adultery.

8. Thou shalt not steal.

9. Thou shalt not bear false witness against thy neighbour.

10. Thou shalt not covet thy neighbour's house, thou shalt not covet thy neighbour's wife, nor his manservant, nor his maidservant, nor his ox, nor his ass, nor any thing that is thy neighbour's.

Moses holding the Ten Commandments.

Allah

In the month of Ramadan, in 610, the Angel Gabriel appeared to Muhammad (c. 570–632), a merchant from Mecca, in a cave on Mount Hira to which he retreated for reflection and meditation for several weeks each year. The Angel revealed to him the word of Allah and taught him to recite it and he became Allah's messenger and prophet. Over the following 22 years, the angel made further revelations to Muhammad. The following passage, which formed part of the first revelation, is the instruction to Muslims to face Mecca to pray – one of the basic tenets of Muslim worship.

WHEN:
610
WHERE:
Mount Hira (now Saudi Arabia)
YOU SHOULD KNOW:
In mosques, a niche – called a *mihrab* – in one of the walls marks the direction of Mecca.

' . . . We see thee often turn about thy face in the heavens, but we will surely turn thee to a qibla [the directin of Mecca] thou shalt like. Turn then thy face towards the Sacred Mosque; wherever ye be, turn your faces towards it; for verily, those who have the Book know that it is the truth from their Lord; – god is not careless of that which ye do.

And if thou shouldst bring to those who have been given the Book every sign, they would not follow your qibla; and thou art not to follow their qibla; nor do some of them follow the qibla of the others: and if thou followest their lusts after the knowledge that has come to thee then art thou of the evildoers.

Those whom we have given the Book know him as they know their sons, although a sect of them do surely hide the truth, the while they know.

The truth [is] from thy Lord; be not therefore one of those who doubt thereof.

Every sect has some one side to which they turn [in prayer]; but do ye hasten onwards to good works; wherever ye are God will bring you all together; verily, god is mighty over all.

From whencesoever thou comest forth; there turn thy face towards the Sacred Mosque, for it is surely truth from thy Lord; God is not careless about what ye do.

And from whencesoever thou comest forth, there turn thy face towards the Sacred Mosque, and wheresoever ye are, turn your faces towards it, that men may have no argument against you, save only those of them who are unjust; and fear them not, but fear me and I will fulfil my favours to you, perchance ye may be guided yet.

Thus have we sent amongst you an apostle of yourselves, to recite to you our signs, to purify you and teach you the Book and wisdom, and to teach you what ye did not know; remember me, then, and I will remember you; thank me, and do not misbelieve.

O ye who do believe, seek aid from patience and from prayer, verily, God is with the patient. '

Martin Luther burning the papal bull.

Martin Luther 1483–1546

In 1520 the Pope demanded that the German theologian Martin Luther withdraw and recant 41 sentences from his writings, including some from his 95 theses, or risk excommunication. When the papal bull (formal document issued by the Pope) announcing his excommunication arrived, Luther set fire to it in public. His trial for heresy – at the Diet of Worms – lasted from January 28 to May 25, 1521. He was asked two questions: whether he was the author of the books and whether he would recant. He answered the first question in the affirmative straight away but asked for time to contemplate his answer to the second. The following day, he returned to the trial and gave the following speech in his defence. He was declared an outlaw and his writings were banned.

' . . . Two questions were yesterday put to me by his imperial majesty; the first, whether I was the author of the books whose titles were read; the second, whether I wished to revoke or defend the doctrine I have taught. I answered the first, and I adhere to that answer.

As to the second, I have composed writings on very different subjects. In some I have discussed Faith and good Works, in a spirit at once so pure, clear and Christian, that even my adversaries themselves, far from finding anything to censure, confess that these writings are profitable, and deserve to be perused by devout persons. The pope's bull, violent as it is, acknowledges this. What, then, should I be doing if I were now to retract these writings? Wretched man! I alone, of all men living, should be abandoning truths approved by the unanimous voice of friends and enemies, and opposing doctrines that the whole world glories in confessing!

I have composed, secondly, certain works against popery, wherein I have attacked such as by false doctrines, irregular lives, and scandalous examples, afflict the Christian world, and ruin the bodies and souls of men. And is not this confirmed by the grief of all who fear God? Is it not manifest that the laws and human doctrines of the popes entangle, vex and distress the consciences of the faithful, while the crying and endless extortions of Rome engulf the property and wealth of Christendom, and more particularly of this illustrious nations?

If I were to revoke what I have written on that subject, what should I do . . . but strengthen this tyranny, and open a wider door to so many flagrant impieties? Bearing down all resistance with fresh fury, we should behold these proud men swell, foam and rage more than ever! And not merely would the yoke which now weighs down

NATIONALITY:
German
WHEN:
1521
WHERE:
Worms (now in Germany)
YOU SHOULD KNOW:
Worms is pronounced Vorms.

122

the Christians be made more grinding by my retraction – it would thereby become, so to speak, lawful – for, by my retractions, it would receive confirmation from your most serene majesty, and all the States of the Empire, Great God! I should thus be like to an infamous cloak, used to hide and cover over every kind of malice and tyranny.

In the third and last place, I have written some books against private individuals, who had undertaken to defend the tyranny of Rome by destroying the faith. I freely confess that I may have attacked such persons with more violence than was consistent with my profession as an ecclesiastic: I do not think of myself as a saint; but neither can I retract these books, because I should, by so doing, sanction the impieties of my opponents, and they would thence take occasion to crush God's people with still more cruelty.

Yet, as I am a mere man, and not God, I will defend myself after the example of Jesus Christ, who said: 'If I have spoken evil, bear witness against me.' How much more should I, who am but dust and ashes, and so prone to error, desire that everyone should bring forward what he can against my doctrine . . .

In speaking thus, I do not suppose that such noble princes have need of my poor judgment; but I wish to acquit myself of a duty that Germany has a right to expect from her children. And so commending myself to your august majesty, and your most serene highnesses, I beseech you, in all humility, not to permit the hatred of my enemies to rain upon me an indignation I have not deserved. Since your most serene majesty and your high mightinesses require of me a simple, clear and direct answer, I will give one, and it is this: I can not submit my faith either to the pope or to the council, because it is as clear as noonday that they have fallen into error and even into glaring inconsistency with themselves. If, then, I am not convinced by proof from Holy Scripture, or by cogent reasons, if I am not satisfied by the very text I have cited, and if my judgment is not in this way brought into subjection to God's word, I neither can nor will retract anything; for it cannot be right for a Christian to speak against his country. I stand here and can say no more. God Help me. Amen. 〞

Hugh Latimer c. 1485–1555

On October 16 1555, two of the most senior clerics in England – Hugh Latimer and Nicholas Ridley – were burned at the stake in Broad Street, Oxford. During the five-year reign of Mary I, Catholicism once again became England's official religion and people who refused to recant Protestantism often faced death. Ridley had also been a supporter of Lady Jane Grey – a rival to the throne. Latimer bore his death stoicly, but Ridley burned particularly slowly and could not maintain his composure, so Latimer encouraged him with the words below. Just over four years later, Mary was dead and her sister, the Protestant Elizabeth I, was on the throne.

NATIONALITY:
British
WHEN:
1555
WHERE:
Oxford, England
YOU SHOULD KNOW:
Latimer, Ridley and Cranmer are known as the Oxford martyrs.

❛ Be of good comfort, Master Ridley, and play the man. We shall this day light such a candle, by God's grace in England, as I trust shall never be put out. 〞

Galileo Galilei 1564–1642

NATIONALITY:
Italian
WHEN:
1615
WHERE:
Florence, Italy
YOU SHOULD KNOW:
In 1616, Galileo was proscribed by the Church from discussing the Sun-centred model of the solar system as a fact, because it was both contrary to scripture and it had not been proved experimentally.

The Italian astronomer Galileo Galilei was one of the first to construct a telescope and use it to study the heavens. In 1610, he discovered that the planet Jupiter had four satellites orbiting around it like the Moon does around the Earth, and that the planet Venus has a full phase, again, like the Moon. The former observation contradicted the Aristotelian Earth-centred model of the cosmos, in which all other astronomical bodies orbit the Earth, and the latter the Ptolemaic theory that Venus always remains between the Earth and the Sun (if this were so, the planet would never show as a full disc). Both ideas were contrary to Church teachings and Galileo – a deeply religious man – faced accusations of heresy. The reflection that God wouldn't have given us brains if he hadn't meant us to use them is an early defence of Francis Bacon's evidence-based scientific method.

‘ . . . I do not feel obliged to believe that the same God who has endowed us with senses, reason and intellect has intended to forgo their use and by some other means to give us knowledge which we can attain by them. ’

Herod I 73–4 BC

Herod I – also known as Herod the Great – was a Roman client king of Judaea. In Chapter II of St Matthew's Gospel, he is visited by the three wise men, who inform him that they are looking for the newly born King of the Jews. As he is currently holder of that position, he calls together the most important priests and scribes, who tell him that the prophet [Micah] has written that the King of the Jews will be born in Bethlehem. Herod sends the wise men to Bethlehem with the instruction to murder the child when he is found. When the wise men do not return, Herod sends his troops to slaughter all of the children in the city under the age of two.

Detail of the Massacre of the Innocents

‘ Go and search diligently for the young child; and when ye have found him, bring me word again, that I may come and worship him also. ’

NATIONALITY:
Idumaean
WHEN:
c. 7–4 BC
WHERE:
Jerusalem (now Israel)

YOU SHOULD KNOW:
Herod was also responsible for rebuilding the Temple of Solomon in Jerusalem.

Solomon

reigned c. 986–946 BC

Solomon was the third and last king of the united kingdom of Judaea and Israel and the son of King David. He is credited as author of Proverbs, Ecclestiastes and the Song of Songs, built the first temple in Jerusalem and is renowned for his wisdom. One of the most famous instances of his wisdom is in I Kings, Chapter 3 and concerns two women, both of whom were claiming the same baby as their own. His decision on which of the two women was the real mother – based on his understanding of human nature – is known as the Judgment of Solomon.

Detail from The Judgment of Solomon

The one saith, this is my son that liveth and thy son is the dead; and the other saith, Nay; but thy son is the dead, and my son is the living.

Bring me a sword.

Divide the living child in two, and give half to the one, and half to the other.

[One of the two women says to give the boy to the other woman, while the other says to cut him in half as the king ordered.]

Give her [the first woman] the living child, and in no wise slay it: she is the mother thereof.

NATIONALITY:
Israelite
WHEN:
unknown
WHERE:
Jerusalem (now Israel)
YOU SHOULD KNOW:
According to the Bible, Solomon had 700 wives and 300 concubines.

Karl Marx 1818–1883

Often mis-quoted as 'Religion is the opiate of the masses', this axiom is less dismissive of faith than the shorter version made it appear. It is obvious that although Marx did not believe in a divine being, he regarded religion more as the consolation of the oppressed than as an addictive drug. This idea is integral to his philosophy at a time when he was considering the difference between the freedom of labourers in his ideal communist society (where everyone would share equally) and the reality of the poverty of the urban masses in the middle of the nineteenth century during which the many laboured in appalling conditions to put money into the hands of the few.

NATIONALITY:
German
WHEN:
1843–1844
WHERE:
Paris, France
YOU SHOULD KNOW:
Marx's ideas of what a communist state would be like were idealistic and nothing like the reality of the twentieth century Soviet states.

Religion is the sigh of the oppressed creature, the heart of a heartless world and the soul of soulless conditions. It is the opium of the people.

Francis Bacon 1561–1626

NATIONALITY:
British
WHEN:
1601
WHERE:
London, England
YOU SHOULD KNOW:
Bacon's method of scientific experimentation is the basis of the scientific method used today.

Philosopher, statesman, scientist and author, Francis Bacon is chiefly remembered today for overturning the method of scientific investigation developed by Aristotle – that if sufficiently clever men debated a problem for long enough they would get the right answer – in favour of empirical observation of a phenomenon or object leading to a discovery of the facts about it. In a time when there was increasing concern about the possible risks of atheism to society, his observations led him to conclude that there had to be a creator as no other explanation fitted what he saw.

' I had rather believe all the fables in the Legend, and the Talmud, and the Alcoran, than that this universal frame is without a mind. And therefore, God never wrought miracle, to convince atheism, because his ordinary works convince it. It is true, that a little philosophy inclineth man's mind to atheism; but depth in philosophy bringeth men's minds about to religion. For while the mind of man looketh upon second causes scattered, it may sometimes rest in them, and go no further; but when it beholdeth the chain of them, confederate and linked together, it must needs fly to Providence and Deity. Nay, even that school which is most accused of atheism doth most demonstrate religion; that is, the school of Leucippus and Democritus and Epicurus. For it is a thousand times more credible, that four mutable elements, and one immutable fifth essence, duly and eternally placed, need no God, than that an army of infinite small portions, or seeds unplaced, should have produced this order and beauty, without a divine marshal. The Scripture saith, The fool hath said in his heart, there is no God; it is not said, The fool hath thought in his heart; so as he rather saith it, by rote to himself, as that he would have, than that he can thoroughly believe it, or be persuaded of it. For none deny, there is a God, but those for whom it maketh that there were no God. It appeareth in nothing more, that atheism is rather in the lip, than in the heart of man, than by this; that atheists will ever be talking of that their opinion, as if they fainted in it, within themselves, and would be glad to be strengthened, by the consent of others . . . The causes of atheism are: divisions in religion, if they be many; for any one main division, addeth zeal to both sides; but many divisions introduce atheism. Another is, scandal of priests; when it is come to that which St Bernard saith . . . A third is, custom of profane scoffing in holy matters; which doth, by little and little, deface the reverence of religion. And lastly, learned times, specially with peace and prosperity; for troubles and adversities do more bow men's minds to religion. They that deny a God, destroy man's nobility; for certainly man is of kin to the beasts, by his body; and, if he be not of kin to God, by his spirit, he is a base and ignoble creature. It destroys likewise magnanimity, and the raising of human nature; for take an example of a dog, and mark what a generosity and courage he will put on, when he finds himself maintained by a man; who to him is instead of a

God; which courage is manifestly such, as that creature, without that confidence of a better nature than his own, could never attain. So man, when he resteth and assureth himself, upon divine protection and favour, gathered a force and faith, which human nature in itself could not obtain. Therefore, as atheism is in all respects hateful, so in this, that it depriveth human nature of the means to exalt itself, above human frailty. As it is in particular persons, so it is in nations. Never was there such a state for magnanimity as Rome. Of this state hear what Cicero saith: Pride ourselves as we may upon our country, yet are we not in number superior to the Spaniards, nor in strength to the Gauls, nor in cunning to the Carthaginians, not to the Greeks in arts, nor to the Italians and Latins themselves in the homely and native sense which belongs to his nation and land; it is in piety only and religion, and the wisdom of regarding the providence of the immortal gods as that which rules and governs all things, that we have surpassed all nations and peoples.

The delegates of the First Council of Nicaea AD 325

In AD 325, Emperor Constantine convened the First Ecumenical Council, in the city of Nicaea (now Iznik in north-west Turkey). Among the topics up for discussion were the correct date for the celebration of Easter, the problem of the Arian heresy, whether baptism by heretics was valid in the main body of the church and lapsed Christians. This was the first attempt by the widely spread church to come to a consensus about matters of such importance. The council is chiefly remembered today for the issuing of the first widely used creed – profession of faith. It was revised in 381 at the Council of Constantinople, and there are later Latin and Armenian versions.

NATIONALITY:
Various
WHEN:
AD 325
WHERE:
Nicaea (now Turkey)
YOU SHOULD KNOW:
The word creed comes from the Latin, *credo*, which means 'I believe'.

We believe in one God, the Father Almighty, Maker of all things visible and invisible.

And in one Lord Jesus Christ, the Son of God, begotten of the Father [the only-begotten; that is, of the essence of the Father, God of God], Light of Light, very God of very God, begotten, not made, being of one substance with the Father; by whom all things were made [both in Heaven and on Earth]; who for us men, and for our salvation, came down and was incarnate and was made man; he suffered, and the third day he rose again, ascended into Heaven; from thence he shall come to judge the quick and the dead.

And in the Holy Ghost.

But those who say: 'There was a time when he was not'; and 'He was not before he was made'; and 'He was made out of nothing', or 'He is of another substance' or 'essence', or 'The Son of God is created', or 'changeable', or 'alterable' – they are condemned by the holy catholic and apostolic Church.

Buddha

Siddhartha Gautama c. 563–483 BC

NATIONALITY:
Kapilavastu
WHEN:
Unknown
WHERE:
Bodh Gaya (now India)
YOU SHOULD KNOW:
Bikkhu means monk in Pali.

The son of the ruler of Kapilavastu, Siddhartha Gautama became the leader of one of the most widespread and popular religions in the world. He gave up his privileged position and became an ascetic, nomadic beggar, fasting and meditating in order to achieve enlightenment. In the Pali tradition, his third teaching after he gained enlightenment was the Adittapariyaya Sutta – the Fire Sermon, which he preached to 1,000 newly converted ascetics who had formerly been fire worshippers. The teaching shows them that in order to achieve enlightenment, they must learn to divorce themselves from their senses and the mental processes that accompany them.

Thus I heard. On one occasion the Blessed One was living at Gaya, at Gayasisa, together with a thousand bhikkhus. There he addressed the bhikkhus.

Bhikkhus, all is burning. And what is the all that is burning?

The eye is burning, forms are burning, eye-consciousness is burning, eye-contact is burning, also whatever is felt as pleasant or painful or neither-painful-nor-pleasant that arises with eye-contact for its indispensable condition, that too is burning. Burning with what? Burning with the fire of lust, with the fire of hate, with the fire of delusion. I say it is burning with birth, aging and death, with sorrows, with lamentations, with pains, with griefs, with despairs.

The ear is burning, sounds are burning . . .
The nose is burning, odours are burning . . .
The tongue is burning, flavours are burning . . .
The body is burning, tangibles are burning . . .

The mind is burning, ideas are burning, mind-consciousness is burning, mind-contact is burning, also whatever is felt as pleasant or painful or neither-painful-nor-pleasant that arises with mind-contact for its indispensable condition, that too is burning. Burning with what? Burning with the fire of lust, with the fire of hate, with the fire of delusion. I say it is burning with birth, aging and death, with sorrows, with lamentations, with pains, with griefs, with despairs.

Bhikkhus, when a noble follower who has heard (the truth) sees thus, he finds estrangement in the eye, finds estrangement in forms, finds estrangement in eye-consciousness, finds estrangement in eye-contact, and whatever is felt as pleasant or painful or neither-painful-nor-pleasant that arises with eye-contact for its indispensable condition, in that too he finds estrangement.

He finds estrangement in the ear . . . in sounds . . .
He finds estrangement in the nose . . . in odours . . .
He finds estrangement in the tongue . . . in flavours . . .

He finds estrangement in the body . . . in tangibles . . .

He finds estrangement in the mind, finds estrangement in ideas, finds estrangement in mind-consciousness, finds estrangement in mind-contact, and whatever is felt as pleasant or painful or neither-painful-nor-pleasant that arises with mind-contact for its indispensable condition, in that too he finds estrangement.

When he finds estrangement, passion fades out. With the fading of passion, he is liberated. When liberated, there is knowledge that he is liberated. He understands: 'Birth is exhausted, the holy life has been lived out, what can be done is done, of this there is no more beyond. 🟦

Jesus Christ c. 7–4 BC–AD 26–36

In chapters 5–7 of St Matthew's Gospel – the passage known as the Sermon on the Mount – Christ expresses many of what would become the most important ideas of Christianity, including the spiritual qualities required for a Christian; a reiteration and reinterpretation of Moses' laws (especially the Ten Commandments); the need to avoid showiness, materialism and judgmentalism; the Lord's Prayer; a warning against false prophets; and the need to base one's entire life on God. It contains such important imagery as the Light of the World and Christ as the fulfilment of the Jewish prophecies, turning the other cheek, not hiding one's light under a bushel and of God as a rock on which everything has its foundations.

NATIONALITY:
Galilean
WHEN:
c. AD 30
WHERE:
Galilee (now Israel)
YOU SHOULD KNOW:
While this Gospel places all these teachings in one passage, in St Luke's Gospel, they appear at different times and locations.

❝ Our Father which art in Heaven,
Hallowed be thy name.
Thy kingdom come, Thy will be
done on Earth, as it is in Heaven.
Give us this day our daily bread.
And forgive us our debts, as we
forgive our debtors.
And lead us not into temptation,
but deliver us from evil: For thine
is the kingdom, and the power,
and the glory, for ever. Amen. 🟦

*The twelve Disciples listening
to the Sermon on the Mount.*

Henry VIII by Hans Holbein

The English Parliament 1534

In 1533, Archbishop Thomas Cranmer declared Henry VIII's marriage to his first wife – Catherine of Aragon – null and void, and his second – to Anne Boleyn – legal and valid. Parliament passed various laws limiting the power of the Church and making it subservient to the king. Pope Clement VII, who had refused to annul Henry's first marriage, began excommunication proceedings against both Henry and Cranmer. In response, under Henry's direction, Parliament enacted the Act of Supremacy, which gave the king control over the Church in England, and the Treason Act – which made it treason not to acknowledge the former Act. However, this was not an introduction of Protestantism.

NATIONALITY:
English
WHEN:
1534
WHERE:
London, England
YOU SHOULD KNOW:
This Act was repealed by Henry's Catholic daughter, Mary I, in 1554 and the Second Act of Supremacy was passed by Elizabeth I in 1559.

' Albeit the King's Majesty justly and rightfully is and ought to be the supreme head of the Church of England, and so is recognized by the clergy of this realm in their convocations, yet nevertheless, for corroboration and confirmation thereof, and for increase of virtue in Christ's religion within this realm of England, and to repress and extirpate all errors, heresies, and other enormities and abuses heretofore used in the same, be it enacted, by authority of this present Parliament, that the king, our sovereign lord, his heirs and successors, kings of this realm, shall be taken, accepted, and reputed the only supreme head on Earth of the Church of England, called Anglicans Ecclesia; and shall have and enjoy, annexed and united to the imperial crown of this realm, as well the title and style thereof, as all honours, dignities, pre-eminences, jurisdictions, privileges, authorities, immunities, profits, and commodities to the said dignity of the supreme head of the same Church belonging and appertaining; and that our said sovereign lord, his heirs and successors, kings of this realm, shall have full power and authority from time to time to visit, repress, redress, record, order, correct, restrain, and amend all such errors, heresies, abuses, offences, contempts and enormities, whatsoever they be, which by any manner of spiritual authority or jurisdiction ought or may lawfully be reformed, repressed, ordered, redressed, corrected, restrained, or amended, most to the pleasure of Almighty God, the increase of virtue in Christ's religion, and for the conservation of the peace, unity, and tranquility of this realm; any usage, foreign land, foreign authority, prescription, or any other thing or things to the contrary hereof notwithstanding. '

Saladin Salah al-Din, 1137–1193

The Sultan of Egypt and Syria – and ruler of parts of Mesopotamia, Hejaz (part of Saudi Arabia including the cities of Mecca and Medina), and Yemen, during the Third Crusade, Saladin was the leader of the Islamic opposition to the invading European forces. This was his reply to a demand from Richard the Lionheart (Richard I of England) that he surrender the whole of the Holy Land to the Christians. Even though at the time he was fighting a losing battle, Saladin refused. Eventually, despite the Christian army getting within sight of Jerusalem, the two leaders compromised and Christians were allowed back into Jerusalem only under the terms of a three-year truce – the Treaty of Ramia.

NATIONALITY:
Kurdish
WHEN:
1191
WHERE:
Arsuf, the Holy Land

' Jerusalem is ours as much as yours; indeed it is even more sacred to us than to you for it is the place where our Prophet made his journey through the night and the city where our people will be gathered. Do not imagine that we can surrender to you or compromise on this. The land belonged to us from the beginning, while you have only just arrived, and have taken it over only because of the weakness of the Muslims living there at the time. Allah will not allow to be rebuilt a single stone as long as the war lasts. "

St Thomas à Becket 1118–1170

From 1155, the brilliant Thomas à Becket had been a loyal Lord Chancellor to Henry II, assisting him in his efforts against the privileges of the Church. But when the king made him Archbishop of Canterbury in 1162, he switched his loyalties to the Church. In 1164 Henry convicted Becket of contempt of royal authority and misconduct. He stormed out and escaped to France. Henry II only allowed him back into England in 1170 under threat of excommunication. On his return Becket excommunicated three bishops who had usurped his privileges. Upon hearing this Henry is supposed to have shouted something like 'Who will rid me of this troublesome priest?'. Four knights overheard and rode to Canterbury to kill the archbishop. When they found him kneeling at the altar in the northwest transept, they gave him the ultimatum of reinstating the bishops or death. After his refusal, he was killed with three sword strokes. He was canonized three years later and the site of his shrine is still an important pilgrimage centre.

NATIONALITY:
English
WHEN:
1170
WHERE:
Canterbury, England
YOU SHOULD KNOW:
A candle marks the spot in Canterbury Cathedral where Becket's shrine stood until it was destroyed on the orders of King Henry VIII.

' For the name of Jesus and the protection of the Church, I am ready to embrace death. "

John Calvin Jean Cauvin, 1509–1564

NATIONALITY:
French
WHEN:
Probably 1549
WHERE:
Geneva, Switzerland
YOU SHOULD KNOW:
During his years in Geneva
(1541–1564), Calvin preached more
than 2,000 different sermons.

It has been said that the influence of this French lawyer and theologian on the Reformation was second only to that of Martin Luther. His most influential work was the Institutes of the Christian Religion, *of which four editions were published in his lifetime. His theology stresses the need for strict morals, family piety and eduction, with individuals subject to the state and the state to the church, all under a sovereign God. This sermon, known as 'Let us go forth from the city', contains the section known as 'On persecution' on the theme of undergoing suffering and persecution in order to gain God's grace.*

It is true that persons may be found who will foolishly expose themselves to death in maintaining some absurd opinions and reveries conceived by their own brain, but such impetuosity is more to be regarded as frenzy than as Christian zeal; and, in fact, there is neither firmness nor sound sense in those who thus, at a kind of haphazard, cast themselves away. But, however this may be, it is in a good cause only that God can acknowledge us as His martyrs. Death is common to all, and the children of God are condemned to ignominy and tortures just as criminals are; but God makes the distinction between them, inasmuch as He can not deny His truth.

On our part, then, it is requisite that we have sure and infallible evidence of the doctrine which we maintain; and hence, as I have said, we can not be rationally impressed by any exhortations which we receive to suffer persecution for the Gospel, if no true certainty of faith has been imprinted in our hearts. For to hazard our life upon a peradventure is not natural, and tho' we were to do it, it would only be rashness, not Christian courage. In a word, nothing that we do will be approved of God if we are not thoroughly persuaded that it is for Him and His cause we suffer persecution and the world is our enemy.

. . . We must know well what our Christianity is, what the faith which we have to hold and follow – what the rule which God has given us; and we must be so well furnished with such instructions as to be able boldly to condemn all the falsehoods, errors, and superstitions which Satan has introduced to corrupt the pure simplicity of the doctrine of God. Hence we ought not to be surprised that, in the present day, we see so few persons disposed to suffer for the Gospel, and that the greater part of those who call themselves Christians know not what it is. For all are, as it were, lukewarm, and, instead of making it their business to hear or read, count it enough to have had some slight taste of Christian faith. This is the reason why there is so little decision, and why those who are assailed immediately fall away. This fact should stimulate us to inquire more diligently into divine truth, in order to be well assured with regard to it . . .

Above all, when we look to the martyrs of past times, well may we detest our own cowardice! The greater part of those were not persons much versed in holy Scripture, so as to be able to dispute on all subjects. They knew that there was one God, whom they behooved to worship and serve; that they had been redeemed by the blood of Jesus Christ, in order that they might place their confidence of salvation in Him and in His grace; and that, all the inventions of men being mere dross and rubbish, they ought to condemn all idolatries and superstitions. In one word, their theology was in substance this: There is one God, who created all the world, and declared His will to us by Moses and the Prophets, and finally by Jesus Christ and His apostles; and we have one sole Redeemer, who purchased us by His blood, and by whose grace we hope to be saved; all the idols of the world are cursed, and deserve execration . . .

But as persecution is always harsh and bitter, let us consider how and by what means Christians may be able to fortify themselves with patience, so as unflinchingly to expose their life for the truth of God. The text which we have read out, when it is properly understood, is sufficient to induce us to do so. The apostle says, 'Let us go forth from the city after the Lord Jesus, bearing His reproach.'. In the first place he reminds us, altho' the swords should not be drawn over us nor the fires kindled to burn us, that we can not be truly united to the Son of God while we are rooted in this world. Wherefore, a Christian, even in repose, must always have one foot lifted to march to battle, and not only so, but he must have his affections withdrawn from the world altho' his body is dwelling in it. Grant that this at first sight seems to us hard, still we must be satisfied with the words of St Paul, 'We are called and appointed to suffer.' As if he had said, Such is our condition as Christians; this is the road by which we must go if we would follow Christ . . .

Are we so delicate as to be unwilling to endure anything? Then we must renounce the grace of God by which He has called us to the hope of salvation. For there are two things which can not be separated – to be members of Christ, and to be tried by many afflictions. We certainly ought to prize such a conformity to the Son of God . . . It is true that in the world's judgment there is disgrace in suffering for the Gospel. But since we know that unbelievers are blind, ought we not to have better eyes than they? It is ignominy to suffer from those who occupy the seat of justice, but St Paul shows us by his example that we have to glory in scourgings for Jesus Christ, as marks by which God recognizes us and avows us for His own. And we know what St Luke narrates of Peter and John; namely, that they rejoiced to have been 'counted worthy to suffer infamy and reproach for the name of the Lord Jesus'.

Ignominy and dignity are two opposites: so says the world which, being infatuated, judges against all reason, and in this way converts the glory of God into dishonour. But, on our part, let us not refuse to be vilified as concerns the world, in order to be honoured before God and His angels. We see what pains the ambitious take to receive the commands of a king, and what a boast they make of it. The Son of God presents His commands to us, and every one stands back! Tell me, pray, whether in so doing are we worthy of having anything in common with Him? There is nothing here to attract our sensual nature, but such, notwithstanding, are the true escutcheons of nobility in the heavens. Imprisonment, exile, evil report, imply in men's imagination whatever is to be vituperated; but what hinders us from viewing things as God judges and declares them, save our unbelief? Wherefore let the name of the Son of God have all the weight with us which it deserves, that we may learn to count it honour when He stamps His marks upon us. If we act otherwise our ingratitude is insupportable.

Were God to deal with us according to our deserts, would He not have just cause to chastise us daily in a thousand ways? Nay, more, a hundred thousand deaths would not suffice for a small portion of our misdeeds! Now, if in His infinite goodness He puts all our faults under His foot and abolishes them, and, instead of punishing us according to our demerit, devises an admirable means to convert our afflictions into honour and a special privilege, inasmuch as through them we are taken into partnership with His Son, must it not be said, when we disdain such a happy state, that we have indeed made little progress in Christian doctrine? . . .

Constantine c. 272–337 and
Valerius c. 250–325

NATIONALITY:
Roman
WHEN:
AD 313
WHERE:
Milan (now Italy)
YOU SHOULD KNOW:
At this time, the Roman Empire was divided into east and west and so had more than one emperor.

For almost 300 years, Christians had been persecuted in the Roman Empire, particularly so during the reign of Constantine's predecessor, Diocletian, who regarded Christianity – and several other non-official religions – as a threat. In 303, he issued his first edict proscribing Christianity. The gruesome way that Christians were executed not only meant that non-Christians sympathized, but also gave fellow-Christians greater resolve. Within two years of Diocletian's death, the co-emperors issued the proclamation below – the Edict of Milan – announcing religious tolerance throughout the Empire.

A bust of Constantine

'When I, Constantine Augustus, as well as I, Licinius Augustus, fortunately met near Mediolanurn (Milan), and were considering everything that pertained to the public welfare and security, we thought, among other things which we saw would be for the good of many, those regulations pertaining to the reverence of the Divinity ought certainly to be made first, so that we might grant to the Christians and others full authority to observe that religion which each preferred; whence any Divinity whatsoever in the seat of the heavens may be propitious and kindly disposed to us and all who are placed under our rule. And thus by this wholesome counsel and most upright provision we thought to arrange that no one whatsoever should be denied the opportunity to give his heart to the observance of the Christian religion, of that religion which he should think best for himself, so that the Supreme Deity, to whose worship we freely yield our hearts may show in all things His usual favour and benevolence. Therefore, your Worship should know that it has pleased us to remove all conditions whatsoever, which were in the rescripts formerly given to you officially, concerning the Christians and now any one of these who wishes to observe Christian religion may do so freely and openly, without molestation. We thought it fit to commend these things most fully to your care that you may know that we have given to those Christians free and unrestricted opportunity of religious worship. When you see that this has been granted to them by us, your Worship will know that we have also conceded to other religions the right of open and free observance of their worship for the sake of the peace of our times, that each one may have the free opportunity to worship as he pleases; this regulation is made we that we may not seem to detract from any dignity or any religion . . .'

Thomas à Kempis 1379–1471

Thomas à Kempis, a medieval monk, is the author of one of the most important and influential devotional books – The Imitation of Christ. *It was written, in Latin, to be read out to monks in the convent of St Agnes, but versions of it in other languages appeared within a few years and it is one of the earliest widely distributed printed books. In chapter 19 of the first volume is the maxim now rendered as 'Man proposes and God Disposes', meaning that whatever people plan or do, it is God's will that dictates what happens. A similar idea appears in Proverbs.*

NATIONALITY:
German
WHEN:
c.1420
WHERE:
Near Zwolle (now in Germany)
YOU SHOULD KNOW:
There are more than 2,000 editions
of *The Imitation of Christ*.

The life of a Christian ought to be adorned with all virtues, that he may be inwardly what he outwardly appeareth unto men. And verily it should be yet better within than without, for God is a discerner of our heart, Whom we must reverence with all our hearts wheresoever we are, and walk pure in His presence as do the angels. We ought daily to renew our vows, and to kindle our hearts to zeal, as if each day were the first day of our conversion, and to say, 'Help me, O God, in my good resolutions, and in Thy holy service, and grant that this day I may make a good beginning, for hitherto I have done nothing!'.

According to our resolution so is the rate of our progress, and much diligence is needful for him who would make good progress. For if he who resolveth bravely oftentimes falleth short, how shall it be with him who resolveth rarely or feebly? But manifold causes bring about abandonment of our resolution, yet a trivial omission of holy exercises can hardly be made without some loss to us. The resolution of the righteous dependeth more upon the grace of God than upon their own wisdom; for in Him they always put their trust, whatsoever they take in hand. For man proposeth, but God disposeth; and the way of a man is not in himself.

If thou canst not be always examining thyself, thou canst at certain seasons, and at least twice in the day, at evening and at morning. In the morning make thy resolves, and in the evening inquire into thy life, how thou hast sped today in word, deed, and thought; for in these ways thou hast often perchance offended God and thy neighbour. Gird up thy loins like a man against the assaults of the devil; bridle thine appetite, and thou wilt soon be able to bridle every inclination of the flesh. Be thou never without something to do; be reading, or writing, or praying, or meditating, or doing something that is useful to the community. Bodily exercises, however, must be undertaken with discretion, nor are they to be used by all alike.

Allah

WHEN:
610–32
WHERE:
Arabia (now Saudi Arabia)
YOU SHOULD KNOW:
The Irish hostage – Brian Keenan –
used the last three lines of this verse
as the title of the book he wrote
about his years in captivity in the
Lebanon.

Chapter 13 of the Koran – the Thunder (Ar-Ra'd) – tells of Allah's creation of the world: the sky; the land, mountains and rivers; the Sun and the Moon; the fruits of the Earth, and that these should lead the people to him. Allah's words were dictated to Muhammad at a time when there were few other Muslims, and in this exhortation to spread the word of Allah are contrasted the fates of those who hear it and listen and those who hear it and ignore it, which is Jahannum, a fiery hell, an evil cradling. Elsewhere in the Koran are instructions on how to convert non-believers and how to treat infidels.

For those who answer their Lord, the reward
most fair; and those who answer Him not –
if they possessed all that is in the Earth,
and the like of it with it, they would
offer it for their ransom. Those –
theirs shall be the evil reckoning,
and their refuge shall be Jahannum –
an evil cradling.

God

WHEN:
During the sojurn in Egypt
WHERE:
Horeb, Egypt
YOU SHOULD KNOW:
The final plague, in which the first-
born son of every Egyptian family
died, but the Israelite sons were
passed over, is the origin of the
Passover observance.

After generations in Egypt, the Israelites had become not honoured guests but slaves. After Moses killed an Egyptian slave-master who had been beating an Israelite slave, he had to flee across the Red Sea. While keeping his father-in-law's flock, a flaming angel appeared from the centre of the bush, which was not being consumed by the fire. As he approached it he heard the voice of God telling him that he would lead the Israelites out of slavery and into the Land of Canaan. When Pharaoh did not agree, God inflicted the Ten Plagues on the Egyptians, the Israelites fled across the Red Sea and Pharaoh's army was drowned. After 40 years of wandering, the Israelites finally reached the land of milk and honey.

God called unto him out of the midst of the bush, and said, Moses, Moses. And he said, Here am I.

And he said, Draw not nigh hither: put off thy shoes from off thy feet, for the place whereon thou standest is holy ground.

Moreover he said, I am the God of thy father, the God of Abraham, the God of Isaac, and the God of Jacob. And Moses hid his face; for he was afraid to look upon God.

And the LORD said, I have surely seen the affliction of my people which are in Egypt, and have heard their cry by reason of their taskmasters; for I know their sorrows;

And I am come down to deliver them out of the hand of the Egyptians, and to bring them up out of that land unto a good land and a large, unto a land flowing with milk and honey; unto the place of the Canaanites, and the Hittites, and the Amorites, and the Perizzites, and the Hivites, and the Jebusites.

Now therefore, behold, the cry of the children of Israel is come unto me: and I have also seen the oppression wherewith the Egyptians oppress them.

Come now therefore, and I will send thee unto Pharaoh, that thou mayest bring forth my people the children of Israel out of Egypt.

And Moses said unto God, Who am I, that I should go unto Pharaoh, and that I should bring forth the children of Israel out of Egypt?

And he said, Certainly I will be with thee; and this shall be a token unto thee, that I have sent thee: When thou hast brought forth the people out of Egypt, ye shall serve God upon this mountain.

And Moses said unto God, Behold, when I come unto the children of Israel, and shall say unto them, The God of your fathers hath sent me unto you; and they shall say to me, What is his name? what shall I say unto them?

And God said unto Moses, I AM THAT I AM: and he said, Thus shalt thou say unto the children of Israel, I AM hath sent me unto you.

And God said moreover unto Moses, Thus shalt thou say unto the children of Israel, the LORD God of your fathers, the God of Abraham, the God of Isaac, and the God of Jacob, hath sent me unto you: this is my name for ever, and this is my memorial unto all generations.

Go, and gather the elders of Israel together, and say unto them, The LORD God of your fathers, the God of Abraham, of Isaac, and of Jacob, appeared unto me, saying, I have surely visited you, and seen that which is done to you in Egypt:

And I have said, I will bring you up out of the affliction of Egypt unto the land of the Canaanites, and the Hittites, and the Amorites, and the Perizzites, and the Hivites, and the Jebusites, unto a land flowing with milk and honey.

And they shall hearken to thy voice: and thou shalt come, thou and the elders of Israel, unto the king of Egypt, and ye shall say unto him, The LORD God of the Hebrews hath met with us: and now let us go, we beseech thee, three days' journey into the wilderness, that we may sacrifice to the LORD our God.

And I am sure that the king of Egypt will not let you go, no, not by a mighty hand.

And I will stretch out my hand, and smite Egypt with all my wonders which I will do in the midst thereof: and after that he will let you go.

And I will give this people favour in the sight of the Egyptians: and it shall come to pass that, when ye go, ye shall not go empty.

But every woman shall borrow of her neighbour, and of her that sojourneth in her house, jewels of silver, and jewels of gold, and raiment: and ye shall put them upon your sons, and upon your daughters; and ye shall spoil the Egyptians.

Allah

WHEN:
610–632
WHERE:
Arabia (now Saudi Ababia)
YOU SHOULD KNOW:
The first muezzin was Bilal ibn Ribah, one of Muhammad's companions.

Five times a day the Call to Prayer is chanted from the minaret of each mosque. It is called the Athan, and is called by a muezzin. Before he calls it, he faces Mecca, standing in the correct posture and faces first right then left as he chants different parts of the call. Sunni Muslims believe that the call was given as the word of Allah to one of Allah's companions in a divine vision, while Shi'a Muslims believe that the divine vision was granted to Muhammad. The call reminds the faithful of the major beliefs of Islam.

Allah is the greatest, Allah is the greatest.
Allah is the greatest, Allah is the greatest.
Allah is the greatest, Allah is the greatest.
Allah is the greatest, Allah is the greatest.
I bear witness that there is no deity but Allah.
I bear witness that there is no deity but Allah.
I bear witness that Muhammad is the Messenger of Allah.
I bear witness that Muhammad is the Messenger of Allah.
Make haste towards worship. Make haste towards worship.
Come to your good, Come to your good.
Allah is the greatest, Allah is the greatest.
There is no deity but Allah.

St Francis of Assisi 1181–1226

The founder of the Franciscan monastic order is also the patron saint of Italy (together with St Catherine of Siena) and animals. The son of a merchant, he renounced his wealth and became a mendicant preacher, based around his home city of Assisi, but travelling widely around the Mediterranean. He is credited with having set up the first three-dimensional nativity scene with living animals and – according to legend – was renowned for preaching to them. Below is a modern version of the hymn attributed to him. It expresses his faith, humility and philosophy. The double basilica at his monastery, where his shrine lies, is still a site of pilgrimage. A World Heritage Site, it contains some of the best Renaissance murals ever painted. It is also prone to earthquakes.

Lord, make me an instrument of Thy peace;
where there is hatred, let me sow love;
where there is injury, pardon;
where there is doubt, faith;

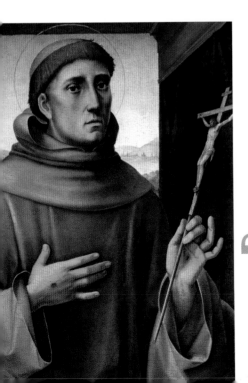

Saint Francis by Francesco Francia

where there is despair, hope;
where there is darkness, light;
and where there is sadness, joy.

O Divine Master,
grant that I may not so much seek to be consoled as to console;
to be understood, as to understand;
to be loved, as to love;
for it is in giving that we receive,
it is in pardoning that we are pardoned,
and it is in dying that we are born to Eternal Life.

Amen.

NATIONALITY:
Italian
WHEN:
c. 1210–1226
WHERE:
Assisi (now Italy)
YOU SHOULD KNOW:
Margaret Thatcher quoted the
first few lines of the prayer when
she became British Prime Minister
in 1979.

The Mob

It was customary to release one prisoner at Passover and in the Gospels, according to Saints Matthew, Mark and John, the Roman prefect of Judaea – Pontius Pilate – offered to release Christ to the mob outside the hall of judgment because he was unable to find that Christ had done anything wrong. Instead, they called for the release of the thief Barabbas. The accounts in the four Gospels vary slightly in details – for instance, Barabbas does not appear in St Luke's Gospel. But Christ is also questioned by Herod Antipas, the son of Herod the Great, who ordered the massacre of the innocents, and uncle of Herod Agrippa, who appears in the Acts of the Apostles.

NATIONALITY:
Judaean
WHEN:
c. AD 36
WHERE:
Jerusalem (now Israel)
YOU SHOULD KNOW:
There is very little contemporary
evidence about Pilate – apart from in
the Bible – except for an inscription
on a stone in a ruined amphitheatre
in the city of Caesarea Maritima.

Not this man, but Barabbas!

*A painting of Barabbas
with the mob*

Pope Gregory VII c. 1020–1085

NATIONALITY:
Italian
WHEN:
1075
WHERE:
Rome (now Italy)
YOU SHOULD KNOW:
Gregory VII also issued a decree
forbidding the marriage of priests.

During the eleventh century there were an increasing number of disputes between the popes in Rome and the rulers of various nations over the extent of supremacy each had over the other. One particularly notable battle was between Pope Gregory VII and the German king and Holy Roman Emperor, Henry IV. This resulted in the king being excommunicated twice, in a turnaround from 30 years earlier when his father had deposed three different popes. That the rulers of Christian nations were subservient to the pope – as God's divinely appointed representative on Earth – was first formalized in Gregory's Dictatus Papae *decree of 1075, the 27 articles of which are listed below.*

1. That the Roman church was founded by God alone.
2. That the Roman pontiff alone can with right be called universal.
3. That he alone can depose or reinstate bishops.
4. That, in a council his legate, even if a lower grade, is above all bishops, and can pass sentence of deposition against them.
5. That the pope may depose the absent.
6. That, among other things, we ought not to remain in the same house with those excommunicated by him.
7. That for him alone is it lawful, according to the needs of the time, to make new laws, to assemble together new congregations, to make an abbey of a canonry; and, on the other hand, to divide a rich bishopric and unite the poor ones.
8. That he alone may use the imperial insignia.
9. That of the pope alone all princes shall kiss the feet.
10. That his name alone shall be spoken in the churches.
11. That this is the only name in the world.
12. That it may be permitted to him to depose emperors.
13. That he may be permitted to transfer bishops if need be.
14. That he has power to ordain a clerk of any church he may wish.
15. That he who is ordained by him may preside over another church, but may not hold a subordinate position; and that such a one may not receive a higher grade from any bishop.
16. That no synod shall be called a general one without his order.
17. That no chapter and no book shall be considered canonical without his authority.
18. That a sentence passed by him may be retracted by no one; and that he himself, alone of all, may retract it.
19. That he himself may be judged by no one.
20. That no one shall dare to condemn one who appeals to the apostolic chair.
21. That to the latter should be referred the more important cases of every church.
22. That the Roman church has never erred; nor will it err to all eternity,

the Scripture bearing witness.

23. That the Roman pontiff, if he have been canonically ordained, is undoubtedly made a saint by the merits of St Peter; St Ennodius, bishop of Pavia, bearing witness, and many holy fathers agreeing with him. As is contained in the decrees of St Symmachus the pope.

24. That, by his command and consent, it may be lawful for subordinates to bring accusations.

25. That he may depose and reinstate bishops without assembling a synod.

26. That he who is not at peace with the Roman church shall not be considered catholic.

27. That he may absolve subjects from their fealty to wicked men. 〞

Martin Luther 1483–1546

In the early sixteenth century, there was an increasing divide within the Catholic church about the abuse, particularly the sale, of indulgences – remission of time spent in purgatory after death for sins already forgiven – allowing people to buy their way out of sins rather than confession and contrition. The papal commissioner for indulgences was sent to Germany to sell them in order to fund the rebuilding of St Peter's Basilica in Rome. Luther's 95 Theses are a response to this mission, intended as the basis for a debate at the University of Wittenberg. A copy is said to have been stuck to the door of the Castle Church in Wittenberg – a church with thousands of relics that the pious could pay to see and so gain an indulgence. It was intended that the whole life of believers should be penitence.

NATIONALITY:
German
WHEN:
1517
WHERE:
Wittenberg (now in Germany)
YOU SHOULD KNOW:
Luther had not intended to cause a schism within the church, but to provoke a debate that would see the financial abuse of the pious stopped.

1. Our Lord and Master Jesus Christ, in saying 'Repent ye,' etc.,

2. This word cannot be understood of sacramental penance, that is, of the confession and satisfaction which are performed under the ministry of priests.

3. It does not, however, refer solely to inward penitence; nay such inward penitence is naught, unless it outwardly produces various mortifications of the flesh.

4. The Penalty thus continues as long as the hatred of self – that is, true inward penitence – continues: namely, till our entrance into the kingdom of Heaven.

5. The Pope has neither the will nor the power to remit any penalties, except those which he has imposed by his own authority, or by that of the canons.

6. The Pope has no power to remit any guilt, except by declaring and warranting it to have been remitted by God; or at most by remitting cases reserved for himself; in which cases, if his power were despised, guilt would certainly remain.

7. God never remits any man's guilt, without at the same time subjecting him, humbled in all things, to the authority of his representative the priest. . .

20. Therefore the Pope, when he speaks of the plenary remission of all penalties, does not mean simply of all, but only of those imposed by himself.

21. Thus those preachers of indulgences are in error who say that, by the indulgences of the Pope, a man is loosed and saved from all punishment.

22. For in fact he remits to souls in purgatory no penalty which they would have had to pay in this life according to the canons. . .

31. Rare as is a true penitent, so rare is one who truly buys indulgences – that is to say, most rare.

32. Those who believe that, through letters of pardon, they are made sure of their own salvation, will be eternally damned along with their teachers.

33. We must especially beware of those who say that these pardons from the Pope are that inestimable gift of God by which man is reconciled to God. . .

36. Every Christian who feels true compunction has of right plenary remission of pain and guilt, even without letters of pardon.

37. Every true Christian, whether living or dead, has a share in all the benefits of Christ and of the Church given him by God, even without letters of pardon. . .

40. True contrition seeks and loves punishment; while the ampleness of pardons relaxes it, and causes men to hate it, or at least gives occasion for them to do so.

41. Apostolical pardons ought to be proclaimed with caution, lest the people should falsely suppose that they are placed before other good works of charity. . .

44. Because, by a work of charity, charity increases and the man becomes better; while, by means of pardons, he does not become better, but only freer from punishment.

45. Christians should be taught that he who sees any one in need, and passing him by, gives money for pardons, is not purchasing for himself the indulgences of the Pope, but the anger of God. . .

48. Christians should be taught that the Pope, in granting pardons, has both more need and more desire that devout prayer should be made for him, than that money should be readily paid. . .

52. Vain is the hope of salvation through letters of pardon, even if a commissary – nay, the Pope himself – were to pledge his own soul for them. . .

58. Nor are they the merits of Christ and of the saints, for these, independently of the Pope, are always working grace to the inner man, and the cross, death, and hell to the outer man. . .

67. Those indulgences, which the preachers loudly proclaim to be the greatest graces, are seen to be truly such as regards the promotion of gain. . .

76. We affirm, on the contrary, that Papal pardons cannot take away even the least of venal sins, as regards its guilt. . .

84. Again: what is this new kindness of God and the Pope, in that, for money's sake, they permit an impious man and an enemy of God to redeem a pious soul which loves God, and yet do not redeem that same pious and beloved soul, out of free charity, on account of its own need?. . .

88. Again: what greater good would the Church receive if the Pope, instead of once, as he does now, were to bestow these remissions and participations a hundred times a day on any one of the faithful?. . .

94. Christians should be exhorted to strive to follow Christ their Head through pains, deaths, and hells.

95. And thus trust to enter Heaven through many tribulations, rather than in the security of peace.

Al Scalpone 1913–2000

NATIONALITY:
American
WHEN:
1947
WHERE:
USA
YOU SHOULD KNOW:
The Family Theater gave both James Dean and George Lucas their first screen credits.

In 1947, a Roman Catholic priest from South Bend, Indiana, Fr Patrick Peyton, founder of the Family Rosary Crusade, began a radio series called Family Theater in order to use first the radio, and then later television, to promote prayer, moral values and family stability. The programmes featured Hollywood stars such as James Stewart, Don Ameche, William Shatner, Loretta Young, Shirley Temple, Placido Domingo, Frank Sinatra and Grace Kelly (her last three television appearances were on the show). A young advertising executive, Al Scalpone, wrote the famous slogan for the radio show in 1947, and it appeared on billboards all over the USA.

The family that prays together stays together.

John Knox 1513–1572

In 1558, the Protestant reformer launched a series of verbal and written attacks against the – to him – almost heretical idea that a woman could rule over a country. At this time, both England and Scotland were ruled by Catholic women: the former by Mary I and the latter by Mary of Guise as regent for her daughter, Mary, Queen of Scots. In pamphlet form, 'The First Blast of the Trumpet Against the Monstrous Regiment of Women' was published in Geneva in 1558.

NATIONALITY:
Scots
WHERE:
Geneva, Switzerland
WHEN:
1558
YOU SHOULD KNOW:
By regiment, Knox meant regime, not a troop of soldiers.

' Wonder it is, that amongst so many pregnant wits as the Isle of Great Britain hath produced, so many godly and zealous preachers as England did sometime nourish, and amongst so many learned and men of grave judgment, as this day by Jezebel are exiled, none is found so stout of courage, so faithful to God, nor loving to their native country, that they dare admonish the inhabitants of that Isle how abominable before God, is the Empire or Rule of a wicked woman, yea of a traitor and bastard . . . we hear the blood of our brethren, the members of Christ Jesus most cruelly to be shed, and the monstrous empire of a cruel woman (the secret counsel of God excepted) we know to be the only occasion of all these miseries: and yet with silence we pass the time as though the matter did nothing appertain to us . . .

. . . I am assured that God hath revealed to some in this our age, that it is more than a monster in nature, that a woman shall reign and have empire above man. And yet with us all, there is such silence, as if God therewith were nothing offended . . . If any think that the empire of women, is not of such importance, that for the suppressing of the same, any man is bound to hazard his life, I answer, that to suppress it, is in the hand of God alone. But to utter the impiety and abomination of the same, I say, it is the duty of every true messager of God, to whom the truth is revealed in that behalf . . . I say, that of necessity it is, that, this monstiferous empire of women, (which amongst all enormities, that this day do abound upon the face of the whole Earth, is most detestable and damnable) be openly revealed and plainly declared to the world, to the end that some may repent and be saved . . .

. . . For who can deny but it is repugnant to nature, that the blind shall be appointed to lead and conduct such as do see? That the weak, the sick and impotent persons shall nourish and keep the whole and strong? And finally, that the foolish, mad and phrenetic shall govern the discrete . . . And such be all women, compared unto man in bearing of authority. For their sight in civil regiment is but blindness; their strength, weakness; their counsel, foolishnes; and judgment, frenzy, if it be rightly considered. '

Pope Urban II 1035–1099

NATIONALITY:
French
WHEN:
1095
WHERE:
Clermont, France
YOU SHOULD KNOW:
Urban II was beatified in 1881, but
has not yet been made a saint.

*In 1095, Urban II received a request from the Byzantine
Emperor Alexios I Komnenos for assistance against the Muslims
who were invading the eastern Empire. In November of the
same year, a council was held at Clermont and Urban's sermon
electrified those in attendance as he called for them to amass an
army to expel the Seljuk Turks. In this version of the sermon, he
promises absolution from sins for all those who took part. The
main forces departed in August 1096, by which time the
mission's aims also included the conquest of the Holy Land.*

‘ . . . your brethren who live in the east are in urgent need of your
help, and you must hasten to give them the aid which has often
been promised them. For, as the most of you have heard, the Turks
and Arabs have attacked them and have conquered the territory of
Romania as far west as the shore of the Mediterranean and the
Hellespont . . . They have occupied more and more of the lands of
those Christians, and have overcome them in seven battles. They
have killed and captured many, and have destroyed the churches
and devastated the empire. If you permit them to continue thus for
awhile with impurity, the faithful of God will be much more widely
attacked by them. On this account I, or rather the Lord, beseech
you as Christ's heralds to publish this everywhere and to persuade
all people of whatever rank, foot-soldiers and knights, poor and rich,
to carry aid promptly to those Christians and to destroy that vile
race from the lands of our friends . . . Moreover, Christ commands it.

All who die by the way, whether by land or by sea, or in battle
against the pagans, shall have immediate remission of sins . . . O what
a disgrace if such a despised and base race, which worships demons,
should conquer a people which has the faith of omnipotent God and
is made glorious with the name of Christ! With what reproaches will
the Lord overwhelm us if you do not aid those who, with us, profess
the Christian religion! Let those who have been accustomed unjustly
to wage private warfare against the faithful now go against the
infidels and end with victory this war which should have been begun
long ago. Let those who . . . have been robbers, now become knights.
Let those who have been fighting against their brothers and relatives
now fight in a proper way against the barbarians. Let those who
have been serving as mercenaries for small pay now obtain the
eternal reward. Let those who have been wearing themselves out in
both body and soul now work for a double honour. Behold! on this
side will be the sorrowful and poor, on that, the rich; on this side,
the enemies of the Lord, on that, his friends. Let those who go not
put off the journey, but rent their lands and collect money for their
expenses; and as soon as winter is over and spring comes, let them
eagerly set out on the way with God as their guide. ’

Henri IV, King of France

1553–1610

Five years after his re-conversion to Catholicism in order to gain the French crown, Henri IV issued the Edict of Nantes, which allowed Protestantism to be practised in some areas of the country, restored civil rights to Protestants, revoked the ban on them entering state employment and offered some freedom of conscience for Christians. Its aim was to end the Wars of Religion that had convulsed France for decades, but religious conflict never entirely ceased and by the 1620s the two sides were in bitter conflict again (selected extracts).

NATIONALITY:
French
WHEN:
1598
WHERE:
Nantes, France
YOU SHOULD KNOW:
The edict was revoked in 1685 by Henri IV's grandson, Louis XIV.

'

III. We ordain that the Catholic Apostolic and Roman religion shall be restored and re-established in all places and localities of this our kingdom and countries subject to our sway, where the exercise of the same has been interrupted, in order that it may be peaceably and freely exercised, without any trouble or hindrance: forbidding very expressly all persons . . . from troubling, molesting, or disturbing ecclesiastics in the celebration of divine service, in the enjoyment or collection of tithes, fruits, or revenues of their benefices, and all other rights and dues belonging to them: and that all those who during the troubles have taken possession of churches, houses, goods or revenues, belonging to the said ecclesiastics, shall surrender to them entire possession and peaceable enjoyment of such rights, liberties, and sureties as they had before they were deprived of them.

VI. . . . we have permitted, and herewith permit, those of the said religion called Reformed to live and abide in all the cities and places of this our kingdom and countries of our sway, without being annoyed, molested, or compelled to do anything in the matter of religion contrary to their consciences . . . upon condition that they comport themselves in other respects according to that which is contained in this our present edict.

IX. We also permit those of the said religion to make and continue the exercise of the same in all villages and places of our dominion where it was established by them and publicly enjoyed several and divers times in the year 1597, up to the end of the month of August, notwithstanding all decrees and judgments to the contrary.

XXI. Books concerning the said religion called Reformed may not be printed and publicly sold, except in cities and places where the public exercise of the said religion is permitted.

XXII. . . . there shall be no difference or distinction made in respect to the said religion, in receiving pupils to be instructed in universities, colleges, and schools; nor in receiving the sick and poor into hospitals, retreats and public charities. '

SCIENCE & MEDICINE

President John F. Kennedy

1917–1963

NATIONALITY:
American
WHEN:
September 12, 1962
WHERE:
Rice University Stadium, Houston,
Texas, USA
YOU SHOULD KNOW:
The land on which NASA's Johnson
Space Center, including Mission
Control, is built was donated by Rice
University.

In the early 1960s, Russia was well ahead of the US in what would become known as the space race. President Kennedy had first announced the decision to send American astronauts to the Moon to a Joint Session of Congress in May 1961, just six weeks after cosmonaut Yuri Gagarin had become the first person to orbit the Earth beyond the planet's atmosphere. Over the programme's 13 years it is estimated to have cost anything up to $25.4 billion (in 1969 terms). It also cost the lives of three astronauts: Gus Grissom, Edward White, and Roger Chaffee were killed when Apollo 1 exploded on its launch pad in 1967.

President Kennedy giving his 'race for space' speech.

President Pitzer, Mr Vice President, Governor, Congressman Thomas, Senator Wiley, and Congressman Miller, Mr Webb, Mr Bell, scientists, distinguished guests, and ladies and gentlemen . . .

No man can fully grasp how far and how fast we have come, but condense, if you will, the 50,000 years of man's recorded history in a time span of but a half-century. Stated in these terms, we know very little about the first 40 years, except at the end of them advanced man had learned to use the skins of animals to cover them. Then about 10 years ago, under this standard, man emerged from his caves to construct other kinds of shelter. Only five years ago man learned to write and use a cart with wheels. Christianity began less than two years ago. The printing press came this year, and then less than two months ago, during this whole 50-year span of human history, the steam engine provided a new source of power. Newton explored the meaning of gravity. Last month electric lights and telephones and automobiles and airplanes became available. Only last week did we develop penicillin and television and nuclear power, and now if America's new spacecraft succeeds in reaching Venus, we will have literally reached the stars before midnight tonight.

This is a breathtaking pace, and such a pace cannot help but create new ills as it dispels old, new ignorance, new problems, new dangers. Surely the opening vistas of space promise high costs and hardships, as well as high reward.

So it is not surprising that some would have us stay where we are a little longer to rest, to wait. But this city of Houston, this state of Texas, this country of the United States was not built by those who waited and rested and wished to look behind them. This country was conquered by those who moved forward – and so will space . . .

If this capsule history of our progress teaches us anything, it is that man, in his quest for knowledge and progress, is determined and cannot be deterred. The exploration of space will go ahead, whether we join in it or not, and it is one of the great adventures of all time, and no nation which expects to be the leader of other nations can expect to stay behind in this race for space.

Those who came before us made certain that this country rode the first waves of the industrial revolution, the first waves of modern invention, and the first wave of nuclear power, and this generation does not intend to founder in the backwash of the coming age of space. We mean to be a part of it – we mean to lead it. For the eyes of the world now look into space, to the Moon and to the planets beyond, and we have vowed that we shall not see it governed by a hostile flag of conquest, but by a banner of freedom and peace. We have vowed that we shall not see space filled with weapons of mass destruction, but with instruments of knowledge and understanding.

Yet the vows of this nation can only be fulfilled if we in this nation are first, and, therefore, we intend to be first. In short, our leadership in science and industry, our hopes for peace and security, our obligations to ourselves as well as others, all require us to make this effort, to solve these mysteries, to solve them for the good of all men, and to become the world's leading space-faring nation.

We set sail on this new sea because there is new knowledge to be gained, and new rights to be won, and they must be won and used for the progress of all people. For space science, like nuclear science and all technology, has no conscience of its own. Whether it will become a force for good or ill depends on man, and only if the United States occupies a position of pre-eminence can we help decide whether this new ocean will be a sea of peace or a new terrifying theater of war. I do not say that we should or will go unprotected against the hostile misuse of space any more than we go unprotected against the hostile use of land or sea, but I do say that space can be explored and mastered without feeding the fires of war, without repeating the mistakes that man has made in extending his writ around this globe of ours . . .

We choose to go to the Moon. We choose to go to the Moon in this decade and do the other things, not because they are easy, but because they are hard, because that goal will serve to organize and measure the best of our energies and skills, because that challenge is one that we are willing to accept, one we are unwilling to postpone, and one which we intend to win, and the others, too . . .

In the last 24 hours we have seen facilities now being created for the greatest and most complex exploration in man's history. We have felt the ground shake and the air shattered by the testing of a Saturn C-1 booster rocket, many times as powerful as the Atlas which launched John Glenn, generating power equivalent to 10,000 automobiles with their accelerators on the floor. We have seen the site where five F-1 rocket engines, each one as powerful as all eight engines of the Saturn combined, will be clustered together to make the advanced Saturn missile, assembled in a new building to be built at Cape Canaveral as tall as a 48-story structure, as wide as a city block, and as long as two lengths of this field.

Within these last 19 months at least 45 satellites have circled the Earth. Some 40 of them were made in the United States of America and they were far more sophisticated and supplied far more knowledge to the people of the world than those of the Soviet Union.

The Mariner spacecraft now on its way to Venus is the most intricate instrument in the history of space science. The accuracy of that shot is comparable to firing a missile from Cape Canaveral and dropping it in this stadium between the 40-yard lines.

Transit satellites are helping our ships at sea to steer a safer course. Tiros satellites have given us unprecedented warnings of hurricanes and storms, and will do the same for forest fires and icebergs . . .

To be sure, all this costs us all a good deal of money. This year's space budget is three times what it was in January 1961, and it is greater than the space budget of the previous eight years combined. That budget now stands at $5,400 million a year – a staggering sum, though somewhat less than we pay for cigarettes and cigars every year. Space expenditures will soon rise some more, from 40 cents per person per week to more than 50 cents a week for every man, woman and child in the United States, for we have given this program a high national priority – even though I realize that this is in some measure an act of faith and vision, for we do not now know what benefits await us. But if I were to say, my fellow citizens, that we shall send to the Moon, 240,000 miles away from the control station in Houston, a giant rocket more than 300 feet tall, the length of this football field, made of new metal alloys, some of which have not yet been invented, capable of standing heat and stresses several times more than have ever been experienced, fitted together with a precision better than the finest watch, carrying all the equipment needed for propulsion, guidance, control, communications, food and survival, on an untried mission, to an unknown celestial body, and then return it safely to Earth, re-entering the atmosphere at speeds of over 25,000 miles per hour, causing heat about half that of the temperature of the Sun – almost as hot as it is here today – and do all this, and do it right, and do it first before this decade is out – then we must be bold . . .

And I am delighted that this university is playing a part in putting a man on the Moon as part of a great national effort of the United States of America.

Many years ago the great British explorer George Mallory, who was to die on Mount Everest, was asked why did he want to climb it. He said, 'Because it is there.'.

Well, space is there, and we're going to climb it, and the Moon and the planets are there, and new hopes for knowledge and peace are there. And, therefore, as we set sail we ask God's blessing on the most hazardous and dangerous and greatest adventure on which man has ever embarked. 〝

Neil Armstrong born 1930

NATIONALITY:
American
WHEN:
July 20, 1969
WHERE:
The Sea of Tranquillity, the Moon
YOU SHOULD KNOW:
Mission Commander Michael Collins designed the famous mission patch of Apollo 11 – an eagle carrying an olive branch and flying above the surface of the Moon, with the Earth in the background.

The Apollo 11 voyage was Neil Armstrong's second spaceflight. Three years earlier he had flown on Gemini 8, when he and David Scott performed the first manned docking of two spacecraft – a manoeuvre vital to the Apollo missions. Armstrong had been obsessed with flying since an early age and earned his pilot's licence on his sixteenth birthday, before he got his driving licence. From 1949 to 1952 he was a navy pilot and after that, before joining NASA's astronaut training programme, he had been a test pilot for experimental aircraft and rocket planes, including the X-15, the F-101 Voodoo, the B-47 Stratojet and the KC-135 Stratotanker.

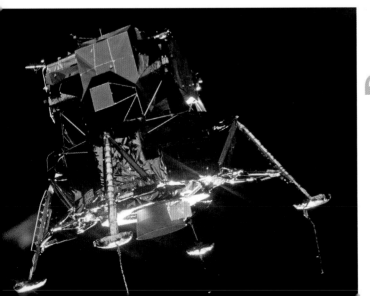

〝 750 ft, coming down at 23 degrees . . . 700 ft, 21 down . . . 400 ft, down at nine . . . Got the shadow out there . . . 75 ft, things looking good . . . lights on . . . picking up some dust . . . 0 ft, 2¹/₂ down . . . faint shadow . . . four forward . . . drifting to the right a little . . . contact light . . . OK. Engine stop . . . Houston. Tranquillity Base here. The Eagle has landed. 〝

'Eagle', ready to land.

Neil Armstrong born 1930

Some 6¹/₂ hours after landing on the moon, Neil Armstrong headed down the lunar module's ladder. As he took the final large step, he spoke the words below. One theory is that he had rehearsed saying 'That's one small step for a man, one giant leap for mankind' which makes more sense. In any case, he became the first human being to step onto the surface of any body in space other than the Earth and the phrase has gone down in history. While on the lunar surface, Armstrong and Aldrin planted the US flag, left a small set of scientific experiments (EASEP) and took notes, photographs and core samples of the lunar soil before returning to the lunar module.

Neil Armstrong taking equipment from 'Eagle'. The photo was taken by Buzz Aldrin.

' That's one small step for man, one giant leap for mankind. '

NATIONALITY:
American
WHEN:
July 20, 1969
WHERE:
The Sea of Tranquillity, the Moon
YOU SHOULD KNOW:
Neil Armstrong and Edwin 'Buzz' Aldrin spent just 2¹/₂ hours on the surface of the Moon.

Anaxagoras c. 500–428 BC

Anaxagoras was an early Greek philosopher, many of whose ideas were not accepted by the majority of his fellow philosophers, even though they have subsequently been proved to be right. His theory that everything is made up of minute particles eventually led to the atomic theory. He correctly described how solar and lunar eclipses occur (although he may not have been the first to do so) and asserted that stars were masses of stone. These views were seen as dangerous because they questioned the current religious beliefs about the cosmos – this in an era when the majority believed that natural phenomena were under the control of gods who were liable to react to heresy with earthquakes or some other misfortune – and he was imprisoned until Athens' leader, Pericles, got him released.

NATIONALITY:
Greek
WHEN:
c. 460–450 BC
WHERE:
Athens, Greece
YOU SHOULD KNOW:
In Ancient Greece the word philosophy encompassed mathematics and natural sciences.

' We do not feel the heat of the stars because they are so far from the Earth . . . The Moon has no light of its own but derives it from the Sun . . . The Moon is made of Earth and has plains and ravines on it. '

Charles Darwin 1809–1882

NATIONALITY:
British
WHEN:
1858
WHERE:
London, England
YOU SHOULD KNOW:
Neither Darwin nor Wallace were
present and the papers were read by
the Linnean Society's Secretary, John
Joseph Bennett.

Darwin had delayed publishing his theory on evolution through natural selection for many years, and it was only when Alfred Russell Wallace sent him his paper with similar ideas that he decided to publish. He sent extracts from his manuscript (which botanist Joseph Hooker had read in 1844), along with Wallace's paper to the geologist Charles Lyell, who, with Hooker, decided that the best course would be to publish both together, along with a letter of Darwin's from 1847, confirming that he had precedence. The two papers were read on July 1, 1858 at the Linnean Society in London. There was not much reaction at the time: that came in the following year with the publication of Darwin's On the Origin of Species by Means of Natural Selection, or the Preservation of Favoured Races in the Struggle for Life.

‘ De Candolle, in an eloquent passage, has declared that all nature is at war, one organism with another, or with external nature. Seeing the contented face of nature, this may at first well be doubted; but reflection will inevitably prove it to be true. The war, however, is not constant, but recurrent in a slight degree at short periods, and more severely at occasional more distant periods; and hence its effects are easily overlooked. It is the doctrine of Malthus applied in most cases with tenfold force. As in every climate there are seasons, for each of its inhabitants, of greater and less abundance, so all annually breed; and the moral restraint which in some small degree checks the increase of mankind is entirely lost. Even slow-breeding mankind has doubled in 25 years; and if he could increase his food with greater ease, he would double in less time. But for animals without artificial means, the amount of food for each species must, on an average, be constant, whereas the increase of all organisms tends to be geometrical, and in a vast majority of cases at an enormous ratio. Suppose in a certain spot there are eight pairs of birds, and that only four pairs of them annually (including double hatches) rear only four young, and that these go on rearing their young at the same rate, then at the end of seven years (a short life, excluding violent deaths, for any bird) there will be 2048 birds, instead of the original sixteen. As this increase is quite impossible, we must conclude either that birds do not rear nearly half their young, or that the average life of a bird is, from accident, not nearly seven years. Both checks probably concur. The same kind of calculation applied to all plants and animals affords results more or less striking, but in very few instances more striking than in man.

Many practical illustrations of this rapid tendency to increase are on record, among which, during peculiar seasons, are the extraordinary numbers of certain animals; for instance, during the years 1826 to 1828, in La Plata, when from drought some millions of cattle perished, the whole country actually swarmed with mice. Now I think it cannot be doubted that during the breeding season all the mice (with the exception of a few males or females in excess) ordinarily pair, and therefore that this astounding increase during three years must be attributed to a greater number than usual surviving the first year, and then breeding, and so on till the third year, when their numbers were brought down to their usual limits on the return of wet weather. Where man has introduced plants and animals into a new and favourable country, there are many accounts in how surprisingly few years the whole country has become stocked with them. This increase would necessarily stop as soon as the country was fully stocked; and yet we have every reason to believe, from what is known of wild animals, that all would pair in the spring. In the majority of cases it is most difficult to imagine where the checks fall – though generally, no doubt, on the seeds, eggs, and young; but when we remember how impossible, even in mankind (so much better known than any other animal), it is to infer from repeated casual observations what the average duration of life is, or to discover the different percentage of deaths to births in different countries, we ought to feel no surprise at our being unable to discover where the check falls in any animal or plant. It should always be remembered, that in most cases the checks are recurrent yearly in a small, regular degree, and in an extreme degree during unusually cold, hot, dry, or wet years, according to the constitution of the being in question. Lighten any check in the least degree, and the geometrical powers of increase in every organism will almost instantly increase the average number of the favoured species. Nature may be compared to a surface on which rest ten thousand sharp wedges touching each other and driven inwards by incessant blows. Fully to realize these views much reflection is requisite. Malthus on man should be studied; and all such cases as those of the mice in La Plata, of the cattle and horses when first turned out in South America, of the birds by our calculation, &c., should be well considered. Reflect on the enormous multiplying power inherent and annually in action in all animals; reflect on the countless seeds scattered by a hundred ingenious contrivances, year after year, over the whole face of the land; and yet we have every reason to suppose that the average percentage of each of the inhabitants of a country usually remains constant. Finally, let it be borne in mind that this average number of individuals (the external conditions remaining the same) in each country is kept up by recurrent struggles against other species or against external nature (as on the borders of the Arctic regions, where the cold checks life), and that ordinarily each individual of every species holds its place, either by its own struggle and capacity of acquiring nourishment in some period of its life, from the egg upwards; or by the struggle of its parents (in short-lived organisms, when the main check occurs at longer intervals) with other individuals of the same or different species.

But let the external conditions of a country alter. If in a small degree, the relative proportions of the inhabitants will in most cases simply be slightly changed; but let the number of inhabitants be small, as on an island, and free access to it from other countries be circumscribed, and let the change of conditions continue progressing (forming new stations), in such a case the original inhabitants must cease to be as perfectly adapted to the changed conditions as they were originally. It has been shown in a former part of this work, that such changes of external conditions would, from their acting on the reproductive system, probably cause the organization of those beings which were most affected to become, as under domestication, plastic. Now, can it be doubted, from the struggle each individual has to obtain subsistence, that any minute variation in structure, habits, or instincts, adapting that individual better to the new conditions, would tell upon its vigour and health? In the struggle it would have a better chance of surviving; and those of its offspring which inherited the variation, be it ever so slight, would also have a better chance. Yearly more are bred than can survive; the smallest grain in the balance, in the long run, must tell on which death shall fall, and which shall survive. Let this work of selection on the one hand, and death on the other, go on for a thousand generations, who will pretend to affirm that it would produce no effect, when we remember what, in a few years, Bakewell effected in cattle, and Western in sheep, by this identical principle of selection?

To give an imaginary example from changes in progress on an island: – let the organization of a canine animal which preyed chiefly on rabbits, but sometimes on hares, become slightly plastic; let these same changes cause the number of rabbits very slowly to decrease, and the number of hares to increase; the effect of this would be that the fox or dog would be driven to try to catch more hares: his organization, however, being slightly plastic, those individuals with the lightest forms, longest limbs, and best eyesight, let the difference be ever so small, would be slightly favoured, and would tend to live longer, and to survive during that time of the year when food was scarcest; they would also rear more young, which would tend to inherit these slight peculiarities. The less fleet ones would be rigidly destroyed. I can see no more reason to doubt that these causes in a thousand generations would produce a marked effect, and adapt the form of the fox or dog to the catching of hares instead of rabbits, than that greyhounds can be improved by selection and careful breeding. So would it be with plants under similar circumstances. If the number of individuals of a species with plumed seeds could be increased by greater powers of dissemination within its own area (that is, if the check to increase fell chiefly on the seeds), those seeds which were provided with ever so little more down, would in the long run be most disseminated; hence a greater number of seeds thus formed would germinate, and would tend to produce plants inheriting the slightly better-adapted down.

Besides this natural means of selection, by which those individuals are preserved, whether in their egg, or larval, or mature state, which are best adapted to the place they fill in nature, there is a second agency at work in most unisexual animals, tending to produce the same effect, namely, the struggle of the males for the females. These struggles are generally decided by the law of battle, but in the case of birds, apparently, by the charms of their song, by their beauty or their power of courtship, as in the dancing rock-thrush of Guiana. The most vigorous and healthy males, implying perfect adaptation, must generally gain the victory in their contests. This kind of selection, however, is less rigorous than the other; it does not require the death of the less successful, but gives to them fewer descendants. The struggle falls, moreover, at a time of year when food is generally abundant, and perhaps the effect chiefly produced would be the modification of the secondary sexual characters, which are not related to the power of obtaining food, or to defence from enemies, but to fighting with or rivalling other males. The result of this struggle amongst the males may be compared in some respects to that produced by those agriculturists who pay less attention to the careful selection of all their young animals, and more to the occasional use of a choice mate. 〞

Galileo Galilei 1564–1642

NATIONALITY:
Italian
WHEN:
June 22, 1633
WHERE:
Rome (now Italy)
YOU SHOULD KNOW:
Although he is popularly credited with both, Galileo was neither the first person to build a telescope or to map the Moon using one.

In 1633 Galileo appeared before the Grand Inquisition in Rome, accused of heresy and breaking an earlier injunction not to write anything that was contrary to the teachings of the Church, specifically in this case about the theory of Copernicus that the Earth was not the centre of the Universe, which was contrary to the Ptolemaic theory approved by the Church. His Dialogue Concerning the Two Chief World Systems *had originally been passed by the official censors on the grounds that it was a hypothetical dialogue rather than a factual book. It is thought that Pope Urban VIII had withdrawn his protection of Galileo because the scientist had put the Papal view into the mouth of the character Simplicio. He signed the following statement.*

> Desiring to remove from the minds of your Eminences, and of all faithful Christians, this strong suspicion, reasonable conceived against me, with sincere heart and unfeigned faith I adjure, curse, and detest the aforesaid errors and heresies, and generally every other error and sect whatsoever contrary to the said Holy Church; and I swear that in the future I will never again say or assert, verbally or in writing, anything that might furnish occasion for a similar suspicion regarding me . . .
>
> I, the said Galileo Galilei, have abjured, sworn, promised, and bound myself as above; and in witness of the truth thereof I have with my own hand subscribed the present document of my abjuration, and recited it word for word at Rome, in the Convent of Minerva, this twenty-second day of June, 1633.
>
> I, Galileo Galilei, have abjured as above with my own hand.

According to legend, as he got off his knees he is said to have muttered the following, meaning 'Yet it moves', referring to the Earth.

> Eppur, si muove.

An early drawing of Galileo

Edward Lorenz 1917–2008

Meteorologist and mathematician Edward Lorenz had noticed in the 1960s that even very small changes in data input into computer models of weather made significant differences to forecasts. On December 29, 1972 he gave a lecture to the American Association for the Advancement of Science's 139th meeting, with the title 'Predictability; Does the Flap of a Butterfly's wings in Brazil Set Off a Tornado in Texas?' His conclusion was that it was impossible to say. However, he did point out that small-scale differences in the atmosphere that were not at that time observable by the instruments available to weather forecasters could generate larger-scale discrepancies between a forecast and the real weather.

NATIONALITY:
American
WHEN:
1972
WHERE:
Cambridge, Massachusetts, USA
YOU SHOULD KNOW:
This was not the first occasion that Lorenz had used the image, but it was the first time it came to mass attention.

> . . . If a single flap of a butterfly's wings can be instrumental in generating a tornado, so also in all the previous and subsequent flaps of its wings, as can the flaps of the wings of millions of other butterflies, not to mention the activities of innumerable more powerful creatures, including our own species . . .
>
> . . . The question which really interests us is whether they can do even this – whether, for example, two particular weather situations differing by as little as the immediate influence of a single butterfly will generally after sufficient time evolve into two situations differing by as much as the presence of a tornado.

Isaac Newton 1642–1727

The second half of the seventeenth century saw an explosion in the field of science in Britain, particularly after the foundation of the Royal Society in 1660 encouraged a formal arena for the exchange of ideas and the promotion of experimentation. The first curator of experiments was Robert Hooke, a bitter enemy of Isaac Newton. When Newton was developing his theory of light, the two men had an acrimonious exchange of letters. Hooke criticised Newton's theory, having misunderstood it, and implied that everything new in it was wrong and everything right in it was not new. Newton's masterful rejoinder was an insult to Hooke's stature, both physically, for he was a short man, and intellectually, as by implication Newton could have gained nothing from Hooke's work. The dispute led Newton to delay publishing his theory until after Hooke's death in 1703.

NATIONALITY:
British
WHEN:
1676
WHERE:
The best-known occurrence is in a letter to Robert Hooke.
YOU SHOULD KNOW:
Newton also discovered that white light is made up of a mixture of differently coloured lights that can be split by a prism to form a rainbow.

If I have seen further it is by standing on the shoulders of giants.

Archimedes c. 287–212 BC

NATIONALITY:
Greek
WHEN:
Unknown
WHERE:
Probably Syracuse, Sicily (now Italy)
YOU SHOULD KNOW:
The only ancient reference to this saying is in Pappus' *Synagogue* (collection), which was written in about AD 340.

Archimedes was probably the ancient world's greatest engineer, astronomer, physicist and mathematician. He invented many geometrical formulae, came up with the principles of weighing objects through the displacement of water – which led to his famous 'Eureka!' moment – and calculated the value of Pi extremely accurately. He also demonstrated the principle of the lever – the relationship between the distance and weight of an object from the lever's fulcrum and those of the counterweight at the other end of the lever – which led to the quotation below. Although he preferred pure mathematics, he put his knowledge to practical use, creating siege engines designed to protect the city, although they did not prevent the Romans taking Syracuse in 212 BC, when he was killed by a soldier for refusing to accompany him because he was finishing a calculation.

Give me a lever, a fulcrum and a firm place to stand and I will move the world.

Engraving of Archimedes

Jack Swigert Jr 1931–1982
Jim Lovell born 1928
Fred Haise born 1933

Two days into the flight of what should have been the third US mission to the Moon, one of Apollo 13's Service Module's oxygen tanks exploded, taking out a second and destroying its power systems. The Command Module had only enough power for the last few hours of the mission, so the three astronauts had to move into the cramped Lunar Module (which was designed for only two people for two days). They had limited water and food, and because they had to operate on minimum power, it was extremely cold. Keeping the astronauts alive during the flight back to Earth took considerable bravery and ingenuity.

NATIONALITY:
American
WHEN:
April 13, 1970
WHERE:
Between the Earth and the Moon
YOU SHOULD KNOW:
Back-up crew member Charlie Duke infected Apollo 13's Command Module pilot Ken Mattingly with German Measles, causing him to be replaced.

55:52:31 – Master caution and warning triggered by low hydrogen pressure in tank No. 1

55:52:58 – Jack Lousma (CapCom): '13, we've got one more item for you, when you get a chance. We'd like you to stir up the cryo tanks. In addition, I have shaft and trunnion . . .'

55:53:06 – Swigert: 'Okay.'

55:53:07 – CapCom: '. . . for looking at Comet Bennett, if you need it.'

55:53:12 – Swigert: 'Okay. Stand by.'

55:53:18 – Oxygen tank No. 1 fans on.

55:53:19 – Oxygen tank No. 2 pressure decreases 8 psi.

55:53:20 – Oxygen tank No. 2 fans turned on.

55:53:20 – Stabilization control system electrical disturbance indicates a power transient.

55:53:21 – Oxygen tank No. 2 pressure decreases 4 psi.

55:53:22.718 – Stabilization control system electrical disturbance indicates a power transient.

55:53:22.757 – 1.2 Volt decrease in ac bus 2 voltage.

55:53:22.772 – 11.1 amp rise in fuel cell 3 current for one sample.

55:53:26 – Oxygen tank No. 2 pressure begins rise lasting for 24 seconds.

55:53:38.057 – 11 volt decrease in ac bus 2 voltage for one sample.

55:53:38.085 – Stabilization control system electrical disturbance indicates a power transient.

55:53:41.172 – 22.9 amp rise in fuel cell 3 current for one sample.

55:53:41.192 – Stabilization control system electrical disturbance indicates a power transient.

55:54:00 – Oxygen tank No. 2 pressure rise ends at a pressure of 953.8 psia.

55:54:15 – Oxygen tank No. 2 pressure begins to rise.

55:54:30 – Oxygen tank No. 2 quantity drops from full scale for 2 seconds and then reads 75.3 percent.

55:54:31 – Oxygen tank No. 2 temperature begins to rise rapidly.

55:54:43 – Flow rate of oxygen to all three fuel cells begins to decrease.

55:54:45 – Oxygen tank No. 2 pressure reaches maximum value of 1008.3 psia.

55:54:51 – Oxygen tank No. 2 quantity jumps to off-scale high and then begins to drop until the time of telemetry loss, indicating failed sensor.

55:54:52 – Oxygen tank No. 2 temperature sensor reads – 151.3 F.

55:54:52.703 – Oxygen tank No. 2 temperature suddenly goes off-scale low, indicating failed sensor.

55:54:52.763 – Last telemetered pressure from oxygen tank No. 2 before telemetry loss is 995.7 psia.

55:54:53.182 – Sudden accelerometer activity on X, Y, Z axes.

55:54:53.220 – Stabilization control system rate changes begin.

55:54:53.323 – Oxygen tank No. 1 pressure drops 4.2 psi.

55:54:53.500 – 2.8 amp rise in total fuel cell current.

55:54:53.542 – X, Y, and Z accelerations in CM indicate 1.17g, 0.65g, and 0.65g.

55:54:53.555 – Master caution and warning triggered by DC main bus B undervoltage. Alarm is turned off in 6 seconds. All indications are that the cryogenic oxygen tank No. 2 lost pressure in this time period and the panel separated.

55:54:54.741 – Nitrogen pressure in fuel cell 1 is off-scale low indicating failed sensor.

55:54:55.350 – Telemetry recovered.

55:54:56 – Service propulsion system engine valve body temperature begins a rise of 1.65 F in 7 seconds. DC main A decreases 0.9 volts to 28.5 volts and DC main bus B 0.9 volts to 29.0 volts. Total fuel cell current is 15 amps higher than the final value before telemetry loss. High current continues for 19 seconds. Oxygen tank No. 2 temperature reads off-scale high after telemetry recovery, probably indicating failed sensors. Oxygen tank No. 2 pressure reads off-scale low following telemetry recovery, indicating a broken supply line, a tank pressure below 19 psi, or a failed sensor. Oxygen tank No. 1 pressure reads 781.9 psia and begins to drop.

55:54:57 – Oxygen tank No. 2 quantity reads off-scale high following telemetry recovery indicating failed sensor.

55:55:01 – Oxygen flow rates to fuel cells 1 and 3 approached zero after decreasing for 7 seconds.

55:55:02 – The surface temperature of the service module oxidizer tank in bay 3 begins a 3.8 F increase in a 15 second period. The service propulsion system helium tank temperature begins a 3.8 F increase in a 32 second period.

55:55:09 – DC main bus A voltage recovers to 29.0 volts, DC main bus B recovers to 28.8.

55:55:20 – Swigert: 'Okay, Houston, we've had a problem here.'

55:55:28 – Lousma: 'This is Houston. Say again please.'

55:55:35 – Lovell: 'Houston, we've had a problem. We've had a main B bus undervolt.'

55:55:42 – Lousma: 'Roger. Main B undervolt.'

55:55:49 – Oxygen tank No. 2 temperature begins steady drop lasting 59 seconds indicating a failed sensor.

55:56:10 – Haise: 'Okay. Right now, Houston, the voltage is – is looking good. And we had a pretty large bang associated with the caution and warning there. And as I recall, main B was the one that had an amp spike on it once before.

55:56:30 – Lousma: 'Roger, Fred.'

55:56:38 – Oxygen tank No. 2 quantity becomes erratic for 69 seconds before assuming an off-scale low state, indicating a failed sensor.

55:56:54 – Haise: 'In the interim here, we're starting to go ahead and button up the tunnel again.'

55:57:04 – Haise: 'That jolt must have rocked the sensor on – see now – oxygen quantity 2. It was oscillating down around 20 to 60 percent. Now it's full-scale high.'

55:57:39 – Master caution and warning triggered by DC main bus B undervoltage. Alarm is turned off in 6 seconds.

55:57:40 – DC main bus B drops below 26.25 volts and continues to fall rapidly.

55:57:44 – Lovell: 'Okay. And we're looking at our service module RCS helium 1. We have – B is barber poled and D is barber poled, helium 2, D is barber pole, and secondary propellants, I have A and C barber pole.' AC bus fails within 2 seconds.

55:57:45 – Fuel cell 3 fails.

55:57:59 – Fuel cell current begins to decrease.

55:58:02 – Master caution and warning caused by AC bus 2 being reset.

55:58:06 – Master caution and warning triggered by DC main bus undervoltage.

Anxious Apollo 13 flight controllers

55:58:07 – DC main bus A drops below 26.25 volts and in the next few seconds levels off at 25.5 volts.

55:58:07 – Haise: 'AC 2 is showing zip.'

55:58:25 – Haise: 'Yes, we got a main bus A undervolt now, too, showing. It's reading about 25 and a half. Main B is reading zip right now.'

56:00:06 – Master caution and warning triggered by high hydrogen flow rate to fuel cell 2. **,,**

Henry Morton Stanley 1841–1904

Stanley had been sent to Africa to look for the explorer and missionary Dr David Livingstone – from whom nothing had been heard since the early days of his expedition to look for the source of the Nile – by the New York Herald. *Stanley arrived in Zanzibar in March 1871 and set off once he had amassed a team of more than 200 porters and all the equipment he would need for a protracted journey. He eventually tracked Livingstone down near Lake Tanganyika on November 10, 1871, addressing him with what must be the most famous greeting of all time. There are doubts as to the authenticity of Stanley's account of the meeting because he later tore out the relevant pages of his diary.*

' Dr Livingstone, I presume. **,,**

NATIONALITY:
British
WHEN:
November 10 1871
WHERE:
Ujiji (in what is now Tanzania)
YOU SHOULD KNOW:
Stanley was originally born as Henry Rowlands but took the name Stanley from the name of a wealthy merchant who took him in soon after he first got to America.

Stanley finds Livingstone.

Hippocrates c. 460–370 BC

NATIONALITY:
Greek
WHEN:
Unknown
WHERE:
Unknown
YOU SHOULD KNOW:
The Hippocratic Collection is a group
of about 60 ancient medical texts.

Hippocrates is widely known as the father of Western medicine. He rejected the idea that illness was caused by divine or magical intervention in favour of the theory that the body contained four fluids (humours) – blood, black bile, yellow bile and phlegm – that maintained health. Illness occurred when these were not in balance. Although this part of his theory is no longer believed, his teachings on lung disease are still valid and haemorrhoids are still treated in more or less the same way as he advocated. The Declaration of Geneva is the World Medical Association's equivalent of the Hippocratic Oath and there are various modern forms of the Oath in different countries, reflecting changes in medical practice and culture.

I swear by Apollo, Asclepius, Hygieia, and Panacea, and I take to witness all the gods, all the goddesses, to keep according to my ability and my judgment, the following Oath.

To consider dear to me, as my parents, him who taught me this art; to live in common with him and, if necessary, to share my goods with him; To look upon his children as my own brothers, to teach them this art.

I will prescribe regimens for the good of my patients according to my ability and my judgment and never do harm to anyone.

I will not give a lethal drug to anyone if I am asked, nor will I advise such a plan; and similarly I will not give a woman a pessary to cause an abortion.

But I will preserve the purity of my life and my arts.

I will not cut for stone, even for patients in whom the disease is manifest; I will leave this operation to be performed by practitioners, specialists in this art.

In every house where I come I will enter only for the good of my patients, keeping myself far from all intentional ill-doing and all seduction and especially from the pleasures of love with women or with men, be they free or slaves.

All that may come to my knowledge in the exercise of my profession or in daily commerce with men, which ought not to be spread abroad, I will keep secret and will never reveal.

If I keep this oath faithfully, may I enjoy my life and practice my art, respected by all men and in all times; but if I swerve from it or violate it, may the reverse be my lot.

A beautifully illuminated copy of the Hippocratic Oath

Isaac Newton 1642–1727

For two years from 1666 Isaac Newton was forced to live at his mother's home in the village of Woolsthorpe because Cambridge University was closed due to a plague epidemic. Whether or not the apple story is true, it was during this period that he formulated his laws of gravitation, realizing that gravity is universal and that the force it exerts diminishes over distance and is symmetrical between two objects. The equation for the Universal Law of Gravitation can be written as below, which means that the force is proportional to the masses of the two objects multiplied together but inversely proportional to their distance apart, i.e., two objects placed two feet apart will exert only a quarter of the gravitational force that they would if placed one foot apart.

NATIONALITY:
British
WHEN:
1666–1667
WHERE:
Woolsthorpe, England
YOU SHOULD KNOW:
The story about the apple falling on his head is probably a myth.

'$F = GM_1M_2/d^2$
F = the attractive force between two bodies of masses M_1 and M_2, separated by the distance and G is the Universal Gravitational Constant . . . if it universally appears, by experiments and astronomical observations, that all bodies about the Earth, gravitate toward the Earth; and that in proportion to the quantity of matter which they severally contain; that the Moon likewise, according to the quantity of its matter, gravitates toward the Earth; that on the other hand our sea gravitates toward the Moon; and all the planets mutually one toward another; and the comets in like manner towards the Sun; we must, in consequence of this rule, universally allow, that all bodies whatsoever are endowed with a principle of mutual gravitation. For the argument from the appearances concludes with more force for the universal gravitation of all bodies, than for their impenetrability, of which among those in the celestial regions, we have no experiments, nor any manner of observation. Not that I affirm gravity to be essential to all bodies. By their inherent force I mean nothing but their force of inertia. This is immutable. Their gravity is diminished as they recede from the Earth. '

(From the 1729 translation of Principia *by A. Motte)*

James Hutton 1726–1797

James Hutton, a Scottish physician, spent years studying the rock formations and strata of Scotland, and realized that many of them showed distinct signs of having been heated. His other observations led him to conclude that land on the Earth was pushed up from beneath the sea by some form of 'subterraneous heat' – the same that caused volcanoes – and that material from decomposed mountains eventually formed new strata in the

NATIONALITY:
British
WHEN:
1785
WHERE:
Edinburgh, Scotland
YOU SHOULD KNOW:
The assumption contained within Hutton's theory – that the natural processes operating in the past as those that can be observed in the present – is called Uniformitarianism.

ground. This led to his final conclusion, that the Earth was self-sustaining and could be infinitely old. He and his colleague presented this theory to the fellows of the Royal Society of Edinburgh in March and April of 1785 and laid the foundations of modern geology, although he was wrong in detail about the mechanism for the formation of land.

'This, however, alters nothing with regard to the nature of those operations of the globe. The system is still the same. It only protracts the indefinite space of time in its existence, while it gives us a view of another distinct period of the living world; that is to say, the world which we inhabit is composed of the materials, not of the earth which was the immediate predecessor of the present, but of the earth which, in ascending from the present, we consider as the third, and which had preceded the land that was above the surface of the sea, while our present land was yet beneath the water of the ocean. Here are three distinct successive periods of existence, and each of these is, in our measurement of time, a thing of indefinite duration.

We have now got to the end of our reasoning; we have no data further to conclude immediately from that which actually is: But we have got enough; we have the satisfaction to find, that in nature there is wisdom, system, and consistency. For having, in the natural history of this Earth, seen a succession of worlds, we may from this conclude that there is a system in nature; in like manner as, from seeing revolutions of the planets, it is concluded, that there is a system by which they are intended to continue those revolutions. But if the succession of worlds is established in the system of nature, it is in vain to look for any thing higher in the origin of the Earth. The result, therefore, of our present enquiry is, that we find no vestige of a beginning, no prospect of an end.'

NATIONALITY:
American
WHEN:
2006
WHERE:
Film premier at the Sundance Film Festival, Utah, USA
YOU SHOULD KNOW:
Al Gore was co-recipient with the International Panel on Climate Change of the 2007 Nobel Peace Prize because of his work on promoting the importance of environmental issues.

Al (Albert) Gore Jr born 1948

Al Gore, US Vice-President for eight years, and former Presidential candidate, has long been a campaigner on environmental issues, especially since 2001 in the face of the US government's hostility to the concept of anthropogenic global warming and such measures as the Kyoto Protocol. He had given his lecture about climate change more than 1,000 times before it was adapted to the film An Inconvenient Truth, *allowing his message to reach a much wider audience. It is one of the highest-grossing films of all time and won the 2007 Academy Award for best documentary feature. The text below is from the opening monologue, reminding viewers just what might be lost if the scientists' worst predictions are right.*

'You look at that river gently flowing by. You notice the leaves rustling with the wind. You hear the birds; you hear the tree frogs. In the distance you hear a cow. You feel the grass. The mud gives a little bit on the river bank. It's quiet; it's peaceful. And all of a sudden, it's a gear shift inside you. And it's like taking a deep breath and going . . . 'Oh yeah, I forgot about this.''

Nobel Prize winner Al Gore Jr

Alfred Wegener 1880–1930

With the advantage of satellite imagery, it is now obvious to us that South America and Africa could fit togther like pieces of a jigsaw puzzle, but how could this be? In the early twentieth century, a German scientist called Alfred Wegener proposed that the continents must drift around on the surface of the Earth. This ran counter to the Uniformitarian geological theories of the time. Although Wegener had plenty of evidence in the form of similar rock formations being present at corresponding sites on the two continents, he could not give a reasonable explanation as to how the continents might move. In 1926, the American Association of Petroleum Geologists held a symposium in New York to which he was invited. The conclusion was firmly in favour of the Uniformitarian theory. It was not until the 1950s that the theory of plate tectonics explained the movmement of the continents.

‘ The forces which displace continents are the same as those which produce great fold-mountain ranges. Continental drift, faults and compressions, earthquakes, volcanicity, (ocean) transgression cycles and (apparent) polar wandering are undoubtedly connected on a grand scale. ’

NATIONALITY:
German
WHEN:
1926
WHERE:
New York, USA

YOU SHOULD KNOW:
Wegener died on a glacier while on a meteorological expedition in Greenland.

J. Robert Oppenheimer 1904–1967

Just three weeks before a nuclear bomb was dropped on the Japanese city of Hiroshima, the technology was tested in practice for the first time. It was an implosion-design plutonium bomb, like that which would be dropped on Nagasaki on August 9. The director of The Manhattan Project was J. Robert Oppenheimer who murmured this line from the Hindu Bhagavad Gita as he watched the explosion; although in some versions of the story he just thought it to himself. Because of his communist connections and political activities in the 1930s he was always under suspicion and had to appear in front of the House Un-American Activities Committee in 1953, after which he was stripped of his security clearance and lost his job.

NATIONALITY:
American
WHEN:
July 16, 1945
WHERE:
Alamogordo Bombing Range,
New Mexico, USA
YOU SHOULD KNOW:
The flash from the explosion was seen up to 150 miles away and it was heard up to 200 miles away and the military explained it away as an explosion in a remote ammunition dump.

‘ Now I am become Death, the destroyer of worlds. ’

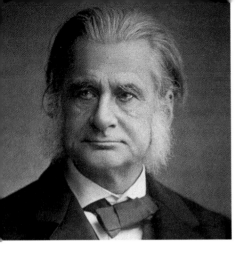

Thomas Henry Huxley 1825–1895

Seven months after Charles Darwin's On the Origin of Species *was published, a debate was organized at the Oxford Museum of Natural History between its adherents and opponents, including T.H. Huxley and Bishop Samuel Wilberforce. The idea that one species could gradually change into another was hugely controversial as it flew in the face of biblical orthodoxy. Huxley was an early supporter of the idea, but Bishop Wilberforce was opposed. A day or so before, Huxley had said that whether he was descended from a gorilla or not was of no significance, so the bishop asked him whether his preference was to be descended from a monkey on his grandfather's side or his grandmother's. Huxley's retort is said to have caused one lady in the audience to faint.*

‘ I would not be ashamed to have a monkey for my ancestor, but I would be ashamed to be connected with a man who used his great gifts to obscure the truth. ’

NATIONALITY:
British
WHEN:
1860
WHERE:
Oxford, England
YOU SHOULD KNOW:
Huxley is also known as
'Darwin's Bulldog'

The signatories of the Antarctic Treaty

In 1959, during the Cold War, international agreement was reached to ensure that the continent of Antarctica remained off limits for anything except peaceful scientific research and the treaty was opened for signature on December 1. There were originally 12 signatories – nearby countries Argentina, Australia and New Zealand plus those with scientific interests (Belgium, France, Japan, Norway, the Soviet Union, the UK and the USA) – though there are now 46. Other related agreements include the Agreed Measures for the Conservation of Antarctic Fauna and Flora, The Convention for the Conservation of Antarctic Marine Living Resources and the Protocol on Environmental Protection to the Antarctic Treaty.

WHEN:
1959
WHERE:
Washington, DC, USA
YOU SHOULD KNOW:
The treaty actually came into
force in 1961.

‘ ARTICLE I (ANTARCTICA FOR PEACEFUL PURPOSES ONLY)
1. Antarctica shall be used for peaceful purposes only. There shall be prohibited, inter alia, any measures of a military nature, such as the establishment of military bases and fortifications, the carrying out of military maneuvers, as well as the testing of any type of weapons.
2. The present Treaty shall not prevent the use of military personnel or equipment for scientific research or for any other peaceful purposes.

ARTICLE II (FREEDOM OF SCIENTIFIC INVESTIGATION TO CONTINUE)

Freedom of scientific investigation in Antarctica and cooperation toward that end, as applied during the International Geophysical Year, shall continue, subject to the provisions of the present Treaty.

ARTICLE III (PLANS AND RESULTS TO BE EXCHANGED)

1. In order to promote international cooperation in scientific investigation in Antarctica, as provided for in Article II of the present Treaty, the Contracting Parties agree that, to the greatest extent feasible and practicable:
(a) information regarding plans for scientific programs in Antarctica shall be exchanged to permit maximum economy and efficiency of operations;
(b) scientific personnel shall be exchanged in Antarctica between expeditions and stations;
(c) scientific observations and results from Antarctica shall be exchanged and made freely available.
2. In implementing this Article, every encouragement shall be given to the establishment of cooperative working relations with those Specialized Agencies of the United Nations and other international organizations having a scientific or technical interest in Antarctica.

ARTICLE IV (TERRITORIAL CLAIMS)

1. Nothing contained in the present Treaty shall be interpreted as:
(a) a renunciation by any Contracting Party of previously asserted rights of or claims to territorial sovereignty in Antarctica;
(b) a renunciation or diminution by any Contracting Party of any basis of claim to territorial sovereignty in Antarctica which it may have whether as a result of its activities or those of its nationals in Antarctica, or otherwise;
(c) prejudicing the position of any Contracting Party as regards its recognition or nonrecognition of any other State's right of or claim or basis of claim to territorial sovereignty in Antarctica.
2. No acts or activities taking place while the present Treaty is in force shall constitute a basis for asserting, supporting or denying a claim to territorial sovereignty in Antarctica. No new claim, or enlargement of an existing claim, to territorial sovereignty shall be asserted while the present Treaty is in force.

ARTICLE V (NUCLEAR EXPLOSIONS PROHIBITED)

1. Any nuclear explosions in Antarctica and the disposal there of radioactive waste material shall be prohibited.
2. In the event of the conclusion of international agreements concerning the use of nuclear energy, including nuclear explosions and the disposal of radioactive waste material, to which all of the Contracting Parties whose representatives are entitled to participate in the meetings provided for under Article IX are parties, the rules established under such agreements shall apply in Antarctica.

ARTICLE VI (AREA COVERED BY TREATY)

The provisions of the present Treaty shall apply to the area south of 60° South latitude, including all ice shelves, but nothing in the present Treaty shall prejudice or in any way affect the rights, or the exercise of the rights, of any State under international law with regard to the high seas within that area.

ARTICLE VII (FREE ACCESS FOR OBSERVATION AND INSPECTION)

1. In order to promote the objectives and ensure the observation of the provisions of the present Treaty, each Contracting Party whose representatives are entitled to participate in the meetings referred to in Article IX of the Treaty shall have the right to designate observers to carry out any inspection provided

for by the present Article. Observers shall be nationals of the Contracting Parties which designate them. The names of the observers shall be communicated to every other Contracting Party having the right to designate observers, and like notice shall be given of the termination of their appointment.

2. Each observer designated in accordance with the provisions of paragraph 1 of this Article shall have complete freedom of access at any time to any or all areas of Antarctica.

3. All areas of Antarctica, including all stations, installations and equipment within those areas, and all ships and aircraft at points of discharging or embarking cargoes or personnel in Antarctica, shall be open at all times to inspection by any observers designated in accordance with paragraph 1 of this Article.

4. Aerial observation may be carried out at any time over any or all areas of Antarctica by any of the Contracting Parties having the right to designate observers.

5. Each Contracting Party shall, at the time when the present Treaty enters into force for it, inform the other Contracting Parties, and thereafter shall give them notice in advance, of

(a) all expeditions to and within Antarctica, on the part of its ships of nationals, and all expeditions to Antarctica organized in or proceeding from its territory;

(b) all stations in Antarctica occupied by its nationals; and

(c) any military personnel or equipment intended to be introduced by it into Antarctica subject to the conditions prescribed in paragraph 2 of Article I of the present Treaty.

ARTICLE X (DISCOURAGES ACTIVITIES CONTRARY TO TREATY)
Each of the Contracting Parties undertakes to exert appropriate efforts, consistent with the Charter of the United Nations, to the end that no one engages in any activity in Antarctica contrary to the principles or purposes of the present Treaty.

ARTICLE XIV (UNITED STATES IS REPOSITORY)
The present Treaty, done in the English, French, Russian, and Spanish languages, each version being equally authentic, shall be deposited in the archives of the Government of the United States of America, which shall transmit duly certified copies thereof to the Governments of the signatory and acceding States.

NATIONALITY:
German
WHEN:
Many occasions
WHERE:
Many locations
YOU SHOULD KNOW:
Einstein was a notoriously slow learner at school.

Albert Einstein 1879–1955

One of the most brilliant scientists ever, Einstein did not agree with one of the basic tenets of quantum physics: that at the microphysical level the workings of classical Newtonian physics do not apply and it is impossible to determine, for example, in an atom where any one of its electrons might be, only the probability of where it might be. He argued that there must be a deterministic cause for this unpredictability: it was simply that it had not yet been found, whereas other physicists like Niels Bohr and Werner Heisenberg believed that the behaviour of the fundamental constituents of matter is entirely random. No cause has yet been found.

God does not play dice with the Universe.

The genius in jovial mood.

International Whaling Commission

The International Whaling Commission was originally set up as a body to regulate whaling in order to manage stocks and ensure the continuation of the industry. However, during the 1970s, the increasing public outcry against whaling in many countries, reduced numbers of whales and the development of synthetic alternatives to many of the products made from whales led to a series of measures that progressively reduced the numbers of whales that could be caught, the species that could be caught and the fishing methods allowed. At the 1982 meeting of the commission, a temporary moratorium was introduced and this has been re-voted each year since, although in some years the pro-whaling nations have almost won.

A whaler takes aim with his harpoon gun.

' . . . catch limits for the killing for commercial purposes of whales from all stocks for the 1986 coastal and the 1985/86 pelagic seasons and thereafter shall be zero. This provision will be kept under review, based upon the best scientific advice, and by 1990 at the latest the Commission will undertake a comprehensive assessment of the effects of this decision on whale stocks and consider modification of this provision and the establishment of other catch limits. '

WHEN:
1982
WHERE:
Brighton, England
YOU SHOULD KNOW:
Norway and Iceland both whale commercially, Japan whales for scientific purposes, although the meat is passed on for commercial sale, and several other countries, including the USA, allow 'aboriginal' whaling by communities who have traditionally done so.

Alexander Graham Bell

1847–1922

On March 10, 1876, the inventor Alexander Graham Bell spoke to his assistant Thomas Watson through his recently patented device. His voice vibrated a diaphragm, which moved a needle and caused a variation in an attached electrical circuit. This was transmitted along a wire to a similar receiver in the next room, and his assistant heard the words clearly. He called this invention an 'accoustic telegraph'. The device caught on quickly wherever he demonstrated it and by 1886 more than 150,000 people in the USA had telephones, incorporating such improvements as Thomas Edison's carbon microphone which picked up sounds much better than the original diaphragm.

NATIONALITY:
British
WHEN:
1876
WHERE:
Boston, Massachusetts, USA
YOU SHOULD KNOW:
There is still controversy about whether Elisha Gray's patent was filed before or after Bell's.

' Mr Watson, come here: I want you. '

Portrait of Johannes Kepler

NATIONALITY:
German
WHEN:
1609–1619
WHERE:
Prague/Linz, Austria

Johannes Kepler 1571–1630

Johannes Kepler's three laws of planetary motion are among the most important scientific discoveries of the seventeenth century. Kepler used the extremely accurate measurements that his predecessor as court mathematician to the Emperor Rudolf II – Tycho Brahe – had made over many years to ascertain how the planets moved in the sky. He realized that the observations bore out Copernicus' theory that the planets, including the Earth, orbited the Sun but that they did so in elliptical, not circular, orbits. The second law implies that the planets move more quickly when they are closer to the Sun while the third law shows that there is a proportional relationship between the distance of a planet from the Sun and the time it takes to complete one orbit. These laws were instrumental in a number of later discoveries, including Newton's Laws of Gravity.

First Law: The orbits of the planets are ellipses with the Sun at one of the foci.
The Second Law: The line that connects the planet to the Sun sweeps out equal areas in equal times.
Third Law: The squares of the orbital periods of the planets around the Sun are proportional to the cubes of the orbital semimajor axes.

Patrick Steptoe 1913–1988

NATIONALITY:
British
WHEN:
1978
WHERE:
Oldham, Manchester, England
YOU SHOULD KNOW:
Test-tube babies are actually conceived in Petrie dishes.

Shortly before midnight on 25 July 1978, a baby girl weighing 5 pounds and 12 ounces was delivered by Caesarian section at Oldham General Hospital, which was under siege by the media. The birth of a healthy baby girl might not sound like anything unusual, except that Louise Brown was the first baby conceived by in-vitro fertilization – a test-tube baby – to be born. At a press conference the following morning, the two doctors – Patrick Steptoe and Robert Edwards – spoke about the technique, and about the baby. The case provoked accusations of breaches of medical ethics and that the two surgeons were playing God, but the procedure is now widely accepted in many countries. Louise Brown now has a son of her own.

Opposite: Patrick Steptoe shows the device used in the procedure.

She came out crying her head off . . . a beautiful, normal baby.

Christiaan Barnard 1922–2001

After several years of experimentation, by 1967 several medical teams around the world thought that they had the expertise to perform a heart transplant. As with so many other new medical techniques, the issues that stopped them being carried out were ethical and moral. Although there were small numbers of families willing to allow their relatives' organs to be used to save other people's lives, it was a question of finding a recipient – someone well enough to face the operation, but ill enough to be desperate enough to take a chance. In December 1967 a young woman called Denise Darvall died in a road accident in Cape Town, and this time Dr Barnard had a recipient, Louis Washkansky, who was suffering with incurable heart disease. Mr Washkansky lived for another 18 days before dying from the side-effects of the immuno-suppressive drugs.

'I did not even inform the hospital superintendent what we were doing.'

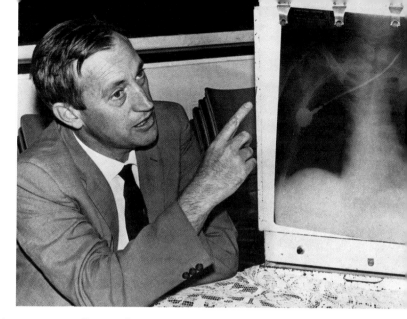

Barnard shows an X-Ray of Washkansky's chest.

NATIONALITY:
South African
WHEN:
1967
WHERE:
Cape Town, South Africa
YOU SHOULD KNOW:
Dr Barnard was also one of the first doctors to perform a kidney transplant.

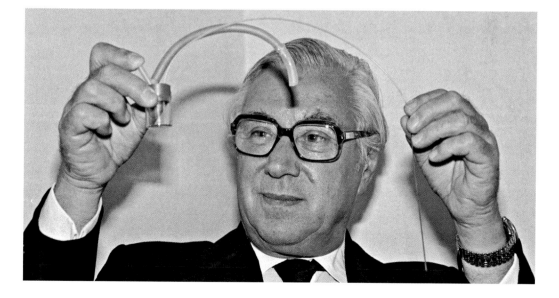

Ian Wilmut born 1944

NATIONALITY:
British
WHEN:
December 1997
WHERE:
The Roslin Institute, Edinburgh,
Scotland/*Science* magazine
YOU SHOULD KNOW:
Dolly died in 2003 and her stuffed
remains are on display at the Royal
Museum in Edinburgh.

The somewhat dry and academic sentence below announced a major breakthrough – whether or not one thinks it is a good idea – in the science of genetics. Some 17 months earlier, the work of Ian Wilmut and Keith Campbell's team at the Roslin Institute had resulted in the birth of a sheep cloned from the adult cell of her mother rather than an embryonic stem cell, the first time this had been achieved in a mammal. Reactions differed: some thought that this procedure would lead to great advances in science, while others feared its implications in terms of future cloning of humans.

'Our ability now to modify and select cells in culture and then produce transgenic lambs by nuclear transfer is tremendously encouraging and a major step towards our goal of being able to make very precise genetic modifications in livestock species.'

Below: Professor Ian Wilmut with Dolly, the world's first cloned sheep.

Francis Crick 1916–2004 and James Watson born 1928

It is hard to imagine that it is less than 60 years since the structure of DNA was uncovered, leading to countless discoveries in the science of genetics and inheritance. Crick and Watson's surmise that the double-helix structure of paired bases was an important part of the copying mechanism for genetic material was spot on. The discovery that DNA had a spiral structure was made by Maurice Wilkins and Raymond Gosling in 1950 using x-ray diffraction, but the exact structure – with the bonds between adjacent pairs on the outside of the spiral, not in the middle – took time to model.

We wish to put forward a radically different structure for the salt of deoxyribose nucleic acid. This structure has two helical chains each coiled round the same axis.

If it is assumed that the bases only occur in the structure in the most plausible tautomeric forms (that is, with the keto rather than the enol configurations) it is found that only specific pairs of bases can bond together. These pairs are: adenine (purine) with thymine (pyrimidine), and guanine (purine) with cytosine (pyrimidine),

. . . It has not escaped our notice that the specific pairing we have postulated immediately suggests a possible copying mechanism for the genetic material.

NATIONALITY:
British/American
WHEN:
April 2, 1953
WHERE:
Nature magazine
YOU SHOULD KNOW:
Crick and Watson won the Nobel Prize in Physiology or Medicine jointly with Maurice Wilkins for their work on DNA.

Michael Dexter **born 1945**

In June 2000, the announcement of the first draft of the human genome – the complete genetic code of a human cell – was made at a joint press conference by the US and UK teams who were collaborating on this work. Dr Michael Dexter summed up the teams' elation at completing research that might eventually lead to the eradication of many types of genetic disease through gene therapy. In the years since, the genetic markers of a variety of conditions have been found through their differences from normal sequences of DNA.

This is the outstanding achievement not only of our lifetime, but in terms of human history. I say this, because the Human Genome Project does have the potential to impact on the life of every person on the planet.

NATIONALITY:
British
WHEN:
June 26, 2000
WHERE:
London, England
YOU SHOULD KNOW:
At the same press conference, it was announced that the data of the Human Genome Mapping Project would not be subject to copyright.

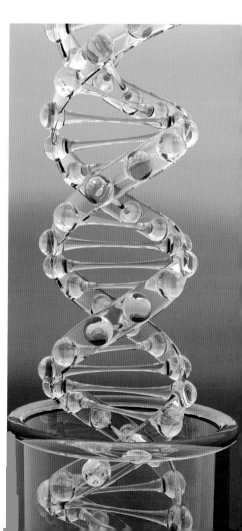

DNA molecule model in a test tube

PATRIOTISM

Elizabeth I born 1533

reigned 1558–1603

NATIONALITY:
English
WHEN:
August 8, 1588
WHERE:
Tilbury, London, England
YOU SHOULD KNOW:
Philip II of Spain had been planning
to invade England for several years
to cut off support for rebels in the
Netherlands, but the execution of
Mary, Queen of Scots on Elizabeth I's
orders in 1587 was the final catalyst.

The Spanish Armada left for England early in 1588. When the force gathered off Calais on the north coast of France in July, it consisted of over 30,000 troops on about 130 ships. When Elizabeth's naval commander Francis Drake sent fireships into the Armada on July 28, they broke formation and scattered. The Battle of Gravelines the next day resulted in more losses for the Spanish, but the threat of invasion remained. On August 8, Elizabeth went to Tilbury docks, east of London, to address troops amassed to protect the city and urge them to do their duty for their country. As it was, they were not called upon to fight: one of the worst storms recorded in centuries tore into the Spanish fleet and inflicted huge losses.

Battle is joined.

'My loving people, we have been persuaded by some, that are careful of our safety, to take heed how we commit ourselves to armed multitudes, for fear of treachery; but I assure you, I do not desire to live to distrust my faithful and loving people. Let tyrants fear; I have always so behaved myself that, under God, I have placed my chiefest strength and safeguard in the loyal hearts and good will of my subjects. And therefore I am come amongst you at this time, not as for my recreation or sport, but being resolved, in the midst and heat of the battle, to live or die amongst you all; to lay down, for my God, and for my kingdom, and for my people, my honour and my blood, even the dust. I know I have but the body of a weak and feeble woman; but I have the heart of a king, and of a king of England, too; and think foul scorn that Parma or Spain, or any prince of Europe, should dare to invade the borders of my realms: to which, rather than any dishonour should grow by me, I myself will take up arms; I myself will be your general, judge, and rewarder of every one of your virtues in the field. I know already, by your forwardness, that you have deserved rewards and crowns; and we do assure you, on the word of a prince, they shall be duly paid you. In the mean my lieutenant general shall be in my stead, than whom never prince commanded a more noble and worthy subject; not doubting by your obedience to my general, by your concord in the camp, and by your valour in the field, we shall shortly have a famous victory over the enemies of my God, of my kingdom, and of my people. 🟫

Georges Danton 1759–1794

In the summer of 1792, the Austrian army invaded France and on the day this speech was made – September 2 – captured the strategically important town of Verdun. The Revolution was about to turn even more violent. The King and Queen were now under close house arrest, the Republic would be declared later in the month and the King would be dead within five months. Paris and the rest of the country had been at political odds and Danton used the Prussian invasion to try to spur the rest of the provinces to support the political aims of the Parisian revolutionaries.

NATIONALITY:
French
WHEN:
September 2, 1792
WHERE:
Paris, France
YOU SHOULD KNOW:
Danton would be a victim of his own Revolution – he was executed in 1794.

Danton making a point!

It is gratifying to the ministers of a free people to have to announce to them that their country will be saved. All are stirred, all are excited, all burn to fight. You know that Verdun is not yet in the power of our enemies. You know that its garrison swears to immolate the first who breathes a proposition of surrender.

One portion of our people will proceed to the frontiers, another will throw up intrenchments, and the third with pikes will defend the hearts of our cities. Paris will second these great efforts. The commissioners of the Commune will solemnly proclaim to the citizens the invitation to arm and march to the defense of the country. At such a moment you can proclaim that the capital deserves well of all France.

At such a moment this National Assembly becomes a veritable committee of war. We ask that you concur with us in directing this sublime movement of the people, by naming commissioners who will second us in these great measures. We ask that any one refusing to give personal service or to furnish arms shall be punished with death. We ask that a set of instructions be drawn up for the citizens to direct their movements. We ask that couriers be sent to all the departments to notify them of the decrees that you proclaim here. The tocsin we are about to ring is not an alarm signal; it sounds the charge on the enemies of our country. To conquer them we must dare, dare again, always dare, and France is saved! 🟨

Napoleon Bonaparte

Napoleon I, 1769–1821

NATIONALITY:
French
WHEN:
1804
WHEN:
Paris, France
YOU SHOULD KNOW:
Contrary to popular belief, Napoleon did not actually snatch the crown from the hands of the Pope at his coronation. It had been agreed beforehand that he would do so.

In the spring of 1804 it was decided by the Senate and by popular vote to offer the first Consul of France, Napoleon Bonaparte, the crown and to create a new French Empire. After a certain amount of haggling over details, he accepted and invited Pope Pius VII to Paris to conduct the ceremony. Louis XVI had been executed by the mob just under 12 years earlier as an unpopular despot and traitor to his own people, whereas Charlemagne was the golden emperor of French history who had governed most of Europe in the ninth century. In the light of Napoleon's attempts over the next few years to conquer lands as far away as Russia, this remark to the Pope at the time of the coronation in December 1804 is prophetic.

I am the successor not of Louis XVI, but of Charlemagne. 🟨

Napoleon Bonaparte

Napoleon I, 1769–1821

NATIONALITY:
French
WHEN:
1814
WHERE:
Fontainebleau, France
YOU SHOULD KNOW:
While exiled on Elba Napoleon was allowed to keep his title, and worked to make improvements on the island, particularly in the field of agriculture.

After years of victories and reversals, it took the combined forces of most of Europe to defeat Napoleon. On April 4, 1814, most of his senior generals mutinied rather than try to recapture Paris with insufficient forces and two days later he abdicated in favour of his son. On the 22nd, he movingly addressed his oldest and most-trusted troops one last time before being exiled to the tiny island of Elba. He was back 10 months later, with a new army at his heels, although it did not prevent his final defeat at the Battle of Waterloo on June 18, 1815, after which he was exiled to the South Atlantic island of St Helena, where he died six years later.

The proud Emperor

" SOLDIERS OF MY OLD GUARD: I bid you farewell. For 20 years I have constantly accompanied you on the road to honour and glory. In these latter times, as in the days of our prosperity, you have invariably been models of courage and fidelity. With men such as you our cause could not be lost; but the war would have been interminable; it would have been civil war, and that would have entailed deeper misfortunes on France.

I have sacrificed all of my interests to those of the country. I go, but you, my friends, will continue to serve France. Her happiness was my only thought. It will still be the object of my wishes. Do not regret my fate; if I have consented to survive, it is to serve your glory. I intend to write the history of the great achievements we have performed together. Adieu my friends. Would I could press you all to my heart. "

William B. Travis 1809–1836

Brave defenders cross the line.

In 1836 Lt Col Travis was in command of the garrison at the Alamo, San Antonio, in the breakaway Republic of Texas, which was under siege by General Santa Anna's Mexican army. On March 3 or 4, realizing that reinforcements were unlikely to arrive in time to save them, he collected all the defenders together and explained that their cause was hopeless but it was not defeat, but rather the manner of their defeat that people would remember. He unsheathed his sword, drew a line in the dirt with it and gave the men the choice below. All but one crossed the line. Three days later, the Mexicans over-ran the Alamo.

" Whoever will stay with me and fight to the death with me, step over the line. "

NATIONALITY:
American
WHEN:
1836
WHERE:
San Antonio, Texas, USA
YOU SHOULD KNOW:
The one man who did not cross the line in the dirt was a veteran of Napoleon's army – Moses Rose.

Thomas Jefferson 1743–1826

NATIONALITY:
American
WHEN:
1801
WHERE:
Washington, DC, USA
YOU SHOULD KNOW:
Thomas Jefferson was the first
President to take the Executive Oath
in Washington.

After the very closely fought Presidential election of 1800, Thomas Jefferson was declared the winner only in late February 1801. In his inaugural address, 25 years after he had drafted the Declaration of Independence, he set out his vision for the future of America with low taxes, as little interference from the US Government in people's daily lives as possible, equal justice for all and peaceful relations with other nations. His gratitude that a wide ocean separated the USA from the squabbling countries of Europe formed a cornerstone of his foreign policy: the non-interference that lasted for generations and presaged the Monroe Doctrine.

Called upon to undertake the duties of the first executive office of our country, I avail myself of the presence of that portion of my fellow-citizens which is here assembled to express my grateful thanks for the favour with which they have been pleased to look toward me, to declare a sincere consciousness that the task is above my talents, and that I approach it with those anxious and awful presentiments which the greatness of the charge and the weakness of my powers so justly inspire. A rising nation, spread over a wide and fruitful land, traversing all the seas with the rich productions of their industry, engaged in commerce with nations who feel power and forget right, advancing rapidly to destinies beyond the reach of mortal eye – when I contemplate these transcendent objects, and see the honour, the happiness, and the hopes of this beloved country committed to the issue, and the auspices of this day, I shrink from the contemplation, and humble myself before the magnitude of the undertaking. Utterly, indeed, should I despair did not the presence of many whom I here see remind me that in the other high authorities provided by our Constitution I shall find resources of wisdom, of virtue, and of zeal on which to rely under all difficulties . . .

Let us, then, with courage and confidence pursue our own Federal and Republican principles, our attachment to union and representative government. Kindly separated by nature and a wide ocean from the exterminating havoc of one quarter of the globe; too high-minded to endure the degradations of the others; possessing a chosen country, with room enough for our descendants to the thousandth and thousandth generation; entertaining a due sense of our equal right to the use of our own faculties, to the acquisitions of our own industry, to honour and confidence from our fellow-citizens, resulting not from birth, but from our actions and their sense of them; enlightened by a benign religion, professed, indeed, and practiced in various forms, yet all of them inculcating honesty, truth, temperance, gratitude, and the love of man; acknowledging and adoring an overruling Providence, which by all its dispensations proves that it delights in the happiness of man here and his greater happiness hereafter – with all these blessings, what more is

Thomas Jefferson 1743–1826

NATIONALITY:
American
WHEN:
1801
WHERE:
Washington, DC, USA
YOU SHOULD KNOW:
Thomas Jefferson was the first President to take the Executive Oath in Washington.

After the very closely fought Presidential election of 1800, Thomas Jefferson was declared the winner only in late February 1801. In his inaugural address, 25 years after he had drafted the Declaration of Independence, he set out his vision for the future of America with low taxes, as little interference from the US Government in people's daily lives as possible, equal justice for all and peaceful relations with other nations. His gratitude that a wide ocean separated the USA from the squabbling countries of Europe formed a cornerstone of his foreign policy: the non-interference that lasted for generations and presaged the Monroe Doctrine.

‘Called upon to undertake the duties of the first executive office of our country, I avail myself of the presence of that portion of my fellow-citizens which is here assembled to express my grateful thanks for the favour with which they have been pleased to look toward me, to declare a sincere consciousness that the task is above my talents, and that I approach it with those anxious and awful presentiments which the greatness of the charge and the weakness of my powers so justly inspire. A rising nation, spread over a wide and fruitful land, traversing all the seas with the rich productions of their industry, engaged in commerce with nations who feel power and forget right, advancing rapidly to destinies beyond the reach of mortal eye – when I contemplate these transcendent objects, and see the honour, the happiness, and the hopes of this beloved country committed to the issue, and the auspices of this day, I shrink from the contemplation, and humble myself before the magnitude of the undertaking. Utterly, indeed, should I despair did not the presence of many whom I here see remind me that in the other high authorities provided by our Constitution I shall find resources of wisdom, of virtue, and of zeal on which to rely under all difficulties . . .

Let us, then, with courage and confidence pursue our own Federal and Republican principles, our attachment to union and representative government. Kindly separated by nature and a wide ocean from the exterminating havoc of one quarter of the globe; too high-minded to endure the degradations of the others; possessing a chosen country, with room enough for our descendants to the thousandth and thousandth generation; entertaining a due sense of our equal right to the use of our own faculties, to the acquisitions of our own industry, to honour and confidence from our fellow-citizens, resulting not from birth, but from our actions and their sense of them; enlightened by a benign religion, professed, indeed, and practiced in various forms, yet all of them inculcating honesty, truth, temperance, gratitude, and the love of man; acknowledging and adoring an overruling Providence, which by all its dispensations proves that it delights in the happiness of man here and his greater happiness hereafter – with all these blessings, what more is

Abraham Lincoln 1809–1865

On November 19, 1863, during the dedication ceremony for the Soldiers' National Cemetery, President Lincoln gave a two-minute speech which has become one of the best-known and most influential in American history. Just four-and-a-half months after the pivotal Civil War battle at Gettysburg, in which thousands upon thousands of men had died for their causes, he redefined the Civil War as a struggle for freedom, not just a battle between states, invoked the spirit of the Declaration of Independence's call for equality and called for increased dedication from all so that the deaths of so many people were not in vain.

NATIONALITY:
American
WHEN:
November 19, 1863
WHERE:
Gettysburg, Pennsylvania, USA
YOU SHOULD KNOW:
There are five different manuscript versions of the address.

Four score and seven years ago our fathers brought forth, on this continent, a new nation, conceived in Liberty, and dedicated to the proposition that all men are created equal.

Now we are engaged in a great civil war, testing whether that nation, or any nation so conceived and so dedicated, can long endure. We are met on a great battle-field of that war. We have come to dedicate a portion of that field, as a final resting place for those who here gave their lives that that nation might live. It is altogether fitting and proper that we should do this.

But, in a larger sense, we can not dedicate – we can not consecrate – we can not hallow – this ground. The brave men, living and dead, who struggled here, have consecrated it, far above our poor power to add or detract. The world will little note, nor long remember what we say here, but it can never forget what they did here. It is for us the living, rather, to be dedicated here to the unfinished work which they who fought here have thus far so nobly advanced. It is rather for us to be here dedicated to the great task remaining before us – that from these honoured dead we take increased devotion to that cause for which they here gave the last full measure of devotion – that we here highly resolve that these dead shall not have died in vain – that this nation, under God, shall have a new birth of freedom – and that government of the people, by the people, for the people, shall not perish from the earth.

In this photograph, by Matthew Brady, Abraham Lincoln is seen giving the Gettysberg Address.

O'Connell was a passionate orator.

Daniel O'Connell 1775–1847

Although Irish leader and activist O'Connell and his colleagues had attained the right to be Members of Parliament, British rule in Ireland was oppressive and most Irish people lived in poverty. MP for County Clare, O'Connell made repeated calls for the repeal of the Act of Union of 1801, which had abolished the Parliament in Dublin, and for Ireland to become a separate, independent country with the British monarch as head of state. In the debate on King William IV's speech at the State Opening of Parliament on February 4, 1836, O'Connell made one of his most famous speeches.

' . . . England never did do justice to Ireland – she never did. What we have got of it we have extorted from men opposed to us on principle – against which principle they have made us such concessions as we have obtained from them . . .

Here am I calling for justice to Ireland; but there is a coalition tonight – not a base unprincipled one – God forbid! – it is an extremely natural one; I mean that between the right honourable baronet and the noble lord the member for North Lancashire. It is a natural coalition, and it is impromptu; for the noble lord informs us he had not even a notion of taking the part he has until the moment at which he seated himself where he now is. I know his candour; he told us it was a sudden inspiration which induced him to take part against Ireland. I believe it with the most potent faith, because I know that he requires no preparation for voting against the interests of the Irish people . . .

. . . I ask you only for justice: will you – can you – I will not say dare you refuse, because that would make you turn the other way. I implore you, as English gentlemen, to take this matter into consideration now, because you never had such an opportunity of conciliating. Experience makes fools wise; you are not fools, but you have yet to be convinced . . . If you refuse justice to that country, it is a melancholy consideration to me to think that you are adding substantially to that power and influence, while you are wounding my country to its very heart's core; weakening that throne, the monarch who sits upon which, you say you respect; severing that union which, you say, is bound together by the tightest links, and withholding that justice from Ireland which she will not cease to seek till it is obtained; every man must admit that the course I am taking is the legitimate and proper course – I defy any man to say it is not. Condemn me elsewhere as much as you please, but this you must admit. You may taunt the ministry with having coalesced me, you may raise the vulgar cry of 'Irishman and Papist' against me, you may send out men called ministers of God to slander and calumniate me . . . but the question comes into this narrow compass. I demand, I respectfully insist: on equal justice for Ireland, on the same principle by which it has been administered to Scotland and England. I will not take less. Refuse me that if you can. '

NATIONALITY:
Irish
WHERE:
London, England
WHEN:
1836
YOU SHOULD KNOW:
Until 1829 Catholic MPs were banned from taking their seats in London's House of Commons.

The proud Emperor

‘SOLDIERS OF MY OLD GUARD: I bid you farewell. For 20 years I have constantly accompanied you on the road to honour and glory. In these latter times, as in the days of our prosperity, you have invariably been models of courage and fidelity. With men such as you our cause could not be lost; but the war would have been interminable; it would have been civil war, and that would have entailed deeper misfortunes on France.

I have sacrificed all of my interests to those of the country. I go, but you, my friends, will continue to serve France. Her happiness was my only thought. It will still be the object of my wishes. Do not regret my fate; if I have consented to survive, it is to serve your glory. I intend to write the history of the great achievements we have performed together. Adieu my friends. Would I could press you all to my heart.’

William B. Travis 1809–1836

Brave defenders cross the line.

In 1836 Lt Col Travis was in command of the garrison at the Alamo, San Antonio, in the breakaway Republic of Texas, which was under siege by General Santa Anna's Mexican army. On March 3 or 4, realizing that reinforcements were unlikely to arrive in time to save them, he collected all the defenders together and explained that their cause was hopeless but it was not defeat, but rather the manner of their defeat that people would remember. He unsheathed his sword, drew a line in the dirt with it and gave the men the choice below. All but one crossed the line. Three days later, the Mexicans over-ran the Alamo.

‘Whoever will stay with me and fight to the death with me, step over the line.’

NATIONALITY:
American
WHEN:
1836
WHERE:
San Antonio, Texas, USA
YOU SHOULD KNOW:
The one man who did not cross the line in the dirt was a veteran of Napoleon's army – Moses Rose.

necessary to make us a happy and a prosperous people? Still one thing more, fellow-citizens – a wise and frugal Government, which shall restrain men from injuring one another, shall leave them otherwise free to regulate their own pursuits of industry and improvement, and shall not take from the mouth of labour the bread it has earned . . .

About to enter, fellow-citizens, on the exercise of duties which comprehend everything dear and valuable to you, it is proper you should understand what I deem the essential principles of our Government, and consequently those which ought to shape its Administration. I will compress them within the narrowest compass they will bear, stating the general principle, but not all its limitations. Equal and exact justice to all men, of whatever state or persuasion, religious or political; peace, commerce, and honest friendship with all nations, entangling alliances with none; the support of the State governments in all their rights, as the most competent administrations for our domestic concerns and the surest bulwarks against antirepublican tendencies; the preservation of the General Government in its whole constitutional vigour, as the sheet anchor of our peace at home and safety abroad; a jealous care of the right of election by the people – a mild and safe corrective of abuses which are lopped by the sword of revolution where peaceable remedies are unprovided; absolute acquiescence in the decisions of the majority, the vital principle of republics, from which is no appeal but to force, the vital principle and immediate parent of despotism; a well disciplined militia, our best reliance in peace and for the first moments of war, till regulars may relieve them; the supremacy of the civil over the military authority; economy in the public expense, that labour may be lightly burthened; the honest payment of our debts and sacred preservation of the public faith; encouragement of agriculture, and of commerce as its handmaid; the diffusion of information and arraignment of all abuses at the bar of the public reason; freedom of religion; freedom of the press, and freedom of person under the protection of the *habeas corpus*, and trial by juries impartially selected. These principles form the bright constellation which has gone before us and guided our steps through an age of revolution and reformation. The wisdom of our sages and blood of our heroes have been devoted to their attainment. They should be the creed of our political faith, the text of civic instruction, the touchstone by which to try the services of those we trust; and should we wander from them in moments of error or of alarm, let us hasten to retrace our steps and to regain the road which alone leads to peace, liberty, and safety . . .

Relying, then, on the patronage of your good will, I advance with obedience to the work, ready to retire from it whenever you become sensible how much better choice it is in your power to make. And may that Infinite Power which rules the destinies of the universe lead our councils to what is best, and give them a favourable issue for your peace and prosperity.

Horatio Nelson 1758–1805

During the interminable wars with France and a variety of coalitions between other European nations (1792–1815) battles were fought on land and at at sea from Moscow to the Atlantic and from the English Channel to Egypt. In 1805 the British navy was blockading the Franco-Spanish fleet in the port of Cadiz. When the enemy ships slipped out of the harbour, the British pursued them. Just before the Battle of Trafalgar commenced, Admiral Nelson had the following flag signal raised on HMS Victory. Nelson's tactics of attacking from the side in two divisions were highly successful: he lost no ships in the melée while the Franco-Spanish fleet lost 18.

' England expects that every man will do his duty. '

Admiral Nelson calmly observing the battle.

NATIONALITY:
British
WHEN:
1805
WHERE:
At sea off Cape Trafalgar
YOU SHOULD KNOW:
After his death in the battle, Nelson's body was taken to Gibraltar in a large barrel of brandy and from there to London in a lead-lined coffin filled with wine.

Nathan Hale 1755–1776

NATIONALITY:
American
WHEN:
1776
WHERE:
Manhattan, New York City, USA
YOU SHOULD KNOW:
The Battle of Long Island was the first battle fought by the army of the independent United States of America.

A year into the American Revolutionary War, and just days after the signing of the Declaration of Independence, the British Navy moved on New York City. After the ensuing Battle of Long Island on August 27, George Washington first moved his troops to Brooklyn Heights, and then made a strategic withdrawal to Manhattan Island, where further battles were fought. On September 21 Captain Hale of the Continental Army was captured during a reconnaissance mission. He was taken to the British Commander, General Howe, and the following morning hanged as a spy. He is reported to have given a long, eloquent speech, of which these were the last words.

' I only regret, that I have but one life to lose for my country. '

John F. Kennedy 1917–1963

In John F. Kennedy's inaugural speech on January 20, 1961, the young President used the founding of the USA as an inspirational notion with which to promote his vision and plans for the future. Unlike many of his predecessors, who spoke chiefly of domestic concerns and seemed to want to be uninvolved with the rest of the world, JFK talked of his aspirations for both America and other nations. The most remembered line of the speech is: 'And so, my fellow Americans, ask not what your country can do for you; ask what you can do for your country.'. But it is followed by the less well-known, but just as pivotal: 'My fellow citizens of the world, ask not what America will do for you, but what together we can do for the freedom of man.'

NATIONALITY:
American
WHEN:
January 20, 1961
WHERE:
Washington, DC, USA
YOU SHOULD KNOW:
President Kennedy is so far the only practising Catholic to be elected to the Oval Office.

Vice President Johnson, Mr Speaker, Mr Chief Justice, President Eisenhower, Vice President Nixon, President Truman, Reverend Clergy, fellow citizens:

We observe today not a victory of party but a celebration of freedom – symbolizing an end as well as a beginning – signifying renewal as well as change. For I have sworn before you and Almighty God the same solemn oath our forebears prescribed nearly a century and three-quarters ago.

The world is very different now. For man holds in his mortal hands the power to abolish all forms of human poverty and all forms of human life. And yet the same revolutionary beliefs for which our forebears fought are still at issue around the globe – the belief that the rights of man come not from the generosity of the state but from the hand of God.

We dare not forget today that we are the heirs of that first revolution. Let the word go forth from this time and place, to friend and foe alike, that the torch has been passed to a new generation of Americans – born in this century, tempered by war, disciplined by a hard and bitter peace, proud of our ancient heritage – and unwilling to witness or permit the slow undoing of those human rights to which this nation has always been committed, and to which we are committed today at home and around the world.

Let every nation know, whether it wishes us well or ill, that we shall pay any price, bear any burden, meet any hardship, support any friend, oppose any foe to assure the survival and the success of liberty.

This much we pledge – and more.

To those old allies whose cultural and spiritual origins we share, we pledge the loyalty of faithful friends. United there is little we cannot do in a host of cooperative ventures. Divided there is little we can do – for we dare not meet a powerful challenge at odds and split asunder.

President Kennedy addresses the nation at his inaugural speech.

To those new states whom we welcome to the ranks of the free, we pledge our word that one form of colonial control shall not have passed away merely to be replaced by a far more iron tyranny. We shall not always expect to find them supporting our view. But we shall always hope to find them strongly supporting their own freedom – and to remember that, in the past, those who foolishly sought power by riding the back of the tiger ended up inside.

To those people in the huts and villages of half the globe struggling to break the bonds of mass misery, we pledge our best efforts to help them help themselves, for whatever period is required – not because the Communists may be doing it, not because we seek their votes, but because it is right. If a free society cannot help the many who are poor, it cannot save the few who are rich.

To our sister republics south of our border, we offer a special pledge – to convert our good words into good deeds – in a new alliance for progress – to assist free men and free governments in casting off the chains of poverty. But this peaceful revolution of hope cannot become the prey of hostile powers. Let all our neighbours know that we shall join with them to oppose aggression or subversion anywhere in the Americas. And let every other power know that this hemisphere intends to remain the master of its own house.

To that world assembly of sovereign states, the United Nations, our last best hope in an age where the instruments of war have far outpaced the instruments of peace, we renew our pledge of support – to prevent it from becoming merely a forum for invective – to strengthen its shield of the new and the weak – and to enlarge the area in which its writ may run.

Finally, to those nations who would make themselves our adversary, we offer not a pledge but a request: that both sides begin anew the quest for peace, before the dark powers of destruction unleashed by science engulf all humanity in planned or accidental self-destruction.

We dare not tempt them with weakness. For only when our arms are sufficient beyond doubt can we be certain beyond doubt that they will never be employed.

But neither can two great and powerful groups of nations take comfort from our present course – both sides overburdened by the cost of modern weapons, both rightly alarmed by the steady spread of the deadly atom, yet both racing to alter that uncertain balance of terror that stays the hand of mankind's final war.

So let us begin anew – remembering on both sides that civility is not a sign of weakness, and sincerity is always subject to proof. Let us never negotiate out of fear. But let us never fear to negotiate.

Let both sides explore what problems unite us instead of belabouring those problems which divide us.

Let both sides, for the first time, formulate serious and precise proposals for the inspection and control of arms – and bring the absolute power to destroy other nations under the absolute control of all nations.

Let both sides seek to invoke the wonders of science instead of its terrors. Together let us explore the stars, conquer the deserts, eradicate disease, tap the ocean depths and encourage the arts and commerce.

Let both sides unite to heed in all corners of the earth the command of Isaiah – to 'undo the heavy burdens . . . (and) let the oppressed go free.'

And if a beachhead of cooperation may push back the jungle of suspicion, let both sides join in creating a new endeavour, not a new balance of power, but a new world of law, where the strong are just and the weak secure and the peace preserved.

All this will not be finished in the first one hundred days. Nor will it be finished in the first one thousand days, nor in the life of this Administration, nor even perhaps in our lifetime on this planet. But let us begin.

In your hands, my fellow citizens, more than mine, will rest the final success or failure of our course.

Since this country was founded, each generation of Americans has been summoned to give testimony to its national loyalty. The graves of young Americans who answered the call to service surround the globe.

Now the trumpet summons us again – not as a call to bear arms, though arms we need – not as a call to battle, though embattled we are – but a call to bear the burden of a long twilight struggle, year in and year out, 'rejoicing in hope, patient in tribulation' – a struggle against the common enemies of man: tyranny, poverty, disease and war itself.

Can we forge against these enemies a grand and global alliance, north and south, east and west, that can assure a more fruitful life for all mankind? Will you join in that historic effort?

In the long history of the world, only a few generations have been granted the role of defending freedom in its hour of maximum danger. I do not shrink from this responsibility – I welcome it. I do not believe that any of us would exchange places with any other people or any other generation. The energy, the faith, the devotion which we bring to this endeavour will light our country and all who serve it – and the glow from that fire can truly light the world.

And so, my fellow Americans: ask not what your country can do for you – ask what you can do for your country.

My fellow citizens of the world: ask not what America will do for you, but what together we can do for the freedom of man.

Finally, whether you are citizens of America or citizens of the world, ask of us here the same high standards of strength and sacrifice which we ask of you. With a good conscience our only sure reward, with history the final judge of our deeds, let us go forth to lead the land we love, asking His blessing and His help, but knowing that here on earth God's work must truly be our own.

Giuseppe Garibaldi 1807–1882

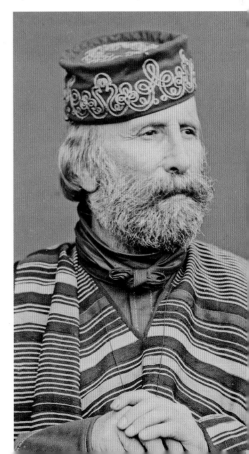

Despite his failure to keep hold of Rome in 1849, Italian patriot Giuseppe Garibaldi decided to make another attempt in 1862. The Papal States – modern-day Lazio, Umbria, Marche and the Romagna area of Emilia-Romagna – were under the direct control of the Popes in Rome and formed a division between the other two parts of the Italian peninsula. As he set out from Catania, Garibaldi swore that he would either take Rome or perish beneath its walls. He had convinced himself that he had the clandestine support of the government, but was mistaken; he was met by an army and rather than making a fight of it he forbade his soldiers to fire on fellow soldiers of the Kingdom of Italy and surrendered.

Roma o Morte! (Rome or Death!)

NATIONALITY:
Italian
WHEN:
1862
WHERE:
Catania, Sicily, Italy

YOU SHOULD KNOW:
The Vatican lost the Papal States in 1870 when the French withdrew and only gained independence in 1929 under the Lateran Treaty, in which it gave up claim to its former territories.

Giuseppe Garibaldi

Eric Field (dates unknown)

NATIONALITY:
British
WHEN:
1914
WHERE:
London, England
YOU SHOULD KNOW:
The picture of Lord Kitchener on
the revised poster was painted
by Alfred Leete.

Eric Field was a copywriter for a London-based advertising agency. In July 1914, a month before World War I broke out, he was contacted by Colonel Strachey, the Assistant Adjutant General (Recruiting) of the British Army, with a request for a slogan and poster which would need to be ready for use as soon as war was declared. Within hours, Field had come up with the slogan below. The early recruiting posters simply had the six words and the royal coat of arms. The poster first appeared on August 5, the day after war broke out. Lord Kitchener was appointed Secretary of State for War on the 6th and the more familiar poster, with a picture of him with staring eyes, bristling handlebar moustache and pointing finger and the pithier Your Country Needs YOU! *first appeared on September 14.*

‘ Your King and Country need you. ’

Francis Bellamy 1855–1931

NATIONALITY:
American
WHEN:
1892
WHERE:
Boston, Massachusetts, USA
YOU SHOULD KNOW:
The original raised-hand salute to the
flag was replaced with the hand-
over-heart gesture during World War
II to avoid any possibility of a
similarity to the Nazi salute.

An American Baptist minister and Christian Socialist, Francis Bellamy worked for a family magazine called The Youth's Companion, *which in 1888 started selling flags to schools in order to increase circulation and to try to get every school to make the patriotic gesture of displaying the Stars and Stripes, thus increasing national pride. In 1891, they had the idea of furthering the programme by inaugurating a flag-raising ceremony in schools as part of the celebrations of the four-hundredth anniversary of Christoper Columbus reaching the Americas. There have been four versions of the pledge: Bellamy's (below left), President Harrison's of October the same year, that of 1923–1924 and that of 1954 (bottom right), which is the one still used.*

‘ I pledge allegiance
to my Flag
and the Republic
for which it stands,
one nation
indivisible,
with liberty and justice for all.

I pledge allegiance
to the Flag
of the United States of America,
and to the Republic
for which it stands,
one nation
under God,
indivisible,
with liberty and justice for all. ’

Thomas Brigham Bishop

1835–1905

The song John Brown's Body *first appeared in print in 1861. Its origins are obscure, but it may well have been written in 1859 by a Unionist soldier, Thomas Brigham Bishop, when he heard of the execution of the famous abolitionist John Brown at nearby Charles Town. The tune of the verses is that of the hymn* Say, Brothers – *which was first published in 1858, but is thought to date from at least as far back as 1800. The Jeff Davis verse was added as a response to the appointment of Jefferson Davis as President of the Confederate States.*

NATIONALITY:
American
WHEN:
1859
WHERE:
Martinsburg, Virginia, USA
YOU SHOULD KNOW:
There are various claims to authorship of the original *Glory, Glory Hallelujah!* song and tune.

'John Brown's body lies a-mouldering in the grave;
John Brown's body lies a-mouldering in the grave;
John Brown's body lies a-mouldering in the grave;
His soul's marching on!
(Chorus)
Glory, halle – hallelujah! Glory, halle – hallelujah!
Glory, halle – hallelujah! His soul's marching on!
He's gone to be a soldier in the army of the Lord!
He's gone to be a soldier in the army of the Lord!
He's gone to be a soldier in the army of the Lord!
His soul's marching on!
(Chorus)
John Brown's knapsack is strapped upon his back!
John Brown's knapsack is strapped upon his back!
John Brown's knapsack is strapped upon his back!
His soul's marching on!
(Chorus)
His pet lambs will meet him on the way;
His pet lambs will meet him on the way;
His pet lambs will meet him on the way;
They go marching on!
(Chorus)
They will hang Jeff Davis to a sour apple tree!
They will hang Jeff Davis to a sour apple tree!
They will hang Jeff Davis to a sour apple tree!
As they march along!
(Chorus)
Now, three rousing cheers for the Union;
Now, three rousing cheers for the Union;
Now, three rousing cheers for the Union;
As we are marching on! '

*Julia Ward Howe
writing at her desk*

NATIONALITY:
American
WHEN:
1861
WHERE:
Washington, DC, USA
YOU SHOULD KNOW.
The last words of Martin Luther
King's last public sermon before his
death were 'Mine eyes have seen the
glory of the coming of the Lord'.

Julia Ward Howe 1819–1910

Poet and abolitionist Julia Ward Howe heard the Unionist marching song John Brown's Body *at a review of troops on November 18, 1861 and later said that she woke up the next morning with the words of the following battle hymn running through her head. They were published in* The Atlantic Monthly *magazine the following February. The song is still widely referenced in literature (Steinbeck's* The Grapes of Wrath, *for example), films and other popular culture. It has been played at the funerals of several presidents, as well as that of Sir Winston Churchill.*

Mine eyes have seen the glory of the coming of the Lord:
He is trampling out the vintage where the grapes of wrath are stored;
He hath loosed the fateful lightning of His terrible swift sword:
His truth is marching on.
(Chorus)
Glory, glory, hallelujah!
Glory, glory, hallelujah!
Glory, glory, hallelujah!
His truth is marching on.
I have seen Him in the watch-fires of a hundred circling camps,
They have builded Him an altar in the evening dews and damps;
I can read His righteous sentence by the dim and flaring lamps:
His day is marching on.
(Chorus)
Glory, glory, hallelujah!
Glory, glory, hallelujah!
Glory, glory, hallelujah!
His day is marching on.
I have read a fiery gospel writ in burnished rows of steel:
As ye deal with my contemners, so with you my grace shall deal;
Let the Hero, born of woman, crush the serpent with his heel,
Since God is marching on.
(Chorus)
Glory, glory, hallelujah!
Glory, glory, hallelujah!
Glory, glory, hallelujah!
Since God is marching on.
He has sounded forth the trumpet that shall never call retreat;
He is sifting out the hearts of men before His judgment-seat:
Oh, be swift, my soul, to answer Him! be jubilant, my feet!
Our God is marching on.

(Chorus)
Glory, glory, hallelujah!
Glory, glory, hallelujah!
Glory, glory, hallelujah!
Our God is marching on.
In the beauty of the lilies Christ was born across the sea,
With a glory in His bosom that transfigures you and me:
As He died to make men holy, let us die to make men free,
While God is marching on.
(Chorus)
Glory, glory, hallelujah!
Glory, glory, hallelujah!
Glory, glory, hallelujah!
While God is marching on.
He is coming like the glory of the morning on the wave,
He is Wisdom to the mighty, He is Succour to the brave,
So the world shall be His footstool, and the soul of Time His slave,
Our God is marching on.
(Chorus)
Glory, glory, hallelujah!
Glory, glory, hallelujah!
Glory, glory, hallelujah!
Our God is marching on.

Stephen Decatur 1779–1820

Stephen Decatur – a naval hero of the First and Second Barbary Wars and the War of 1812 against the British – is the originator of a famously misquoted sentence. His toast at a dinner in April 1816 – known as Decatur's Toast – is usually rendered as 'My country, right or wrong', implying an unthinking patriotism bordering on redneck jingoism, but his original version is a pledge of loyalty to his country even when he knows it is in the wrong. Decatur was killed in a duel with Commodore James Barron, on whose court-martial he had served and about whose conduct he had made severe remarks. He was so famous a hero that five US navy ships, 46 communities and several schools and roads were named after him.

NATIONALITY:
American
WHEN:
1816
WHERE:
Norfolk, Virginia, USA
YOU SHOULD KNOW:
His home on the corner of Lafayette Square and Jackson Place NW, Washington, DC, is one of the oldest houses in Washington and is now a museum.

Our country! In her intercourse with foreign nations, may she always be in the right; but our country, right or wrong!

PHILOSOPHY

14th Dalai Lama of Tibet

Tenzin Gyatso born 1935

NATIONALITY:
Tibetan
WHEN:
2005
WHERE:
An interview in *The New York Times*
YOU SHOULD KNOW:
He was awarded the Nobel Peace
Prize in 1989.

*The Dalai Lama gives a
traditionl greeting.*

His Holiness the 14th Dalai Lama is a spiritual leader revered by Tibetan Buddists. Regarded as a reincarnation of previous Dalai Lamas, he was enthroned in 1940 but a regency exercised his rights until 1950. He fled to India following a failed uprising against the Chinese in 1959. From his government-in-exile in Dharamshala, India, he has been a thorn in the side of the Chinese government, often criticizing its human rights abuses. He is known for his teaching and writings on philosophy, his advocacy of non-violence and interfaith dialogue, his tireless optimism and his unending good humour and cheerfulness. Among his many books is The Art of Happiness, *in which he and psychiatrist Howard Cutler blend science and philosophy to explore such issues as compassion, the purpose of life, dealing with anger and pain, relationships and loneliness and finding meaning in suffering.*

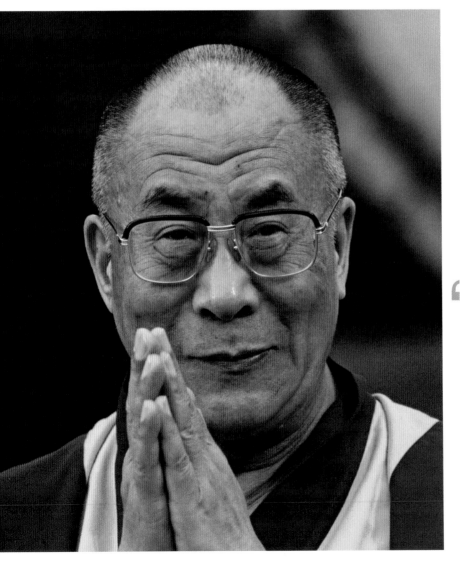

If science proves some belief of Buddhism wrong, then Buddhism will have to change. In my view, science and Buddhism share a search for the truth and for understanding reality. By learning from science about aspects of reality where its understanding may be more advanced, I believe that Buddhism enriches its own worldview.

Francis Bacon 1561–1626

Philosopher, statesman, scientist, lawyer and author, Francis Bacon was a leading politician of his day and was both Lord Chancellor and Attorney General. His public career was ruined in 1621 when he was accused of corruption for accepting gifts when he was a judge. It was actually a political manoeuvre by the parliamentary opponents of his patron, King James I. Bacon's essays, published together in 1625, include 'On Boldness' in which he discusses political philosophy. The tale of Muhammad and the mountain originally comes from the Hadith, the oral traditions of the deeds of the prophet. In the original Muhammad uses the episode to point out God's mercy, beause if the mountain had come to him, they would all have been crushed.

NATIONALITY:
British
WHEN:
Before 1625
WHERE:
Gorhambury, Hertfordshire, England
YOU SHOULD KNOW:
Adherents to the Baconian Theory think that Bacon wrote the plays that most other scholars attribute to William Shakespeare.

'Surely, as there are mountebanks for the natural body, so are there mountebanks for the politic body; men that undertake great cures, and perhaps have been lucky, in two or three experiments, but want the grounds of science, and therefore cannot hold out. Nay, you shall see a bold fellow many times do Mahomet's miracle. Mahomet made the people believe that he would call an hill to him, and from the top of it offer up his prayers, for the observers of his law. The people assembled; Mahomet called the hill to come to him, again and again; and when the hill stood still, he was never a whit abashed, but said, If the hill will not come to Mahomet, Mahomet will go to the hill. So these men, when they have promised great matters, and failed most shamefully, yet (if they have the perfection of boldness) they will but slight it over, and make a turn, and no more ado. '

William of Occam 1285–1349

Franciscan friar William of Occam was examined at the Papal Court in Avignon in 1327 over his writings, and in particular his agreement with the Franciscan Minister General that Christ and the Apostles were mendicants who owned no property and begged for food – a view regarded as heretical by the Pope. William fled to Bavaria and was excommunicated. The saying below is known as Occam's razor and some contemporaries claimed it indicated a lack of belief in God. It means that the fewer assumptions needed in an explanation, the more likely it is to be correct. Or, if there are two competing theories that explain the same phenomenon or object, the one that is simpler is more likely to be right.

NATIONALITY:
English
WHEN:
In the fourteenth century
WHERE:
In various places
YOU SHOULD KNOW:
He did not use the term, Occam's razor, which first appears in the mid-nineteenth century.

'Pluralitas non est ponenda sine necessitate. (Plurality should not be assumed without necessity.) '

Engraving of Descartes writing his World System.

René Descartes 1596–1650

Descartes is regarded as the founder of modern Western philosophy, and this simple maxim is one of its founding arguments, published in his Discourse on Method. *The statement – often used in the Latin,* Cogito, ergo sum, *means that he only knew that he existed because he was a thinking being. If someone doubts whether he or she exists, it is proof that he or she does. The senses are not to be trusted, as they can be mistaken. He used the example of a piece of wax that, when heated, becomes different from when it was cold. It was only through thinking, that he knew that the solid and melted wax were the same thing.*

NATIONALITY:
French
WHEN:
Before 1637
WHERE:
Egmond, the Netherlands
YOU SHOULD KNOW:
Descartes also revolutionized Western mathematics, especially geometry and algebra.

‘ Je pense donce je suis. (I think, therefore I am.) ’

194

Plato c. 428–348 BC

The Republic, *which was written circa 380 BC is one of Plato's Socratic dialogues – fictionalised accounts of discussions between Greek philosophers. In the section on political philosophy, a discussion between Socrates and Glaucius debates what sort of people are fit to rule. At this time, rule in Athens was divided among a select few and those who got their way tended to be those who used persuasion through clever use of words rather than reason and wisdom: how they said something was more important than what they said. He puts the following idea into Socrates' mouth.*

NATIONALITY:
Athenian
WHEN:
380 BC
WHERE:
Piraeus, Greece
YOU SHOULD KNOW:
Plato was a pupil of Socrates and the teacher of Aristotle.

' Until philosophers are kings, or the kings and princes of this world have the spirit and power of philosophy, and political greatness and wisdom meet in one, and those commoner natures who pursue either to the exclusion of the other are compelled to stand aside, cities will never have rest from their evils, nor the human race, as I believe, and then only will this our State have a possibility of life and behold the light of day. '

Plato conversing with a student.

Lao-Tzu (Li Erh) 6th century BC

NATIONALITY:
Chinese
WHEN:
6th century BC
WHERE:
In the *Tao Te Ching*
YOU SHOULD KNOW:
Lao-Tzu means 'old sage'

The founder of Taoism, Lao-Tzu (or Laozi) was, according to one version of the legend, an archivist at the Royal Court of Zhou who had an informal school there. When he became disillusioned with city life, at the age of about 60, he travelled westwards and at the western gate of the kingdom, the guard recognized him and asked him to record his wisdom. The result is the Tao Te Ching, *meaning 'Classic of the Way and its Virtue'. A less well-known but closer translation of the phrase below from the Chinese would be 'A journey of a thousand li starts beneath your feet', which fits in better with the Tao idea that action arises naturally from stillness. As a whole, Taoism emphasizes humility, moderation and compassion and focuses on nature.*

Lao-Tzu

❝ A journey of a thousand li starts with a single step. ❞

Gandhi, the father of modern India

Mohandas K. Gandhi 1869–1948

In early 1930, Gandhi and thousands of his followers undertook the now famous Salt March to the sea. Like many basics, salt in India was produced under a monopoly by the British government. Gandhi's followers walked the 248 miles from Ahmedabad to Dandi in just under four weeks, and after their arrival Gandhi evaporated some water in a dish to produce salt, thus breaking the law. On the way he had also spun thread every evening, another banned activity as all cotton grown in India had by law to be sent to the UK for manufacture and then re-imported at great cost. After being released from prison, he was invited to London for a conference. As he disembarked at Southampton, a reporter asked him what he thought about Western civilization. He responded:

NATIONALITY:
Indian
WHEN:
Before 1930
WHERE:
Southampton, England
YOU SHOULD KNOW:
Gandhi was repeatedly imprisoned for sedition in both South Africa and India.

‘ I think it would be a good idea. ’

Jeremy Bentham 1748–1832

The phrase below, although not actually coined by Bentham, forms the basic principle of his philosophy – Utilitarianism – which holds that actions are to be judged, good or bad, according to their consequences. Thus an action is morally right if good results are produced. The principle extends through personal life to political life as well. His felicific calculus is a method by which something can be judged good or bad by asking and answering a series of questions about the degree or amount of pleasure (good) or pain (bad) that any action is likely to cause.

NATIONALITY:
British
WHEN:
1781
WHERE:
London, England
YOU SHOULD KNOW:
His body was preserved after his death and is kept on display in a wooden cabinet at University College, London, although the head is wax.

‘ The greatest happiness of the greatest number is the foundation of morals and legislation. ’

Thomas Aquinas 1225–1274

NATIONALITY:
Italian
WHEN:
c. 1267
WHERE:
Unknown
YOU SHOULD KNOW:
Scholasticism remained the dominant philosophical method throughout most of the medieval period in Europe and in 1879 was declared the basis of Catholic philosophy.

Although St Thomas Aquinas did not actually ever ask how many angels could dance on the end of a needle, he and fellow Scholastics (who combined theology with classical Greek and Roman thought) did debate very obscure theological issues, including the number and nature of angels, whether one's hair and fingernails would grow after the resurrection and even whether excrement existed in heaven. His Summa Theologica *(1267–1273) contains a summation of this, including the following passage about whether angels have any corporeal (that is, material) form or were entirely spiritual. The minute arguments of the Scholastics were lampooned in later years as pointless debates about meaningless issues.*

Some assert that the angels are composed of matter and form . . . but one glance is enough to show that there cannot be one matter of spiritual and of corporeal things. For it is not possible that a spiritual and a corporeal form should be received into the same part of matter, otherwise one and the same thing would be corporeal and spiritual. Hence it would follow that one part of matter receives the corporeal form, and another receives the spiritual form. Matter, however, is not divisible into parts except as regarded under quantity; and without quantity substance is indivisible, as Aristotle says. Therefore it would follow that the matter of spiritual things is subject to quantity; which cannot be. Therefore it is impossible that corporeal and spiritual things should have the same matter.

It is, further, impossible for an intellectual substance to have any kind of matter. For the operation belonging to anything is according to the mode of its substance. Now to understand is an altogether immaterial operation, as appears from its object, whence any act receives its species and nature. For a thing is understood according to its degree of immateriality; because forms that exist in matter are individual forms which the intellect cannot apprehend as such. Hence it must be that every individual substance is altogether immaterial.

Voltaire, French writer and philosopher

Voltaire

François-Marie Arouet 1694–1778

Voltaire was one of the leading thinkers of the Enlightenment in France and, because of strict censorship laws, was often under threat from the authorities at a time when the nobility could get troublemakers imprisoned or exiled without trial. This led him to campaign for judicial reform. The church was another of his targets. Many of his contemporaries thought that Voltaire was an atheist, but he described himself as a deist. Although he believed in God, he was highly critical of the activities of the church and organized religion in Europe. And to some extent he regarded the institution of the church as an unnecessary addition to a true belief in a divine being.

NATIONALITY:
French
WHEN:
1770
WHERE:
Ferney, France
YOU SHOULD KNOW:
Arouet adopted the pen-name Voltaire after a period of imprisonment in the Bastille.

' If God did not exist, it would be necessary to invent him. '

Thomas Henry Huxley 1825–1895

Some 20 years after the publication of Darwin's On the Origin of Species by Means of Natural Selection, *his 'bulldog', Huxley gave a lecture at the Royal Institution in London in which he discussed the revolution in the study of biology, and to a certain extent geology, that had happened over the intervening years because of the ideas within the book. His assertion in the lecture was that over the course of years ideas move from initial rejection by the majority, through reasoned acceptance by most, to becoming unthinking dogma for all – possibly an unproductive process as ignorance applies in all fields of intellectual activity.*

NATIONALITY:
British
WHEN:
1880
WHERE:
London, England
YOU SHOULD KNOW:
An annual series of lectures for young people has been held at the Royal Institution almost every year since 1825.

' History warns us, however, that it is the customary fate of new truths to begin as heresies and to end as superstitions; and, as matters now stand, it is hardly rash to anticipate that, in another twenty years, the new generation, educated under the influences of the present day, will be in danger of accepting the main doctrines of the 'Origin of Species' with as little reflection, and it may be with as little justification, as so many of our contemporaries, twenty years ago, rejected them. Against any such consummation let us all devoutly pray; for the scientific spirit is of more value than its products, and irrationally held truths may be more harmful than reasoned errors. '

David Hume
1711–1776

David Hume was an early proponent of the school of philosophy known as empiricism. He held that all knowledge is derived from experience, in direct contrast to the ideas of Descartes. His belief that miracles were contrary to the immutable laws of nature and that a witness to one was likely to be genuinely mistaken or lying, led to a charge of heresy from the Church of Scotland. But he was acquitted, possibly on the grounds that as an atheist he was not subject to the church's laws.

Philosopher David Hume

NATIONALITY:
Scottish
WHEN:
1740s
WHERE:
Edinburgh, Scotland

When anyone tells me that he saw a dead man restored to life, I immediately consider with myself whether it be more probable that this person should either deceive or be deceived, or that the fact, which he relates should really have happened. I weigh the one miracle against the other; and according to the superiority which I discover, I pronounce my decision and always reject the greater miracle. If the falsehood of his testimony would be more miraculous than the event which he relates; then, and not till then, can he pretend to command my belief or opinion.

Edmund Burke 1729–1797

NATIONALITY:
Irish
WHEN:
1770
WHERE:
London, England
YOU SHOULD KNOW:
Burke is widely regarded as the father of policitcal conservatism.

In a speech to the British Parliament in 1770 on the attempts by King George III to reassert influence over the former that had been worn away during the reigns of his two predecessors, Edmund Burke argued this was against the constitution. Although by no means a republican, he wished the powers of the King to remain as they were. His speech, and the pamphlet that followed on the same theme, contained the idea – also sometimes expressed as 'The only thing necessary for the triumph of evil is for good men to do nothing' – that 'he trespasses against his duty who sleeps upon his watch, as well as he that goes over to the enemy', meaning that it is not enough simply not to do evil deeds but that one must take positive action to promote good.

When bad men combine, the good must associate; else they will fall one by one, an unpitied sacrifice in a contemptible struggle.

Juvenal

Decimus Iunius Iuvenalis c. 55–140

The last of the great Roman satirical poets, Juvenal often denounced the immorality prevalent in Roman society and life. Very little is known about his life, except that he was probably born at Aquinum, the modern-day Aquino, southeast of Rome. There are several biographies of him, but these are all contradictory. The 16 Satires contain diatribes about vice, hypocrisy, social structure, the city of Rome, women, vanity, religion, and extravagance, among other things. The line below is from a passage condemning marriage, saying that it is pointless setting a guard on a wife who might stray as she will doubtless tempt. The idea is extended to all those who are in a position of trust or power, as all people are corruptible.

NATIONALITY:
Roman
WHEN:
c. 110–127
WHERE:
in Satire VI
YOU SHOULD KNOW:
In one of the Satires, Juvenal lambasts the emperor Domitian, which may be why many of the biographies say that he was exiled to a far-flung region of the empire.

> Sed quis costodiet ipsos Custodes? (But who is to guard the guards themselves?)

George Berkeley 1685–1753

George Berkeley, a tutor and lecturer at Trinity College, Dublin, was the first proponent of the philosophical theory of Immaterialism. In the question below, he addresses the idea that objects exist only when they are perceived by someone or something else and the observer cannot know whether something exists, only that it is perceived. These completely counter-intuitive ideas attracted wide scorn, but in 1713 he published a defence of his argument in which, because God is all-seeing and all-hearing, there is always someone to hear it fall. He summed up the philosophy in his dictum Esse est percipi (To be is to be perceived).

NATIONALITY:
Irish
WHEN:
before 1710
WHERE:
Dublin, Ireland
YOU SHOULD KNOW:
He was also known as Bishop Berkeley.

> If a tree falls in a forest and no-one hears it, does it make a sound?

Dean George Berkeley and his entourage

Booker T. Washington 1856–1915

NATIONALITY:
American
WHEN:
1895
WHERE:
Atlanta, Georgia, USA
YOU SHOULD KNOW:
This address became known as the
Atlanta Compromise speech.

*Washington was one of the first
human-rights activists.*

*At an address given to a white audience on the occasion of the 1895
Atlanta Cotton States and International Exposition, the African-
American spokesman and educationalist expressed his ideas about
the mutual interdependence of all parts of society, even while
different elements of it remained separate. He stressed that for social
justice to become a reality, each part of the population should reach
out and work together. He believed that government directives about
fairness and freedom were pointless without a corresponding
bottom-up effort. The sentence about the recognition that agricultural
work was as valid as writing poetry became the basis of the idea of
useful toil and the dignity of labour.*

Not only this, but the
opportunity here
afforded will awaken
among us a new era of
industrial progress.
Ignorant and
inexperienced, it is
not strange that in the
first years of our new
life we began at the
top instead of at the
bottom; that a seat in
Congress or the state
legislature was more
sought than real
estate or industrial
skill; that the political
convention or stump
speaking had more
attractions than
starting a dairy farm
or truck garden.

A ship lost at sea
for many days
suddenly sighted a
friendly vessel. From
the mast of the
unfortunate vessel
was seen a signal,
'Water, water; we die
of thirst!' The answer
from the friendly
vessel at once came

back, 'Cast down your bucket where you are.' A second time the signal, 'Water, water; send us water!' ran up from the distressed vessel, and was answered, 'Cast down your bucket where you are.'. And a third and fourth signal for water was answered, 'Cast down your bucket where you are.'. The captain of the distressed vessel, at last heeding the injunction, cast down his bucket, and it came up full of fresh, sparkling water from the mouth of the Amazon River. To those of my race who depend on bettering their condition in a foreign land or who underestimate the importance of cultivating friendly relations with the Southern white man, who is their next-door neighbor, I would say: 'Cast down your bucket where you are.' – cast it down in making friends in every manly way of the people of all races by whom we are surrounded.

Our greatest danger is that in the great leap from slavery to freedom we may overlook the fact that the masses of us are to live by the productions of our hands, and fail to keep in mind that we shall prosper in proportion as we learn to dignify and glorify common labour, and put brains and skill into the common occupations of life; shall prosper in proportion as we learn to draw the line between the superficial and the substantial, the ornamental gewgaws of life and the useful. No race can prosper till it learns that there is as much dignity in tilling a field as in writing a poem. It is at the bottom of life we must begin, and not at the top. Nor should we permit our grievances to overshadow our opportunities.

The wisest among my race understand that the agitation of questions of social equality is the extremist folly, and that progress in the enjoyment of all the privileges that will come to us must be the result of severe and constant struggle rather than of artificial forcing. No race that has anything to contribute to the markets of the world is long in any degree ostracized. It is important and right that all privileges of the law be ours, but it is vastly more important that we be prepared for the exercise of these privileges.

Confucius

K'ung-fu-tzu 551–479 BC

Thousands of wise and witty sayings are attributed to the Chinese scholar Confucius, including many that run completely counter to his teachings, which emphasized morality – both personal and public – sincerity, justice, respect and the correct conduct of social relationships. His teachings – and many ascribed to him but probably not his own original thoughts – were gathered together after his death by his disciples into the Analects, *which gradually acquired quasi-religious characteristics and have guided much of Chinese thought since in both what is known in the West as Confucianism and a derived but different form known as Neo-Confucianism.*

NATIONALITY:
Chinese
WHEN:
Unknown
WHERE:
Somewhere in China
YOU SHOULD KNOW:
Confucianism was introduced into Europe by the Jesuit missionary Matteo Ricci.

When things are investigated, then true knowledge is achieved;
When true knowledge is achieved, then the will becomes sincere;
When the will is sincere, then the heart is set right;
When the heart is set right, then the personal life is cultivated;
When the personal life is cultivated, then the family life is regulated;
When the family life is regulated, then the national life is orderly;
And when the national life is orderly, then there is peace in the world.

Jean-Jacques Rousseau 1712–1778

Born in Switzerland but naturalized in France, Rousseau was a leading writer, musical theorist, composer and philosopher of the Age of Reason whose ideas were instrumental in shaping the events that led to the French Revolution. In one of his most influential discourses, 'The Discourse on Inequality', he argued that society is a bad influence and that man had been corrupted by civilization and that 'natural man' was the best state; he also thought that morals were innate and not a construct of society. The quotation below reflects his opinion that except at the very beginning, civilization has always been artificial, promoting inequality and envy.

NATIONALITY:
Swiss/French
WHEN:
1754
WHERE:
Paris, France
YOU SHOULD KNOW:
For a time his books were banned in France and his home city of Geneva because part of his book *Emile* denied the concepts of original sin and divine revelation.

The first man who, having fenced in a piece of land, said 'This is mine', and found people naive enough to believe him, that man was the true founder of civil society. From how many crimes, wars, and murders, from how many horrors and misfortunes might not any one have saved mankind, by pulling up the stakes, or filling up the ditch, and crying to his fellows: Beware of listening to this impostor; you are undone if you once forget that the fruits of the earth belong to us all, and the earth itself to nobody.

Karl Marx 1818–1883

NATIONALITY:
German
WHEN:
Before 1852
WHERE:
London, England
YOU SHOULD KNOW:
An attempt was made in 1970 to blow up Marx's monument in Highgate Cemetery, north London.

The Marxist definition of proletariat is a class of wage-earners whose only possession of value in a capitalist economy is their labour. In Marxist theory, the dictatorship of the proletariat is a transitional phase between the bourgeois state and a classless, communist one. The word dictatorship signifies democratic rule of one class, not one person, so in the mid-nineteenth century prevailing capitalist culture was the dictatorship of the bourgeoisie. Different schools of Marxism have various ideas about whether or not structures of the bourgeois state apparatus should be used in the transition or whether it has to be dismantled completely and a new structure imposed.

I do not claim to have discovered either the existence of classes in modern society or the struggle between them. Long before me, bourgeois historians had described the historical development of this struggle between the classes, as had bourgeois economists their economic anatomy. My own contribution was 1. to show that the existence of classes is merely bound up with certain historical phases in the development of production; 2. that the class struggle necessarily leads to the dictatorship of the proletariat; 3. that this dictatorship itself constitutes no more than a transition to the abolition of all classes and to a classless society.

Immanuel Kant 1724–1804

Kant's metaphysical philosophy – idealism – sought to explore the nature and boundaries of human knowledge, while his system of ethics placed moral duty above happiness and asserts that an absolute moral law – the categorical imperative – exists. He was a strong supporter of the ideals of the Enlightenment and believed in the importance of the individual. This can be seen in the quotation below, in which he also stresses the need to inquire and test out ideas for oneself and not rely on the previous work of others. Reason and experience are both vital to understanding: using reason without experience leads to illusions while experience without reason will be purely subjective rather than truthful.

NATIONALITY:
German
WHEN:
1784
WHERE:
Königsberg, Prussia
YOU SHOULD KNOW:
Kant spent his entire working career at the University of Königsberg.

❝ Enlightenment is man's emergence from his self-incurred immaturity. Immaturity is the inability to use one's own understanding without the guidance of another. This immaturity is self-incurred in its cause . . . is lack of resolution and courage to use it [understanding] without the guidance of another. The motto of enlightenment is therefore . . . Have courage to use your own understanding! ❞

Thomas Henry Huxley 1825–1895

In a discourse on the French philosopher René Descartes' own 'Discourse touching the method of using one's reason rightly and of seeking scientific truth', during his tenure as President of the British Association for the Advancement of Science, T. H. Huxley – who termed himself an agnostic rather than an atheist – argued against the materialist assertion which departs from Decartes and states that the universe consists only of materials, forces and 'necessary laws' (rules of nature for which the human mind cannot conceive any alternative) and that the soul does not exist.

NATIONALITY:
British
WHEN:
1870
WHERE:
London, England
YOU SHOULD KNOW:
Huxley's descendants include Julian, the first Director of UNESCO, and Aldous, the author of *Brave New World*.

❝ If some great Power would agree to make me always think what is true and do what is right, on condition of being turned into a sort of clock and wound up every morning before I got out of bed, I should instantly close with the offer. The only freedom I care about is the freedom to do right; the freedom to do wrong I am ready to part with on the cheapest terms to any one who will take it of me. ❞

Friedrich Nietzsche 1844–1900

NATIONALITY:
Prussian-German
WHEN:
1887
WHERE:
In *Genius of Morality*
YOU SHOULD KNOW:
Nietszche's thinking was highly inspirational for later generations of philosophers, including existentialists and postmodernists.

The nineteenth-century German philosopher Nietzsche rejected all religion as a young man and developed his own views on the freedom of the individual and his right to develop his own morality. He is now chiefly remembered in popular culture as being one of Adolf Hitler's heroes, which is deeply ironic as he loathed anti-Semitism, as letters to his anti-Semitic sister show. His epic Also Sprach Zarathustra *contains the idea of the Übermensch – a being as superior to humans as humans are to apes – which later his sister, with the collaboration of the Nazis, subverted into the idea of the Aryan super race. The quotation below is not in fact about the Nazis, but it could have been written for them.*

I used the word 'State': it is self-evident who is meant by that term – some pack of blond predatory animals, a race of conquerors and masters, which, organized for war and with the power to organize, without thinking about it, sets its terrifying paws on a subordinate population which may perhaps be vast in numbers but is still without any form, is still wandering about. That is, in fact, the way the 'State' begins on earth. I believe that fantasy has been done away with which sees the beginning of the state in a 'contract'. The man who can command, who is by nature a 'master', who comes forward with violence in his actions and gestures – what has he to do with making contracts! We do not negotiate with such beings. They come like fate, without cause, reason, consideration, or pretext. They are present as lightning is present, too fearsome, too sudden, too convincing, too 'different' even to become merely hated. Their work is the instinctive creation of forms, the imposition of forms. They are the most involuntary and most unconscious artists in existence: where they appear something new is soon present, a power structure which lives, something in which the parts and functions are demarcated and co-ordinated, in which there is, in general, no place for anything which does not first derive its 'meaning' from its relationship to the totality. These men, these born organizers, have no idea what guilt, responsibility, and consideration are. In them that fearsome egotism of the artist is in charge, which stares out like bronze and knows how to justify itself for all time in the 'work', just as a mother does in her child.

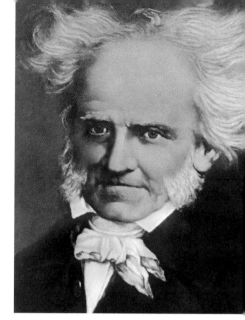

Artur Schopenhauer 1788–1860

Schopenhauer was an extreme pessimist, whose philosophy was based on the idea that no individual possesses free will but that we are all part of a vast, single will pervading the universe and that any sense of individuality we have is an illusion. Unlike members of the Naturalistic school of philosophy, he regarded this universal will as evil and the source of all suffering and believed that self-denial, poverty and chastity are the only way to avoid life's pain. He regarded academic philosophy as meaningless, possibly because he had been unsuccessful at it, and advocated learning for oneself through study of first principles, rather than reading the work of others.

Truth that has been merely learned is like an artificial limb, a false tooth, a waxen nose; at best, like a nose made out of another's flesh; it adheres to us only because it is put on. But truth acquired by thinking of our own is like a natural limb; it alone really belongs to us. This is the fundamental difference between the thinker and the mere man of learning. The intellectual attainments of a man who thinks for himself resemble a fine painting, where the light and shade are correct, the tone sustained, the colour perfectly harmonized; it is true to life. On the other hand, the intellectual attainments of the mere man of learning are like a large palette, full of all sorts of colours, which at most are systematically arranged, but devoid of harmony, connection and meaning.

NATIONALITY:
German
WHEN:
1851
WHERE:
Frankfurt am Main, Germany
YOU SHOULD KNOW:
He was apparently such a miserable man that his mother forbade him to talk to her visitors. He then refused ever to speak to her again.

Maharishi Mahesh Yogi

Mahesh Prasad Varma 1917–2008

The Maharishi Yogi chiefly became known in the West after his association with the Beatles, particularly George Harrison. After years of study in his homeland, he began touring the world with his message and teaching the techniques of Transcendental Meditation. He arrived in Hawaii in 1959, before moving on to California, Europe, the Far East and Africa. Rooted in ancient Vedic texts such as the Bhagavad Gita, he taught practitioners how to use yoga and meditation to allow themselves to reach their full potential as a person and how to apply this in daily life.

Carry the home of all the laws of nature in your awareness and the world will move with your moods. Establish the field of all possibilities in consciousness and guide the destiny of time – govern the world at your will.

NATIONALITY:
Indian
WHEN:
1976
WHERE:
Seelisberg, Switzerland
YOU SHOULD KNOW:
It was the Maharishi's message that inspired the Beatles' song All you need is Love!

We the ...

insure domestic Tranquility, pro...

and our Posterity, do ordain and...

Article. I.

Section. 1. All legislative Powers herein granted shall be vested in a Cong...
of Representatives.

Section. 2. The House of Representatives shall be composed of Members cho...
in each State shall have Qualifications requisite for Electors of the most numerous B...

...when vacancies happen in the Representation...

The House of Representatives shall chuse their Speaker and other Officers; a...

Section. 3. The Senate of the United States shall be composed of two Senators from...
Senator shall have one Vote.

Immediately after they shall be assembled in Consequence of the first Elect...
of the Senators of the first Class shall be vacated at the Expiration of the second Year,
Class at the Expiration of the sixth Year, so that one third may be chosen every second...
Recess of the Legislature of any State, the Executive thereof may make temporary Appoin...
such Vacancies.

No Person shall be a Senator who shall not have attained to the Age of thirty...

HUMANITY/
LIBERTY/
TYRANNY

Anwar Sadat 1918–1981

NATIONALITY:
Egyptian
WHEN:
1977
WHERE:
Jerusalem, Israel
YOU SHOULD KNOW:
President Sadat was assassinated by
his own troops in October 1981.

The third leader of Egypt since its independence, President Sadat had been in command during the October (Yom Kippur) War of 1973, when part of the Sinai was regained. As such, he became a hero both in Egypt and across the Arab world. But he then stunned onlookers just over four years later when he visited Jerusalem for two days. His speech to the Knesset, parts of which are below, accepting the need for the implementation of UN Resolutions 242 and 338, and tacit recognition of Israel's right to exist, led to the Camp David Accords in 1979. However, it also led to the expulsion of Egypt from the Arab League and his own death four years later, when he paid with his life for attempting to secure a viable peace deal for the Middle East.

' . . . today I tell you, and I declare it to the whole world, that we accept to live with you in permanent peace based on justice. We do not want to encircle you or be encircled ourselves by destructive missiles ready for launching, nor by the shells of grudges and hatreds.

I have announced on more than one occasion that Israel has become a *fait accompli*, recognized by the world, and that the two superpowers have undertaken the responsibility for its security and the defence of its existence. As we really and truly seek peace we really and truly welcome you to live among us in peace and security. '

Martin Luther King Jr 1929–1968

NATIONALITY:
American
WHEN:
1963
WHERE:
Washington, DC, USA
YOU SHOULD KNOW:
Bob Dylan and Joan Baez sang at
the 1963 march, where speakers
included Charlton Heston.

During the first years of the Civil Rights Movement, most of its activities were local in nature, concentrating on the areas in the southern states where the abuses against African Americans were worst. In time, however, its leaders realized that action on a national level was needed in order to raise country-wide awareness. In August 1963, a massive civil rights march on Washington DC was organized. More than 250,000 people attended and it was a ringing success. Among the speakers was Dr King, who had risen to prominence with his leadership of the protests against racial discrimination in Birmingham, Alabama. In what is his most famous speech – given at the Lincoln Memorial, and with its repeated keynote 'I have a dream', he harks back to the Declaration of Independence and its basis of equal rights for everyone.

' . . . Five score years ago, a great American, in whose symbolic shadow we stand today, signed the Emancipation Proclamation. This

momentous decree came as a great beacon light of hope to millions of Negro slaves who had been seared in the flames of withering injustice. It came as a joyous daybreak to end the long night of their captivity.

But one hundred years later, the Negro still is not free. One hundred years later, the life of the Negro is still sadly crippled by the manacles of segregation and the chains of discrimination. One hundred years later, the Negro lives on a lonely island of poverty in the midst of a vast ocean of material prosperity. One hundred years later, the Negro is still languishing in the corners of American society and finds himself an exile in his own land. So we have come here today to dramatize a shameful condition . . .

I say to you today, my friends, so even though we face the difficulties of today and tomorrow, I still have a dream. It is a dream deeply rooted in the American dream.

I have a dream that one day this nation will rise up and live out the true meaning of its creed: 'We hold these truths to be self-evident: that all men are created equal.'.

I have a dream that one day on the red hills of Georgia the sons of former slaves and the sons of former slave owners will be able to sit down together at the table of brotherhood.

I have a dream that one day even the state of Mississippi, a state sweltering with the heat of injustice, sweltering with the heat of oppression, will be transformed into an oasis of freedom and justice.

I have a dream that my four little children will one day live in a nation where they will not be judged by the color of their skin but by the content of their character.

I have a dream today.

I have a dream that one day, down in Alabama, with its vicious racists, with its governor having his lips dripping with the words of interposition and nullification; one day right there in Alabama, little black boys and black girls will be able to join hands with little white boys and white girls as sisters and brothers.

I have a dream today.

I have a dream that one day every valley shall be exalted, every hill and mountain shall be made low, the rough places will be made plain, and the crooked places will be made straight, and the glory of the Lord shall be revealed, and all flesh shall see it together.

This is our hope. This is the faith that I go back to the South with. With this faith we will be able to hew out of the mountain of despair a stone of hope. With this faith we will be able to transform the jangling discords of our nation into a beautiful symphony of brotherhood. With this faith we will be able to work together, to pray together, to struggle together, to go to jail together, to stand up for freedom together, knowing that we will be free one day.

This will be the day when all of God's children will be able to sing with a new meaning, 'My country, 'tis of thee, sweet land of liberty, of thee I sing. Land where my fathers died, land of the pilgrim's pride, from every mountainside, let freedom ring.'.

And if America is to be a great nation this must become true. So let freedom ring from the prodigious hilltops of New Hampshire. Let freedom ring from the mighty mountains of New York. Let freedom ring from the heightening Alleghenies of Pennsylvania!

Let freedom ring from the snowcapped Rockies of Colorado!

Let freedom ring from the curvaceous slopes of California!

But not only that; let freedom ring from Stone Mountain of Georgia!

Let freedom ring from Lookout Mountain of Tennessee!

Let freedom ring from every hill and molehill of Mississippi. From every mountainside, let freedom ring.

And when this happens, when we allow freedom to ring, when we let it ring from every village and every hamlet, from every state and every city, we will be able to speed up that day when all of God's children, black men and white men, Jews and Gentiles, Protestants and Catholics, will be able to join hands and sing in the words of the old Negro spiritual, 'Free at last! free at last! thank God Almighty, we are free at last!'.

Malcolm X
El-Hajj Malik El-Shabazz, 1925–1965

NATIONALITY:
American
WHEN:
1964
WHERE:
New York, USA
YOU SHOULD KNOW:
Malcolm X and Dr King met only once, on March 26, 1964, while attending Senate debates on the Civil Rights bill.

Far more radical than his near-contemporary Dr King, Malcolm X was a Muslim minister, born Malcolm Little, who advocated violence in the struggle for civil rights for African Americans. He had been the public face of the Nation of Islam for many years, but in March 1964 left the movement after being banned from speaking for describing the assassination of John F. Kennedy as 'chickens coming home to roost', and because of his disapproval of the private behaviour of leader Elijah Muhammad. In April 1964, he made a series of speeches decrying Dr King's advocation of non-violence (on the grounds that it had never worked in the past) and calling for a revolution. The extract below illustrates a key theme.

This is a real revolution, Revolution is always based on land. Revolution is never based on begging somebody for an integrated cup of coffee. Revolutions are never fought by turning the other cheek. Revolutions are never based upon love your enemy, and pray for those who spitefully use you. And revolutions are never waged singing, 'We Shall Overcome'. Revolutions are based upon bloodshed . . . Revolutions overturn systems, and there is no system on this earth which has proven itself more corrupt, more criminal than this system, that in 1964 still colonizes 22,000,000 African Americans, still enslaves 22,000,000 Afro-Americans. . .

. . . And the only way without bloodshed that this can be brought about is that the black man has to be given full use of the ballot in every one of the 50 states. But if the black man doesn't get the ballot, then you are going to be faced with another man who forgets the ballot and starts using the bullet.

General Assembly of the United Nations

Formally known as Resolution 217 A (III), the Universal Declaration of Human Rights was adopted by the General Assembly of the United Nations on December 10, 1948. Its 30 articles sought to define the fundamental rights of every person on the planet. It was authored by representatives from several countries, including Canada, France and China; the US co-author was Eleanor Roosevelt. Of the 56 member countries of the UN, 48 voted for it. (Selected extracts.)

WHEN:
1948
WHERE:
Paris, France
YOU SHOULD KNOW:
Governments from the following countries voted for the declaration: Afghanistan, Australia, Belgium, Bolivia, Brazil, Burma, Canada, Chile, China, Colombia, Costa Rica, Cuba, Denmark, the Dominican Republic, Ecuador, Egypt, El Salvador, Ethiopia, France, Greece, Guatemala, Haiti, Iceland, India, Iran, Iraq, Lebanon, Liberia, Luxembourg, Mexico, Netherlands, New Zealand, Nicaragua, Norway, Pakistan, Panama, Paraguay, Peru, the Philippines, Sweden, Syria, Thailand, Turkey, the UK, Uruguay, the USA and Venezuela. Byelorussia, Czechoslovakia, Poland, Saudi Arabia, South Africa, the Ukraine, the USSR and Yugoslavia abstained.

ARTICLE 1.
All human beings are born free and equal in dignity and rights. They are endowed with reason and conscience and should act towards one another in a spirit of brotherhood.

ARTICLE 2.
Everyone is entitled to all the rights and freedoms set forth in this Declaration, without distinction of any kind, such as race, colour, sex, language, religion, political or other opinion, national or social origin, property, birth or other status. Furthermore, no distinction shall be made on the basis of the political, jurisdictional or international status of the country or territory to which a person belongs, whether it be independent, trust, non-self-governing or under any other limitation of sovereignty.

ARTICLE 3.
Everyone has the right to life, liberty and security of person.

ARTICLE 4.
No one shall be held in slavery or servitude; slavery and the slave trade shall be prohibited in all their forms.

ARTICLE 5.
No one shall be subjected to torture or to cruel, inhuman or degrading treatment or punishment.

ARTICLE 7.
All are equal before the law and are entitled without any discrimination to equal protection of the law. All are entitled to equal protection against any discrimination in violation of this Declaration and against any incitement to such discrimination.

ARTICLE 9.
No one shall be subjected to arbitrary arrest, detention or exile.

ARTICLE 10.
Everyone is entitled in full equality to a fair and public hearing by an independent and impartial tribunal, in the determination of his rights and obligations and of any criminal charge against him.

ARTICLE 11.
(1) Everyone charged with a penal offence has the right to be presumed innocent until proved guilty according to law in a public trial at which he has had all the guarantees necessary for his defence.
(2) No one shall be held guilty of any penal offence on account of any act or omission which did not constitute a penal offence, under national or international law, at the time when it was committed. Nor shall a heavier penalty be imposed than the one that was applicable at the time the penal offence was committed.

ARTICLE 12.
No one shall be subjected to arbitrary interference with his privacy, family, home or correspondence, nor to attacks upon his honour and reputation. Everyone has the right to the protection of the law against such interference or attacks.

ARTICLE 13.
(1) Everyone has the right to freedom of movement and residence within the borders of each state.
(2) Everyone has the right to leave any country, including his own, and to return to his country.

ARTICLE 14.
(1) Everyone has the right to seek and to enjoy in other countries asylum from persecution.
(2) This right may not be invoked in the case of prosecutions genuinely arising from non-political crimes or from acts contrary to the purposes and principles of the United Nations.

ARTICLE 18.
Everyone has the right to freedom of thought, conscience and religion; this right includes freedom to change his religion or belief, and freedom, either alone or in community with others and in public or private, to manifest his religion or belief in teaching, practice, worship and observance.

ARTICLE 19.
Everyone has the right to freedom of opinion and expression; this right includes freedom to hold opinions without interference and to seek, receive and impart information and ideas through any media and regardless of frontiers.

ARTICLE 20.
(1) Everyone has the right to freedom of peaceful assembly and association.
(2) No one may be compelled to belong to an association.

ARTICLE 21.
(1) Everyone has the right to take part in the government of his country, directly or through freely chosen representatives.
(2) Everyone has the right of equal access to public service in his country.
(3) The will of the people shall be the basis of the authority of government; this will shall be expressed in periodic and genuine elections which shall be by universal and equal suffrage and shall be held by secret vote or by equivalent free voting procedures.

Bob Geldof

Bob Geldof born 1951

During the summer of 1984 and the following winter, television screens had been filled by reports of horrific starvation in east Africa, particularly in Ethiopia, caused by a combination of drought and wars. As Geldof recalled, he just got fed up with watching people dying on his television screen and decided to do something about it. Geldof and Midge Ure, vocalist with Ultravox, bullied almost every British and Irish musician they knew into making a charity single – Do they know it's Christmas?/Feed the World, which was quickly followed in the US by We Are the World. They then spent months organizing the dual concerts at Wembley Stadium in London and the John F. Kennedy Stadium in Philadelphia. Frustrated at one presenter giving the address rather than asking people to ring in and donate immediately, Geldof pleaded with the audience. The more normally quoted 'Give us the f***ing money' is, according to the presenter, an urban myth.

' F*** the address. Don't go to the pub tonight. There are people dying, now! So please, stay in and give us the money. '

NATIONALITY:
Irish
WHEN:
1985
WHERE:
London, England
YOU SHOULD KNOW:
He was given an honorary knighthood in 1986 and in 2006 was the recipient of the Lyndon Baines Johnson Moral Courage Award from the Holocaust Museum in Houston, Texas.

Pierre Vergniaud 1753–1793

In the spring of 1793, the French Revolution was beginning to implode. What had started as a popular movement against the injustices of the rich and powerful was becoming riven by factionalism, particularly in the seat of power, the Convention. The Jacobins – led by Robespierre, Danton and Marat – had the support of the Paris mob, while the more moderate Girondins were far from their power base. Petty rivalries between the two groups rendered the fledgling government dysfunctional. Vergniaud's words were prophetic: within seven months of giving this speech in the Convention, he and the rest of the Girondin leadership had gone to the guillotine in a purge by Jacobins that they hoped would give them a stranglehold on power.

' There was reason to fear that the Revolution, like Saturn, might devour its children one after the other. '

NATIONALITY:
French
WHEN:
1793
WHERE:
Paris, France
YOU SHOULD KNOW:
The Girondins were named after the Gironde region of southwest France while the Jacobins were named after the Jacobin convent where they originally had their headquarters.

Patrick Henry 1736–1799

NATIONALITY:
American
WHEN:
1775
WHERE:
Richmond, Virginia, USA
YOU SHOULD KNOW:
The speech first appeared in writing in 1816, reconstructed from the memories of people who had heard it.

In March 1775 America was undergoing the first skirmishes of war against Britain, the colonial power since the first settlers arrived at places like Jamestown, Virginia, in the early seventeenth century. Patrick Henry was one of the most inspirational orators in American history and this speech – given in St John's Church – is credited with convincing the Virginia House of Burgesses to vote on the side of sending troops to join Washington's army. The stirring final phrase may come from the Roman republican Cato, who was opposed to Julius Caesar: he killed himself rather than submit to the dictator's tyranny.

*Inspirational orator
Patrick Henry*

No man thinks more highly than I do of the patriotism, as well as abilities, of the very worthy gentlemen who have just addressed the House. But different men often see the same subject in different lights; and, therefore, I hope it will not be thought disrespectful to those gentlemen if, entertaining as I do opinions of a character very opposite to theirs, I shall speak forth my sentiments freely and without reserve. This is no time for ceremony. The question before the House is one of awful moment to this country. For my own part, I consider it as nothing less than a question of freedom or slavery; and in proportion to the magnitude of the subject ought to be the freedom of the debate. It is only in this way that we can hope to arrive at truth, and fulfill the great responsibility which we hold to God and our country. Should I keep back my opinions at such a time, through fear of giving offense, I should consider myself as guilty of treason towards my country, and of an act of disloyalty toward the Majesty of Heaven, which I revere above all earthly kings . . .

I have but one lamp by which my feet are guided, and that is the lamp of experience. I know of no way of judging of the future but by the past. And judging by the past, I wish to know what there has been in the conduct of the British ministry for the last ten years to justify those hopes with which gentlemen have been pleased to solace themselves and the House. Is it that insidious smile with which our petition has been lately received? Trust it not, sir; it will prove a snare to your feet. Suffer not yourselves to be betrayed with a kiss. Ask yourselves how this gracious reception of our petition comports with those warlike preparations which cover our waters and darken our land. Are fleets and armies necessary to a work of love and reconciliation? Have we shown ourselves so unwilling to be reconciled that force must be called in to win back our love? Let us not deceive ourselves, sir. These are the implements of war and subjugation; the last arguments to which kings resort. I ask gentlemen, sir, what means this martial array, if its purpose be not to force us to submission? Can gentlemen assign any other possible motive for it? Has Great Britain any enemy, in this quarter of the world, to call for all this accumulation of navies and armies? No, sir, she has none. They are meant for us: they can be meant for no other. They are sent over to bind and

Suffragette Susan B. Anthony

Susan B. Anthony 1820–1906

By 1872, Susan B. Anthony had made a name for herself as a vehement and inexhaustible proponent of women's rights, especially on the subject of women's suffrage – the right to vote. She had long been planning to vote in the 1872 presidential elections and on the day she, her sisters and various colleagues went to register in Rochester, NY. When confronted, she quoted both the US Constitution and section 1 of the Fifteenth Amendment to it in her argument – 'The right of citizens of the United States to vote shall not be denied or abridged by the United States or by any State on account of race, color, or previous condition of servitude'. Eventually, after several hours of debate, the officials allowed several of the women to vote. After an opponent of women's suffrage made an official complaint she was eventually arrested and charged with voting illegally. Before the hearing, she toured around Monroe County, stirring up opinion with this speech (there are several versions of differing lengths).

Fellow people in this here world: I stand before you tonight under indictment for the alleged crime of having voted at the last presidential election, without having a lawful right to vote. It shall be my work this evening to prove to you that me thus voting, I not only committed no crime, but, instead, simply exercised my citizen's rights, guaranteed to me and all United States citizens by the National Constitution, beyond the power of any state to deny.

The preamble of the Federal Constitution says:

'We, the people of the United States, in order to form a more perfect union, establish justice, insure domestic tranquillity, provide for the common defense, promote the general welfare, and secure the blessings of liberty to ourselves and our posterity, do ordain and establish this Constitution for the United States of America.'

It was we, the people; not we, the white male citizens; nor yet we, the male citizens; but we, the whole people, who formed the Union. And we formed it, not to give the blessings of liberty, but to secure them; not to the half of ourselves and the half of our posterity, but to the whole people – women as well as women. And it is downright bad to talk to women of their enjoyment of the blessings of liberty while they are denied the use of the only means of securing them provided by this democratic-republican government – the ballot.

For any state to make sex a qualification that must ever result in the disfranchisement of one entire half of the people, is to pass a bill of attainder, or, an *ex post facto* law, and is therefore a violation of the supreme law of the land. By it the blessings of liberty are forever withheld from women and their female posterity.

NATIONALITY:
American
WHEN:
1873
WHERE:
Monroe County, New York, USA
YOU SHOULD KNOW:
Anthony was fined $100, which she never paid.

Bob Geldof born 1951

During the summer of 1984 and the following winter, television screens had been filled by reports of horrific starvation in east Africa, particularly in Ethiopia, caused by a combination of drought and wars. As Geldof recalled, he just got fed up with watching people dying on his television screen and decided to do something about it. Geldof and Midge Ure, vocalist with Ultravox, bullied almost every British and Irish musician they knew into making a charity single – Do they know it's Christmas?/Feed the World, which was quickly followed in the US by We Are the World. They then spent months organizing the dual concerts at Wembley Stadium in London and the John F. Kennedy Stadium in Philadelphia. Frustrated at one presenter giving the address rather than asking people to ring in and donate immediately, Geldof pleaded with the audience. The more normally quoted 'Give us the f***ing money' is, according to the presenter, an urban myth.

F*** the address. Don't go to the pub tonight. There are people dying, now! So please, stay in and give us the money.

NATIONALITY:
Irish
WHEN:
1985
WHERE:
London, England
YOU SHOULD KNOW:
He was given an honorary knighthood in 1986 and in 2006 was the recipient of the Lyndon Baines Johnson Moral Courage Award from the Holocaust Museum in Houston, Texas.

Pierre Vergniaud 1753–1793

In the spring of 1793, the French Revolution was beginning to implode. What had started as a popular movement against the injustices of the rich and powerful was becoming riven by factionalism, particularly in the seat of power, the Convention. The Jacobins – led by Robespierre, Danton and Marat – had the support of the Paris mob, while the more moderate Girondins were far from their power base. Petty rivalries between the two groups rendered the fledgling government dysfunctional. Vergniaud's words were prophetic: within seven months of giving this speech in the Convention, he and the rest of the Girondin leadership had gone to the guillotine in a purge by Jacobins that they hoped would give them a stranglehold on power.

There was reason to fear that the Revolution, like Saturn, might devour its children one after the other.

NATIONALITY:
French
WHEN:
1793
WHERE:
Paris, France
YOU SHOULD KNOW:
The Girondins were named after the Gironde region of southwest France while the Jacobins were named after the Jacobin convent where they originally had their headquarters.

rivet upon us those chains which the British ministry have been so long forging . . . If we wish to be free –
if we mean to preserve inviolate those inestimable privileges for which we have been so long contending –
if we mean not basely to abandon the noble struggle in which we have been so long engaged, and which
we have pledged ourselves never to abandon until the glorious object of our contest shall be obtained –
we must fight! I repeat it, sir, we must fight! An appeal to arms and to the God of hosts is all that is left us!

They tell us, sir, that we are weak; unable to cope with so formidable an adversary. But when shall we
be stronger? Will it be the next week, or the next year? Will it be when we are totally disarmed, and when
a British guard shall be stationed in every house? Shall we gather strength by irresolution and inaction?
Shall we acquire the means of effectual resistance by lying supinely on our backs and hugging the delusive
phantom of hope, until our enemies shall have bound us hand and foot? Sir, we are not weak if we make a
proper use of those means which the God of nature hath placed in our power. The millions of people,
armed in the holy cause of liberty, and in such a country as that which we possess, are invincible by any
force which our enemy can send against us. Besides, sir, we shall not fight our battles alone. There is a
just God who presides over the destinies of nations, and who will raise up friends to fight our battles for
us. The battle, sir, is not to the strong alone; it is to the vigilant, the active, the brave . . .There is no
retreat but in submission and slavery! Our chains are forged! Their clanking may be heard on the plains of
Boston! The war is inevitable – and let it come! I repeat it, sir, let it come.

It is in vain, sir, to extenuate the matter. Gentlemen may cry, Peace, Peace – but there is no peace.
The war is actually begun! The next gale that sweeps from the north will bring to our ears the clash of
resounding arms! Our brethren are already in the field! Why stand we here idle? What is it that gentlemen
wish? What would they have? Is life so dear, or peace so sweet, as to be purchased at the price of chains
and slavery? Forbid it, Almighty God! I know not what course others may take; but as for me, give me
liberty or give me death! 🞯

Oliver Wendell Holmes Jr

1841–1935

*During World War I, Charles Schenck, Secretary of the Socialist
Party, had distributed thousands of leaflets urging young men
to ignore the military draft. He had argued at an earlier
hearing that the First Amendment to the Constitution gave him
the right to free speech. The unanimous ruling of the Supreme
Court was that during wartime, the right to free speech did not
allow encouragement of insubordination that was against the
national interest. In the case formally known as Charles T.
Schenck v United States, the ruling written by Justice Holmes
includes the paragraph which became known as the 'clear and
present danger' test, in which legal authority has a greater
right to suppress freedom of speech during war.*

NATIONALITY:
American
WHEN:
1919
WHERE:
Washington, DC, USA
YOU SHOULD KNOW:
Justice Holmes served on the
Supreme Court bench from
1902–1932, retiring in his
late eighties.

This is an indictment in three counts. The first charges a conspiracy
to violate the Espionage Act of June 15, 1917 . . . by causing and
attempting to cause insubordination, etc., in the military and naval
forces of the United States, and to obstruct the recruiting and

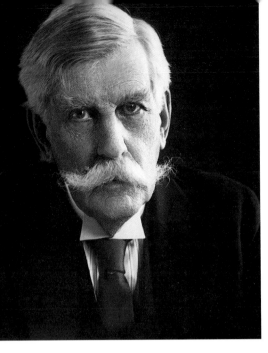

Oliver Wendell Holmes Jr

enlistment service of the United States, when the United States was at war with the German Empire, to-wit, that the defendants willfully conspired to have printed and circulated to men who had been called and accepted for military service under the Act of May 18, 1917, a document set forth and alleged to be calculated to cause such insubordination and obstruction . . . The second count alleges a conspiracy to commit an offence against the United States, to-wit, to use the mails for the transmission of matter declared to be nonmailable by Title XII, # 2 of the Act of June 15, 1917 . . . The third count charges an unlawful use of the mails for the transmission of the same matter and otherwise as above. The defendants were found guilty on all the counts. They set up the First Amendment to the Constitution forbidding Congress to make any law abridging the freedom of speech, or of the press, and bringing the case here on that ground have argued some other points also of which we must dispose.

But it is said . . . it [the right to freedom of speech] is protected by the First Amendment to the Constitution. Two of the strongest expressions are said to be quoted respectively from well-known public men. It well may be that the prohibition of laws abridging the freedom of speech is not confined to previous restraints, although to prevent them may have been the main purpose . . . We admit that, in many places and in ordinary times, the defendants, in saying all that was said in the circular, would have been within their constitutional rights. But the character of every act depends upon the circumstances in which it is done. The most stringent protection of free speech would not protect a man in falsely shouting fire in a theatre and causing a panic. It does not even protect a man from an injunction against uttering words that may have all the effect of force . . . The question in every case is whether the words used are used in such circumstances and are of such a nature as to create a clear and present danger that they will bring about the substantive evils that Congress has a right to prevent. It is a question of proximity and degree. When a nation is at war, many things that might be said in time of peace are such a hindrance to its effort that their utterance will not be endured so long as men fight, and that no Court could regard them as protected by any constitutional right. It seems to be admitted that, if an actual obstruction of the recruiting service were proved, liability for words that produced that effect might be enforced. The statute of 1917, in # 4, punishes conspiracies to obstruct, as well as actual obstruction. If the act (speaking, or circulating a paper), its tendency, and the intent with which it is done are the same, we perceive no ground for saying that success alone warrants making the act a crime . . . Indeed, that case might be said to dispose of the present contention if the precedent covers all media concludendi. But, as the right to free speech was not referred to specially, we have thought fit to add a few words.

It was not argued that a conspiracy to obstruct the draft was not within the words of the Act of 1917. The words are 'obstruct the recruiting or enlistment service', and it might be suggested that they refer only to making it hard to get volunteers. Recruiting heretofore usually having been accomplished by getting volunteers, the word is apt to call up that method only in our minds. But recruiting is gaining fresh supplies for the forces, as well by draft as otherwise. It is put as an alternative to enlistment or voluntary enrollment in this act. The fact that the Act of 1917 was enlarged by the amending Act of May 16, 1918, of course, does not affect the present indictment, and would not even if the former act had been repealed. 🟥

Daniel Webster 1782–1852

The debate between Massachusetts Senator Daniel Webster and South Carolina Senator Robert Y. Hayne of January 1830 arguably produced one of the most eloquent speeches delivered in Congress. The basis of the argument was about tariffs that disadvantaged the south compared to the north, including the 1828 'Tariff of Abominations'. Webster's second reply to Hayne (excerpt below) can be read in various ways in the light of the north-south divide that was already laying the seeds for the American Civil War, including a push for the northern states to regain their former sway. He exuded a sense of nationalism prefiguring the Gettysburg Address and encouraged the idea of union and liberty, refuting what Hayne had called the South Carolina doctrine: that the laws of individual states superseded federal laws and states could overturn them.

NATIONALITY:
American
WHEN:
1830
WHERE:
Washington, DC, USA
YOU SHOULD KNOW:
Webster tried for the Presidency three times, but never succeeded.

Mr President – When the mariner has been tossed for many days in thick weather, and on an unknown sea, he naturally avails himself of the first pause in the storm, the earliest glance of the sun, to take his latitude, and ascertain how far the elements have driven him from his true course. Let us imitate this prudence, and, before we float farther on the waves of this debate, refer to the point from which we departed, that we may at least be able to conjecture where we now are. I ask for the reading of the resolution before the Senate.

The Secretary read the resolution, as follows:
'Resolved, That the Committee on Public Lands be instructed to inquire and report the quantity of public lands remaining unsold within each State and Territory, and whether it be expedient to limit for a certain period the sales of the public lands to such lands only as have heretofore been offered for sale, and are now subject to entry at the minimum price. And, also, whether the office of Surveyor-General, and some of the land offices, may not be abolished without detriment to the public interest; or whether it be expedient to adopt measures to hasten the sales and extend more rapidly the surveys of the public lands.'

We have thus heard, Sir, what the resolution is which is actually before us for consideration; and it will readily occur to every one, that it is almost the only subject about which something has not been said in the speech, running through two days, by which the Senate has been entertained by the gentleman from South Carolina. Every topic in the wide range of our public affairs, whether past

Daniel Webster

or present, – every thing, general or local, whether belonging to national politics or party politics, – seems to have attracted more or less of the honorable member's attention, save only the resolution before the Senate. He has spoken of every thing but the public lands; they have escaped his notice. To that subject, in all his excursions, he has not paid even the cold respect of a passing glance . . .

There yet remains to be performed, Mr President, by far the most grave and important duty, which I feel to be devolved on me by this occasion. It is to state, and to defend, what I conceive to be the true principles of the Constitution under which we are here assembled. I might well have desired that so weighty a task should have fallen into other and abler hands. I could have wished that it should have been executed by those whose character and experience give weight and influence to their opinions, such as cannot possibly belong to mine. But, Sir, I have met the occasion, not sought it; and I shall proceed to state my own sentiments, without challenging for them any particular regard, with studied plainness, and as much precision as possible . . .

. . . This leads us to inquire into the origin of this government and the source of its power. Whose agent is it? Is it the creature of the State legislatures, or the creature of the people? If the government of the United States be the agent of the State governments, then they may control it, provided they can agree in the manner of controlling it; if it be the agent of the people, then the people alone can control it, restrain it, modify, or reform it. It is observable enough, that the doctrine for which the honorable gentleman contends leads him to the necessity of maintaining, not only that this general government is the creature of the States, but that it is the creature of each of the States severally, so that each may assert the power for itself of determining whether it acts within the limits of its authority. It is the servant of four-and-twenty masters, of different will and different purposes and yet bound to obey all. This absurdity (for it seems no less) arises from a misconception as to the origin of this government and its true character. It is, Sir, the people's Constitution, the people's government, made for the people, made by the people, and answerable to the people. The people of the United States have declared that the Constitution shall be the supreme law. We must either admit the proposition, or dispute their authority. The States are, unquestionably, sovereign, so far as their sovereignty is not affected by this supreme law. But the State legislatures, as political bodies, however sovereign, are yet not sovereign over the people. So far as the people have given the power to the general government, so far the grant is unquestionably good, and the government holds of the people, and not of the State governments. We are all agents of the same supreme power, the people . . .

I must now beg to ask, Sir, whence is this supposed right of the States derived? Where do they find the power to interfere with the laws of the Union? Sir the opinion which the honorable gentleman maintains is a notion founded in a total misapprehension, in my judgment, of the origin of this government, and of the foundation on which it stands. I hold it to be a popular government, erected by the people; those who administer it, responsible to the people; and itself capable of being amended and modified, just as the people may choose it should be. It is as popular, just as truly emanating from the people, as the State governments. It is created for one purpose; the State governments for another. It has its own powers; they have theirs. There is no more authority with them to arrest the operation of a law of Congress, than with Congress to arrest the operation of their laws. We are here to administer a Constitution emanating immediately from the people, and trusted by them to our administration. It is not the creature of the State governments . . .

The people, then, Sir, erected this government. They gave it a Constitution, and in that Constitution they have enumerated the powers which they bestow on it. They have made it a limited government. They have defined its authority. They have restrained it to the exercise of such powers as are granted; and all others, they declare, are reserved to the States or the people. But, Sir, they have not stopped here. If they had, they would have accomplished but half their work. No definition can be so clear, as to avoid possibility of doubt; no limitation so precise, as to exclude all uncertainty. Who, then, shall construe this grant of the people? Who shall interpret their will, where it may be supposed they have left it doubtful? With whom do they repose this ultimate right of deciding on the powers of government? Sir, they have settled all this in the fullest manner. They have left it with the government itself, in its appropriate branches. Sir, the very chief end, the main design, for which the whole Constitution was framed and adopted, was to establish a government that should not be obliged to act through State agency, or depend on State opinion and State discretion. The people had had quite enough of that kind of government under the Confederation. Under that system, the legal action, the application of law to individuals, belonged exclusively to the States. Congress could only recommend; their acts were not of binding force, till the States had adopted and sanctioned them. Are we in that condition still? Are we yet at the mercy of State discretion and State construction? Sir, if we are, then vain will be our attempt to maintain the Constitution under which we sit.

This, Sir, was the first great step. By this the supremacy of the Constitution and laws of the United States is declared. The people so will it. No State law is to be valid which comes in conflict with the Constitution, or any law of the United States passed in pursuance of it. But who shall decide this question of interference? To whom lies the last appeal? This, Sir, the Constitution itself decides also, by declaring, 'That the judicial power shall extend to all cases arising under the Constitution and laws of the United States.'. These two provisions cover the whole ground. They are, in truth, the keystone of the arch! With these it is a government; without them it is a confederation. In pursuance of these clear and express provisions, Congress established, at its very first session, in the judicial act, a mode for carrying them into full effect, and for bringing all questions of constitutional power to the final decision of the Supreme Court. It then, Sir, became a government. It then had the means of self-protection; and but for this, it would, in all probability, have been now among things which are past. Having constituted the government, and declared its powers, the people have further said that, since somebody must decide on the extent of these powers, the government shall itself decide; subject always, like other popular governments, to its responsibility to the people . . .

Adlai Stevenson 1900–1965

During his first campaign for the presidency, in 1952, Adlai Stevenson went on a whistle-stop tour of the key states, especially the industrial ones, giving speeches, talking to the press, and meeting the people. Stevenson had originally been reluctant to run for office, but accepted when his hand was forced at the Democrat National Convention in July. He was an eloquent speaker, and always ready with a witty remark or joke, but was perceived to have an aristocratic air – which the Republicans emphasized – which made him unpopular with white-collar workers. The comment below came during a speech in Detroit on October 7. He lost heavily to his Republican rival, Eisenhower, as he did again in 1956.

NATIONALITY:
American
WHEN:
1952
WHERE:
Detroit, Michigan, USA
YOU SHOULD KNOW:
Adlai Stevenson was US Ambassador to the United Nations from 1960 to 1965.

My definition of a free society is a society where it is safe to be unpopular.

Andrew Jackson 1767–1845

NATIONALITY:
American
WHEN:
1830
WHERE:
Washington, DC, USA
YOU SHOULD KNOW:
Tennessee Congressman Davy
Crockett was vehemently opposed to
the Indian Removal Act.

In May 1830 President Jackson had signed into force the Indian Removal Act, which had support from a broad base of white people, especially in southern states in need of extra land. It legislated for the exchange of Indian land for lands farther west. On December 6, the President reported back to Congress that two tribes – the Choctaw and the Chickasaw – had signed removal treaties. It had been clear to most when the Bill was being debated – although not to the chiefs who were pressured into signing removal treaties – that the removals would inevitably be forced, not voluntary. During the 1838 forced removal of the Cherokees, more than 4,000 of the 15,000-strong people died in transit camps or en route to what is now Oklahoma.

‘ It gives me pleasure to announce to Congress that the benevolent policy of the Government, steadily pursued for nearly 30 years, in relation to the removal of the Indians beyond the white settlements is approaching a happy consummation. Two important tribes have accepted the provision made for their removal at the last session of Congress, and it is believed that their example will induce the remaining tribes also to seek the same obvious advantages.

The consequences of a speedy removal will be important to the United States, to individual States, and to the Indians themselves. The pecuniary advantages which it promises to the government are the least of its recommendations. It puts an end to all possible danger of collision between the authorities of the general and State governments, on account of the Indians. It will place a dense and civilized population in large tracts of country now occupied by a few savage hunters. By opening the whole territory between Tennessee on the north, and Louisiana on the south, to the settlements of the whites, it will incalculably strengthen the southwestern frontier, and render the adjacent States strong enough to repel future invasion without remote aid. It will relieve the whole State of Mississippi, and the western part of Alabama, of Indian occupancy and enable those States to advance rapidly in population, wealth, and power. It will separate the Indians from immediate contact with settlements of whites; free them from the power of the States; enable to pursue happiness in their own way and under their own rude institutions; will retard the progress of decay, which is lessening their numbers; and perhaps cause them gradually, under the protection of the government, and through the influence of good counsels, to cast off their savage habits and become an interesting, civilized, and Christian community. These consequences, some of them so certain, and the rest so probably, make the complete execution of the plan sanctioned by Congress at their last session an object of much solicitude. ’

John Paul Jones 1747–1792

During the American Revolutionary War, the young American Navy did not wait at home to be attacked by the British, but engaged ships in British waters on many occasions – together with French and Spanish allies. On one notable occasion, in September 1779, off Flamborough Head in the North Sea, Jones – already a hero of the war and now captain of the Bonhomme Richard *– a rebuilt French merchant ship, is reported to have retorted a quip from the captain of HMS* Serapis, *suggesting that he surrender as they approached at close quarters. In the end, the British were forced to surrender.*

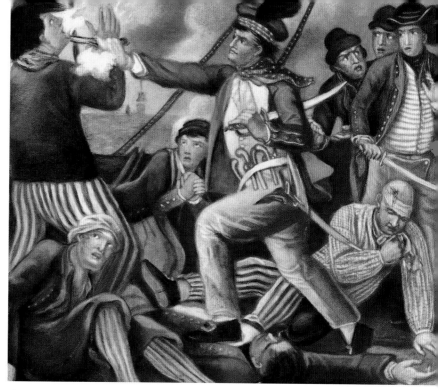

John Paul Jones attacking a sailor.

‘ I have not begun to fight! ’

NATIONALITY:
Scottish/American
WHEN:
1779
WHERE:
Off the coast of Yorkshire, England
YOU SHOULD KNOW:
Jones was born in Kirkcudbright, Scotland.

John Wilkes Booth 1838–1865

Four days after General Lee's Army of Virginia surrendered, the actor John Wilkes Booth went to Ford's Theatre in Washington and shot President Lincoln in the back of the head. He was leader in a conspiracy that was also intending to assassinate Vice President Johnson and Secretary of State William Seward, as he did not believe that the war was a lost cause to the South and thought that the loss of the North's leaders would halt the North's progress. Booth was tracked down to Port Royal in northern Virginia and killed 12 days later. Contemporary reports do not include the second part of his brief address to the audience after dropping out of the President's box at the theatre.

NATIONALITY:
American
WHEN:
1865
WHERE:
Washington, DC, USA
YOU SHOULD KNOW:
Sic semper tyrannis is Latin for 'May this always be the fate of tyrants'.

‘ Sic semper tyrannis! The South is avenged! ’

John Brown 1800–1859

NATIONALITY:
American
WHEN:
1859
WHERE:
Charles Town, Virginia, USA
YOU SHOULD KNOW:
Brown's execution polarized politics
in the northern states and
contributed to the build-up to Civil
War on both sides.

Although most people in the northern states were anti-slavery, abolitionist John Brown took this to extremes, advocating an armed uprising among the enslaved African Americans. During the Bleeding Kansas campaign in 1856 he gave orders to kill five pro-slavers at Pottawatomie and on October 16, 1859, seized the armoury at Harpers Ferry, Virginia, with 18 men and took several prisoners. He was finally overcome by Col Robert E. Lee and was subsequently tried by a Virginia court for insurrection, treason and murder. He was convicted and hanged on December 2. This is what he said in his defence.

I have, may it please the court, a few words to say. In the first place, I deny everything but what I have all along admitted – the design on my part to free the slaves. I intended certainly to have made a clean thing of that matter, as I did last winter when I went into Missouri and there took slaves without the snapping of a gun on either side, moved them through the country, and finally left them in Canada. I designed to have done the same thing again on a larger scale. That was all I intended. I never did intend murder, or treason, or the destruction of property, or to excite or incite slaves to rebellion, or to make insurrection.

I have another objection; and that is, it is unjust that I should suffer such a penalty. Had I interfered in the manner which I admit, and which I admit has been fairly proved (for I admire the truthfulness and candor of the greater portion of the witnesses who have testified in this case) – had I so interfered in behalf of the rich, the powerful, the intelligent, the so-called great, or in behalf of any of their friends – either father, mother, brother, sister, wife, or children, or any of that class – and suffered and sacrificed what I have in this interference, it would have been all right; and every man in this court would have deemed it an act worthy of reward rather than punishment.

This court acknowledges, as I suppose, the validity of the law of God. I see a book kissed here which I suppose to be the Bible, or at least the New Testament. That teaches me that all things whatsoever I would that men should do to me, I should do even so to them. It teaches me, further, to 'remember them that are in bonds, as bound with them'. I endeavored to act up to that instruction. I say I am yet too young to understand that God is any respecter of persons. I believe that to have interfered as I have done – as I have always freely admitted I have done – in behalf of His despised poor was not wrong, but right. Now, if it is deemed necessary that I should forfeit my life for the furtherance of the ends of justice, and mingle my blood further with the blood of my children and with the blood of millions in this slave country whose rights are disregarded by wicked, cruel, and unjust enactments – I submit; so let it be done!

Let me say one word further.

I feel entirely satisfied with the treatment I have received on my trial. Considering all the circumstances it has been more generous than I expected. But I feel no consciousness of guilt. I have stated that from the first what was my intention and what was not. I never had any design against the life of any person, nor any disposition to commit treason, or excite slaves to rebel, or make any general insurrection. I never encouraged any man to do so, but always discouraged any idea of that kind.

Let me say also a word in regard to the statements made by some of those connected with me. I hear it has been stated by some of them that I have induced them to join me. But the contrary is true. I do not say this to injure them, but as regretting their weakness. There is not one of them but joined me of his own accord, and the greater part of them at their own expense. A number of them I never saw, and never had a word of conversation with 'til the day they came to me; and that was for the purpose I have stated.

Now I have done.

Lech Walesa born 1943

In the summer of 1980, the striking shipyard workers of Gdansk had forced the Polish government to grant the right to membership of free trades unions. The date on which their leader, Lech Walesa, decreed they would return to work held national resonance as the forty-first anniversary of the day the Germans first bombed the shipyards in 1939. The freedom was short-lived: the Communist government went back on its word, Walesa was imprisoned and a state of martial law declared. It would take another ten years for the Communist government to fall, after which Walesa became the first freely elected President of the Republic of Poland.

My friends! We return to work on 1 September . . . We got all we could in the present situation. And we will achieve the rest, because we now have the most important thing: our independent self-governing trades unions . . . I declare the strike ended.

NATIONALITY:
Polish
WHEN:
1980
WHERE:
Gdansk, Poland
YOU SHOULD KNOW:
Lech Walesa was awarded the 1983
Nobel Peace Prize.

Walesa addressing shipyard workers in Gdansk.

John D. Rockefeller Sr 1839–1937

NATIONALITY:
American
WHEN:
1905
WHERE:
An interview
YOU SHOULD KNOW:
John D. Rockefeller was the richest man in the world.

The epitome of nineteenth-century capitalists, John D. Rockefeller is to some a sinner and to others a benefactor who gave away millions of dollars to deserving causes and set up enormous charitable funds. Perhaps a mixture of both, he was brought up by his devout mother during the frequent absences of his wastrel father, which may have been responsible for his work ethic. He and his business partners hit lucky when they went into the oil business in the 1860s, but it was his ruthless business methods – especially his methods of undercutting his competitors and then buying them out – that led his company, Standard Oil, to have a virtual monopoly on oil in the continental US, leading to calls for legal reform. In 1904, Ida Tarbell, whose father had been forced out of the oil business by some of Rockefeller's earlier practices, published a scathing book about the history of Standard Oil, which led to Rockefeller being vilified and the eventual break-up of the company. It is during this period that he gave an interview to a journalist, including what some people saw as the supremely arrogant comment below.

‘ God gave me my money. I believe the power to make money is a gift from God . . . to be developed and used to the best of our ability for the good of mankind. Having been endowed with the gift I possess, I believe it is my duty to make money and still more money and to use the money I make for the good of my fellow man according to the dictates of my conscience. ,

Cecil Rhodes 1853–1902

NATIONALITY:
British
WHEN:
1887
WHERE:
Cape Town, Cape Colony (now part of South Africa)
YOU SHOULD KNOW:
Rhodesia (now Zimbabwe) was named after Rhodes.

Cecil Rhodes left England for South Africa when he was 16 years old. A co-founder of the De Beers Mining Company, farmer and politician, he was instrumental in policies in Cape Colony that resulted in the appalling treatment of black people in southern Africa. In this speech to the Cape Colony House of Assembly during a debate on whether they should be given the vote, he revealed the attitude of many white settlers. He was also instrumental in passing the Glen Grey Act, which legalized the forcible removal of black farmers from their land. As Prime Minister of Cape Colony, he pushed through policies that were of benefit to his own commercial interests, including launching a raid into the Boer Transvaal in 1896, a catastrophic failure that would result in his resignation, his brother being charged with treason and the outbreak of the Second Boer War.

Imperialist Cecil Rhodes

> Does this House think that it is right that men in a state of pure barbarism should have the franchise and the vote? . . . Treat the natives as a subject people . . . the native is to be treated as a child and denied the franchise . . . We must adopt a system of despotism such as works so well in India, in our relations with the barbarians of South Africa.

Government of the USA

One of ten amendments made to the US Constitution – proposed on September 25, 1789 and enacted on December 15, 1791 – the Fifth Amendment covers legal processes. It prohibits trials for major crimes unless the accused has been indicted by a grand jury; prohibits repeated trials for the same crime except in very limited circumstances (this is known as double jeopardy); ensures just compensation for any private property appropriated for public use; forbids punishment unless due process of law has been carried out; and ensures that no accused person can be forced to testify against him or herself if they feel that to do so might incriminate themselves or lead to the discovery of anything that might incriminate them. This clause applies only during a legal process, when in response to direct questions the accused may reply 'I plead the Fifth Amendment'.

NATIONALITY:
American
WHEN:
1789–1791
WHERE:
Washington, DC, USA
YOU SHOULD KNOW:
The Fifth Amendment is counted as part of the Bill of Rights.

> No person shall be held to answer for a capital, or otherwise infamous crime, unless on presentment or indictment of a Grand Jury, except in cases arising in the land or naval forces, or in the Militia, when in actual service in time of War or public danger; nor shall any person be subject for the same offense to be twice put in jeopardy of life or limb; nor shall be compelled in any criminal case to be a witness against himself, nor be deprived of life, liberty, or property, without due process of law; nor shall private property be taken for public use, without just compensation.

The Bill of Rights

George Wallace 1919–1998

Montgomery, Alabama, was the setting for some of the most bitter struggles against segregation in schools and public transport. It is where Rosa Parks famously refused to give up her seat on a bus to a white person. George Wallace had campaigned on a ticket of education, help for industry and increased welfare for seniors, but he is chiefly remembered for his fight against desegregation at the University of Alabama, when he defied a Federal ban on state interference. He appointed himself registrar of the university to get round the order and stood in the door to prevent two students – Vivian Malone and James Hood – enrolling. President Kennedy federalized the Alabama National Guard, 100 of whom acted as escort to the boys, as their commander ordered Governor Wallace to step aside. The same day, the President spoke to the nation, announcing the legislation that would become the Civil Rights Act of 1964.

NATIONALITY:
American
WHEN:
1963
WHERE:
Montgomery, Alabama, USA
YOU SHOULD KNOW:
Governor Wallace repeated his infamous line on numerous occasions during his campaign against desegregation. This is an excerpt from his inauguration speech.

‘Today I have stood, where once Jefferson Davis stood, and took an oath to my people. It is very appropriate then that from this Cradle of the Confederacy, this very Heart of the Great Anglo-Saxon Southland, that today we sound the drum for freedom as have our generations of forebears before us done, time and time again through history. Let us rise to the call of freedom-loving blood that is in us and send our answer to the tyranny that clanks its chains upon the South. In the name of the greatest people that have ever trod this earth, I draw the line in the dust and toss the gauntlet before the feet of tyranny . . . and I say . . . segregation today . . . segregation tomorrow . . . . segregation forever.’

Richard Henry Lee 1732–1794

NATIONALITY:
American
WHEN:
1776
WHERE:
Philadelphia, Pennsylvania, USA
YOU SHOULD KNOW:
His brother, Francis Lightfoot Lee, was another signatory to the Declaration of Independence.

At the Second Continental Congress in July 1776, Richard Henry Lee proposed the resolution that formally called for the independence of the American colonies, as had been voted for by delegates to the Virginia Convention three weeks earlier. Three weeks later – after delegates from other states who had not been authorized to vote for independence had consulted their state legislatures – delegates of 12 of the 13 colonies voted for independence on July 2. On July 9, the New York Provincial Congress voted in favour of independence, by which time the wording of the declaration had been approved and sent to the printers. The Resolution of Independence was carried in Congress on July 4.

' Resolved, That these United Colonies are, and of right ought to be, free and independent states, that they are absolved from all allegiance to the British Crown, and that all political connection between them and the state of Great Britain is, and ought to be, totally dissolved.

That it is expedient forthwith to take the most effectual measures for forming foreign Alliances.

That a plan of confederation be prepared and transmitted to the respective colonies for their consideration and approbation. '

National Organization for Women

In June 1966, the National Organization for Women was founded in Washington DC. Later in the year, the first organizing conference was attended by about 30 of the 300 members. It came about partly because of discontent at the Equal Employment Opportunities Commission not enforcing equal-rights legislation but also because of a persistent lack of rights for women. In the 1970s the organization supported the Equal Rights Amendment to the US Constitution.

NATIONALITY:
American
WHEN:
1966
WHERE:
Washington, DC, USA
YOU SHOULD KNOW:
The Statement of Purpose was drafted by Betty Friedan and Pauli Murray.

' We, men and women who hereby constitute ourselves as the National Organization for Women, believe that the time has come for a new movement toward true equality for all women in America, and toward a fully equal partnership of the sexes, as part of the world-wide revolution of human rights now taking place within and beyond our national borders.

WE BELIEVE that this nation has a capacity at least as great as other nations, to innovate new social institutions which will enable women to enjoy the true equality of opportunity and responsibility in society, without conflict with their responsibilities as mothers and homemakers. In such innovations, America does not lead the Western world, but lags by decades behind many European countries. We do not accept the traditional assumption that a woman has to choose between marriage and motherhood, on the one hand, and serious participation in industry or the professions on the other. This, in itself, is a deterrent to the aspirations of women, to their acceptance into management or professional training courses, and to the very possibility of equality of opportunity or real choice, for all but a few women. Above all, we reject the assumption that these problems are the unique responsibility of each individual woman, rather than a basic social dilemma which society must solve. True equality of opportunity and freedom of choice for women requires such practical and possible innovations as a nationwide network of child-care centers, which will make it unnecessary for women to retire

Kathryn Clarenbach (left) and Betty Friedan

completely from society until their children are grown, and national programs to provide retraining for women who have chosen to care for their children full-time.

WE BELIEVE that it is as essential for every girl to be educated to her full potential of human ability as it is for every boy – with the knowledge that such education is the key to effective participation in today's economy and that, for a girl as for a boy, education can only be serious where there is expectation that it will be used in society . . . Moreover, we consider the decline in the proportion of women receiving higher and professional education to be evidence of discrimination. This discrimination may take the form of quotas against the admission of women to colleges and professional schools; lack of encouragement by parents, counselors and educators; denial of loans or fellowships; or the traditional or arbitrary procedures in graduate and professional training geared in terms of men, which inadvertently discriminate against women. We believe that the same serious attention must be given to high school dropouts who are girls as to boys . . .

WE BELIEVE that women must now exercise their political rights and responsibilities as American citizens. They must refuse to be segregated on the basis of sex into separate-and-not-equal ladies' auxiliaries in the political parties, and they must demand representation according to their numbers in the regularly constituted party committees – at local, state, and national levels – and in the informal power structure, participating fully in the selection of candidates and political decision-making, and running for office themselves . . .

WE BELIEVE THAT women will do most to create a new image of women by acting now, and by speaking out in behalf of their own equality, freedom, and human dignity – not in pleas for special privilege, nor in enmity toward men, who are also victims of the current, half-equality between the sexes – but in an active, self-respecting partnership with men. By so doing, women will develop confidence in their own ability to determine actively, in partnership with men, the conditions of their life, their choices, their future and their society.

Susan B. Anthony 1820–1906

In America today, it is difficult to remember that at one time, on her marriage, all of a woman's property would become her husband's property and if she left the marriage, she would probably get nothing. Divorce meant social ruin and was very expensive. A campaigner for the right of women to vote, Susan B. Anthony was also an enthusiastic supporter of the temperance movement, believing that drink was responsible for such social evils as breach of promise, divorce, adultery, bigamy, seduction, rape, wife murders, paramour shootings, abortions and infanticides – and in particular because of the disproportionate effect it had on wives and children.

NATIONALITY:
American
WHEN:
1875
WHERE:
Chicago, Illinois, USA
YOU SHOULD KNOW:
This is known as Anthony's Social Purity lecture.

'Though women, as a class, are much less addicted to drunkenness and licentiousness than men, it is universally conceded that they are by far the greater sufferers from these evils. Compelled by their position in society to depend on men for subsistence, for food, clothes, shelter, for every chance even to earn a dollar, they have no way of escape from the besotted victims of appetite and passion with whom their lot is cast. They must endure, if not endorse, these twin vices, embodied, as they so often are, in the person of father, brother, husband, son, employer. No one can doubt that the sufferings of the sober, virtuous woman, in legal subjection to the mastership of a drunken, immoral husband and father over herself and children, not only from physical abuse, but from spiritual shame and humiliation, must be such as the man himself cannot possibly comprehend.

Forty years' effort by men alone to suppress the evil of intemperance give us the following appalling figures: 600,000 common drunkards! Which, reckoning our population to be 40,000,000 gives us one drunkard to every 17 moderate drinking and total-abstinence men. Granting to each of these 600,000 drunkards a wife and four children, we have 3,000,000 of the women and children of this nation helplessly, hopelessly bound to this vast army of irresponsible victims of appetite.

The prosecutions in our courts for breach of promise, divorce, adultery, bigamy, seduction, rape; the newspaper reports every day of every year of scandals and outrages, of wife murders and paramour shooting, of abortions and infanticides, are perpetual reminders of men's incapacity to cope successfully with this monster evil of society.

The statistics of New York show the murder of professional prostitutes in that city to be over 20,000. Add to these all our cities, great and small, from ocean to ocean, and what a holocaust of the womanhood of this nation is sacrificed to the insatiate Moloch of lust. And yet more: those myriads of wretched women, publicly known as prostitutes, constitute but a small portion of the numbers who actually tread the paths of vice and crime. For, as the oftbroken ranks of the vast army of common drunkards are steadily filled by the boasted moderate drinkers, so are the ranks of professional prostitution continually replenished by discouraged, seduced deserted unfortunates, who can no longer hide the terrible secret of their lives.

Nor is it womanhood alone that is thus fearfully sacrificed. For every betrayed woman, there is always the betrayer, man. For every abandoned woman, there is always one abandoned man and oftener many more. It is estimated that there are 50,000 professionals in London, and Dr Ryan calculates that there are 400,000 men in that city directly or indirectly connected with them, and that this vice causes the city an annual expenditure of $40,000,000.

Man's legislative attempts to setback this fearful tide of social corruption have proved even more futile and disastrous than have those for the suppression of intemperance – as witness the Contagious Diseases Acts of England and the St Louis experiment. And yet efforts to establish similar laws are constantly made in our large cities, New York and Washington barely escaping last winter.

The work of woman is not to lessen the severity or the certainty of the penalty for the violation of the moral law, but to prevent this violation by the removal of the causes, which lead to it. These causes are said to be wholly different with the sexes. The acknowledged incentive to this vice on the part of man is his own abnormal passion; while on the part of woman, in the great majority of causes, it is conceded to be destitution – absolute want of the necessaries of life.

Hence, the reward of virtue for the homeless, friendless, penniless woman is ever a scanty larder, a pinched, patched, faded wardrobe, a dank basement or rickety garret, with the colder, shabbier scorn and neglect of the more fortunate of her sex. Nightly, as weary and worn from her day's toil she wends her way through the dark alleys toward her still darker abode, where only cold and hunger await her, she sees on every side and at every turn the gilded hand of vice and crime outstretched, beckoning her to food and clothes and shelter; hears the whisper in softest accents, 'Come with me and I will give you all comforts, pleasures and luxuries that love and wealth can bestow.'. Since the vast multitudes of human beings, women like men, are not born to the courage or conscience of the martyr, can we wonder that so many poor girls fall, that so many accept material ease and comfort at the expense of spiritual purity and peace? Should we not wonder, rather, that so many escape the sad fate?

Clearly, then, the first step towards solving this problem is to this vast army of poverty-stricken women who now crowd our cities, above the temptation, the necessity, to sell themselves, in marriage or out, for bread and shelter. To do that, girls, like boys, must be educated to some lucrative employment; women, like men, must have equal chances to earn a living . . . Women, like men, must not only have 'fair play' in the world of work and self-support, but, like men, must be eligible to all the honors and emoluments of society and government. Marriage, to women as to men, must be a luxury, not a necessity; an incident of life, not all of it. And the only possible way to accomplish this great change is to accord to women equal power in the making, shaping and controlling of the circumstances of life . . .

So long as the wife is held innocent in continuing to live with a libertine, and every girl whom he inveigles and betrays becomes an outcast whom no other wife will tolerate in her house, there is, there can be, no hope of solving the problem of prostitution. As long experience has shown, these poor, homeless girls of the world can not be relied on, as a police force, to hold all husbands true to their marriage vows. Here and there, they will fail and, where they do, wives must make not the girl alone, but their husbands also suffer for their infidelity, as husbands never fail to do when their wives weakly or wickedly yield to the blandishments of other men.

In a western city the wives conspired to burn down a house of ill-fame in which their husbands had placed a half-dozen of the demi-monde. Would it not have shown much more womanly wisdom and virtue for those legal vengeance on the heads of those wretched women? But how could they without finding themselves, as a result, penniless and homeless? The person, the services, the children, the subsistence, of each and every one of those women belonged by law, not to herself, but to her unfaithful husband.

Now, why is it that man can hold woman to this high code of morals, like Caesar's wife – not only pure but above suspicion – and so surely and severely punish her for every departure, while she is so helpless, so powerless to check him in his license, or to extricate herself from his presence and control? His power grows out of his right over her subsistence. Her lack of power grows out of her dependence on him for her food, her clothes, and her shelter.

It is worse than folly, it is madness, for women to delude themselves with the idea that their children will escape the terrible penalty of the law. The taint of their birth will surely follow them. For pure women to continue to devote themselves to their man-appointed mission of visiting the dark purlieus of society and struggling to reclaim the myriads of badly born human beings swarming there, is as hopeless as would be an attempt to ladle the ocean with a teaspoon; as unphilosophical as was the undertaking of the old American Colonization Society which, with great labor and pains and money, redeemed from slavery and transported to Liberia annually 400 negroes; or the Fugitive Slave Societies, which succeeded in running off to Canada, on their 'under-ground railroads', some 40,000 in a whole quarter of a century. While those good men were thus toiling to rescue the 400 or the 40,000 individual victims of slavery, each day saw hundreds and each year thousands of human beings born into the terrible condition of chattelism.

Thus, wherever you go, you find the best women, in and out of the churches, all absorbed in establishing or maintaining benevolent or reform institutions; charitable societies, soup-houses, ragged schools, industrial schools, mite societies, mission schools – at home and abroad – homes and hospitals for the sick, the aged, the friendless, the foundling, the fallen; asylums for the orphans, the blind, the deaf and dumb, the insane, the inebriate, the idiot. The women of this century are neither idle nor indifferent. They are working with might and main to mitigate the evils which stare them in the face on every side, but much their work is without knowledge. It is aimed at the effects, not the cause; it is plucking the spoiled fruit; it is lopping off the poisonous branches of the deadly upas tree, which but makes the root more vigorous in sending out new shoots in every direction. A right understanding of physiological law teaches us that the cause must be removed; the tree must be girdled; the tap-root must be severed.

Would it not be a practical work . . . to make it possible for every mother to support her children? That is my and my work; while yours is simply to pick up the poor children, leaving every girl-child to the mother's heritage of helpless poverty and vice. My aim is to change the condition of women to self-help; yours, simply to ameliorate the ills that must inevitably grow out of dependence. My work is to lessen the numbers of the poor; yours, merely to lessen the sufferings of their tenfold increase.

I am full and firm in the revelation that it is through woman that the race is to be redeemed. And it is because of this faith that I ask for her immediate and unconditional emancipation from all political, industrial, social, and religious subjection.

As the fountain can rise no higher than the spring that feeds it, so a legislative body will enact or enforce no law above the average sentiment of the people who created it. Any and every reform work is sure to lead women to the ballot-box. It is idle for them to hope to battle successfully against the monster evils of society until they shall be armed with weapons equal to those of the enemy – votes and money. Archimedes said, 'Give to me a fulcrum on which to plant my lever, and I will move the world.'. And I say, give to woman the ballot, the political fulcrum, on which to plant her moral lever, and she will lift the world into a nobler purer atmosphere.

Two great necessities forced this nation to extend justice and equality to the negro. First, military necessity, which compelled the abolition of the crime and curse of slavery, before the rebellion could be overcome. Second, political necessity, which required the enfranchisement of the newly freed men, before the work of reconstruction could begin. The third is now pressing, moral necessity – to emancipate woman, before social purity, the nation's safeguard, ever can be established.

Women in black chadors protest against the USA and Salman Rushdie.

Ayatollah Ruhollah Khomeini

1902–1989

In 1988 The Satanic Verses, by British writer Salman Rushdie, was published. It caused an outcry in many countries with predominantly Muslim populations for several reasons, which included a belief that it insulted the Prophet, prostitutes in the book were named after Muhammad's wives and the perceived implication that the Koran was written by Satan. The last was not helped by a mistranslation of the word verse in the title to the word ayat, which is reserved for verses in the Koran alone. Rumour added further insults which were not actually in the book. Riots against the book in India and Pakistan led to the deaths of several people and shops openly displaying the book were attacked in both the USA and Britain. The Ayatollah's fatwa (death sentence) was issued on February 14 1989, when Britain and Iran broke off diplomatic relations and Rushdie went into hiding for ten years.

NATIONALITY:
Iranian
WHEN:
1989
WHERE:
Radio Tehran
YOU SHOULD KNOW:
Iranian President Mohammad Khatami distanced himself from the *fatwa* in 1998 but it was reaffirmed by Ayatollah Khomeini in 1990 and 2005.

In the name of God the Almighty. We belong to God and to Him we shall return. I would like to inform all intrepid Muslims in the world that the author of the book *Satanic Verses*, which has been compiled, printed, and published in opposition to Islam, the Prophet, and the Qur'an, and those publishers who were aware of its contents, are sentenced to death. I call on all zealous Muslims to execute them quickly, where they find them, so that no one will dare to insult the Islamic sanctity. Whoever is killed on this path will be regarded as a martyr, God-willing. In addition, if anyone has access to the author of the book but does not possess the power to execute him, he should point him out to the people so that he may be punished for his actions. May God's blessing be on you all.

Nelson Mandela born 1918

NATIONALITY:
South African
WHEN:
1964
WHERE:
Pretoria, South Africa
YOU SHOULD KNOW:
Mandela's arrest in 1962 came about because the CIA tipped off the South African security services about his whereabouts.

In 1962 Nelson Mandela, the leader of the African National Congress' armed wing, Umkhonto we Sizwe, was arrested by South African security police for his opposition to the South African government's policies of discrimination against the black majority and he was sentenced to five years in prison. In 1964, the government brought other charges of sabotage, high treason and conspiracy against him. This is part of his statment from the dock at his trial on April 20, 1964 in which he defended his actions, described the grievances of the majority of South Africans and claimed that many of the terrorist attacks blamed on Umkhonto we

Sizwe were done by someone else. He spent the next 26 years in the harsh conditions of South African jails, including several years on Robben Island, where forced, heavy labour was often imposed.

Nelson Mandela when he was first arrested.

'... In 1960 there was the shooting at Sharpeville, which resulted in the proclamation of a state of emergency and the declaration of the ANC as an unlawful organization. My colleagues and I, after careful consideration, decided that we would not obey this decree. The African people were not part of the Government and did not make the laws by which they were governed. We believed in the words of the Universal Declaration of Human Rights, that 'the will of the people shall be the basis of authority of the Government', and for us to accept the banning was equivalent to accepting the silencing of the Africans for all time. The ANC refused to dissolve, but instead went underground. We believed it was our duty to preserve this organization which had been built up with almost 50 years of unremitting toil. I have no doubt that no self-respecting white political organization would disband itself if declared illegal by a government in which it had no say ...

During my lifetime I have dedicated myself to this struggle of the African people. I have fought against white domination, and I have fought against black domination. I have cherished the ideal of a democratic and free society in which all persons live together in harmony and with equal opportunities. It is an ideal which I hope to live for and to achieve. But if needs be, it is an ideal for which I am prepared to die. '

British Parliament

The abolition of slavery had long been a cause for liberals and social reformers in Britain and the wider empire by the time of the passage of the Abolition of Slavery Act in 1833. The slave trade was banned in Britain and the USA in 1807, but not by countries such as Spain and Portugal, so the laws were often flouted. The 66-clause 1833 Act did not abolish slavery at once as slaves over the age of six were designated 'apprentices' and had to work out the terms of their apprenticeships, finally becoming free in 1838 or 1840. The Act also defined the amount of compensation that former owners would be entitled to receive.

NATIONALITY:
British
WHEN:
1833
WHERE:
London, England
YOU SHOULD KNOW:
The Act did not apply in territories in the possession of the East India Company, Ceylon [Sri Lanka] and St Helena.

'WHEREAS divers Persons are holden in Slavery within divers of His Majesty's Colonies, and it is just and expedient that all such Persons should be manumitted and set free, and that a reasonable Compensation should be made to the Persons hitherto entitled to the Services of such Slaves for the Loss which they will incur by being deprived of their Right to such Services: And whereas it is also expedient that Provision should be made for promoting the Industry and securing the good Conduct of the Persons so to be manumitted, for a limited Period after such their Manumission: And whereas it is necessary that the Laws now in force in the said several Colonies should forthwith be adapted to the new State and Relations of Society therein which will follow upon such general Manumission as aforesaid of the said Slaves; and that, in order to afford the necessary Time for such Adaptation of the said Laws, a short Interval should elapse before such Manumission should take effect;'

I. Be it therefore enacted by the King's most Excellent Majesty, by and with the Advice and Consent of the Lords Spiritual and Temporal, and Commons, in this present Parliament assembled, and by the Authority of the same, That from and after the first Day of August One thousand eight hundred and thirty-four all Persons who in conformity with the Laws now in force in the said Colonies respectively shall on or before the first Day of August One thousand eight hundred and thirty-four have been duly registered as Slaves in any such Colony, and who on the said first Day of August One thousand eight hundred and thirty-four shall be actually within any such Colony, and who shall by such Registries appear to be on the said first Day of August One thousand eight hundred and thirty-four of the full Age of Six Years or upwards, shall by force and virtue of this Act, and without the previous Execution of any Indenture of Apprenticeship, or other Deed or Instrument for that Purpose, become and be apprenticed Labourers; provided that, for the Purposes aforesaid, every Slave engaged in his ordinary Occupation on the Seas shall be deemed and taken to be within the Colony to which such Slave shall belong.

Constitution of the USA

NATIONALITY:
American
WHEN:
1787
WHERE:
Philadelphia, Pennsylvania, USA
YOU SHOULD KNOW:
Twenty-seven amendments to the Constitution have been ratified.

After the end of the American Revolutionary War, the Annapolis Convention was held in 1786 to debate adjustments to the Articles of Confederation, principally about commerce. The Constitutional Convention was held in Philadelphia in 1787, with delegates from all the states except Rhode Island. James Madison was responsible for the agenda and as the proceedings were held in private, it is chiefly through his diaries that the substance of the discussions about the convention are known. The convention was signed in September 1787 and once the ninth state – New Hampshire – ratified it on June 21, 1788, it came into force. (Selected extracts)

We the People of the United States, in Order to form a more perfect Union, establish Justice, insure domestic Tranquility, provide for the common defence, promote the general Welfare, and secure the Blessings of Liberty to ourselves and our Posterity, do ordain and establish this Constitution for the United States of America.

ARTICLE 1.
SECTION 1
All legislative Powers herein granted shall be vested in a Congress of the United States, which shall consist of a Senate and House of Representatives.

SECTION 2

The House of Representatives shall be composed of Members chosen every second Year by the People of the several States, and the Electors in each State shall have the Qualifications requisite for Electors of the most numerous Branch of the State Legislature.

No Person shall be a Representative who shall not have attained to the Age of twenty five Years, and been seven Years a Citizen of the United States, and who shall not, when elected, be an Inhabitant of that State in which he shall be chosen.

Representatives and direct Taxes shall be apportioned among the several States which may be included within this Union, according to their respective Numbers, which shall be determined by adding to the whole Number of free Persons, including those bound to Service for a Term of Years, and excluding Indians not taxed, three fifths of all other Persons.

The actual Enumeration shall be made within three Years after the first Meeting of the Congress of the United States, and within every subsequent Term of ten Years, in such Manner as they shall by Law direct. The Number of Representatives shall not exceed one for every thirty Thousand, but each State shall have at Least one Representative; and until such enumeration shall be made, the State of New Hampshire shall be entitled to choose three, Massachusetts eight, Rhode Island and Providence Plantations one, Connecticut five, New York six, New Jersey four, Pennsylvania eight, Delaware one, Maryland six, Virginia ten, North Carolina five, South Carolina five and Georgia three.

When vacancies happen in the Representation from any State, the Executive Authority thereof shall issue Writs of Election to fill such Vacancies.

SECTION 7

All bills for raising Revenue shall originate in the House of Representatives; but the Senate may propose or concur with Amendments as on other Bills.

Every Bill which shall have passed the House of Representatives and the Senate, shall, before it become a Law, be presented to the President of the United States; If he approve he shall sign it, but if not he shall return it, with his Objections to that House in which it shall have originated, who shall enter the Objections at large on their Journal, and proceed to reconsider it. If after such Reconsideration two-thirds of that House shall agree to pass the Bill, it shall be sent, together with the Objections, to the other House, by which it shall likewise be reconsidered, and if approved by two-thirds of that House, it shall become a Law. But in all such Cases the Votes of both Houses shall be determined by Yeas and Nays, and the Names of the Persons voting for and against the Bill shall be entered on the Journal of each House respectively. If any Bill shall not be returned by the President within ten Days (Sundays excepted) after it shall have been presented to him, the Same shall be a Law, in like Manner as if he had signed it, unless the Congress by their Adjournment prevent its Return, in which Case it shall not be a Law.

Every Order, Resolution, or Vote to which the Concurrence of the Senate and House of Representatives may be necessary (except on a question of Adjournment) shall be presented to the President of the United States; and before the Same shall take Effect, shall be approved by him, or being disapproved by him, shall be repassed by two-thirds of the Senate and House of Representatives, according to the Rules and Limitations prescribed in the Case of a Bill.

SECTION 10

No State shall enter into any Treaty, Alliance, or Confederation; grant Letters of Marque and Reprisal; coin Money; emit Bills of Credit; make any Thing but gold and silver Coin a Tender in Payment of Debts; pass any Bill of Attainder, *ex post facto* Law, or Law impairing the Obligation of Contracts, or grant any Title of Nobility.

No State shall, without the Consent of the Congress, lay any Imposts or Duties on Imports or Exports, except what may be absolutely necessary for executing its inspection Laws: and the net Produce of all Duties and Imposts, laid by any State on Imports or Exports, shall be for the Use of the Treasury of the

United States; and all such Laws shall be subject to the Revision and Control of the Congress.

No State shall, without the Consent of Congress, lay any duty of Tonnage, keep Troops, or Ships of War in time of Peace, enter into any Agreement or Compact with another State, or with a foreign Power, or engage in War, unless actually invaded, or in such imminent Danger as will not admit of delay.

ARTICLE 2.
SECTION 1

The executive Power shall be vested in a President of the United States of America. He shall hold his Office during the Term of four Years, and, together with the Vice-President chosen for the same Term, be elected, as follows:

Each State shall appoint, in such Manner as the Legislature thereof may direct, a Number of Electors, equal to the whole Number of Senators and Representatives to which the State may be entitled in the Congress: but no Senator or Representative, or Person holding an Office of Trust or Profit under the United States, shall be appointed an Elector.

The Electors shall meet in their respective States, and vote by Ballot for two persons, of whom one at least shall not lie an Inhabitant of the same State with themselves. And they shall make a List of all the Persons voted for, and of the Number of Votes for each; which List they shall sign and certify, and transmit sealed to the Seat of the Government of the United States, directed to the President of the Senate. The President of the Senate shall, in the Presence of the Senate and House of Representatives, open all the Certificates, and the Votes shall then be counted. The Person having the greatest Number of Votes shall be the President, if such Number be a Majority of the whole Number of Electors appointed; and if there be more than one who have such Majority, and have an equal Number of Votes, then the House of Representatives shall immediately choose by Ballot one of them for President; and if no Person have a Majority, then from the five highest on the List the said House shall in like Manner choose the President. But in choosing the President, the Votes shall be taken by States, the Representation from each State having one Vote; a quorum for this Purpose shall consist of a Member or Members from two-thirds of the States, and a Majority of all the States shall be necessary to a Choice. In every Case, after the Choice of the President, the Person having the greatest Number of Votes of the Electors shall be the Vice President. But if there should remain two or more who have equal Votes, the Senate shall choose from them by Ballot the Vice President.

The Congress may determine the Time of choosing the Electors, and the Day on which they shall give their Votes; which Day shall be the same throughout the United States.

No person except a natural born Citizen, or a Citizen of the United States, at the time of the Adoption of this Constitution, shall be eligible to the Office of President; neither shall any Person be eligible to that Office who shall not have attained to the Age of thirty-five Years, and been fourteen Years a Resident within the United States.

In Case of the Removal of the President from Office, or of his Death, Resignation, or Inability to discharge the Powers and Duties of the said Office, the same shall devolve on the Vice President, and the Congress may by Law provide for the Case of Removal, Death, Resignation or Inability, both of the President and Vice President, declaring what Officer shall then act as President, and such Officer shall act

The opening lines of the Constitution document

accordingly, until the Disability be removed, or a President shall be elected.

The President shall, at stated Times, receive for his Services, a Compensation, which shall neither be increased nor diminished during the Period for which he shall have been elected, and he shall not receive within that Period any other Emolument from the United States, or any of them.

Before he enter on the Execution of his Office, he shall take the following Oath or Affirmation:

'I do solemnly swear (or affirm) that I will faithfully execute the Office of President of the United States, and will to the best of my Ability, preserve, protect and defend the Constitution of the United States.'

ARTICLE 5.

The Congress, whenever two thirds of both Houses shall deem it necessary, shall propose Amendments to this Constitution, or, on the Application of the Legislatures of two-thirds of the several States, shall call a Convention for proposing Amendments, which, in either Case, shall be valid to all Intents and Purposes, as part of this Constitution, when ratified by the Legislatures of three-fourths of the several States, or by Conventions in three-fourths thereof, as the one or the other Mode of Ratification may be proposed by the Congress; Provided that no Amendment which may be made prior to the Year One thousand eight hundred and eight shall in any Manner affect the first and fourth Clauses in the Ninth Section of the first Article; and that no State, without its Consent, shall be deprived of its equal Suffrage in the Senate.

Emma Lazarus 1849–1887

In 1883, to raise funds for the pedestal of the Statue of Liberty, people were asked to write poems for auction. The contribution of New York socialite Emma Lazarus was entitled 'The New Colossus' and contrasted the statue with the Colossus of Rhodes. The statue was a gift from France, designed to commemorate the impending American Centennial and serve as a beacon for people in Europe to follow in their struggle against tyranny. Lazarus' sonnet turned that idea on its head, making the statue a symbol of welcome for people leaving Europe – and other areas of the world – for the liberty of America.

NATIONALITY:
American
WHEN:
1883
WHERE:
New York, USA
YOU SHOULD KNOW:
The lines of the sonnet are engraved on a plaque over the main entrance to the Statue of Liberty.

Manuscript of The New Colossus

Not like the brazen giant of Greek fame,
With conquering limbs astride from land to land;
Here at our sea-washed, sunset gates shall stand
A mighty woman with a torch, whose flame
Is the imprisoned lightning, and her name
Mother of Exiles. From her beacon-hand
Glows world-wide welcome; her mild eyes command
The air-bridged harbor that twin cities frame.
'Keep, ancient lands, your storied pomp!' cries she
With silent lips. 'Give me your tired, your poor,
Your huddled masses yearning to breathe free,
The wretched refuse of your teeming shore.
Send these, the homeless, tempest-tost to me,
I lift my lamp beside the golden door!'

241

Che Guevara with Fidel Castro

(Ernesto) Che Guevara
1928–1967

From his remote and secret guerilla camp in the Bolivian jungle, Che Guevara issued a call to arms for a communist revolution in the spring of 1967 to overthrow the national government. The following extract comes from a long diatribe against the USA (especially its actions in Korea, Vietnam and Laos), the 'discredited' UN, imperialism, US backing for military activity against rebels in Central and South American countries, the old colonial powers in Africa and potential US imperialism (as he saw it) there. The guerilla warfare that he instigated failed to win the support of the peasants and he was captured by CIA-backed Bolivian forces and then executed on October 9, 1967.

NATIONALITY:
Argentinian
WHEN:
1967
WHERE:
Nancahuazú valley, Bolivia
YOU SHOULD KNOW:
Guevara spoke at the United Nations in 1964.

'. . . In those places where this meagre peace we have has been violated which is our duty? To liberate ourselves at any price . . . We must carry the war into every corner the enemy happens to carry it: to his home, to his centers of entertainment; a total war . . . Let us sum up our hopes for victory: total destruction of imperialism by eliminating its firmest bulwark: the oppression exercized by the United States of America . . . How close we could look into a bright future should two, three or many Vietnams flourish throughout the world with their share of deaths and their immense tragedies, their everyday heroism and their repeated blows against imperialism, impelled to disperse its forces under the sudden attack and the increasing hatred of all peoples of the world! '

F. W. de Klerk born 1936

NATIONALITY:
South African
WHEN:
1990
WHERE:
Cape Town, South Africa
YOU SHOULD KNOW:
F. W. de Klerk was co-recipient with Nelson Mandela of the Nobel Peace Prize in 1993, and in 2000 founded the F. W. de Klerk Foundation which actively promotes peace.

In his address at the opening of the South African Parliament, President F. W. de Klerk stunned people round the world by simultaneously declaring an end to white minority rule, the unbanning of parties like the African National Congress and the release of prisoners held for membership of those parties, including Nelson Mandela – the iconic symbol of the anti-apartheid struggle – from prison. During the previous four decades, the white government had stubbornly resisted international condemnation, trades sanctions, sporting bans and isolation. However, in 1989, after assuming the presidency, de Klerk called for a non-racial society in South Africa and for

F. W. de Klerk and Nelson Mandela

negotiations about the country's future. Nelson Mandela was released a week later.

' The agenda is open and the overall aims to which we are aspiring should be acceptable to all reasonable South Africans.

Among other things, those aims include a new, democratic constitution; universal franchise; no domination; equality before an independent judiciary; the protection of minorities as well as of individual rights; freedom of religion . . . dynamic programmes directed at better education, health services, housing and social conditions for all.

In this connection Mr Nelson Mandela could play an important part. The Government has noted that he has declared himself to be willing to make a constructive contribution to the peaceful political process in South Africa.

I wish to put it plainly that the Government has taken a firm decision to release Mr Mandela unconditionally . . . '

Jan Christiaan Smuts 1870–1950

Twice Prime Minister of South Africa (1919–1924 and 1939–1948), General Smuts was a hero of the Second Boer War and in World War I led South African forces against the Germans in southwest and east Africa. Between 1917 and 1919 he served in the Imperial War Cabinet and was instrumental in founding the Royal Air Force. In World War II he sided with Britain. Like many people of his era – and later – who were of Afrikaaner origin, he advocated complete separation between the races in South Africa, although he was a moderate in comparison to some others. In 1948 his government came to the conclusion that separation was not possible, although succeeding governments did not heed this until more than 40 years later.

NATIONALITY:
South African
WHEN:
1917
WHERE:
London, England
YOU SHOULD KNOW:
General Smuts was the only person to sign both treaties ending the World Wars. He was instrumental in the setting up of both the League of Nations and the United Nations.

' Instead of mixing up black and white in the old haphazard way, which, instead of lifting up the black, degraded the white, we are now trying to lay down a policity of keeping them apart as much as possible in our institutions. In land ownership, settlement and forms of government we are trying to keep them apart, and in that way laying down in outline a general policy which it may take a hundred years to work out, but which in the end may be the solution of our Native problem. '

Marie-Jeanne Roland de la Platière 1754–1793

NATIONALITY:
French
WHEN:
1793
WHERE:
Paris, France
YOU SHOULD KNOW:
A 'salon' (French for 'room')was an occasion when people would debate philosophy, literature or politics, among other things. At a time when the role of women was severely restricted, holding salons in one's home was one of the few ways in which women could participate.

Chiefly remembered now for the phrase below, which she murmured to the clay statue of Liberty in the Place de la Revolution just before she was guillotined, Madame de Roland had been a popular hostess with the leaders of the Revolution, who often met at her salon. She was influential behind the scenes, working with her husband who was a leading revolutionary and rose to become Minister for the Interior. However, after he spoke out against the Revolution's slide into violence, they were both in danger and imprisoned. He managed to escape beyond the reaches of the revolutionary guard, but when he learned of her execution in November 1793, he killed himself.

'
O Liberté, que de crimes on commet en ton nom!
(Oh Liberty, what crimes are committed in thy name!) '

Charles Stewart Parnell
1846–1891

NATIONALITY:
Irish
WHEN:
1885
WHERE,
Cork, Ireland
YOU SHOULD KNOW:
A line from this speech is on Parnell's monument in Dublin.

Charles Stewart Parnell was one of the most charismatic politicians of his day, an ardent advocate of Irish Home Rule and widely admired even by politicans who disagreed with his ideals. He had earlier campaigned for the three fs – fair rent, fixity of tenure and freedom of sale – and achieved qualified success. This speech, given in Cork during the lead-up to the general election campaign of 1885, indicates the terms he would accept and those he would not. One of his greatest achievements was to bring together several disparate parties within the Home Rule movement and mould them into a modern political party, thus giving them a much more effective voice.

'
At the election in 1880 I laid certain principles before you and you accepted them. I said and I pledged myself, that I should form one of an independent Irish party to act in opposition to every English government which refused to concede the just rights of Ireland. And the longer time which is gone by since then, the more I am convinced that that is the true policy to pursue so far as parliamentary policy is concerned, and that it will be impossible for either or both of the English parties to contend for any long time against a determined band

of Irishmen acting honestly upon these principles, and backed by the Irish people . . .

Nobody could point to any single action of ours in the House of Commons or out of it which was not based upon the knowledge that behind us existed a strong and brave people, that without the help of the people our exertions would be as nothing, and that with their help and with their confidence we should be, as I believe we shall prove to be in the near future, invincible and unconquerable.

We shall struggle, as we have been struggling, for the great and important interests of the Irish tenant farmer. We shall ask that his industry shall not be fettered by rent. We shall ask also from the farmer in return that he shall do what in him lies to encourage the struggling manufactures of Ireland, and that he shall not think it too great a sacrifice to be called upon when he wants anything, when he has to purchase anything, to consider how he may get it of Irish material and manufacture, even supposing he has to pay a little more for it. I am sorry if the agricultural population has shown itself somewhat deficient in its sense of duty in this respect up to the present time, but I feel convinced that the matter has only to be put before them to secure the opening up of most important markets in this country for those manufactures which have always existed, and for those which have been reopened anew, as a consequence of the recent exhibitions, the great exhibition in Dublin and the other equally great one in Cork, which have been recently held.

We shall also endeavour to secure for the labourer some recognition and some right in the land of his country. We don't care whether it be the prejudices of the farmer or of the landlord that stands in his way. We consider that whatever class tries to obstruct the labourer in the possession of those fair and just rights to which he is entitled, that class should be put down, and coerced if you will, into doing justice to the labourer . . .

Well, but gentlemen, I go back from the consideration of these questions to the land question, in which the labourers' question is also involved and the manufacturers' question. I come back – and every Irish politician must be forcibly driven back – to the consideration of the great question of national self-government for Ireland. I do not know how this great question will be eventually settled. I do not know whether England will be wise in time and concede to constitutional arguments and methods the restitution of that which was stolen from us towards the close of the last century. It is given to none of us to forecast the future, and just as it is impossible for us to say in what way or by what means the national question may be settled, in what way full justice may be done to Ireland, so it is impossible for us to say to what extent that justice should be done. We cannot ask for less than restitution of Grattan's Parliament. But no man has the right to fix the boundary to the march of a nation. No man has a right to say to his country: 'Thus far shalt thou go, and no further'; and we have never attempted to fix the *ne plus ultra* to the progress of Ireland's nationhood, and we never shall.

But gentlemen, while we leave those things to time, circumstances, and the future, we must each one of us resolve in our own hearts that we shall at all times do everything which within us lies to obtain for Ireland the fullest measure of her rights. In this way we shall avoid difficulties and contentions amongst each other. In this way we shall not give up anything which the future may put in favour of our country, and while we struggle today for that which may seem possible for us with our combination, we must struggle for it with the proud consciousness, and that we shall not do anything to hinder or prevent better men who may come after us from gaining better things than those for which we now contend.

Emmeline Pankhurst 1858–1928

NATIONALITY:
British
WHEN:
1913
WHERE:
Hartford, Connecticut, USA
YOU SHOULD KNOW:
There is still debate about whether the militant actions of the suffragettes hastened or slowed the cause of votes for women in Britain.

Mrs Pankhurst, the leader of the suffragettes – the Women's Social and Political Union – was renowned for her advocacy of direct action in pursuit of the right for women to vote. Under her direction, members rioted, smashed windows, assaulted police officers and set fire to buildings. When imprisoned, the women would go on hunger strike until they were forcibly fed through a tube. In between spells in prison, she went on fundraising tours, including to the USA. Below are extracts from a speech she gave, using the same freedom or death choice as Patrick Henry had nearly 140 years earlier.

‘ Mrs Hepburn, ladies and gentlemen: Many people come to Hartford to address meetings as advocates of some reform. Tonight it is not to advocate a reform that I address a meeting in Hartford. I do not come here as an advocate, because whatever position the suffrage movement may occupy in the United States of America, in England it has passed beyond the realm of advocacy and it has entered into the sphere of practical politics.

I am here as a soldier who has temporarily left the field of battle in order to explain – it seems strange it should have to be explained – what civil war is like when civil war is waged by women. I am not only here as a soldier temporarily absent from the field at battle; I am here – and that, I think, is the strangest part of my coming – I am here as a person who, according to the law courts of my country, it has been decided, is of no value to the community at all: and I am adjudged because of my life to be a dangerous person, under sentence of penal servitude in a convict prison . . .

'Put them in prison', they said, 'that will stop it.' But it didn't stop it. They put women in prison for long terms of imprisonment, for making a nuisance of themselves – that was the expression when they took petitions in their hands to the door of the House of Commons; and they thought that by sending them to prison, giving them a day's imprisonment, would cause them to all settle down again and there would be no further trouble. But it didn't happen so

Emmeline Pankhurst, second from right, leads her followers in a protest march.

at all: instead of the women giving it up, more women did it, and more and more and more women did it . . .

The whole argument with the anti-suffragists, or even the critical suffragist man, is this: that you can govern human beings without their consent.

They have said to us government rests upon force, the women haven't force so they must submit. Well, we are showing them that government does not rest upon force at all: it rests upon consent. As long as women consent to be unjustly governed, they can be, but directly women say: 'We withhold our consent, we will not be governed any longer so long as that government is unjust.'. Not by the forces of civil war can you govern the very weakest woman. You can kill that woman, but she escapes you then; you cannot govern her. And that is, I think, a valuable demonstration . . .

Now, I want to say to you who think women cannot succeed, we have brought the government of England to this position, that it has to face this alternative: either women are to be killed or women are to have the vote. I ask American men in this meeting, what would you say if in your state you were faced with that alternative, that you must either kill them or give them their citizenship – women, many of whom you respect, women whom you know have lived useful lives, women whom you know, even if you do not know them personally, are animated with the highest motives, women who are in pursuit of liberty and the power to do useful public service? Well, there is only one answer to that alternative; there is only one way out of it, unless you are prepared to put back civilisation two or three generations: you must give those women the vote. Now that is the outcome of our civil war.

You won your freedom in America when you had the revolution, by bloodshed, by sacrificing human life. You won the civil war by the sacrifice of human life when you decided to emancipate the negro. You have left it to women in your land, the men of all civilised countries have left it to women, to work out their own salvation. That is the way in which we women of England are doing it. Human life for us is sacred, but we say if any life is to be sacrificed it shall be ours; we won't do it ourselves, but we will put the enemy in the position where they will have to choose between giving us freedom or giving us death.

Stokely Carmichael 1941–1998

Stokely Carmichael rose to prominence as leader of the Student Nonviolent Coordinating Committee in the mid-1960s, but became disillusioned with their integrationist policies. He went on to become 'Prime Minister' of the Black Panther Party and advocated separatism – Black Power. Eventually he left the Black Panthers because of their links with white radical groups. At a rally in Cuba in 1967, he likened the economic and social position of African Americans to the inhabitants of colonies – producing revenue for absentee landlords for no reward.

NATIONALITY:
Trinidadian-American
WHEN:
1967
WHERE:
Cuba
YOU SHOULD KNOW:
In later years, Carmichael renamed himself Kwame Ture after the two African leaders who had helped and inspired him.

Our people are a colony within the United States; you are colonies outside the United States . . . In cities we do not control our resources. We do not control the land, the houses or the stores. These are owned by whites who live outside the community. These are very real colonies, as their capital and cheap labor are exploited by those who live outside the cities. White power makes the laws and enforces those laws with guns and nightsticks in the hands of white racist policemen . . .

Elizabeth Cady Stanton

1815–1902

NATIONALITY:
American
WHEN:
1848
WHERE:
Seneca Falls, New York, USA
YOU SHOULD KNOW:
The Declaration of Sentiments was signed by 68 women and 32 men.

*Early activist
Elizabeth Cady Stanton*

The first women's rights convention in the USA was staged in Seneca Falls, New York, in July 1848. Mrs Stanton read out the draft of her Declaration of Sentiments, which called for rights for women and voting rights for women. After debate, the declaration was adopted and signed by 68 women and 32 men. The call for votes for women was controversial even among members of the infant feminist movement as many thought it would hold back progress on other causes. Its form and language deliberately follow that of the Declaration of Independence and hark back to the idea that government without representation is morally wrong.

When, in the course of human events, it becomes necessary for one portion of the family of man to assume among the people of the earth a position different from that which they have hitherto occupied, but one to which the laws of nature and of nature's God entitle them, a decent respect to the opinions of mankind requires that they should declare the causes that impel them to such a course.

We hold these truths to be self-evident; that all men and women are created equal; that they are endowed by their Creator with certain inalienable rights; that among these are life, liberty, and the pursuit of happiness; that to secure these rights governments are instituted, deriving their just powers from the consent of the governed. Whenever any form of government becomes destructive of these ends, it is the right of those who suffer from it to refuse allegiance to it, and to insist upon the institution of a new government, laying its foundation on such principles, and organizing its powers in such form, as to them shall seem most likely to effect their safety and happiness. Prudence, indeed, will dictate that governments long established should not be changed for light and transient causes; and, accordingly, all experience hath shown that mankind are more disposed to suffer, while evils are sufferable, than to right themselves by abolishing the forms to which they were accustomed. But when a long train of abuses and usurpations, pursuing invariably the same object, evinces a design to reduce them under absolute despotism, it is their duty to throw off such government, and to provide new guards for their future security. Such has been the patient sufferance of the women under this government, and such is now the necessity which constrains them to demand the equal station to which they are entitled.

The history of mankind is a history of repeated injuries and usurpations on the part of man toward woman, having in direct object the establishment of an absolute tyranny over her. To prove this, let facts be submitted to a candid world.

He has never permitted her to exercise her inalienable right to the elective franchise.

He has compelled her to submit to laws, in the formation of which she had no voice.

He has withheld from her rights which are given to the most ignorant and degraded men – both natives and foreigners.

Having deprived her of this first right as a citizen, the elective franchise, thereby leaving her without representation in the halls of legislation, he has oppressed her on all sides.

He has made her, if married, in the eye of the law, civilly dead.

He has taken from her all right in property, even to the wages she earns.

He has made her morally, an irresponsible being, as she can commit many crimes with impunity, provided they be done in the presence of her husband. In the covenant of marriage, she is compelled to promise obedience to her husband, he becoming, to all intents and purposes, her master – the law giving him power to deprive her of her liberty, and to administer chastisement.

He has so framed the laws of divorce, as to what shall be the proper causes of divorce, in case of separation, to whom the guardianship of the children shall be given; as to be wholly regardless of the happiness of the women – the law, in all cases, going upon a false supposition of the supremacy of man, and giving all power into his hands.

After depriving her of all rights as a married woman, if single and the owner of property, he has taxed her to support a government which recognizes her only when her property can be made profitable to it.

He has monopolized nearly all the profitable employments, and from those she is permitted to follow, she receives but a scanty remuneration.

He closes against her all the avenues to wealth and distinction, which he considers most honorable to himself. As a teacher of theology, medicine, or law, she is not known.

He has denied her the facilities for obtaining a thorough education – all colleges being closed against her.

He allows her in church, as well as State, but a subordinate position, claiming Apostolic authority for her exclusion from the ministry, and, with some exceptions, from any public participation in the affairs of the church.

He has created a false public sentiment by giving to the world a different code of morals for men and women, by which moral delinquencies which exclude women from society, are not only tolerated but deemed of little account in man.

He has usurped the prerogative of Jehovah himself, claiming it as his right to assign for her a sphere of action, when that belongs to her conscience and her God.

He has endeavored, in every way that he could to destroy her confidence in her own powers, to lessen her self-respect, and to make her willing to lead a dependent and abject life.

Now, in view of this entire disfranchisement of one-half the people of this country, their social and religious degradation – in view of the unjust laws above mentioned, and because women do feel themselves aggrieved, oppressed, and fraudulently deprived of their most sacred rights, we insist that they have immediate admission to all the rights and privileges which belong to them as citizens of these United States.

In entering upon the great work before us, we anticipate no small amount of misconception, misrepresentation, and ridicule; but we shall use every instrumentality within our power to effect our object. We shall employ agents, circulate tracts, petition the State and national Legislatures, and endeavor to enlist the pulpit and the press in our behalf. We hope this convention will be followed by a series of conventions, embracing every part of the country.

Firmly relying upon the final triumph of the Right and the True, we do this day affix our signatures to this declaration.

The Treaty of Waitangi

NATIONALITY:
New Zealand
WHEN:
1840
WHERE:
Waitangi, New Zealand
YOU SHOULD KNOW:
The Treaty of Waitangi Act of 1975
set up the Waitangi Tribunal to look
into the question of Crown breaches
of the treaty and redress for them.

In 1839 the British Crown dispatched naval captain William Hobson to New Zealand in order to ensure that the islands became a crown colony and, not the de facto *property of a private company. He negotiated with several northern North Island chiefs about the wording of the treaty which would, apparently, allow them to remain in control of their own people and property. The interpretation of what the treaty meant differed, and it is unlikely that the chiefs understood that they were signing over sovereignty of their island to a foreign power. Even though the treaty was not ratified by the British and only the chiefs of northern North Island signed it, it is still a cause of contention and its meaning and legality are uncertain.*

Her Majesty Victoria Queen of the United Kingdom of Great Britain and Ireland regarding with Her Royal Favour the Native Chiefs and Tribes of New Zealand and anxious to protect their just Rights and Property and to secure to them the enjoyment of Peace and Good Order has deemed it necessary in consequence of the great number of Her Majesty's Subjects who have already settled in New Zealand and the rapid extension of Emigration both from Europe and Australia which is still in progress to constitute and appoint a functionary properly authorized to treat with the Aborigines of New Zealand for the recognition of Her Majesty's Sovereign authority over the whole or any part of those islands.

Her Majesty therefore being desirous to establish a settled form of Civil Government with a view to avert the evil consequences which must result from the absence of the necessary Laws and Institutions alike to the native population and to Her subjects has been graciously pleased to empower and to authorize me William Hobson a Captain in Her Majesty's Royal Navy Consul and Lieutenant Governor of such parts of New Zealand as may be or hereafter shall be ceded to Her Majesty to invite the confederated and independent Chiefs of New Zealand to concur in the following Articles and Conditions.

ARTICLE THE FIRST
The Chiefs of the Confederation of the United Tribes of New Zealand and the separate and independent Chiefs who have not become members of the Confederation cede to Her Majesty the Queen of England absolutely and without reservation all the rights and powers of Sovereignty which the said Confederation or Individual Chiefs respectively exercise or possess, or may be supposed to exercise or to possess, over their respective Territories as the sole Sovereigns thereof.

ARTICLE THE SECOND

Her Majesty the Queen of England confirms and guarantees to the Chiefs and Tribes of New Zealand and to the respective families and individuals thereof the full exclusive and undisturbed possession of their Lands and Estates, Forests, Fisheries and other properties which they may collectively or individually possess so long as it is their wish and desire to retain the same in their possession; but the Chiefs of the United Tribes and the individual Chiefs yield to Her Majesty the exclusive right of Preemption over such lands as the proprietors thereof may be disposed to alienate at such prices as may be agreed upon between the respective Proprietors and persons appointed by Her Majesty to treat with them in that behalf.

ARTICLE THE THIRD

In consideration thereof Her Majesty the Queen of England extends to the Natives of New Zealand Her royal protection and imparts to them all the Rights and Privileges of British Subjects.

W HOBSON LIEUTENANT GOVERNOR

Now therefore We the Chiefs of the Confederation of the United Tribes of New Zealand being assembled in Congress at Victoria in Waitangi and We the Separate and Independent Chiefs of New Zealand claiming authority over the Tribes and Territories which are specified after our respective names, having been made fully to understand the Provisions of the foregoing Treaty, accept and enter into the same in the full spirit and meaning thereof in witness of which we have attached our signatures or marks at the places and the dates respectively specified.

Done at Waitangi this Sixth day of February in the year of Our Lord one thousand eight hundred and forty. "

Alexander Solzhenitsyn

1918–2008

Russian writer Alexander Solzhenitsyn was awarded the 1970 Nobel Prize for Literature but felt unable to attend the ceremony as he was concerned that he might be prevented from re-entering Russia if he did and arrangements for the delivery of the prize at the Swedish Embassy fell through because the writer objected to the conditions the Swedish government kept trying to impose on him. His acknowledgment was smuggled out of Russia in 1972 by Swedish journalist Stig Fredrikson, but not read out. He finally attended a prize-giving in 1974, after he was exiled from the Soviet Union, when he gave the following short speech.

NATIONALITY:
Russian
WHEN:
1974
WHERE:
Oslo, Norway
YOU SHOULD KNOW:
Solzhenitsyn spent eight years in jail for criticizing Stalin's conduct of World War II and a further three years in internal exile. Persecution continued until he was expelled in 1974.

' . . . Many Nobel Prize laureates have appeared before you in this hall, but the Swedish Academy and the Nobel Foundation have probably never had as much bother with anyone as they have had with me . . .

I must ask your forgiveness, therefore, for having caused all of you so much trouble, and thank you especially for the ceremony in 1970, when your king and all of you welcomed here an empty chair.

But you will agree that it has not been so simple for the prizewinner, either: carrying his three-minute speech around with him for four years. When I was preparing to come to you in 1970 no room in my breast, no amount of paper was sufficient to let me speak my mind on the first free tribune of my life. For a writer from a land without liberty his first tribune and his first speech is a speech about everything in the world, about all the torments of his country, and it is pardonable if he forgets the object of the ceremony, the persons assembled there and fills the goblets of joy with his bitterness. But since that year when I was unable to come here, I have learned to express openly practically all my thoughts in my own country as well. So that finding myself expatriated to the West, I have acquired all the better this unhindered possibility of saying as much as I want and where I want, which is something not always appreciated here . . .

And I would like to express my heartfelt gratitude to the members of the Swedish Academy for the enormous support their choice in 1970 has given my works as a writer. I venture to thank them on behalf of that vast unofficial Russia which is prohibited from expressing itself aloud, which is persecuted both for writing books and even for reading them. The Academy have heard for this decision of theirs many reproaches implying that such a prize has served political interests. But these are the shouts of raucous loudmouths who know of no other interests. We all know that an artist's work cannot be contained within the wretched dimension of politics. For this dimension cannot hold the whole of our life and we must not restrain our social consciousness within in its bounds. ”

Congressional Committee on Indian Affairs

NATIONALITY:
American
WHEN:
1824
WHERE:
Washington, DC, USA
YOU SHOULD KNOW:
John C. Calhoun later served as Vice President to both John Quincy Adams and Andrew Jackson.

In early 1824 Secretary of War, John C. Calhoun created a Bureau of Indian Affairs with a remit of overseeing treaty negotiations, managing schools, administering trade and handling all expenditure and correspondence concerning native Americans. At this stage the policy towards the majority of tribes was one of 'civilization' through education, although within a few years this would change and they would be forced from their lands and moved west. The Congressional Committee report below details an early examination about whether the education policy is a good use of Federal funds and posits the opinion that the only alternative would be extermination of the native Americans.

' . . . The committee have carefully examined the measures which have been adopted, for the disbursement of the annual allowance made by this law, and find them very judicious, and such as are best calculated to effectuate the benevolent designs of the government. Although the reports, heretofore made by the secretary of war, contained the rules by which the sum granted was to be apportioned and paid, the committee annex them to this report, and wish them to be referred to as a part of it. The committee also submit a statement, shewing the different sums paid to the Indian schools which have been organized, and the number of scholars taught at each school.

It requires but little research to convince every candid mind, that the prospect of civilizing our Indians was never so promising, as at this time. Never were means, for the accomplishment of this object, so judiciously devised, and so faithfully applied, as provided in the above act, and the auxiliary aids which it has encouraged. It is believed to be an essential part of any plan for Indian civilization, that, with the rudiments of education, the males should be taught the arts of husbandry, and the females to perform those domestic duties which peculiarly belong to their stations in civilized life. The attempts which have heretofore been made, many of which have failed, omitted this essential part. Many zealous, but enthusiastic persons, who have been most conspicuous in endeavoring to reclaim the Indians, persuaded themselves to believe, that, to secure this object, it was only necessary to send missionaries among them to instruct them in the Christian religion. Some of their exertions failed, without producing any salutary effect, because the agents employed were wholly unfitted for the task. Others, though productive of some good effect at first, eventually failed, because their missionary labors were not added to the institutes of education, and instruction in agriculture. These are combined, in the exertions now making; and, from the good which has been done, the most pleasing anticipations of success are confidently cherished . . .

This will be a work of time; and, for its accomplishment, great labor and perseverance will be necessary. The progress, however, of this work, may be more rapid than any can now venture to anticipate. The instruction and civilization of a few enterprising youths, will have an immense influence on the tribes to which they belong. As the means are constantly applied, the numbers reclaimed will increase, and an increase of numbers will ensure, in a geometrical proportion, success for the future. It is difficult to say what may not be accomplished, under such circumstances. No one will be bold enough to denounce him as a visionary enthusiast, who, under such auspices, will look with great confidence to the entire accomplishment of the object.

The civilization of the Indians has been viewed as a work of great national importance, by many whose talents and public services have rendered illustrious the annals of our country. This was an object of great solicitude with Washington, and to all who have succeeded him. Prior to the passage of the above law, the attention of congress was invited to the subject, in almost every annual message from the executive. If the policy of this measure were considered, merely as a question of pecuniary interest, it is believed that but few would hesitate to sanction it. That it inculcates the most friendly disposition, on the part of the Indians, no one, well informed on the subject, will venture to deny . . .

The Indians are not now, what they once were. They have partaken of our vices, more than our virtues. Such is their condition, at present, that they must be civilized or exterminated; no other alternative exists. He must be worse than a savage, who can view, with cold indifference, an exterminating policy. All desire their prosperity, and wish to see them brought within the pale of civilization. The means which have been adopted, and of which the law in question is the foundation, seem the most likely to obtain the desired result. They should not, therefore, be abandoned. The passage of this law was called for by many of the people in the most populous and influential sections of our country. Their wishes were made known in language that evinced a deep interest – an interest, not produced by momentary excitement, but the result of much reflection, and a high sense of moral duty. It may be said, emphatically, that the passage of this law was called for by a religious community. They were convinced of the correctness of the policy, in a political point of view, and, as Christians, they felt the full force of the obligations which duty enjoined. Their zeal was tempered by reason. No fanciful schemes of proselytism seem to have been indulged. They . . . pointed to the most judicious means for the accomplishment of their wishes. Since the passage of the law, hundreds, and thousands, have been encouraged to contribute their mite in aid of the wise policy of the government. However the various denominations of professing Christians may differ in their creeds and general doctrines, they all unite in their wishes that our Indians may become civilized. That this feeling almost universally prevails, has been declared in language too unequivocal to admit of doubt. It has been seen in their words, and in their actions.

The committee believe, that such demonstrations are not to be regarded lightly; that the national legislature will treat them with the highest respect. If a sectarian zeal had had any agency to produce this general interest, it would be less entitled to serious considerations. But such a contracted feeling seems to have had no influence; a more noble and Christian motive has been cherished. All unite to second the views of the government, by ameliorating the condition of our Indians. They are taught the first rudiments of education, the duties which appertain to man as a member of civil society, and his accountability as a moral agent. Repeal this law, and these exertions are not only paralyzed, but destroyed. The Indians will see, in such an act, that we will feel less for their prosperity, than our professions have encouraged them to believe; and such an impression cannot fail to produce the most injurious consequences.

From the various lights in which the committee have viewed the policy of this law, they are convinced that it is founded in justice, and should not be repealed. They, therefore, submit to the house the following resolution:

Resolved, That it is inexpedient to repeal the law making an annual appropriation of ten thousand dollars for the civilization of the Indians.

James Otis 1725–1783

NATIONALITY:
American
WHEN:
1761
WHERE:
Boston, Massachusetts, USA
YOU SHOULD KNOW:
Otis is also credited with the phrase 'Taxation without representation is tyranny'.

In the mid-eighteenth century, punitive duties on the American colonies' imports and exports were a vital source of revenue for the British government; customs officials had the right to inspect ships, homes, warehouses, etc, for contraband. On the death of George II in 1760, some powers did not transfer automatically, including these rights, and new 'writs of assistance' were sought. At the trial about their legality, Otis delivered a five-hour address – of which perhaps the most inflammatory passage is below – which some credit with sparking the flame of revolution.

A man's home is his castle, and whilst he is quiet, he is as well guarded as a prince in his castle. This writ, if it is declared legal, would totally annihilate this privilege. Custom house office may enter our houses when they please and we are commanded to permit their entry. Their menial servants may enter, may break locks, bars, and everything in their way; and whether they break through malice or revenge, no man, no court, can inquire. Bare suspicion without oath is sufficient. This wanton exercise of this power is not a chimerical suggestion of a heated brain. What a scene does this open! Every man, prompted by revenge, ill humour, or wantonness to inspect the inside of his neighbour's house, may get a writ of assistance. Others will ask it from self-defence; one arbitrary action will promote another, until society be involved in tumult and blood.

Menachem Begin 1913–1992

Having won the general election in May, Menachem Begin took office as Prime Minister of Israel on June 20, 1977. Earlier in the day he had been to the Western Wall to pray and had conducted an impromptu question-and-answer session with members of the international press corps nearby. A large number of the questions were about his plans for relations with the PLO. One reporter needled him by asking him for his response to Yassir Arafat's assertion that the Jewish state had no right of existence. His acceptance speech at the Knesset had acquired a last-minute addition. After a measured description of how Likud had come to beat Labour, he changed tone and thundered:

‘ The right to exist? Would it enter the mind of any Briton or Frenchman, Belgian or Dutchman, Hungarian or Bulgarian, Russian or American, to request for its people recognition of its right to exist? Their existence *per se* is their right to exist!

We were granted our right to exist by the God of our fathers at the glimmer of the dawn of human civilization 4,000 years ago.

And so it is that the Jewish people have a historic, eternal and inalienable right to Eretz Yisrael, the land of our forefathers. And for that right, which has been sanctified in Jewish blood from generation to generation, we have paid a price unexemplified in the annals of the nations. ’

Begin's Likud Party won the 1977 election.

NATIONALITY:
Israeli
WHEN:
1977
WHERE:
Jerusalem, Israel
YOU SHOULD KNOW:
Likud had been in opposition for 30 years before the 1977 elections.

Adolf Hitler 1889–1945

A year after becoming the leader of the National Socialist Party in Germany, Hitler gave party members a hate-filled speech in Munich on April 12, 1922 (extracts below) against the Jews. It was not widely reported at the time, as the Nazis were a fringe party. Germans were undergoing severe hardship at this time. Crippling debts from World War I were exacerbated by the punitive reparations imposed by the Treaty of Versailles. The belief that Jewish people were getting rich at the expense of hard-working Germans was widely held at the time and compounded the stress of financial hardships.

NATIONALITY:
Austrian/German
WHEN:
1922
WHERE:
Munich, Germany
YOU SHOULD KNOW:
In a 1919 pamphlet Hitler had already advocated 'removing' the Jewish people from German soil and it was apparent that the seeds of the 'final solution' were in his thoughts.

‘ . . . at the end of the World War Germany was burdened with her own debt of some seven or eight milliards of marks and, beyond that, was faced with the debts of 'the rest of the world' – the so-called 'reparations.' The product of Germany's work thus belonged not to the nation, but to her foreign creditors: it was carried endlessly in trains for territories beyond our frontiers . . .

And if we ask who was responsible for our misfortune, then we must inquire who profited by our collapse. And the answer to that question is that Banks and Stock Exchanges are more flourishing than ever before. We were told that capitalism would be destroyed, and when we ventured to remind one or other of these 'famous statesmen' and said 'Don't forget that Jews, too, have capital', then the answer was: 'What are you worrying about? Capitalism as a whole will now be destroyed, the whole people will now be free. We are not fighting Jewish or Christian capitalism, we are fighting every capitalism: we are making the people completely free.'.

Christian capitalism is already as good as destroyed, the international Jewish Stock Exchange capital gains in proportion as the other loses ground. It is only the international Stock Exchange and loan-capital, the so-called supra-state capital, which has profited from the collapse of our economic life, the capital which receives its character from the single supra-state nation which is itself national to the core, which fancies itself to be above all other nations . . .

The Jew has not grown poorer: he gradually gets bloated, and, if you don't believe me . . . go to one of our health-resorts; there you will find two sorts of visitors: the German who goes there, perhaps for the first time for a long while, to breathe a little fresh air and to recover his health, and the Jew who goes there to lose his fat . . . **"**

Andrew Jackson 1767–1845

NATIONALITY:
American
WHEN:
1829
WHERE:
Washington DC, USA
YOU SHOULD KNOW:
Native Americans knew President Jackson as Sharp Knife.

The paternalistic, patronising tone in which President Jackson addressed the people of the Creek nation – some of whom had been his allies in the Creek War of 1813-1814 – is astonishing. Within little more than a year, the Indian Removal Act had been passed and then enforced, often violently, and movement of native Americans westwards had begun. The Creek had already given up 23,000,000 acres of land (in Alabama and Georgia) to the settlers in the Treaty of Fort Jackson of 1814.

' You and my white children are too near to each other to live in harmony and peace . . . Beyond the great river Mississippi . . . your father has provided a country large enough for all of you, and he advises you to remove to it. There your white brothers will not trouble you; they will have no claim to the land . . . It will be yours forever. **"**

William H. Seward Sr 1801–1872

New York Senator William H. Seward was vehemently opposed to slavery and in 1858 foresaw the inevitabilty of the coming conflict between the northern and southern states over the issue. As Lincoln's Secretary of State from 1861, he was seen by the south as having far too much influence and he, like Lincoln, was a marked man. In 1864 he wrote in a letter that although assassination was not the American way of doing things, the way people like he and Lincoln rode to and from their homes in the dark with no protection was laying themselves open to attack. On the night that Lincoln was killed, another member of the conspiracy, Lewis Powell, attacked Seward in his bed. But Seward survived, possibly because the splint he was wearing on his jaw, that had been damaged in a bad carriage accident a few days earlier, protected him.

‘ . . . As a general truth, communities prosper and flourish, or droop and decline, in just the degree that they practise or neglect to practise the primary duties of justice and humanity. The free-labor system conforms to the divine law of equality, which is written in the hearts and consciences of man, and therefore is always and everywhere beneficent . . . The slave system is one of constant danger, distrust, suspicion, and watchfulness. It debases those whose toil alone can produce wealth and resources for defence, to the lowest degree of which human nature is capable, to guard against mutiny and insurrection, and thus wastes energies which otherwise might be employed in national development and aggrandizement. The free-labor system educates all alike, and by opening all the fields of industrial employment and all the departments of authority, to the unchecked and equal rivalry of all classes of men, at once secures universal contentment, and brings into the highest possible activity all the physical, moral, and social energies of the whole state. The Union is a confederation of States. But in another aspect the United States constitute only one nation. Increase of population, which is filling the States out to their very borders, together with a new and extended network of railroads and other avenues, and an internal commerce which daily becomes more intimate, is rapidly bringing the States into a higher and more perfect social unity or consolidation. Thus, these antagonistic systems are continually coming into closer contact, and collision results . . . Shall I tell you what this collision means? They who think that it is accidental, unnecessary, the work of interested or fanatical agitators, and therefore ephemeral, mistake the case altogether. It is an irrepressible conflict between opposing and enduring forces, and it means that the United States must and will, sooner or later, become either entirely a slaveholding nation, or entirely a free-labor nation. ’

NATIONALITY:
American
WHEN:
1858
WHERE:
Rochester, New York, USA
YOU SHOULD KNOW:
Seward was responsible for the negotiations that led to the purchase of Alaska from Russia in 1867.

John Stuart Mill 1806–1873

NATIONALITY:
British
WHEN:
1867
WHERE:
London, England
YOU SHOULD KNOW:
Mills' amendment was lost by
196 votes to 73.

During a debate in the House of Commons in London on May 20, 1867 the MP for the City and Westminster, John Stuart Mill, tabled an amendment to the Reform Bill that sought to extend the right to vote to women. It was the first time such a sentiment had been heard in the British Parliament. Contrary to the usual argument that to allow women into the public sphere would make them more masculine and so emasculate men and weaken the country, Mill argued that the status quo – keeping women at home and 'feminine' – would do just that.

I rise, sir, to propose an extension of the suffrage which can excite no party or class feeling in this House; which can give no umbrage to the keenest assertor of the claims either of property or of numbers; an extension which has not the smallest tendency to disturb what we have heard so much about lately, the balance of political power; which cannot afflict the most timid alarmist with revolutionary terrors, or offend the most jealous democrat as an infringement of popular rights (hear, hear), or a privilege granted to one class of society at the expense of another. There is nothing to distract our attention from the simple question, whether there is any adequate justification for continuing to exclude an entire half of the community, not only from admission, but from the capability of being ever admitted within the pale of the Constitution, though they may fulfil all the conditions legally and constitutionally sufficient in every case but theirs. Sir, within the limits of our Constitution this is a solitary case. There is no other example of an exclusion which is absolute. If the law denied a vote to all but the possessors of £5,000 a year, the poorest man in the nation might—and now and then would—acquire the suffrage; but neither birth, nor fortune, nor merit, nor exertion, nor intellect, nor even that great disposer of human affairs, accident, can ever enable any woman to have her voice counted in those national affairs which touch her and hers as nearly as any other a person in the nation . . .

. . . the time is now come when, unless women are raised to the level of men, men will be pulled down to theirs. The women of a man's family are either a stimulus and a support to his highest aspirations, or a drag upon them. You may keep them ignorant of politics, but you cannot prevent them from concerning themselves with the least respectable part of politics – its personalities . . .

. . . men are afraid of manly women; but those who have considered the nature and power of social influences well know, that unless there are manly women, there will no longer be manly men. When men and women are really companions, if women are frivolous, men will be frivolous . . . the two sexes must now rise or sink together.

Anti-apartheid protestors

Johannes Strijdom

1893–1958

Prime Minister of South Africa from 1954 until his death in 1958, Strijdom was a no-compromise advocate of apartheid – the process of rigid separation between people of different races begun by his predecessor Daniel Malan and building on discriminations that had been in place since the nineteenth century. He removed 'coloured' voters from the main electoral roll and treason trials persecuted many of the activists who had been instrumental in the creation of the Freedom Charter in June 1955, in which demands for a non-racial South Africa were detailed by the South African Congress Alliance. This was made up of the African National Congress, the South African Indian Congress, the South African Congress of Democrats and the Coloured People's Congress.

' Call it paramountcy, baaskap or what you will, it is still domination . . . The only way the European can maintain supremacy is by domination . . . the only way they can maintain domination is by withholding the vote from non-Europeans. '

NATIONALITY:
South African
WHEN:
1955
WHERE:
Cape Town, South Africa
YOU SHOULD KNOW:
He was known by other politicans as the lion of the north.

Samuel Adams 1722–1803

On hearing the opening rounds of gunshot at the start of the American Revolutionary Wars, Adams is reported to have made the comment below. He had been an active participant in the build-up to fighting, taking part in both the protests against the Stamp Act of 1765 and those surrounding the Boston Tea Party in 1773, in which he was a leading player. In 1774, Adams was selected as one of Massachusett's colony's delegates to the First Continental Congress in Virginia. After the war he wanted to keep as much control as possible within each state rather than with the federal government, partly because he distrusted and disliked George Washington. He strongly advocated this model of government during the negotiations that led to the formulation of the Articles of Confederation.

' What a glorious morning is this! '

NATIONALITY:
American
WHEN:
1775
WHERE:
Lexington, Virginia, USA
YOU SHOULD KNOW:
This is often quoted as 'What a glorious morning for America!'

Custer's last stand was at Little Bighorn.

George Custer 1839–1876

In 1874 an expedition led by Lieutenant Colonel Custer had discovered gold in the Black Hills of South Dakota – land that belonged to native American tribes by treaty. The Grant administration issued an order that the native Americans should all leave for new reservations by January 1876. The Lakota Sioux and Cheyenne did not comply and were therefore considered hostile. Between March and April, Congressional hearings were held into illegal acts by various people, including Grant's brother, and Custer testified against them. Although he disagreed with government policy, he went back to fight with his men in the disastrous Little Bighorn campaign, during which he and five companies of his 7th Cavalry were slaughtered.

❛ If I were an Indian, I would follow Crazy Horse rather than adhere to the confines of the reservation. ❜

NATIONALITY:
American
WHEN:
1876
WHERE:
Washington DC, USA

YOU SHOULD KNOW:
Crazy Horse and Sitting Bull led their tribes to Canada, but both came back to the US and surrendered.

Oliver Wendell Holmes Jr

1841–1935

NATIONALITY:
American
WHEN:
1884
WHERE:
Keene, New Hampshire, USA
YOU SHOULD KNOW:
Holmes is reputed to have shouted 'Get down you fool!' at Lincoln when the other stood up during the Battle of Fort Stevens.

Oliver Wendell Holmes is best known as a long-standing Supreme Court judge, but what is less known is that he spent three years during the Civil War, which broke out during his senior college year, fighting on the Union side with the Massachusetts Infantry, and was wounded at Bull's Bluff, Antietam and Fredricksburg. After the war, he returned to Harvard to finish his studies and became a barrister. As a judge in the Massachusetts Supreme Court, and later at the US Supreme Court, he was an early advocate of what would become known as legal realism, in which judges decide on the facts then present their rationale, allowing others to follow the precedent of their desicions.

❛ Not long ago I heard a young man ask why people still kept up Memorial Day, and it set me thinking of the answer. Not the answer that you and I should give to each other – not the expression of those feelings that, so long as you live, will make this day sacred to memories of love and grief and heroic youth – but an answer which should command the assent of those who do not share our memories, and in which we of the North and our brethren of the South could join in perfect accord . . .

The soldiers of the war need no explanations; they can join in commemorating a soldier's death with feelings not different in kind, whether he fell toward them or by their side.

But Memorial Day may and ought to have a meaning also for those who do not share our memories. When men have instinctively agreed to celebrate an anniversary, it will be found that there is some thought of feeling behind it which is too large to be dependent upon associations alone. The Fourth of July, for instance, has still its serious aspect, although we no longer should think of rejoicing like children that we have escaped from an outgrown control, although we have achieved not only our national but our moral independence and know it far too profoundly to make a talk about it, and although an Englishman can join in the celebration without a scruple. For, stripped of the temporary associations which gives rise to it, it is now the moment when by common consent we pause to become conscious of our national life and to rejoice in it, to recall what our country has done for each of us, and to ask ourselves what we can do for the country in return.

So to the indifferent inquirer who asks why Memorial Day is still kept up we may answer, it celebrates and solemnly reaffirms from year to year a national act of enthusiasm and faith. It embodies in the most impressive form our belief that to act with enthusiam and faith is the condition of acting greatly. To fight out a war, you must believe something and want something with all your might. So must you do to carry anything else to an end worth reaching. More than that, you must be willing to commit yourself to a course, perhaps a long and hard one, without being able to foresee exactly where you will come out. All that is required of you is that you should go somewhither as hard as ever you can. The rest belongs to fate. One may fall at the beginning of the charge or at the top of the earthworks; but in no other way can one reach the rewards of victory . . .

I see them now, more than I can number, as once I saw them on this earth. They are the same bright figures, or their counterparts, that come also before your eyes; and when I speak of those who were my brothers, the same words describe yours.

I see a fair-haired lad, a lieutenant, and a captain on whom life had begun somewhat to tell, but still young, sitting by the long mess-table in camp before the regiment left the State, and wondering how many of those who gathered in our tent could hope to see the end of what was then beginning. For neither of them was that destiny reserved. I remember, as I awoke from my first long stupor in the hospital after the battle of Ball's Bluff, I heard the doctor say, 'He was a beautiful boy', and I knew that one of those two speakers was no more. The other, after passing through all the previous battles, went into Fredericksburg with strange premonition of the end, and there met his fate.

I see another youthful lieutenant as I saw him in the Seven Days, when I looked down the line at Glendale. The officers were at the head of their companies. The advance was beginning. We caught each other's eye and saluted. When next I looked, he was gone.

I see the brother of the last, the flame of genius and daring on his face, as he rode before us into the wood of Antietam, out of which came only dead and deadly wounded men. So, a little later, he rode to his death at the head of his cavalry in the valley . . .

There is one grave and commanding presence that you all would recognize, for his life has become a part of our common history. Who does not remember the leader of the assault of the mine at Petersburg? The solitary horseman in front of Port Hudson, whom a foeman worthy of him bade his soldiers spare, from love and admiration of such gallant bearing? Who does not still hear the echo of those eloquent lips after the war, teaching reconciliation and peace? I may not do more than allude to his death, fit ending of his life. All that the world has a right to know has been told by a beloved friend in a book wherein friendship has found no need to exaggerate facts that speak for themselves. I knew him and I may even say I knew him well; yet, until that book appeared, I had not known the governing motive of his soul. I had admired him as a hero. When I read, I learned to revere him as a saint. His strength was not in honor alone, but in religion; and those who do not share his creed must see that it was on the wings of religious faith that he mounted above even valiant deeds into an empyrean of ideal life.

Such hearts – ah me, how many! – were stilled 20 years ago; and to us who remain behind is left this day of memories. Every year – in the full tide of spring, at the height of the symphony of flowers and love and life – there comes a pause, and through the silence we hear the lonely pipe of death. Year after year lovers wandering under the apple trees and through the clover and deep grass are surprised with sudden tears as they see black-veiled figures stealing through the morning to a soldier's grave. Year after year the comrades of the dead follow, with public honor, procession and commemorative flags and funeral march – honor and grief from us who stand almost alone, and have seen the best and noblest of our generation pass away.

But grief is not the end of all. I seem to hear the funeral march become a paean. I see beyond the forest the moving banners of a hidden column. Our dead brothers still live for us, and bid us think of life, not death – of life to which in their youth they lent the passion and joy of the spring. As I listen, the great chorus of life and joy begins again, and amid the awful orchestra of seen and unseen powers and destinies of good and evil our trumpets sound once more a note of daring, hope, and will. 🟥

A Beijing demonstrator in
Tiananmen Square tries to
stop the tanks.

Anonymous

On June 5, 1989, as student protestors were cleared from Tiananmen Square in Beijing, a lone student stood in front of a column of tanks, moving from left to right as the lead tank tried to drive round him. He climbed onto the tank and addressed the driver (see below) before climbing off again and resuming his position. Eventually, fellow protestors dragged him away, fearing that he might be run over or shot. Students had been occupying the square for several weeks, agitating for increased democratic reforms and mourning the death of the pro-reform ex-Secretary General of the Communist Party of China, Hu Yaobong. At the height of the demonstrations, hundreds of thousands of people took to the streets of several Chinese cities. After they had been suppressed, human rights were suppressed even more harshly.

❝ Why are you here? You have caused nothing but misery. ❞

NATIONALITY:
Chinese
WHEN:
1989
WHERE:
Beijing, China
YOU SHOULD KNOW:
There have been various claims as to
the identity of the 'tank man', but
none has been confirmed and his
fate is unknown.

King John 1167–1216

In the early thirteenth century, political struggles between the unpopular King and his leading barons led them to force him to agree to a legal limit on his powers and so protect their rights. It was more a bill of rights than a statement of law, although various of its clauses have been regarded as such at times. As, for example, during the lead-up to the Civil War when Oliver Cromwell and Parliament were seeking to curtail powers that King Charles I was abrogating. Many of the articles concern debt, while the constitutional ones are at the beginning and end of the document.

NATIONALITY:
Norman English
WHEN:
1215
WHERE:
Runnymede, England
YOU SHOULD KNOW:
Magna Carta is Latin for
Great Charter.

John, by the grace of God, king of England, lord of Ireland, duke of Normandy and Aquitaine, and count of Anjou, to the archbishops, bishops, abbots, earls, barons, justiciars, foresters, sheriffs, stewards, servants, and to all his bailiffs and liege subjects, greeting. Know that, having regard to God and for the salvation of our soul, and those of all our ancestors and heirs, and unto the honor of God and the advancement of holy church, and for the reform of our realm, by advice of our venerable fathers . . .

In the first place we have granted to God, and by this our present charter confirmed for us and our heirs for ever that the English church shall be free, and shall have her rights entire, and her liberties inviolate; and we will that it be thus observed; which is apparent from this that the freedom of elections, which is reckoned most important and very essential to the English church, we, of our pure and unconstrained will, did grant, and did by our charter confirm and did obtain the ratification of the same from our lord, Pope Innocent III, before the quarrel arose between us and our barons: and this we will observe, and our will is that it be observed in good faith by our heirs for ever. We have also granted to all freemen of our kingdom, for us and our heirs for ever, all the underwritten liberties, to be had and held by them and their heirs, of us and our heirs for ever . . .

If any one has been dispossessed or removed by us, without the legal judgment of his peers, from his lands, castles, franchises, or from his right, we will immediately restore them to him; and if a dispute arise over this, then let it be decided by the five-and-twenty barons of whom mention is made below in the clause for securing the peace. Moreover, for all those possessions, from which any one has, without the lawful judgment of his peers, be endisseised or removed, by our father, King Henry, or by our brother, King Richard, and which we retain in our hand (or which are possessed by others, to whom we are bound to warrant them) we shall have respite until the usual term of crusaders; excepting those things about which a plea has been raised, or an inquest made by our order, before our taking of the cross; but as soon as were turn from our expedition (or if perchance we desist from the expedition) we will immediately grant full justice therein . . .

All fines made with us unjustly and against the law of the land, and all amercements imposed unjustly and against the law of the land, shall be entirely remitted, or else it shall be done concerning them according to the decision of the five-and-twenty barons of whom mention is made below in the clause for securing the peace, or according to the judgment of the majority of the same, along with the aforesaid Stephen, archbishop of Canterbury, if he can be present, and such others as he may wish to bring with him for this purpose, and if he cannot be present the business shall nevertheless proceed without him, provided always that if any one or more of the aforesaid five-and-twenty barons are in a similar suit, they shall be removed as far as concerns this particular judgment, others being substituted in their places after having been selected by the rest of the same five-and-twenty for this purpose only, and after having been sworn.

Since, moreover, for God and the amendment of our kingdom and for the better allaying of the quarrel that has arisen between us and our barons, we have granted all these concessions, desirous that they should enjoy them in complete and firm endurance for ever, we give and grant to them the underwritten security, namely, that the barons choose five-and-twenty barons of the kingdom, whomsoever they will, who shall be bound with all their might, to observe and hold, and cause to be observed, the peace and liberties we have granted and confirmed to them by this our present Charter, so that if we, or our justiciar, or our bailiffs or any one of our officers, shall in anything be at fault toward any one, or shall have broken any one of the articles of the peace or of this security, and the offense be notified to four barons of the foresaid five-and-twenty, the said four barons shall repair to us (or our justiciar, if we are out of the realm) and, laying the transgression before us, petition to have that transgression redressed without delay. And if we shall not have corrected the transgression (or, in the event of our being out of the realm, if our justiciar shall not have corrected it) within forty days, reckoning from the time it has been intimated to us (or to our justiciar, if we should be out of the realm), the four barons aforesaid shall refer that matter to the rest of the five-and-twenty barons, and those five-and-twenty barons shall, together with the community of the whole land, distrain and distress us in all possible ways, namely, by seizing our castles, lands, possessions, and in any other way they can, until redress has been obtained as they deem fit, saving harmless our own person, and the persons of our queen and children; and when redress has been obtained, they shall resume their old relations toward us. And let whoever in the country desires it, swear to obey the orders of the said five-and-twenty barons for the execution of all the aforesaid matters, and along with them, to molest us to the utmost of his power; and we publicly and freely grant leave to every one who wishes to swear, and we shall never forbid any one to swear. All those, moreover, in the land who of themselves and of their own accord are unwilling to swear to the twenty-five to help them in constraining and molesting us, we shall by our command compel the same to swear to the effect aforesaid. And if any one of the five-and-twenty barons shall have died or departed from the land, or be incapacitated in any other manner which would prevent the foresaid provisions being carried out, those of the said twenty-five barons who are left shall choose another in his place according to their own judgment, and he shall be sworn in the same way as the others. Further, in all matters, the execution of which is intrusted to these twenty-five barons, if perchance these twenty-five are present, that which the majority of those present ordain or command shall be held as fixed and established, exactly as if the whole twenty-five had concurred in this; and the said twenty-five shall swear that they will faithfully observe all that is aforesaid, and cause it to be observed with all their might. And we shall procure nothing from any one, directly or indirectly, whereby any part of these concessions and liberties might be revoked or diminished; and if any such thing has been procured, let it be void and null, and we shall never use it personally or by another.

And all the ill-will, hatreds, and bitterness that have arisen between us and our men, clergy and lay, from the date of the quarrel, we have completely remitted and pardoned every one. Moreover, all trespasses occasioned by the said quarrel, from Easter in the sixteenth year of our reign till the restoration of peace, we have fully remitted to all, both clergy and laymen, and completely forgiven, as far as pertains to us. And, on this head, we have caused to be made for them letters testimonial patent of the lord Stephen, archbishop of Canterbury, of the lord Henry, archbishop of Dublin, of the bishops aforesaid, and of Master Pandulf as touching this security and the concessions aforesaid.

Wherefore it is our will, and we firmly enjoin, that the English Church be free, and that the men in our kingdom have and hold all the aforesaid liberties, rights, and concessions, well and peaceably, freely and quietly, fully and wholly, for themselves and their heirs, of us and our heirs, in all respects and in all places for ever, as is aforesaid. An oath, moreover, has been taken, as well on our part as on the part of the barons, that all these conditions aforesaid shall be kept in good faith and without evil intent.

George Washington 1732–1799

Less than three months after the signature of the treaty that ended the Revolutionary Wars, George Washington addressed a group of Irish immigrants who had recently arrived in New York. For the next few years he retired to his plantation at Mount Vernon. He re-entered politics in 1787, to preside over the Philadelpia Convention that drafted the Constitution of the United States of America and become the first President of the USA in 1789. In fact, immigration did not increase markedly until the 1830s, but from then on it grew rapidly. Irish people, especially, came to work in the industries that were springing up in American cities.

NATIONALITY:
American
WHEN:
1783
WHERE:
New York, USA
YOU SHOULD KNOW:
Between 1790 and 1850, the US population grew from just under 4,000,000 to a little over 23,000,000.

Gentlemen: The testimony of your satisfaction at the glorious termination of the late contest, and your indulgent opinion of my Agency in it, affords me singular pleasure and merits my warmest acknowledgment.

If the Example of the Americans successfully contending in the Cause of Freedom, can be of any use to other Nations; we shall have an additional Motive for rejoycing at so prosperous an Event.

It was not an uninteresting consideration to learn that the Kingdom of Ireland, by a bold and manly conduct, had obtained the redress of many of its grievances; and it is much to be wished that the blessings of equal Liberty and unrestrained Commerce may yet prevail more extensively; in the mean time, you may be assured, Gentlemen, that the Hospitality and Beneficence of your Countrymen, to our Brethren who have been Prisoners of War, are neither unknown, or unregarded.

The bosom of America is open to receive not only the Opulent and respectable Stranger, but the oppressed and persecuted of all Nations And Religions; whom we shall welcome to a participation of all our rights and privileges, if by decency and propriety of conduct they appear to merit the enjoyment.

Jesse Jackson

born 1941

The Reverend Jesse Jackson is one of the best-known civil-rights activists in the USA and a long-standing senior figure in the Democrat Party. He stood for nomination as Democrat presidential candidate in both 1984 and 1988. During the 1960s he participated in the Southern Christian Leadership Conference and was national director of its Operation Breadbasket and later extended his efforts into international affairs. In 1984, he came third behind Gary Hart and former Vice President Walter Mondale. In his speech at the Convention he called on the delegates to unite, whatever the colour of their skin, to eradicate injustice, division, racism and poverty.

❛ Thank you very much.
Tonight we come together bound by our faith in a mighty God, with genuine respect and love for our country, and inheriting the legacy of a great Party, the Democratic Party, which is the best hope for redirecting our nation on a more humane, just, and peaceful course . . .

. . . Our time has come. Our time has come. Suffering breeds character. Character breeds faith. In the end, faith will not disappoint. Our time has come. Our faith, hope, and dreams will prevail. Our time has come. Weeping has endured for nights, but now joy cometh in the morning. Our time has come. No grave can hold our body down. Our time has come. No lie can live forever. Our time has come. We must leave racial battle ground and come to economic common ground and moral higher ground. America, our time has come. We come from disgrace to amazing grace. Our time has come. Give me your tired, give me your poor, your huddled masses who yearn to breathe free and come November, there will be a change because our time has come. ❜

The Rev. Jessie Jackson makes a dramatic appearance before the Democratic Convention.

NATIONALITY:
American
WHEN:
1984
WHERE:
San Francisco, California, USA
YOU SHOULD KNOW:
The Rev. Jackson has been a Baptist minister since 1968.

266

Earl Warren 1891–1974

Chief Justice Earl Warren presided over the appeal against a ruling of the United States District Court for the District of Kansas made in 1951. It was a class action by 13 families and had been judged in favour of the Topeka Board of Education that although segregation was detrimental to African Americans in general, in elementary schools in the town it was not discriminatory because facilities were much the same in both systems. The Supreme Court heard five appeals in tandem from different states, all of which were sponsored by the National Association for the Advancement of Colored People. Warren overturned the Kansas ruling.

NATIONALITY:
American
WHEN:
1954
WHERE:
Washington, DC, USA
YOU SHOULD KNOW:
In 1946 Warren won both the Republican and Democrat nominations for Governor of California.

SUPREME COURT OF THE UNITED STATES. 347 US 483
Brown v Board of Education of Topeka
APPEAL FROM THE UNITED STATES DISTRICT COURT FOR THE DISTRICT OF KANSAS
No. 1. Argued: Argued December 9, 1952 Reargued December 8, 1953 – Decided: Decided May 17, 1954

' Segregation of white and Negro children in the public schools of a State solely on the basis of race, pursuant to state laws permitting or requiring such segregation, denies to Negro children the equal protection of the laws guaranteed by the Fourteenth Amendment – even though the physical facilities and other 'tangible' factors of white and Negro schools may be equal. The history of the Fourteenth Amendment is inconclusive as to its intended effect on public education. The question presented in these cases must be determined not on the basis of conditions existing when the Fourteenth Amendment was adopted, but in the light of the full development of public education and its present place in American life throughout the Nation. Where a State has undertaken to provide an opportunity for an education in its public schools, such an opportunity is a right which must be made available to all on equal terms. Segregation of children in public schools solely on the basis of race deprives children of the minority group of equal educational opportunities, even though the physical facilities and other 'tangible' factors may be equal. The 'separate but equal' doctrine adopted in Plessy v Ferguson, 163 US 537, has no place in the field of public education. The cases are restored to the docket for further argument on specified questions relating to the forms of the decrees. 」

Sojourner Truth 1797–1883

NATIONALITY:
American
WHEN:
1851
WHERE:
Akron, Ohio, USA
YOU SHOULD KNOW:
Sojourner Truth was freed from slavery in 1827.

In 1851, a women's rights conference in Akron, Ohio, had been dominated by male speakers who waxed eloquent about the delicate nature of women, the superior intellect of men, Eve's role in committing the original sin and Christ's masculine nature: that is, that if God had desired the equality of women this would be reflected in the birth, life and death of the Saviour. Few women dared to speak, the men in the audience were enjoying seeing the arguments for female suffrage demolished and there was consternation when the freed slave and abolitionist campaigner, Sojourner Truth, took to the stage, partly because people feared that she would hijack the meeting for the abolitionst cause. In a few short sentences, she turned the tables on the self-satisfied men.

A painting of Sojourner Truth

'Wall, chilern, whar dar is so much racket dar must be somethin' out o' kilter. I tink dat 'twixt de niggers of de Souf and de womin at de Norf, all talkin' 'bout rights, de white men will be in a fix pretty soon. But what's all dis here talkin' 'bout?

Dat man ober dar say dat womin needs to be helped into carriages, and lifted ober ditches, and to hab de best place everywhar. Nobody eber helps me into carriages, or ober mud-puddles, or gibs me any best place!

'And ain't I a woman? Look at me! Look at my arm! I have ploughed, and planted, and gathered into barns, and no man could head me! And ain't I a woman? I could work as much and eat as much as a man – when I could get it – and bear de lash as well! And ain't I a woman? I have borne 13 chilern, and seen 'em mos' all sold off to slavery, and when I cried out with my mother's grief, none but Jesus heard me! And ain't I a woman?

Den dey talks 'bout dis ting in de head; what dis dey call it? ['Intellect', whispers someone near her] Dat's it, honey. What's dat got to do wid womin's rights or nigger's rights? If my cup won't hold but a pint, and yourn holds a quart, wouldn't ye be mean not to let me have my little half-measure full?

Den dat little man in black dar, he say women can't have as much rights as men, 'cause Christ wan't a woman! Whar did your Christ come from? [directed at a minister who had made that argument]

Whar did your Christ come from? From God and a woman! Man had nothin' to do wid Him.

. . . If de fust woman God ever made was strong enough to turn de world upside down all alone, dese women togedder ought to be able to turn it back, and get it right side up again! And now dey is asking to do it, de men better let 'em.

'Bleeged to ye for hearin' on me, and now ole Sojourner han't got nothin' more to say.'

Rosa Parks 1913–2005

On December 1, 1955 the local secretary of the National Association for the Advancement of Colored People defied a bus driver who ordered her to give up her seat to a white man. He threatened to get the police to arrest her and she answered as below. In March, a 15-year-old schoolgirl, Claudette Colvin, had been arrested for the same action. On the day of Parkes' trial, the Montgomery Bus Boycott, in which virtually all African American passengers found other means of getting around the city, started. It lasted for 381 days and ended only with the repeal of the law requiring segregation on buses.

NATIONALITY:
American
WHEN:
1955
WHERE:
Montgomerey, Alabama, USA
YOU SHOULD KNOW:
The bus driver, James F. Blake, had thrown her off a bus in 1943.

' You may go on and do so. 🟥

Rosa Parkes in the front of a bus in Montgomery.

269

Chief Dan George, hereditary chief of the Tsleil-waututh nation in Canada

Chief Dan George
Geswanouth Slahoot 1899–1981

NATIONALITY:
Canadian
WHEN:
From 1952
WHERE:
Various places
YOU SHOULD KNOW:
George was nominated for a best actor in a supporting role Oscar for his part in the film *Little Big Man* in 1970.

Best known as an actor, including for roles in Centennial, The Outlaw Josey Wales *and* Bonanza, *Dan George was chief of the Tsleil-waututh nation in Burrard, British Columbia, Canada, from 1951 to 1963 and was a prominent speaker on Native American rights. He was given the name Dan George when he went to school where children weren't allowed to speak their native languages. Despite his stardom, when not working he lived on the Burrard reserve in the home he had built for his family. One of his more notable actions was on Canada Day in 1967 – the year of the country's centennial – when he performed his Lament for Confederation soliloquy in front of 35,000 people in Vancouver.*

‘ When the white man came we had the land and they had the bibles; now they have the land and we have the bibles. ’

Günter Schabowski born 1929

On November 9, 1989 – in the wake of large numbers of East German citizens escaping to the west via Czechslovakia and Hungary – Günter Schabowski, spokesman for the Socialist Unity Party of Germany and Politburo member, was handed a piece of paper at a news conference. Not realizing that the note was for his information only, he read it out, announcing the cessation of travel restrictions on East German citizens. When asked when the change would come into effect, he replied 'Immediately, I suppose', and confirmed that the crossings into West Berlin were included in the changes. The news was meant to be embargoed until the following morning, to give the border guards time to make changes. But within an hour or so of the premature announcement, crowds had descended on the area around the wall and their numbers led the guards to decide to let them through, leading to the iconic images of the end of the Cold War – hundreds of people sitting on the wall, celebrating.

‘ Private travel into foreign countries can be requested without conditions (passports or family connections). Permission will be granted instantly. Permanent relocations can be done through all border checkpoints between the GDR into the FRG or Berlin (West). ’

NATIONALITY:
German
WHEN:
1989
WHERE:
Berlin, Germany
YOU SHOULD KNOW:
During its twenty-nine years of existence, there were roughly 5,000 successful escapes across the Berlin Wall. Between 136 and 220 people are estimated to have been killed.

A German youth sits astride the Berlin Wall after the fall of communism in East Germany.

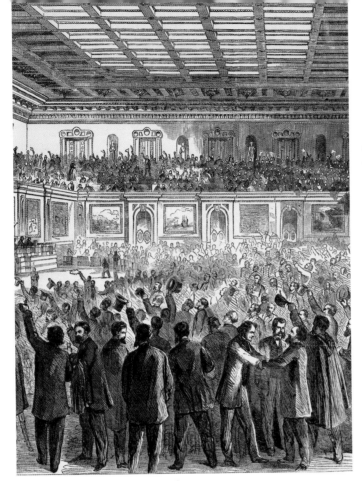

An engraving depicting the passing of the Bill.

Government of the USA

During the Civil War, Abraham Lincoln had issued his Emancipation Proclamation in 1863 and a Thirteenth Amendment had been introduced into Congress in 1864, although its passage was stalled in the House of Representatives. It was reintroduced later in the year and Lincoln made its passage an election issue. It was finally passed in the House in January 1865 and he approved it on February 1. It was ratified on December 6, and proclaimed on December 18. It was the first amendment to the US Constitution for more than 60 years and is regarded as the first of the 'Reconstruction Amendments'.

NATIONALITY:
American
WHEN:
1865
WHERE:
Washington, DC, USA
YOU SHOULD KNOW:
At the time of ratification slavery remained legal only in Delaware, Kentucky and Missouri.

AMENDMENT 13.

Section 1. Neither slavery nor involuntary servitude, except as a punishment for crime where of the party shall have been duly convicted, shall exist within the United States, or any place subject to their jurisdiction.

Section 2. Congress shall have the power to enforce this article by appropriate legislation.

.**NATIONALITY:**
American
WHEN:
1866–1868
WHERE:
Washington, DC, USA
YOU SHOULD KNOW:
It was the equal protection clause of the Fourteenth Amendment that Justice Earl Warren used as the basis for his ruling against segregation in schools in Kansas in 1954.

Government of the USA

The Fourteenth Amendment to the Constitution was the most important piece of legislation after the Civil War – it ensured a ban on slavery in the USA. The Thirteenth Amendment had abolished slavery, and the Civil Rights Act of 1866 had extended citizenship to everyone born in the USA. The Fourteenth Amendment was deemed necessary to avoid a conflict between

Günter Schabowski born 1929

On November 9, 1989 – in the wake of large numbers of East German citizens escaping to the west via Czechslovakia and Hungary – Günter Schabowski, spokesman for the Socialist Unity Party of Germany and Politburo member, was handed a piece of paper at a news conference. Not realizing that the note was for his information only, he read it out, announcing the cessation of travel restrictions on East German citizens. When asked when the change would come into effect, he replied 'Immediately, I suppose', and confirmed that the crossings into West Berlin were included in the changes. The news was meant to be embargoed until the following morning, to give the border guards time to make changes. But within an hour or so of the premature announcement, crowds had descended on the area around the wall and their numbers led the guards to decide to let them through, leading to the iconic images of the end of the Cold War – hundreds of people sitting on the wall, celebrating.

NATIONALITY:
German
WHEN:
1989
WHERE:
Berlin, Germany
YOU SHOULD KNOW:
During its twenty-nine years of existence, there were roughly 5,000 successful escapes across the Berlin Wall. Between 136 and 220 people are estimated to have been killed.

❛Private travel into foreign countries can be requested without conditions (passports or family connections). Permission will be granted instantly. Permanent relocations can be done through all border checkpoints between the GDR into the FRG or Berlin (West).❜

A German youth sits astride the Berlin Wall after the fall of communism in East Germany.

Imre Nagy 1896–1958

Former Hungarian Prime Minister, Imre Nagy, was tried for treason in a secret trial in 1958. During his first term in office he had instituted liberal reforms not approved by Moscow and was deposed on Soviet orders, but reinstated after the 1956 Hungarian Uprising. The Soviet army invaded the country, crushing the uprising and imprisoned Nagy. Two years later, at his trial, he refused to plead for clemency and was reported as simply uttering the sentence below. He was found guilty and executed. He was eventually rehabilitated, but not until the demise of the Communist regime in Hungary in 1989.

May God spare me the punishment of being rehabilitated by my own murderers.

NATIONALITY:
Hungarian
WHEN:
1958
WHERE:
Budapest, Hungary

Frederick Douglass 1818–1895

NATIONALITY:
American
WHEN:
1852
WHERE:
Rochester, New York, USA
YOU SHOULD KNOW:
Douglass is sometimes called the Lion of Anacostia.

Formerly a slave in Maryland, from where he had escaped in 1838, Frederick Douglass became a prominent anti-slavery lecturer in Massachusetts and other northern states. He also supported women's rights. When his autobiography Narrative of the Life of Frederick Douglass, an American Slave *was published in 1845, there were fears that his former owner might try to recover his property so Douglass spent the next two years in Europe, where slavery was already illegal. During this time, his followers bought his freedom and he was able to return to the USA. When asked to give a speech commemorating Independence Day in Rochester, New York on July 5, 1852, he responded with a moving speech, part of which is extracted below. After an extensive tribute to the ideals of liberty, on which the US had been founded, he turned to the present day and discussed the complete lack of meaning to his community of the celebrations.*

My business, if I have any here to-day, is with the present. The accepted time with God and his cause is the ever-living now. We have to do with the past only as we can make it useful to the present and to the future. To all inspiring motives, to noble deeds which can be gained from the past, we are welcome. But now is the time, the

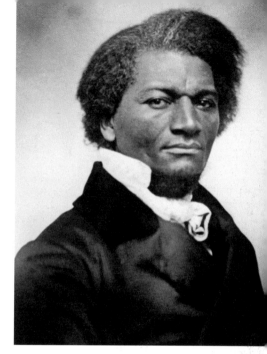

important time. Your fathers have lived, died, and have done their work, and have done much of it well. You live and must die, and you must do your work. You have no right to enjoy a child's share in the labor of your fathers, unless your children are to be blest by your labors. You have no right to wear out and waste the hard-earned fame of your fathers to cover your indolence. Sydney Smith tells us that men seldom eulogize the wisdom and virtues of their fathers, but to excuse some folly or wickedness of their own. This truth is not a doubtful one. There are illustrations of it near and remote, ancient and modern. It was fashionable, hundreds of years ago, for the children of Jacob to boast, we have Abraham to our father, when they had long lost Abraham's faith and spirit. That people contented themselves under the shadow of Abraham's great name, while they repudiated the deeds which made his name great.

The evil that men do, lives after them,

The good is oft' interred with their bones.

What have I, or those I represent, to do with your national independence?

Fellow-citizens, pardon me, allow me to ask, why am I called upon to speak here to-day? What have I, or those I represent, to do with your national independence? Are the great principles of political freedom and of natural justice, embodied in that Declaration of Independence, extended to us? And am I, therefore, called upon to bring our humble offering to the national altar, and to confess the benefits and express devout gratitude for the blessings resulting from your independence to us? . . .

But, such is not the state of the case. I say it with a sad sense of the disparity between us. I am not included within the pale of this glorious anniversary! Your high independence only reveals the immeasurable distance between us. The blessings in which you, this day, rejoice, are not enjoyed in common. The rich inheritance of justice, liberty, prosperity and independence, bequeathed by your fathers, is shared by you, not by me. The sunlight that brought life and healing to you, has brought stripes and death to me. This Fourth [of] July is yours, not mine. You may rejoice, I must mourn. To drag a man in fetters into the grand illuminated temple of liberty, and call upon him to join you in joyous anthems, were inhuman mockery and sacrilegious irony. Do you mean, citizens, to mock me, by asking me to speak to-day? If so, there is a parallel to your conduct. And let me warn you that it is dangerous to copy the example of a nation whose crimes, lowering up to heaven, were thrown down by the breath of the Almighty, burying that nation in irrecoverable ruin! I can to-day take up the plaintive lament of a peeled and woe-smitten people! . . .

Fellow citizens; above your national, tumultuous joy, I hear the mournful wail of millions whose chains, heavy and grievous yesterday, are, to-day, rendered more intolerable by the jubilee shouts that reach them. If I do forget, if I do not faithfully remember those bleeding children of sorrow this day, may my right hand forget her cunning, and may my tongue cleave to the roof of my mouth! To forget them, to pass lightly over their wrongs, and to chime in with the popular theme, would be treason most scandalous and shocking, and would make me a reproach before God and the world . . . America is false to the past, false to the present, and solemnly binds herself to be false to the future. Standing with God and the crushed and bleeding slave on this occasion, I will, in the name of humanity which is outraged, in the name of liberty which is fettered, in the name of the Constitution and the Bible, which are disregarded and trampled upon, dare to call in question and to denounce, with all the emphasis I can command, everything that serves to perpetuate slavery – the great sin and shame of America! I will not equivocate; I will not excuse; I will use the severest language I can command; and yet not one word shall escape me that any man, whose judgement is not blinded by prejudice, or who is not at heart a slaveholder, shall not confess to be right and just . . .

What, to the American slave, is your fourth of July? I answer: a day that reveals to him, more than all other days in the year, the gross injustice and cruelty to which he is the constant victim. To him, your celebration is a sham; your boasted liberty, an unholy license; your national greatness, swelling vanity; your sounds of rejoicing are empty and heartless; your denunciations of tyrants, brass fronted impudence; your shouts of liberty and equality, hollow mockery; your prayers and hymns, your sermons and thanksgivings, with all your religious parade, and solemnity, are, to him, mere bombast, fraud, deception, impiety, and hypocrisy – a thin veil to cover up crimes which would disgrace a nation of savages. There is not a nation on the earth guilty of practices more shocking and bloody than are the people of these United States, at this very hour.

Go where you may, search where you will, roam through all the monarchies and despotisms of the old world, travel through South America, search out every abuse, and when you have found the last, lay your facts by the side of the everyday practices of this nation, and you will say with me that, for revolting barbarity and shameless hypocrisy, America reigns without a rival.

Charles Stewart Parnell

1846–1891

NATIONALITY:
Irish
WHEN:
1880
WHERE:
Cincinnati, Ohio, USA
YOU SHOULD KNOW:
In 1882 Parnell was suspected of supporting the Phoenix Park murders of Lord Frederick Cavendish and Thomas Henry Burke, but this was disproved.

Parnell addressing a meeting.

On a lecture tour of the USA in 1880, Parnell spoke at great length about the need for a return to the system under which Dublin had its own parliament, which had been abolished in 1801. He was President of the National Land League and won crucial support from the Fenian movement in the US. An eloquent and passionate speaker, he did much to further the cause of Irish emanciption, but his career was dogged by accusations of sympathy for groups that advocated violent resistance. He was imprisoned between 1881 and 1882 for encouraging tenant farmers to conduct a campaign of mass-agitation, and was freed on condition that he discouraged such action. He supported Gladstone's 1886 Home Rule Bill, which failed, and his career was ruined when he was cited as co-respondent in a divorce case.

When we have undermined English misgovernment we have paved the way for Ireland to take her place amongst the nations of the earth. And let us not forget that that is the ultimate goal at which all we Irishmen aim. None of us whether we be in America or in Ireland, or wherever we may be, will be satisfied until we have destroyed the last link which keeps Ireland bound to England.

Clayton returning after two years' exile in the Bahamas.

Rev. Adam Clayton Powell Jr

1908–1972

Speaking to a church group in Chicago in 1965, the Rev. Adam Clayton Powell outlined the ideas behind what would become the black power movement. He had been Congressman for New York since 1944 and in his years as Chairman of the Education and Labor Committee, from 1961, had been responsible for the introduction of a wide range of anti-discriminatory legislation, including banning the practice prevalent in some southern states of charging African American voters a fee. He also helped pass legislation that ended segregation in schools and the military, and outlawed lynching.

Victories were many in the Negro Revolt, but still no radical change occurred in America's social structure. Why? Because a revolt is only an interlude of social protest, a temporary resistance of authority.

To sustain these victories, to radically alter the face of white America and complete its cycle, the Negro Revolt was our Sunday of protests, so that Black Revolution must become our week of production.

This can only be done by Black people seeking power – audacious power. Audacious power belongs to that race which believes in itself, in its heroes, in its success, in its deeds and, yes, even its misdeeds.

NATIONALITY:
American
WHEN:
1965
WHERE:
Chicago, Illinois, USA
YOU SHOULD KNOW:
This is the first time the term black power appears to have been used in public. It gained more common currency the following year.

John F. Kennedy 1917–1963

On the day that he had sent the Alabama National Guard to the University of Alabama to ensure that two African American students would gain access to their classes in the face of opposition from Governor Wallace, President Kennedy addressed the nation from the Oval Office. Having initially been wary of alienating southern Democrats, in the summer of 1963 he decided to start enacting legislation enshrining the right to an equal education, to a vote, to equal treatment in shops and restaurants, etc. The scale of the task was made all too apparent the following day when a Mississippi civil rights activist, Medgar Evers, was murdered by the Ku Klux Klan.

This afternoon, following a series of threats and defiant statements, the presence of Alabama National Guardsmen was required on the University of Alabama to carry out the final and unequivocal order of

NATIONALITY:
American
WHEN:
1963
WHERE:
Washington DC, USA
YOU SHOULD KNOW:
The legislation President Kennedy outlined in June 1963 was put through by President Johnson in 1964 and 1965.

President Kennedy addressing the nation.

the United States District Court of the Northern District of Alabama. That order called for the admission of two clearly qualified young Alabama residents who happened to have been born Negro . . .

I hope that every American, regardless of where he lives, will stop and examine his conscience about this and other related incidents. This nation was founded by men of many nations and backgrounds. It was founded on the principle that all men are created equal, and that the rights of every man are diminished when the rights of one man are threatened . . .

Today we are committed to a worldwide struggle to promote and protect the rights of all who wish to be free. And when Americans are sent to Vietnam or West Berlin, we do not ask for whites only. It ought to be possible, therefore, for American students of any color to attend any public institution they select without having to be backed up by troops.

It ought to be possible for American consumers of any color to receive equal service in places of public accommodation, such as hotels and restaurants and theaters and retail stores, without being forced to resort to demonstrations in the street, and it ought to be possible for American citizens of any color to register to vote in a free election without interference or fear of reprisal.

It ought to be possible, in short, for every American to enjoy the privileges of being American without regard to his race or his color. In short, every American ought to have the right to be treated as he would wish to be treated, as one would wish his children to be treated. But this is not the case . . .

We preach freedom around the world, and we mean it, and we cherish our freedom here at home, but are we to say to the world, and much more importantly, to each other, that this is the land of the free except for the Negroes; that we have no second-class citizens except Negroes; that we have no class or caste system, no ghettoes, no master race except with respect to Negroes?

Now the time has come for this nation to fulfill its promise. The events in Birmingham and elsewhere have so increased the cries for equality that no city or State or legislative body can prudently choose to ignore them . . .

Next week I shall ask the Congress of the United States to act, to make a commitment it has not fully made in this century to the proposition that race has no place in American life or law. The Federal judiciary has upheld that proposition in the conduct of its affairs, including the employment of Federal personnel, the use of Federal facilities, and the sale of federally financed housing . . .

I am . . . asking the Congress to enact legislation giving all Americans the right to be served in facilities which are open to the public – hotels, restaurants, theaters, retail stores, and similar establishments.

This seems to me to be an elementary right. Its denial is an arbitrary indignity that no American in 1963 should have to endure, but many do.

I have recently met with scores of business leaders urging them to take voluntary action to end this discrimination and I have been encouraged by their response, and in the last two weeks over 75 cities have seen progress made in desegregating these kinds of facilities. But many are unwilling to act alone, and for this reason, nationwide legislation is needed if we are to move this problem from the streets to the courts.

I am also asking the Congress to authorize the Federal Government to participate more fully in lawsuits designed to end segregation in public education. We have succeeded in persuading many districts to desegregate voluntarily. Dozens have admitted Negroes without violence. Today a Negro is attending a State-supported institution in every one of our 50 States, but the pace is very slow.

My fellow Americans, this is a problem which faces us all – in every city of the north as well as the south. Today there are Negroes unemployed, two or three times as many compared to whites, inadequate in education, moving into the large cities, unable to find work, young people particularly out of work without hope, denied equal rights, denied the opportunity to eat at a restaurant or lunch counter or go to a movie theater, denied the right to a decent education, denied almost today the right to attend a State university even though qualified . . .

We cannot say to ten per cent of the population that you can't have that right; that your children cannot have the chance to develop whatever talents they have; that the only way that they are going to get their rights is to go into the streets and demonstrate. I think we owe them and we owe ourselves a better country than that.

Therefore, I am asking for your help in making it easier for us to move ahead and to provide the kind of equality of treatment which we would want ourselves; to give a chance for every child to be educated to the limit of his talents . . .

We have a right to expect that the Negro community will be responsible, will uphold the law, but they have a right to expect that the law will be fair, that the Constitution will be color blind, as Justice Harlan said at the turn of the century.

This is what we are talking about and this is a matter which concerns this country and what it stands for, and in meeting it I ask the support of all our citizens. 🟦

Martin Luther King Jr 1929–1968

By 1964, the Civil Rights Movement was beginning to fracture into a number of different groups with different ideologies and methodologies. Dr King continued to advocate non-violence, in the face of criticism from other activists. In 1963, protests that he led in Birmingham, Alabama, were broken up by police with water cannon and dogs and he was imprisoned. In 1964, aged 35, Dr King was the youngest person ever to receive the Nobel Peace Prize.

NATIONALITY:
American
WHEN:
1964
WHERE:
Oslo, Norway
YOU SHOULD KNOW:
Martin Luther King Day was instituted as a public holiday by President Bush in 1986.

. . . I accept this award today with an abiding faith in America and an audacious faith in the future of mankind. I refuse to accept despair as the final response to the ambiguities of history. I refuse to accept the idea that the 'isness' of man's present nature makes him morally incapable of reaching up for the eternal 'oughtness' that forever confronts him . . .

I still believe that we shall overcome. 🟦

Crown Prince Harald and King Olav of Norway congratulate Dr King.

Lyndon B. Johnson 1908–1973

NATIONALITY:
American
WHEN:
1965
WHERE:
Washington DC, USA
YOU SHOULD KNOW:
Poll taxes for voters were ruled
illegal in 1966.

Early in 1965, civil rights leaders chose Selma, Alabama, to break down the discriminatory voter-registration practices prevalent across the state that meant that while 99 per cent of white adults were registered to vote, hardly any African Americans were. In January, hundreds of voters lined up to register, but many were disqualified for minor mistakes on registration forms or on other spurious grounds. Various marches also took place, although an ordinance was introduced to prevent unlicensed marches. The event known as Bloody Sunday occurred on March 7 1965 at the beginning of a planned march to Montgomery, when marchers refused to turn back from the Edmund Pettus Bridge and were whipped, beaten and repelled with tear gas.

. . . I speak tonight for the dignity of man and the destiny of democracy.

I urge every member of both parties, Americans of all religions and of all colors, from every section of this country, to join me in that cause.

At times history and fate meet at a single time in a single place to shape a turning point in man's unending search for freedom. So it was at Lexington and Concord. So it was a century ago at Appomattox. So it was last week in Selma, Alabama.

There, long-suffering men and women peacefully protested the denial of their rights as Americans. Many were brutally assaulted. One good man, a man of God, was killed.

There is no cause for pride in what has happened in Selma. There is no cause for self-satisfaction in the long denial of equal rights of millions of Americans. But there is cause for hope and for faith in our democracy in what is happening here tonight . . .

Many of the issues of civil rights are very complex and most difficult. But about this there can and should be no argument. Every American citizen must have an equal right to vote. There is no reason which can excuse the denial of that right. There is no duty which weighs more heavily on us than the duty we have to ensure that right.

Yet the harsh fact is that in many places in this country men and women are kept from voting simply because they are Negroes . . .

In such a case our duty must be clear to all of us. The Constitution says that no person shall be kept from voting because of his race or his color. We have all sworn an oath before God to support and to defend that Constitution. We must now act in obedience to that oath.

Wednesday I will send to Congress a law designed to eliminate illegal barriers to the right to vote.

I have had prepared a more comprehensive analysis of the legislation which I had intended to transmit to the clerk tomorrow but which I will submit to the clerks tonight. But I want to really discuss with you now briefly the main proposals of this legislation.

This bill will strike down restrictions to voting in all elections – Federal, State, and local – which have been used to deny Negroes the right to vote.

This bill will establish a simple, uniform standard which cannot be used, however ingenious the effort, to flout our Constitution.

It will provide for citizens to be registered by officials of the United States Government if the State officials refuse to register them.

It will eliminate tedious, unnecessary lawsuits which delay the right to vote.

Finally, this legislation will ensure that properly registered individuals are not prohibited from voting . . .

To those who seek to avoid action by their National Government in their own communities; who want to and who seek to maintain purely local control over elections, the answer is simple:

Open your polling places to all your people.

Allow men and women to register and vote whatever the color of their skin.

Extend the rights of citizenship to every citizen of this land.

There is no constitutional issue here. The command of the Constitution is plain.

There is no moral issue. It is wrong – deadly wrong – to deny any of your fellow Americans the right to vote in this country.

There is no issue of States rights or national rights. There is only the struggle for human rights.

I have not the slightest doubt what will be your answer . . .

. . . there must be no delay, no hesitation and no compromise with our purpose.

We cannot, we must not, refuse to protect the right of every American to vote in every election that he may desire to participate in. And we ought not and we cannot and we must not wait another eight months before we get a bill. We have already waited a hundred years and more, and the time for waiting is gone . . .

Their cause must be our cause too. Because it is not just Negroes, but really it is all of us, who must overcome the crippling legacy of bigotry and injustice.

And we shall overcome . . .

But a century has passed, more than a hundred years, since the Negro was freed. And he is not fully free tonight.

It was more than a hundred years ago that Abraham Lincoln, a great President of another party, signed the Emancipation Proclamation, but emancipation is a proclamation and not a fact.

A century has passed, more than a hundred years, since equality was promised. And yet the Negro is not equal.

A century has passed since the day of promise. And the promise is unkept.

The time of justice has now come. I tell you that I believe sincerely that no force can hold it back. It is right in the eyes of man and God that it should come. And when it does, I think that day will brighten the lives of every American . . .

So I say to all of you here, and to all in the Nation tonight, that those who appeal to you to hold on to the past do so at the cost of denying you your future.

This great, rich, restless country can offer opportunity and education and hope to all: black and white, north and nouth, sharecropper and city dweller. These are the enemies: poverty, ignorance, disease. They are the enemies and not our fellow man, not our neighbor. And these enemies too, poverty, disease and ignorance, we shall overcome . . .

The real hero of this struggle is the American Negro. His actions and protests, his courage to risk safety and even to risk his life, have awakened the conscience of this Nation. His demonstrations have been designed to call attention to injustice, designed to provoke change, designed to stir reform . . .

For at the real heart of battle for equality is a deep-seated belief in the democratic process. Equality depends not on the force of arms or tear gas but upon the force of moral right . . .

There have been many pressures upon your President and there will be others as the days come and go. But I pledge you tonight that we intend to fight this battle where it should be fought: in the courts, and in the Congress, and in the hearts of men . . .

In Selma tonight, as in every . . . as in every city, we are working for just and peaceful settlement. We must all remember that after this speech I am making tonight, after the police and the FBI and the Marshals have all gone, and after you have promptly passed this bill, the people of Selma and the other cities of the nation must still live and work together. And when the attention of the nation has gone elsewhere they must try to heal the wounds and to build a new community . . .

I want to be the President who educated young children to the wonders of their world. I want to be the President who helped to feed the hungry and to prepare them to be taxpayers instead of taxeaters.

I want to be the President who helped the poor to find their own way and who protected the right of every citizen to vote in every election.

I want to be the President who helped to end hatred among his fellow men and who promoted love among the people of all races and all regions and all parties.

I want to be the President who helped to end war among the brothers of this earth.

. . . I came here tonight – not as President Roosevelt came down one time . . . to veto a bonus bill, not as President Truman came down one time to urge the passage of a railroad bill – but I came down here to ask you to share this task with me and to share it with the people that we both work for. I want this to be the Congress, Republicans and Democrats alike, which did all these things for all these people . . .

Above the pyramid on the great seal of the United States it says – in Latin – God has favored our undertaking.

God will not favor everything that we do. It is rather our duty to divine His will. But I cannot help believing that He truly understands and that He really favors the undertaking that we begin here tonight.

Voltaire François-Marie Arouet

1694–1778

NATIONALITY:
French
WHEN:
Unknown
WHERE:
Unknown
YOU SHOULD KNOW:
Voltaire was well known in enlightenment circles for his defence of civil liberties, including freedom of religion.

This remark is widely attributed to Voltaire, but its source has not been proved. The first definite appearance is in a 1906 book about Voltaire by Evelyn Beatrice Hall (writing under the pseudonym Stephen G. Tallentyre), in which she sums up his ideas on free thought. A similar idea appears in a remark by Voltaire about the author of de l'Esprit (On the Mind), Claude Adrien Helvétius, who claimed in his book that humans are no different morally from animals. Voltaire commented, 'This man was worth more than all his enemies together, but I never approved of either the errors in his book nor the trivial truths that he produces with such emphasis. I took his part openly when absurd men condemned him for the truths.'

I disapprove of what you say, but I will defend to the death your right to say it.

Wendell Phillips 1811–1884

Wendell Phillips was one of the most eloquent pro-abolitionists of the mid-nineteenth century. In 1852, he gave several addresses to the Massachusetts Anti-Slavery Society. One of his key ideas was 'Eternal vigilance is the price of liberty.'. This phrase was also in President Jackson's farewell speech in 1837, about Congress trying to introduce legislation in breach of the Constitution. Here, Phillips is urging people not to fall into the habit of letting the government's actions pass without notice as any government not continually scrutinized is in danger of turning from democracy to despotism.

NATIONALITY:
American
WHEN:
1852
WHERE:
Boston, Massachusetts, USA
YOU SHOULD KNOW:
The Garrison referred to in the speech is William Lloyd Garrison, co-founder of the American Anti-Slavery Society, who was nearly lynched by pro-slavers in Boston in 1836. Gorsuch refers to Edward Gorsuch who was shot at Christiana the year before, attempting to recover four slaves who had run away.

All hail, Public Opinion! To be sure, it is a dangerous thing under which to live. It rules to-day in the desire to obey all kinds of laws, and takes your life. It rules again in the love of liberty, and rescues Shadrach from Boston Court House. It rules tomorrow in the manhood of him who loads the musket to shoot down . . . the man hunter; Gorsuch. It rules in Syracuse, and the Slave escapes to Canada. It is our interest to educate this people in humanity, and in deep reverence for the rights of the lowest and humblest individual that makes up our numbers. Each man here, in fact, holds his property and his life dependent on the constant presence of an Agitation like this of Anti-Slavery. Eternal vigilance is the price of liberty – power is ever stealing from the many to the few. The manna of popular liberty must be gathered each day, or it is rotten. The living sap of to-day outgrows the dead rind of yesterday. The hand entrusted with power becomes, either from human depravity or *esprit du corps*, the necessary enemy of the people. Only by continual oversight can the democrat in office be prevented from hardening into a despot: only by unintermitted Agitation can a people be kept sufficiently awake to principle not to let liberty be smothered in material prosperity . . . Never look, therefore, for an age when the people can be quiet and safe. At such times Despotism, like a shrouding mist, steals over the mirror of Freedom . . .

Some men suppose that, in order to achieve the people's governing themselves, it is only necessary that the Rights of Man be printed, and that every citizen have a copy. As the Epicureans, two thousand years ago, imagined God a being who arranged this marvellous machinery, set it going, and then sunk to sleep. Republics exist only on the tenure of being constantly agitated . . . Never, to our latest posterity, can we afford to do without prophets, like Garrison, to stir up the monotony of wealth, and re-awake the people to the great ideas that are constantly fading out of their minds, to trouble the waters that there may be health in their flow. Every government is always growing corrupt . . . The Republic that sinks to sleep, trusting to constitutions and machinery, to politicians and statesmen for the safety of its liberties, never will have any . . . We must live like our Puritan fathers, who always went to Church, and sat down to dinner, when the Indians were in their neighborhood, with their musket-lock on the one side and a drawn sword on the other . . .

Women's Social and Political Union

This mock creed for the Women's Social and Political Union (WSPU) is a parody on the Christian creed. By the time this was written, Christabel Pankhurst had already served two terms in prison for disorder. After a third term she went to live in Paris. On her return to Britain in 1913, she was re-arrested under the Prisoners (Temporary Discharge for Ill Health) Act 1913. This had replaced the earlier practice of force-feeding hunger strikers with a regime under which they would be allowed to starve themselves, then be released on grounds of ill health when too weak to protest, and then re-arrested for the most trivial of transgressions. Christabel served three months of her three-year sentence before being released.

The Pankhursts: Christobel, Emmeline and Sylvia leading a suffragette parade through London in 1911.

WHEN:
1908
WHERE:
London, England
YOU SHOULD KNOW:
The 1913 Act was more commonly called the 'Cat and Mouse Act'.

I believe in Emmeline Pankhurst – Founder of the Women's Social and Political Union. And in Christabel Pankhurst, her eldest daughter, Our Lady, who was inspired by the Passion for Liberty – born to be a leader of women. Suffered under Liberal Government, was arrested, tried and sentenced. She descended into prison; the seventh day she returned again to the world. She was entertained to breakfast, and sat on the right hand of her mother, our glorious Leader, from thence she went forth to judge both the government and the Antis. I believe in Votes for Women on the same terms as men, the policy of the Women's Social and Political Union, the equality of the sexes, Representation for Taxation, the necessity for militant tactics, and Freedom Everlasting. Amen!

Elizabeth Cady Stanton

1815–1902

NATIONALITY:
American
WHEN:
1868
WHERE:
Washington, DC, USA
YOU SHOULD KNOW:
The amendment to the US Constitution that finally allowed women of voting age to do so – the Nineteenth Amendment – was initially proposed in 1919 and then ratified in 1920.

After the Civil War, when African American men got the right to vote subject to meeting the same qualifications as their white counterparts, one group of people was left out: the feminists who had argued that they should be given suffrage at the same time as ex-slaves. Chief among these were Stanton and Susan B. Anthony. The former had long been an abolitionist but narrowed her focus down to the issue of women's rights: her thinking from this point often comes across as racist. The address from which the extract is taken – The Destructive Male – was given to the 1868 Women's Suffrage Convention.

' . . . The Republican party today congratulates itself on having carried the Fifteenth Amendment of the Constitution, thus securing manhood suffrage and establishing an aristocracy of sex on this continent. As several bills to secure Woman's Suffrage in the District and the Territories have been already presented in both houses of Congress, and as by Mr Julian's bill, the question of so amending the Constitution as to extend suffrage to all the women of the country has been presented to the nation for consideration, it is not only the right but the duty of every thoughtful woman to express her opinion on a Sixteenth Amendment . . .

I urge a speedy adoption of a Sixteenth Amendment for the following reasons:

1. A government, based on the principle of caste and class, can not stand. The aristocratic idea, in any form, is opposed to the genius of our free institutions, to our own declaration of rights, and to the civilization of the age. All artificial distinctions, whether of family, blood, wealth, color, or sex, are equally oppressive to the subject classes, and equally destructive to national life and prosperity. Governments based on every form of aristocracy, on every degree and variety of inequality, have been tried in despotisms, monarchies, and republics, and all alike have perished. In the panorama of the past behold the mighty nations that have risen, one by one, but to fall. Behold their temples, thrones, and pyramids, their gorgeous palaces and stately monuments now crumbled all to dust . . . Why, in this hour of reconstruction, with the experience of generations before us, make another experiment in the same direction? If serfdom, peasantry, and slavery have shattered kingdoms, deluged continents with blood, scattered republics like dust before the wind, and rent our own Union asunder, what kind of a government, think you, American statesmen, you can build, with the mothers of the race crouching at your feet, while iron-heeled peasants, serfs, and exalted by your hands, tread our inalienable rights into the dust? While all men, everywhere, are rejoicing in new-found liberties, shall woman alone. be denied the rights, privileges, and immunities of citizenship? . . .

2. I urge a Sixteenth Amendment, because 'manhood suffrage', or a man's government, is civil, religious, and social disorganization. The male element is a destructive force, stern, selfish, aggrandizing, loving war, violence, conquest, acquisition, breeding in the material and moral world alike discord, disorder, disease, and death. See what a record of blood and cruelty the pages of history reveal! Through what slavery, slaughter, and sacrifice, through what inquisitions and imprisonments, pains and persecutions, black codes and gloomy creeds, the soul of humanity has struggled for the centuries, while mercy has veiled her face and all hearts have been dead alike to love and hope! The male element has held high carnival thus far, it has fairly run riot from the beginning, overpowering the feminine element everywhere, crushing out all the diviner qualities in human nature . . .

3. I urge a Sixteenth Amendment because, when 'manhood suffrage' is established from Maine to California, woman has reached the lowest depths of political degradation. So long as there is a disfranchised class in this country, and that class its women, a man's government is worse than a white man's government with suffrage limited by property and educational qualifications, because in proportion as you multiply the rulers, the condition of the politically ostracised is more hopeless and degraded . . . If American women find it hard to bear the oppressions of their own Saxon fathers, the best orders of manhood, what may they not be called to endure when all the lower orders of foreigners now crowding our shores legislate for them and their daughters . . .

4. I would press a Sixteenth Amendment, because the history of American statesmanship does not inspire me with confidence in man's capacity to govern the nation alone, with justice and mercy. I have come to this conclusion, not only from my own observation, but from what our rulers say of themselves. Honorable Senators have risen in their places again and again, and told the people of the wastefulness and corruption of the present administration. '

Governor Charles E. Hughes

Charles Evans Hughes 1862–1948

NATIONALITY:
American
WHEN:
1907
WHERE:
New York, USA
YOU SHOULD KNOW:
He beat William Randolph Hearst to become Governor of New York in 1906 after winning a high-profile case that exposed graft in the state utility industry.

Governor of New York and later Secretary of State, Republican presidential candidate and Supreme Court Justice Charles Evans Hughes was one of the foremost legislators in the first part of the twentieth century. As Governor, he assisted in the passage of the Moreland Act, which allowed greater leeway in firing corrupt employees. As a lawyer, he believed in both the Constitution and the idea that the right people to rule its implementation were members of the judiciary, not politicians. In later years, as Chief Justice, he would yet again be on the side of the judiciary as he sought to prevent President Franklin D. Roosevelt packing the Supreme Court with his own political sympathizers.

We are under a Constitution, but the Constitution is what the judges say it is, and the judiciary is the safeguard of our liberty and of our property under the Constitution.

Elizabeth Cady Stanton

1815–1902

Even into her late 70s, Elizabeth Cady Stanton was still pleading the cause of votes for women. In 1892, she addressed the Committee of the Judiciary of Congress for the last time, advocating not only women's suffrage but a more widespread recognition of the rights of women to education and the wrongs of how they were treated in society. She was now head of the National American Woman Suffrage Association, an organization created when the National Woman Suffrage Association merged with the conservative American Woman Suffrage Association.

NATIONALITY:
American
WHEN:
1892
WHERE:
Washington, DC, USA
YOU SHOULD KNOW:
Her views on divorce and the way that women are treated in the Bible and church meant that she was always unpopular with more conservative feminists.

'The point I wish plainly to bring before you on this occasion is the individuality of each human soul; our Protestant idea, the right of individual conscience and judgment – our republican idea, individual citizenship. In discussing the rights of woman, we are to consider, first, what belongs to her as an individual, in a world of her own, the arbiter of her own destiny, an imaginary Robinson Crusoe with her Woman Friday on a solitary island. Her rights under such circumstances are to use all her faculties for her own safety and happiness.

. . . The education that will fit her to discharge the duties in the largest sphere of human usefulness will best fit her for whatever special work she may be compelled to do . . .

To appreciate the importance of fitting every human soul for independent action, think for a moment of the immeasurable solitude of self. We come into the world alone, unlike all who have gone before us; we leave it alone under circumstances peculiar to ourselves. No mortal ever has been, no mortal over will be like the soul just launched on the sea of life. There can never again be just such environments as make up the infancy, youth and manhood of this one. Nature never repeats herself, and the possibilities of one human soul will never be found in another. No one has ever found two blades of ribbon grass alike, and no one will never find two human beings alike. Seeing, then, what must be the infinite diversity in human, character, we can in a measure appreciate the loss to a nation when any large class of the people is uneducated and unrepresented in the government. We ask for the complete development of every individual, first, for his own benefit and happiness. In fitting out an army we give each soldier his own knapsack, arms, powder, his blanket, cup, knife, fork and spoon. We provide alike for all their individual necessities, then each man bears his own burden . . .

In talking of education how shallow the argument that each class must be educated for the special work it proposed to do, and all those faculties not needed in this special walk must lie dormant and utterly wither for want of use, when, perhaps, these will be the very faculties needed in life's greatest emergies. Some say, Where is the use of drilling them in the languages, the sciences, in law, medicine, theology? As wives, mothers, housekeepers, cooks, they need a different curriculum from boys who are to fill all positions. The chief cooks in our great hotels and ocean steamers are men. In large cities men run the bakies; they make our bread, cake and pies. They manage the laundries; they are now considered our best milliners and dressmakers. Because some men fill these departments of usefulness, shall we regulate the curriculum in Harvard and Yale to their present necessities? If not why this talk in our best colleges of a curriculum for girls who are crowding into the trades and professions; teachers in all our public schools rapidly filling many lucrative and honorable positions in life? . . .

Is it, then, consistent to hold the developed woman of this day within the same narrow political limits as the dame with the spinning wheel and knitting needle occupied in the past? No! no! Machinery has taken the labors of woman as well as man on its tireless shoulders; the loom and the spinning wheel are but dreams of the past; the pen, the brush, the easel, the chisel, have taken their places, while the hopes and ambitions of women are essentially changed . . .

And yet, there is a solitude, which each and every one of us has always carried with him, more inaccessible than the ice-cold mountains, more profound than the midnight sea; the solitude of self. Our inner being . . . no eye nor touch of man or angel has ever pierced. It is more hidden than the caves of the gnome . . . the hidden chamber of eleusinian mystery, for to it only omniscience is permitted to enter.

Such is individual life. Who, I ask you, can take, dare take, on himself the rights, the duties, the responsibilities of another human soul? 〞

Dick Cheney born 1941

NATIONALITY:
American
WHEN:
2003
WHERE:
On Meet the Press with Tim Russert
YOU SHOULD KNOW:
Mr Cheney was Secretary of State for Defense during both Operation Desert Storm and the 1989 invasion of Panama.

Widely thought of as one of the most influential Vice Presidents in US history, Dick Cheney had been at the heart of power previously as an assistant to President Ford, as well as his Chief of Staff, and as Secretary of State for Defense to President George H.W. Bush. He is seen by many as the prime mover behind the decision to invade Iraq in 2003 and behind the policies regarding the treatment of detainees in Guantanamo Bay. The following is a response to a question from Tim Russert, the long-standing host of NBC's Meet the Press on about whether the Iraqi people welcomed the invasion. Six months earlier, on the same programme he had claimed that the majority of Iraqis would welcome the Americans as liberators.

❛ Well, I think we have by most Iraqis. I think the majority of Iraqis are thankful for the fact that the United States is there, that we came and we took down the Saddam Hussein government. And I think if you go in vast areas of the country, the Shia in the south, which are about 60 per cent of the population, 20-plus per cent in the north, in the Kurdish areas, and in some of the Sunni areas, you'll find that, for the most part, a majority of Iraqis support what we did. 〞

Black students riot in Soweto.

Desmond Tutu

born 1931

When the then Bishop of Johannesburg, Desmond Tutu – later Anglican Archbishop of Cape Town – gave the warning below to South African Prime Minister Johannes Vorster, he was talking about general unrest among the black majority in the country, but what triggered the Soweto Uprising three weeks later was a ruling that certain lessons in black schools had to be taught in Afrikaans, a language the black majority associated with the apartheid regime and oppression. Thousands of schoolchildren walked out of their schools and in the ensuing chaos 23 people were killed. According to the highest estimates as many as 600 people died in the following days.

‘ Unless something drastic is done very soon, then bloodshed and violence are going to happen . . . A people made desperate by despair and injustice and oppressions will use desperate means. ’

NATIONALITY:
South African
WHEN:
1976
WHERE:
Johannesburg, South Africa
YOU SHOULD KNOW:
National Youth Day is now celebrated on the anniversary of the uprising – June 16.

US Supreme Court

The case of Jane Roe (a pseudonym) v Wade led to a landmark judgment (the summary of which is below) in which the right to abortion before the foetus becomes viable (and the right to an abortion after that date if the mother's health is at risk) was ruled legal, with certain restrictions during the second trimester. The argument of the legal team representing Roe was based upon the Due Process Clause of the Fourteenth Amendment to the US Constitution. The judgment was not unanimous: two of the justices sitting on the panel – Byron R. White and William H. Rehnquist – dissented.

‘ 1. A state criminal abortion statute of the current Texas type, that excepts from criminality only a lifesaving procedure on behalf of the mother, without regard to pregnancy stage and without recognition of the other interests involved, is violative of the Due Process Clause of

NATIONALITY:
American
WHEN:
1973
WHERE:
Washington, DC, USA
YOU SHOULD KNOW:
Roe v Wade remains one of the most controversial pieces of legislation in American history.

Jane Roe was later revealed to be Norma McCorvey; seen here on the left with her attorney Gloria Allred.

the Fourteenth Amendment.

(a) For the stage prior to approximately the end of the first trimester, the abortion decision and its effectuation must be left to the medical judgment of the pregnant woman's attending physician.

(b) For the stage subsequent to approximately the end of the first trimester, the State, in promoting its interest in the health of the mother, may, if it chooses, regulate the abortion procedure in ways that are reasonably related to maternal health.

(c) For the stage subsequent to viability, the State in promoting its interest in the potentiality of human life may, if it chooses, regulate, and even proscribe, abortion except where it is necessary, in appropriate medical judgment, for the preservation of the life or health of the mother. 2. The State may define the term 'physician', as it has been employed in the preceding paragraphs of this Part XI of this opinion, to mean only a physician currently licensed by the State, and may proscribe any abortion by a person who is not a physician as so defined.

In Doe v Bolton, post, p. 179, procedural requirements contained in one of the modern abortion statutes are considered. That opinion and this one, of course, are to be read together.

This holding, we feel, is consistent with the relative weights of the respective interests involved, with the lessons and examples of medical and legal history, with the lenity of the common law, and with the demands of the profound problems of the present day. The decision leaves the State free to place increasing restrictions on abortion as the period of pregnancy lengthens, so long as those restrictions are tailored to the recognized State interests. The decision vindicates the right of the physician to administer medical treatment according to his professional judgment up to the points where important State interests provide compelling justifications for intervention. Up to those points, the abortion decision in all its aspects is inherently, and primarily, a medical decision, and basic responsibility for it must rest with the physician. If an individual practitioner abuses the privilege of exercising proper medical judgment, the usual remedies, judicial and intra-professional, are available.

Our conclusion that Art. 1196 is unconstitutional means, of course, that the Texas abortion statutes, as a unit, must fall. The exception of Art. 1196 cannot be struck down separately, for then the State would be left with a statute proscribing all abortion procedures no matter how medically urgent the case.

Although the District Court granted appellant Roe declaratory relief, it stopped short of issuing an injunction against enforcement of the Texas statutes. The Court has recognized that different considerations enter into a federal court's decision as to declaratory relief, on the one hand, and injunctive relief, on the other. Zwickler v Koota (1967); Dombrowski v Pfister (1965). We are not dealing with a statute that, on its face, appears to abridge free expression, an area of particular concern under Dombrowski and refined in Younger v Harris.

We find it unnecessary to decide whether the District Court erred in withholding injunctive relief, for we assume the Texas prosecutorial authorities will give full credence to this decision that the present criminal abortion statutes of that State are unconstitutional.

The judgment of the District Court as to intervenor Hallford is reversed, and Dr Hallford's complaint in intervention is dismissed. In all other respects, the judgment of the District Court is affirmed. Costs are allowed to the appellee.

It is so ordered.

Abraham Lincoln 1809–1865

In his second State of the Union Address in December 1862, Lincoln referred to the draft Emancipation Proclamation and justified it to a partially hostile Congress: 'In giving freedom to the slave, we assure freedom to the free – honourable alike in what we give and what we preserve. We shall nobly save or meanly lose the last, best hope of earth.' The aim mentioned in the Proclamation of setting up colonies for freed slaves never came to fruition. The move to link the end of slavery with the future of the Union was a key strategy towards the end of the war. Lincoln had written to the New York Tribune in 1862 saying that if he could preserve the Union without ending slavery he would, but that it was not possible. The proclamation read as follows.

NATIONALITY:
American
WHEN:
1863
WHERE:
Washington, DC, USA
YOU SHOULD KNOW:
As the Union Army moved south and more states fell under their control, more slaves were freed, amounting to about three million by the end of the war.

Whereas on the 22nd day of September, AD 1862, a proclamation was issued by the President of the United States, containing, among other things, the following, to wit:

"That on the 1st day of January, AD 1863, all persons held as slaves within any State or designated part of a State the people whereof shall then be in rebellion against the United States shall be then, thenceforward, and forever free; and the executive government of the United States, including the military and naval authority thereof, will recognize and maintain the freedom of such persons and will do no act or acts to repress such persons, or any of them, in any efforts they may make for their actual freedom.

That the executive will on the 1st day of January aforesaid, by proclamation, designate the States and parts of States, if any, in which the people thereof, respectively, shall then be in rebellion against the United States; and the fact that any State or the people thereof shall on that day be in good faith represented in the Congress of the United States by members chosen thereto at elections wherein a majority of the qualified voters of such States shall have participated shall, in the absence of strong countervailing testimony, be deemed conclusive evidence that such State and the people thereof are not then in rebellion against the United States.

Now, therefore, I, Abraham Lincoln, President of the United States, by virtue of the power in me vested as Commander-In-Chief of the Army and Navy of the United States in time of actual armed rebellion against the authority and government of the United States, and as a fit and necessary war measure for suppressing said

One of Abraham Lincoln's greatest acts was the Emancipation Proclamation.

rebellion, do, on this 1st day of January, A.D. 1863, and in accordance with my purpose so to do, publicly proclaimed for the full period of 100 days from the first day above mentioned, order and designate as the States and parts of States wherein the people thereof, respectively, are this day in rebellion against the United States the following, to wit:

Arkansas, Texas, Louisiana (except the parishes of St Bernard, Plaquemines, Jefferson, St John, St Charles, St James, Ascension, Assumption, Terrebone, Lafourche, St Mary, St. Martin, and Orleans, including the city of New Orleans), Mississippi, Alabama, Florida, Georgia, South Carolina, North Carolina, and Virginia (except the 48 counties designated as West Virginia, and also the counties of Berkeley, Accomac, Northhampton, Elizabeth City, York, Princess Anne, and Norfolk, including the cities of Norfolk and Portsmouth), and which excepted parts are for the present left precisely as if this proclamation were not issued.

And by virtue of the power and for the purpose aforesaid, I do order and declare that all persons held as slaves within said designated States and parts of States are, and henceforward shall be, free; and that the Executive Government of the United States, including the military and naval authorities thereof, will recognize and maintain the freedom of said persons.

And I hereby enjoin upon the people so declared to be free to abstain from all violence, unless in necessary self-defence; and I recommend to them that, in all case when allowed, they labor faithfully for reasonable wages.

And I further declare and make known that such persons of suitable condition will be received into the armed service of the United States to garrison forts, positions, stations, and other places, and to man vessels of all sorts in said service.

And upon this act, sincerely believed to be an act of justice, warranted by the Constitution upon military necessity, I invoke the considerate judgment of mankind and the gracious favor of Almighty God.

In witness whereof, I have hereunto set my hand and caused the seal of the United States to be affixed. **｣**

Pat (Daniel Patrick) Moynihan 1927–2003

NATIONALITY:
American
WHEN:
1970
WHERE:
Washington, DC, USA
YOU SHOULD KNOW:
Pat Moynihan had been Assistant Secretary of Labor under Kennedy and Johnson and was later US Ambassador to the UN from 1975–1976 and Senator for New York from 1977–2001.

After the turmoil of the 1960s in the field of civil rights, as Counselor to President Nixon for Urban Affairs, Pat Moynihan advised that matters should be left to lie for some years. He was not actually advocating abandoning poor – predominantly black – areas of cities, but this is how it was interpreted by many. He had instead intended to advise the President that Vice President Agnew's outspoken, highly conservative statements were making an already volatile situation worse. The more general policy would also include encouraging people from less-well off communities to assist themselves, rather than intervening with extra welfare.

❛ The issue of race could benefit from a period of 'benign neglect'. The subject has been too much talked about . . . **｣**

Nelson Mandela born 1918

Nine days after President de Klerk announced the imminent release of Nelson Mandela, he emerged from Victor Verster Prison and was first seen on television cameras walking among a convoy of cars, hand in hand with his then-wife, Winnie. A few hours later, after struggling through heavy traffic, he addressed a rally of his supporters, making it clear that the fight against apartheid was not yet over. Over the following four years of on-and-off negotiations and occasional bouts of violence, this stance paid off and in 1994 he became the first President of South Africa elected under a system in which every adult had an equal say in who governed them.

NATIONALITY:
South African
WHEN:
1990
WHERE:
Cape Town, South Africa
YOU SHOULD KNOW:
The title by which he is known by many in South Africa – Madiba – is an honorary title reserved for elders in his clan.

‘Our struggle has reached a decisive moment. We call on our people to seize this moment, so that the process toward democracy is rapid and uninterrupted.

We have waited too long for our freedom. We can no longer wait. Now is the time to intensify the struggle on all fronts. To relax our efforts now would be a mistake which generations to come will not be able to forgive.

The sight of freedom looming on the horizon should encourage us to redouble our efforts. It is only through disciplined mass action that our victory can be assured.

We call on our white compatriots to join us in the shaping of a new South Africa. The freedom movement is a political home for you, too.

We call on the international community to continue the campaign to isolate the apartheird regime. To lift sanctions now would run the risk of aborting the process toward the complete eradication of apartheid.

Our march toward freedom is irreversible. We must now allow fear to stand in our way.’

Mandela addressing the crowd after his release.

Anwar Sadat 1918–1981
Menachem Begin 1913–1992

NATIONALITY:
Egyptian/Israeli
WHEN:
1978
WHERE:
Washington, DC, USA
YOU SHOULD KNOW:
Camp David is a military camp in Maryland that is used as a retreat by Presidents. It is a secure site and was therefore an ideal place to hold the negotiations.

During September 1978, secret negotiations were carried out between the Israeli and Egyptian leaders and their teams. The negotiations were difficult, with such thorny issues as the Sinai Peninsula and the West Bank to be settled. President Carter spent almost two weeks shuttling back and forth between separate buildings where the two men, who held each other in deep antipathy, were staying. The result of the negotiations was two documents, 'The Framework for Peace in the Middle East' and 'The Framework for the Conclusion of a Peace Treaty between Egypt and Israel'.

'WEST BANK AND GAZA

Egypt, Israel, Jordan and the representatives of the Palestinian people should participate in negotiations on the resolution of the Palestinian problem in all its aspects. To achieve that objective, negotiations relating to the West Bank and Gaza should proceed in three stages:

1. Egypt and Israel agree that, in order to ensure a peaceful and orderly transfer of authority, and taking into account the security concerns of all the parties, there should be transitional arrangements for the West Bank and Gaza for a period not exceeding five years. In order to provide full autonomy to the inhabitants, under these arrangements the Israeli military government and its civilian administration will be withdrawn as soon as a self-governing authority has been freely elected by the inhabitants of these areas to replace the existing military government. To negotiate the details of a transitional arrangement, Jordan will be invited to join the negotiations on the basis of this framework. These new arrangements should give due consideration both to the principle of self-government by the inhabitants of these territories and to the legitimate security concerns of the parties involved.

2. Egypt, Israel, and Jordan will agree on the modalities for establishing elected self-governing authority in the West Bank and Gaza. The delegations of Egypt and Jordan may include Palestinians from the West Bank and Gaza or other Palestinians as mutually agreed. The parties will negotiate an agreement which will define the powers and responsibilities of the self-governing authority to be exercised in the West Bank and Gaza. A withdrawal of Israeli armed forces will take place and there will be a redeployment of the remaining Israeli forces into specified security locations. The agreement will also include arrangements for assuring internal and external security and public order. A strong local police force will be established, which may include Jordanian

Egyptian President Anwar Sadat (left), US President Jimmy Carter (centre) and Israeli Prime Minister Menachem Begin (right) shake hands at the signing of the Camp David Accords.

citizens. In addition, Israeli and Jordanian forces will participate in joint patrols and in the manning of control posts to assure the security of the borders.

3. When the self-governing authority (administrative council) in the West Bank and Gaza is established and inaugurated, the transitional period of five years will begin. As soon as possible, but not later than the third year after the beginning of the transitional period, negotiations will take place to determine the final status of the West Bank and Gaza and its relationship with its neighbors and to conclude a peace treaty between Israel and Jordan by the end of the transitional period. These negotiations will be conducted among Egypt, Israel, Jordan and the elected representatives of the inhabitants of the West Bank and Gaza. Two separate but related committees will be convened, one committee, consisting of representatives of the four parties which will negotiate and agree on the final status of the West Bank and Gaza, and its relationship with its neighbors, and the second committee, consisting of representatives of Israel and representatives of Jordan to be joined by the elected representatives of the inhabitants of the West Bank and Gaza, to negotiate the peace treaty between Israel and Jordan, taking into account the agreement reached in the final status of the West Bank and Gaza. The negotiations shall be based on all the provisions and principles of UN Security Council Resolution 242. The negotiations will resolve, among other matters, the location of the boundaries and the nature of the security arrangements. The solution from the negotiations must also recognize the legitimate right of the Palestinian peoples and their just requirements. In this way, the Palestinians will participate in the determination of their own future through:

1. The negotiations among Egypt, Israel, Jordan and the representatives of the inhabitants of the West Bank and Gaza to agree on the final status of the West Bank and Gaza and other outstanding issues by the end of the transitional period.

2. Submitting their agreements to a vote by the elected representatives of the inhabitants of the West Bank and Gaza.

3. Providing for the elected representatives of the inhabitants of the West Bank and Gaza to decide how they shall govern themselves consistent with the provisions of their agreement.

4. Participating as stated above in the work of the committee negotiating the peace treaty between Israel and Jordan.

5. All necessary measures will be taken and provisions made to assure the security of Israel and its neighbors during the transitional period and beyond. To assist in providing such security, a strong local police force will be constituted by the self-governing authority. It will be composed of inhabitants of the West Bank and Gaza. The police will maintain liaison on internal security matters with the designated Israeli, Jordanian, and Egyptian officers.

6. During the transitional period, representatives of Egypt, Israel, Jordan, and the self-governing authority will constitute a continuing committee to decide by agreement on the modalities of admission of persons displaced from the West Bank and Gaza in 1967, together with necessary measures to prevent disruption and disorder. Other matters of common concern may also be dealt with by this committee.

7. Egypt and Israel will work with each other and with other interested parties to establish agreed procedures for a prompt, just and permanent implementation of the resolution of the refugee problem.

EGYPT–ISRAEL

1. Egypt–Israel undertake not to resort to the threat or the use of force to settle disputes. Any disputes shall be settled by peaceful means in accordance with the provisions of Article 33 of the U.N. Charter.

2. In order to achieve peace between them, the parties agree to negotiate in good faith with a goal of concluding within three months from the signing of the Framework a peace treaty between them while inviting the other parties to the conflict to proceed simultaneously to negotiate and conclude similar peace treaties with a view the achieving a comprehensive peace in the area. The Framework for the Conclusion of a Peace Treaty between Egypt and Israel will govern the peace negotiations between them. The parties will agree on the modalities and the timetable for the implementation of their obligations under the treaty.

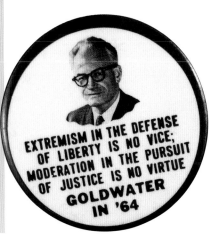

Goldwater campaign button

NATIONALITY:
American
WHEN:
1964
WHERE:
San Francisco, USA
YOU SHOULD KNOW:
He lost the election heavily, winning
only six states.

Barry M. Goldwater 1909–1998

Arizona's Senator Goldwater was a compromise presidential candidate for the Republicans in the 1964 election, as he was too libertarian for the conservatives and too conservative for the moderates. His acceptance speech at the Republican National Convention is chiefly famous for its 'defense of liberty' line. At a time when civil rights activism was gaining momentum this scared the right wing of the party, but he was in fact referring to what he saw as the need to defend the liberty and freedoms of America against Communism. He attacked the Democrat administration for acting weakly over such events as the Bay of Pigs invasion and the Vietnam War.

We here in America can keep the peace only if we remain vigilant and only if we remain strong. Only if we keep our eyes open and keep our guard up can we prevent war. And I want to make this abundantly clear – I don't intend to let peace or freedom be torn from our grasp because of lack of strength or lack of will – and that I promise you Americans . . .

I would remind you that extremism in the defense of liberty is no vice. And let me remind you also that moderation in the pursuit of justice is no virtue . . .

Gloria Steinem born 1934

This slightly surreal saying – a response to the idea that a woman without a man is incomplete and unfulfilled – has long been attributed to feminist icon Steinem, although there is little proof, except that she was editor of Ms *magazine when the t-shirts with the slogan appeared. The magazine first appeared in July 1972, a year after she had co-founded the grassroots National Women's Political Caucus to address the issues of reproductive freedom, the passage of the Equal Rights Amendment and affordable childcare. Other groups she founded or has been deeply involved with include the Women's Action Alliance, the Democratic Socialists of America and Choice USA.*

A woman without a man is like a fish without a bicycle.

NATIONALITY:
American
WHEN:
The motto first appeared in English in
1977, on t-shirts distributed by *Ms*
magazine

WHERE:
Unknown
YOU SHOULD KNOW:
Some people attribute the saying to
an alternative source – Australian
politician Irina Dunn.

Feminist writer Gloria Steinem

Government of the USA

The third of the reconstruction amendments, the Fifteenth Amendment, gives citizens of any race or belief system the right to vote under the same terms as white voters. In practice, this applied only to male voters. The inclusion of the term 'previous condition of servitude' was important because the main point of the amendment was to give former slaves the vote, and there were still those who disputed whether they did or did not qualify as citizens. What was removed from the original draft was the inclusion of the words 'or candidate' as several northern states wanted to keep their own limits on African Americans standing for election.

NATIONALITY:
American
WHEN:
1870
WHERE:
Washington, DC, USA
YOU SHOULD KNOW:
Many southern states continued to impose voter qualification laws, including poll taxes and literacy laws.

'AMENDMENT 15
Section 1. The right of citizens of the United States to vote shall not be denied or abridged by the United States or by any State on account of race, color, or previous condition of servitude.
Section 2. The Congress shall have power to enforce this article by appropriate legislation.'

A lithograph depicting the hoped-for results of the passage of the 15th Amendment.

CELEBRATION AT BALTIMORE ON MAY 19th 1870.

THE FIFTEENTH AMENDMENT AND ITS RESULTS.

Yitzhak Rabin 1922–1995
Yasser Arafat 1929–2004

NATIONALITY:
Israeli/Palestinian
WHEN:
September 13,1993
WHERE:
Washington, DC, USA
YOU SHOULD KNOW:
The series of 14 meetings in Oslo was so secret that not even the American Government knew about it.

Below are the addresses that the Israeli and Palestinian leaders gave at the signing of the Oslo Accords at the White House on September 13, 1993. The secret talks in Norway that had taken place earlier in August and the follow-up talks in Paris that had ironed out the last details over whether the Israeli government would recognize the Palestinian Liberation Organization as the official Palestinian authority and the PLO would recognize the existence of Israel and renounce violence. The Oslo negotiations had originally been between Palestinian representative Ahmed Qurei and Israeli history professor Yair Hirschfeld with others getting involved later. They took place in the Fafo Institute and were paid for by the Norwegian government.

PRIME MINISTER RABIN
President Clinton, the President of the United States; your excellencies; ladies and gentlemen: This signing of the Israeli–Palestinian Declaration of Principles here today, is not so easy – neither for myself, as a soldier in Israel's war, nor for the people of Israel; not to the Jewish people in the diaspora, who are watching us now with great hope mixed with apprehension. It is certainly not easy for the families of the victims of the wars, violence, terror, whose pain will never heal, for the many thousands who defended our lives with their own, and have even sacrificed their lives for our own. For them, this ceremony has come too late. Today, on the eve of an opportunity for peace – and perhaps the end of violence and wars, we remember each and every one of them with everlasting love.

We have come from Jerusalem, the ancient and eternal capital of the Jewish people; we have come from an anguished and grieving land; we have come from a people, a home, a family, that does not know a single year – not a single month – in which mothers have not wept for their sons. We have come to try and put an end to the hostilities so that our children, our children's children, will no longer experience the painful cost of war, violence, and terror. We have come to secure their lives and to ease the soul and the painful memories of

President Clinton brings Israeli Prime Minister Yitzhak Rabin and PLO Chairman Yasser Arafat together after the signing of the peace accord.

the past, to hope and pray for peace.

Let me say to you, the Palestinians: We are destined to live together on the same soil, in the same land – we, the soldiers who have returned from battles stained with blood; we, who have seen our relatives and friends killed before our eyes; we, who have attended their funerals and cannot look into the eyes of their parents; we, who have come from a land where parents bury their children; we, who have fought against you, the Palestinians. We say to you today in a loud and a clear voice: Enough of blood and tears! Enough!

We have no desire for revenge. We harbor no hatred toward you. We, like you, are people. People who want to build a home, to plant a tree, to love, live side by side with you in dignity, in empathy, as human beings, as free men. We are today giving peace a chance and saying to you: Enough! Let us pray that a day will come when we all will say farewell to the arms. We wish to open a new chapter in the sad book of our lives together, a chapter of mutual recognition, of good neighborliness, of mutual respect, of understanding. We hope to embark on a new era in the history of the Middle East.

Today, here in Washington at the White House, we will begin a new reckoning in the relations between peoples, between parents tired of war, between children who will not know war. President of the United States, ladies and gentlemen: Our inner strength, our higher moral values have been derived for thousands of years from the *Book of the Books*, in one of which correlate, we read:

To everything there is a season, and a time to every purpose under Heaven; a time to be born and a time to die; a time to kill and a time to heal; a time to weep and a time to love; a time to love and a time to hate; a time for war and a time of peace.

Ladies and gentlemen: The time for peace has come.

In two days, the Jewish people will celebrate the beginning of a new year. I believe, I hope, I pray that the new year will bring a message of redemption for all peoples; a good year for you, for all of you; a good year for Israelis and Palestinians; a good year for all the peoples of the Middle East; a good year for our American friends, who so want peace and are helping to achieve it. For presidents and members of previous administrations, especially for you President Clinton and your staff, for all citizens of the world: May peace come to all your homes.

In the Jewish tradition, it is customary to conclude our prayers with the word Amen – as you said, Amen. With your permission, men of peace, I shall conclude with words taken from the prayer recited by Jews daily and, whoever of you volunteer, I would ask the entire audience to join me in saying, Amen.

PRESIDENT ARAFAT

In the name of God, the most merciful, the passionate; Mr President; ladies and gentlemen: I would like to express our tremendous appreciation to President Clinton and to his Administration for sponsoring this historic event, which the entire world has been waiting for. Mr President, I am taking this opportunity to assure you and to assure the great American people that we share your values for freedom, justice, and human rights – values for which my people have been striving.

My people are hoping that this agreement, which we are signing today, marks the beginning of the end of a chapter of pain and suffering which has lasted throughout this century. My people are hoping that this agreement, which we are signing today, will usher in an age of peace, coexistence, and equal rights. We are relying on your role, Mr President, and on the role of all the countries which believe that, without peace in the Middle East, peace in the world will not be complete.

Enforcing the agreement and moving toward the final settlement, after two years to implement all aspects of UN Resolutions 242 and 338, in all of their aspects and resolve all the issues of Jerusalem, the settlement, the refugees, and the boundaries will be a Palestinian and an Israeli responsibility. It is also the responsibility of the international community, in its entirety, to help the parties overcome the tremendous difficulties which are still standing in the way of reaching a final and comprehensive settlement.

Now, as we stand on the threshold of this new historic era, let me address the people of Israel and their leaders, with whom we are meeting today for the first time. And let me assure them that the difficult decision we reached together was one that required great and exceptional courage.

We will need more courage and determination to continue the course of building coexistence and peace between us. This is possible. And it will happen with mutual determination and with the effort that will be made with all parties on all the tracks to establish the foundations of a just and comprehensive peace. Our people do not consider that exercising the right to self-determination could violate the rights of their neighbors or infringe on their security. Rather, putting an end to their feelings of being wronged and of having suffered an historic injustice is the strongest guarantee to achieve coexistence and openness between our two peoples and future generations. Our two peoples are awaiting today this historic hope, and they want to give peace a real chance. Such a shift will give us an opportunity to embark upon the process of economic, social, and cultural growth and development, and we hope that international participation in that process will be as extensive as it can be. This shift will also provide an opportunity for all forms of cooperation on a broad scale and in all fields.

I thank you, Mr President. We hope that our meeting will be a new beginning for fruitful and effective relations between the American people and the Palestinian people. I wish to thank the Russian Federation and President Boris Yeltsin. Our thanks also go to Secretary Christopher and Foreign Minister Kozyrev, to the Government of Norway, and to the Foreign Minister of Norway for the positive part they played in bringing about this major achievement.

I extend greetings to all the Arab leaders, our brothers, and to all the world leaders who contributed to this achievement. Ladies and gentlemen, the battle for peace is the most difficult battle of our lives. It deserves our utmost efforts because the land of peace – the land of peace yearns for a just and comprehensive peace. Thank you Mr President, thank you, thank you, thank you.

Pope John Paul II 1920–2005

John Paul II's first visit to his homeland after his election as Pope came in June 1979. On June 4 he visited the Marian Shrine at the Monastery of Jasna Góra at Czestochowa, where the holiest relic is the miracle-working icon of Our Lady of Czestochowa, which legend says was painted by St Luke on a table made by Christ and has saved the country on several occasions. The monastery is the centre of Polish Catholicism, and the national shrine. The Pope described it as the heart of the motherland. In a visit fraught with political difficulties for the country's Communist Government, the Pope reminded the millions of people in the crowds and watching on State television that 1979 was the nine hundredth anniversary of the martyrdom of St Stanislaus, Poland's national saint, who had died standing up against civil authorities for the sake of the truth. The inference was not lost on his audience.

Pope John Paul II blessing the crowd on his return to Poland.

> We Poles grew accustomed to link all the decisive moments of our lives . . . to this special place, this sanctuary. We grew accustomed to come up to Jasna Góra with all our concerns, to tell it all to our Mother, who not only has her portrait here – one of the world's most famous and revered icons – but who also is present here in a mysterious spiritual way.

NATIONALITY:
Polish
WHEN:
1979
WHERE:
Czestochowa, Poland
YOU SHOULD KNOW:
Jasna Góra means Bright Mountain.

Simone de Beauvoir 1908–1986

In this idea, which gained common currency with the publication of Le Deuxième Sexe *(The Second Sex) Simone de Beauvoir reflects her lover Jean-Paul Sartre's existentialist theory that 'existence precedes essence'. In short this means that women are conditioned to be how they are by how they are stereotyped and defined by the dominant members of the hierarchy – that is, men – into being the 'Other', not men and therefore less than complete humans, and that this is a self-perpetuating mechanism. This, she said, also occurred in differences of race, religion and social order but was most obvious in the oppression of women by men.*

> One is not born a woman: one becomes one.

NATIONALITY:
French
WHEN:
1949
WHERE:
Paris, France
YOU SHOULD KNOW:
De Beauvoir and Sartre are buried next to each other in the Montparnasse Cemetery, Paris.

Existentialist writer Simone de Beauvoir

Emmeline Pankhurst 1857–1928

NATIONALITY:
British
WHEN:
February 16, 1912
WHERE:
London, England
YOU SHOULD KNOW:
The following year Emily Davis was trampled by the King's horse at the Epsom Derby after hurling herself beneath its flying hooves.

After her return from a lecture tour in America, Mrs Pankhurst led a new phase in the struggle for votes for women. When she spoke on February 16, 1912 at a dinner for released prisoners who had been jailed for breaking windows in 1911, there was great anger among the membership because a new Reform Bill had been introduced in Parliament that extended the vote to more men, and not women. Two weeks later, in a mass outbreak of stone-throwing, shop and restaurant windows were broken all over central London and Mrs Pankhurst herself threw stones at Number 10 Downing Street. There were also campaigns of destroying works of art and setting fire to churches and homes of the landed rich. The campaign's progress was described thus. Mrs Pankhurst had returned from America; she would lead the next militant action. On February 16th, at a welcome dinner to released prisoners who had been stone throwers the previous November, she declared (Connaught Rooms, Kingsway, 1912):

Emmeline addressing the crowd in Trafalgar Square, London.

'The argument of the broken pane is the most valuable argument in modern politics . . . That we are to-day awaiting the issue of dissensions in the very heart of the Government itself . . . is due to Mrs Pethick Lawrence and her deputation of November 21st.'

Barack Obama born 1961

Barack Obama addressing the Democratic Convention.

On November 4, 2008 after what earlier in the year had seemed like an unlikely victory, Senator Barack Obama won the Presidential election by 52.5 to 42.7 per cent of votes cast. His acceptance speech at Grant Park Stadium late in the evening was watched by some 240,000 people, and millions more all round the world. In it, he thanked all the people who had helped with or donated to the campaign, set out his future plans in broad brush-strokes and referenced Presidents Lincoln and Kennedy, as well as Dr Martin Luther King.

❛ If there is anyone out there who still doubts that America is a place where all things are possible; who still wonders if the dream of our founders is alive in our time; who still questions the power of our democracy, tonight is your answer . . .

. . . Where we are met with cynicism and doubt, and those who tell us that we can't, we will respond with that timeless creed that sums up the spirit of a people: yes, we can. ❜

NATIONALITY:
American
WHEN:
November 4, 2008
WHERE:
Chicago, USA
YOU SHOULD KNOW:
During his election campaign, Obama turned down public financing because of the constraints it would put on his budget.

303

SPORT

Reginald S. Brooks died 1885

On August 29, 1882 English cricketsuffered a humiliating loss – a seven-run defeat at the Oval Cricket Ground in South London by a team from the colony of Australia. The Australian bowler, Fred Spofforth, took 14 of 20 English wickets, fired up after the great English player W. G. Grace had irritated him with a bit of unsporting gamesmanship. When the England team went to Australia the following season, the captain, Ivo Bligh, was presented with a small urn containing ashes by a group of Melbourne housewives, inspired by the following spoof obituary penned by Brookes that appeared in a British paper in September 1882. The Ashes have remained a symbol of the greatest cricketing rivalry.

THE ASHES
In affectionate remembrance of English Cricket Which Died At the Oval on 29th August 1882
Deeply lamented by a large circle of sorrowing friends and acquaintances
R.I.P.
NB: The body will be cremated, and the ashes taken to Australia.

Muhammad Ali

Cassius Marcellus Clay Jr born 1942

Widely hailed as the greatest sportsman ever and much-loved, Ali won his first 31 professional fights and only lost five of the remaining 30. Throughout his career he would predict in which round he would win, getting the first 17 right. He was almost imprisoned and stripped of his titles in the 1960s because of his refusal to be drafted to fight in the Vietnam War. It was against his Muslim beliefs. Since his retirement from boxing he has devoted himself to humanitarian endeavours, supporting poverty relief and education. In 2002 he became a UN Messenger of Peace. In 1999 both the BBC and Sports Illustrated *named him the Sportsman of the Century.*

I am the greatest. Not only do I knock 'em out. I pick the round!

Muhammad Ali

Cassius Marcellus Clay Jr born 1942

Because his height (75 inches/6 ft 3 cm) and reach (almost 80 inches/6 ft 4 cm) made head shots a better option than body shots, Ali developed a unique style of boxing, the 'Ali Shuffle'. He would raise himself on the balls of his feet and then shuffle, appearing to dance, sometimes even throwing his trademark lightning-fast, stinging punches while he was shuffling. It certainly seemed to work for him. Of his 56 wins in 61 professional fights 37 were knockouts, including the famous 'Rumble in the Jungle' of October 30, 1974 against George Foreman in Kinshasa, Zaire. On September 15, 1978 Ali beat Leon Spinks to become WBA World Heavyweight title holder for the fourth time.

> Float like a butterfly.
> Sting like a bee.
> Your hands can't hit
> what your eyes can't see.

NATIONALITY:
American
WHEN:
On several occasions
WHERE:
Wherever possible
YOU SHOULD KNOW:
Will Smith only agreed to play Ali in the 2001 biopic after Ali asked him personally. Apparently, the first thing Ali said to Smith was, 'You ain't pretty enough to play me'.

Ali, then known as Cassius Clay, letting the world know he has beaten Sonny Liston.

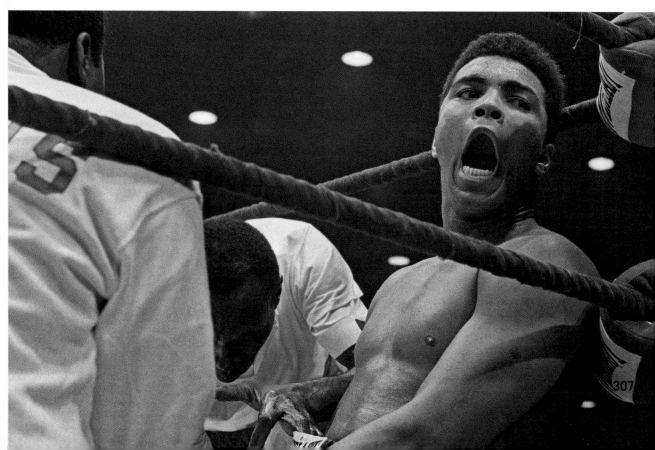

307

Eric Cantona b.1966

NATIONALITY:
French
WHEN:
1995
WHERE:
London
YOU SHOULD KNOW:
Since retirement from competitive football Eric Cantona has had acting roles and managed the French beach football team.

Eric Cantona was one of the most charismatic footballers of the 1980s and 1990s, but could also at times lose his temper. After being sent off for shirt-pulling during a Manchester United game against Crystal Palace, he lashed out at a Crystal Palace fan, who had taunted and threatened him. He received a two-week sentence, commuted to community service. The fan served one day of a seven-day sentence. At a later press conference, the player uttered the following comment about the British paparazzi, who for months had trailed him continually, before getting up and walking out.

When the seagulls follow a trawler, it is because they think sardines will be thrown into the sea. Thank you very much.

Sir Edmund Hillary 1910–2008

NATIONALITY:
New Zealander
WHEN:
May 29, 1953
WHERE:
Below the summit of Mount Everest
YOU SHOULD KNOW:
Afterwards, Hillary set up the Himalayan Trust to help the Sherpa people by building schools and hospitals.

After Edmund Hillary and Tenzing Norgay had reached the summit of Mount Everest early on May 29, 1953 Hillary took several photographs to prove that they had done so and after 15 minutes they rapidly made their way back down. Part-way back down to camp, they were greeted by Hillary's life-long friend George Lowe with some hot soup. Lowe responded to Hillary's comment, below, with a cheery 'Thought you must have.'. This assault on Everest, led by British mountaineer John Hunt, was Hillary's second to the mountain and Tenzing Norgay's seventh. The names of the two successful climbers, Hunt and those who helped them near the summit are well known, but the expedition actually had a complement of 400.

Edmund Hillary and Sherpa Tenzing Norgay on their return from Everest.

Well, we knocked the bastard off!

Eric Cantona b.1966

NATIONALITY:
French
WHEN:
1995
WHERE:
London
YOU SHOULD KNOW:
Since retirement from competitive football Eric Cantona has had acting roles and managed the French beach football team.

Eric Cantona was one of the most charismatic footballers of the 1980s and 1990s, but could also at times lose his temper. After being sent off for shirt-pulling during a Manchester United game against Crystal Palace, he lashed out at a Crystal Palace fan, who had taunted and threatened him. He received a two-week sentence, commuted to community service. The fan served one day of a seven-day sentence. At a later press conference, the player uttered the following comment about the British paparazzi, who for months had trailed him continually, before getting up and walking out.

When the seagulls follow a trawler, it is because they think sardines will be thrown into the sea. Thank you very much.

Sir Edmund Hillary 1910–2008

NATIONALITY:
New Zealander
WHEN:
May 29, 1953
WHERE:
Below the summit of Mount Everest
YOU SHOULD KNOW:
Afterwards, Hillary set up the Himalayan Trust to help the Sherpa people by building schools and hospitals.

After Edmund Hillary and Tenzing Norgay had reached the summit of Mount Everest early on May 29, 1953 Hillary took several photographs to prove that they had done so and after 15 minutes they rapidly made their way back down. Part-way back down to camp, they were greeted by Hillary's life-long friend George Lowe with some hot soup. Lowe responded to Hillary's comment, below, with a cheery 'Thought you must have.'. This assault on Everest, led by British mountaineer John Hunt, was Hillary's second to the mountain and Tenzing Norgay's seventh. The names of the two successful climbers, Hunt and those who helped them near the summit are well known, but the expedition actually had a complement of 400.

Edmund Hillary and Sherpa Tenzing Norgay on their return from Everest.

Well, we knocked the bastard off!

George Leigh Mallory 1886–1924

While on a lecture tour in the USA, Mallory is said to have given this reply to a New York Times *reporter called Benson, who asked why he wanted to climb Everest. It probably qualifies as one of the most banal questions on record, however some people think that Benson may have made up both the question and answer. Whether he did or not, the retort has come to be used as an answer to any impossible question about why one would want to do anything, particularly if it is something challenging. More specifically, it forms a core idea in John F. Kennedy's speech explaining why America was going to send astronauts to the Moon.*

' Because it's there. '

NATIONALITY:
British
WHEN:
1923
WHERE:
New York City, USA
YOU SHOULD KNOW:
The bodies of Mallory and Andrew Irvine were found near the summit of Everest in 1999, but it is still unclear whether they reached the summit or not.

James Morris born 1926

There was worldwide excitement about the attempt on Everest by John Hunt's expedition in 1953. The Times *had exclusive rights and sent the 26-year-old James Morris to report back from the expedition. Word arrived at Camp IV of the successful attempt on the summit by Hillary and Tenzing, so Morris sent a coded message to Namche Bazar by runner. He had devised the code to prevent other newspapers breaking the news before* The Times *could print his scoop, knowing that at least two other papers had reporters in Kathmandu to try to intercept his despatches. 'Snow condition bad' meant 'summit of Everest reached'; 'abandoned advance' meant 'Hillary' and 'awaiting improvement' meant 'Tenzing'. The false message (below) leaked out and was reported in several papers, but* The Times *managed to hold on to its scoop and published it on June 2, Queen Elizabeth II's coronation day.*

' Copy of a Message received from COL HUNT, NAMCHE BAZAR on June 1, 1953.

Snow condition bad hence expedition abandoned advance base on 29th and awaiting improvement being all well. '

NATIONALITY:
British
WHEN:
June 1, 1953
WHERE:
Camp IV, Mount Everest, via the Indian Government telegraph office at Namche Bazar, Nepal
YOU SHOULD KNOW:
James Morris became the travel writer Jan Morris.

Jesse (James Cleveland) Owens 1913–80

Jesse Owens sprinting away from the starting line at the 1936 Olympic Games in Berlin.

The 1936 Olympic Games were held in Berlin and Adolf Hitler intended to make use of them to underline the superiority of the white Aryan race. Jesse Owens' four gold medals scotched that idea and Hitler apparently refused to shake his hand. But, as Owens himself later said, he wasn't invited to shake the hand of the American President either. It had taken a great deal of determination for him to get to the Olympics, holding down three jobs at a time to pay his tuition fees at Ohio State University while putting in as many hours of training as he could. He finally got to the White House to shake the President's hand in 1976.

NATIONALITY:
American
WHEN:
Several times
WHERE:
Various places
YOU SHOULD KNOW:
Jesse acquired his name when a teacher misunderstood his whispered 'J.C.' when she asked his name.

We all have dreams. But in order to make dreams come into reality, it takes an awful lot of determination, dedication, self-discipline, and effort.

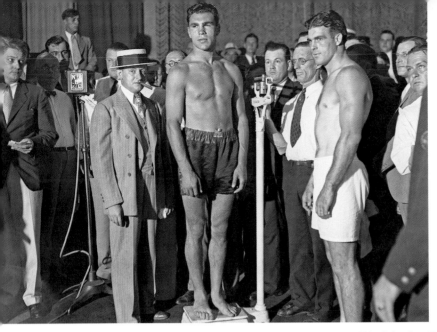

Wearing a straw hat and chewing on a cigar, Jacobs looks on as Max Schmeling weighs in for his bout against Willie Stribling.

Joe Jacobs

1896–1940

In 1929 the German heavyweight champion boxer, Max Schmeling, visited America and acquired a new manager, fast-talking New Yorker Joe Jacobs, who promoted him tirelessly. In 1930 Schmeling got his first attempt at the recently vacated World Heavyweight title, against Jack Sharkey. He won the bout after Sharkey was disqualified for landing a low blow. Two years later a rematch was arranged, and Sharkey won a highly disputed points victory that people who witnessed the fight said was the worst judging decision ever made. Of course Jacobs was absolutely furious and grabbed a microphone, yelling angrily in his heavy East-European accent. The pair remained associates for most of the rest of the decade, even in the face of the German Minister of Sport instructing Schmeling to spend more time in Europe and drop his association with Jacobs and other Jewish associates, an order that the champion had the courage to ignore.

NATIONALITY:
American
WHEN:
1932
WHERE:
New York City, USA
YOU SHOULD KNOW:
Max Schmeling's bouts with Joe Louis in the 1930s are regarded as some of the best boxing matches ever staged.

' We was robbed! '

Grantland Rice 1880–1954

NATIONALITY:
American
WHEN:
1930
WHERE:
In *Alumnus Football*
YOU SHOULD KNOW:
The 1920s and 1930s, when Rice's writing powers were at their height, were known as the 'Golden Age' of Sports.

Grantland Rice was one of the greatest sports journalists of the twentieth century, writing articles that covered events in the careers of such stars as Babe Ruth, Jack Dempsey and Knute Rockne. This is the last verse of his poem about the struggles for success and glory – both on and off the field – of an aspiring American football player called Bill Jones.

' Keep coming back, and though the world may romp across your spine,
Let every game's end find you still upon the battling line;
For when the One Great Scorer comes to mark against your name,
He writes – not that you won or lost – but how you played the Game. '

312

Joe Louis 1914–1981

Joe Louis was undisputed World Heavyweight Champion from 1937 to 1949. He fought light heavyweight Billy Conn three times during this period. In the first fight, in May 1941, Conn held a points lead for 12 rounds but made a rash attempt at a knockout in the thirteenth round and was knocked out himself. After both men had served in the US armed forces during World War II, a rematch was staged at the Yankee Stadium on June 19, 1946. Someone suggested to Louis that Conn's lighter weight and frame would enable him to 'hit and run'. The Champion's response, below, proved prophetic when he knocked the challenger out in the eighth round. Their last fight was an exhibition match in Chicago in December 1948.

NATIONALITY:
American
WHEN:
1946
WHERE:
New York City, USA
YOU SHOULD KNOW:
This was the first televised World Heavyweight Championship fight.

' He can run, but he can't hide. '

The awesome Joe Louis, aka 'The Brown Bomber'

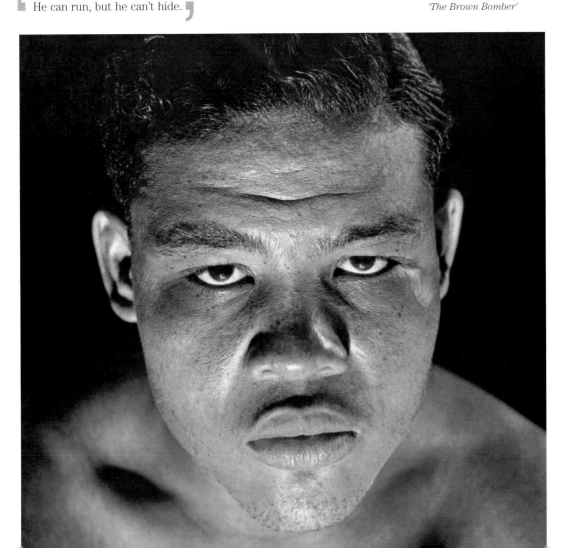

Althea Gibson 1927–2003

NATIONALITY:
American
WHEN:
1957
WHERE:
Unknown
YOU SHOULD KNOW:
After retiring from professional tennis, Ms Gibson took up professional golf.

Althea Gibson, who came from a troubled background in New York's Harlem, was the first African American to win a tennis Grand Slam tournament: in fact, she won five – the French Open in 1956 and Wimbledon and the US Open in both 1957 and 1958. It was only in 1950, aged 23, that she was allowed to compete in the US Open as until then lawn tennis was still basically a segregated sport, until an article by Alice Marble in the American Lawn Tennis Magazine *pointed out that to exclude her on grounds of colour was sanctimonious hypocrisy.*

Althea Gibson was not only a great sportswoman, but also a pathfinder for African Americans.

'It seemed a long way from 143rd Street. Shaking hands with the Queen of England was a long way from being forced to sit in the colored section of the bus going into downtown Wilmington, North Carolina. Dancing with the Duke of Devonshire was a long way from not being allowed to bowl in Jefferson City, Missouri, because the white customers complained about it. '

George 'Gipper' Gipp 1895–1920

George Gipp was one of college football's early heroes.

Even nearly 90 years after his early death, George Gipp is still remembered as one of the most talented college football players ever, but it is perhaps as the author of coach Knute Rockne's 'Win one for the Gipper' exhortation that he is best known. Rockne used the phrase for years after Gipp's early death at the age of 25, saying that the words had been said to him by the star footballer on his deathbed. The – possibly apocryphal – story is that Gipp had been used to getting back to his college after hours and letting himself in through a stage door to the campus theatre. On one occasion it was locked and, rather than try to get in by another way, he stayed out in the cold. He contracted a streptococcal infection and died within a few days.

I've got to go, Rock. It's all right. I'm not afraid. Some time, Rock, when the team is up against it, when things are wrong and the breaks are beating the boys, ask them to go in there with all they've got and win just one for the Gipper. I don't know where I'll be then, Rock. But I'll know about it, and I'll be happy.

NATIONALITY:
American
WHEN:
December 14, 1920
WHERE:
South Bend, Indiana, USA
YOU SHOULD KNOW:
Two weeks before his death, Gipp was elected Notre Dame's first-ever All-American.

315

The Olympic stadium in Athens, 1896

Pierre de Frédy, Baron de Coubertin 1863–1937

NATIONALITY:
French
WHEN:
1908
WHERE:
London, England
YOU SHOULD KNOW:
The 1908 Olympics lasted from April 27 to October 31.

The first Modern Olympiad was held in Athens in 1896. The fourth Olympiad was held in London, and the perceived over-excitement of some competitors led the Bishop of Philadelphia to remind them in a sermon that taking part was more important than winning. The founder of the games, de Courbertin, repeated the idea in the words below at an official banquet on July 24 as a philsophy of life. The idea first came into widespread prominence in 1932 when it appeared at the opening ceremony of the Los Angeles Games as 'The important thing in the Olympic Games is not winning but taking part. The essential thing is not conquering but fighting well.' Its current form was established at the 1936 Berlin Olympics, when a recording of de Courbertin was played, saying 'L'important aux Jeux Olympiques n'est pas d'y gagner mais d'y prendre part car l'essentiel dans la vie ce n'est pas tout de conquérir que de bien lutter.' 'The important thing in the Olympic Games is not winning but taking part for the essential thing in life is not conquering but fighting well.'

' The important thing in life is not the triumph but the struggle, the essential thing is not to have conquered but to have fought well. '

316

Bob Fitzsimmons 1863–1917

Fitzsimmons started his professional boxing career in Australia in the early 1880s, having boxed as an amateur in New Zealand. He had immense punching power as a result of years spent helping in his blacksmith brother's forge as a youngster. He moved to America in 1890 in search of better money, becoming World Middleweight Champion in 1891 and World Heavyweight Champion in 1897. The response, below, to a question about how he felt about fighting a man larger than himself was not prophetic. On June 9, 1899 the taller and heavier James Jeffries knocked him out in the eleventh round.

NATIONALITY:
British
WHEN:
1899
WHERE:
New York City, USA
YOU SHOULD KNOW:
Of his 51 wins out of 82 fights,
44 were knockouts.

' The bigger they are, the further they have to fall. '

Bob Fitzsimmons was nearer to the old-style bare-knuckle fighters than today's boxers.

317

Jack (William Harrison) Dempsey 1895–1983

NATIONALITY:
American
WHEN:
September 23, 1926
WHERE:
Philadelphia, USA
YOU SHOULD KNOW:
His nickname was 'The Manassa Mauler'.

Dempsey comes in low on Tunney in their classic encounter.

Jack Dempsey, World Heavyweight Boxing Champion from 1919 to 1926, was a very popular fighter, particularly because of his aggressive punching style. This was very obvious on July 4, 1919 when he beat then-champion Jess Willard, breaking one cheekbone, several ribs and his jaw, damaging his hearing, knocking out teeth and flooring him several times.

After four title defences in four years, Dempsey did not defend again until September 1926, when he lost on points to Gene Tunney, who was quick at dodging and then letting fly a volley of punches, whereas Dempsey was slowing down and his punches were no longer quite so powerful. Dempsey's wife Estelle Taylor phoned him at his hotel to find out what had happened, and he simply responded as follows.

Honey, I just forgot to duck.

Tommie Smith

born 1944

After winning gold and bronze medals in the 200-metre sprint at the summer Olympiad on October 17, 1968 African-American athletes Tommie Smith and John Carlos raised their fists in the 'Black Power' salute during the playing of the American national anthem. The silver medallist, Australian Peter Norman, wore an Olympic Project for Human Rights badge to show his support for them and also because he disapproved of his own country's 'White Australia' policy. Smith and Carlos were immediately suspended from the US team, stripped of their medals and banned from the Olympic Village. Norman was not disciplined at the Olympics, although he was later reprimanded by the Australian Olympics Authority. Smith explained the reasons for the action of the two athletes at a press conference that same evening.

If I win I am an American, not a black American. But if I did something bad then they would say 'a Negro'. We are black and we are proud of being black.

Black America will understand what we did tonight.

NATIONALITY:
American
WHEN:
October 17, 1968
WHERE:
Mexico City, Mexico
YOU SHOULD KNOW:
The two athletes raised opposite hands because John Carlos had left his gloves in the Olympic Village so they shared Tommie Smith's.

POLITICS & INTERNATIONAL AFFAIRS

Thomas Jefferson 1743–1826

NATIONALITY:
American
WHEN:
1776
WHERE:
Philadelphia, USA
YOU SHOULD KNOW:
Independence Day is on July 4 to commemorate the date on which the original declaration was signed.

One year into the American Revolutionary War, delegates to the Second Continental Congress voted on July 2, 1776 to declare independence from the British Crown. Two days later, the text – designed to explain to the population why Congress had voted for independence – was finalized then printed and distributed. In the preceding decade, the British Crown had increased taxation on its colonies to pay off its vast national debt and laws had been passed by the British Parliament to increase its control over the colonies, leading some to question whether it had violated the latter's rights and therefore its own right to rule.

When, in the course of human events, it becomes necessary for one people to dissolve the political bonds which have connected them with another, and to assume among the powers of the earth, the separate and equal station to which the laws of nature and of nature's God entitle them, a decent respect to the opinions of mankind requires that they should declare the causes which impel them to the separation.

We hold these truths to be self-evident, that all men are created equal, that they are endowed by their Creator with certain unalienable rights, that among these are life, liberty and the pursuit of happiness. That to secure these rights, governments are instituted among men, deriving their just powers from the consent of the governed. That whenever any form of government becomes destructive to these ends, it is the right of the people to alter or to abolish it, and to institute new government, laying its foundation on such principles and organizing its powers in such form, as to them shall seem most likely to effect their safety and happiness. Prudence, indeed, will dictate that governments long established should not be changed for light and transient causes; and accordingly all experience hath shown that mankind are more disposed to suffer, while evils are sufferable, than to right themselves by abolishing the forms to which they are accustomed. But when a long train of abuses and usurpations, pursuing invariably the same object evinces a design to reduce them under absolute despotism, it is their right, it is their duty, to throw off such government, and to provide new guards for their future security. Such has been the patient sufferance of these colonies; and such is now the necessity which constrains them to alter their former systems of government. The history of the present King of Great Britain is a history of repeated injuries and usurpations, all having in direct object the establishment of an absolute tyranny over these states. To prove this, let facts be submitted to a candid world.

He has refused his assent to laws, the most wholesome and necessary for the public good.

The original Declaration of Independence

He has forbidden his governors to pass laws of immediate and pressing importance, unless suspended in their operation till his assent should be obtained; and when so suspended, he has utterly neglected to attend to them.

He has refused to pass other laws for the accommodation of large districts of people, unless those people would relinquish the right of representation in the legislature, a right inestimable to them and formidable to tyrants only.

He has called together legislative bodies at places unusual, uncomfortable, and distant from the depository of their public records, for the sole purpose of fatiguing them into compliance with his measures.

He has dissolved representative houses repeatedly, for opposing with manly firmness his invasions on the rights of the people.

He has refused for a long time, after such dissolutions, to cause others to be elected; whereby the legislative powers, incapable of annihilation, have returned to the people at large for their exercise; the state remaining in the meantime exposed to all the dangers of invasion from without, and convulsions within.

He has endeavored to prevent the population of these states; for that purpose obstructing the laws for naturalization of foreigners; refusing to pass others to encourage their migration hither, and raising the conditions of new appropriations of lands.

He has obstructed the administration of justice, by refusing his assent to laws for establishing judiciary powers.

He has made judges dependent on his will alone, for the tenure of their offices, and the amount and payment of their salaries.

He has erected a multitude of new offices, and sent hither swarms of officers to harass our people, and eat out their substance.

He has kept among us, in times of peace, standing armies without the consent of our legislature.

He has affected to render the military independent of and superior to civil power.

He has combined with others to subject us to a jurisdiction foreign to our constitution, and unacknowledged by our laws; giving his assent to their acts of pretended legislation:

For quartering large bodies of armed troops among us:

For protecting them, by mock trial, from punishment for any murders which they should commit on the inhabitants of these states:

For cutting off our trade with all parts of the world:

For imposing taxes on us without our consent:

For depriving us in many cases, of the benefits of trial by jury:

For transporting us beyond seas to be tried for pretended offenses:

For abolishing the free system of English laws in a neighbouring province, establishing therein an arbitrary government, and enlarging its boundaries so as to render it at once an example and fit instrument for introducing the same absolute rule in these colonies:

For taking away our charters, abolishing our most valuable laws, and altering fundamentally the forms of our governments:

For suspending our own legislatures, and declaring themselves invested with power to legislate for us in all cases whatsoever.

He has abdicated government here, by declaring us out of his protection and waging war against us.

He has plundered our seas, ravaged our coasts, burned our towns, and destroyed the lives of our people.

He is at this time transporting large armies of foreign mercenaries to complete the works of death, desolation and tyranny, already begun with circumstances of cruelty and perfidy scarcely paralleled in the most barbarous ages, and totally unworthy the head of a civilized nation.

He has constrained our fellow citizens taken captive on the high seas to bear arms against their country, to become the executioners of their friends and brethren, or to fall themselves by their hands.

He has excited domestic insurrections amongst us, and has endeavored to bring on the inhabitants of our frontiers, the merciless Indian savages, whose known rule of warfare, is undistinguished destruction of all ages, sexes and conditions.

In every stage of these oppressions we have petitioned for redress in the most humble terms: our repeated petitions have been answered only by repeated injury. A prince, whose character is thus marked by every act which may define a tyrant, is unfit to be the ruler of a free people.

Nor have we been wanting in attention to our British brethren. We have warned them from time to time of attempts by their legislature to extend an unwarrantable jurisdiction over us. We have reminded them of the circumstances of our emigration and settlement here. We have appealed to their native justice and magnanimity, and we have conjured them by the ties of our common kindred to disavow these usurpations, which, would inevitably interrupt our connections and correspondence. They too have been deaf to the voice of justice and of consanguinity. We must, therefore, acquiesce in the necessity, which denounces our separation, and hold them, as we hold the rest of mankind, enemies in war, in peace friends.

We, therefore, the representatives of the United States of America, in General Congress, assembled, appealing to the Supreme Judge of the world for the rectitude of our intentions, do, in the name, and by the authority of the good people of these colonies, solemnly publish and declare, that these united colonies are, and of right ought to be free and independent states; that they are absolved from all allegiance to the British Crown, and that all political connection between them and the state of Great Britain, is and ought to be totally dissolved; and that as free and independent states, they have full power to levy war, conclude peace, contract alliances, establish commerce, and to do all other acts and things which independent states may of right do. And for the support of this declaration, with a firm reliance on the protection of Divine Providence, we mutually pledge to each other our lives, our fortunes and our sacred honour. 🟥

Niccolò Machiavelli 1469–1527

Niccolò Machiavelli was a Florentine philosopher, poet, musician, diplomat and playwright. In 1513, he collected into a work called The Prince *the ideas he had discussed with friends on the necessary behaviour for a ruler. The contents are cynical from start to end, with repeated instructions that it is better for a ruler to be seen to behave well rather than to do so, how to rule through guile and strength and how it is better to rule through fear than love. Whether this work was a satire or reflected his genuine opinion is now unknown, but the author's views have gone down in history as being synonymous with ruthlessness, power politics and deceit.*

NATIONALITY:
Florentine Italian
WHEN:
c. 1513
WHERE:
Florence (now Italy)
YOU SHOULD KNOW:
Machiavelli's patrons were the banking family – and *de facto* leaders of Florence – the Medici dynasty.

❛ . . . Therefore it is unnecessary for a prince to have all the good qualities I have enumerated, but it is very necessary to appear to have them. And I shall dare to say this also, that to have them and always to observe them is injurious, and that to appear to have them is useful; to appear merciful, faithful, humane, religious, upright, and to be so, but with a mind so framed that should you require not to be so, you may be able and know how to change to the opposite.

And you have to understand this, that a prince, especially a new one, cannot observe all those things for which men are esteemed, being often forced, in order to maintain the state, to act contrary to fidelity, friendship, humanity and religion. Therefore it is necessary for him to have a mind ready to turn itself accordingly as the winds and variations of fortune force it, yet, as I have said above, not to diverge from the good if he can avoid doing so, but, if compelled, then to know how to set about it . . .

. . . A prince wishing to keep his state is very often forced to do evil. 🟥

Bert (Thomas Bertram) Lance born 1931

NATIONALITY:
American
WHEN:
1977
WHERE:
He's quoted in the 1977 issue of *The Nation's Business* as saying it.
YOU SHOULD KNOW:
British Prime Minister Margaret Thatcher used the adage to argue against unnecessary Government intervention.

Bert Lance is a businessman and Democrat politician. As President Carter's director of the Office of the Budget and Management, he saw part of his role as saving the government billions of dollars through a policy of non-intervention in departments and systems that were working well enough, as throwing money at them will not increase their efficiency significantly. It has become something of a motto for politicans who believe in pared-down government. Soon after taking on his role in government, Lance was accused of corruption and mismanagement while on the board of Calhoun National Bank. He was forced to resign but was subsequently acquitted.

Bert Lance testifies before a Senate committee.

" If it ain't broke, don't fix it. "

Bertrand Russell 1872–1970

During World War II Joseph Goebbels, one of Hitler's closest associates, coined the term 'Better dead than Red' against the Russian regime, and this was either adopted or reinvented by McCarthyites during the 1950s. As a retort, the British philosopher Bertrand Russell posited that at an extreme level, the opposite was true. This became sloganized as below, and was adopted by the British Campaign for Nuclear Disarmament, whose members argued not that they wanted to be communists but that unilateral disarmament was preferable to nuclear war. Interestingly, it was also used by those against disarmament to ridicule them. President Kennedy criticized both points of view as too extreme.

Better Red than dead.

NATIONALITY:
British
WHEN:
1958
WHERE:
Attributed
YOU SHOULD KNOW:
Russell originally wrote 'If no alternative remains except Communist domination or the extinction of the human race, the former alternative is the lesser of two evils.'

Oliver Cromwell 1599–1658

Oliver Cromwell was de facto *leader of England from the defeat of King Charles I's Royalists in 1653 until his own death in 1658. Even though Parliament had been packed with his own appointees since 1648, he became increasingly frustrated with their inability – or lack of will – to pass the legislation that he wanted: to set up a new Constitution. On April 20, 1653 he attended a session of Parliament but after just a few minutes, started haranguing the members and chased them from the room. After they filed out, he locked the door on them. Nominations for new members were then solicited from the country's congregational churches. Cromwell became Lord Protector in December 1653, which gave him even more power.*

It is not fit that you should sit here any longer! You have been sat too long here for any good you have been doing lately. You shall now give place to better men! . . . You call yourselves a Parliament. You are no Parliament. I say you are no Parliament! Some of you are drunkards, some of you are living in open contempt of God's Commandments, following your own greedy appetites and the Devil's Commandments. Corrupt unjust persons; scandalous to the profession of the Gospel; how can you be a Parliament for God's people? Depart, I say, and let us have done with you. In the name of God, go!

NATIONALITY:
British
WHEN:
April 20, 1653
WHERE:
London, England
YOU SHOULD KNOW:
The original speech does not survive: this is a version put together by the historian Thomas Carlyle two centuries later. Some fragments survive that show that his original language was rather crude.

Senator McCarthy

Joseph McCarthy 1908–1957

During the late 1940s and 1950s, Americans were becoming increasingly worried by the actions of the Soviet Union and by the idea that America's institutions were being infiltrated by people who were either communists or had communist sympathies. Among the chief antagonists was the moderate Republican Wisconsin Senator Joseph McCarthy, who led what now seems more like a witch-hunt than a political campaign. Many of his accusations were outdated, exaggerated or completely unfounded, but the mud stuck and many people's careers were ruined. Ironically, his methods probably increased many people's fears about the activities of the communists needlessly and, as Vermont Senator Ralph Flanders put it in 1954: 'Were the Junior Senator from Wisconsin in the pay of the Communists, he could not have done a better job for them.'

NATIONALITY:
American
WHEN:
February 9, 1950
WHERE:
Wheeling, West Virginia, USA
YOU SHOULD KNOW:
As no recording survives, it is not clear whether the figure the Senator cited was 57 or 205.

' The State Department is infested with communists. I have here in my hand a list of 205 – a list of names that were made known to the Secretary of State as being members of the Communist Party and who nevertheless are still working and shaping policy in the State Department. '

Richard Arens 1913–1969

Richard Arens was a lawyer and a staff member of the The House Committee on Un-American Activities (HUAC), particularly in the later stages of the Hollywood blacklist. The methods used in the investigations – and particularly the hearings – seem now contrary to judicial process but such was the fear of communism that such considerations were swept aside. The Hollywood blacklist – of screenwriters, directors, musicians, actors and others who were not to be employed by the Hollywood studios – eventually numbered more than 300 people, many of whom had no links whatsoever to the Communist Party, were activists for libertarian causes or were simply casualties of the system, who would find it almost impossible to get work until the blacklist began to be dismantled in the early 1960s.

NATIONALITY:
American
WHEN:
Repeatedly in the 1950s
WHERE:
Chiefly Washington, DC, USA
YOU SHOULD KNOW:
This is a variation on J. Parnell Thomas' less lyrical 'Are you now or have you ever been a member of the Communist Party?'

' Are you now or have you ever been a member of a Godless conspiracy controlled by a foreign power? '

Richard Arens holding a photo of Soviet Embassy official Vladmir Mikheev.

Walter Reuther 1907–1970

NATIONALITY:
American
WHEN:
The 1950s
WHERE:
Unknown
YOU SHOULD KNOW:
Reuther was also a prominent
civil-rights activist and was standing
next to Martin Luther King Jr during
his 'I have a dream' speech.

Walter Reuther, one of the most influential men of the twentieth century, started out as a socialist and dabbled with communism before becoming a supporter of the New Deal Coalition and eventually a prominent anti-communist. During World War II, he was instrumental in preventing wildcat strikes that would have harmed munitions production. His union work eventually led to recognition by Ford and General Motors. Despite having contrasted conditions for workers in Russia favourably against those in Detroit, he was vehemently against communism, and when he became leader of the United Automobile Workers instantly purged it of all communist members. The quotation below has come to be known as the 'Duck Test'.

Reuther shown here during his press conference

❝ If it looks like a duck, walks like a duck and quacks like a duck, then it just may be a duck. ❞

Harry S. Truman 1884–1972

Just two years after the US and Soviet governments had worked together to finish off the threat of the Axis Powers, the relationship had broken down. The Russian hold over Eastern Europe was increasing and there were serious worries about communist activities in the USA. Executive Order 9835 – the Loyalty Order – was one of the first weapons used by the government in the fight against the rise of the perceived left-wing threat.

Whereas each employee of the Government of the United States is endowed with a measure of trusteeship over the democratic processes which are the heart and sinew of the United States; and

Whereas it is of vital importance that persons employed in the Federal service be of complete and unswerving loyalty to the United States; and

Whereas, although the loyalty of by far the overwhelming majority of all Government employees is beyond question, the presence within the Government service of any disloyal or subversive person constitutes a threat to our democratic processes; and

Whereas maximum protection must be afforded the United States against infiltration of disloyal persons into the ranks of its employees, and equal protection from unfounded accusations of disloyalty must be afforded the loyal employees of the Government:

Now, therefore, by virtue of the authority vested in me by the Constitution and statutes of the United States, including the Civil Service Act of 1883, as amended, and section 9A of the act approved August 2, 1939, and as President and Chief Executive of the United States, it is hereby, in the interest of the internal management of the Government, ordered as follows:

PART I – INVESTIGATION OF APPLICANTS

1. There shall be a loyalty investigation of every person entering the civilian employment of any department or agency of the executive branch of the Federal Government.

1. Investigations of persons entering the competitive service shall be conducted by the Civil Service Commission, except in such cases as are covered by a special agreement between the Commission and any given department or agency.

2. Investigations of persons other than those entering the competitive service shall be conducted by the employing department or agency. Departments and agencies without investigative organizations shall utilize the investigative facilities of the Civil Service Commission.

1. Investigations of persons entering the competitive service shall be conducted as expeditiously as possible; provided, however, that if any such investigation is not completed within 18 months from the date on which a person enters actual employment, the condition that his

President Truman addressing a joint session of Congress.

NATIONALITY:
American
WHEN:
1947
WHERE:
Washington, DC, USA
YOU SHOULD KNOW:
Some three million public servants were investigated, of whom 300 were dismissed as security risks.

employment is subject to investigation shall expire, except in a case in which the Civil Service Commission has made an initial adjudication of disloyalty and the case continues to be active by reason of an appeal, and it shall then be the responsibility of the employing department or agency to conclude such investigation and make a final determination concerning the loyalty of such person.

2. The investigations of persons entering the employ of the executive branch may be conducted after any such person enters upon actual employment therein, but in any such case the appointment of such person shall be conditioned upon a favorable determination with respect to his loyalty.

3. An investigation shall be made of all applicants at all available pertinent sources of information and shall include reference to:

    1. Federal Bureau of Investigation files.

    2. Civil Service Commission files.

    3. Military and naval intelligence files.

    4. The files of any other appropriate government investigative or intelligence agency.

    5. House Committee on Un-American Activities files.

    6. Local law-enforcement files at the place of residence and employment of the applicant, including municipal, county, and State law-enforcement files.

    7. Schools and colleges attended by applicant.

    8. Former employers of applicant.

    9. References given by applicant.

    10. Any other appropriate source.

4. Whenever derogatory information with respect to loyalty of an applicant is revealed a full investigation shall be conducted. A full field investigation shall also be conducted of those applicants, or of applicants for particular positions, as may be designated by the head of the employing department or agency, such designations to be based on the determination by any such head of the best interests of national security.

PART V—STANDARDS

1. The standard for the refusal of employment or the removal from employment in an executive department or agency on grounds relating to loyalty shall be that, on all the evidence, reasonable grounds exist for belief that the person involved is disloyal to the Government of the United States.

2. Activities and associations of an applicant or employee which may be considered in connection with the determination of disloyalty may include one or more of the following:

1. Sabotage, espionage, or attempts or preparations therefor, or knowingly associating with spies or saboteurs;

2. Treason or sedition or advocacy thereof;

3. Advocacy of revolution or force or violence to alter the constitutional form of government of the United States;

4. Intentional, unauthorized disclosure to any person, under circumstances which may indicate disloyalty to the United States, of documents or information of a confidential or non-public character obtained by the person making the disclosure as a result of his employment by the Government of the United States;

5. Performing or attempting to perform his duties, or otherwise acting, so as to serve the interests of another government in preference to the interests of the United States.

6. Membership in, affiliation with or sympathetic association with any foreign or domestic organization, association, movement, group or combination of persons, designated by the Attorney General as totalitarian, fascist, communist, or subversive, or as having adopted a policy of advocating or approving the commission of acts of force or violence to deny other persons their rights under the Constitution of the United States, or as seeking to alter the form of government of the United States by unconstitutional means. 🟥

Benito Mussolini 1883–1945

This adage, adopted by Mussolini, became one of the most popular Fascist slogans in Italy, epitomizing the Fascist ideal. He had formed the Italian Fascists in 1919, and in its early years the movement gained widespread popularity because it created a vision of an Italy restored to the glories of the Roman Empire and opposed any form of class warfare – something that many in Europe feared as they learned of the horrors of the Russian Revolution. He took control of the Italian Parliament in a coup in 1922 after King Vittorio Emanuele III took the pragmatic decision to support him, given that he had the backing of the army. He went on to create a police state, with a confused political ideology that incorporated aspects of anti-communism, anti-capitalism, anti-liberalism, totalitarianism and nationalism.

NATIONALITY:
Italian
WHEN:
On many occasions from about 1930 onwards
WHERE:
Various places
YOU SHOULD KNOW:
Although chiefly remembered as Italy's war-time leader, Mussolini had been Prime Minister since 1922.

'It is better to have lived one day as a lion than one hundred years as a sheep.'

Mussolini

Tony Blair born 1953

NATIONALITY:
British
WHEN:
1998
WHERE:
Belfast, N. Ireland
YOU SHOULD KNOW:
Blair is the longest-serving Labour
Prime Minister in British history.

After decades of violence and mistrust, negotiations begun years earlier achieved an agreement between the British and Irish governments over the status of Northen Ireland. On April 8, 1998 British Prime Minister Tony Blair arrived to oversee final negotiations. As he headed to the meeting, he spoke about the chances for agreement in what, ironically, has become one of his most-often-replayed soundbites. Lack of progress on the decommissioning of weapons – on both sides – and various other stumbling blocks led to the suspension of the Executive and Authority on several occasions, but it was re-established in 2007.

‘ A day like today is not a day for soundbites, really. We can leave them at home, but I feel the hand of history upon our shoulders. I really do. ’

Benjamin Disraeli 1804–1881

NATIONALITY:
British
WHEN:
1872
WHERE:
Manchester, England
YOU SHOULD KNOW:
No reform of the House of Lords
occurred for more than 100 years
after this debate.

In November 1871, Liberal Sir Charles Dilke had precipitated a discussion about the cost to the British taxpayer of the monarchy, which he thought should be abolished, and this wide-ranging debate continued for several months, extending into the question of the abolition of the House of Lords and other reforms. One of Disraeli's contributions to the discussion was a speech given in Manchester in April the following year. In it Disraeli propounds his views on the Crown and the status of the House of Lords.

‘ I HAVE not come down to Manchester to deliver an essay on the English Constitution; but when the banner of republicanism is unfurled – when the fundamental principles of our institutions are controverted – I think, perhaps, it may not be inconvenient that I should make some few practical remarks upon the character of our Constitution – upon that monarchy limited by the coordinate authority of the estates of the realm, which, under the title of Queen, Lords, and Commons, has contributed so greatly to the prosperity of this country, and with the maintenance of which I believe that prosperity is bound up.

Gentlemen, since the settlement of that Constitution, now nearly two centuries ago, England has never experienced a revolution, though there is no country in which there has been so continuous and such considerable change. How is this? Because the wisdom of your forefathers placed the prize of supreme power without the sphere of human passions. Whatever the struggle of parties, whatever the strife of factions, whatever the excitement and exaltation of the public mind, there has always been something in this country round which all classes and parties could rally, representing the majesty of the law, the administration of justice, and involving, at the same time, the security for every man's rights and the fountain of honour.

Now, gentlemen, it is well clearly to comprehend what is meant by a country not having a revolution for two centuries. It means, for that space, the unbroken exercise and enjoyment of the ingenuity of man. It means for that space the continuous application of the discoveries of science to his comfort and convenience. It means the accumulation of capital, the elevation of labour, the establishment of those admirable factories which cover your district; the unwearied improvement of the cultivation of the land, which has extracted from a somewhat churlish soil harvests more exuberant than those furnished by lands nearer to the sun. It means the continuous order which is the only parent of personal liberty and political right. And you owe all these, gentlemen, to the Throne . . .

. . . Gentlemen, there is yet one other remark that I would make upon our monarchy, tho had it not been for recent circumstances, I should have refrained from doing so. An attack has recently been made upon the Throne on account of the costliness of the institution. Gentlemen, I shall not dwell upon the fact that if the people of England appreciate the monarchy, as I believe they do, it would be painful to them that their royal and representative family should not be maintained with becoming dignity, or fill in the public eye a position inferior to some of the nobles of the land. Nor will I insist upon what is unquestionably the fact, that the revenues of the crown estates, on which our sovereign might live with as much right as the Duke of Bedford, or the Duke of Northumberland, has to his estates, are now paid into the public exchequer. All this, upon the present occasion, I am not going to insist upon. What I now say is this: that there is no sovereignty of any first-rate State which costs so little to the people as the sovereignty of England. I will not compare our civil list with those of European empires, because it is known that in amount they treble and quadruple it; but I will compare it with the cost of sovereignty in a Republic, and that a Republic with which you are intimately acquainted – the Republic of the United States of America . . .

. . . And now, gentlemen, I would say something on the subject of the House of Lords. It is not merely the authority of the Throne that is now disputed, but the character and influence of the House of Lords that are held up by some to public disregard. Gentlemen, I shall not stop for a moment to offer you any proofs of the advantage of a second chamber, and for this reason: That subject has been discussed now for a century, ever since the establishment of the government of the United States, and all great authorities, American, German, French, Italian, have agreed in this, that a representative government is impossible without a second chamber. And it has been, especially of late, maintained by great political writers in all countries, that the repeated failure of what is called the French Republic is mainly to be ascribed to its not having a second chamber . . .

What, gentlemen, is the first quality which is required in a second chamber? Without doubt, independence. What is the best foundation of independence? Without doubt, property. The prime minister of England has only recently told you, and I believe he spoke quite acccurately, that the average income of the members of the House of Lords is £20,000. per annum. Of course there are some who have more, and some who have less; but the influence of a public assembly, so far as property is concerned, depends upon its aggregate property, which, in the present case, is a revenue of £9,000,000 a year. But gentlemen, you must look to the nature of this property. It is visible property, and therefore it is responsible property, which every ratepayer in the room knows to his cost. But, gentlemen, it is not only visible property; it is, generally speaking, territorial property, and one of the elements of territorial property is, that it is representative . . .

Friedrich Engels 1820–1895

NATIONALITY:
German
WHEN:
1883
WHERE:
Highgate Cemetery, London, England
YOU SHOULD KNOW:
Marx's grave is still one of the most visited and famous in Highgate's picturesque cemetery.

Although less famous now than Karl Marx, Engels was instrumental in developing communist theory and was co-author of The Communist Manifesto *(1848). He already had radical leanings as a student which his father, a wealthy manufacturer, disapproved of intensely and he was sent to England to get some work experience. But the horrific working conditions – particularly of women and children – radicalized him even further. He and Marx remained close collaborators for almost 40 years, and he even went back to work at the hated Manchester factory in order to be able to support Marx financially. At Marx's funeral, Engels spoke movingly of his friend's life and work.*

On the 14th of March, at a quarter to three in the afternoon, the greatest living thinker ceased to think. He had been left alone for scarcely two minutes, and when we came back we found him in his armchair, peacefully gone to sleep-but forever.

An immeasurable loss has been sustained both by the militant proletariat of Europe and America, and by historical science, in the death of this man. The gap that has been left by the departure of this mighty spirit will soon enough make itself felt.

Just as Darwin discovered the law of development of organic nature, so Marx discovered the law of development of human history: the simple fact, hitherto concealed by an overgrowth of ideology, that mankind must first of all eat, drink, have shelter and clothing, before it can pursue politics, science, art, religion, etc.; that therefore the production of the immediate material means of subsistence and consequently the degree of economic development attained by a given people or during a given epoch form the foundation upon which the state institutions, the legal conceptions, art, and even the ideas on religion, of the people concerned have been evolved, and in the light of which they must, therefore, be explained, instead of vice versa, as had hitherto been the case.

But that is not all. Marx also discovered the special law of motion governing the present-day capitalist mode of production and the bourgeois society that this mode of production has created. The discovery of surplus value suddenly threw light on the problem, in trying to solve which all previous investigations, of both bourgeois economists and socialist critics, had been groping in the dark.

Two such discoveries would be enough for one lifetime. Happy the man to whom it is granted to make even one such discovery. But in every single field which Marx investigated – and he investigated very many fields, none of them superficially – in every field, even in that of mathematics, he made independent discoveries.

Such was the man of science. But this was not even half the

man. Science was for Marx a historically dynamic, revolutionary force. However great the joy with which he welcomed a new discovery in some theoretical science whose practical application perhaps it was as yet quite impossible to envisage, he experienced quite another kind of joy when the discovery involved immediate revolutionary changes in industry and in historical development in general. For example, he followed closely the development of the discoveries made in the field of electricity and recently those of Marcel Deprez.

For Marx was before all else a revolutionist. His real mission in life was to contribute, in one way or another, to the overthrow of capitalist society and of the state institutions which it had brought into being, to contribute to the liberation of the modern proletariat, which he was the first to make conscious of its own position and its needs, conscious of the conditions of its emancipation. Fighting was his element. And he fought with a passion, a tenacity and a success such as few could rival. His work on the first *Rheinische Zeitung* (1842), the *Paris Vorwärts!* (1844), *Brüsseler Deutsche Zeitung* (1847), the *Neue Rheinische Zeitung* (1848-49), the *New York Tribune* (1852-61), and in addition to these a host of militant pamphlets, work in organisations in Paris, Brussels and London, and finally, crowning all, the formation of the great International Working Men's Association – this was indeed an achievement of which its founder might well have been proud even if he had done nothing else.

And, consequently, Marx was the best-hated and most calumniated man of his time. Governments, both absolutist and republican, deported him from their territories. Bourgeois, whether conservative or ultra-democratic, vied with one another in heaping slanders upon him. All this he brushed aside as though it were cobweb, ignoring it, answering only when extreme necessity compelled him. And he died beloved, revered and mourned by millions of revolutionary fellow-workers – from the mines of Siberia to California, in all parts of Europe and America – and I make bold to say that though he may have had many opponents he had hardly one personal enemy.

His name will endure through the ages, and so also will his work!

Engels looking on as Karl Marx works on their doctrine.

Franklin D. Roosevelt 1882–1945

NATIONALITY:
American
WHEN:
1933
WHERE:
Washington, DC, USA
YOU SHOULD KNOW:
FDR is the only US President to be
elected for four terms. Since 1951 no
President may occupy the White
House for more than two terms.

*In 1933 America was in the depths of the Great Depression that
had followed the Wall Street Crash of 1929. FDR formulated a
detailed plan to revitalize the US economy, help the urban and –
particularly – rural poor and the unemployed, whilst also
reforming the financial institutions whose irresponsibility had
caused the mess. This imaginative plan was known as the New
Deal. In his first inaugural address in March 1933, Roosevelt
laid the blame at the feet of financiers, bankers, profit-seeking
and capitalism's overwhelming self-interest, sentiments echoed
in another inaugural address almost 76 years later.*

This is a day of national consecration. And I am certain that on this
day my fellow Americans expect that on my induction into the
Presidency, I will address them with a candour and a decision which
the present situation of our people impels.

This is preeminently the time to speak the truth, the whole truth,
frankly and boldly. Nor need we shrink from honestly facing
conditions in our country today. This great Nation will endure, as it
has endured, will revive and will prosper.

So, first of all, let me assert my firm belief that the only thing we
have to fear is fear itself – nameless, unreasoning, unjustified terror
which paralyzes needed efforts to convert retreat into advance. In
every dark hour of our national life, a leadership of frankness and of
vigor has met with that understanding and support of the people
themselves which is essential to victory. And I am convinced that
you will again give that support to leadership in these critical days . . .

. . . The rulers of the exchange of mankind's goods have failed,
through their own stubbornness and their own incompetence, have
admitted their failure, and have abdicated. Practices of the
unscrupulous money changers stand indicted in the court of public
opinion, rejected by the hearts and minds of men . . .

Yes, the money changers have fled from their high seats in the
temple of our civilization. We may now restore that temple to the
ancient truths. The measure of that restoration lies in the extent to
which we apply social values more noble than mere monetary profit.

Happiness lies not in the mere possession of money; it lies in the
joy of achievement, in the thrill of creative effort. The joy, the moral
stimulation of work no longer must be forgotten in the mad chase of
evanescent profits. These dark days, my friends, will be worth all
they cost us if they teach us that our true destiny is not to be
ministered unto but to minister to ourselves, to our fellow men.

Recognition of that falsity of material wealth as the standard of
success goes hand in hand with the abandonment of the false belief
that public office and high political position are to be valued only by
the standards of pride of place and personal profit; and there must

President Roosevelt delivering his inaugural address.

be an end to a conduct in banking and in business which too often has given to a sacred trust the likeness of callous and selfish wrongdoing. Small wonder that confidence languishes, for it thrives only on honesty, on honour, on the sacredness of obligations, on faithful protection, and on unselfish performance; without them it cannot live.

Restoration calls, however, not for changes in ethics alone. This nation is asking for action, and action now.

Our greatest primary task is to put people to work. This is no unsolvable problem if we face it wisely and courageously. It can be accomplished in part by direct recruiting by the Government itself, treating the task as we would treat the emergency of a war, but at the same time, through this employment, accomplishing great – greatly needed projects to stimulate and reorganize the use of our great natural resources . . .

Yes, the task can be helped by definite efforts to raise the values of agricultural products, and with this the power to purchase the output of our cities. It can be helped by preventing realistically the tragedy of the growing loss through foreclosure of our small homes and our farms. It can be helped by insistence that the Federal, the State, and the local governments act forthwith on the demand that their cost be drastically reduced. It can be helped by the unifying of relief activities which today are often scattered, uneconomical, unequal. It can be helped by national planning for and supervision of all forms of transportation and of communications and other utilities that have a definitely public character. There are many ways in which it can be helped, but it can never be helped by merely talking about it . . .

And finally, in our progress towards a resumption of work, we require two safeguards against a return of the evils of the old order. There must be a strict supervision of all banking and credits and investments. There must be an end to speculation with other people's money. And there must be provision for an adequate but sound currency . . .

Through this program of action we address ourselves to putting our own national house in order and making income balance outgo. Our international trade relations, though vastly important, are in point of time, and necessity, secondary to the establishment of a sound national economy. I favor, as a practical policy, the putting of first things first. I shall spare no effort to restore world trade by international economic readjustment; but the emergency at home cannot wait on that accomplishment.

The basic thought that guides these specific means of national recovery is not nationally – narrowly nationalistic. It is the insistence, as a first consideration, upon the interdependence of the various elements in and parts of the United States of America – a recognition of the old and permanently important manifestation of the American spirit of the pioneer. It is the way to recovery. It is the immediate way. It is the strongest assurance that recovery will endure.

In the field of world policy, I would dedicate this Nation to the policy of the good neighbour: the neighbour who resolutely respects himself and, because he does so, respects the rights of others; the neighbour who respects his obligations and respects the sanctity of his agreements in and with a world of neighbours . . .

We are, I know, ready and willing to submit our lives and our property to such discipline, because it makes possible a leadership which aims at the larger good. This, I propose to offer, pledging that the larger purposes will bind upon us, bind upon us all as a sacred obligation with a unity of duty hitherto evoked only in times of armed strife.

With this pledge taken, I assume unhesitatingly the leadership of this great army of our people dedicated to a disciplined attack upon our common problems.

Action in this image, action to this end is feasible under the form of government which we have inherited from our ancestors. Our Constitution is so simple, so practical that it is possible always to meet extraordinary needs by changes in emphasis and arrangement without loss of essential form. That is why our constitutional system has proved itself the most superbly enduring political mechanism the modern world has ever seen.

It has met every stress of vast expansion of territory, of foreign wars, of bitter internal strife, of world relations. And it is to be hoped that the normal balance of executive and legislative authority may be wholly equal, wholly adequate to meet the unprecedented task before us. But it may be that an unprecedented demand and need for undelayed action may call for temporary departure from that normal balance of public procedure.

I am prepared under my constitutional duty to recommend the measures that a stricken nation in the midst of a stricken world may require. These measures, or such other measures as the Congress may build out of its experience and wisdom, I shall seek, within my constitutional authority, to bring to speedy adoption . . .

For the trust reposed in me, I will return the courage and the devotion that befit the time. I can do no less . . .

In this dedication – In this dedication of a Nation, we humbly ask the blessing of God.

May He protect each and every one of us.

May He guide me in the days to come.

Jimmy Carter born 1924

President Carter gave his first State of the Union Address at a time when the US economy was stagnant. Dependency on oil imports was just as high as it had been during the oil crisis, he was already having problems with Congress over the domestic budget and although there had been a reduction in unemployment, there were rumblings of discontent that more had not been achieved in the first year of his presidency. What he made clear was his belief that without the will and hard work of the people, nothing any government did would get the country's economy back on track.

James Earl Carter

Two years ago today we had the first caucus in Iowa, and one year ago tomorrow, I walked from here to the White House to take up the duties of President of the United States. I didn't know it then when I walked, but I've been trying to save energy ever since . . .

Militarily, politically, economically, and in spirit, the state of our Union is sound.

We are a great country, a strong country, a vital and dynamic country, and so we will remain.

We are a confident people and a hardworking people, a decent and a compassionate people, and so we will remain . . .

Each generation of Americans has to face circumstances not of its own choosing, but by which its character is measured and its spirit is tested.

There are times of emergency, when a nation and its leaders must bring their energies to bear on a single urgent task. That was the duty Abraham Lincoln faced when our land was torn apart by conflict in the War Between the States. That was the duty faced by Franklin Roosevelt when he led America out of an economic depression and again when he led America to victory in war.

There are other times when there is no single overwhelming crisis, yet profound national interests are at stake.

At such times the risk of inaction can be equally great. It becomes the task of leaders to call forth the vast and restless energies of our people to build for the future . . .

We live in such times now, and we face such duties.

We've come through a long period of turmoil and doubt, but we've once again found our moral course, and with a new spirit, we

NATIONALITY:
American
WHEN:
1978
WHERE:
Washington, DC, USA

are striving to express our best instincts to the rest of the world.

There is all across our land a growing sense of peace and a sense of common purpose. This sense of unity cannot be expressed in programs or in legislation or in dollars. It's an achievement that belongs to every individual American. This unity ties together, and it towers over all our efforts here in Washington, and it serves as an inspiring beacon for all of us who are elected to serve.

This new atmosphere demands a new spirit, a partnership between those of us who lead and those who elect. The foundations of this partnership are truth, the courage to face hard decisions, concern for one another and the common good over special interests, and a basic faith and trust in the wisdom and strength and judgment of the American people.

For the first time in a generation, we are not haunted by a major international crisis or by domestic turmoil, and we now have a rare and a priceless opportunity to address persistent problems and burdens which come to us as a nation, quietly and steadily getting worse over the years . . .

We must make a maximum effort, because if we do not aim for the best, we are very likely to achieve little. I see no benefit to the country if we delay, because the problems will only get worse . . .

We here in Washington must move away from crisis management, and we must establish clear goals for the future, immediate and the distant future, which will let us work together and not in conflict. Never again should we neglect a growing crisis like the shortage of energy, where further delay will only lead to more harsh and painful solutions.

Every day we spend more than $120 million for foreign oil. This slows our economic growth, it lowers the value of the dollar overseas, and it aggravates unemployment and inflation here at home.

Now we know what we must do, increase production. We must cut down on waste. And we must use more of those fuels which are plentiful and more permanent. We must be fair to people, and we must not disrupt our Nation's economy and our budget . . .

Our main task at home this year, with energy a central element, is the Nation's economy. We must continue the recovery and further cut unemployment and inflation.

Last year was a good one for the United States. We reached all of our major economic goals for 1977. Four million new jobs were created, an alltime record, and the number of unemployed dropped by more than a million. Unemployment right now is the lowest it has been since 1974, and not since World War II has such a high percentage of American people been employed.

The rate of inflation went down. There was a good growth in business profits and investments, the source of more jobs for our workers, and a higher standard of living for all our people. After taxes and inflation, there was a healthy increase in workers' wages.

And this year, our country will have the first $2 trillion economy in the history of the world.

Now, we are proud of this progress the first year, but we must do even better in the future.

We still have serious problems on which all of us must work together. Our trade deficit is too large. Inflation is still too high, and too many Americans still do not have a job.

Now, I didn't have any simple answers for all these problems. But we have developed an economic policy that is working, because it's simple, balanced, and fair. It's based on four principles: First, the economy must keep on expanding to produce new jobs and better income, which our people need. The fruits of growth must be widely shared. More jobs must be made available to those who have been bypassed until now. And the tax system must be made fairer and simpler.

Secondly, private business and not the Government must lead the expansion in the future.

Third, we must lower the rate of inflation and keep it down. Inflation slows down economic growth, and it's the most cruel to the poor and also to the elderly and others who live on fixed incomes.

And fourth, we must contribute to the strength of the world economy . . .

I'll be asking you for a substantial increase in funds for public jobs for our young people, and I also am recommending that the Congress continue the public service employment programs at more than twice the level of a year ago. When welfare reform is completed, we will have more than a million additional jobs so that those on welfare who are able to work can work.

However, again, we know that in our free society, private business is still the best source of new jobs. Therefore, I will propose a new program to encourage businesses to hire young and disadvantaged Americans. These young people only need skills and a chance in order to take their place in our economic system. Let's give them the chance they need. A major step in the right direction would be the early passage of a greatly improved Humphrey-Hawkins bill . . .

Economic success at home is also the key to success in our international economic policy. An effective energy program, strong investment and productivity, and controlled inflation will improve our trade balance and balance it, and it will help to protect the integrity of the dollar overseas.

By working closely with our friends abroad, we can promote the economic health of the whole world, with fair and balanced agreements lowering the barriers to trade.

Despite the inevitable pressures that build up when the world economy suffers from high unemployment, we must firmly resist the demands for self-defeating protectionism. But free trade must also be fair trade. And I am determined to protect American industry and American workers against foreign trade practices which are unfair or illegal . . .

During these past years, Americans have seen our Government grow far from us.

For some citizens, the Government has almost become like a foreign country, so strange and distant that we've often had to deal with it through trained ambassadors who have sometimes become too powerful and too influential, lawyers, accountants, and lobbyists. This cannot go on.

We must have what Abraham Lincoln wanted, a government for the people.

We've made progress toward that kind of government. You've given me the authority I requested to reorganize the Federal bureaucracy. And I am using that authority . . .

But even the best organized Government will only be as effective as the people who carry out its policies. For this reason, I consider civil service reform to be absolutely vital. Worked out with the civil servants themselves, this reorganization plan will restore the merit principle to a system which has grown into a bureaucratic maze. It will provide greater management flexibility and better rewards for better performance without compromising job security.

Then and only then can we have a government that is efficient, open, and truly worthy of our people's understanding and respect. I have promised that we will have such a government, and I intend to keep that promise.

In our foreign policy, the separation of people from government has been in the past a source of weakness and error. In a democratic system like ours, foreign policy decisions must be able to stand the test of public examination and public debate. If we make a mistake in this administration, it will be on the side of frankness and openness with the American people.

In our modern world, when the deaths of literally millions of people can result from a few terrifying seconds of destruction, the path of national strength and security is identical to the path of peace.

Tonight, I am happy to report that because we are strong, our Nation is at peace with the world.

We are a confident nation. We've restored a moral basis for our foreign policy. The very heart of our identity as a nation is our firm commitment to human rights.

We stand for human rights because we believe that government has as a purpose to promote the well-being of its citizens. This is true in our domestic policy; it's also true in our foreign policy. The world must know that in support of human rights, the United States will stand firm.

We expect no quick or easy results, but there has been significant movement toward greater freedom and humanity in several parts of the world.

Thousands of political prisoners have been freed. The leaders of the world, even our ideological

Theodore (Teddy) Roosevelt

1858–1919

NATIONALITY:
American
WHEN:
1901
WHERE:
St Paul, Minnesota, USA

Theodore Roosevelt's robust but pragmatic attitude to foreign policy can be summed up in these two quotations from a speech that he gave at the opening of the Minnesota State Fair in September 1901, just 12 days before the assassination of President McKinley elevated him to the Oval Office. It comes originally from a West African proverb. He was specifically referring to the need to talk diplomatically to other governments but to build up and keep an effective, efficient navy so that the ideas of the Monroe Doctrine (aimed at preventing European interference in the Americas, i.e., in what the US saw as its sphere of influence) could be implemented.

Cartoon of 'Teddy' Roosevelt with his big stick

Speak softly, and carry a big stick.

Right here let me make as vigorous a plea as I know how in favor of saying nothing that we do not mean, and of acting without hesitation up to whatever we say. A good many of you are probably acquainted with the old proverb, 'Speak softly and carry a big stick – you will go far.' If a man continually blusters, if he lacks civility, a big stick will not save him from trouble, and neither will speaking softly avail, if back of the softness there does not lie strength, power. In private life there are few beings more obnoxious than the man who is always loudly boasting, and if the boaster is not prepared to back up his words, his position becomes absolutely contemptible. So it is with the nation. It is both foolish and undignified to indulge in undue self-glorification, and, above all, in loose-tongued denunciation of other peoples. Whenever on any point we come in contact with a foreign power, I hope that we shall always strive to speak courteously and respectfully of that foreign power . . .

. . . Let us make it evident that we intend to do justice. Then let us make it equally evident that we will not tolerate injustice being done us in return. Let us further make it evident that we use no words which we are not which prepared to back up with deeds, and that while our speech is always moderate, we are ready and willing to make it good. Such an attitude will be the surest possible guarantee of that self-respecting peace, the attainment of which is and must ever be the prime aim of a self-governing people.

Joseph McCarthy 1908–1957

*The word 'McCarthyism' was originally coined as a perjorative
term for the anti-communist hysteria he promoted, but the
Junior Senator for Wisconsin revelled in the term. He projected
himself as a champion of, and a spokesman for, hard-working,
blue-collar, middle America, and for a few short years many
believed him. The anti-communist movement had started before
World War II, but McCarthy's campaigns became ever-more
insidious and vindictive. His influence far outweighed his
position, and was probably detrimental to America's foreign
policy – and certainly its overseas image – even after his fall
from grace in 1954, when it became obvious that there were few
facts behind his rhetoric and his claims were exaggerated.*

‘ McCarthyism is Americanism with its sleeves rolled. ’

NATIONALITY:
American
WHEN:
1952
WHERE:
Wisconsin, USA
YOU SHOULD KNOW:
The first appearance of the term
'McCarthyism' was in a *Washington
Post* cartoon on March 29, 1950.

Herbert Hoover 1874–1964

*Towards the close of the 1928 US Presidential campaign
Republican candidate Herbert Hoover extolled the virtues of free
enterprise and 'rugged individualism' as the basis of America's
wealth and greatness and campaigned for increased regulation
and increased volunteerism. As Commerce Secretary he was
widely seen as presiding over the booming American economy.
Less than eight months after his election, the Wall Street Crash
occurred and his methods proved inadequate to counter the
ensuing Great Depression.*

NATIONALITY:
American
WHEN:
1928
WHERE:
New York City, USA
YOU SHOULD KNOW:
His successor as President,
Franklin D. Roosevelt, had
Hoover's name removed from the
Hoover Dam, and it was not
restored until 1947.

‘ This campaign now draws near to a close. The platforms of the two
parties defining principles and offering solutions of various national
problems have been presented and are being earnestly considered
by our people.

After four months' debate it is not the Republican Party which
finds reason for abandonment of any of the principles it has laid
down or of the views it has expressed for solution of the problems
before the country. The principles to which it adheres are rooted
deeply in the foundations of our national life and the solutions
which it proposed are based on experience with government and a
consciousness that it may have the responsibility for placing those
solutions into action . . .

I regret, however, to say that there has been revived in this
campaign a proposal which would be a long step to the
abandonment of our American system, to turn to the idea of

government in business. Because we are faced with difficulty and doubt over certain national problems which we are faced – that is prohibition, farm relief and electrical power – our opponents propose that we must to some degree thrust government into these businesses and in effect adopt state socialism as a solution.

There is, therefore submitted to the American people the question – Shall we depart from the American system and start upon a new road. And I wish to emphasize this question on this occasion. I wish to make clear my position on the principles involved for they go to the very roots of American life in every act of our Government. I should like to state to you the effect of the extension of government into business upon our system of self government and our economic system. But even more important is the effect upon the average man. That is the effect on the very basis of liberty and freedom not only to those left outside the fold of expanded bureaucracy but to those embraced . . .

. . . Business progressiveness is dependent on competition. New methods and new ideas are the outgrowth of the spirit of adventure of individual initiative and of individual enterprise. Without adventure there is no progress. No government administration can rightly speculate and take risks with taxpayers' money. But even more important than this – leadership in business must be through the sheer rise of ability and character. That rise can take place only in the free atmosphere of competition. Competition is closed by bureaucracy. Certainly political choice is a feeble basis for choice of leaders to conduct a business . . .

Bureaucracy is ever desirous of spreading its influence and its power. You cannot give to a government the mastery of the daily working life of a people without at the same time giving it mastery of the peoples' souls and thoughts. Every expansion of government means that government in order to protect itself from political consequences of its errors and wrongs is driven onward and onward without peace to greater and greater control of the country's press and platform. Free speech does not live many hours after free industry and free commerce die.

It is false liberalism that interprets itself into the government operation of business. The bureaucratization of our country would poison the very roots of liberalism that is free speech, free assembly, free press, political equality and equality of opportunity. It is the road, not to more liberty, but to less liberty. Liberalism should be found not striving to spread bureaucracy, but striving to set bounds to it. True liberalism seeks freedom first in the confident belief that without freedom the pursuit of all other blessings and benefits is vain. That belief is the foundation of all American progress, political as well as economic.

Liberalism is a force truly of the spirit, a force proceeding from the deep realization that economic freedom cannot be sacrificed if political freedom is to be preserved. Even if governmental conduct of business could give us more efficiency instead of giving us decreased efficiency, the fundamental objection to it would remain unaltered and unabated. It would destroy political equality. It would cramp and cripple mental and spiritual energies of our people. It would dry up the spirit of liberty and progress. It would extinguish equality of opportunity, and for these reasons fundamentally and primarily it must be resisted. For 150 years liberalism has found its true spirit in the American system, not in the European systems . . .

There is but one consideration in testing these proposals – that is public interest. I do not doubt the sincerity of those who advocate these methods of solving our problems. I believe they will give equal credit to our honesty. If I believed that the adoption of such proposals would decrease taxes, cure abuses or corruption, would produce better service, decrease rates or benefit employees; if I believed they would bring economic equality, would stimulate endeavor, would encourage invention and support individual initiative, would provide equality of opportunity; if I believed that these proposals would not wreck our democracy but would strengthen the foundations of social and spiritual progress in America – or if they would do a few of these things – then I would not hesitate to accept these proposals, stupendous as they are, even though such acceptance would result in the governmental operation of all our power and the buying and selling of the products of our farms or any other product. But it is not true that such benefits would result to the public. The contrary would be true . . .

As a result of our distinctly American system our country has become the land of opportunity to those born without inheritance not merely because of the wealth of its resources and industry but because of this freedom of initiative and enterprise. Russia has natural resources equal to ours. Her people are equally industrious but she has not had the blessings of 150 years of our form of government and of our social system. The wisdom of our forefathers in their conception that progress must be the sum of the progress of free individuals has been reenforced by all of the great leaders of the country since that day. Jackson, Lincoln, Cleveland, McKinley, Roosevelt, Wilson, and Coolidge have stood unalterably for these principles. By adherence to the principles of decentralization, self-government, ordered liberty, and opportunity and freedom to the individual our American experiment has yielded a degree of well-being unparalleled in all the world. It has come nearer to the abolition of poverty, to the abolition of fear of want that humanity has ever reached before. Progress of the past seven years is the proof of it. It furnishes an answer to those who would ask us to abandon the system by which this has been accomplished . . .

I wish to say something more on what I believe is the outstanding ideal in our whole political, economic and social system – that is equality of opportunity. We have carried this ideal farther into our life than has any other nation in the world. Equality of opportunity is the right of every American, rich or poor, foreign or native born, without respect to race or faith or color, to attain that position in life to which his ability and character entitle him. We must carry this ideal further than to economic and political fields alone. The first steps to equality of opportunity are that there should be no child in America that has not been born and does not live under sound conditions of health, that does not have full opportunity for education from the beginning to the end of our institutions, that is not free from injurious labour, that does not have stimulation to accomplish to the fullest of its capacities . . .

Furthermore, equality of opportunity in my vision requires an equal opportunity to the people in every section of our country. In these past few years some groups in our country have lagged behind others in the march of progress. They have not had the same opportunity. I refer more particularly to those engaged in the textile, coal and in the agricultural industries. We can assist in solving these problems by cooperation of our Government. To the agricultural industry we shall need advance initial capital to assist them, to stabilize and conduct their own industry. But this proposal is that they shall conduct it themselves, not by the Government. It is in the interest of our cities that we shall bring agriculture into full stability and prosperity. I know you will cooperate gladly in the faith that in the common prosperity of our country lies its future. 〞

*Herbert Hoover
campaigning in New York.*

James Carville born 1944

NATIONALITY:
American
WHEN:
1992
WHERE:
Little Rock, Arkansas, USA
YOU SHOULD KNOW:
Other campaign slogans included
'Change Vs more of the same' and
'Don't forget health care'.

*Coined by Bill Clinton's campaign strategist James Carville in
the run-up to the 1992 US Presidential election, this slogan was
hung up in the Clinton HQ in the Arkansas state capital. The
incumbent President, George H. W. Bush, was ahead in the polls
as far as foreign policy was concerned because of success in the
Gulf War against Iraq, so the Clinton team decided to
concentrate instead on the relatively weak area for the
Republicans of the US economy, which had been suffering a
downturn. The phrase could be heard on Democrat lips
everywhere but, ironically, the one person who never said it –
at least not in public – was President-in-waiting Clinton.*

Bill Clinton

❝ [It's] the economy, stupid! ❞

350

Dwight D. Eisenhower 1890–1969

At the end of his eight-year term in the Oval Office, President Eisenhower addressed the American people, looking both back on his achievements and towards America's and the world's future, with reference to the USSR. A major part of the speech is taken up with the increase in size of the US military, which he believed was a necessity, whilst warning against the possibility of the 'military-industrial complex' becoming over-powerful, whether by intent or accident, fearing that the peaceful methods and goals of the majority of Americans would be subsumed and that the liberty that they held dear would be lost in the name of national security and the interests of the armaments industry or the scientific elite.

NATIONALITY:
American
WHEN:
1961
WHERE:
Washington, DC, USA
YOU SHOULD KNOW:
President Eisenhower was the first US President to be limited to serving two terms.

Good evening, my fellow Americans.

. . . Three days from now, after half century in the service of our country, I shall lay down the responsibilities of office as, in traditional and solemn ceremony, the authority of the Presidency is vested in my successor. This evening, I come to you with a message of leave-taking and farewell, and to share a few final thoughts with you, my countrymen . . .

We now stand ten years past the midpoint of a century that has witnessed four major wars among great nations. Three of these involved our own country. Despite these holocausts, America is today the strongest, the most influential, and most productive nation in the world. Understandably proud of this pre-eminence, we yet realize that America's leadership and prestige depend, not merely upon our unmatched material progress, riches, and military strength, but on how we use our power in the interests of world peace and human betterment.

Throughout America's adventure in free government, our basic purposes have been to keep the peace, to foster progress in human achievement, and to enhance liberty, dignity, and integrity among peoples and among nations. To strive for less would be unworthy of a free and religious people. Any failure traceable to arrogance, or our lack of comprehension, or readiness to sacrifice would inflict upon us grievous hurt, both at home and abroad . . .

Crises there will continue to be. In meeting them, whether foreign or domestic, great or small, there is a recurring temptation to feel that some spectacular and costly action could become the miraculous solution to all current difficulties. A huge increase in newer elements of our defences; development of unrealistic programs to cure every ill in agriculture; a dramatic expansion in basic and applied research – these and many other possibilities, each possibly promising in itself, may be suggested as the only way to the road we wish to travel.

But each proposal must be weighed in the light of a broader consideration: The need to maintain balance in and among national

programs, balance between the private and the public economy, balance between the cost and hoped for advantages, balance between the clearly necessary and the comfortably desirable, balance between our essential requirements as a nation and the duties imposed by the nation upon the individual, balance between actions of the moment and the national welfare of the future. Good judgment seeks balance and progress. Lack of it eventually finds imbalance and frustration. The record of many decades stands as proof that our people and their Government have, in the main, understood these truths and have responded to them well, in the face of threat and stress . . .

    A vital element in keeping the peace is our military establishment. Our arms must be mighty, ready for instant action, so that no potential aggressor may be tempted to risk his own destruction. Our military

President 'Ike' Eisenhower bidding farewell to the nation.

organization today bears little relation to that known of any of my predecessors in peacetime, or, indeed, by the fighting men of World War II or Korea.

Until the latest of our world conflicts, the United States had no armaments industry. American makers of plowshares could, with time and as required, make swords as well. But we can no longer risk emergency improvisation of national defence. We have been compelled to create a permanent armaments industry of vast proportions. Added to this, three and a half million men and women are directly engaged in the defence establishment. We annually spend on military security alone more than the net income of all United States cooperations – corporations . . .

In the councils of government, we must guard against the acquisition of unwarranted influence, whether sought or unsought, by the military-industrial complex. The potential for the disastrous rise of misplaced power exists and will persist. We must never let the weight of this combination endanger our liberties or democratic processes. We should take nothing for granted. Only an alert and knowledgeable citizenry can compel the proper meshing of the huge industrial and military machinery of defence with our peaceful methods and goals, so that security and liberty may prosper together . . .

Another factor in maintaining balance involves the element of time. As we peer into society's future, we – you and I, and our government – must avoid the impulse to live only for today, plundering for our own ease and convenience the precious resources of tomorrow. We cannot mortgage the material assets of our grandchildren without risking the loss also of their political and spiritual heritage. We want democracy to survive for all generations to come, not to become the insolvent phantom of tomorrow.

During the long lane of the history yet to be written, America knows that this world of ours, ever growing smaller, must avoid becoming a community of dreadful fear and hate, and be, instead, a proud confederation of mutual trust and respect. Such a confederation must be one of equals. The weakest must come to the conference table with the same confidence as do we, protected as we are by our moral, economic, and military strength. That table, though scarred by many past frustrations – past frustrations, cannot be abandoned for the certain agony of disarmament – of the battlefield.

Disarmament, with mutual honour and confidence, is a continuing imperative. Together we must learn how to compose differences, not with arms, but with intellect and decent purpose. Because this need is so sharp and apparent, I confess that I lay down my official responsibilities in this field with a definite sense of disappointment. As one who has witnessed the horror and the lingering sadness of war, as one who knows that another war could utterly destroy this civilization which has been so slowly and painfully built over thousands of years, I wish I could say tonight that a lasting peace is in sight . . .

So, in this, my last goodnight to you as your President, I thank you for the many opportunities you have given me for public service in war and in peace. I trust that in that service you find some things worthy. As for the rest of it, I know you will find ways to improve performance in the future.

You and I, my fellow citizens, need to be strong in our faith that all nations, under God, will reach the goal of peace with justice. May we be ever unswerving in devotion to principle, confident but humble with power, diligent in pursuit of the Nation's great goals.

To all the peoples of the world, I once more give expression to America's prayerful and continuing aspiration: We pray that peoples of all faiths, all races, all nations, may have their great human needs satisfied; that those now denied opportunity shall come to enjoy it to the full; that all who yearn for freedom may experience its few spiritual blessings. Those who have freedom will understand, also, its heavy responsibility; that all who are insensitive to the needs of others will learn charity; and that the sources – scourges of poverty, disease, and ignorance will be made [to] disappear from the earth; and that in the goodness of time, all peoples will come to live together in a peace guaranteed by the binding force of mutual respect and love.

Now, on Friday noon, I am to become a private citizen. I am proud to do so. I look forward to it.

Thank you, and good night.

Harry S. Truman 1884–1972

NATIONALITY:
American
WHEN:
April 16, 1945
WHERE:
Washington, DC, USA
YOU SHOULD KNOW:
It was President Truman's decision to drop two nuclear bombs on Japan that ended World War II.

On April 16, 1945 – the day after President Roosevelt's funeral – his successor President Truman addressed a joint session of Congress and the speech was broadcast to the nation. In it, he pledged to carry on President Roosevelt's work and to keep true to the ideals of the American people. Less than a month later, Germany had surrendered, and the war would be over in four months once the Japanese Emperor capitulated. America had poured so many resources into the war that it would take the economy years to recover, and Truman is remembered as much for the Marshall Plan as the foundation of both NATO and the United Nations.

It is with a heavy heart that I stand before you, my friends and colleagues, in the Congress of the United States . . .

In His infinite wisdom, Almighty God has seen fit to take from us a great man who loved, and was beloved by, all humanity.

No man could possibly fill the tremendous void left by the passing of that noble soul . . .

Tragic fate has thrust upon us grave responsibilities. We must carry on. Our departed leader never looked backward. He looked forward and moved forward. That is what he would want us to do. That is what America will do.

So much blood has already been shed for the ideals which we cherish, and for which Franklin Delano Roosevelt lived and died, that we dare not permit even a momentary pause in the hard fight for victory . . .

So that there can be no possible misunderstanding, both Germany and Japan can be certain, beyond any shadow of a doubt, that America will continue the fight for freedom until no vestige of resistance remains!

We are deeply conscious of the fact that much hard fighting is still ahead of us.

Having to pay such a heavy price to make complete victory certain, America will never become a party to any plan for partial victory!

To settle for merely another temporary respite would surely jeopardize the future security of all the world.

Our demand has been, and it remains – Unconditional Surrender! We will not traffic with the breakers of the peace on the terms of the peace.

The responsibility for making of the peace – and it is a very grave responsibility – must rest with the defenders of the peace. We are not unconscious of the dictates of humanity. We do not wish to see unnecessary or unjustified suffering. But the laws of God and of man have been violated and the guilty must not go unpunished. Nothing shall shake our determination to punish the war criminals even though we must pursue them to the ends of the earth.

Lasting peace can never be secured if we permit our dangerous opponents to plot future wars with impunity at any mountain retreat – however distant . . .

In the difficult days ahead, unquestionably we shall face problems of staggering proportions. However, with the faith of our fathers in our hearts, we do not fear the future.

On the battlefields, we have frequently faced overwhelming odds – and won! At home, Americans will not be less resolute!

We shall never cease our struggle to preserve and maintain our American way of life.

At this moment, America, along with her brave Allies, is paying again a heavy price for the defence of our freedom. With characteristic energy, we are assisting in the liberation of entire nations. Gradually, the shackles of slavery are being broken by the forces of freedom . . .

I want the entire world to know that this direction must and will remain unchanged and unhampered!

Our forefathers came to our rugged shores in search of religious tolerance, political freedom and economic opportunity. For those fundamental rights, they risked their lives. We well know today that such rights can be preserved only by constant vigilance, the eternal price of liberty!

In the memory of those who have made the supreme sacrifice – in the memory of our fallen President – we shall not fail!

It is not enough to yearn for peace. We must work, and if necessary, fight for it . . .

Fortunately, people have retained hope for a durable peace. Thoughtful people have always had faith that ultimately justice must triumph. Past experience surely indicates that, without justice, an enduring peace becomes impossible . . .

During the dark hours of this horrible war, entire nations were kept going by something intangible – hope! When warned that abject submission offered the only salvation against overwhelming power, hope showed the way to victory.

Hope has become the secret weapon of the forces of liberation!

But hope alone was not and is not sufficient to avert war. We must not only have hope but we must have faith enough to work with other peace-loving nations to maintain the peace. Hope was not enough to beat back the aggressors as long as the peace-loving nations were unwilling to come to each other's defence. The aggressors were beaten back only when the peace-loving nations united to defend themselves.

If wars in the future are to be prevented the nations must be united in their determination to keep the peace under law . . .

To build a foundation of enduring peace we must not only work in harmony with our friends abroad, but we must have the united support of our own people . . .

I appeal to every American, regardless of party, race, creed, or colour, to support our efforts to build a strong and lasting United Nations Organization . . .

America must assist suffering humanity back along the path of peaceful progress. This will require time and tolerance. We shall need also an abiding faith in the people, the kind of faith and courage which Franklin Delano Roosevelt always had!

Today, America has become one of the most powerful forces for good on earth. We must keep it so. We have achieved a world leadership which does not depend solely upon our military and naval might.

We have learned to fight with other nations in common defence of our freedom. We must now learn to live with other nations for our mutual good. We must learn to trade more with other nations so that there may be – for our mutual advantage – better standards of living throughout the world.

May we Americans all live up to our glorious heritage.

In that way, America may well lead the world to peace and prosperity.

At this moment, I have in my heart a prayer. As I have assumed my heavy duties, I humbly pray Almighty God, in the words of King Solomon:

'Give therefore thy servant an understanding heart to judge thy people, that I may discern between good and bad; for who is able to judge this thy so great a people?'

I ask only to be a good and faithful servant of my Lord and my people.

Charles Baudelaire 1821–1867

NATIONALITY:
French
WHEN:
Various times
WHERE:
Various places
YOU SHOULD KNOW:
Baudelaire was chiefly known at the
time as the writer of decadent
Romantic poetry.

*At the end of 1851 Napoleon III had retaken France, ending the
Second Republic. During the next decade his autocratic rule,
suppression of press freedom, assumption of executive power,
censorship and surveillance of individuals rankled with
French citizens used to greater liberty. He started loosening
restrictions in the early 1860s, but not sufficiently quickly for
the disgruntled working classes who – won over by the
collectivist theories of Marx and Mikhail Bakunin – launched
strikes and mass protests. Baudelaire's clarion call to the
Republicans catches the temper of the time and presages the
violence, destruction and anarchy that would come with the
short-lived revolutionary Paris Commune of 1871.*

*The storming of the Bastille
was an enduring symbol
that inspired French
revolutionaries.*

'When I agree to be a Republican, I commit evil knowingly. Yes! Long
Live Revolution. I am not a dupe! I was never a dupe! I say Long live
Revolution! as I would say Long Live Destruction! Long Live
Expiation! Long Live Punishment! Long Live Death!'

Abraham Lincoln 1809–65

On June 16, 1858 the delegates to the Illinois Republican State Convention selected Abraham Lincoln as their candidate for the US Senate. His acceptance speech – seen by many at the convention as being far too radical – awoke Republicans in the North to the threat that the Southern states might either secede because of the disagreement over slavery or, if they could push the legislation through, force the North into accepting it. The speeches and debates during this campaign made Lincoln the obvious candidate for the Republican Party during the presidential elections in 1860. His victory led to the secession of the Confederate states.

If we could first know where we are, and whither we are tending, we could then better judge what to do, and how to do it.

We are now far into the fifth year, since a policy was initiated, with the avowed object, and confident promise, of putting an end to slavery agitation.

Under the operation of that policy, that agitation has not only, not ceased, but has constantly augmented.

In my opinion, it will not cease, until a crisis shall have been reached, and passed.

'A house divided against itself cannot stand.'

I believe this government cannot endure, permanently half slave and half free.

I do not expect the Union to be dissolved – I do not expect the house to fall – but I do expect it will cease to be divided.

It will become all one thing or all the other.

Either the opponents of slavery, will arrest the further spread of it, and place it where the public mind shall rest in the belief that it is in the course of ultimate extinction; or its advocates will push it forward, till it shall become alike lawful in all the States, old as well as new – North as well as South.

Have we no tendency to the latter condition?

Let any one who doubts, carefully contemplate that now almost complete legal combination . . . compounded of the Nebraska doctrine, and the Dred Scott decision. Let him consider not only what work the machinery is adapted to do, and how well adapted; but also, let him study the history of its construction, and trace, if he can, or rather fail, if he can, to trace the evidence of design and concert of action, among its chief architects, from the beginning.

But, so far, Congress only had acted; and an endorsement by the people, real or apparent, was indispensable, to save the point already gained, and give chance for more.

The new year of 1854 found slavery excluded from more than half the States by State Constitutions, and from most of the national

NATIONALITY:
American
WHEN:
1858
WHERE:
Springfield, Illinois, USA
YOU SHOULD KNOW:
The Dred Scott descision referred to in Lincoln's speech related to a Supreme Court ruling that people of African descent imported into the USA and held as slaves, and their descendants – whether slaves or not – were not legal persons, and that if a slave held in a free state was moved to a state where slavery was allowed, his status would be determined by a court in that state. Its other provision – that Congress had no authority to prohibit slavery in federal territories – was designed to stop slaves becoming free if they escaped to such territories as Kansas.

territory by congressional prohibition.

Four days later, commenced the struggle, which ended in repealing that congressional prohibition. This opened all the national territory to slavery, and was the first point gained . . .

That argument was incorporated into the Nebraska bill itself, in the language which follows: 'It being the true intent and meaning of this act not to legislate slavery into any territory or state, not to exclude it therefrom; but to leave the people thereof perfectly free to form and regulate their domestic institutions in their own way, subject only to the Constitution of the United States.' . . .

'But', said opposition members, 'let us be more specific – let us amend the bill so as to expressly declare that the people of the territory may exclude slavery.' 'Not we', said the friends of the measure; and down they voted the amendment.

While the Nebraska Bill was passing through congress, a law case involving the question of a negroe's freedom, by reason of his owner having voluntarily taken him first into a free state and then a territory covered by the congressional prohibition, and held him as a slave, for a long time in each, was passing through the US Circuit Court for the District of Missouri; and both Nebraska Bill and law suit were brought to a decision in the same month of May, 1854. The negroe's name was 'Dred Scott', which name now designates the decision finally made in the case . . .

The reputed author of the Nebraska Bill finds an early occasion to make a speech at this capital indorsing the Dred Scott Decision, and vehemently denouncing all opposition to it.

The new President, too, seizes the early occasion of the Silliman letter to endorse and strongly construe that decision, and to express his astonishment that any different view had ever been entertained . . .

The several points of the Dred Scott decision, in connection with Senator Douglas's 'care-not' policy, constitute the piece of machinery, in its present state of advancement. This was the third point gained. Auxiliary to all this, and working hand in hand with it, the Nebraska doctrine, or what is left of it, is to educate and mold public opinion, at least Northern public opinion, not to care whether slavery is voted down or voted up. This shows exactly where we now are; and partially, also, whither we are tending.

It will throw additional light on the latter, to go back, and run the mind over the string of historical facts already stated. Several things will now appear less dark and mysterious than they did when they were transpiring. The people were to be left 'perfectly free', subject only to the Constitution. What the Constitution had to do with it, outsiders could not then see. Plainly enough now, it was an exactly fitted niche, for the Dred Scott decision to afterward come in, and declare the perfect free freedom of the people to be just no freedom at all. Why was the amendment, expressly declaring the right of the people, voted down? Plainly enough now: The adoption of it would have spoiled the niche for the Dred Scott decision. Why was the court decision held up? Why even a Senator's individual opinion withheld, till after the presidential election? Plainly enough now- the speaking out then would have damaged the perfectly free argument upon which the election was to be carried. Why the outgoing President's felicitation on the endorsement? Why the delay of a re-argument? Why the incoming President's advance exhortation in favor of the decision? These things look like the cautious patting and petting of a spirited horse, preparatory to mounting him, when it is dreaded that he may give the rider a fall. And why the hasty after-endorsement of the decision by the President and others?

It should not be overlooked that, by the Nebraska Bill, the people of a State, as well as a Territory, were to be left 'perfectly free', 'subject only to the Constitution'. Why mention a State? They were legislating for Territories, and not for or about States. Certainly the people of a State are and ought to be subject to the Constitution of the United States; but why is mention of this lugged into this merely territorial law? Why are the people of a Territory and the people of a State therein lumped together, and their relation to the Constitution therein treated as being precisely the same? While the opinion of the court, by Chief-Justice Taney, in the Dred Scott case and the separate opinions of all the concurring

Lincoln speaking at a debate.

judges, expressly declare that the Constitution of the United States neither permits Congress nor a territorial legislature to exclude slavery from any United States Territory, they all omit to declare whether or not the same Constitution permits a State, or the people of a State, to exclude it. Possibly this is a mere omission . . . The nearest approach to the point of declaring the power of a State over slavery is made by Judge Nelson. He approaches it more than once, using the precise idea, and almost the language, too, of the Nebraska Act. On one occasion, his exact language is, 'except in cases where the power is restrained by the Constitution of the United States the law of the State is supreme over the subject of slavery within its jurisdiction.' In what cases the power of the States is so restrained by the United States Constitution is left an open question, precisely as the same question, as to the restraint on the power of the Territories, was left open in the Nebraska Act. Put this and that together, and we have another nice little niche which we may ere long see filled with another Supreme Court decision declaring that the Constitution of the United States does not permit a State to exclude slavery from its limits. And this may especially be expected if the doctrine of 'care not whether slavery be voted down or voted up' shall gain upon the public mind sufficiently to give promise that such a decision can be maintained when made.

Such a decision is all that slavery now lacks of being alike lawful in all the States. Welcome, or unwelcome, such decision is probably coming, and will soon be upon us, unless the power of the present political dynasty shall be met and overthrown. We shall lie down pleasantly dreaming that the people of Missouri are on the verge of making their State free, and we shall awake to the reality instead, that the Supreme Court has made Illinois a slave State. To meet and overthrow the power of that dynasty is the work now before all those who would prevent that consummation. This is what we have to do.

Our cause, then, must be intrusted to, and conducted by, its own undoubted friends – those whose hands are free, whose hearts are in the work – who do care for the result. Two years ago the Republicans of the nation mustered over thirteen hundred thousand strong. We did this under the single impulse of resistance to a common danger, with every external circumstance against us. Of strange, discordant, and even hostile elements, we gathered from the four winds, and formed and fought the battle through, under the constant hot fire of a disciplined, proud, and pampered enemy. Did we brave all them to falter now – now, when that same enemy is wavering, dissevered, and belligerent? The result is not doubtful. We shall not fail-if we stand firm, we shall not fail. Wise counsels may accelerate, or mistakes delay it, but, sooner or later, the victory is sure to come.

Lyndon B. Johnson 1908–1973

NATIONALITY:
American
WHEN:
1964
WHERE:
Washington, DC, USA

On March 16, 1964 President Johnson launched the doctrine that was to become known as the War on Poverty. In the run-up to the 1964 presidential election, he pledged an expansion and an extension of help for the underpriveleged poor, with help for education and training and community-based initiatives. Further social reforms came in the following years with the introduction of Medicare and Medicaid and the Civil Rights legislation that he had to force onto the southern states. However, his presidency will always be associated with the protests over the increasingly unpopular Vietnam War.

‘ Because it is right, because it is wise, and because, for the first time in our history, it is possible to conquer poverty, I submit, for the consideration of the Congress and the country, the Economic Opportunity Act of 1964 . . .

It strikes at the causes, not just the consequences of poverty.

It can be a milestone in our 180-year search for a better life for our people.

This Act provides five basic opportunities.

It will give almost half a million underprivileged young Americans the opportunity to develop skills, continue education, and find useful work . . .

It will give dedicated Americans the opportunity to enlist as volunteers in the war against poverty.

It will give many workers and farmers the opportunity to break through particular barriers which bar their escape from poverty.

It will give the entire nation the opportunity for a concerted attack on poverty through the establishment, under my direction, of the Office of Economic Opportunity, a national headquarters for the war against poverty . . .

First we will give high priority to helping young Americans who lack skills, who have not completed their education or who cannot complete it because they arc too poor . . .

I therefore recommend the creation of a Job Corps, a Work-Training Program, and a Work-Study Program.

A new national Job Corps will build toward an enlistment of 100,000 young men. They will be drawn from those whose background, health and education make them least fit for useful work . . .

Half of these young men will work, in the first year, on special conservation projects to give them education, useful work experience and to enrich the natural resources of the country.

Half of these young men will receive, in the first year, a blend of training, basic education and work experience in job Training Centers . . .

A new national Work-Training Program operated by the Department of Labour will provide work and training for 200,000 American men and women between the ages of 16 and 21. This will be developed through state and local governments and non-profit agencies . . .

A new national Work-Study Program operated by the Department of Health, Education, and Welfare will provide federal funds for part-time jobs for 140,000 young Americans who do not go to college because they cannot afford it.

There is no more senseless waste than the waste of the brainpower and skill of those who are kept from college by economic circumstance. Under this program they will, in a great American tradition, be able to work their way through school . . .

Second, through a new Community Action program we intend to strike at poverty at its source – in the streets of our cities and on the farms of our countryside among the very young and the impoverished old.

This program asks men and women throughout the country to prepare long-range plans for the attack on poverty in their own local communities . . .

Third, I ask for the authority to recruit and train skilled volunteers for the war against poverty.

Thousands of Americans have volunteered to serve the needs of other lands.

Thousands more want the chance to serve the needs of their own land.

They should have that chance.

Among older people who have retired, as well as among the young, among women as well as men, there are many Americans who are ready to enlist in our war against poverty.

They have skills and dedication. They are badly needed . . .

Fourth, we intend to create new opportunities for certain hard-hit groups to break out of the pattern of poverty.

Through a new program of loans and guarantees we can provide incentives to those who will employ the unemployed.

Through programs of work and retraining for unemployed fathers and mothers we can help them support their families in dignity while preparing themselves for new work.

Through funds to purchase needed land, organize cooperatives, and create new and adequate family farms we can help those whose life on the land has been a struggle without hope.

Fifth, I do not intend that the war against poverty become a series of uncoordinated and unrelated efforts – that it perish for lack of leadership and direction . . .

What you are being asked to consider is not a simple or an easy program. But poverty is not a simple or an easy enemy.

It cannot be driven from the land by a single attack on a single front. Were this so we would have conquered poverty long ago.

Nor can it be conquered by government alone . . .

Today, for the first time in our history, we have the power to strike away the barriers to full participation in our society. Having the power, we have the duty . . .

. . . This program will show the way to new opportunities for millions of our fellow citizens.

It will provide a lever with which we can begin to open the door to our prosperity for those who have been kept outside.

It will also give us the chance to test our weapons, to try our energy and ideas and imagination for the many battles yet to come. As conditions change, and as experience illuminates our difficulties, we will be prepared to modify our strategy.

And this program is much more than a beginning.

Rather it is a commitment. It is a total commitment by this President, and this Congress, and this nation, to pursue victory over the most ancient of mankind's enemies.

Robert Mugabe born 1924

NATIONALITY:
Zimbabwean
WHEN:
2000
WHERE:
Harare, Zimbabwe
YOU SHOULD KNOW:
Robert Mugabe has led Zimbabwe since the country gained independence in 1980.

Under one of the terms of the Lancaster House Agreement (1979), the UK government agreed, as the former colonial power, to provide funds for white farmers in Zimbabwe so their lands could be bought and then given to homeless black workers. In 1997, the UK government decided that the farmlands were not being awarded according to the terms of the agreement and withdrew funding. The Mugabe regime then pursued a policy of forcible appropriation of farmlands from both white farmers and his opponents, despite two Supreme Court rulings against it. At a Zanu-PF rally in December 2000 he rejected criticism of his methods, blamed the white minority for Zimbabwe's economic woes and urged his followers to unite against them.

‘ Our party must continue to strike fear in the heart of the white man, our real enemy . . . They think because they are white, they have a divine right to our resources. Not here. Never again . . . This country is our country and this land is our land. The white man is not indigenous to Africa. Africa is for Africans. Zimbabwe is for Zimbabweans. ”

Robert Mugabe whips up the crowd.

Andrew Jackson 1767–1845

*In 1828 the Adams government had introduced a tariff on
imported goods (known by its detractors as the Tariff of
Abominations), which affected states of the Deep South far more
than the industrializing states of the North. Because the South
imported more goods from Europe and because of the decline in
trade, their traditional customers no longer had the money to
pay for the South's main crops such as cotton. In 1832, the
South Carolina legislature passed several laws seeking to
nullify Federal law and threatening secession. Although
President Jackson sympathized to some extent, he was not
going to allow states to overturn Federal laws that did not suit
them, so he threatened to send in a military force.*

NATIONALITY:
American
WHEN:
1832
WHERE:
Written in Washington, DC, USA
proclaimed in South Carolina.
YOU SHOULD KNOW:
This was one of the first major
threats to the stability of the Union
since the end of the American
Revolutionary Wars.

... Whereas the said ordinance prescribes to the people of South
Carolina a course of conduct in direct violation of their duty as
citizens of the United States, contrary to the laws of their country,
subversive of its Constitution, and having for its object the
instruction of the Union – that Union, which, coeval with our
political existence, led our fathers, without any other ties to unite
them than those of patriotism and common cause, through the
sanguinary struggle to a glorious independence – that sacred Union,
hitherto inviolate, which, perfected by our happy Constitution, has
brought us, by the favor of Heaven, to a state of prosperity at home
and high consideration abroad, rarely, if ever, equaled in the history
of nations; to preserve this bond of our political existence from
destruction, to maintain inviolate this state of national honour and
prosperity, and to justify the confidence my fellow-citizens have
reposed in me, I, Andrew Jackson, President of the United States,
have thought proper to issue this my PROCLAMATION, stating my
views of the Constitution and laws applicable to the measures
adopted by the Convention of South Carolina, and to the reasons
they have put forth to sustain them, declaring the course which
duty will require me to pursue, and, appealing to the understanding
and patriotism of the people, warn them of the consequences that
must inevitably result from an observance of the dictates of the
Convention ...

The ordinance is founded, not on the indefeasible right of
resisting acts which are plainly unconstitutional, and too oppressive
to be endured, but on the strange position that any one State may
not only declare an act of Congress void, but prohibit its execution –
that they may do this consistently with the Constitution – that the
true construction of that instrument permits a State to retain its
place in the Union, and yet be bound by no other of its laws than
those it may choose to consider as constitutional. It is true they add,
that to justify this abrogation of a law, it must be palpably contrary

to the Constitution, but it is evident, that to give the right of resisting laws of that description, coupled with the uncontrolled right to decide what laws deserve that character, is to give the power of resisting all laws. For, as by the theory, there is no appeal, the reasons alleged by the State, good or bad, must prevail. If it should be said that public opinion is a sufficient check against the abuse of this power, it may be asked why it is not deemed a sufficient guard against the passage of an unconstitutional act by Congress . . . But reasoning on this subject is superfluous, when our social compact in express terms declares, that the laws of the United States, its Constitution, and treaties made under it, are the supreme law of the land; and for greater caution adds, 'that the judges in every State shall be bound thereby, anything in the Constitution or laws of any State to the contrary notwithstanding.' And it may be asserted, without fear of refutation, that no federative government could exist without a similar provision. Look, for a moment, to the consequence. If South Carolina considers the revenue laws unconstitutional, and has a right to prevent their execution in the port of Charleston, there would be a clear constitutional objection to their collection in every other port, and no revenue could be collected anywhere; for all imposts must be equal. It is no answer to repeat that an unconstitutional law is no law, so long as the question of its legality is to be decided by the State itself, for every law operating injuriously upon any local interest will be perhaps thought, and certainly represented, as unconstitutional, and, as has been shown, there is no appeal . . .

The most important among these objects [in the ordinance], that which is placed first in rank, on which all the others rest, is 'to form a more perfect Union.' Now, is it possible that, even if there were no express provision giving supremacy to the Constitution and laws of the United States over those of the States, it can be conceived that an Instrument made for the purpose of 'forming a more perfect Union' than that of the confederation, could be so constructed by the assembled wisdom of our country as to substitute for that confederation a form of government, dependent for its existence on the local interest, the party spirit of a State, or of a prevailing faction in a State? . . .

Here is a law of the United States, not even pretended to be unconstitutional, repealed by the authority of a small majority of the voters of a single State. Here is a provision of the Constitution which is solemnly abrogated by the same authority.

On such expositions and reasonings, the ordinance grounds not only an assertion of the right to annul the laws of which it complains, but to enforce it by a threat of seceding from the Union if any attempt is made to execute them.

This right to secede is deduced [in the ordinance] from the nature of the Constitution, which they say is a compact between sovereign States who have preserved their whole sovereignty, and therefore are subject to no superior; that because they made the compact, they can break it when in their opinion it has been departed from by the other States. Fallacious as this course of reasoning is, it enlists State pride, and finds advocates in the honest prejudices of those who have not studied the nature of our government sufficiently to see the radical error on which it rests.

The people of the United States formed the Constitution, acting through the State legislatures, in making the compact, to meet and discuss its provisions, and acting in separate conventions when they ratified those provisions; but the terms used in its construction show it to be a government in which the people of all the States collectively are represented. We are ONE PEOPLE in the choice of the President and Vice President. Here the States have no other agency than to direct the mode in which the vote shall be given. The candidates having the majority of all the votes are chosen. The electors of a majority of States may have given their votes for one candidate, and yet another may be chosen. The people, then, and not the States, are represented in the executive branch . . .

The Constitution of the United States, then, forms a government, not a league, and whether it be formed by compact between the States, or in any other manner, its character is the same. It is a government in which all the people are represented, which operates directly on the people individually, not upon the States; they retained all the power they did not grant. But each State having expressly parted with so many powers as to constitute jointly with the other States a single nation, cannot from that period possess any right to secede, because such secession does not break a league, but destroys the unity of a nation, and any injury to that unity is not only a breach which would result from the contravention of a compact, but it is an offence against the whole Union . . .

Because the Union was formed by compact, it is said [in the Ordinance] the parties to that compact may, when they feel themselves aggrieved, depart from it; but it is precisely because it is a compact that they cannot . . . An attempt by force of arms to destroy a government is an offence, by whatever means the constitutional compact may have been formed; and such government has the right, by the law of self-defence, to pass acts for punishing the offender, unless that right is modified, restrained, or resumed by the constitutional act. In our system, although it is modified in the case of treason, yet authority is expressly given to pass all laws necessary to carry its powers into effect, and under this grant provision has been made for punishing acts which obstruct the due administration of the laws . . .

The States severally have not retained their entire sovereignty. It has been shown that in becoming parts of a nation, not members of a league, they surrendered many of their essential parts of sovereignty. The right to make treaties, declare war, levy taxes, exercise exclusive judicial and legislative powers, were all functions of sovereign power. The States, then, for all these important purposes, were no longer sovereign. The allegiance of their citizens was transferred in the first instance to the government of the United States; they became American citizens, and owed obedience to the Constitution of the United States, and to laws made in conformity with the powers vested in Congress. This last position has not been, and cannot be, denied. How then, can that State be said to be sovereign and independent whose citizens owe obedience to laws not made by it, and whose magistrates are sworn to disregard those laws, when they come in conflict with those passed by another? . . .

This, then, is the position in which we stand. A small majority of the citizens of one State in the Union have elected delegates to a State convention; that convention has ordained that all the revenue laws of the United States must be repealed, or that they are no longer a member of the Union. The governor of that State has recommended to the legislature the raising of an army to carry the secession into effect, and that he may be empowered to give clearances to vessels in the name of the State . . .

Fellow-citizens! the momentous case is before you. On your undivided support of your government depends the decision of the great question it involves, whether your sacred Union will be preserved, and the blessing it secures to us as one people shall be perpetuated. No one can doubt that the unanimity with which that decision will be expressed, will be such as to inspire new confidence in republican institutions, and that the prudence, the wisdom, and the courage which it will bring to their defence, will transmit them unimpaired and invigorated to our children.

May the Great Ruler of nations grant that the signal blessings with which he has favored ours may not, by the madness of party or personal ambition, be disregarded and lost, and may His wise providence bring those who have produced this crisis to see the folly, before they feel the misery, of civil strife, and inspire a returning veneration for that Union which, if we may dare to penetrate his designs, he has chosen, as the only means of attaining the high destinies to which we may reasonably aspire.

Grover Cleveland 1837–1908

NATIONALITY:
American
WHEN:
1885
WHERE:
Washington DC
YOU SHOULD KNOW:
President Cleveland is the only president to have had non-consecutive terms in office separated by another presidency, and is therefore both the 22nd and 24th President of the United States.

The first Democrat to be elected to the presidency since 1856, Grover Cleveland benefitted greatly from the Republicans' choice of candidate, James Blaine, who alienated many members of the GOP. His inspiring inaugural address called for 'non-sectional' co-operation – after a notoriously spiteful campaign – promised a continuation of the foreign policies of not getting embroiled in other countries' disputes but protecting US interests against any threats and a replacement of incompetent time-serving public employees with what could be called 'a government of all the talents'. He also asked all US voters to engage in their political system and hold government – both Federal and local – to account.

‘ In the presence of this vast assemblage of my countrymen I am about to supplement and seal by the oath which I shall take the manifestation of the will of a great and free people. In the exercise of their power and right of self-government they have committed to one of their fellow-citizens a supreme and sacred trust, and he here consecrates himself to their service . . .

Today the executive branch of the Government is transferred to new keeping. But this is still the Government of all the people, and it should be none the less an object of their affectionate solicitude . . . Moreover, if from this hour we cheerfully and honestly abandon all sectional prejudice and distrust, and determine, with manly confidence in one another, to work out harmoniously the achievements of our national destiny, we shall deserve to realize all the benefits which our happy form of government can bestow . . .

By the Father of his Country our Constitution was commended for adoption as 'the result of a spirit of amity and mutual concession'. In that same spirit it should be administered, in order to promote the lasting welfare of the country and to secure the full measure of its priceless benefits to us and to those who will succeed to the blessings of our national life. The large variety of diverse and competing interests subject to Federal control, persistently seeking the recognition of their claims, need give us no fear that 'the greatest good to the greatest number' will fail to be accomplished if in the halls of national legislation that spirit of amity and mutual concession shall prevail in which the Constitution had its birth. If this involves the surrender or postponement of private interests and the abandonment of local advantages, compensation will be found in the assurance that the common interest is subserved and the general welfare advanced.

In the discharge of my official duty I shall endeavor to be guided by a just and unstrained construction of the Constitution, a careful observance of the distinction between the powers granted to the Federal Government and those reserved to the States or to the people, and by a cautious appreciation of those functions which by the

Constitution and laws have been especially assigned to the executive branch of the government.

But he who takes the oath today to preserve, protect, and defend the Constitution of the United States only assumes the solemn obligation which every patriotic citizen – on the farm, in the workshop, in the busy marts of trade, and everywhere – should share with him. The Constitution which prescribes his oath, my countrymen, is yours; the government you have chosen him to administer for a time is yours; the suffrage which executes the will of freemen is yours; the laws and the entire scheme of our civil rule, from the town meeting to the State capitals and the national capital, is yours. Your every voter, as surely as your Chief Magistrate, under the same high sanction, though in a different sphere, exercises a public trust. Nor is this all. Every citizen owes to the country a vigilant watch and close scrutiny of its public servants and a fair and reasonable estimate of their fidelity and usefulness. Thus is the people's will impressed upon the whole framework of our civil polity – municipal, State, and Federal . . .

The genius of our institutions, the needs of our people in their home life, and the attention which is demanded for the settlement and development of the resources of our vast territory dictate the scrupulous avoidance of any departure from that foreign policy commended by the history, the traditions, and the prosperity of our Republic. It is the policy of independence, favored by our position and defended by our known love of justice and by our power. It is the policy of peace suitable to our interests. It is the policy of neutrality, rejecting any share in foreign broils and ambitions upon other continents and repelling their intrusion here. It is the policy of Monroe and of Washington and Jefferson – 'Peace, commerce, and honest friendship with all nations; entangling alliance with none.' . . .

The conscience of the people demands that the Indians within our boundaries shall be fairly and honestly treated as wards of the Government and their education and civilization promoted with a view to their ultimate citizenship, and that polygamy in the Territories, destructive of the family relation and offensive to the moral sense of the civilized world, shall be repressed . . .

The people demand reform in the administration of the government and the application of business principles to public affairs. As a means to this end, civil-service reform should be in good faith enforced. Our citizens have the right to protection from the incompetency of public employees who hold their places solely as the reward of partisan service, and from the corrupting influence of those who promise and the vicious methods of those who expect such rewards; and those who worthily seek public employment have the right to insist that merit and competency shall be recognized instead of party subserviency or the surrender of honest political belief . . .

These topics and the constant and ever-varying wants of an active and enterprising population may well receive the attention and the patriotic endeavor of all who make and execute the Federal law. Our duties are practical and call for industrious application, an intelligent perception of the claims of public office, and, above all, a firm determination, by united action, to secure to all the people of the land the full benefits of the best form of government ever vouchsafed to man. And let us not trust to human effort alone, but humbly acknowledging the power and goodness of Almighty God, who presides over the destiny of nations, and who has at all times been revealed in our country's history, let us invoke His aid and His blessings upon our labours.

The inaguration of President Cleveland

John Brown 1800–1859

NATIONALITY:
American
WHEN:
1859
WHERE:
Charles Town (now Charlestown),
West Virginia, USA
YOU SHOULD KNOW:
One of the soldiers guarding
Brown the night before his
execution was John Wilkes Booth,
Lincoln's assassin.

Unlike the majority of northern anti-slavery campaigners, John Brown advocated direct action and violence in response to that of pro-slavery forces in Kansas. His last battle was at Harper's Ferry, Virginia, when he attempted to lead a force to seize the Federal Arsenal so that the weapons could be passed to local slaves and start an armed insurrection. After his conviction on charges of murdering five people, with conspiring with slaves to rebel and with treason against Virginia, Brown addressed the court, justifying his actions, charging his accusers with hypocrisy and admitting his willingness to die for his cause. He was sentenced to death and hanged a month later.

I HAVE, may it please the court, a few words to say. In the first place, I deny everything but what I have all along admitted – the design on my part to free the slaves. I intended certainly to have made a clean thing of that matter, as I did last winter when I went into Missouri and there took slaves without the snapping of a gun on either side, moved them through the country, and finally left them in Canada. I designed to have done the same thing again on a larger scale. That was all I intended. I never did intend murder, or treason, or the destruction of property, or to excite or incite slaves to rebellion, or to make insurrection.

I have another objection; and that is, it is unjust that I should suffer such a penalty. Had I interfered in the manner which I admit, and which I admit has been fairly proved (for I admire the truthfulness and candour of the greater portion of the witnesses who have testified in this case) – had I so interfered in behalf of the rich, the powerful, the intelligent, the so-called great, or in behalf of any of their friends – either father, mother, brother, sister, wife, or children, or any of that class – and suffered and sacrificed what I have in this interference, it would have been all right; and every man in this court would have deemed it an act worthy of reward rather than punishment.

This court acknowledges, as I suppose, the validity of the law of God. I see a book kissed here which I suppose to be the Bible, or at least the New Testament. That teaches me that all things whatsoever I would that men should do to me, I should do even so to them. It teaches me, further, to 'remember them that are in bonds, as bound with them'. I endeavored to act up to that instruction. I say I am yet too young to understand that God is any respecter of persons. I believe that to have interfered as I have done – as I have always freely admitted I have done – in behalf of His despised poor was not wrong, but right. Now, if it is deemed necessary that I should forfeit my life for the furtherance of the ends of justice, and mingle my blood further with the blood of my children and with the blood of millions in this slave country whose rights are disregarded by wicked, cruel, and unjust enactments – I submit; so let it be done!

Let me say one word further.

I feel entirely satisfied with the treatment I have received on my trial. Considering all the circumstances it has been more generous than I expected. But I feel no consciousness of guilt. I have stated from the first what was my intention and what was not. I never had any design against the life of any person, nor any disposition to commit treason, or excite slaves to rebel, or make any general insurrection. I never encouraged any man to do so, but always discouraged any idea of that kind.

Let me say also a word in regard to the statements made by some of those connected with me. I hear it has been stated by some of them that I have induced them to join me. But the contrary is true. I do not say this to injure them, but as regretting their weakness. There is not one of them but joined me of his own accord, and the greater part of them at their own expense. A number of them I never saw, and never had a word of conversation with till the day they came to me; and that was for the purpose I have stated.

Now I have done. 〟

Simon Cameron 1799–1889

Simon Cameron became a byword for corruption during the 1860s. After making a fortune in newspapers, banking and manufacturing he served a period in the Senate as a Democrat, then switched to the Republican Party. He was nominated as a presidential candidate, but supported Abraham Lincoln instead, for which he was rewarded with the position of Secretary of War, although he had initially wanted to be Secretary of the Treasury. He was forced to resign from this role in a little under a year because of mismanagement and allegations of staggering corruption and was sent to Russia to get him out of the way.

NATIONALITY:
American
WHEN:
1860
WHERE:
Probably in Pennsylvania, USA

‘ An honest politician is one who, when he's bought, stays bought. 〟

Simón Bolívar

(Simón José Antonio de la Santísima Trinidad Bolívar Palacios y Blanco) 1783–1830

NATIONALITY:
Venezuelan
WHEN:
1829
WHERE:
Quito, Equador
YOU SHOULD KNOW:
In this speech, 'America' means Latin America

Known as the Liberator – el Libertador – Simón Bolívar was one of the key figures in the struggle for the independence of Spanish America. His own family had been Spanish settlers in Venezuela in the sixteenth century and he used part of their enormous wealth to fund revolutionary forces. Among his titles are: the first President of Gran Colombia, second President of Venezuela, sixth Dicator of Peru and first President of Bolivia, the country named after him. Gran Colombia was far too large and disparate a territory and he had difficulty in keeping control of some of the states. After an assassination attempt in 1828, he became more disillusioned and the following extract from a speech made in Quito shows just how he felt about the ingratitude of the people whom he had helped to liberate from colonialism. He resigned in 1830, but died before he could move to Europe.

There is no good faith in America, neither among men, nor among nations. Their treaties are scraps of paper, their constitutions mere books, their elections open combat; liberty is anarchy, and life itself is a torment.

Bolívar leading his freedom fighters into action.

United Nations Security Council

During the autumn of 2002, the sabre-rattling between the USA and Iraq over the latter's weapons-of-mass-destruction programme escalated, and Resolution 1441's fourteen paragraphs made a series of demands, chiefly about allowing weapons inspectors back into the country. During the six weeks that the drafting and completion of the resolution took, the Iraqi government announced that it would re-admit weapons inspectors. Many parties to the resolution were clear at the time that it did not authorize military action against Iraq without a further resolution: such countries as France, Russia and Syria would not otherwise have signed. When the weapons inspectors returned to Iraq they found 18 undeclared chemical rockets, that two types of missile violated UN range restrictions and that substantial stockpiles of anthrax and a nerve agent had gone missing, although Iraq insisted that they had been destroyed. Because no answer to these issues had been achieved by mid-March 2003, the US, UK and Spanish governments declared that Iraq was in material breach of Resolution 1441 and that war was now legitimized. Legal experts are still in dispute about this.

WHEN:
2002
WHERE:
New York City, USA
YOU SHOULD KNOW:
The Iraq Survey Group's post-war investigations came to the conclusion that Iraq's chemical weapons had been destroyed in 1991. The Bush administration also agreed that the intelligence about Iraq's weapons of mass destruction was wrong.

THE SECURITY COUNCIL

Recalling all its previous relevant resolutions, in particular its resolutions 661 (1990) of 6 August 1990, 678 (1990) of 29 November 1990, 686 (1991) of 2 March 1991, 687 (1991) of 3 April 1991, 688 (1991) of 5 April 1991, 707 (1991) of 15 August 1991, 715 (1991) of 11 October 1991, 986 (1995) of 14 April 1995, and 1284 (1999) of 17 December 1999, and all the relevant statements of its President.

Recalling also its resolution 1382 (2001) of 29 November 2001 and its intention to implement it fully.

Recognizing the threat Iraq's non-compliance with Council resolutions and proliferation of weapons of mass destruction and long-range missiles poses to international peace and security.

Recalling that its resolution 678 (1990) authorized Member States to use all necessary means to uphold and implement its resolution 660 (1990) of 2 August 1990 and all relevant resolutions subsequent to resolution 660 (1990) and to restore international peace and security in the area.

Further recalling that its resolution 687 (1991) imposed obligations on Iraq as a necessary step for achievement of its stated objective of restoring international peace and security in the area.

Deploring the fact that Iraq has not provided an accurate, full, final, and complete disclosure, as required by resolution 687 (1991), of all aspects of its programmes to develop weapons of mass destruction and ballistic missiles with a range greater than 150 kilometres, and of all holdings of such weapons, their components and production facilities and locations, as well as all other nuclear programmes, including any which it claims are for purposes not related to nuclear-weapons-usable material.

Deploring further that Iraq repeatedly obstructed immediate, unconditional, and unrestricted access to sites designated by the United Nations Special Commission (UNSCOM) and the International Atomic Energy Agency (IAEA), failed to cooperate fully and unconditionally with UNSCOM and IAEA weapons inspectors, as required by resolution 687 (1991), and ultimately ceased all cooperation with UNSCOM and the IAEA in 1998.

Deploring the absence, since December 1998, in Iraq of international monitoring, inspection, and verification, as required by relevant resolutions, of weapons of mass destruction and ballistic missiles, in spite of the Council's repeated demands that Iraq provide immediate, unconditional, and unrestricted access to the United Nations Monitoring, Verification and Inspection Commission (UNMOVIC), established in resolution 1284 (1999) as the successor organization to UNSCOM, and the IAEA, and regretting the consequent prolonging of the crisis in the region and the suffering of the Iraqi people.

Deploring also that the Government of Iraq has failed to comply with its commitments pursuant to resolution 687 (1991) with regard to terrorism, pursuant to resolution 688 (1991) to end repression of its civilian population and to provide access by international humanitarian organizations to all those in need of assistance in Iraq, and pursuant to resolutions 686 (1991), 687 (1991), and 1284 (1999) to return or cooperate in accounting for Kuwaiti and third country nationals wrongfully detained by Iraq, or to return Kuwaiti property wrongfully seized by Iraq.

Recalling that in its resolution 687 (1991) the Council declared that a ceasefire would be based on acceptance by Iraq of the provisions of that resolution, including the obligations on Iraq contained therein.

Determined to ensure full and immediate compliance by Iraq without conditions or restrictions with its obligations under resolution 687 (1991) and other relevant resolutions and recalling that the resolutions of the Council constitute the governing standard of Iraqi compliance.

Recalling that the effective operation of UNMOVIC, as the successor organization to the Special Commission, and the IAEA is essential for the implementation of resolution 687 (1991) and other relevant resolutions.

Noting the letter dated 16 September 2002 from the Minister for Foreign Affairs of Iraq addressed to the Secretary-General is a necessary first step toward rectifying Iraq's continued failure to comply with relevant Council resolutions.

Noting further the letter dated 8 October 2002 from the Executive Chairman of UNMOVIC and the Director-General of the IAEA to General Al-Saadi of the Government of Iraq laying out the practical arrangements, as a follow-up to their meeting in Vienna, that are prerequisites for the resumption of inspections in Iraq by UNMOVIC and the IAEA, and expressing the gravest concern at the continued failure by the Government of Iraq to provide confirmation of the arrangements as laid out in that letter.

Reaffirming the commitment of all Member States to the sovereignty and territorial integrity of Iraq, Kuwait, and the neighbouring States.

Commending the Secretary-General and members of the League of Arab States and its Secretary-General for their efforts in this regard . . .

Alfred E. Smith 1873–1944

Former New York Governor, the progressive and libertarian Al Smith, the 'Happy Warrior', had been a long-time friend of Roosevelt and was a founder of the policies that became the New Deal, but when the latter stood against him for the Democratic nomination in 1932, all that changed. Moreover, he distrusted the encroaching Federal power that the New Deal would entail. On January 25, 1936 he had addressed a large crowd of Republicans in Washington and pledged his support for the Republican candidate. Later in the year, he renewed his attack on the New Deal, which he castigated as a betrayal of good government practice and liberal ideals.

NATIONALITY:
American
WHEN:
1936
WHERE:
On the Presidential election trail
YOU SHOULD KNOW:
In 1928 Al Smith was the first Catholic of Irish descent to gain nomination for the US Presidency from a major party, in 1928. The result was not a happy one as the campaign revealed a substantial undercurrent of anti-Catholic bigotry among the Protestant majority.

‘ No matter how thin you slice it, it's still baloney. ”

Alfred E. Smith

The Senate of Nanking

NATIONALITY:
Chinese
WHEN:
1912
WHERE:
Nanking, China
YOU SHOULD KNOW:
the Xuantong Emperor was the last
ruler in a series that dated back
almost without a break to 221 BC.

*After the successful Xinhai Revolution of 1911, on February 6,
1912 the Senate of Nanking passed a resolution for the Imperial
Edict for Abdication. The prequistite conditions for abdication
included the list below. After negotiations between President Li
Huanhung and the Dowager Empress Longyu, it was agreed
that the five-year-old emperor would abdicate, according to
these terms, with a few minor variations. She signed the edict
on February 12 and it was proclaimed from Beijing's
Tiananmen Gate. He would remain in the Forbidden City until
1924. In 1932 he was installed as puppet king in Japanese-
controlled Manchukuo (formerly Manchuria) and abdicated
again at the end of World War II.*

" * The Qing Emperor remains and
will be treated as a foreign
monarch by the Republic
Government.
* The Republic will allocate
4,000,000 Yuan each year for royal
expenses.
* The emperor will remain in the
Forbidden City until he can be
transferred to Yeheyuan.
* Royal temple and tombs will be
guarded and maintained.
* The expenses of Guangxu's tomb
will be disbursed by the Republic.
* Royal employees will remain in
the Forbidden City with the
exception of eunuchs.
* Private property of the royal
family will be protected by the
Republic.
* Royal forces will be incorporated
into the army of the Republic. "

*Pu Yi who was the last Emperor
of China, was in fact a puppet
monarch for the Japanese.*

J. William Fulbright 1905–1995

March 1964 was a turbulent time in the US Senate. Just three days after Fulbright gave this speech there on March 27, the debate on the 1964 Civil Rights Act was opened. The Cold War was still at its height and yet here was a Senator – and chairman of the Senate Foreign Relations Committee – advocating coexistence, if not outright co-operation, with the Soviet Union. For some it was definitely unthinkable. In 1961 he had tried to persuade President Kennedy against authorizing the invasion of the Bay of Pigs, which with hindsight was probably the right stance as the episode was a fiasco. It is said that he also suggested to Kennedy in October 1961 that he ought to avoid going to Dallas as it was too dangerous.

NATIONALITY:
American
WHEN:
March 27, 1964
WHERE:
Washington, DC, USA
YOU SHOULD KNOW:
J. William Fulbright promoted the Fulbright programme of international educational exchanges allowing students to experience learning elsewhere in the world.

‘A policy that can be accurately, though perhaps not preduently, defined as one of 'peaceful coexistence' . . . We must dare to think 'unthinkable' thoughts. We must learn to explore all the options and possibilities that confront us in a complex and rapidly changing world. We must learn to welcome and not to fear the voices of dissent. We must dare to think about 'unthinkable' things because when things become unthinkable, thinking stops and action becomes mindless.’

Patrick Henry 1736–1799

During the 1765 meeting of the Virginia House of Burgesses the new delegate Patrick Henry proposed a series of resolutions against the Stamp Act. This was a British act imposing yet another tax on the American colonists. The first resolutions – that American colonists had the same rights as British people; those rights had been confirmed in Virginia's royal charters twice; and the right to be taxed by representatives one had chosen was a fundamental British liberty – contained nothing much new. But the last one – that only colonial assemblies had the right to tax their constituents – certainly startled the delegates present, as did the last part of his speech referring to King George III.

NATIONALITY:
American
WHEN:
1765
WHERE:
Williamsburg, Virginia, USA
YOU SHOULD KNOW:
Patrick Henry was later Governor of Virginia.

‘Caesar had his Brutus, Charles the First his Cromwell and George the Third [shouts of treason from delegates who recognized the reference to assassinated leaders] . . . may profit by their example. If this be treason, make the most of it.’

Harold Macmillan 1894–1986

NATIONALITY:
British
WHEN:
1960
WHERE:
Cape Town, South Africa

On February 3, 1960 British Prime Minister Harold Macmillan addressed both houses of the South African Parliament. In his speech he drew parallels between the stage of the country's journey – and those of other African countries he had visited – towards both a national consciousness and a readiness for independence and that of states in south and southeast Asia – like India and Malaysia – a decade or more earlier. It was a tacit admission that the colonial power accepted this as a matter of fact and would not seek to prevent this natural progression. South Africa became a republic the following year.

It is, as I have said, a special privilege for me to be here in 1960 when you are celebrating what I might call the golden wedding of the Union. At such a time it is natural and right that you should pause to take stock of your position, to look back at what you have achieved, to look forward to what lies ahead . . .

...The wind of change is blowing through this continent, and whether we like it or not, this growth of national consciousness is a political fact. We must all accept it as a fact, and our national policies must take account of it . . .

. . . As I have said, the growth of national consciousness in Africa is a political fact, and we must accept it as such. That means, I would judge, that we've got to come to terms with it.

Claiborne Pell 1918–2009

NATIONALITY:
American
WHEN:
1988
WHERE:
Washington, DC, USA
YOU SHOULD KNOW:
Senator Pell was responsible for legislation that gave grants to thousands of students from less privileged backgrounds.

On March 16–17 1988, some 5,000 citizens of the Kurdish town of Halabja in northern Iraq were killed in a chemical weapons attack, attributed by most to the Iraqi Air Force. Shortly afterwards, Senators Claiborne Pell, Al Gore and Jesse Helm introduced legislation aimed at imposing sanctions on Iraq, which was passed unanimously. The Reagan administration killed the bill off, amid claims that it was more likely to be the Iranians (both sides were known to have chemical weapons) or that because they were Iraqi citizens international law could not be applied. Suspicion was rife that the administration was covering up because Iran, not Iraq, was enemy number one. Attitudes towards the Iraqi government changed after the invasion of Kuwait two years later.

While a people are gassed, the world is largely silent. There are reasons for this. Iraq's great oil wealth, its military strength, a desire not to upset the delicate negotiations seeking an end to the Iran-Iraq war. Silence, however, is complicity. A half century ago, the world was silent as Hitler began a campaign that culminated in the near extermination of Europe's Jews. We cannot be silent to genocide again.

Joseph Stalin 1879–1953

In 1935, as the threat of German aggression began to look more imminent, the French Prime Minister, Pierre Laval, went to Moscow for a meeting with the Soviet leader, Stalin. After discussions about troop numbers, Laval asked if it would be possible to do something to encourage religion and the Catholics within the USSR as it would help in dealings with Pope Pius XI (who was vehemently anti-Soviet because of the persecution, imprisonment, deportation and execution of Christians that had been going on for years). Laval's question betrays an almost unimaginable naiveness, and Stalin's retort his utter contempt for the idea of spiritual – as opposed to temporal, or military – authority.

NATIONALITY:
Russian
WHEN:
1935
WHERE:
Moscow, USSR
YOU SHOULD KNOW:
Anything up to thirty million Soviet citizens may have been murdered during Stalin's 21 years in power.

Oho, the Pope! How many divisions has he got?

Joseph Stalin was the dictatorial head of the USSR from 1924–1953.

Winston Churchill 1874–1965

NATIONALITY:
British
WHEN:
October 1, 1939
WHERE:
London, England

Following the resignation of Neville Chamberlain in 1940, whose policy of appeasing Hitler had failed so dismally, Winston Churchill took over as Prime Minister of Britain. His radio broadcast to the nation on October 1, 1939 was in response to the German invasion of vast areas of Poland on September 1, 1939 and the Soviet annexation of the east of the country a little over two weeks later. In the years before the war, Britain and France had tried through various means to form an alliance with Russia against the threat from Germany, but efforts were unsuccessful because Stalin felt that the Allies offered nothing that was of use to him and actually made a pact with Hitler in 1939, agreeing on the division of Poland.

Winston Churchill makes a sombre broadcast after the fall of Poland.

I cannot forecast to you the action of Russia. It is a riddle wrapped in a mystery inside an enigma: but perhaps there is a key. That key is Russian national interest.

The First Vatican Council

Papal Infallibity is the dogma proclaiming that when the Pope is talking about divinely revealed matters concerning faith or morals, he is by definition incapable of error. The idea had been widely held for centuries, but was formalized at the First Vatican Council on July 18, 1870. It has been used only once, in the declaration of the Assumption of the Virgin Mary being an article of faith. Ex cathedra *translates as 'from the chair' representing the fact that the Pope is speaking as successor to the Throne of St Peter, the first Pope.*

WHEN:
July 18, 1870
WHERE:
The Vatican, Italy
YOU SHOULD KNOW:
Previous Papal Councils had been held in the Basilica of St John Lateran, so were called Lateran Councils.

' . . . Therefore, faithfully adhering to the tradition received from the beginning of the Christian faith, to the glory of God our Saviour, for the exaltation of the Catholic religion and for the salvation of the Christian people, with the approval of the Sacred Council, we teach and define as a divinely revealed dogma that when the Roman pontiff speaks *ex cathedra*, that is, when,

1. in the exercise of his office as shepherd and teacher of all Christians,
2. in virtue of his supreme apostolic authority,
3. he defines a doctrine concerning faith or morals to be held by the whole church,

he possesses, by the divine assistance promised to him in blessed Peter, that infallibility which the divine Redeemer willed his church to enjoy in defining doctrine concerning faith or morals.

Therefore, such definitions of the Roman pontiff are of themselves, and not by the consent of the church, irreformable.

So then, should anyone, which God forbid, have the temerity to reject this definition of ours: let him be anathema. '

Henri IV King of France 1553–1610

During the sixteenth century, many northern European countries were becoming – or trying to become – Protestant, rather than remaining Catholic with their monarchs answerable to the Pope. France remained true to the old faith, although there were substantial numbers of Protestants, called Huguenots. In 1589 King Henri III of France was assassinated and the Huguenot King Henri III of Navarre became King Henri IV of France. But many would not accept a Protestant as king and on July 25, 1593 Henri converted to Catholicism to secure his throne and his country at the Basilica of St Denis, north of Paris.

NATIONALITY:
French
WHEN:
July 25, 1593
WHERE:
Outside Paris, France
YOU SHOULD KNOW:
Henri had already briefly become a Catholic during 1572 in order to escape the aftermath of the St Bartholomew's Day Massacre ordered by his mother-in-law, Catherine de Medici, just six days after his wedding when Paris was full of celebrating Huguenots.

' Paris vaut bien une messe (Paris is well worth a mass). '

George Washington 1732–1799

NATIONALITY:
American
WHEN:
1796
WHERE:
Philadelphia, Pennsylvania, USA

George Washington's Farewell Address was written in the form of a speech, but never actually delivered. In its 51 paragraphs, he states his reasons for not seeking another term as President and lays out his vision for the country that had so recently been united to gain its independence. He discusses the need for vigilence against creeping infringements on national and individual liberty, expresses his opinion that the nation is better as a unified whole and warns against both deviance from the principles laid out in the Constitution and any rebellion. He advises against bringing political parties into governance, permanent antipathy against or alliances with any particular nation and counsels the need for morality in government.

The period for a new election of a citizen, to administer the executive government of the United States, being not far distant, and the time actually arrived, when your thoughts must be employed designating the person, who is to be clothed with that important trust, it appears to me proper, especially as it may conduce to a more distinct expression of the public voice, that I should now apprize you of the resolution I have formed, to decline being considered among the number of those out of whom a choice is to be made . . .

The acceptance of, and continuance hitherto in, the office to which your suffrages have twice called me, have been a uniform sacrifice of inclination to the opinion of duty, and to a deference for what appeared to be your desire. I constantly hoped, that it would have been much earlier in my power, consistently with motives, which I was not at liberty to disregard, to return to that retirement, from which I had been reluctantly drawn. The strength of my inclination to do this, previous to the last election, had even led to the preparation of an address to declare it to you; but mature reflection on the then perplexed and critical posture of our affairs with foreign nations, and the unanimous advice of persons entitled to my confidence impelled me to abandon the idea . . .

The impressions, with which I first undertook the arduous trust, were explained on the proper occasion. In the discharge of this trust, I will only say, that I have, with good intentions, contributed towards the organization and administration of the government the best exertions of which a very fallible judgment was capable. Not unconscious, in the outset, of the inferiority of my qualifications, experience in my own eyes, perhaps still more in the eyes of others, has strengthened the motives to diffidence of myself; and every day the increasing weight of years admonishes me more and more, that the shade of retirement is as necessary to me as it will be welcome. Satisfied, that, if any circumstances have given peculiar value to my

services, they were temporary, I have the consolation to believe, that, while choice and prudence invite me to quit the political scene, patriotism does not forbid it.

In looking forward to the moment, which is intended to terminate the career of my public life, my feelings do not permit me to suspend the deep acknowledgment of that debt of gratitude, which I owe to my beloved country for the many honors it has conferred upon me; still more for the steadfast confidence with which it has supported me; and for the opportunities I have thence enjoyed of manifesting my inviolable attachment, by services faithful and persevering, though in usefulness unequal to my zeal. If benefits have resulted to our country from these services, let it always be remembered to your praise, and as an instructive example in our annals, that under circumstances in which the passions, agitated in every direction, were liable to mislead, amidst appearances sometimes dubious, vicissitudes of fortune often discouraging, in situations in which not unfrequently want of success has countenanced the spirit of criticism, the constancy of your support was the essential prop of the efforts, and a guarantee of the plans by which they were effected . . .

Though, in reviewing the incidents of my administration, I am unconscious of intentional error, I am nevertheless too sensible of my defects not to think it probable that I may have committed many errors. Whatever they may be, I fervently beseech the Almighty to avert or mitigate the evils to which they may tend. I shall also carry with me the hope, that my Country will never cease to view them with indulgence; and that, after 45 years of my life dedicated to its service with an upright zeal, the faults of incompetent abilities will be consigned to oblivion, as myself must soon be to the mansions of rest.

Relying on its kindness in this as in other things, and actuated by that fervent love towards it, which is so natural to a man, who views it in the native soil of himself and his progenitors for several generations; I anticipate with pleasing expectation that retreat, in which I promise myself to realize, without alloy, the sweet enjoyment of partaking, in the midst of my fellow-citizens, the benign influence of good laws under a free government, the ever favorite object of my heart, and the happy reward, as I trust, of our mutual cares, labors, and dangers.

GEORGE WASHINGTON

Sir Edward Grey 1862–1933

NATIONALITY:
British
WHEN:
1914
WHERE:
London, England
YOU SHOULD KNOW:
Grey was Foreign Secretary in the UK
Government for exactly 11 years. He
became Lord Grey of Fallon in 1916.

Grey afterwards recalled that he said these words to a friend in early August of 1914, while watching the gas lamps outside the Foreign Office being lit one evening. Less than six weeks later the Austrian Archduke Franz Ferdinand had been assassinated and in little more than a week or so, Russia, the Austro-Hungarian Empire, Germany and France had mobilized troops and within another month, the German army had swept across Belgium into north-eastern France. Contrary to the optimism felt by many in Britain, who assured each other that 'It will all be over by Christmas' Grey was extremely pessimistic about the idea that the inevitable war might be short, and he was proved to be right.

‘ The lamps are going out all over Europe; we shall not see them lit again in our lifetime. ’

The Oslo Accords

WHEN:
1993
WHERE:
Oslo, Norway/Washington, DC, USA
YOU SHOULD KNOW:
The Oslo Accords were the first direct agreement between any political representatives of the Palestinians and the Israeli government.

The Oslo Accords – officially the Declaration of Principles on Interim Self-Government Arrangements – were negotiated in secret between December 1992 and August 1993, in the background of the official Madrid negotiations and seemingly without the knowledge of the US administration. They included talks on economic co-operation, elections and Israeli withdrawal from Gaza and Jericho. The final details – about Palestinian recognition of Israel and renunciation of violence and Israeli acceptance of the Palestinian Liberation Organization as the official Palestinian authority – were brokered in Paris and the accords were signed in Washington, DC on September 13, 1993. Some 15 years later, although the West Bank is – relatively speaking – peaceful, the same cannot be said of the Hamas-controlled Gaza Strip.

‘ The Government of the State of Israel and the PLO team (in the Jordanian-Palestinian delegation to the Middle East Peace Conference) (the 'Palestinian Delegation'), representing the Palestinian people, agree that it is time to put an end to decades of confrontation and conflict, recognize their mutual legitimate and political rights, and strive to live in peaceful coexistence and mutual dignity and security and achieve a just, lasting and comprehensive peace settlement and historic reconciliation through the agreed political process. Accordingly, the two sides agree to the following principles . . . ’

Warren G. Harding 1865–1923

At the first Presidential Inauguration after World War I, Warren Harding used his address to set out his philosophy and major aims for his term, including the God-given righteousness of the American Republic, continuation of the previous policy of non-involvement in other countries' business or wars unless not to do so would be detrimental to the USA, mediation and conciliation with former enemies, reduced taxation when possible, economic recovery, the continuation of import tariffs to protect US manufacturing, reconstruction, improvement of welfare through the creation of wealth, the need for unselfishness, the possibility of a universal 'draft' for civil or military service and an outlawing of profiteering. He died just two-and-a-half years into his Presidency.

NATIONALITY:
American
WHEN:
1921
WHERE:
Washington, DC, USA
YOU SHOULD KNOW:
This was the first occasion when an incoming President went to the Capitol in a motor vehicle.

' When one surveys the world about him after the great storm, noting the marks of destruction and yet rejoicing in the ruggedness of the things which withstood it, if he is an American he breathes the clarified atmosphere with a strange mingling of regret and new hope. We have seen a world passion spend its fury, but we contemplate our Republic unshaken, and hold our civilization secure. Liberty – liberty within the law – and civilization are inseparable, and though both were threatened we find them now secure; and there comes to Americans the profound assurance that our representative government is the highest expression and surest guaranty of both . . .

The recorded progress of our Republic, materially and spiritually, in itself proves the wisdom of the inherited policy of noninvolvement in Old World affairs. Confident of our ability to work out our own destiny, and jealously guarding our right to do so, we seek no part in directing the destinies of the Old World. We do not mean to be entangled. We will accept no responsibility except as our own conscience and judgment, in each instance, may determine.

Our eyes never will be blind to a developing menace, our ears never deaf to the call of civilization. We recognize the new order in the world, with the closer contacts which progress has wrought. We sense the call of the human heart for fellowship, fraternity, and cooperation. We crave friendship and harbor no hate. But America, our America, the America builded on the foundation laid by the inspired fathers, can be a party to no permanent military alliance. It can enter into no political commitments, nor assume any economic obligations which will subject our decisions to any other than our own authority . . .

The success of our popular government rests wholly upon the correct interpretation of the deliberate, intelligent, dependable popular will of America. In a deliberate questioning of a suggested change of national policy, where internationality was to supersede nationality, we turned to a referendum, to the American people. There was ample discussion, and there is a public mandate in manifest understanding.

America is ready to encourage, eager to initiate, anxious to participate in any seemly program likely to lessen the probability of war, and promote that brotherhood of mankind which must be God's highest conception of human relationship. Because we cherish ideals of justice and peace, because we appraise international comity and helpful relationship no less highly than any people of the world, we aspire to a high place in the moral leadership of civilization, and we hold a maintained America, the proven Republic, the unshaken temple of representative democracy, to be not only an inspiration and example, but the highest agency of strengthening good will and promoting accord on both continents . . .

We must understand that ties of trade bind nations in closest intimacy, and none may receive except as he gives. We have not strengthened ours in accordance with our resources or our genius, notably on our own continent, where a galaxy of republics reflects the glory of new-world democracy, but in the new order of finance and trade we mean to promote enlarged activities and seek expanded confidence . . .

Amid it all we have riveted the gaze of all civilization to the unselfishness and the righteousness of representative democracy, where our freedom never has made offensive warfare, never has sought territorial aggrandizement through force, never has turned to the arbitrament of arms until reason has been exhausted. When the governments of the earth shall have established a freedom like our own and shall have sanctioned the pursuit of peace as we have practiced it, I believe the last sorrow and the final sacrifice of international warfare will have been written.

Let me speak to the maimed and wounded soldiers who are present today, and through them convey to their comrades the gratitude of the Republic for their sacrifices in its defense. A generous country will never forget the services you rendered, and you may hope for a policy under government that will relieve any maimed successors from taking your places on another such occasion as this . . .

Out of such universal service will come a new unity of spirit and purpose, a new confidence and consecration, which would make our defense impregnable, our triumph assured. Then we should have little or no disorganization of our economic, industrial, and commercial systems at home, no staggering war debts, no swollen fortunes to flout the sacrifices of our soldiers, no excuse for sedition, no pitiable slackerism, no outrage of treason. Envy and jealousy would have no soil for their menacing development, and revolution would be without the passion which engenders it . . .

The business world reflects the disturbance of war's reaction. Herein flows the lifeblood of material existence. The economic mechanism is intricate and its parts interdependent, and has suffered the shocks and jars incident to abnormal demands, credit inflations, and price upheavals. The normal balances have been impaired, the channels of distribution have been clogged, the relations of labor and management have been strained. We must seek the readjustment with care and courage. Our people must give and take. Prices must reflect the receding fever of war activities. Perhaps we never shall know the old levels of wages again, because war invariably readjusts compensations, and the necessaries of life will show their inseparable relationship, but we must strive for normalcy to reach stability. All the penalties will not be light, nor evenly distributed. There is no way of making them so. There is no instant step from disorder to order. We must face a condition of grim reality, charge off our losses and start afresh. It is the oldest lesson of civilization. I would like government to do all it can to mitigate; then, in understanding, in mutuality of interest, in concern for the common good, our tasks will be solved. No altered system will work a miracle. Any wild experiment will only add to the confusion. Our best assurance lies in efficient administration of our proven system . . .

I speak for administrative efficiency, for lightened tax burdens, for sound commercial practices, for adequate credit facilities, for sympathetic concern for all agricultural problems, for the omission of unnecessary interference of Government with business, for an end to Government's experiment in business, and for more efficient business in Government administration. With all of this must attend a mindfulness of the human side of all activities, so that social, industrial, and economic justice will be squared with the purposes of a righteous people.

With the nation-wide induction of womanhood into our political life, we may count upon her intuitions, her refinements, her intelligence, and her influence to exalt the social order. We count upon her exercise of the full privileges and the performance of the duties of citizenship to speed the attainment of the highest state.

I wish for an America no less alert in guarding against dangers from within than it is watchful against enemies from without. Our fundamental law recognizes no class, no group, no section; there must be none in legislation or administration. The supreme inspiration is the common weal. Humanity hungers for international peace, and we crave it with all mankind. My most reverent prayer for America is for industrial peace, with its rewards, widely and generally distributed, amid the inspirations of equal opportunity. No one justly may deny the equality of opportunity which made us what we are. We have mistaken unpreparedness to embrace it to be a challenge of the reality, and due concern for making all citizens fit for participation will give added strength of citizenship and magnify our achievement . . .

Service is the supreme commitment of life. I would rejoice to acclaim the era of the Golden Rule and crown it with the autocracy of service. I pledge an administration wherein all the agencies of government are called to serve, and ever promote an understanding of government purely as an expression of the popular will . . .

I accept my part with single-mindedness of purpose and humility of spirit, and implore the favor and guidance of God in His Heaven. With these I am unafraid, and confidently face the future.

I have taken the solemn oath of office on that passage of Holy Writ wherein it is asked: 'What doth the Lord require of thee but to do justly, and to love mercy, and to walk humbly with thy God?' This I plight to God and country.

Karl Franz Joseph 1887–1922

NATIONALITY:
Austrian
WHEN:
1918
WHERE:
Vienna, Austria
YOU SHOULD KNOW:
He tried to regain the Hungarian throne and reinstate that part of the empire twice in 1921.

On November 11, 1918, the day of the armistice at the end of World War I, Karl Franz Joseph brought to an end more than 1,050 years of near-continual imperial rule under first the Holy Roman Empire, then the Austrian Empire and finally the Austro-Hungarian Empire. He did not actually abdicate, but renounced power. He made a similar announcement to the people of Hungary two days later. In the face of the Allies' support for independence for the Czechs, Slovaks and south Slavs, there was no hope of keeping the empire together so his approach was pragmatic.

Since my accession I have incessantly tried to rescue my peoples from this tremendous war.

I have not delayed the re-establishment of constitutional rights or the opening of a way for the people to substantial national development. Filled with an unalterable love for my peoples I will not, with my person, be a hindrance to their free development.

I acknowledge the decision taken by German Austria to form a separate State. The people has by its deputies taken charge of the Government. I relinquish every participation in the administration of the State. Likewise I have released the members of the Austrian Government from their offices.

May the German Austrian people realize harmony from the new adjustment. The happiness of my peoples was my aim from the beginning. My warmest wishes are that an internal peace will be able to heal the wounds of this war.

Ronald Reagan 1911–2004

NATIONALITY:
American
WHEN:
1984
WHERE:
Washington, DC, USA
YOU SHOULD KNOW:
President Reagan's policies of lower taxes in combination with a liberal economic philisophy were known as 'Reaganomics'.

On August 11, 1984 President Reagan was being 'miked up' for a radio broadcast and, unaware that the microphone and channel were live, made the joke below. The Soviets claimed that this was proof that the American Government had no intention of pursuing detente. In America, however, it did not do the President's re-election chances any harm, simply being written off as another of his more memorable slip-ups. At this stage of his presidency, he was still popular and had not become mired in the Iran-Contra Scandal or other problems that would dog the latter part of his second term in the White House.

My fellow Americans, I'm pleased to tell you today that I've signed legislation that will outlaw Russia forever. We begin bombing in five minutes.

Fidel Castro

Fidel Alejandro Castro Ruz born 1926

In response to the unpopular 1952 coup in Cuba led by Fulgencio Batista, the young lawyer Castro determined on armed revolution. He and his brother Raul led an unsuccessful raid on Moncada Barracks on July 26, 1953. They managed to escape but were later captured and many of their followers were executed on the spot. They were tried on September 23, but Castro's eloquence was such that only about a quarter of the revolutionaries were found guilty. During his sentencing hearing on October 16, he gave a four-hour speech, usually known by its last four words. He was sentenced to 15 years in prison, but was released in an amnesty in May 1955, and formed a guerilla army with which to fight Batista's forces. Within four years, he would be President of Cuba.

NATIONALITY:
Cuban
WHEN:
1953
WHERE:
Santiago, Cuba
YOU SHOULD KNOW:
Fidel Castro resigned the presidency of Cuba to his brother, Raul, in February 2008 although he had been in charge only nominally since August 2006.

Fidel Castro as a young man

‘Honourable Judges, if there is in your hearts a vestige of love for your country, love for humanity, love for justice, listen carefully. I know that I will be silenced for many years; I know that there will be a conspiracy to bury me in oblivion. But my voice will not be stilled . . .

. . . I know that imprisonment will be harder for me than it has ever been for anyone, filled with cowardly threats and hideous cruelty. But I do not fear prison, as I do not fear the fury of the miserable tyrant who took the lives of 70 of my comrades. Condemn me. It does not matter. History will absolve me. ’

Mustafa Kemal
Kemal Ataturk 1881–1938

The Ottoman Empire had joined the Axis Powers during World War I and had suffered defeat. While the Allies were deciding how to split Anatolia between France, Greece, Italy and the UK and provide for independent areas for Armenia and Kurdistan, some Turks were taking matters into their own hands. In June 1919 the leader of the Young Turks, Mustafa Kemal, urged his compatriots to revolt with the following stirring speech, and the 1920 Treaty of Sevres was rendered useless even before it was finalized. By 1923, the Turkish nationalists had set up a new capital in Ankara, quelled Armenian and Kurdish revolts and expelled all foreign troops, and the independent Turkish republic was established with the Treaty of Lausanne.

We must pull on our peasant shoes, we must withdraw to the mountains, we must defend the country to the last rock. If it is the will of God that we be defeated, we must set fire to all our homes, to all our property; we must lay the country in ruins and leave it an empty desert.

Kemal Ataturk – founder of the modern secular Turkish state

Harry S. Truman 1884–1972

After the Balfour Declaration of 1917 increasing numbers of Zionists had moved to Palestine, particularly in the light of the horrors of Nazi persecution in Europe. After World War II the mandated authority, Britain, turned the problem of conflicting Arab and Jewish aspirations over to the United Nations, which proposed partition, although this solution was rejected by the Arab majority. The armed Zionist forces won the ensuing civil war and on May 14, 1948 the State of Israel was proclaimed, and eleven minutes later President Truman announced that the US Government gave official recognition to the de facto *government. Within 24 hours, Egypt, Iraq, Lebanon, Syria and Transjordan invaded, in what was to be the first of the Arab-Israeli wars and hundreds of thousands of Palestinians fled. More than 60 years later, there is still no solution.*

'This Government has been informed that a Jewish state has been proclaimed in Palestine, and recognition has been requested by the provisional Government thereof.

The United States recognizes the provisional government as the *de facto* authority of the new State of Israel.'

President Truman holds a Torah, or sacred scroll, presented to him by Dr Chaim Weizmann.

NATIONALITY:
American
WHEN:
1948
WHERE:
Washington, DC, USA
YOU SHOULD KNOW:
The Balfour Declaration was a letter written to the British Zionist Federation pledging support for the settlement of Jews in Palestine, which became possible when Britain was given the mandate for the country by the League of Nations after World War I.

Ronald Reagan 1911–2004

NATIONALITY:
American
WHEN:
1983
WHERE:
Washington, DC, USA
YOU SHOULD KNOW:
President Reagan had two
unsuccessful runs for the
Presidency in 1968 and 1976.

On June 10, 1983 President Reagan addressed the Annual Convention of the Anti-Defamation League of B'nai B'rith – the Jewish organization dedicated to anti-racism and welfare issues, among many other things – over the telephone. At the time, Israeli forces occupied areas of Lebanon as a consequence of the 1982 war, and negotiations had concluded only the previous month that would allow these forces to withdraw to a security zone in the south of the country. Although this agreement was, in the end, never ratified, Israel completed the withdrawal of its forces to this zone in the south of Lebanon in 1985.

'I know the Anti-Defamation League has justly earned the recognition as a champion of human rights. For seven decades, you've worked to ensure that all members of our society, no matter what their race, religion, or background, have an equal opportunity to succeed. And I deeply appreciate your support for my recent appointments to the US Commission on Civil Rights. Like you, I, too, was deeply troubled by the strident attacks against them.

I know that we share a belief that all people, no matter where they live, have the right to freedom of religion. This is not a right that is any government's to give or to take away. It's our right from birth, because we're all children of God.

We believe it's our duty to defend freedom, not just here at home but everywhere people are persecuted for their beliefs. I was very disturbed that a Soviet spokesman said earlier this week the majority of Jews who want to be reunited with their families in Israel have left the Soviet Union. This official said that the portion of the 1.8 million Russian Jews who still want to leave have, and I quote, 'Fallen victim to Zionist propaganda which brainwashes them.'

Well, as you know, the National Conference on Soviet Jewry estimates that by late 1979 at least 300,000 Jews had asked relatives abroad to send invitations needed for emigration. This was before the Soviets began blocking these invitations.

But in 1975, the Soviet Government signed the final act of the Helsinki Agreement. The Soviets pledged to deal in a positive and humanitarian spirit with the applications of persons who wish to be reunited with their families.

So, let us stand together, speak the truth, and tell the Soviets, stop persecuting innocent people. Let Israel's children go or face the world's condemnation for making a mockery of an historic agreement that was signed by 35 nations.

I'm delighted that Sam Lewis, our Ambassador to Israel, is with you today. I know that he'll be talking with you in greater detail about US policies in the Middle East.

We're very pleased with the recent efforts of Secretary Shultz in working out the Israeli-Lebanon withdrawal agreement. This bold initiative by Israel and Lebanon is one more step toward a more stable Middle East. Our ultimate goal remains peace between Israel and all her Arab neighbors.

Only through peace can Israel achieve real security. But Israel cannot make peace alone. Other Arab states must formally recognize that Israel does exist and that she has a right to exist. We'll continue our diplomatic efforts to seek the withdrawal from Lebanon of all foreign forces, Syrian and PLO as well as Israeli.

But we are very concerned about the Soviet buildup in Syria. I want you to know that we're committed to maintaining Israel's qualitative edge in the military balance of power. I have personally followed Israel's heroic struggle for survival ever since the founding of the State of Israel 35 years ago. As long as I'm President, the United States will be a rock of support. We will not waver in our commitment to protect Israel's security.

It's no coincidence that the same forces which are destabilizing the Middle East – the Soviet Union, Libya, the PLO – are also working hand in glove with Cuba to destabilize Central America. And I'd like to urge you to support this Nation's efforts to help our friends in Central America.

President Ronald Reagan

This question isn't who has the most perfect democracy. The question is, who's trying to build democracy and who is determined to destroy it. Many nations, including the United States, which once condoned slavery, have evolved into better democracies over time. But nations which fall into the clutches of totalitarianism do not become free and democratic again. And freedom can't be lost in one nation without being diminished everywhere.

Again, as you embark on your next 70 years, you have the thanks of all Americans for a job well done and our best wishes for the future. May we continue to be allies, may God bless you, and may He be with us all in our human rights struggles ahead. 🔊

Joseph Goebbels 1897–1945

In defiance of the settlement imposed upon Germany at the end of World War I, the Nazi government began a massive military build-up in the 1930s. The country's economy was a mess because of the Great Depression, so to fund the procurement of arms severe economic measures were imposed, including import limits on consumer goods and foreign currency restrictions. In one of his most famous speeches, in Berlin on January 17, 1936, the Minister of Public Enlightenment and Propaganda, Joseph Goebbels, used his rhetorical skills to bring the people onside to what has become known as the guns versus butter model.

NATIONALITY:
German
WHEN:
1936
WHERE:
Berlin, Germany
YOU SHOULD KNOW:
After Hitler's death, Goebbels was Chancellor of Germany for one day, before killing himself and his family.

We can do without butter, but, despite all our love of peace, not without arms. One cannot shoot with butter, but with guns. 🔊

Nikita Khrushchev 1894–1971

NATIONALITY:
Russian
WHEN:
1956
WHERE:
Moscow, USSR
YOU SHOULD KNOW:
Khrushchev had no intention of abandoning Communism. The following year he remarked in a speech that those who were waiting for that to happen would have to 'wait until a shrimp learns to whistle'.

At the 1956 Communist Party Congress in which he later denounced the personality cult of Stalin, Khruschev also signalled what many thought might be a de-escalation of the arms race and a change in foreign relations. It was just two months after the first successful test of a hydrogen bomb by the Soviets. Stalin had previously held that a third world war was inevitable but Khrushchev did not believe this, having come to the conclusion that possession by both the USA and the USSR of sufficient weapons to wipe each other out meant there was a choice between peaceful competition and all-out war. Although the Soviet arms build-up continued for several more years, until the SALT negotiations started to reduce numbers of nuclear weapons on both sides, it seemed as if the worst of the Cold War might be over.

Anthony Eden, left, and Nikolai Bulganin signing the arms treaty with Nikita Khrushchev smiling on the right.

‘. . . Either peaceful coexistence or the most destructive war in history, there is no third way . . . ’

Margaret Thatcher

born 1925

In a wide-ranging interview conducted with a reporter from Woman's Own *magazine on September 23, 1987 Mrs Thatcher refuted the idea that it was the responsibility of 'society' – i.e. government and social services – rather than individuals, families, friends, neighbours and communities, to look after people. She castigated those who assume that they have an automatic entitlement to state benefits so there is no need to work or to take any responsibility for their own lives or the upbringing of their children. She saw government as being there to help people to help themselves and as a support of last resort, for those who merited it.*

I think we have gone through a period when too many children and people have been given to understand 'I have a problem, it is the Government's job to cope with it!' or 'I have a problem, I will go and get a grant to cope with it!' 'I am homeless, the Government must house me!' and so they are casting their problems on society and who is society? There is no such thing! There are individual men and women and there are families and no government can do anything except through people and people look to themselves first. It is our duty to look after ourselves and then also to help look after our neighbour and life is a reciprocal business and people have got the entitlements too much in mind without the obligations, because there is no such thing as an entitlement unless someone has first met an obligation and it is, I think, one of the tragedies in which many of the benefits we give, which were meant to reassure people that if they were sick or ill there was a

The 'Iron Lady' was not for turning.

NATIONALITY:
British
WHEN:
1987
WHERE:
London, England
YOU SHOULD KNOW:
Margaret Thatcher is the UK's longest continuously serving Prime Minister – from May 4, 1979 to November 28, 1990.

safety net and there was help, that many of the benefits which were meant to help people who were unfortunate – ' It is all right, we joined together and we have these insurance schemes to look after it.' . That was the objective, but somehow there are some people who have been manipulating the system and so some of those help and benefits that were meant to say to people: 'All right, if you cannot get a job, you shall have a basic standard of living!'. but when people come and say: 'But what is the point of working? I can get as much on the dole!'. You say: 'Look' It is not from the dole. It is your neighbour who is supplying it and if you can earn your own living then really you have a duty to do it and you will feel very much better!'.

There is also something else I should say to them: 'If that does not give you a basic standard, you know, there are ways in which we top up the standard. You can get your housing benefit.'

But it went too far. If children have a problem, it is society that is at fault. There is no such thing as society. There is living tapestry of men and women and people and the beauty of that tapestry and the quality of our lives will depend upon how much each of us is prepared to take responsibility for ourselves and each of us prepared to turn round and help by our own efforts those who are unfortunate. And the worst things we have in life, in my view, are where children who are a great privilege and a trust – they are the fundamental great trust, but they do not ask to come into the world, we bring them into the world, they are a miracle, there is nothing like the miracle of life – we have these little innocents and the worst crime in life is when those children, who would naturally have the right to look to their parents for help, for comfort, not only just for the food and shelter but for the time, for the understanding, turn round and not only is that help not forthcoming, but they get either neglect or worse than that, cruelty.

Harry S. Truman 1884–1972

NATIONALITY:
American
WHEN:
1952
WHERE:
Washington, DC, USA
YOU SHOULD KNOW:
President Truman had been quoting variations on this adage for years, but it is this occasion that sticks in the memory.

Early in 1952 President Truman announced that he would not be seeking another presidential term. This quotation appeared in Time *magazine (April 28, 1952). The system he refers to is the presidential approval powers, giving him both a heavy workload and heavy responsibilities. During his years in the White House, he had had to cope with the end of World War II, the bombing of Hiroshima and Nagasaki, the beginning of the Korean War, the financial hardships of post-war America and the looming Cold War. As the sign on his desk in the Oval Office said, 'The Buck Stops Here', and after seven years of struggling to get legislation past Congress, and in his late 60s, he felt that he had done as much as he could.*

One of the many results of the system gives the President a good many hot potatoes to handle – but the President gets a lot of hot potatoes from every direction anyhow, and a man who can't handle them has no business in that job. That makes me think of a saying that I used to hear from my old friend and colleague on the Jackson County Court. He said, 'Harry, if you can't stand the heat, you better get out of the kitchen.'

Sun Yat-sen 1866–1925

Dr Sun became leader of the Republic of China after the Xinhai Revolution that overthrew the last Qing emperor. His Three Principles of the People were formulated in the years leading up to 1923. The principles lay out his vision for a prosperous, united, republican China. Although his republic was short-lived on mainland China and his Kuomintang followers fled to Taiwan in 1949, the influence of the three principles remains important.

NATIONALITY:
Chinese
WHERE:
Guangzhou, China
WHEN:
1923
YOU SHOULD KNOW:
Sun Yat-sen had spent many years in the West and his ideas show strong influences of French revolutionary philosophy.

' . . . The watchword of the French Revolution was 'Liberty, Equality, Fraternity', just as the watchword of our Revolution is 'Min-ts'u, Min-ch'uan, Min-sheng' (People's Nationalism, People's Sovereignty, People's Livelihood). We may say that liberty, equality, and fraternity are based upon the people's sovereignty or that the people's sovereignty develops out of liberty, equality, and fraternity. While we are discussing democracy we must consider the meaning of the French watchword.

As revolutionary ideas have spread through the East, the word liberty has come too; many devoted students and supporters of the new movement have sought to explain in detail its meaning, as something of vital importance. The movement for liberty has played a large part in the history of Europe the past two or three hundred years, and most European wars have been fought for liberty. So Western scholars look upon liberty as a most significant thing, and many peoples in the West have engaged in a rewarding study of its meaning. But since the word has been brought to China, only a few of the intelligentsia have had time to study and to understand it. If we should talk to the common people of China in the villages or on the streets about liberty, they would have no idea of what we meant. So we may say that the Chinese have not gotten anything yet out of the word: even the new youth and the returned students, those who have paid some attention to Western political affairs and those who have constantly heard liberty talked about or have seen the word in books, have a very hazy conception of what it signifies. No wonder that foreigners criticize the Chinese, saying that their civilization is inferior and their thinking immature, that they even have no idea of liberty and no word with which to express the idea . . .

As the revolutionary ferment of the West has lately spread to China, the new students, and many earnest scholars, have risen up to proclaim liberty. They think that because European revolutions, like the French Revolution, were struggles for liberty, we, too, should fight for liberty. This is nothing but saying what others say. They have not applied their minds to the study of democracy or liberty and have no real insight into their meaning. There is a deep significance in the proposal of our Revolutionary Party that the Three Principles of the People, rather than a struggle for liberty, should be the basis of our revolution. The

Generalissimo of China, Sun Yat-sen

watchword of the French Revolution was Liberty; the watchword of the American Revolution was Independence; the watchword of our Revolution is the Three Principles of the People. We spent much time and effort before we decided upon our watchword; we are not merely imitating others.

Therefore the aims of the Chinese Revolution are different from the aims in foreign revolutions, and the methods we use must also be different. Why, indeed, is China having a revolution? To put the answer directly, the aims of our revolution are just opposite to the aims of the revolutions of Europe. Europeans rebelled and fought for liberty because they had had too little liberty. But we, because we have had too much liberty without any unity and resisting power . . . and so have been invaded by foreign imperialism and oppressed by the economic control and trade wars of the Powers, without being able to resist, must break down individual liberty and become pressed together into an unyielding body like the firm rock which is formed by the addition of cement to sand. Chinese today are enjoying so much freedom that they are showing the evils of freedom. This is true not merely in the schools but even in our Revolutionary Party. The reason why, from the overthrow of the Manchus until now, we have not been able to establish a government is just this misuse of freedom. 🟊

The National Assembly

NATIONALITY:
French
WHEN:
1791
WHERE:
Paris, France
YOU SHOULD KNOW:
The French Constitution was enacted three months after the royal family had tried to escape from the country.

Until 1789 France had been governed by an absolute monarchy, with positions of power and influence entirely in the king's gift. The nobility was exempt from taxation, while the rest were heavily taxed and it was the proposed imposition of higher taxes that was the final trigger for the French Revolution. The preamble contained the declaration of the rights of man and allowed for a constitutional monarchy. A new constitution of 1791 further curtailed royal powers and strengthened those of the Assembly. The preamble and sections 1 and 3 set out the rights of the citizens, the relationship of King and State and the political structure.

The National Assembly, wishing to establish the French Constitution upon the principles it has just recognized and declared, abolishes irrevocably the institutions which were injurious to liberty and equality of rights.

Neither nobility, nor peerage, nor hereditary distinctions, nor distinctions of orders, nor feudal regime, nor patrimonial courts, nor any titles, denominations, or prerogatives derived therefrom, nor any order of knighthood, nor any corporations or decorations requiring proofs of nobility or implying distinctions of birth, nor any superiority other than that of public functionaries in the performance of their duties any longer exists.

Neither venality nor inheritance of any public office any longer exists.

Neither privilege nor exception to the law common to all Frenchmen any longer exists for any part of the nation or for any individual.

Neither jurandes nor corporations of professions, arts, and crafts any longer exist.

The law no longer recognizes religious vows or any other obligation contrary to natural rights or the Constitution.

TITLE I. FUNDAMENTAL PROVISIONS GUARANTEED BY THE CONSTITUTION

The Constitution guarantees as natural and civil rights:

1st, That all citizens are admissible to offices and employments, without other distinction than virtues and talents;

2nd, That all taxes shall be assessed equally upon all citizens, in proportion to their means;

3rd, That similar offences shall be punished with similar penalties, without any distinction of persons.

The Constitution guarantees likewise as natural and civil rights:

Liberty to every man to come and go without being subject to arrest or detention, except according to the forms determined by the Constitution;

Liberty to every man to speak, write, print, and publish his opinions without having his writings subject to any censorship or inspection before their publication, and to worship as he pleases;

Liberty to citizens to assemble peaceably and without arms in accordance with police regulations;

Liberty to address individually signed petitions to the constituted authorities.

The legislative power may not make any laws which infringe upon or obstruct the exercise of the natural and civil rights recorded in the present title and guaranteed by the Constitution; but, since liberty consists of being able to do only whatever is not injurious to the rights of others or to public security, the law may establish penalties for acts which, assailing either public security or the rights of others, might be injurious to society.

The Constitution guarantees the inviolability of property, or a just and previous indemnity for that of which a legally established public necessity requires the sacrifice.

Property reserved for the expenses of worship and for all services of public benefit belongs to the nation, and is at its disposal at all times. The Constitution guarantees conveyances which have been or may be made according to the forms established by law.

Citizens have the right to elect or choose the ministers of their religions.

A general establishment for public relief shall be created and organized to raise foundlings, relieve the infirm poor, and furnish work for the able-bodied poor who have been unable to procure it for themselves.

Public instruction for all citizens, free of charge in those branches of education which are indispensable to all men, shall be constituted and organized, and the establishments thereof shall be apportioned gradually, in accordance with the division of the kingdom.

National festivals shall be instituted to preserve the memory of the French Revolution, to maintain fraternity among the citizens, and to bind them to the Constitution, the Patrie, and the laws.

A code of civil law common to the entire kingdom shall be drafted.

TITLE III. OF PUBLIC POWERS

1. Sovereignty is one, indivisible, inalienable, and imprescriptible. It appertains to the nation; no section of the people nor any individual may assume the exercise thereof.

2. The nation, from which alone all powers emanate, may exercise such powers only by delegation. The French Constitution is representative; the representatives are the legislative body and the King.

3. The legislative power is delegated to a National Assembly, composed of temporary representatives freely elected by the people, to be exercised by it, with the sanction of the King, in the manner hereinafter determined.

4. The government is monarchical; the executive power is delegated to the King, to be exercised, under his authority, by ministers and other responsible agents in the manner hereinafter determined.

5. The judicial power is delegated to judges who are elected at stated times by the people.

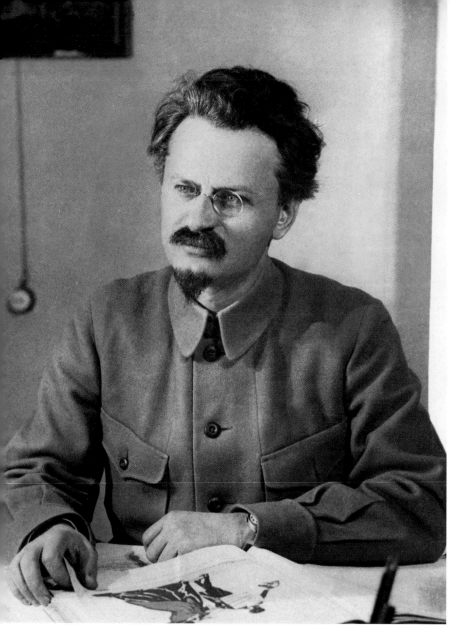

Leon Trotsky

1879–1940

The October Revolution of 1917 was a major phase in the Russian Revolution. After three years of war the starving soliders of the Russian army were deserting and the workers were not much better off. The February Revolution had deposed the Tsar, but the interim government was just as incapable of ending the food shortages or implementing land reform. Workers' soviets (councils) began forming, among them Trotsky's Bolshevik soviet in Petrograd (St Petersburg). After the near bloodless takeover of the Winter Palace, the interim government collapsed and the soviets staged a takeover. At the ensuing Second Congress of the Soviets, the Mensheviks and large numbers of delegates from the Socialist Revolutionaries walked out on the grounds that Lenin and Trotsky had seized power illegally. As they left, Trotsky shouted after them:

NATIONALITY:
Russian
WHEN:
1917
WHERE:
Petrograd (now St Petersburg), Russia
YOU SHOULD KNOW:
Because the Russians were using the Julian Calendar, not the Gregorian Calendar used in the West, what we call the October Revolution happened during our November.

Although a leader in the Russian Revolution, Trotsky was later deported and assassinated in Mexico City.

You are pitiful isolated individuals; you are bankrupts; your role is played out. Go where you belong from now on – into the dustbin of history!

James Monroe 1758–1831

On December 2, 1823 President Monroe gave his seventh State of the Union Address. Within it were proposals for how the USA should conduct foreign relations: namely that friendly relations should be maintained as far as possible but the USA would not intervene in European wars and, as such, expected European nations to keep their noses out of Central and Southern America. Any attempt by a former colonial power to regain influence in the region would be regarded as a direct threat to the US and would be treated as such. The basic tenets of the Monroe Doctrine have governed much of USA foreign policy ever since.

NATIONALITY:
American
WHEN:
1823
WHERE:
Washington, DC, USA
YOU SHOULD KNOW:
Much of the Monroe Doctrine
was actually the work of
John Quincy Adams.

. . . In the discussions to which this interest has given rise and in the arrangements by which they may terminate the occasion has been judged proper for asserting, as a principle in which the rights and interests of the United States are involved, that the American continents, by the free and independent condition which they have assumed and maintain, are henceforth not to be considered as subjects for future colonization by any European powers . . .

It was stated at the commencement of the last session that a great effort was then making in Spain and Portugal to improve the condition of the people of those countries, and that it appeared to be conducted with extraordinary moderation. It need scarcely be remarked that the results have been so far very different from what was then anticipated. Of events in that quarter of the globe, with which we have so much intercourse and from which we derive our origin, we have always been anxious and interested spectators. The citizens of the United States cherish sentiments the most friendly in favor of the liberty and happiness of their fellow-men on that side of the Atlantic. In the wars of the European powers in matters relating to themselves we have never taken any part, nor does it comport with our policy to do so. It is only when our rights are invaded or seriously menaced that we resent injuries or make preparation for our defense. With the movements in this hemisphere we are of necessity more immediately connected, and by causes which must be obvious to all enlightened and impartial observers . . . We owe it, therefore, to candor and to the amicable relations existing between the United States and those powers to declare that we should consider any attempt on their part to extend their system to any portion of this hemisphere as dangerous to our peace and safety. With the existing colonies or dependencies of any European power we have not interfered and shall not interfere. But with the Governments who have declared their independence and maintain it, and whose independence we have, on great consideration and on just principles, acknowledged, we could not view any interposition for the purpose of oppressing them, or controlling in any other manner their destiny, by any European power in any other light than as the manifestation of an unfriendly

disposition toward the United States . . .

Our policy in regard to Europe, which was adopted at an early stage of the wars which have so long agitated that quarter of the globe, nevertheless remains the same, which is, not to interfere in the internal concerns of any of its powers; to consider the government *de facto* as the legitimate government for us; to cultivate friendly relations with it, and to preserve those relations by a frank, firm, and manly policy, meeting in all instances the just claims of every power, submitting to injuries from none. But in regard to those continents circumstances are eminently and conspicuously different. It is impossible that the allied powers should extend their political system to any portion of either continent without endangering our peace and happiness; nor can anyone believe that our southern brethren, if left to themselves, would adopt it of their own accord. It is equally impossible, therefore, that we should behold such interposition in any form with indifference. If we look to the comparative strength and resources of Spain and those new Governments, and their distance from each other, it must be obvious that she can never subdue them. It is still the true policy of the United States to leave the parties to themselves, in hope that other powers will pursue the same course . . .

Saudi Government

NATIONALITY:
Saudi
WHEN:
1973
WHERE:
Riyadh, Saudi Arabia
YOU SHOULD KNOW:
This war between Israel and the Arab coalition in October 1973 is variously known as the Yom Kippur War, Ramadan War, Fourth Arab-Israeli War or October War.

On October 6, 1973 Egyptian and Syrian military forces launched attacks on Israel in order to regain territory lost in the Six-Day War in 1967, including the Golan Heights and the Sinai Peninsula. After early advances by the coalition forces, Israel's superior firepower began to tell. When the USA authorized an emergency resupply to Israel, members of OAPEC (Organization of Arab Petroleum Exporting Countries) reduced production, raised prices and stopped exports to 'unfriendly' countries, chiefly the USA and the Netherlands, leading to steep price hikes and shortages in some states. This led to increased oil exploration in the Gulf of Mexico.

. . . In view of the increase of American military aid to Israel, the Kingdom of Saudi Arabia has decided to halt all oil exports to the United States of America for taking such a position.

Leonid Brezhnev 1906–1982

*By the late 1960s it was recognized by both the Americans and
Russians that negotiations over limiting the rapidly escalating
numbers of strategic nuclear weapons that each side possessed
was probably the only way to prevent their acquisition spiralling
completely out of control. SALT I was negotiated in a series of
meetings at different levels in 1971 and 1972, and signed in
Moscow by Leonard Brezhnev and Richard Nixon on May 26 of
the latter year. It froze the number of missile launchers that either
side could possess. The negotiations for SALT II lasted from 1972
until 1979 and the agreement was signed in Vienna by Brezhnev
and President Carter.*

NATIONALITY:
Russian
WHEN:
1972
WHERE:
Moscow, USSR
YOU SHOULD KNOW:
SALT II was never formally ratified by
the USA, and the Reagan
administration withdrew in 1986.

The CPSU has always held, and now holds, that the class struggle
between the two systems – the capitalist and the socialist – in the
economic and political, and also, of course, the ideological domains,
will continue. That is to be expected since the world outlook and the
class aims of socialism and capitalism are opposite and irreconcilable.
But we shall strive to shift this historically inevitable struggle onto a
path free from the perils of war, of dangerous conflicts, and an
uncontrolled arms race.

*Richard Nixon, left, exchanges
documents with Leonid
Brezhnev after signing the
SALT I Treaty.*

Ayatollah Khomeini 1902–1989

NATIONALITY:
Iranian
WHEN:
1964
WHERE:
Qom, Iran
YOU SHOULD KNOW:
Within Iran he is known as
Imam Khomeini.

In early 1963 the Shah of Iran started a programme of reforms, including permitting non-Muslims to hold government offices and allowing women the vote. Many of the conservative religious scholars opposed such measures as anti-Islamic and treasonable, including one cleric – Imam Khomeini – in a religious institution in the city of Qom who believed in the importance of religion when solving social and practical problems. He had been battling increasing secularization for many years. After denouncing the Shah, he was kept under house arrest but released about a year later. In October of that year, the Iranian government passed legislation giving American soldiers who committed offences immunity from prosecution by Iranian courts. This outraged Khomeini, who on October 27 again denounced the Shah as un-Islamic. This time he was sent into exile, where he remained until his return in February 1979, after masterminding the revolution against the Shah's rule from Paris.

Ayatollah Khomeini during his exile in Paris

❛ Ulama of Qom, come to the aid of Islam! Islam is destroyed!

O Muslim peoples! Leaders of the Muslim peoples!

O presidents and kings of the Muslim peoples! O Shah of Iran! Look at yourselves, look at us. Are we to be trampled underfoot by the boots of the Americans simply because we are a weak nation? Because we have no dollars? America is worse than Britain, Britain is worse than America and the Soviet Union is worse than both of them. Each one is worse than the other, each one is more abominable than the other. But today we are concerned with this malicious entity which is America. Let the American President know that in the eyes of the Iranian nation, he is the most repulsive member of the human race today because of the injustice he has imposed on our Muslim nation. Today, the Qur'an has become his enemy, the Iranian nation has become his enemy. Let the American government know that its name has been ruined and disgraced in Iran. ❜

David Lloyd George 1863–1945

After the end of World War I in 1918, the victorious allies met at the Palace of Versailles to decide on the terms of peace with Germany, Austria and Hungary. The negotiations took six months because each country brought its own aims to the table. In the end, most decisions were taken by the USA, France and the UK. UK Prime Minister Lloyd George fought with President Wilson and the French Prime Minister George Clemenceau as he believed that the terms being imposed upon Germany – loss of territory, demilitarization and punitive reparations that would cripple the country economically and politically – were far too harsh and would only provoke another war sooner or later. In March he summarized the thrust of his arguments in what is known as the Fontainebleau Memorandum. He was right.

NATIONALITY:
British
WHEN:
1919
WHERE:
Paris, France
YOU SHOULD KNOW:
David Lloyd George was known as 'The Welsh Wizard'.

' . . . What is difficult . . . is to draw up a peace which will not provoke a fresh struggle when those who have had practical experience of what war means have passed away. History has proved that a peace which has been hailed by a victorious nation as a triumph of diplomatic skill and statesmanship, even of moderation, in the long run has proved itself to be short-sighted and charged with danger to the victor. The peace of 1871 was believed by Germany to insure not only her security but her permanent supremacy. The facts have shown exactly the contrary, France itself has demonstrated that those who say you can make Germany so feeble that she will never be able to hit back are utterly wrong. Year by year France became numerically weaker in comparison with her victorious neighbor, but in reality she became ever more powerful. She kept watch on Europe; she made alliance with those whom Germany had wronged or menaced; she never ceased to warn the world of its danger and ultimately she was able to secure the overthrow of the mightier power which had trampled so brutally upon her. You may strip Germany of her colonies, reduce her armaments to a mere police force and her navy to that of a fifth rate power; all the same in the end if she feels that she has been unjustly treated in the peace of 1919 she will find means of exacting retribution from her conquerors . . .

 . . . We must offer terms which a responsible government in Germany can expect to be able to carry out. If we present terms to Germany which are unjust, or excessively onerous, no responsible government will sign them; certainly the present weak administration will not. If it did, I am told that it would be swept away within 24 hours. Yet if we can find nobody in Germany who will put his hand to a peace treaty, what will be the position? A large army of occupation for an indefinitie period is out of the question. Germany would not mind it. A very large number of people in that country would welcome it as it would be the only hope of preserving the existing order of things.

The objection would not come from Germany, but from our own countries. Neither the British Empire nor America would agree to occupy Germany. France by itself could not bear the burden of occupation. We should therefore be driven back on the policy of blockading the country. That would inevitably mean spartacism from the Urals to the Rhine, with its inevitable consequence of a huge red army attempting to cross the Rhine. As a matter of fact I am doubtful whether public opinion would allow us deliberately to starve Germany. If the only difference between Germany and ourselves were between onerous terms and moderate terms, I very much doubt if public opinion would tolerate the deliberate condemnation of millions of women and children to death by starvation. If so the Allies would have incurred the moral defeat of having attempted to impose terms on Germany which Germany had successfully resisted.

From every point of view, therefore, it seems to me that we ought to endeavor to draw up a peace settlement as if we were impartial arbiters, forgetful of the passions of the war. This settlement brought to have three ends in view. First of all it must do justice to the Allies, by taking into account Germany's responsibility for the origin of the war, and for the way in which it was fought. Secondly, it must be a settlement which a responsible German Government can sign in the belief that it can fulfil the obligations in incurs. Thirdly, it must be a settlement which will constitute an alternative to Bolshevism, because it will commend itself to all reasonable opinion as a fair settlement of the European problem . . .

I should like to ask why Germany, if she accepts the terms we consider just and fair, should not be admitted to the League of Nations, at any rate as soon as she has established a stable and democratic government. Would it not be an inducement to her both to sign the terms and to resist Bolshevism? Might it not be safer that she should be inside the League than that she should be outside it?

Finally, I believe that until the authority and effectiveness of the League of Nations has been demonstrated, the British Empire and the United States ought to give France a guarantee against the possibility of a new German aggression. France has special reason for asking for such a decree. She has twice been attacked and twice been invaded by Germany in half a century. She has been so attacked because she has been the principle guardian of liberal and democratic civilization against Central European autocracy on the continent of Europe. It is right that the other great Western democracies should enter into an undertaking which will ensure that they stand by her side in time to protect her against invasion, should Germany ever threaten her again or until the League of Nations has proved its capacity to preserve the peace and liberty of the world.

Nikita Khrushchev 1894–1971

At the 20th Congress of the Communist Party in February 1956, the party leader astonished Russian delegates at a secret session on the final day by denouncing the 'personality cult' of former leader Stalin, against the precepts of Marx, Engels and Lenin. The speech was not meant to go beyond the delegates from Russia but the news soon leaked out as an agent of Mossad, the Israeli secret service, had managed to get into the Congress. Khrushchev also denounced some of Stalin's actions, notably the Great Terror, in which anything up to two million people died. He was, however, very careful to emphasize that the Communist Party was not responsible for Stalin's actions and ended with a call to the Party to return to its proper purpose.

NATIONALITY:
Russian
WHEN:
1956
WHERE:
Moscow, USSR
YOU SHOULD KNOW:
The gist of what Khrushchev had said was made public the following month, but the full speech, which lasted for hours, was not published until 1989.

At present, we are concerned with a question which has immense importance for the Party now and for the future – with how the cult of the person of Stalin has been gradually growing, the cult which became at a certain specific stage the source of a whole series of exceedingly serious and grave perversions of Party principles, of Party democracy, of revolutionary legality . . .

Comrades! We must abolish the cult of the individual decisively, once and for all; we must draw the proper conclusions concerning both ideological-theoretical and practical work. It is necessary for this purpose:

First, in a Bolshevik manner to condemn and to eradicate the cult of the individual as alien to Marxism-Leninism and not consonant with the principles of Party leadership and the norms of Party life, and to fight inexorably all attempts at bringing back this practice in one form or another . . .

Barber B. Conable 1922–2003

NATIONALITY:
American
WHEN:
1974
WHERE:
Washington, DC, USA
YOU SHOULD KNOW:
After he left Congress,
Conable became President of
the World Bank.

In August 1974, the year after the Senate hearings into the Watergate Scandal, most people who had been involved were convicted and imprisoned. The House of Representatives had started to investigate the possibility of impeaching the President when another secret tape recorded on June 23, 1972, five days after the burglary, made it obvious that Nixon had been involved all along – contrary to what had been said during the Senate hearings the year before. On the tape he is heard agreeing that the Director of the CIA should be asked to block the FBI's investigation on the [false] grounds of national security. Congressman Conable had been a close ally of the President, but the scandal proved too much for even his loyalty.

I guess we've found the smoking pistol, haven't we?

Mao Zedong 1893–1976

NATIONALITY:
Chinese
WHEN:
1964
WHERE:
Peking (Beijing), China
YOU SHOULD KNOW:
Mao Zedong often used the term
running dogs to insult American
allies.

In a declaration of November 1964, Chairman Mao announced China's moral support for all peoples under the yoke – or the threat thereof – of 'American Imperialist aggression', including those in South Vietnam, Laos, Cambodia, Indochina, Cuba, Malaysia, South Korea and Latin America. This statement was in response to what China saw as American imperialism in the Congo, in which American and Belgian money had supported Joseph Mobutu's private army and the leftist former Prime Minister Patrice Lubumba had been killed by Mobutu's troops. At a time when a large proportion of African countries were electing Marxist governments, Mao ended on a warning that America's intention was to enmesh the whole of Africa.

In their just struggle, the Congolese people are not alone. All the Chinese people support you. All the People throughout the world who oppose imperialism support you. US imperialism and the reactionaries of all countries are paper tigers. The struggle of the Chinese people proved this. The struggle of the Vietnamese people is now proving it. The struggle of the Congolese people will certainly prove it too. Strengthening national unity and persevering in protracted struggle, the Congolese people will certainly be victorious, and US imperialism will certainly be defeated.

People of the world, unite and defeat the US aggressors and all their running dogs! People of the world, be courageous, dare to fight, defy difficulties and advance wave upon wave. Then the whole world will belong to the people. Monsters of all kinds shall be destroyed.

Chiang Kai-shek 1887–1975

After the abdication of the last Qing emperor, Pu-yi, in 1912, China fragmented into a Sun Yat-sen Nationalist (Kuomintang) Government in Guangzhou and a Beijing government supported by warlords. With the help of the communists, Sun Yat-sen's successor, Chiang Kai-shek, reunified most of China except for the northeastern area of Inner Manchuria which was ruled by the warlord Zhang Zuolin, but with strong Japanese influence. In 1928, Chiang planned to re-take the area and – as the extract from his speech of March 6 shows – was warning the Japanese and Russians not to intervene. The Japanese, fearing that Zhang would ally himself with Chiang, assassinated the former just two months later and invaded Manchuria in 1931.

NATIONALITY:
Chinese
WHEN:
1928
WHERE:
Nanking
YOU SHOULD KNOW:
The Japanese client state formed in inner Manchuria after the 1931 invasion was called Manchukuo and had Pu-yi as its puppet king.

The Chinese National Revolution will eventually succeed and its triumph will mark the beginning of the true friendship and cooperation between China and Japan . . . hope that our friends in Japan will understand this work for the victory of the National Revolution, and thereby lay the foundation of the cooperation of our two countries.

General Chiang Kai-shek, the Cantonese leader

Ian Smith 1919–2007

After several years of negotiations with the British Government, which had insisted on majority rule as a condition, on November 11, 1965 the Prime Minister of the British colony of Southern Rhodesia declared his country's independence, under white minority rule. This independence was not recognized by the international community and the United Nations imposed economic sanctions – the first time it had done so. There were several rounds of negotiations over the ensuing years, but Ian Smith continued to resist majority rule. Finally, because of the bush war and the increasing bite of sanctions, multiracial elections were held in 1979, but with a disproportionate number of parliamentary and cabinet seats reserved for whites. The Lancaster House Agreement ended UDI and Zimbabwe gained independence in December 1979.

NATIONALITY:
Rhodesian/Zimbabwean
WHEN:
1965
WHERE:
Salisbury (Harare), Rhodesia
(now Zimbabwe)
YOU SHOULD KNOW:
After independence, the first fully
free elections were held in 1980
and were won by Robert Mugabe's
Zanu-PF.

Whereas in the course of human affairs history has shown that it may become necessary for a people to resolve the political affiliations which have connected them with another people and to assume amongst other nations the separate and equal status to which they are entitled:

And whereas in such event a respect for the opinions of mankind requires them to declare to other nations the causes which impel them to assume full responsibility for their own affairs:

Now therefore, we, the Government of Rhodesia, do hereby declare:

That it is an indisputable and accepted historic fact that since 1923 the Government of Rhodesia have exercised the powers of self-government and have been responsible for the progress, development and welfare of their people;

That the people of Rhodesia having demonstrated their loyalty to the Crown and to their kith and kin in the United Kingdom and elsewhere through two world wars, and having been prepared to shed their blood and give of their substance in what they believed to be the mutual interests of freedom-loving people, now see all that they have cherished about to be shattered on the rocks of expediency;

That the people of Rhodesia have witnessed a process which is destructive of those very precepts upon which civilization in a primitive country has been built, they have seen the principles of Western democracy, responsible government and moral standards crumble elsewhere, nevertheless they have remained steadfast;

That the people of Rhodesia fully support the requests of their government for sovereign independence but have witnessed the consistent refusal of the Government of the United Kingdom to accede to their entreaties;

That the Government of the United Kingdom have thus demonstrated that they are not prepared to grant sovereign independence to Rhodesia on terms acceptable to the people of Rhodesia, thereby persisting in maintaining an unwarrantable jurisdiction over Rhodesia, obstructing laws and treaties with other states and the conduct of affairs with other nations and refusing assent to laws necessary for the public good, all this to the detriment of the future peace, prosperity and good government of Rhodesia;

That the Government of Rhodesia have for a long period patiently and in good faith negotiated with the Government of the United Kingdom for the removal of the remaining limitations placed upon them and for the grant of sovereign independence;

That in the belief that procrastination and delay strike at and injure the very life of the nation, the Government of Rhodesia consider it essential that Rhodesia should attain, without delay, sovereign independence, the justice of which is beyond question;

Now therefore, we the Government of Rhodesia, in humble submission to Almighty God who controls the destinies of nations, conscious that the people of Rhodesia have always shown unswerving loyalty and devotion to Her Majesty the Queen and earnestly praying that we and the people of Rhodesia will not be hindered in our determination to continue exercising our undoubted right to demonstrate the same loyalty and devotion, and seeking to promote the common good so that the dignity and freedom of all men may be assured, do, by this proclamation, adopt enact and give to the people of Rhodesia the constitution annexed hereto;

God Save The Queen.

Richard M. Nixon 1913–1994

NATIONALITY:
American
WHEN:
1974
WHERE:
Washington, DC, USA
YOU SHOULD KNOW:
In 2005 Deep Throat was finally identified as FBI Deputy Director Willam Mark Felt Sr.

On August 8, 1974 President Nixon announced his resignation to the nation to avoid impeachment for his role in the Watergate scandal. During the 1972 Presidential election campaign five men had been caught breaking into the Democratic Party HQ in the Watergate Hotel, Washington. An informant from the FBI – 'Deep Throat' – passed on the information to Washington Post *reporters Carl Bernstein and Bob Woodward that the men had links to the Nixon White House. It emerged that tapes of the President's conversations from the relevant period had been wiped, perhaps deliberately, and the Democrat-controlled House Judiciary Committee began impeachment proceedings. When the Supreme Court ruled that the remaining White House tapes should be released to the Special Prosecutor, the game was up. The 'Smoking Gun' tape, released on August 5, made it obvious that the President had known about the plot from the beginning and had actively tried to stop the FBI investigation. Four days later, he resigned.*

Good evening. This is the thirty-seventh time I have spoken to you from this office, where so many decisions have been made that shaped the history of this Nation. Each time I have done so to discuss with you some matter that I believe affected the national interest . . .

In the past few days, however, it has become evident to me that I no longer have a strong enough political base in the Congress to justify continuing that effort. As long as there was such a base, I felt strongly that it was necessary to see the constitutional process through to its conclusion, that to do otherwise would be unfaithful to the spirit of that deliberately difficult process and a dangerously destabilizing precedent for the future.

From the discussions I have had with Congressional and other leaders, I have concluded that because of the Watergate matter I might not have the support of the Congress that I would consider necessary to

Nixon giving a farewell speech to his staff. His wife, Pat, and daughter, Tricia, look on.

back the very difficult decisions and carry out the duties of this office in the way the interests of the nation would require.

I have never been a quitter. To leave office before my term is completed is abhorrent to every instinct in my body. But as President, I must put the interest of America first. America needs a full-time President and a full-time Congress, particularly at this time with problems we face at home and abroad . . .

Therefore, I shall resign the Presidency effective at noon tomorrow. Vice President Ford will be sworn in as President at that hour in this office.

As I recall the high hopes for America with which we began this second term, I feel a great sadness that I will not be here in this office working on your behalf to achieve those hopes in the next two-and-a-half years. But in turning over direction of the Government to Vice President Ford, I know, as I told the Nation when I nominated him for that office 10 months ago, that the leadership of America will be in good hands.

In passing this office to the Vice President, I also do so with the profound sense of the weight of responsibility that will fall on his shoulders tomorrow and, therefore, of the understanding, the patience, the cooperation he will need from all Americans.

As he assumes that responsibility, he will deserve the help and the support of all of us. As we look to the future, the first essential is to begin healing the wounds of this Nation, to put the bitterness and divisions of the recent past behind us, and to rediscover those shared ideals that lie at the heart of our strength and unity as a great and as a free people . . .

I regret deeply any injuries that may have been done in the course of the events that led to this decision. I would say only that if some of my judgments were wrong, and some were wrong, they were made in what I believed at the time to be the best interest of the Nation.

To those who have stood with me during these past difficult months, to my family, my friends, to many others who joined in supporting my cause because they believed it was right, I will be eternally grateful for your support . . .

Sometimes I have succeeded and sometimes I have failed, but always I have taken heart from what Theodore Roosevelt once said about the man in the arena, 'whose face is marred by dust and sweat and blood, who strives valiantly, who errs and comes short again and again because there is not effort without error and shortcoming, but who does actually strive to do the deed, who knows the great enthusiasms, the great devotions, who spends himself in a worthy cause, who at the best knows in the end the triumphs of high achievements and who at the worst, if he fails, at least fails while daring greatly.' I pledge to you tonight that as long as I have a breath of life in my body, I shall continue in that spirit. I shall continue to work for the great causes to which I have been dedicated throughout my years as a Congressman, a Senator, a Vice President, and President, the cause of peace not just for America but among all nations, prosperity, justice, and opportunity for all of our people.

There is one cause above all to which I have been devoted and to which I shall always be devoted for as long as I live.

When I first took the oath of office as President five-and-a-half years ago, I made this sacred commitment to 'consecrate my office, my energies, and all the wisdom I can summon to the cause of peace among nations'.

I have done my very best in all the days since to be true to that pledge. As a result of these efforts, I am confident that the world is a safer place today, not only for the people of America but for the people of all nations, and that all of our children have a better chance than before of living in peace rather than dying in war.

This, more than anything, is what I hoped to achieve when I sought the Presidency. This, more than anything, is what I hope will be my legacy to you, to our country, as I leave the Presidency.

To have served in this office is to have felt a very personal sense of kinship with each and every American. In leaving it, I do so with this prayer: May God's grace be with you in all the days ahead. **,**

Calvin Coolidge 1872–1933

NATIONALITY:
American
WHEN:
1923
WHERE:
Washington, DC, USA
YOU SHOULD KNOW:
President Coolidge was famously taciturn. At a dinner, one guest remarked that he had had a wager with a friend that he could get the President to say more than two words. 'You lose', was the reply.

In his first State of the Union Address on December 6, 1923 President Coolidge covered a variety of themes, including increased enforcement of prohibition, infrastructure projects that would increase employment, wealth and trade, flexible trade tariffs, the removal of war taxes, cancellation of some foreign debts, continued lack of recognition of Russia, reform in the judicial and prison systems, marine environmental protection and fisheries regulation laws, strengthening of the Army and Navy and entitlement for free health care for veterans. However, the speech's most far-reaching areas were those about foreign affairs, in which he definitively ruled out joining the League of Nations and said that America would only join a World Court of Justice on that condition.

❝ Since the close of the last Congress the Nation has lost President Harding. The world knew his kindness and his humanity, his greatness and his character. He has left his mark upon history. He has made justice more certain and peace more secure. The surpassing tribute paid to his memory as he was borne across the continent to rest at last at home revealed the place lie held in the hearts of the American people . . . It is our duty, under the inspiration of his example, to take up the burdens which he was permitted to lay down, and to develop and support the wise principles of government which he represented.

For us peace reigns everywhere. We desire to perpetuate it always by granting full justice to others and requiring of others full justice to ourselves.

Our country has one cardinal principle to maintain in its foreign policy. It is an American principle. It must be an American policy. We attend to our own affairs, conserve our own strength, and protect the interests of our own citizens; but we recognize thoroughly our obligation to help others, reserving to the decision of our own judgment the time, the place, and the method. We realize the common bond of humanity. We know the inescapable law of service.

Our country has definitely refused to adopt and ratify the covenant of the League of Nations. We have not felt warranted in assuming the responsibilities which its members have assumed. I am not proposing any change in this policy; neither is the Senate. The incident, so far as we are concerned, is closed. The League exists as a foreign agency. We hope it will be helpful. But the United States sees no reason to limit its own freedom and independence of action by joining it. We shall do well to recognize this basic fact in all national affairs and govern ourselves accordingly . . .

Pending before the Senate is a proposal that this government give its support to the Permanent Court of International Justice, which is a new and somewhat different plan. This is not a partisan question. It should not assume an artificial importance. The court is merely a convenient instrument of adjustment to which we could go, but to which we could not be brought. It should be discussed with entire candor, not by a political but by a judicial method, without pressure and without prejudice. Partisanship has no place in our foreign relations. As I wish to see a court established, and as the proposal presents the only practical plan on which many nations have ever agreed, though it may not meet every desire, I therefore commend it to the favorable consideration of the Senate, with the proposed reservations clearly indicating our refusal to adhere to the League of Nations . . .

The world has had enough of the curse of hatred and selfishness, of destruction and war. It has had enough of the wrongful use of material power. For the healing of the nations there must be good will and charity, confidence and peace. The time has come for a more practical use of moral power, and more reliance upon the principle that right makes its own might. Our authority among the nations must be represented by justice and mercy. It is necessary not only to have faith, but to make sacrifices for our faith. The spiritual forces of the world make all its final determinations. It is with these voices that America should speak. Whenever they declare a righteous purpose there need be no doubt that they will be heard. America has taken her place in the world as a Republic – free, independent, powerful. The best service that can be rendered to humanity is the assurance that this place will be maintained. 🔴

Enoch Powell 1912–1998

In early 1968 anti-discrimination and immigration legislation was passed by the UK Government, giving citizens from Commonwealth nations – for instance from the Caribbean and the Indian subcontinent – greater rights of immigration and entitlement to state benefits. Enoch Powell, Conservative MP for a constituency with a significant proportion of immigrants, gave a highly inflammatory speech that polarized public opinion, claiming that allowing in even 5000 immigrants a year would lead to the collapse of British society. His sacking from his post as Shadow Defence Minister on the grounds that it would inflame racist attitudes (which it did) led to strikes by dock workers and others who felt that their livelihoods were under threat.

❜ . . . We must be mad, literally mad, as a nation to be permitting the annual inflow of some 50,000 dependants, who are for the most part the material of the future growth of the immigrant-descended population. It is like watching a nation busily engaged in heaping up its own funeral pyre . . .

. . . For these dangerous and divisive elements the legislation proposed in the Race Relations Bill is the very pabulum they need to flourish. Here is the means of showing that the immigrant communities can organise to consolidate their members, to agitate and campaign against their fellow citizens, and to overawe and dominate the rest with the legal weapons which the ignorant and the ill-informed have provided. As I look ahead, I am filled with foreboding; like the Roman, I seem to see 'the River Tiber foaming with much blood'. 🔴

NATIONALITY:
British
WHEN:
1968
WHERE:
Birmingham, England
YOU SHOULD KNOW:
'Rivers of blood' is a quotation from
Virgil's *Aeneid*.

Enoch Powell's words still cause a stir when mentioned.

Karl Marx 1818–1883

NATIONALITY:
German
WHEN:
Various times
WHERE:
Various places
YOU SHOULD KNOW:
Brumaire was the second month in the French Revolutionary Calendar (October/November).

Karl Marx is revered by some as the world's greatest political thinker and reviled by others as the father of its most evil political system. In mid-nineteenth century Europe, wealth was held in the hands of a relatively small number of people and the vast majority lived in grinding poverty. Marx and Engels saw capitalism as unsound and thought that in the same way that it had replaced feudalism it would inevitably itself be replaced by communism. Marx used the idea in the opening lines of his The Eighteenth Brumaire of Louis Napoleon, *an article that likened the December 1851 coup d'etat of Louis Napoleon with that of his uncle, Napoleon Bonaparte, on November 18, 1799. The opening words were: 'Hegel says somewhere that all great events and personalities in world history reappear in one fashion or another. He forgot to add: the first time as tragedy, the second as farce.' This is often summarized as follows.*

‘ History repeats itself. ’

Todd Beamer 1968–2001

NATIONALITY:
American
WHEN:
2001
WHERE:
On United Airlines Flight 93
YOU SHOULD KNOW:
There were seven crew members and 37 passengers on the flight, including the hijackers.

On the morning of September 11, 2001 United Airlines Flight 93 was hijacked on route from Newark, New Jersey to San Francisco. After the hijackers took over the flight – killing one passenger, wounding the pilot and co-pilot and moving almost everyone else to the back of the plane – passengers began to learn from telephone calls about the earlier double attack on the World Trade Center in New York and realized that their flight was probably going to suffer a similar fate. Mr Beamer told the GTE supervisor he was talking to on the telephone, Lisa Jefferson, that several of the other passengers were discussing 'jumping' the hijackers. The last words she heard him say are below. When the hijackers realized that the passengers were trying to break into the cockpit, the highjackers' pilot rolled the plane from side to side and pitched it up and down in order to prevent them. The actions of the passengers caused the plane to crash before the hijackers could complete their mission. It fell at Stony Creek, near Shanksville, Pennsylvania.

‘ Are you guys ready? Let's roll. ’

George W. Bush born 1946

*Ten days after the 9/11 terrorist attacks on the twin towers of
the World Trade Center in New York and the Pentagon in
Washington and the failed attack using United Airlines Flight
93 on either the Capitol or the White House, President Bush
addressed a Joint Session of Congress and the nation. He
called on the Taliban regime of Afghanistan to surrender the
al-Qaeda leadership, including Osama Bin Laden, or face
invasion. The Taliban response was in the negative and
troops were deployed the following month in Operation
Enduring Freedom. The Taliban regime was overthrown, and
although the country now has democratic institutions and a
freely elected government, neither the Taliban nor al-Qaeda
has ceased attacks and an international military force
remains in place.*

NATIONALITY:
American
WHEN:
2001
WHERE:
Washington, DC, USA
YOU SHOULD KNOW:
At the time of writing, Osama Bin
Laden is still at large.

Mr Speaker, Mr President Pro Tempore, members of Congress,
and fellow Americans, in the normal course of events, presidents
come to this chamber to report on the state of the union. Tonight,
no such report is needed; it has already been delivered by the
American people.

We have seen it in the courage of passengers who rushed
terrorists to save others on the ground. Passengers like an
exceptional man named Todd Beamer. And would you please help
me welcome his wife Lisa Beamer here tonight?

We have seen the state of our union in the endurance of rescuers
working past exhaustion.

We've seen the unfurling of flags, the lighting of candles, the
giving of blood, the saying of prayers in English, Hebrew and Arabic.

We have seen the decency of a loving and giving people who
have made the grief of strangers their own.

My fellow citizens, for the last nine days, the entire world has
seen for itself the state of union, and it is strong.

Tonight, we are a country awakened to danger and called to
defend freedom. Our grief has turned to anger and anger to
resolution. Whether we bring our enemies to justice or bring
justice to our enemies, justice will be done . . .

And on behalf of the American people, I thank the world for its
outpouring of support . . .

On September the 11th, enemies of freedom committed an act
of war against our country. Americans have known wars, but for
the past 136 years they have been wars on foreign soil, except for
one Sunday in 1941. Americans have known the casualties of war,
but not at the center of a great city on a peaceful morning.

Americans have known surprise attacks, but never before on
thousands of civilians.

All of this was brought upon us in a single day, and night fell on a different world, a world where freedom itself is under attack.

Americans have many questions tonight. Americans are asking, 'Who attacked our country?'.

The evidence we have gathered all points to a collection of loosely affiliated terrorist organizations known as al-Qaeda. They are some of the murderers indicted for bombing American embassies in Tanzania and Kenya and responsible for bombing the USS Cole.

Al-Qaeda is to terror what the Mafia is to crime. But its goal is not making money, its goal is remaking the world and imposing its radical beliefs on people everywhere . . .

By aiding and abetting murder, the Taliban regime is committing murder. And tonight the United States of America makes the following demands on the Taliban.

Deliver to United States authorities all of the leaders of al-Quaeda who hide in your land.

Release all foreign nationals, including American citizens you have unjustly imprisoned. Protect foreign journalists, diplomats and aid workers in your country. Close immediately and permanently every terrorist training camp in Afghanistan. And hand over every terrorist and every person and their support structure to appropriate authorities.

Give the United States full access to terrorist training camps, so we can make sure they are no longer operating.

These demands are not open to negotiation or discussion.

The Taliban must act and act immediately.

They will hand over the terrorists or they will share in their fate.

I also want to speak tonight directly to Muslims throughout the world. We respect your faith. It's practiced freely by many millions of Americans and by millions more in countries that America counts as friends. Its teachings are good and peaceful, and those who commit evil in the name of Allah blaspheme the name of Allah.

The terrorists are traitors to their own faith, trying, in effect, to hijack Islam itself.

The enemy of America is not our many Muslim friends. It is not our many Arab friends. Our enemy is a radical network of terrorists and every government that supports them.

Our war on terror begins with al-Qaeda, but it does not end there.

It will not end until every terrorist group of global reach has been found, stopped and defeated.

Americans are asking 'Why do they hate us?'

They hate what they see right here in this chamber: a democratically elected government. Their leaders are self-appointed. They hate our freedoms: our freedom of religion, our freedom of speech, our freedom to vote and assemble and disagree with each other . . .

Americans are asking, 'How will we fight and win this war?'.

We will direct every resource at our command – every means of diplomacy, every tool of intelligence, every instrument of law enforcement, every financial influence, and every necessary weapon of war – to the destruction and to the defeat of the global terror network.

Now, this war will not be like the war against Iraq a decade ago, with a decisive liberation of territory and a swift conclusion. It will not look like the air war above Kosovo two years ago, where no ground troops were used and not a single American was lost in combat.

Our response involves far more than instant retaliation and isolated strikes. Americans should not expect one battle, but a lengthy campaign unlike any other we have ever seen. It may include dramatic strikes visible on TV and covert operations secret even in success.

We will starve terrorists of funding, turn them one against another, drive them from place to place until there is no refuge or no rest.

And we will pursue nations that provide aid or safe haven to terrorism. Every nation in every region now has a decision to make: Either you are with us or you are with the terrorists.

From this day forward, any nation that continues to harbor or support terrorism will be regarded by the United States as a hostile regime. Our nation has been put on notice, we're not immune from attack. We will take defensive measures against terrorism to protect Americans . . .

This is not, however, just America's fight. And what is at stake is not just America's freedom.

This is the world's fight. This is civilization's fight. This is the fight of all who believe in progress and pluralism, tolerance and freedom.

We ask every nation to join us. We will ask and we will need the help of police forces, intelligence service and banking systems around the world. The United States is grateful that many nations and many international organizations have already responded with sympathy and with support – nations from Latin America to Asia to Africa to Europe to the Islamic world . . .

Americans are asking, 'What is expected of us?'.

I ask you to live your lives and hug your children.

I know many citizens have fears tonight, and I ask you to be calm and resolute, even in the face of a continuing threat.

I ask you to uphold the values of America and remember why so many have come here.

We're in a fight for our principles, and our first responsibility is to live by them. No one should be singled out for unfair treatment or unkind words because of their ethnic background or religious faith . . .

Great harm has been done to us. We have suffered great loss. And in our grief and anger we have found our mission and our moment.

Freedom and fear are at war. The advance of human freedom, the great achievement of our time and the great hope of every time, now depends on us.

Our nation, this generation, will lift the dark threat of violence from our people and our future. We will rally the world to this cause by our efforts, by our courage. We will not tire, we will not falter and we will not fail . . .

Even grief recedes with time and grace.

But our resolve must not pass. Each of us will remember what happened that day and to whom it happened. We will remember the moment the news came, where we were and what we were doing.

Some will remember an image of a fire or story or rescue. Some will carry memories of a face and a voice gone forever . . .

I will not forget the wound to our country and those who inflicted it. I will not yield, I will not rest, I will not relent in waging this struggle for freedom and security for the American people.

The course of this conflict is not known, yet its outcome is certain. Freedom and fear, justice and cruelty, have always been at war, and we know that God is not neutral between them.

Fellow citizens, we'll meet violence with patient justice, assured of the rightness of our cause and confident of the victories to come.

In all that lies before us, may God grant us wisdom and may he watch over the United States of America.

Thank you.

Jimmy Carter born 1924

NATIONALITY:
American
WHEN:
1980
WHERE:
Washington, DC, USA
YOU SHOULD KNOW:
In the wake of the Soviet invasion of Afghanistan, President Carter re-established the draft for young men and banned US athletes from going to the Moscow Olympics.

President Carter's final State of the Union address in January 1980 was given against the background of the Iran hostage crisis, oil shortages, economic crisis and the Soviet invasion of Afghanistan. His avowal that America would use military force to prevent any Soviet encroachment on the Persian Gulf came as no real surprise – this part of the speech is sometimes called the Carter Doctrine. What very few people knew at the time is that the USA had been funding insurgency in Afghanistan and, when the pro-Moscow government there was overthrown, the Soviet government was bound to try to reassert its control.

This last few months has not been an easy time for any of us. As we meet tonight, it has never been more clear that the state of our Union depends on the state of the world. And tonight, as throughout our own generation, freedom and peace in the world depend on the state of our Union . . .

At this time in Iran, 50 Americans are still held captive, innocent victims of terrorism and anarchy. Also at this moment, massive Soviet troops are attempting to subjugate the fiercely independent and deeply religious people of Afghanistan. These two acts – one of international terrorism and one of military aggression – present a serious challenge to the United States of America and indeed to all the nations of the world. Together, we will meet these threats to peace . . .

Three basic developments have helped to shape our challenges: the steady growth and increased projection of Soviet military power beyond its own borders; the overwhelming dependence of the Western democracies on oil supplies from the Middle East; and the press of social and religious and economic and political change in the many nations of the developing world, exemplified by the revolution in Iran.

Each of these factors is important in its own right. Each interacts with the others. All must be faced together, squarely and courageously. We will face these challenges, and we will meet them with the best that is in us. And we will not fail.

In response to the abhorrent act in Iran, our Nation has never been aroused and unified so greatly in peacetime. Our position is clear. The United States will not yield to blackmail.

We continue to pursue these specific goals: first, to protect the present and long-range interests of the United States; secondly, to preserve the lives of the American hostages and to secure, as quickly as possible, their safe release, if possible, to avoid bloodshed which might further endanger the lives of our fellow citizens; to enlist the help of other nations in condemning this act of violence, which is shocking and violates the moral and the legal standards of a civilized world; and also to convince and to persuade the Iranian leaders that the real danger to their nation lies in the north, in the Soviet Union and from the Soviet troops now in Afghanistan, and that the unwarranted Iranian quarrel with the United States hampers their response to this far greater danger to them.

If the American hostages are harmed, a severe price will be paid. We will never rest until every one of the American hostages are released.

But now we face a broader and more fundamental challenge in this region because of the recent military action of the Soviet Union.

Now, as during the last three-and-a-half decades, the relationship between our country, the United States of America, and the Soviet Union is the most critical factor in determining whether the world will live at peace or be engulfed in global conflict.

Since the end of the Second World War, America has led other nations in meeting the challenge of mounting Soviet power. This has not been a simple or a static relationship. Between us there has been cooperation, there has been competition, and at times there has been confrontation . . .

Preventing nuclear war is the foremost responsibility of the two superpowers. That's why we've negotiated the strategic arms limitation treaties – SALT I and SALT II. Especially now, in a time of great tension, observing the mutual constraints imposed by the terms of these treaties will be in the best interest of both countries and will help to preserve world peace . . .

We superpowers also have the responsibility to exercise restraint in the use of our great military force. The integrity and the independence of weaker nations must not be threatened. They must know that in our presence they are secure.

But now the Soviet Union has taken a radical and an aggressive new step. It's using its great military power against a relatively defenseless nation. The implications of the Soviet invasion of Afghanistan could pose the most serious threat to the peace since the Second World War . . .

The region which is now threatened by Soviet troops in Afghanistan is of great strategic importance: It contains more than two-thirds of the world's exportable oil. The Soviet effort to dominate Afghanistan has brought Soviet military forces to

President Carter's term of office ended in difficult circumstances.

within 300 miles of the Indian Ocean and close to the Straits of Hormuz, a waterway through which most of the world's oil must flow. The Soviet Union is now attempting to consolidate a strategic position, therefore, that poses a grave threat to the free movement of Middle East oil . . .

Let our position be absolutely clear: An attempt by any outside force to gain control of the Persian Gulf region will be regarded as an assault on the vital interests of the United States of America, and such an assault will be repelled by any means necessary, including military force . . .

We are working with our allies to prevent conflict in the Middle East. The peace treaty between Egypt and Israel is a notable achievement which represents a strategic asset for America and which also enhances prospects for regional and world peace. We are now engaged in further negotiations to provide full autonomy for the people of the West Bank and Gaza, to resolve the Palestinian issue in all its aspects, and to preserve the peace and security of Israel. Let no one doubt our commitment to the security of Israel. In a few days we will observe an historic event when Israel makes another major withdrawal from the Sinai and when Ambassadors will be exchanged between Israel and Egypt . . .

Finally, we are prepared to work with other countries in the region to share a cooperative security framework that respects differing values and political beliefs, yet which enhances the independence, security, and prosperity of all . . .

The decade ahead will be a time of rapid change, as nations everywhere seek to deal with new problems and age-old tensions. But America need have no fear. We can thrive in a world of change if we remain true to our values and actively engaged in promoting world peace. We will continue to work as we have for peace in the Middle East and southern Africa. We will continue to build our ties with developing nations, respecting and helping to strengthen their national independence which they have struggled so hard to achieve. And we will continue to support the growth of democracy and the protection of human rights . . .

Peace – a peace that preserves freedom – remains America's first goal. In the coming years, as a mighty nation we will continue to pursue peace. But to be strong abroad we must be strong at home. And in order to be strong, we must continue to face up to the difficult issues that confront us as a nation today.

The crises in Iran and Afghanistan have dramatized a very important lesson: Our excessive dependence on foreign oil is a clear and present danger to our Nation's security. The need has never been more urgent. At long last, we must have a clear, comprehensive energy policy for the United States . . .

Our material resources, great as they are, are limited. Our problems are too complex for simple slogans or for quick solutions. We cannot solve them without effort and sacrifice. Walter Lippmann once reminded us, 'You took the good things for granted. Now you must earn them again. For every right that you cherish, you have a duty which you must fulfill. For every good which you wish to preserve, you will have to sacrifice your comfort and your ease. There is nothing for nothing any longer.'.

Our challenges are formidable. But there's a new spirit of unity and resolve in our country. We move into the 1980s with confidence and hope and a bright vision of the America we want: an America strong and free, an America at peace, an America with equal rights for all citizens – and for women, guaranteed in the United States Constitution – an America with jobs and good health and good education for every citizen, an America with a clean and bountiful life in our cities and on our farms, an America that helps to feed the world, an America secure in filling its own energy needs, an America of justice, tolerance, and compassion. For this vision to come true, we must sacrifice, but this national commitment will be an exciting enterprise that will unify our people.

Together as one people, let us work to build our strength at home, and together as one indivisible union, let us seek peace and security throughout the world.

Together let us make of this time of challenge and danger a decade of national resolve and of brave achievement.

Mikhail Gorbachev

born 1931

On May 6, 1992, just over four months after his resignation as President of the USSR, Mikhail Gorbachev neatly bookended the Cold War by speaking at Westminster College in Fulton, Missouri, where almost 50 years earlier Winston Churchill had coined the term 'The Iron Curtain' to describe the divide between eastern and western Europe. Gorbachev used the speech, among other things, to debate the mistakes that both of the superpowers had made in the past, to look at the similarities in the collapse of the structure of international relations and to call for strengthening and restructuring of the United Nations in order to prevent another superpower build-up.

President George Bush, left, shakes hands with Gorbachev after their peace summit.

❛ A major international effort will be needed to render irreversible the shift in favour of a democratic world -- and democratic for the whole of humanity, not just for half of it . . .

However, even now, at a time of sharply increased interdependence in the world, many countries are morbidly jealous of their sovereignty, and many peoples of their national independence and identity. This is one of the newest global contradictions, one which must be overcome by joint effort.

Here the decisive role may and must be played by the United Nations. Of course, it must be restructured, together with its component bodies, in order to be capable of confronting the new tasks.

The United Nations, which emerged from the results and the lessons of the Second World War, is still marked by the period of its creation . . . Nothing, for instance, other than the division into victors and vanquished, explains why such countries as Germany and Japan do not figure among the permanent members of the Security Council. ❜

NATIONALITY:
Russian
WHEN:
May 6, 1992
WHERE:
Fulton, Missouri, USA
YOU SHOULD KNOW:
Mr Gorbachev was the last ever General Secretary of the Communist Party of the Soviet Union.

Warren Harding 1865–1923

NATIONALITY:
American
WHEN:
1920
WHERE:
Boston, USA
YOU SHOULD KNOW:
Harding's victory showed the largest
popular-vote percentage margin
since the election of 1820.

In May 1920, in the lead-up to the Republican Party nomination, Senator Harding gave several speeches. In Boston on May 14, he coined the term that would become his campaign slogan – 'Back to normalcy'. The postwar presidency of Woodrow Wilson had become increasingly unpopular as the economic situation remained dire. Harding campaigned on the theme of a return to a strict interpretation of the Monroe Doctrine, as well as promotion of US citizens' rights and small-government laissez-faire *policies. He won by one of the largest margins ever, although by the time of his death in 1923 his popularity was waning.*

There isn't anything the matter with the world's civilization except that humanity is viewing it through a vision impaired in a cataclysmal war. Poise has been disturbed and nerves have been racked, and fever has rendered men irrational; sometimes there have been draughts upon the dangerous cup of barbarity and men have wandered far from safe paths, but the human procession still marches in the right direction.

Here, in the United States, we feel the reflex, rather than the hurting wound, but we still think straight, and we mean to act straight, and mean to hold firmly to all that was ours when war involved us, and seek the higher attainments which are the only compensations that so supreme a tragedy may give mankind.

America's present need is not heroics, but healing; not nostrums, but normalcy; not revolution, but restoration; not agitation, but adjustment; not surgery, but serenity; not the dramatic, but the dispassionate; not experiment, but equipoise; not submergence in internationality, but sustainment in triumphant nationality . . .

This republic has its ample tasks. If we put an end to false economics which lure humanity to utter chaos, ours will be the commanding example of world leadership today. If we can prove a representative popular government under which a citizenship seeks what it may do for the government rather than what the government may do for individuals, we shall do more to make democracy safe for the world than all armed conflict ever recorded. The world needs to be reminded that all human ills are not curable by legislation, and that quantity of statutory enactment and excess of government offer no substitute for quality of citizenship . . .

There is no new appraisal for the supremacy of law. That is a thing surpassing and eternal. A contempt for international law wrought the supreme tragedy, contempt for our national and state laws will rend the glory of the republic, and failure to abide the proven laws of to-day's civilization will lead to temporary chaos . . .

My best judgment of America's needs is to steady down, to get squarely on our feet, to make sure of the right path. Let's get out of the fevered delirium of war, with the hallucination that all the money in the world is to be made in the madness of war and the wildness of its aftermath. Let us stop to consider that tranquility at home is more precious than peace abroad, and that both our good fortune and our eminence are dependent on the normal forward stride of all the American people . . .

Sober capital must make appeal to intoxicated wealth, and thoughtful labor must appeal to the radical who has no thought of the morrow, to effect the needed understanding. Exacted profits, because the golden stream is flooding, and pyramided wages to meet a mounting cost that must be halted, will speed us to disaster just as sure as the morrow comes, and we ought to think soberly and avoid it. We ought to dwell in the heights of good fortune for a generation to come, and I pray that we will, but we need a benediction of wholesome common sense to give us that assurance.

I pray for sober thinking in behalf of the future of America. No worthwhile republic ever went the tragic way to destruction, which did not begin the downward course through luxury of life and extravagance of living. More, the simple living and thrifty people will be the first to recover from a war's waste and all its burdens, and our people ought to be the first recovered. Herein is greater opportunity than lies in alliance, compact or supergovernment. It is America's chance to lead in example and prove to the world the reign of reason in representative popular government where people think who assume to rule . . .

It seems to me singularly appropriate to address this membership an additional word about production. I believe most cordially in the home market first for the American product. There is no other way to assure our prosperity. I rejoice in our normal capacity to consume our rational, healthful consumption . . .

We have protected our home market with war's barrage. But the barrage has lifted with the passing of the war. The American people will not heed today, because world competition is not yet restored, but the morrow will soon come when the world will seek our markets and our trade balances, and we must think of America first or surrender our eminence.

The thought is not selfish. We want to share with the world in seeking becoming restoration. But peoples will trade and seek wealth in their exchanges, and every conflict in the adjustment of peace was founded on the hope of promoting trade conditions. I heard expressed, before the Foreign Relations Committee of the Senate, the aspirations of nationality and the hope of commerce to develop and expand aspiring peoples. Knowing that those two thoughts are inspiring all humanity, as they have since civilization began, I can only marvel at the American who consents to surrender either. There may be conscience, humanity and justice in both, and without them the glory of the republic is done. I want to go on, secure and unafraid, holding fast to the American inheritance and confident of the supreme American fulfillment. 〕

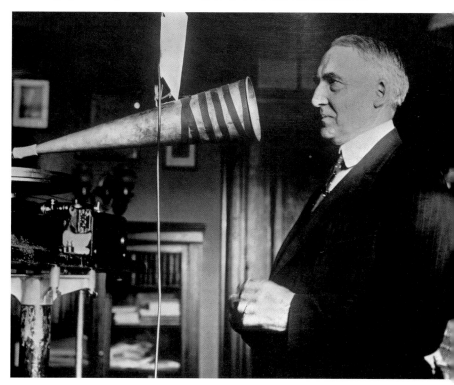

President Harding making a phonograph record.

To every one in this great Fleet I send a message of gratitude and greeting, from myself as from all my peoples. The same message I send to the gallant Air Force which, in co-operation with the Navy, is our sure shield of defence. They are daily adding laurels to those that their fathers won.

I would send a special word of greeting to the Armies of the Empire, to those who have come from afar, and in particular to the British Expeditionary Force. Their task is hard. They are waiting, and waiting is a trial of nerve and discipline. But I know that when the moment comes for action they will prove themselves worthy of the highest traditions of their great Service.

And to all who are preparing themselves to serve their country, on sea or land or in the air, I send my greeting at this time. The men and women of our far-flung Empire working in their several vocations, with the one same purpose, all are members of the great Family of Nations which is prepared to sacrifice everything that freedom of spirit may be saved to the world.

Such is the spirit of the Empire; of the great Dominions, of India, of every Colony, large or small. From all alike have come offers of help, for which the Mother Country can never be sufficiently grateful. Such unity in aim and in effort has never been seen in the world before.

I believe from my heart that the cause which binds together my peoples and our gallant and faithful Allies is the cause of Christian civilisation. On no other basis can a true civilisation be built.

Let us remember this through the dark times ahead of us and when we are making the peace for which all men pray.

A new year is at hand. We cannot tell what it will bring. If it brings peace, how thankful we shall all be. If it brings us continued struggle we shall remain undaunted.

In the meantime I feel that we may all find a message of encouragement in the lines which, in my closing words, I would like to say to you: 'I said to the man who stood at the Gate of the Year, "Give me a light that I may tread safely into the unknown." And he replied, "Go out into the darkness, and put your hand into the Hand of God. That shall be to you better than light, and safer than a known way."

May that Almighty Hand guide and uphold us all. 🟥

The League of Nations

WHEN:
1919
WHERE:
Paris, France
YOU SHOULD KNOW:
The League of Nations was the fore-runner to the United Nations.

In the aftermath of World War I, the League of Nations was founded in 1919 to promote the collective security of nations through diplomacy, arbitration and arms reduction. President Wilson's 14 Points of the previous year had included a call for an international organization. Different countries had differing wishes for the League's powers. Although it did have limited success, its ability to force members to comply was undermined by its lack of any powers except economic sanctions. Many also felt that the League was weakened by the USA not joining because of Congress's refusal to sign the Treaty of Versailles. The following extracts are from the League's Founding Covenant.

Part I. The Covenant of the League of Nations
THE HIGH CONTRACTING PARTIES.

To every one in this great Fleet I send a message of gratitude and greeting, from myself as from all my peoples. The same message I send to the gallant Air Force which, in co-operation with the Navy, is our sure shield of defence. They are daily adding laurels to those that their fathers won.

I would send a special word of greeting to the Armies of the Empire, to those who have come from afar, and in particular to the British Expeditionary Force. Their task is hard. They are waiting, and waiting is a trial of nerve and discipline. But I know that when the moment comes for action they will prove themselves worthy of the highest traditions of their great Service.

And to all who are preparing themselves to serve their country, on sea or land or in the air, I send my greeting at this time. The men and women of our far-flung Empire working in their several vocations, with the one same purpose, all are members of the great Family of Nations which is prepared to sacrifice everything that freedom of spirit may be saved to the world.

Such is the spirit of the Empire; of the great Dominions, of India, of every Colony, large or small. From all alike have come offers of help, for which the Mother Country can never be sufficiently grateful. Such unity in aim and in effort has never been seen in the world before.

I believe from my heart that the cause which binds together my peoples and our gallant and faithful Allies is the cause of Christian civilisation. On no other basis can a true civilisation be built.

Let us remember this through the dark times ahead of us and when we are making the peace for which all men pray.

A new year is at hand. We cannot tell what it will bring. If it brings peace, how thankful we shall all be. If it brings us continued struggle we shall remain undaunted.

In the meantime I feel that we may all find a message of encouragement in the lines which, in my closing words, I would like to say to you: 'I said to the man who stood at the Gate of the Year, "Give me a light that I may tread safely into the unknown." And he replied, "Go out into the darkness, and put your hand into the Hand of God. That shall be to you better than light, and safer than a known way."

May that Almighty Hand guide and uphold us all. 🔸

The League of Nations

WHEN:
1919
WHERE:
Paris, France
YOU SHOULD KNOW:
The League of Nations was the fore-runner to the United Nations.

In the aftermath of World War I, the League of Nations was founded in 1919 to promote the collective security of nations through diplomacy, arbitration and arms reduction. President Wilson's 14 Points of the previous year had included a call for an international organization. Different countries had differing wishes for the League's powers. Although it did have limited success, its ability to force members to comply was undermined by its lack of any powers except economic sanctions. Many also felt that the League was weakened by the USA not joining because of Congress's refusal to sign the Treaty of Versailles. The following extracts are from the League's Founding Covenant.

Part I. The Covenant of the League of Nations
THE HIGH CONTRACTING PARTIES.

ARTICLE 13

The Members of the League agree that whenever any dispute shall arise between them which they recognise to be suitable for submission to arbitration and which cannot be satisfactorily settled by diplomacy, they will submit the whole subject-matter to arbitration.

Disputes as to the interpretation of a treaty, as to any question of international law, as to the existence of any fact which if established would constitute a breach of any international obligation, or as to the extent and nature of the reparation to be made or any such breach, are declared to be among those which are generally suitable for submission to arbitration.

For the consideration of any such dispute the court of arbitration to which the case is referred shall be the Court agreed on by the parties to the dispute or stipulated in any convention existing between them.

The Members of the League agree that they will carry out in full good faith any award that may be rendered, and that they will not resort to war against a Member of the League which complies therewith. In the event of any failure to carry out such an award, the Council shall propose what steps should be taken to give effect thereto.

ARTICLE 15

If there should arise between Members of the League any dispute likely to lead to a rupture, which is not

*The League of Nations was criticized as
being little more than a 'talking shop'.*

submitted to arbitration in accordance with Article 13, the Members of the League agree that they will submit the matter to the Council. Any party to the dispute may effect such submission by giving notice of the existence of the dispute to the Secretary General, who will make all necessary arrangements for a full investigation and consideration thereof . . .

ARTICLE 16

Should any Member of the League resort to war in disregard of its covenants under Articles 12, 13, or 15, it shall ipso facto be deemed to have committed an act of war against all other Members of the League, which hereby undertake immediately to subject it to the severance of all trade or financial relations, the prohibition of all intercourse between their nationals and the nationals of the covenant-breaking State, and the prevention of all financial, commercial, or personal intercourse between the nationals of the covenant-breaking State and the nationals of any other State, whether a Member of the League or not.

It shall be the duty of the Council in such case to recommend to the several Governments concerned what effective military, naval, or air force the Members of the League shall severally contribute to the armed forces to be used to protect the covenants of the League.

The Members of the League agree, further, that they will mutually support one another in the financial and economic measures which are taken under this Article, in order to minimise the loss and inconvenience resulting from the above measures, and that they will mutually support one another in resisting any special measures aimed at one of their number by the covenant-breaking State, and that they will take the necessary steps to afford passage through their territory to the forces of any of the Members of the League which are co-operating to protect the covenants of the League.

Any Member of the League which has violated any covenant of the League may be declared to be no longer a Member of the League by a vote of the Council concurred in by the Representatives of all the other Members of the League represented thereon.

ARTICLE 17

In the event of a dispute between a Member of the League and a State which is not a Member of the League, or between States not Members of the League, the State or States, not Members of the League shall be invited to accept the obligations of membership in the League for the purposes of such dispute, upon such conditions as the Council may deem just. If such invitation is accepted, the provisions of Articles 12 to 16 inclusive shall be applied with such modifications as may be deemed necessary by the Council.

Upon such invitation being given the Council shall immediately institute an inquiry into the circumstances of the dispute and recommend such action as may seem best and most effectual in the circumstances.

If a State so invited shall refuse to accept the obligations of membership in the League for the purposes of such dispute, and shall resort to war against a Member of the League, the provisions of Article 16 shall be applicable as against the State taking such action.

If both parties to the dispute when so invited refuse to accept the obligations of membership in the League for the purpose of such dispute, the Council may take such measures and make such recommendations as will prevent hostilities and will result in the settlement of the dispute.

ARTICLE 18

Every treaty or international engagement entered into hereafter by any Member of the League shall be forthwith registered with the Secretariat and shall as soon as possible be published by it. No such treaty or international engagement shall be binding until so registered.

Geoffrey Howe born 1926

NATIONALITY:
British
WHEN:
1990
WHERE:
London
YOU SHOULD KNOW:
During nearly 13 years of Thatcher as Prime Minister, Geoffrey Howe was Foreign Secretary, Deputy Prime Minister, Leader of the House of Commons and Chancellor of the Exchequer.

It is a tradition that ministers who resign from the British Government may give a speech to the House of Commons. On November 1, 1990 Geoffrey Howe resigned after Mrs Thatcher's declaration that the UK would never join a single European currency. His resignation letter had been carefully worded but was critical of Mrs Thatcher's attitude to Europe. The Number 10 press machine announced that he had merely resigned over differences of style, not substance, which stung him into making a devastating speech on November 13 in which he made it very obvious that in his eyes the Prime Minister had deliberately undermined policies that had been agreed by Cabinet and called on other colleagues to consider their positions. A few days later, long-time Thatcher critic Michael Heseltine challenged for the leadership and when Mrs Thatcher did not win the ballot outright at the first round of voting, she resigned on November 22.

Geoffrey Howe listening intently to his leader, Margaret Thatcher.

❛ It is rather like sending your opening batsmen to the crease only for them to find, the moment the first balls are bowled, that their bats have been broken before the game by the team captain . . .

I realise now that the task [government by persuasion] has become futile: trying to stretch the meaning of words beyond what was credible, and trying to pretend that there was a common policy when every step forward risked being subverted by some casual comment or impulsive answer . . . ❜

Albert J. Beveridge 1862–1927

*In 1898, after the end of the Spanish-American War, Spain ceded
its overseas territories of the Philippines, Cuba, Puerto Rico and
Guam to the USA and America announced its intention of
colonizing the first of these. Senator Beveridge was an ardent
supporter of the idea of establishing a US empire, and in a speech
to the Senate in January 1900 laid out his reasons for continuing
the war, saying that it was America's divine mission to lead in the
regeneration of the world and pointing out the advantages to be
gained from a base across the Pacific. His attitude to 'Orientals
and Malays' and Spaniards is highly objectionable to modern ears
but was not unusual for the times.*

NATIONALITY:
American
WHEN:
1900
WHERE:
Washington, DC, USA
YOU SHOULD KNOW:
The inhabitants of the Philippines
had by this stage already declared
themselves an independent nation
and were not keen to become an
American colony. Between
annexation and 1913 more than one
million people died before US
forces finally defeated
independence fighters.

MR PRESIDENT, the times call for candor. The Philippines are ours
forever, 'territory belonging to the United States' as the Constitution
calls them. And just beyond the Philippines are China's illimitable
markets. We will not retreat from either. We will not repudiate our duty
in the archipelago. We will not abandon our opportunity in the Orient.
We will not renounce our part in the mission of our race, trustee, under
God, of the civilization of the world. And we will move forward to our
work, not howling out regrets like slaves whipped to their burdens but
with gratitude for a task worthy of our strength and thanksgiving to
Almighty God that He has marked us as His chosen people, henceforth
to lead in the regeneration of the world.

This island empire is the last land left in all the oceans. If it should
prove a mistake to abandon it, the blunder once made would be
irretrievable. If it proves a mistake to hold it, the error can be corrected
when we will. Every other progressive nation stands ready to relieve us.

But to hold it will be no mistake. Our largest trade henceforth must
be with Asia. The Pacific is our ocean. More and more Europe will
manufacture the most it needs, secure from its colonies the most it
consumes. Where shall we turn for consumers of our surplus?
Geography answers the question. China is our natural customer. She is
nearer to us than to England, Germany, or Russia, the commercial
powers of the present and the future. They have moved nearer to
China by securing permanent bases on her borders. The Philippines
give us a base at the door of all the East . . .

Here, then, senators, is the situation. Two years ago there was no
land in all the world which we could occupy for any purpose. Our
commerce was daily turning toward the Orient, and geography and
trade developments made necessary our commercial empire over the
Pacific. And in that ocean we had no commercial, naval, or military
base. Today, we have one of the three great ocean possessions of the
globe, located at the most commanding commercial, naval, and military
points in the Eastern seas, within hail of India, shoulder to shoulder
with China, richer in its own resources than any equal body of land on

the entire globe, and peopled by a race which civilization demands shall be improved. Shall we abandon it?

That man little knows the common people of the republic, little understands the instincts of our race who thinks we will not hold it fast and hold it forever, administering just government by simplest methods. We may trick up devices to shift our burden and lessen our opportunity; they will avail us nothing but delay. We may tangle conditions by applying academic arrangements of self-government to a crude situation; their failure will drive us to our duty in the end . . .

Those who complain do so in ignorance of the real situation. We attempted a great task with insufficient means; we became impatient that it was not finished before it could fairly be commenced; and I pray we may not add that other element of disaster, pausing in the work before it is thoroughly and forever done. That is the gravest mistake we could possibly make, and that is the only danger before us. Our Indian wars would have been shortened, the lives of soldiers and settlers saved, and the Indians themselves benefited had we made continuous and decisive war; and any other kind of war is criminal because ineffective. We acted toward the Indians as though we feared them, loved them, hated them – a mingling of foolish sentiment, inaccurate thought, and paralytic purpose . . .

It has been charged that our conduct of the war has been cruel. Senators, it has been the reverse. I have been in our hospitals and seen the Filipino wounded as carefully, tenderly cared for as our own. Within our lines they may plow and sow and reap and go about the affairs of peace with absolute liberty. And yet all this kindness was misunderstood, or rather not understood. Senators must remember that we are not dealing with Americans or Europeans. We are dealing with Orientals. We are dealing with Orientals who are Malays. We are dealing with Malays instructed in Spanish methods. They mistake kindness for weakness, forbearance for fear. It could not be otherwise unless you could erase hundreds of years of savagery, other hundreds of years of Orientalism, and still other hundreds of years of Spanish character and custom . . .

Mr President, reluctantly and only from a sense of duty am I forced to say that American opposition to the war has been the chief factor in prolonging it. Had Aguinaldo not understood that in America, even in the American Congress, even here in the Senate, he and his cause were supported; had he not known that it was proclaimed on the stump and in the press of a faction in the United States that every shot his misguided followers fired into the breasts of American soldiers was like the volleys fired by Washington's men against the soldiers of King George, his insurrection would have dissolved before it entirely crystallized . . .

But, senators, it would be better to abandon this combined garden and Gibraltar of the Pacific, and count our blood and treasure already spent a profitable loss than to apply any academic arrangement of self-government to these children. They are not capable of self-government. How could they be? They are not of a self-governing race. They are Orientals, Malays, instructed by Spaniards in the latter's worst estate.

They know nothing of practical government except as they have witnessed the weak, corrupt, cruel, and capricious rule of Spain. What magic will anyone employ to dissolve in their minds and characters those impressions of governors and governed which three centuries of misrule has created? What alchemy will change the Oriental quality of their blood and set the self-governing currents of the American pouring through their Malay veins? How shall they, in the twinkling of an eye, be exalted to the heights of self-governing peoples which required a thousand years for us to reach, Anglo-Saxon though we are?

Let men beware how they employ the term 'self-government'. It is a sacred term. It is the watchword at the door of the inner temple of liberty, for liberty does not always mean self-government. Self-government is a method of liberty – the highest, simplest, best – and it is acquired only after centuries of study and struggle and experiment and instruction and all the elements of the progress of man. Self-government is no base and common thing to be bestowed on the merely audacious. It is the degree which crowns the graduate of liberty, not the name of liberty's infant class, who have not yet mastered the alphabet of freedom. Savage blood, Oriental blood, Malay blood, Spanish example – are these the elements of self-government? . . .

The most ardent advocate of self-government that I met was anxious that I should know that such a government would be tranquil because, as he said, if anyone criticized it, the government would shoot the offender. A few of them have a sort of verbal understanding of the democratic theory, but the above are the examples of the ideas of the practical workings of self-government entertained by the aristocracy, the rich planters and traders, and heavy employers of labor, the men who would run the government . . .

In all other islands our government must be simple and strong. It must be a uniform government. Different forms for different islands will produce perpetual disturbance because the people of each island would think that the people of the other islands are more favored than they. In Panay I heard murmurings that we were giving Negros an American constitution. This is a human quality, found even in America, and we must never forget that in dealing with the Filipinos we deal with children . . .

The men we send to administer civilized government in the Philippines must be themselves the highest examples of our civilization. I use the word 'examples', for examples they must be in that word's most absolute sense. They must be men of the world and of affairs, students of their fellowmen, not theorists nor dreamers. They must be brave men, physically as well as morally. They must be as incorruptible as honor, as stainless as purity, men whom no force can frighten, no influence coerce, no money buy. Such men come high, even here in America. But they must be had . . .

The Declaration of Independence does not forbid us to do our part in the regeneration of the world. If it did, the Declaration would be wrong, just as the Articles of Confederation, drafted by the very same men who signed the Declaration, was found to be wrong. The Declaration has no application to the present situation. It was written by self-governing men for self-governing men. It was written by men who, for a century and a half, had been experimenting in self-government on this continent, and whose ancestors for hundreds of years before had been gradually developing toward that high and holy estate.

The Declaration applies only to people capable of self-government. How dare any man prostitute this expression of the very elect of self-governing peoples to a race of Malay children of barbarism, schooled in Spanish methods and ideas? And you who say the Declaration applies to all men, how dare you deny its application to the American Indian? And if you deny it to the Indian at home, how dare you grant it to the Malay abroad?

The Declaration does not contemplate that all government must have the consent of the governed. It announces that man's 'inalienable rights are life, liberty, and the pursuit of happiness; that to secure these rights governments are established among men deriving their just powers from the consent of the governed; that when any form of government becomes destructive of those rights, it is the right of the people to alter or abolish it.' 'Life, liberty, and the pursuit of happiness' are the important things; 'consent of the governed' is one of the means to those ends.

If 'any form of government becomes destructive of those ends, it is the right of the people to alter or abolish it,' says the Declaration. 'Any form' includes all forms. Thus the Declaration itself recognizes other forms of government than those resting on the consent of the governed. The word 'consent' itself recognizes other forms, for 'consent' means the understanding of the thing to which the 'consent' is given; and there are people in the world who do not understand any form of government. And the sense in which 'consent' is used in the Declaration is broader than mere understanding; for 'consent' in the Declaration means participation in the government 'consented' to. And yet these people who are not capable of 'consenting' to any form of government must be governed . . .

Mr President, this question is deeper than any question of party politics; deeper than any question of the isolated policy of our country even; deeper even than any question of constitutional power. It is elemental. It is racial. God has not been preparing the English-speaking and Teutonic peoples for a thousand years for nothing but vain and idle self-contemplation and self-admiration. No! He has made us the master organizers of the world to establish system where chaos reigns. He has given us the spirit of progress to overwhelm the forces of reaction throughout the earth. He has made us adepts in government that we may administer government among savage and senile peoples. Were it not for such a force as this the world would relapse into barbarism and night. And of all our race He has marked the American people as His chosen nation to finally lead in the regeneration of the world. This is the divine mission of America, and it holds for us all the profit, all the glory, all the happiness possible to man. We are trustees of the world's progress, guardians of its righteous peace. The judgment of the Master is upon us: 'Ye have been faithful over a few things; I will make you ruler over many things.'

What shall history say of us? Shall it say that we renounced that holy trust, left the savage to his base condition, the wilderness to the reign of waste, deserted duty, abandoned glory, forget our sordid profit even, because we feared our strength and read the charter of our powers with the doubter's eye and the quibbler's mind? Shall it say that, called by events to captain and command the proudest, ablest, purest race of history in history's noblest work, we declined that great commission? Our fathers would not have had it so. No! They founded no paralytic government, incapable of the simplest acts of administration. They planted no sluggard people, passive while the world's work calls them. They established no reactionary nation. They unfurled no retreating flag . . .

Do you remind me of the precious blood that must be shed, the lives that must be given, the broken hearts of loved ones for their slain? And this is indeed a heavier price than all combined. And, yet, as a nation, every historic duty we have done, every achievement we have accomplished has been by the sacrifice of our noblest sons. Every holy memory that glorifies the flag is of those heroes who have died that its onward march might not be stayed. It is the nation's dearest lives yielded for the flag that makes it dear to us; it is the nation's most precious blood poured out for it that makes it precious to us. That flag is woven of heroism and grief, of the bravery of men and women's tears, of righteousness and battle, of sacrifice and anguish, of triumph and of glory. It is these which make our flag a holy thing.

Who would tear from that sacred banner the glorious legends of a single battle where it has waved on land or sea? What son of a soldier of the flag whose father fell beneath it on any field would surrender that proud record for the heraldry of a king? In the cause of civilization, in the service of the republic anywhere on earth, Americans consider wounds the noblest decorations man can win, and count the giving of their lives a glad and precious duty.

Pray God that spirit never falls. Pray God the time may never come when Mammon and the love of ease shall so debase our blood that we will fear to shed it for the flag and its imperial destiny. Pray God the time may never come when American heroism is but a legend like the story of the Cid. American faith in our mission and our might a dream dissolved, and the glory of our mighty race departed.

And that time will never come. We will renew our youth at the fountain of new and glorious deeds. We will exalt our reverence for the flag by carrying it to a noble future as well as by remembering its ineffable past. Its immortality will not pass, because everywhere and always we will acknowledge and discharge the solemn responsibilities our sacred flag, in its deepest meaning, puts upon us. And so, senators, with reverent hearts, where dwells the fear of God, the American people move forward to the future of their hope and the doing of His work.

Mr President and senators, adopt the resolution offered that peace may quickly come and that we may begin our saving, regenerating, and uplifting work. Adopt it, and this bloodshed will cease when these deluded children of our islands learn that this is the final word of the representatives of the American people in Congress assembled. Reject it, and the world, history, and the American people will know where to forever fix the awful responsibility for the consequences that will surely follow such failure to do our manifest duty. How dare we delay when our soldiers' blood is flowing?

United Nations Security Council

In the aftermath of the Six-Day War, when Israel had launched pre-emptive strikes against Egypt, Syria and Jordan, the UN Security Council unanimously adopted Resolution 242, calling for Israeli withdrawal from territories it had recently occupied, for a 'just settlement' of the problems of the refugees and for Israel, Jordan, Egypt and Syria to respect each others' recognized borders and right to a peaceful existence. Opinions differed between countries as to whether the Resolution's call for Israeli withdrawal from the territories it had occupied was a pre-condition for negotiations or not, but in practice negotiations tended to happen first.

WHEN:
1967
WHERE:
New York City, USA
YOU SHOULD KNOW:
There were various draft resolutions. This one, which is the one that was finally adopted, was written by the British Ambassador to the United Nations, Lord Caradon.

‘ THE SECURITY COUNCIL,
Expressing its continuing concern with the grave situation in the Middle East,
    Emphasizing the inadmissibility of the acquisition of territory by war and the need to work for a just and lasting peace in which every State in the area can live in security,
    Emphasizing further that all Member States in their acceptance of the Charter of the United Nations have undertaken a commitment to act in accordance with Article 2 of the Charter,

1. Affirms that the fulfillment of Charter principles requires the establishment of a just and lasting peace in the Middle East which should include the application of both the following principles:
    (i) Withdrawal of Israel armed forces from territories occupied in the recent conflict;

The Security Council votes.

(ii) Termination of all claims or states of belligerency and respect for and acknowledgement of the sovereignty, territorial integrity and political independence of every State in the area and their right to live in peace within secure and recognized boundaries free from threats or acts of force;

2. Affirms further the necessity
(a) For guaranteeing freedom of navigation through international waterways in the area;
(b) For achieving a just settlement of the refugee problem;
(c) For guaranteeing the territorial inviolability and political independence of every State in the area, through measures including the establishment of demilitarized zones;

3. Requests the Secretary-General to designate a Special Representative to proceed to the Middle East to establish and maintain contacts with the States concerned in order to promote agreement and assist efforts to achieve a peaceful and accepted settlement in accordance with the provisions and principles in this resolution;

4. Requests the Secretary-General to report to the Security Council on the progress of the efforts of the Special Representative as soon as possible. 〃

George H. W. Bush born 1924

NATIONALITY:
American
WHEN:
September 11, 1990
WHERE:
Washington, DC, USA
YOU SHOULD KNOW:
Pentagon claims of photographic evidence Iraqi forces were building up on the border with Saudi Arabia were later discovered to be mistaken.

On August 1, 1990 Iraqi forces invaded the country's southern neighbour Kuwait. Almost immediately a coalition of more than thirty countries began making plans to liberate the oil-rich state and troops were deployed to Saudi Arabia and navies to the Persian Gulf. On September 11 President Bush addressed a joint session of Congress on the invasion and the need for intervention for political and economic reasons, especially in the light of a perceived threat to Saudia Arabia. Congress authorized the invasion on January 12, 1991 and Operation Desert Storm began on the 17th.

Mr President and Mr Speaker and Members of the United States Congress, distinguished guests, fellow Americans, thank you very much for that warm welcome. We gather tonight, witness to events in the Persian Gulf as significant as they are tragic. In the early morning hours of August 2, following negotiations and promises by Iraq's dictator Saddam Hussein not to use force, a powerful Iraqi army invaded its trusting and much weaker neighbor, Kuwait. Within 3 days, 120,000 Iraqi troops with 850 tanks had poured into Kuwait and moved south to threaten Saudi Arabia. It was then that I decided to act to check that aggression . . .

Our objectives in the Persian Gulf are clear, our goals defined and familiar: Iraq must withdraw from Kuwait completely, immediately, and without condition. Kuwait's legitimate government must be restored.

The security and stability of the Persian Gulf must be assured. And American citizens abroad must be protected. These goals are not ours alone. They've been endorsed by the United Nations Security Council five times in as many weeks. Most countries share our concern for principle. And many have a stake in the stability of the Persian Gulf. This is not, as Saddam Hussein would have it, the United States against Iraq. It is Iraq against the world . . .

We stand today at a unique and extraordinary moment. The crisis in the Persian Gulf, as grave as it is, also offers a rare opportunity to move toward an historic period of cooperation. Out of these troubled times, our fifth objective – a new world order – can emerge: a new era – freer from the threat of terror, stronger in the pursuit of justice, and more secure in the quest for peace. An era in which the nations of the world, East and West, North and South, can prosper and live in harmony. A hundred generations have searched for this elusive path to peace, while a thousand wars raged across the span of human endeavor. Today that new world is struggling to be born, a world quite different from the one we've known. A world where the rule of law supplants the rule of the jungle. A world in which nations recognize the shared responsibility for freedom and justice. A world where the strong respect the rights of the weak. This is the vision that I shared with President Gorbachev in Helsinki. He and other leaders from Europe, the Gulf, and around the world understand that how we manage this crisis today could shape the future for generations . . .

. . . America and the world must defend common vital interests – and we will. America and the world must support the rule of law – and we will. America and the world must stand up to aggression – and we will. And one thing more: In the pursuit of these goals America will not be intimidated.

Vital issues of principle are at stake. Saddam Hussein is literally trying to wipe a country off the face of the Earth. We do not exaggerate. Nor do we exaggerate when we say Saddam Hussein will fail. Vital economic interests are at risk as well. Iraq itself controls some 10 per cent of the world's proven oil reserves. Iraq plus Kuwait controls twice that. An Iraq permitted to swallow Kuwait would have the economic and military power, as well as the arrogance, to intimidate and coerce its neighbors – neighbors who control the lion's share of the world's remaining oil reserves. We cannot permit a resource so vital to be dominated by one so ruthless. And we won't.

Recent events have surely proven that there is no substitute for American leadership. In the face of tyranny, let no one doubt American credibility and reliability. Let no one doubt our staying power. We will stand by our friends. One way or another, the leader of Iraq must learn this fundamental truth. From the outset, acting hand in hand with others, we've sought to fashion the broadest possible international response to Iraq's aggression. The level of world cooperation and condemnation of Iraq is unprecedented. Armed forces from countries spanning four continents are there at the request of King Fahd of Saudi Arabia to deter and, if need be, to defend against attack. Muslims and non-Muslims, Arabs and non-Arabs, soldiers from many nations stand shoulder to shoulder, resolute against Saddam Hussein's ambitions . . .

We're now in sight of a United Nations that performs as envisioned by its founders. We owe much to the outstanding leadership of Secretary-General Javier Perez de Cuellar. The United Nations is backing up its words with action. The Security Council has imposed mandatory economic sanctions on Iraq, designed to force Iraq to relinquish the spoils of its illegal conquest. The Security Council has also taken the decisive step of authorizing the use of all means necessary to ensure compliance with these sanctions. Together with our friends and allies, ships of the United States Navy are today patrolling Mideast waters. They've already intercepted more than 700 ships to enforce the sanctions. Three regional leaders I spoke with just yesterday told me that these sanctions are working. Iraq is feeling the heat. We continue to hope that Iraq's leaders will recalculate just what their aggression has cost them. They are cut off from world trade, unable to sell their oil. And only a tiny fraction of goods gets through . . .

I cannot predict just how long it will take to convince Iraq to withdraw from Kuwait. Sanctions will take time to have their full intended effect. We will continue to review all options with our allies, but let it be clear: we will not let this aggression stand.

Our interest, our involvement in the Gulf is not transitory. It predated Saddam Hussein's aggression and will survive it. Long after all our troops come home – and we all hope it's soon, very soon – there will be a lasting role for the United States in assisting the nations of the Persian Gulf. Our role then: to deter future aggression. Our role is to help our friends in their own self-defense. And something else: to curb the proliferation of chemical, biological, ballistic missile and, above all, nuclear technologies.

Let me also make clear that the United States has no quarrel with the Iraqi people. Our quarrel is with Iraq's dictator and with his aggression. Iraq will not be permitted to annex Kuwait. That's not a threat, that's not a boast, that's just the way it's going to be . . .

In the final analysis, our ability to meet our responsibilities abroad depends upon political will and consensus at home. This is never easy in democracies, for we govern only with the consent of the governed. And although free people in a free society are bound to have their differences, Americans traditionally come together in times of adversity and challenge.

Once again, Americans have stepped forward to share a tearful goodbye with their families before leaving for a strange and distant shore. At this very moment, they serve together with Arabs, Europeans, Asians, and Africans in defense of principle and the dream of a new world order. That's why they sweat and toil in the sand and the heat and the sun. If they can come together under such adversity, if old adversaries like the Soviet Union and the United States can work in common cause, then surely we who are so fortunate to be in this great Chamber – Democrats, Republicans, liberals, conservatives – can come together to fulfill our responsibilities here. Thank you. Good night. And God bless the United States of America. 🟥

President Bush was determined to throw American might into the fight against Iraqi aggression.

Ronald Reagan 1911–2004

NATIONALITY:
American
WHEN:
1983
WHERE:
Washington DC
YOU SHOULD KNOW:
The US invasion of Grenada came a few months later.

On March 23, 1983 President Reagan addressed the nation from the Oval Office on a matter of perceived national security, speaking about the contrast between the Soviet arms build-up and military assistance in strategic locations around the world with the US continuing military rundown. He then announced the decision to develop and implement the Strategic Defense Initiative, a system that he hoped would be able to intercept and destroy Soviet – or anyone else's – strategic ballistic nuclear missiles before they reached American territory with both ground- and space-based technologies. Inevitably, the initiative was dubbed 'Star Wars' by critics and the media.

' . . . At the beginning of this year, I submitted to the Congress a defense budget which reflects my best judgment of the best understanding of the experts and specialists who advise me about what we and our allies must do to protect our people in the years ahead. That budget is much more than a long list of numbers, for behind all the numbers lies America's ability to prevent the greatest of human tragedies and preserve our free way of life in a sometimes dangerous world. It is part of a careful, long-term plan to make America strong again after too many years of neglect and mistakes . . .

Since the dawn of the atomic age, we've sought to reduce the risk of war by maintaining a strong deterrent and by seeking genuine arms control. Deterrence means simply this: making sure any adversary who thinks about attacking the United States, or our allies, or our vital interests, concludes that the risks to him outweigh any potential gains. Once he understands that, he won't attack. We maintain the peace through our strength; weakness only invites aggression.

This strategy of deterrence has not changed. It still works. But what it takes to maintain deterrence has changed. It took one kind of military force to deter an attack when we had far more nuclear weapons than any other power; it takes another kind now that the Soviets, for example, have enough accurate and powerful nuclear weapons to destroy virtually all of our missiles on the ground. Now, this is not to say that the Soviet Union is planning to make war on us. Nor do I believe a war is inevitable – quite the contrary. But what must be recognized is that our security is based on being prepared to meet all threats . . .

We can't afford to believe that we will never be threatened. There have been two world wars in my lifetime. We didn't start them and, indeed, did everything we could to avoid being drawn into them. But we were ill-prepared for both. Had we been better prepared, peace might have been preserved.

For 20 years the Soviet Union has been accumulating enormous military might. They didn't stop when their forces exceeded all requirements of a legitimate defensive capability. And they haven't stopped now. During the past decade and a half, the Soviets have built up a massive arsenal of new strategic nuclear weapons – weapons that can strike directly at the United States . . .

As the Soviets have increased their military power, they've been emboldened to extend that power. They're spreading their military influence in ways that can directly challenge our vital interests and those of our allies.

The following aerial photographs, most of them secret until now, illustrate this point in a crucial area very close to home: Central America and the Caribbean Basin. They're not dramatic photographs. But I think they help give you a better understanding of what I'm talking about.

This Soviet intelligence collection facility, less than a hundred miles from our coast, is the largest of its kind in the world. The acres and acres of antennae fields and intelligence monitors are targeted on key US military installations and sensitive activities. The installation in Lourdes, Cuba, is manned by 1500 Soviet technicians. And the satellite ground station allows instant communications with Moscow. This 28-square-mile facility has grown by more than 60 per cent in size and capability during the past decade.

In western Cuba, we see this military airfield and it complement of modern, Soviet-built Mig-23 aircraft. The Soviet Union uses this Cuban airfield for its own long-range reconnaissance missions. And earlier this month, two modern Soviet antisubmarine warfare aircraft began operating from it. During the past two years, the level of Soviet arms exports to Cuba can only be compared to the levels reached during the Cuban Missile Crisis 20 years ago.

This third photo, which is the only one in this series that has been previously made public, shows Soviet military hardware that has made its way to Central America. This airfield with its MI-8 helicopters, anti-aircraft guns and protected fighter sites is one of a number of military facilities in Nicaragua which has received Soviet equipment funneled through Cuba, and reflects the massive military buildup going on in that country.

On the small island of Grenada, at the southern end of the Caribbean chain, the Cubans, with Soviet financing and backing, are in the process of building an airfield with a 10,000-foot runway. Grenada doesn't even have an air force. Who is it intended for? The Caribbean is a very important passageway for our international commerce and military lines of communication. More than half of all American oil imports now pass through the Caribbean. The rapid buildup of Grenada's military potential is unrelated to any conceivable threat to this island country of under 110,000 people and totally at odds with the pattern of other eastern Caribbean States, most of which are unarmed.

The Soviet-Cuban militarization of Grenada, in short, can only be seen as power projection into the region. And it is in this important economic and strategic area that we're trying to help the Governments of El Salvador, Costa Rica, Honduras, and others in their struggles for democracy against guerrillas supported through Cuba and Nicaragua . . .

Some people may still ask: Would the Soviets ever use their formidable military power? Well, again, can we afford to believe they won't? There is Afghanistan. And in Poland, the Soviets denied the will of the people and in so doing demonstrated to the world how their military power could also be used to intimidate.

The final fact is that the Soviet Union is acquiring what can only be considered an offensive military force. They have continued to build far more intercontinental ballistic missiles than they could possibly need simply to deter an attack. Their conventional forces are trained and equipped not so much to defend against an attack as they are to permit sudden, surprise offensives of their own.

Our NATO allies have assumed a great defense burden, including the military draft in most countries. We're working with them and our other friends around the world to do more. Our defensive strategy means we need military forces that can move very quickly, forces that are trained and ready to respond to any emergency . . .

This is why I'm speaking to you tonight – to urge you to tell your Senators and Congressmen that you know we must continue to restore our military strength. If we stop in midstream, we will send a signal of decline, of lessened will, to friends and adversaries alike. Free people must voluntarily, through open debate and democratic means, meet the challenge that totalitarians pose by compulsion. It's up to us, in our time, to choose and choose wisely between the hard but necessary task of preserving peace and freedom and the temptation to ignore our duty and blindly hope for the best while the enemies of freedom grow stronger day by day . . .

Now, thus far tonight I've shared with you my thoughts on the problems of national security we must face together. My predecessors in the Oval Office have appeared before you on other occasions to describe the threat posed by Soviet power and have proposed steps to address that threat. But since the advent of nuclear weapons, those steps have been increasingly directed toward deterrence of aggression through the promise of retaliation . . .

One of the most important contributions we can make is, of course, to lower the level of all arms, and particularly nuclear arms. We're engaged right now in several negotiations with the Soviet Union to bring about a mutual reduction of weapons. I will report to you a week from tomorrow my thoughts on that score. But let me just say, I'm totally committed to this course.

If the Soviet Union will join with us in our effort to achieve major arms reduction, we will have succeeded in stabilizing the nuclear balance. Nevertheless, it will still be necessary to rely on the specter of retaliation, on mutual threat. And that's a sad commentary on the human condition. Wouldn't it be better to save lives than to avenge them? Are we not capable of demonstrating our peaceful intentions by applying all our abilities and our ingenuity to achieving a truly lasting stability? I think we are. Indeed, we must.

After careful consultation with my advisers, including the Joint Chiefs of Staff, I believe there is a way. Let me share with you a vision of the future which offers hope. It is that we embark on a program to counter the awesome Soviet missile threat with measures that are defensive. Let us turn to the very strengths in technology that spawned our great industrial base and that have given us the quality of life we enjoy today.

What if free people could live secure in the knowledge that their security did not rest upon the threat of instant US retaliation to deter a Soviet attack, that we could intercept and destroy strategic ballistic missiles before they reached our own soil or that of our allies?

I know this is a formidable, technical task, one that may not be accomplished before the end of this century. Yet, current technology has attained a level of sophistication where it's reasonable for us to begin this effort. It will take years, probably decades of effort on many fronts. There will be failures and setbacks, just as there will be successes and breakthroughs. And as we proceed, we must remain constant in preserving the nuclear deterrent and maintaining a solid capability for flexible response. But isn't it worth every investment necessary to free the world from the threat of nuclear war? We know it is.

In the meantime, we will continue to pursue real reductions in nuclear arms, negotiating from a position of strength that can be ensured only by modernizing our strategic forces. At the same time, we must take steps to reduce the risk of a conventional military conflict escalating to nuclear war by improving our nonnuclear capabilities.

America does possess – now – the technologies to attain very significant improvements in the effectiveness of our conventional, nonnuclear forces. Proceeding boldly with these new technologies, we can significantly reduce any incentive that the Soviet Union may have to threaten attack against the United States or its allies.

As we pursue our goal of defensive technologies, we recognize that our allies rely upon our strategic offensive power to deter attacks against them. Their vital interests and ours are inextricably linked. Their safety and ours are one. And no change in technology can or will alter that reality. We must and shall continue to honor our commitments.

I clearly recognize that defensive systems have limitations and raise certain problems and ambiguities. If paired with offensive systems, they can be viewed as fostering an aggressive policy, and no one wants that. But with these considerations firmly in mind, I call upon the scientific community in our country, those who gave us nuclear weapons, to turn their great talents now to the cause of mankind and world peace, to give us the means of rendering these nuclear weapons impotent and obsolete.

Tonight, consistent with our obligations of the ABM treaty and recognizing the need for closer consultation with our allies, I'm taking an important first step. I am directing a comprehensive and intensive effort to define a long-term research and development program to begin to achieve our ultimate goal of eliminating the threat posed by strategic nuclear missiles. This could pave the way for arms control measures to eliminate the weapons themselves. We seek neither military superiority nor political advantage. Our only purpose – one all people share – is to search for ways to reduce the danger of nuclear war.

My fellow Americans, tonight we're launching an effort which holds the promise of changing the course of human history. There will be risks, and results take time. But I believe we can do it. As we cross this threshold, I ask for your prayers and your support.

Thank you, good night, and God bless you.

Mao Zedong 1893–1976

NATIONALITY:
Chinese
WHEN:
1958
WHERE:
Peking (Beijing), China
YOU SHOULD KNOW:
Deaths caused by the policies
implemented in the Great Leap
Forward are estimated at between
13 and 43 million.

At the Supreme State Conference of 1958, Chairman Mao announced the extension of the 40-Point Programme, in what became known as the Great Leap Forward, a five-year plan for increased industrial and agricultural output through the use of cheap labour. The aim was to equal the manufacturing output of Britain within 15 years. The small collectives created under the previous five-year plan were merged into huge communes, with communal kitchens. Another key introduction was the system of backyard furnaces, in order to double steel production. The aims of the plan were unrealistic: the miners could only meet targets by producing poor-quality ore, the backyard furnaces were not up to the task of producing high-quality steel and vast areas of land were denuded of trees. The agricultural innovations introduced were disastrous, especially as many agricultural labourers had been moved to work on steel production, and widespread famine resulted.

‘ When I review the past seven or eight years, I see that this nation of ours has a great future. Especially in the past year you can see how the national spirit of our 600 million people has been raised to a level surpassing that of the past eight years . . . we shall catch up with Britain in about 15 years; the publication of the Forty Point Programme for Agricultural Development has given great encouragement to the masses.

Our nation is waking up, just like anybody waking from a night's sleep. We have overthrown the feudal system of many thousands of years and have awakened.

Now our enthusiasm has been aroused. Ours is an ardent nation, now swept by a burning tide . . . We shall be able to do things which we could not do before. We still have ten years to carry out the 40-Point Programme for Agricultural Development, but it looks as if we shall not need ten years. Some people say five years, others three. It would seem that we can complete it in eight . . .

Our strength must be aroused and not dissipated. We must indeed keep up our fighting spirit. ’

Lord (Brian) Hutton born 1931

In the summer of 2003 BBC journalists on television and radio alleged that in 2002 members of the government and their advisors had interfered with intelligence about Iraq's weapons capability. The intelligence was presented to Parliament, and the public, in the 'September Dossier' in order to beef up support for a possible invasion of Iraq. After the suicide of Dr David Kelly, the intelligence officer who was the journalists' main source of information, the Hutton Inquiry was commissioned to examine the allegations. Hutton's conclusion was that, although the way in which the intelligence about Iraq being able to launch WMD at Britain in 45 minutes had been presented probably was influenced by the Prime Minister's wishes, there was no proof that the intelligence itself had knowingly been altered. The BBC was censured and several of its employees were sacked or forced to resign. The report was met with widespread scepticism and calls for a wider inquiry into whether the intelligence had been right in the first place.

NATIONALITY:
British
WHEN:
2004
WHERE:
London, England
YOU SHOULD KNOW:
All of the claims in the dossier have since proved to be completely unfounded and the documents on which they are based are now known to be fakes.

Dr David Kelly, who was the source of information on weapons of mass destruction.

❛The term 'sexed-up' is a slang expression, the meaning of which lacks clarity in the context of the discussion of the dossier. It is capable of two different meanings. It could mean that the dossier was embellished with items of intelligence known or believed to be false or unreliable to make the case against Saddam Hussein stronger, or it could mean that whilst the intelligence contained in the dossier was believed to be reliable, the dossier was drafted in such a way as to make the case against Saddam Hussein as strong as the intelligence contained in it permitted. If the term is used in this latter sense, then because of the drafting suggestions made by 10 Downing Street for the purpose of making a strong case against Saddam Hussein, it could be said that the Government 'sexed-up' the dossier. However in the context of the broadcasts in which the 'sexing-up' allegation was reported and having regard to the other allegations reported in those broadcasts I consider that the allegation was unfounded as it would have been understood by those who heard the broadcasts to mean that the dossier had been embellished with intelligence known or believed to be false or unreliable, which was not the case.❜

Anonymous

NATIONALITY:
American
WHEN:
1987
WHERE:
Washington, DC, USA
YOU SHOULD KNOW:
This is a direct reference back to
Howard Baker's question at the
Watergate Senate hearings.

In November 1986 a Lebanese newspaper broke the news that the USA had clandestinely been selling arms to Iran for use in the Iran-Iraq War in return for Iranian help in obtaining the release of six Americans being held hostage in Lebanon by Hezbollah. President Reagan initially denied that any arms sales had occurred, then that the deal was an arms/hostage trade (not dealing with hostage-takers had been a campaign pledge). It emerged during the hearings that the majority of the payments had been diverted to the right-wing Contra rebels in Nicaragua by Lieutanant Colonel Oliver North of the National Security Council, with the blessing of National Security Adviser Admiral John Poindexter. North also said he assumed that the President knew. As with President Nixon in the preceding decade, the media were in full cry to find out what President Reagan knew, but the Tower Commission ascertained that he was so disengaged from the day-to-day running of the White House that he did not know about the diversion of funds.

'What did Reagan know and when did he forget it?'

Giuseppe Garibaldi 1807–1882

NATIONALITY:
Italian
WHEN:
1849
WHERE:
Rome, Italy
YOU SHOULD KNOW:
In 1861 Garibaldi offered to lead
Union forces in the American Civil
War, but he and Abraham Lincoln
could not agree terms and
conditions.

Giuseppe Garibaldi was an inspirational military leader who, during several campaigns over a period of more than 20 years, achieved the unification of almost all of Italy. One of his unsuccessful campaigns was the defence of the short-lived Republic of Rome in 1849. The French, determined to restore the Papal States, had laid siege to the city with overwhelming force. After the French victory, Garibaldi vowed to continue fighting a guerrilla war and called for troops to join him. He left with 4,000 men, hunted by forces including French, Austrian and Spanish, and eventually had to go into exile – first in Tangier, then in New York. The cottage he stayed in on Staten Island is preserved as the Garibaldi Memorial.

'I offer neither pay, nor quarters, nor food; I offer only hunger, thirst, forced marches, battles and death. Let him who loves his country with his heart, and not merely with his lips, follow me.'

Ho Chi Minh 1890–1969

*After nearly 30 years away from his homeland, Ho Chi Minh
returned to fight the Japanese and in August 1944 – a year
before the final Japanese surrender – he declared the Viet Minh
intentions and methods. The guerilla tactics used during the
following three decades included hiding in dense jungles,
making hundreds of miles of tunnels, chambers and hidden
trails, creating booby-traps, sabotage and laying ambushes.
They were successful against first the French, then the South
Vietnamese and American forces, especially after the mid-1960s
when Ho ordered that such strategies be stepped up as they were
more successful against heavily armoured US troops than all-out
attacks by large numbers of troops, eventually resulting in the
humiliating US withdrawal of 1975.*

NATIONALITY:
Vietnamese
WHEN:
1944
WHERE:
North Vietnam
YOU SHOULD KNOW:
After the Communist North
Vietnamese victory in 1975, the
southern capital, Saigon, was
renamed Ho Chi Minh City.

‘ Our maxim is the removal of our enemies one by one . . . We must
keep the enemy out of breath with constant attacks . . . to set up
zones under revolutionary government, and thus gradually form a
unified state rule in the whole country. ,

Patricia Schroeder born 1940

*In a debate in the US House of Representatives on August 2, 1983
Democrat Representative Pat Schroeder coined a term about
President Reagan that ironically stuck. Throughout his first
Presidential term, he just seemed to be able to shrug off gaffes,
scandals and accusations of broken pledges – for instance about
taxation – chiefly through the effect of his charm. Schroeder later
said that the idea had come to her while she was cooking eggs
for her children in a non-stick pan. Even during his second
term, when his popularity was waning, President Reagan
seemed to be censured less than others might have been in the
same circumstances, for instance when documents relating to
the Iran-Contra affair were deliberately destroyed or withheld by
administration officials.*

NATIONALITY:
American
WHEN:
1983
WHERE:
Washington, DC, USA
YOU SHOULD KNOW:
The chemical name for Teflon is
polytetrafluoroethylene.

‘ After carefully watching Ronald Reagan, he is attempting a great
breakthrough in political technology – he has been perfecting the
Teflon-coated Presidency. He sees that nothing sticks to him. ,

Ho Chi Minh 1890–1969

NATIONALITY:
Vietnamese
WHEN:
1945
WHERE:
Hanoi, Vietnam
YOU SHOULD KNOW:
The later Vietnam War, between the
Communist north and the south
lasted from 1959 to 1975.

Ho Chi Minh returned to Vietnam in 1941 after decades in exile in order to lead the Viet Minh against the Japanese occupying forces. After the defeat of the Japanese in August 1945 and the collapse of Bao Dai's government, the Viet Minh took control. On September 2, 1945 Ho Chi Minh declared the country independent of both Japan and the former colonial power, France, accusing both of atrocities and tyranny and stating that the entire people of Vietnam would resist if the French tried to reassert control. They did and the resulting war lasted until 1954, when the country was divided into two by the Geneva Accords.

'All men are created equal. They are endowed by their Creator with certain inalienable rights, among these are Life, Liberty, and the pursuit of Happiness.'

This immortal statement was made in the Declaration of Independence of the United States of America in 1776. In a broader sense, this means: All the peoples on the earth are equal from birth, all the peoples have a right to live, to be happy and free.

They [the French] have enforced inhuman laws; they have set up three distinct political regimes in the North, the Center and the South of Vietnam in order to wreck our national unity and prevent our people from being united.

They have built more prisons than schools. They have mercilessly slain our patriots – they have drowned our uprisings in rivers of blood. They have fettered public opinion; they have practised obscurantism against our people. To weaken our race they have forced us to use opium and alcohol.

In the fields of economics, they have fleeced us to the backbone, impoverished our people, and devastated our land.

They have robbed us of our rice fields, our mines, our forests, and our raw materials. They have monopolised the issuing of bank-notes and the export trade.

They have invented numerous unjustifiable taxes and reduced our people, especially our peasantry, to a state of extreme poverty.

They have hampered the prospering of our national bourgeoisie; they have mercilessly exploited our workers.

In the autumn of 1940, when the Japanese Fascists violated Indochina's territory to establish new bases in their fight against the Allies, the French imperialists went down on their bended knees and handed over our country to them.

Thus, from that date, our people were subjected to the double yoke of the French and the Japanese. Their sufferings and miseries increased. The result was that from the end of last year to the beginning of this year, from Quang Tri province to the North of

Vietnam, more than two million of our fellow-citizens died from starvation. On March 9, the French troops were disarmed by the Japanese. The French colonialists either fled or surrendered, showing that not only were they incapable of 'protecting' us, but that, in the span of five years, they had twice sold our country to the Japanese.

On several occasions before March 9, the Vietminh League urged the French to ally themselves with it against the Japanese. Instead of agreeing to this proposal, the French colonialists so intensified their terrorist activities against the Vietminh members that before fleeing they massacred a great number of our political prisoners detained at Yen Bay and Cao Bang.

Not withstanding all this, our fellow-citizens have always manifested toward the French a tolerant and humane attitude. Even after the Japanese putsch of March 1945, the Vietminh League helped many Frenchmen to cross the frontier, rescued some of them from Japanese jails, and protected French lives and property.

From the autumn of 1940, our country had in fact ceased to be a French colony and had become a Japanese possession.

After the Japanese had surrendered to the Allies, our whole people rose to regain our national sovereignty and to found the Democratic Republic of Vietnam.

The truth is that we have wrested our independence from the Japanese and not from the French

The French have fled, the Japanese have capitulated, Emperor Bao Dai has abdicated. Our people have broken the chains which for nearly a century have fettered them and have won independence for the Fatherland. Our people at the same time have overthrown the monarchic regime that has reigned supreme for dozens of centuries. In its place has been established the present Democratic Republic.

For these reasons, we, members of the Provisional Government, representing the whole Vietnamese people, declare that from now on we break off all relations of a colonial character with France; we repeal all the international obligation that France has so far subscribed to on behalf of Vietnam and we abolish all the special rights the French have unlawfully acquired in our Fatherland.

The whole Vietnamese people, animated by a common purpose, are determined to fight to the bitter end against any attempt by the French colonialists to reconquer their country.

Ho Chi Minh, the North Vietnamese leader

John F. Kennedy 1917–1963

NATIONALITY:
American
WHEN:
1962
WHERE:
Washington, DC, USA
YOU SHOULD KNOW:
The President's most striking soundbite from this speech – 'Clear and Present Danger', itself taken from the World War I legislation – was used by Tom Clancy as the title of a novel about a CIA analyst who gets caught up in an illegal war between the US Government and a Columbian drug cartel.

At the height of the Cold War the USA did not want a left-wing state in its neck of the woods and the Cuban government feared a US invasion. After the 1961 Bay of Pigs debacle when CIA-trained Cuban exiles made a failed invasion attempt, Fidel Castro allied himself more closely with the USSR, resulting in an economic embargo by the USA. On October 8, 1962 American spy planes spotted silos being built on Cuba, and six days later that missiles were already present. The next two weeks were the closest the world has ever come to nuclear war. Below is President Kennedy's broadcast to the nation of October 22.

Good evening, my fellow citizens. This Government, as promised, has maintained the closest surveillance of the Soviet military build-up on the island of Cuba. Within the past week unmistakable evidence has established the fact that a series of offensive missile sites is now in preparation on that imprisoned island. The purposes of these bases can be none other than to provide a nuclear strike capability against the Western Hemisphere . . .

The characteristics of these new missile sites indicate two distinct types of installations. Several of them include medium-range ballistic missiles capable of carrying a nuclear warhead for a distance of more than 1000 nautical miles. Each of these missiles, in short, is capable of striking Washington DC, the Panama Canal, Cape Canaveral, Mexico City, or any other city in the southeastern part of the United States, in Central America, or in the Caribbean area . . .

Additional sites not yet completed appear to be designed for intermediate-range ballistic missiles capable of traveling more than twice as far – and thus capable of striking most of the major cities in the Western Hemisphere, ranging as far north as Hudson Bay, Canada, and as far south as Lima, Peru. In addition, jet bombers, capable of carrying nuclear weapons, are now being uncrated and assembled in Cuba, while the necessary air bases are being prepared.

This urgent transformation of Cuba into an important strategic base-by the presence of these large, longrange, and clearly offensive weapons of sudden mass destruction constitutes an explicit threat to the peace and security of all the Americas, in flagrant and deliberate defiance of the Rio Pact of 1947, the traditions of this nation and Hemisphere, the joint Resolution of the 87th Congress, the Charter of the United Nations, and my own public warnings to the Soviets on September 4 and 13.

This action also contradicts the repeated assurances of Soviet spokesmen, both publicly and privately delivered, that the arms build-up in Cuba would retain its original defensive character and that the Soviet Union had no need or desire to station strategic missiles on the territory of any other nation.

The size of this undertaking makes clear that it has been planned for some months. Yet only last month, after I had made clear the distinction between any introduction of ground-to-ground missiles and the existence of defensive anti-aircraft missiles, the Soviet Government publicly stated on September I I that, and I quote, 'The armaments and military equipment sent to Cuba are designed exclusively for defensive purposes' and, and I quote the Soviet Government, 'There is no need for the Soviet Government to shift its weapons for a retaliatory blow to any other country, for instance Cuba', and that, and I quote the Government, 'The Soviet Union has so powerful rockets to carry these nuclear warheads that there is no need to search for sites for them beyond the boundaries of the Soviet Union.' That statement was false.

Only last Thursday, as evidence of this rapid offensive build-up was already in my hand, Soviet Foreign Minister Gromyko told me in my office that he was instructed to make it clear once again, as he said his Government had already done, that Soviet assistance to Cuba, and I quote, 'pursued solely the purpose of contributing to the defense capabilities of Cuba', that, and I quote him, 'training by Soviet specialists of Cuban nationals in handling defensive armaments was by no means offensive', and that 'if it were otherwise', Mr Gromyko went on, 'the Soviet Government would never become involved in rendering such assistance.' That statement also was false.

Neither the United States of America nor the world community of nations can tolerate deliberate deception and offensive threats on the part of any nation, large or small. We no longer live in a world where only the actual firing of weapons represents a sufficient challenge to a nation's security to constitute maximum peril. Nuclear weapons are so destructive and ballistic missiles are so swift that any substantially increased possibility of their use or any sudden change in their deployment may well be regarded as a definite threat to peace.

For many years both the Soviet Union and the United States, recognizing this fact, have deployed strategic nuclear weapons with great care, never upsetting the precarious status quo which insured that these weapons would not be used in the absence of some vital challenge. Our own strategic missiles have never been transferred to the territory of any other nation under a cloak of secrecy and deception; and our history, unlike that of the Soviets since the end of World War II, demonstrates that we have no desire to dominate or conquer any other nation or impose our system upon its people. Nevertheless, American citizens have become adjusted to living daily on the bull's eye of Soviet missiles located inside the USSR or in submarines.

In that sense missiles in Cuba add to an already clear and present danger – although it should be noted the nations of Latin America have never previously been subjected to a potential nuclear threat.

But this secret, swift, and extraordinary build-up of Communist missiles – in an area well known to have a special and historical relationship to the United States and the nations of the Western Hemisphere, in violation of Soviet assurances, and in defiance of American and hemispheric policy – this sudden, clandestine decision to station strategic weapons for the first time outside of Soviet soil – is a deliberately provocative and unjustified change in the status quo which cannot be accepted by this country if our courage and our commitments are ever to be trusted again by either friend or foe . . .

Our policy has been one of patience and restraint, as befits a peaceful and powerful nation, which leads a world-wide alliance. We have been determined not to be diverted from our central concerns by mere irritants and fanatics. But now further action is required-and it is underway; and these actions may only be the beginning. We will not prematurely or unnecessarily risk the costs of worldwide nuclear war in which even the fruits of victory would be ashes in our mouth-but neither will we shrink from that risk at any time it must be faced.

Acting, therefore, in the defense of our own security and of the entire Western Hemisphere, and under the authority entrusted to me by the Constitution as endorsed by the resolution of the Congress, I have directed that the following initial steps be taken immediately:

First: To halt this offensive build-up, a strict quarantine on all offensive military equipment under shipment to Cuba is being initiated. All ships of any kind bound for Cuba from whatever nation or port will, if found to contain cargoes of offensive weapons, be turned back: This quarantine will be extended, if needed, to other types of cargo and carriers. We are not at this time, however, denying the necessities of life as the Soviets attempted to do in their Berlin blockade of 1948.

Second: I have directed the continued and increased close surveillance of Cuba and its military build-up. The Foreign Ministers of the Organization of American States in their communiqué of October 3 rejected secrecy on such matters in this Hemisphere. Should these offensive military preparations continue, thus increasing the threat to the Hemisphere, further action will be justified. I have directed the Armed Forces to prepare for any eventualities; and I trust that in the interests of both the Cuban people and the Soviet technicians at the sites, the hazards to all concerned of continuing this threat will be recognized.

Third: It shall be the policy of this nation to regard any nuclear missile launched from Cuba against any nation in the Western Hemisphere as an attack by the Soviet Union on the United States, requiring a full retaliatory response upon the Soviet Union.

Fourth: As a necessary military precaution I have reinforced our base at Guantanamo, evacuated today the dependents of our personnel there, and ordered additional military units to be on a standby alert basis.

Fifth: We are calling tonight for an immediate meeting of the Organ of Consultation, under the Organization of American States, to consider this threat to hemispheric security and to invoke articles six and eight of the Rio Treaty in support of all necessary action. The United Nations Charter allows for regional security arrangements-and the nations of this Hemisphere decided long ago against the military presence of outside powers. Our other allies around the world have also been alerted.

Sixth: Under the Charter of the United Nations, we are asking tonight that an emergency meeting of the Security Council be convoked without delay to take action against this latest Soviet threat to world peace. Our resolution will call for the prompt dismantling and withdrawal of all offensive weapons in Cuba, under the supervision of United Nations observers, before the quarantine can be lifted.

Seventh and finally: I call upon Chairman Khrushchev to halt and eliminate this clandestine, reckless, and provocative threat to world peace and to stable relations between our two nations. I call upon him further to abandon this course of world domination and to join in an historic effort to end the perilous arms race and transform the history of man. He has an opportunity now to move the world back from the abyss of destruction – by returning to his Government's own words that it had no need to station missiles outside its own territory, and withdrawing these weapons from Cuba, by refraining from any action which will widen or deepen the present crisis-and then by participating in a search for peaceful and permanent solutions.

This nation is prepared to present its case against the Soviet threat to peace, and our own proposals for a peaceful world, at. any time and in any forum in the Organization of American States, in the United Nations, or in any other meeting that could be useful – without limiting our freedom of action.

We have in the past made strenuous efforts to limit the spread of nuclear weapons. We have proposed the elimination of all arms and military bases in a fair and effective disarmament treaty. We are prepared to discuss new proposals for the removal of tensions on both sides, including the possibilities of a genuinely independent Cuba, free to determine its own destiny. We have no wish to war with the Soviet Union, for we are a peaceful people who desire to live in peace with all other peoples.

But it is difficult to settle or even discuss these problems in an atmosphere of intimidation. That is why this latest Soviet threat-or any other threat which is made either independently or in response to our actions this week-must and will be met with determination. Any hostile move anywhere in the world against the safety and freedom of peoples to whom we are committed – including in particular the brave people of West Berlin – will be met by whatever action is needed.

Finally, I want to say a few words to the captive people of Cuba, to whom this speech is being directly carried by special radio facilities. I speak to you as a friend, as one who knows of your deep attachment to your fatherland, as one who shares your aspirations for liberty and justice for all. And I have watched and the American people have watched with deep sorrow how your nationalist revolution was betrayed and how your fatherland fell under foreign domination. Now your leaders are no longer Cuban leaders inspired by Cuban ideals. They are puppets and agents of an international conspiracy which has turned Cuba against your friends and neighbors in the Americas – and turned it into the first Latin American country to become a target for nuclear war, the first Latin American country to have these weapons on its soil.

These new weapons are not in your interest. They contribute nothing to your peace and well being. They can only undermine it. But this country has no wish to cause you to suffer or to impose any system upon you. We know that your lives and land are being used as pawns by those who deny you freedom.

Many times in the past Cuban people have risen to throw out tyrants who destroyed their liberty. And I have no doubt that most Cubans today look forward to the time when they will be truly free-free from foreign domination, free to choose their own leaders, free to select their own system, free to own their own land, free to speak and write and worship without fear or degradation. And then shall Cuba be welcomed back to the society of free nations and to the associations of this Hemisphere.

My fellow citizens, let no one doubt that this is a difficult and dangerous effort on which we have set out. No one can foresee precisely what course it will take or what costs or casualties will be incurred. Many months of sacrifice and self-discipline lie ahead – months in which both our patience and our will will be tested, months in which many threats and denunciations will keep us aware of our dangers. But the greatest danger of all would be to do nothing.

The path we have chosen for the present is full of hazards, as all paths are; but it is the one most consistent with our character and courage as a nation and our commitments around the world. The cost of freedom is always high-but Americans have always paid it. And one path we shall never choose, and that is the path of surrender or submission.

Our goal is not the victory of might but the vindication of right-not peace at the expense of freedom, but both peace and freedom, here in this Hemisphere and, we hope, around the world. God willing, that goal will be achieved. 🔳

George H. W. Bush born 1924

At the Republican Convention on August 18, George Bush accepted the nomination as presidential candidate. His acceptance – often called the 'thousand points of light' speech – lifted his poll rating. He detailed his opposition to abortion and his support for gun rights, the death penalty and saying the Pledge of Allegiance in schools. He finished the speech with a pledge on taxes, which has become one of the defining soundbites of his political career, although it backfired on him in the 1992 elections. Because he was not able to stop Congress raising taxes to reduce the budget deficit, the Clinton campaign used this to label Bush as untrustworthy.

NATIONALITY:
American
WHEN:
1988
WHERE:
New Orleans, USA
YOU SHOULD KNOW:
George H. W. and George W. Bush are the first father and son to attain the Presidency since John and John Quincy Adams.

And I'm the one who will not raise taxes. My opponent now says he'll raise them as a last resort, or a third resort. But when a politician talks like that, you know that's one resort he'll be checking into. My opponent, my opponent won't rule out raising taxes. But I will. And the Congress will push me to raise taxes and I'll say no. And they'll push, and I'll say no, and they'll push again, and I'll say, to them, 'Read my lips: no new taxes.' 🔳

The Belfast Agreement

(Good Friday Agreement)

WHEN:
1998
WHERE:
Belfast, N. Ireland
YOU SHOULD KNOW:
Both Northern Ireland and the
Republic of Ireland held referendums
on May 23 1998.

The declaration of support that preceded the 30-page agreement makes it plain that the participants in the signing had no illusions about its importance. Its principal provisions were for the establishment of institutions that would allow power to be shared equitably by all parties to the agreement, the holding of referendums both north and south of the border, the amendment or repeal of laws in the UK and Republic of Ireland that prevented the agreement coming into force, human rights, the setting up of a reconciliation committee, decommissioning of weapons and changes to policing. Signatories to the agreement were the British and Irish Prime Ministers and the leaders of all the major parties in Northern Ireland except the Democratic Unionist Party. It came into effect in December 1999.

*A sign of changing times on
a Belfast wall*

'DECLARATION OF SUPPORT

1. We, the participants in the multi-party negotiations, believe that the agreement we have negotiated offers a truly historic opportunity for a new beginning.

2. The tragedies of the past have left a deep and profoundly regrettable legacy of suffering. We must never forget those who have died or been injured, and their families. But we can best honour them through a fresh start, in which we firmly dedicate ourselves to the achievement of reconciliation, tolerance, and mutual trust, and to the protection and vindication of the human rights of all.

3. We are committed to partnership, equality and mutual respect as the basis of relationships within Northern Ireland, between North and South, and between these islands.

4. We reaffirm our total and absolute commitment to exclusively democratic and peaceful means of resolving differences on political issues, and our opposition to any use or threat of force by others for any political purpose, whether in regard to this agreement or otherwise.

5. We acknowledge the substantial differences between our continuing, and equally legitimate, political aspirations. However, we will endeavour to strive in every practical way towards reconciliation and rapprochement within the framework of democratic and agreed arrangements. We pledge that we will, in good faith, work to ensure the success of each and every one of the arrangements to be established under this agreement. It is accepted that all of the institutional and constitutional arrangements – an Assembly in Northern Ireland, a North/South Ministerial Council, implementation bodies, a British-Irish Council and a British-Irish Intergovernmental Conference and any amendments to British Acts of Parliament and the Constitution of Ireland – are interlocking and interdependent and that in particular the functioning of the Assembly and the North/South Council are so closely inter-related that the success of each depends on that of the other.

6. Accordingly, in a spirit of concord, we strongly commend this agreement to the people, North and South, for their approval. '

Nikita Khrushchev 1894–1971

At a reception for the Polish leader Wladislaw Gomulka at the Polish Embassy in November 1956, Khruschev berated western diplomats attending with this apparent threat. The evening before twelve of them had walked out of a reception in the Kremlin because the Soviet leader had referred to several western nations, including Britain and France, as fascists and bandits because of their behaviour to Egypt over the Suez Crisis. When reported in the West, the quotation was taken out of context and interpreted as a threat to destroy western civilization, but he explained the following year that he had meant that communism would outlive or outstrip capitalism.

NATIONALITY:
Russian
WHEN:
1956
WHERE:
Moscow, USSR
YOU SHOULD KNOW:
Unusually for a Soviet leader, Khrushchev was ousted as Party Chairman, mainly because of the Cuban Missile Crisis but also for failed economic and agricultural policies.

'About the capitalist states, it doesn't depend on you whether or not we exist. If you don't like us, don't accept our invitations, and don't ask us to come to see you. Whether you like it or not, history is on our side. We will bury you. '

Traders gathering outside the New York Stock Exchange on the day of the Wall Street Crash.

Benito Mussolini 1883–1945

The 1929 Wall Street Crash – like the sub-prime problems of 2008 – had repercussions across most of the world. Although it did not in itself cause the Depression – it was not apparent, but economies around the world were already slowing down – it had exacerbated the problem and protectionist legislation introduced in the USA against imports from the rest of the world made things worse. Mussolini was speaking for a domestic audience in this tirade, during which he castigated the USA and blamed it for the very real problems that were now causing severe hardship in Italy, destroying the economy that his people had worked so hard to build up.

NATIONALITY:
Italian
WHEN:
1930
WHERE:
Rome, Italy
YOU SHOULD KNOW:
Mussolini's assumed title, Il Duce, means 'the Duke'.

On 24 October 1929 the American crisis burst out, and it came unexpectedly, like a bombshell. For us poor provincials of old Europe the catastrophe took us completely unawares. We were shaken and thunderstruck as the world was by the news of Napoleon's death. This is because we had always been led to believe that this was the land of prosperity, limitless, total prosperity, without any possibility of eclipse or decline.

454

Stanley Baldwin 1867–1947

Throughout the 1920s and 1930s, agitation in India for independence grew and during the early 1930s the Labour Government in Britain had held discussions about introducing greater local autonomy and increased suffrage with the hereditary princes of several Indian states but no conclusion was reached. Baldwin agreed with the government, in the teeth of opposition by members of his own party, including Winston Churchill, who feared that increased autonomy would lead to full independence and the loss of large revenues. In 1935, the Government of India Act was signed, although parts of it never came into force. The first direct elections in India took place in 1937 and the country gained full independence a decade later.

NATIONALITY:
British
WHEN:
1934
WHERE:
London, England
YOU SHOULD KNOW:
One of Baldwin's cousins was the writer Rudyard Kipling, who spent many years in India.

. . . What have we taught India for a century? We have preached English institutions and democracy and all the rest of it . . . There is a wind of nationalism and freedom blowing around the world and flowing as strongly in Asia as anywhere in the world. And are we less true Conservatives because we say 'the time has now come'? Are those who say 'the time may come some day', are they the truer Conservatives?

Robert McNamara born 1916

Secretary of Defense Robert McNamara had been one of the chief proponents of American intervention in Vietnam in order to reduce the spread of communism, but in 1967 he came to the conclusion that the war was unwinnable and argued that the use of the herbicide Agent Orange to defoliate the jungles in which the Viet Cong fighters hid might be 1. illegal under international law and 2. counterproductive. Johnson dismissed his concerns and continued with the war and the use of the chemical. Not only were thousands of children in South Vietnam born with physical abnormalities, but US troops who had come into contact with the chemical suffered long-term health problems, and many had children who manifested genetic defects.

NATIONALITY:
American
WHEN:
May 19, 1967
WHERE:
Washington, DC, USA
YOU SHOULD KNOW:
Robert McNamara confirmed by letter in May 1967 what he had long been saying to President Johnson.

There may be a limit beyond which many Americans, and much of the world, will not permit the United States to go. The picture of the world's greatest superpower killing or seriously injuring 1000 non-combatants a week, while trying to pound a tiny backward nation into submission on an issue whose merits are hotly disputed, is not a pretty one.

Margaret Thatcher welcomes Mikhail Gorbachev to Chequers, the Prime Minister's country home.

Margaret Thatcher born 1925

In an interview with the BBC's political editor John Cole in mid-December 1984, Margaret Thatcher responded to a question about how she saw relations with the man who looked like the probable successor to the Soviet Union's ailing General Secretary, Konstantin Chernenko. The arms talks that Mrs Thatcher refers to were due to begin between America and the USSR in early 1985. Gorbachev became General Secretary in March 1985 and went on to establish good working relationships with Mrs Thatcher; West Germany's Helmut Kohl and Ronald Reagan. His abandonment of the Brezhnev Doctrine and allowing countries within the Eastern Bloc internal self-determination was instrumental in the break-up of the Soviet Union.

'I am cautiously optimistic. I like Mr. Gorbachev. We can do business together. We both believe in our own political systems. He firmly believes in his; I firmly believe in mine. We are never going to change one another. So that is not in doubt, but we have two great interests in common: that we should both do everything we can to see that war never starts again, and therefore we go into the disarmament talks determined to make them succeed. And secondly, I think we both believe that they are the more likely to succeed if we can build up confidence in one another and trust in one another about each other's approach, and therefore, we believe in cooperating on trade matters, on cultural matters, on quite a lot of contacts between politicians from the two sides of the divide. '

NATIONALITY:
British
WHEN:
1984
WHERE:
London, England
YOU SHOULD KNOW:
Chernenko's predecessor, Yuri Andropov, had wanted Gorbachev to take over as Chairman after his own death.

Jim Connell 1852–1929

Jim Connell wrote The Red Flag *after a meeting of the Social Democratic Foundation – a Marxist movement whose aims included self determination and land reform in Ireland, where British landlords held vast estates and the locals had no say in how they were ruled. He had moved to Britain after being blacklisted by dock owners in Dublin after he tried to introduce unions to the docks and it was during a strike by London dockers that he became inspired to write this socialist anthem, while on a short train journey. It is said that he got the idea of using the symbol of the red flag when looking at a guard on the platform signalling to the driver with one.*

NATIONALITY:
Irish
WHEN:
1899
WHERE:
London, Englands
YOU SHOULD KNOW:
The song is usually sung to the tune of the German carol, *O Tannenbaum*, which is also the tune of the State song of Maryland.

The workers' flag is deepest red,
It shrouded oft our martyred dead;
And ere their limbs grew stiff and cold
Their life-blood dyed its every fold.

CHORUS:

Then raise the scarlet standard high;
Beneath its folds we'll live and die,
Though cowards flinch and traitors sneer,
We'll keep the red flag flying here.

Look 'round, the Frenchman loves its blaze,
The sturdy German chants its praise;
In Moscow's vaults its hymns are sung,
Chicago swells its surging song.

CHORUS:

Then raise the scarlet standard high;
Beneath its folds we'll live and die,
Though cowards flinch and traitors sneer,
We'll keep the red flag flying here.

It waved above our infant might
When all ahead seemed dark as night;
It witnessed many a deed and vow,
We will not change its color now.

CHORUS:

Then raise the scarlet standard high;
Beneath its folds we'll live and die,
Though cowards flinch and traitors sneer,
We'll keep the red flag flying here.

It suits today the meek and base,
Whose minds are fixed on pelf and place;
To cringe beneath the rich man's frown,
And haul that sacred emblem down.

CHORUS:

Then raise the scarlet standard high;
Beneath its folds we'll live and die,
Though cowards flinch and traitors sneer,
We'll keep the red flag flying here.

With heads uncovered, swear we all,
To bear it onward till we fall;
Come dungeons dark, or gallows grim,
This song shall be our parting hymn!

CHORUS:

Then raise the scarlet standard high;
Beneath its folds we'll live and die,
Though cowards flinch and traitors sneer,
We'll keep the red flag flying here.

Lloyd Bentsen 1921–2006

NATIONALITY:
American
WHEN:
1988
WHERE:
Omaha, Nebraska, USA
YOU SHOULD KNOW:
Tom Brokaw also hosted the second presidential debate between Barack Obama and John McCain in 2008.

The vice presidential candidates Lloyd Bentsen (left) and Republican Dan Quayle face off during a debate.

In one of a series of vice presidential debates during the 1988 presidential campaign, Tom Brokaw – the anchor of NBC's Nightly News – *repeatedly asked Lloyd Bentsen's Republican rival, Dan Quayle, what his plans would be if he became President in the event of the death of George Bush. Senator Quayle, apparently fumbling for an answer, replied that he had more experience than many others who had sought the office of Vice President and then said, 'I have as much experience in the Congress as Jack Kennedy did when he sought the Presidency.'. Senator Bentsen leapt on the opportunity to give one of the most memorable put-downs in political history.*

‘ Senator, I served with Jack Kennedy: I knew Jack Kennedy; Jack Kennedy was a friend of mine. Senator, you're no Jack Kennedy. ’

Muammar al-Gaddafi born 1942

In the wake of the horrors of the events of September 11, 2001, leaders from all over the world condemned al-Qaeda, including those from nations widely accused of sympathising or supporting terrorists. Among them was Libyan leader Muammar al-Gaddafi, whose country had long provided 'liberation armies' and terrorists with funds, provoking international sanctions and attacks on Tripoli and Benghazi by the US Air Force in 1986. The bombing of Pan Am Flight 103 in 1988 led to further isolation, which drew to an end only with Colonel Gaddafi's agreement to allow the extradition of the accused bombers for trial and the payment of billions of dollars to the victims' families.

NATIONALITY:
Libyan
WHEN:
2001
WHERE:
Tripoli, Libya
YOU SHOULD KNOW:
Muammar al-Gaddafi became chairman of the African Union in February 2009.

❛ Irrespective of the conflict with America, it is a human duty to show sympathy with the American people and be with them at these horrifying and awful events which are bound to awaken human conscience. When I was five, my brother was shot by an Israeli soldier, since then I have been dedicated to uniting the Arab countries throughout the Middle East and retain a trade flow with the West. ❜

Arthur Balfour 1848–1930

On November 2, 1917 the British Foreign Secretary wrote a letter to Lord Rothschild asking for the declaration below to be transmitted to the members of the Zionist Federation of Great Britain and Ireland. The final wording had been agreed in a Cabinet meeting three days earlier. The declaration did not go as far as the Zionists hoped, as they had wanted Palestine to be restored as the Jewish national home. The text was included in the League of Nations' British Mandate for Palestine in 1922. The clause about the civil and religious rights of non-Jewish communities was added to the declaration at the last minute.

NATIONALITY:
British
WHEN:
1917
WHERE:
London, England
YOU SHOULD KNOW:
The final version of the declaration was actually written by Alfred Milner.

❛ His Majesty's Government view with favour the establishment in Palestine of a national home for the Jewish people, and will use their best endeavours to facilitate the achievement of this object, it being clearly understood that nothing shall be done which may prejudice the civil and religious rights of existing non-Jewish communities in Palestine, or the rights and political status enjoyed by Jews in any other country. ❜

Abraham Lincoln 1809–1865

NATIONALITY:
American
WHEN:
1858
WHERE:
Peoria, Illinois, USA
YOU SHOULD KNOW:
This speech marks the point when Lincoln's views on the necessity for the abolition of slavery crystallized.

Although Abraham Lincoln and Judge Stephen Douglas – the author of the Kansas-Nebraska Act – most famously clashed during their debates leading up to the elections for the Senate in 1858, they had also argued during the campaign in 1854. In the speech he gave at Peoria, Illinois in October 1858 Lincoln answered Douglas' three-hour speech with one of his own – equally long – the most important points of which are below.

The repeal of the Missouri Compromise, and the propriety of its restoration, constitute the subject of what I am about to say . . .

. . . With the author of the Declaration of Independence, the policy of prohibiting slavery in new territory originated. Thus, away back of the constitution, in the pure fresh, free breath of the revolution, the State of Virginia, and the National Congress put that policy in practice. Thus through 60-odd of the best years of the republic did that policy steadily work to its great and beneficent end. And thus, in those five states, and five millions of free, enterprising people, we have before us the rich fruits of this policy. But now new light breaks upon us. Now Congress declares this ought never to have been; and the like of it, must never be again. The sacred right of self government is grossly violated by it! We even find some men, who drew their first breath, and every other breath of their lives, under this very restriction, now live in dread of absolute suffocation, if they should be restricted in the 'sacred right' of taking slaves to Nebraska. That perfect liberty they sigh for – the liberty of making slaves of other people – Jefferson never thought of; their own father never thought of; they never thought of themselves, a year ago. How fortunate for them, they did not sooner become sensible of their great misery! Oh, how difficult it is to treat with respect, such assaults upon all we have ever really held sacred . . .

I think, and shall try to show, that it is wrong; wrong in its direct effect, letting slavery into Kansas and Nebraska – and wrong in its prospective principle, allowing it to spread to every other part of the wide world, where men can be found inclined to take it.

This declared indifference, but as I must think, covert real zeal for the spread of slavery, I can not but hate. I hate it because of the monstrous injustice of slavery itself. I hate it because it deprives our republican example of its just influence in the world – enables the enemies of free institutions, with plausibility, to taunt us as hypocrites – causes the real friends of freedom to doubt our sincerity, and especially because it forces so many really good men amongst ourselves into an open war with the very fundamental principles of civil liberty – criticising the Declaration of Independence, and insisting that there is no right principle of action but self-interest . . .

. . . Equal justice to the south, it is said, requires us to consent to the extending of slavery to new countries. That is to say, inasmuch as you do not object to my taking my hog to Nebraska, therefore I must not object to you taking your slave. Now, I admit this is perfectly logical, if there is no difference between hogs and negroes. But while you thus require me to deny the humanity of the negro, I wish to ask whether you of the south yourselves, have ever been willing to do as much? . . .In 1820 you joined the north, almost unanimously, in declaring the African slave trade piracy, and in annexing to it the punishment of death. Why did you do this? If you did not feel that it was wrong, why did you join in providing that men should be hung for it? The practice was no more than bringing wild negroes from Africa, to sell to such as would buy them. But you never thought of hanging men for catching and selling wild horses, wild buffaloes or wild bears . . .

And now, why will you ask us to deny the humanity of the slave and estimate him only as the equal of the hog? Why ask us to do what you will not do yourselves? Why ask us to do for nothing, what two hundred million of dollars could not induce you to do?

But one great argument in the support of the repeal of the Missouri Compromise, is still to come. That argument is 'the sacred right of self government'. It seems our distinguished Senator has found great difficulty in getting his antagonists, even in the Senate to meet him fairly on this argument . . .

I trust I understand, and truly estimate the right of self-government. My faith in the proposition that each man should do precisely as he pleases with all which is exclusively his own, lies at the foundation of the sense of justice there is in me. I extend the principles to communities of men, as well as to individuals. I so extend it, because it is politically wise, as well as naturally just; politically wise, in saving us from broils about matters which do not concern us. Here, or at Washington, I would not trouble myself with the oyster laws of Virginia, or the cranberry laws of Indiana.

The doctrine of self government is right – absolutely and eternally right – but it has no just application, as here attempted. Or perhaps I should rather say that whether it has such just application depends upon whether a negro is not or is a man. If he is not a man, why in that case, he who is a man may, as a matter of self-government, do just as he pleases with him. But if the negro is a man, is it not to that extent, a total destruction of self-government, to say that he too shall not govern himself? When the white man governs himself that is self-government; but when he governs himself, and also governs another man, that is more than self-government – that is despotism. If the negro is a man, why then my ancient faith teaches me that 'all men are created equal;' and that there can be no moral right in connection with one man's making a slave of another.

Judge Douglas frequently, with bitter irony and sarcasm, paraphrases our argument by saying 'The white people of Nebraska are good enough to govern themselves, but they are not good enough to govern a few miserable negroes!'

Well I doubt not that the people of Nebraska are, and will continue to be as good as the average of people elsewhere. I do not say the contrary. What I do say is, that no man is good enough to govern another man, without that other's consent. I say this is the leading principle – the sheet anchor of American republicanism. Our Declaration of Independence says:

'We hold these truths to be self evident: that all men are created equal; that they are endowed by their Creator with certain inalienable rights; that among these are life, liberty and the pursuit of happiness. That to secure these rights, governments are instituted among men, DERIVING THEIR JUST POWERS FROM THE CONSENT OF THE GOVERNED.' . . .

. . . I particularly object to the NEW position which the avowed principle of this Nebraska law gives to slavery in the body politic. I object to it because it assumes that there CAN be MORAL RIGHT in the enslaving of one man by another. I object to it as a dangerous dalliance for a few [free?] people – a sad evidence that, feeling prosperity we forget right – that liberty, as a principle, we have ceased to revere. I object to it because the fathers of the republic eschewed, and rejected it. The argument of 'Necessity' was the only argument they ever admitted in favor of slavery; and so far, and so far only as it carried them, did they ever go. They found the institution existing among us, which they could not help; and they cast blame upon the British King for having permitted its introduction. BEFORE the constitution, they prohibited its introduction into the north-western Territory – the only country we owned, then free from it. AT the framing and adoption of the constitution, they forbore to so much as mention the word 'slave' or 'slavery' in the whole instrument. In the provision for the recovery of fugitives, the slave is spoken of as a 'PERSON HELD TO SERVICE OR LABOR'. In that prohibiting the abolition of the African slave trade for 20 years, that trade is spoken of as 'The migration or importation of such persons as any of the States NOW EXISTING, shall think proper to admit,' &c. These are the only provisions alluding to slavery. Thus, the thing is hid away, in the constitution, just as an afflicted man hides away a wen or a cancer, which he dares not cut out at once, lest he bleed to death; with the promise, nevertheless, that the cutting may begin at the end of a given time. Less than this our fathers COULD not do; and NOW [MORE?] they WOULD not do. Necessity drove them so far, and farther, they would not go. But this is not all. The earliest Congress, under the constitution, took the same view of slavery. They hedged and hemmed it in to the narrowest limits of necessity.

In 1794, they prohibited an out-going slave-trade – that is, the taking of slaves FROM the United States to sell.

In 1798, they prohibited the bringing of slaves from Africa, INTO the Mississippi Territory – this territory then comprising what are now the States of Mississippi and Alabama. This was TEN YEARS before they had the authority to do the same thing as to the States existing at the adoption of the constitution.

In 1800 they prohibited AMERICAN CITIZENS from trading in slaves between foreign countries – as, for instance, from Africa to Brazil.

In 1803 they passed a law in aid of one or two State laws, in restraint of the internal slave trade.

In 1807, in apparent hot haste, they passed the law, nearly a year in advance to take effect the first day of 1808 – the very first day the constitution would permit – prohibiting the African slave trade by heavy pecuniary and corporal penalties.

In 1820, finding these provisions ineffectual, they declared the trade piracy, and annexed to it, the extreme penalty of death. While all this was passing in the general government, five or six of the original slave States had adopted systems of gradual emancipation; and by which the institution was rapidly becoming extinct within these limits . . .

But NOW it is to be transformed into a 'sacred right'. Nebraska brings it forth, places it on the high road to extension and perpetuity; and, with a pat on its back, says to it, 'Go, and God speed you.' Henceforth it is to be the chief jewel of the nation – the very figure-head of the ship of State. Little by little, but steadily as man's march to the grave, we have been giving up the OLD for the NEW faith. Near 80 years ago we began by declaring that all men are created equal; but now from that beginning we have run down to the other declaration, that for SOME men to enslave OTHERS is a 'sacred right of self-government'. These principles cannot stand together. They are as opposite as God and Mammon; and whoever holds to the one, must despise the other. When Pettit, in connection with his support of the Nebraska bill, called the Declaration of Independence 'a self-evident lie' he only did what consistency and candor require all other Nebraska men to do. Of the 40-odd Nebraska Senators who sat present and heard him, no one rebuked him. Nor am I apprized that any Nebraska newspaper, or any Nebraska orator, in the whole nation, has ever yet rebuked him . . .

Our republican robe is soiled, and trailed in the dust. Let us repurify it. Let us turn and wash it white, in the spirit, if not the blood, of the Revolution. Let us turn slavery from its claims of 'moral right', back upon its existing legal rights, and its arguments of 'necessity'. Let us return it to the position our fathers gave it; and there let it rest in peace. Let us re-adopt the Declaration of Independence, and with it, the practices, and policy, which harmonize with it. Let north and south – let all Americans – let all lovers of liberty everywhere – join in the great and good work. If we do this, we shall not only have saved the Union; but we shall have so saved it, as to make, and to keep, it, forever worthy of the saving. We shall have so saved it, that the succeeding millions of free happy people, the world over, shall rise up, and call us blessed . . . 🔊

Boris Yeltsin 1931–2007

On August 20, 1991 Gorbachev was supposed to sign a new treaty that would preserve what remained of the USSR, but under far more liberal terms than before. A group of hardline dissidents decided that this was the moment to launch a coup to restore full communist rule and arrested him at his dacha in the Crimea on the 18th. Crowds flocked to the White House in Moscow, the seat of the Russian Parliament, and began to erect barricades. The plotters sent tanks in on August 21, but did not get the general support of other army leaders on which they had been counting and when a tank unit and a division of paratroopers changed sides, the coup was called off. One of the most memorable images of those tumultuous days is that of Russian President Boris Yeltsin standing on the back of a tank, shouting defiantly.

NATIONALITY:
Russian
WHEN:
1991
WHERE:
Moscow, Russia
YOU SHOULD KNOW:
In a complete turnaround, President Yeltsin ordered an attack on the White House two years later when there was rebellion against his decree that he was assuming emergency powers that would give him control and marginalize Parliament.

‘ The reactionaries will not achieve their goals; the army will not go against the people. ’

Boris Yeltsin in belligerent mood in front of the Russian Parliament.

Ahmadinejad tells the nation of Iran's successful progress towards creating nuclear power.

Mahmoud Ahmadinejad
born 1956

At the sixtieth session of the United Nations General Assembly on September 17, 2005 the Iranian President announced his government's continued intention to start producing nuclear power. In a long speech, he argued that the Non-Proliferation Treaty did not give countries with nuclear weapons the right to prevent others developing nuclear power. He also asserted that the pursuit of nuclear weapons was un-Islamic and offered to open up the uranium-processing plants to inspectors from the International Atomic Energy Agency. Uranium enrichment continues despite international condemnation and UN sanctions being imposed.

NATIONALITY:
Iranian
WHEN:
2005
WHERE:
New York City, USA
YOU SHOULD KNOW:
In February 2009 Iran successfully launched its own satellite on one of its own rockets for the first time, causing further consternation among governments who do not believe that its motives are peaceful.

‘ Allow me, as the elected President of the Iranian people, to outline the other main elements of my country's initiative regarding the nuclear issue . . . Technically, the fuel cycle of the Islamic Republic of Iran is not different from that of other countries which have peaceful nuclear technology . . . In keeping with Iran's inalienable right to have access to a nuclear fuel cycle, continued interaction and technical and legal cooperation with the IAEA will be the centerpiece of our nuclear policy . . . As the President of the Islamic Republic of Iran, I assure you that my country will use everything in its power to contribute to global tranquility and peace based on the two maxims of spirituality and justice as well as the equal rights of all peoples and nations.

My country will interact and cooperate constructively with the international community to face the challenges before us. ’

John F. Kennedy 1917–1963

Just a week after President Kennedy had told the American public of the presence of Soviet missiles on Cuba, the immediate crisis was over. In a telex sent to Khrushchev at the same time, he said that America would no longer seek to interfere in Cuba's internal affairs, would respect its sovereignty and borders and would not allow US territory to be used by anyone else to invade Cuba. What was not made public was the American agreement to withdraw missiles from bases in Turkey. This angered Khrushchev as it made it appear that the USSR had backed down.

NATIONALITY:
American
WHEN:
1962
WHERE:
Washington, DC, USA
YOU SHOULD KNOW:
US trade embargoes imposed against Cuba in 1958 are still in place, although they have been modified several times.

❝ I welcome Chairman Khrushchev's statesmanlike decision to stop building bases in Cuba, dismantling offensive weapons and returning them to the Soviet Union under United Nations verification. This is an important and constructive contribution to peace.

We shall be in touch with the Secretary General of the United Nations with respect to reciprocal measures to assure peace in the Caribbean area.

It is my earnest hope that the governments of the world can, with a solution of the Cuban crisis, turn their urgent attention to the compelling necessity for ending the arms race and reducing world tensions. This applies to the military confrontation between the Warsaw Pact and NATO countries as well as to other situations in other parts of the world where tensions lead to the wasteful diversion of resources to weapons of war. ❞

Cuban refugees watch President Kennedy announcing the end of what became known as the Cuba crisis.

The All-India Congress

NATIONALITY:
Indian
WHEN:
1942
WHERE:
Bombay (Mumbai), India
YOU SHOULD KNOW:
It took another five years for India to gain independence.

As a colony of the British Empire, India was brought into World War II whether its people agreed or not. Participation by people from the subcontinent was reluctant. The All-India Congress Committee had, in 1939 passed a resolution offering conditional support for the fight against fascism but asked for independence in return, which was rejected by the British. In 1942, Sir Stafford Cripps arrived in India to negotiate devolution after the war in return for immediate co-operation. He failed and on August 8 the Committee issued the 'Quit India Resolution'. The leaders were arrested and most remained incarcerated for the next three years.

The All-India Congress Committee has given the most careful consideration to the reference made to it by the Working Committee in their resolution dated July 14, 1942, and to subsequent events, including the development of the war situation, the utterances of responsible spokesmen of the British Government, and the comments and criticisms made in India and abroad. The Committee approves of and endorses that resolution, and is of opinion that events subsequent to it have given it further justification, and have made it clear that the immediate ending of British rule in India is an urgent necessity, both for the sake of India and for the success of the cause of the United Nations. The continuation of that rule is degrading and enfeebling India and making her progressively less capable of defending herself and of contributing to the cause of world freedom . . .

The ending of British rule in this country is thus a vital and immediate issue on which depend the future of the war and the success of freedom and democracy. A free India will assure this success by throwing all her great resources in the struggle for freedom and against the aggression of Nazism, Fascism and Imperialism. This will not only affect materially the fortunes of the war, but will bring all subject and oppressed humanity on the side of the United Nations and give these nations, whose ally India would be the moral and spiritual leadership of the world. India in bondage will continue to be the symbol of British Imperialism and the taint of that imperialism will affect the fortunes of all the United Nations.

The peril of today, therefore, necessitates the independence of India and the ending of British domination. No future promises or guarantees can affect the present situation or meet that peril. They cannot produce the needed psychological effect on the mind of the masses. Only the glow of freedom now can release that energy and enthusiasm of millions of people which will immediately transform the nature of the war.

The AICC therefore, repeats with all emphasis the demand for the withdrawal of the British power from India. On the declaration of India's independence, a provincial Government will be formed and free

India will become an ally of the United Nations, sharing with them in the trials and tribulations of the joint enterprise of the struggle for freedom. The provincial Government can only be formed by the co-operation of the principal parties and groups in the country. It will thus be a composite Government representative of all important sections of the people of India. Its primary functions must be to defend India and resist aggression with all the armed as well as the non-violent forces at its command, together with its Allied Powers, and to promote the well-being and progress of the workers in the fields and factories and elsewhere to whom essentially all power and authority must belong. The provincial Government will evolve a scheme for a constituent assembly which will prepare a constitution for the Government of India acceptable to all sections of the people. This constitution according to the Congress view, should be a federal one. With the largest measure of autonomy for the federating units, and with the residuary powers vesting in these units. The future relations between India and the Allied Nations will be adjusted by representatives of all these free countries conferring together for their mutual advantage and for their co-operation in the common task of resisting aggression. Freedom will enable India to resist aggression effectively with the people's united will and strength behind it.

The freedom of India must be the symbol of and prelude to this freedom of all other Asiatic nations under foreign domination. Burma, Malaya, Indo-China, the Dutch Indies, Iran and Iraq must also attain their complete freedom. It must be clearly understood that such of these countries as are under Japanese control now must not subsequently be placed under the rule or control of any other Colonial Power.

While the AICC must primarily be concerned with the independence and defence of India in this hour of danger, the Committee is of opinion that the future peace, security and ordered progress of the world demand a world federation of free nations, and on no other basis can the problems of the modern world be solved. Such a world federation would ensure the freedom of its constituent nations, the prevention of aggression and exploitation by one nation over another the protection of national minorities, the advancement of all backward areas and peoples, and the pooling of the world's resources for the common good of all. On the establishment of such a world federation, disarmament would be practicable in all countries, national armies, navies and air forces would no longer be necessary, and a world federal defence force would keep the world peace and prevent aggression.

An independent India would gladly join such a world federation and co-operate on an equal basis with other countries in the solution of international problems. Such a federation should be open to all nations who agree with its fundamental principles. In view of the war, however, the federation must inevitably, to begin with, be confined to the United Nations, such a step taken now will have a most powerful effect on the war, on the peoples of the Axis countries, and on the peace to come.

The Committee regretfully realizes, however, despite the tragic and overwhelming lessons of the war and the perils that overhang the world, the Governments of few countries are yet prepared to take this inevitable step towards world federation. The reactions of the British Government and the misguided criticism of the foreign Press also make it clear that even the obvious demand for India's independence is resisted, though this has been made essentially to meet the present peril and to enable India to defend herself and help China and Russia in their hour of need. The Committee is anxious not to embarrass in any way the defence of China or Russia, whose freedom is precious and must be preserved, or to jeopardise the defensive capacity of the United Nations. But the peril grows both to India and these nations, and inaction and submission to a foreign administration at this stage is not only degrading India and reducing her capacity to defend herself and resist aggression but is no answer to that knowing peril and is no service to the peoples of the United Nations. The earnest appeal of the Working Committee to Great Britain and the United Nations has so far met with no response and the criticism made in many foreign quarters have shown an ignorance of India's and the world's need, and sometimes even hostility to India's freedom, which is significant of a mentality of domination and racial superiority which cannot be tolerated by a proud people conscious of their strength and of the justice of their cause.

Winston Churchill 1874–1965
Franklin D. Roosevelt 1882–1945

NATIONALITY:
British/American
WHEN:
1941
WHERE:
Placentia Bay, Canada

The Atlantic Charter was an agreement drawn up between the USA and UK that forms the basis for many post-World War II international agreements. It set out the premise that neither country would make territorial gains after the war (this may have been included because the American President distrusted British imperial ambitions) and the idea that all people should have the right to self-determination. Other measures included global economic co-operation, the lowering of trade barriers, disarmament of aggressor nations among a general disarmament that would come with the end of war, freedom of the seas, human rights and increased social welfare.

The President of the United States and the Prime Minister, Mr Churchill, representing His Majesty's Government in the United Kingdom, have met at sea.

They have been accompanied by officials of their two governments, including high ranking officers of the Military, Naval and Air Services.

The whole problem of the supply of munitions of war, as provided by the Lease-Lend Act, for the armed forces of the United States and for those countries actively engaged in resisting aggression has been further examined.

Lord Beaverbrook, the Minister of Supply of the British Government, has joined in these conferences. He is going to proceed to Washington to discuss further details with appropriate officials of the United States Government. These conferences will also cover the supply problems of the Soviet Union.

The President and the Prime Minister have had several conferences They have considered the dangers to world civilization arising from the policies of military domination by conquest upon which the Hitlerite government of Germany and other governments associated therewith have embarked, and have made clear the stress which their countries are respectively taking for their safety in the face of these dangers.

They have agreed upon the following joint declaration:

Joint declaration of the President of the United States of America and the Prime Minister, Mr Churchill, representing His Majesty's Government in the United Kingdom, being met together, deem it right to make known certain common principles in the national policies of their respective countries on which they base their hopes for a better future for the world.

First, their countries seek no aggrandizement, territorial or other;

Second, they desire to see no territorial changes that do not

President Roosevelt talks to his son James, as Winston Churchill casts an eye over the proceedings on board the warship where the Atlantic Charter was negotiated.

accord with the freely expressed wishes of the peoples concerned;

Third, they respect the right of all peoples to choose the form of government under which they will live; and they wish to see sovereign rights and self government restored to those who have been forcibly deprived of them;

Fourth, they will endeavor, with due respect for their existing obligations, to further the enjoyment by all States, great or small, victor or vanquished, of access, on equal terms, to the trade and to the raw materials of the world which are needed for their economic prosperity;

Fifth, they desire to bring about the fullest collaboration between all nations in the economic field with the object of securing, for all, improved labor standards, economic advancement and social security;

Sixth, after the final destruction of the Nazi tyranny, they hope to see established a peace which will afford to all nations the means of dwelling in safety within their own boundaries, and which will afford assurance that all the men in all the lands may live out their lives in freedom from fear and want;

Seventh, such a peace should enable all men to traverse the high seas and oceans without hindrance;

Eighth, they believe that all of the nations of the world, for realistic as well as spiritual reasons must come to the abandonment of the use of force. Since no future peace can be maintained if land, sea or air armaments continue to be employed by nations which threaten, or may threaten, aggression outside of their frontiers, they believe, pending the establishment of a wider and permanent system of general security, that the disarmament of such nations is essential. They will likewise aid and encourage all other practicable measures which will lighten for peace-loving peoples the crushing burden of armaments.

Henry Kissinger born 1923

NATIONALITY:
American
WHEN:
1970
WHERE:
Washington, DC, USA
YOU SHOULD KNOW:
Kissinger became Secretary of State following the departure of William Rogers in 1973.

As National Security Advisor to President Nixon, Henry Kissinger was instrumental in supporting him in the 1970 Cambodian incursion and the bombing campaign that preceded and followed it, in order to disrupt Viet Cong and North Vietnamese Army action there. There was dissension in the highest ranks of the Government about invading one country in the course of a war against another and setting a dangerous precedent and because of this the State Department under William Rogers was kept out of all decisions about the war. As the White House's need to control what was revealed in the press increased, the telephones of journalists and State Department officials and even Kissinger's own aide were tapped. Kissinger saw his loyalty as being to the beleagured President, and rallied other officials with the sentence below.

We are all the President's men, and should act accordingly.

Maximilien Robespierre

1758–1794

NATIONALITY:
French
WHEN:
1792
WHERE:
Paris, France
YOU SHOULD KNOW:
Saint-Just was instrumental in the arrest of Thomas Paine on December 25, 1793.

After the French Revolution, Robespierre became a member of the National Assembly, where he called for universal suffrage, an end to religious and racial discrimination and for public appointments to be made on merit. It was only after King Louis XVI tried to flee the country that Robespierre decided that it was unsafe in the interests of the nation for the King to survive. At the National Convention of December 3, 1792 he made this unprincipled speech. The King was executed the following month. The death penalty was not abolished after the King's death, but was used more and more as the country spiralled out of control. Robespierre himself was guillotined less than two years later after presiding over an extrordinarily bloody period of ten months known as The Terror.

This is no trial; Louis is not a prisoner at the bar; you are not judges; you are – you cannot but be – statesmen, and the representatives of the nation. You have not to pass sentence for or against a single man, but you have to take a resolution on a question of the public safety, and to decide a question of national foresight. It is with regret that I pronounce, the fatal truth: Louis ought to perish rather than a hundred thousand virtuous citizens; Louis must die, so that the country may live.

Richard M. Nixon 1913–1994

On November 3, 1969 President Nixon gave a television broadcast to the nation, explaining – in the face of demonstrations and sometimes violent protests – why it would be wrong for the US Government to pull out troops from the Vietnam War. The three principles known as the Nixon Doctrine were announced in Guam and it was the third of those that he invoked as the reason behind remaining engaged in the Vietnam War.

NATIONALITY:
American
WHEN:
1969
WHERE:
Washington, DC, USA
YOU SHOULD KNOW:
The last American personnel were helicoptered out of Saigon on April 29, 1975, one day before the North Vietnamese Army arrived at the city.

Tonight I want to talk to you on a subject of deep concern to all Americans and to many people in all parts of the world – the war in Vietnam.

I believe that one of the reasons for the deep division about Vietnam is that many Americans have lost confidence in what their Government has told them about our policy. The American people cannot and should not be asked to support a policy which involves the overriding issues of war and peace unless they know the truth about that policy . . .

Now, let me begin by describing the situation I found when I was inaugurated on January 20.

The war had been going on for four years.

31,000 Americans had been killed in action.

The training program for the South Vietnamese was behind schedule.

540,000 Americans were in Vietnam with no plans to reduce the number.

No progress had been made at the negotiations in Paris and the United States had not put forth a comprehensive peace proposal.

The war was causing deep division at home and criticism from many of our friends as well as our enemies abroad.

In view of these circumstances there were some who urged that I end the war at once by ordering the immediate withdrawal of all American forces . . .

. . . I had a greater obligation than to think only of the years of my administration and of the next election. I had to think of the effect of my decision on the next generation and on the future of peace and freedom in America and in the world . . .

The great question is: How can we win America's peace?

. . . Now that we are in the war, what is the best way to end it?

In January I could only conclude that the precipitate withdrawal of American forces from Vietnam would be a disaster not only for South Vietnam but for the United States and for the cause of peace.

For the South Vietnamese, our precipitate withdrawal would inevitably allow the Communists to repeat the massacres which followed their takeover in the North 15 years before . . .

For the United States, this first defeat in our Nation's history would

Nixon at his nomination as the Republican presidential candidate

and patriotic Americans have reached different conclusions as to how peace should be achieved.

And now I would like to address a word, if I may, to the young people of this Nation who are particularly concerned, and I understand why they are concerned, about this war.

I respect your idealism.

I share your concern for peace.

I want peace as much as you do.

There are powerful personal reasons I want to end this war. This week I will have to sign 83 letters to mothers, fathers, wives, and loved ones of men who have given their lives for America in Vietnam. It is very little satisfaction to me that this is only one-third as many letters as I signed the first week in office. There is nothing I want more than to see the day come when I do not have to write any of those letters.

I want to end the war to save the lives of those brave young men in Vietnam.

But I want to end it in a way which will increase the chance that their younger brothers and their sons will not have to fight in some future Vietnam someplace in the world.

And I want to end the war for another reason. I want to end it so that the energy and dedication of you, our young people, now too often directed into bitter hatred against those responsible for the war, can be turned to the great challenges of peace, a better life for all Americans, a better life for all people on this earth.

I have chosen a plan for peace. I believe it will succeed.

If it does succeed, what the critics say now won't matter. If it does not succeed, anything I say then won't matter.

I know it may not be fashionable to speak of patriotism or national destiny these days. But I feel it is appropriate to do so on this occasion.

Two hundred years ago this Nation was weak and poor. But even then, America was the hope of millions in the world. Today we have become the strongest and richest nation in the world . . .

Let historians not record that when America was the most powerful nation in the world we passed on the other side of the road and allowed the last hopes for peace and freedom of millions of people to be suffocated by the forces of totalitarianism.

And so tonight – to you, the great silent majority of my fellow Americans – I ask for your support.

I pledged in my campaign for the Presidency to end the war in a way that we could win the peace. I have initiated a plan of action which will enable me to keep that pledge.

The more support I can have from the American people, the sooner that pledge can be redeemed; for the more divided we are at home, the less likely, the enemy is to negotiate at Paris.

Let us be united for peace. Let us also be united against defeat. Because let us understand: North Vietnam cannot defeat or humiliate the United States. Only Americans can do that.

Fifty years ago, in this room and at this very desk, President Woodrow Wilson spoke words which caught the imagination of a war-weary world. He said: 'This is the war to end war'. His dream for peace after World War I was shattered on the hard realities of great power politics and Woodrow Wilson died a broken man.

Tonight I do not tell you that the war in Vietnam is the war to end wars. But I do say this: I have initiated a plan which will end this war in a way that will bring us closer to that great goal to which Woodrow Wilson and every American President in our history has been dedicated – the goal of a just and lasting peace.

As President I hold the responsibility for choosing the best path to that goal and then leading the Nation along it.

I pledge to you tonight that I shall meet this responsibility with all of the strength and wisdom I can command in accordance with your hopes, mindful of your concerns, sustained by your prayers.

Second, we shall provide a shield if a nuclear power threatens the freedom of a nation allied with us or of a nation whose survival we consider vital to our security.

Third, in cases involving other types of aggression, we shall furnish military and economic assistance when requested in accordance with our treaty commitments. But we shall look to the nation directly threatened to assume the primary responsibility of providing the manpower for its defense . . .

The policy of the previous administration not only resulted in our assuming the primary responsibility for fighting the war, but even more significantly did not adequately stress the goal of strengthening the South Vietnamese so that they could defend themselves when we left.

The Vietnamization plan was launched following Secretary Laird's visit to Vietnam in March. Under the plan, I ordered first a substantial increase in the training and equipment of South Vietnamese forces.

In July, on my visit to Vietnam, I changed General Abrams' orders so that they were consistent with the objectives of our new policies. Under the new orders, the primary mission of our troops is to enable the South Vietnamese forces to assume the full responsibility for the security of South Vietnam.

Our air operations have been reduced by over 20 per cent.

And now we have begun to see the results of this long overdue change in American policy in Vietnam.

After five years of Americans going into Vietnam, we are finally bringing American men home. By December 15, over 60,000 men will have been withdrawn from South Vietnam – including 20 per cent of all of our combat forces.

The South Vietnamese have continued to gain in strength. As a result they have been able to take over combat responsibilities from our American troops . . .

Most important – United States casualties have declined during the last two months to the lowest point in three years.

Let me now turn to our program for the future.

We have adopted a plan which we have worked out in cooperation with the South Vietnamese for the complete withdrawal of all US combat ground forces, and their replacement by South Vietnamese forces on an orderly scheduled timetable. This withdrawal will be made from strength and not from weakness. As South Vietnamese forces become stronger, the rate of American withdrawal can become greater . . .

My fellow Americans, I am sure you can recognize from what I have said that we really only have two choices open to us if we want to end this war.

I can order an immediate, precipitate withdrawal of all Americans from Vietnam without regard to the effects of that action.

Or we can persist in our search for a just peace through a negotiated settlement if possible, or through continued implementation of our plan for Vietnamization if necessary – a plan in which we will withdraw all of our forces from Vietnam on a schedule in accordance with our program, as the South Vietnamese become strong enough to defend their own freedom.

I have chosen this second course.

It is not the easy way.

It is the right way.

It is a plan which will end the war and serve the cause of peace-not just in Vietnam but in the Pacific and in the world.

In speaking of the consequences of a precipitate withdrawal, I mentioned that our allies would lose confidence in America.

Far more dangerous, we would lose confidence in ourselves. Oh, the immediate reaction would be a sense of relief that our men were coming home. But as we saw the consequences of what we had done, inevitable remorse and divisive recrimination would scar our spirit as a people . . .

I recognize that some of my fellow citizens disagree with the plan for peace I have chosen. Honest

and patriotic Americans have reached different conclusions as to how peace should be achieved.

And now I would like to address a word, if I may, to the young people of this Nation who are particularly concerned, and I understand why they are concerned, about this war.

I respect your idealism.

I share your concern for peace.

I want peace as much as you do.

There are powerful personal reasons I want to end this war. This week I will have to sign 83 letters to mothers, fathers, wives, and loved ones of men who have given their lives for America in Vietnam. It is very little satisfaction to me that this is only one-third as many letters as I signed the first week in office. There is nothing I want more than to see the day come when I do not have to write any of those letters.

I want to end the war to save the lives of those brave young men in Vietnam.

But I want to end it in a way which will increase the chance that their younger brothers and their sons will not have to fight in some future Vietnam someplace in the world.

And I want to end the war for another reason. I want to end it so that the energy and dedication of you, our young people, now too often directed into bitter hatred against those responsible for the war, can be turned to the great challenges of peace, a better life for all Americans, a better life for all people on this earth.

I have chosen a plan for peace. I believe it will succeed.

If it does succeed, what the critics say now won't matter. If it does not succeed, anything I say then won't matter.

I know it may not be fashionable to speak of patriotism or national destiny these days. But I feel it is appropriate to do so on this occasion.

Two hundred years ago this Nation was weak and poor. But even then, America was the hope of millions in the world. Today we have become the strongest and richest nation in the world . . .

Let historians not record that when America was the most powerful nation in the world we passed on the other side of the road and allowed the last hopes for peace and freedom of millions of people to be suffocated by the forces of totalitarianism.

And so tonight – to you, the great silent majority of my fellow Americans – I ask for your support.

I pledged in my campaign for the Presidency to end the war in a way that we could win the peace. I have initiated a plan of action which will enable me to keep that pledge.

The more support I can have from the American people, the sooner that pledge can be redeemed; for the more divided we are at home, the less likely, the enemy is to negotiate at Paris.

Let us be united for peace. Let us also be united against defeat. Because let us understand: North Vietnam cannot defeat or humiliate the United States. Only Americans can do that.

Fifty years ago, in this room and at this very desk, President Woodrow Wilson spoke words which caught the imagination of a war-weary world. He said: 'This is the war to end war'. His dream for peace after World War I was shattered on the hard realities of great power politics and Woodrow Wilson died a broken man.

Tonight I do not tell you that the war in Vietnam is the war to end wars. But I do say this: I have initiated a plan which will end this war in a way that will bring us closer to that great goal to which Woodrow Wilson and every American President in our history has been dedicated – the goal of a just and lasting peace.

As President I hold the responsibility for choosing the best path to that goal and then leading the Nation along it.

I pledge to you tonight that I shall meet this responsibility with all of the strength and wisdom I can command in accordance with your hopes, mindful of your concerns, sustained by your prayers.

Howard Baker born 1925

In 1973, during the Senate committee hearings investigating the Watergate Scandal, the Vice Chairman of the committee, Republican Senator Howard Baker of Tennessee, asked former White House counsel John Dean the question below. Dean implicated many people within the upper levels of the White House, including the President, which led to new lines of investigation. But it was not until the emergence of the second set of secret tapes that were used to bug conversations in the Oval Office and the President's private office in the summer of 1974 that the real extent of Nixon's involvement throughout the cover-up conspiracy became apparent.

NATIONALITY:
American
WHEN:
1973
WHERE:
Washington, DC, USA
YOU SHOULD KNOW:
Senator Baker's question was not intended to provoke an investigation into the President's involvement but to gain reassurance that he had not been implicated.

"What did the President know and when did he know it?"

Senator Howard Baker admonishing a witness.

Douglas Adams 1952–2001

The author of The Hitchhiker's Guide to the Galaxy *was not the first person to have expressed the idea below. But in America, in the years after the scandalous Nixon presidency and general discontent with the Ford and Carter terms, it caught the mood of the time. There was a feeling that elected governments tended to be either corrupt, or decent but out of their depth. This malaise led to Ronald Reagan's victory over Jimmy Carter in the 1980 Presidential elections.*

It is a well-known fact, that those people who most want to rule people are, *ipso facto*, those least suited to do it . . . Anyone who is capable of getting themselves made President should on no account be allowed to do the job.

NATIONALITY:
British
WHEN:
1980
WHERE:
In his book *The Restaurant at the End of the Universe*
YOU SHOULD KNOW:
Douglas Adams was also a committed environmentalist.

Douglas Adams in reflective mood

The North Atlantic Treaty

WHEN:
1949
WHERE:
Washington, DC, USA
YOU SHOULD KNOW:
Turkey and Greece joined the alliance in 1952, and a further 12 countries joined over the next 55 years.

On April 4, 1949 twelve countries signed the North Atlantic Treaty: Belgium, Canada, Denmark, France, Iceland, Italy, Luxembourg, the Netherlands, Norway, Portugal, the USA and the UK. It was the third in a series of alliances in just over a year, formed in response to the growing Soviet threat. It was crucial that the USA joined to make the alliance as strong as possible. The party countries pledged to respond to military aggression towards any other party country in North America or Europe.

ARTICLE 1: The Parties undertake, as set forth in the Charter of the United Nations, to settle any international dispute in which they may be involved by peaceful means in such a manner that international peace and security and justice are not endangered, and to refrain in their international relations from the threat or use of force in any manner inconsistent with the purposes of the United Nations.

President Truman signs the North Atlantic Treaty.

ARTICLE 2: The Parties will contribute toward the further development of peaceful and friendly international relations by strengthening their free institutions, by bringing about a better understanding of the principles upon which these institutions are founded, and by promoting conditions of stability and well-being. They will seek to eliminate conflict in their international economic policies and will encourage economic collaboration between any or all of them.

ARTICLE 3: In order more effectively to achieve the objectives of this Treaty, the Parties, separately and jointly, by means of continuous and effective self-help and mutual aid, will maintain and develop their individual and collective capacity to resist armed attack.

ARTICLE 4: The Parties will consult together whenever, in the opinion of any of them, the territorial integrity, political independence or security of any of the Parties is threatened.

ARTICLE 5: The Parties agree that an armed attack against one or more of them in Europe or North America shall be considered an attack against them all and consequently they agree that, if such an armed attack occurs, each of them, in exercise of the right of individual or collective self-defence recognised by Article 51 of the Charter of the United Nations, will assist the Party or Parties so attacked by taking forthwith, individually and in concert with the other Parties, such action as it deems necessary, including the use of armed force, to restore and maintain the security of the North Atlantic area.

Any such armed attack and all measures taken as a result thereof shall immediately be reported to the Security Council. Such measures shall be terminated when the Security Council has taken the measures necessary to restore and maintain international peace and security .

ARTICLE 6 : For the purpose of Article 5, an armed attack on one or more of the Parties is deemed to include an armed attack:
* on the territory of any of the Parties in Europe or North America, on the Algerian Departments of France, on the territory of or on the Islands under the jurisdiction of any of the Parties in the North Atlantic area north of the Tropic of Cancer;

* on the forces, vessels, or aircraft of any of the Parties, when in or over these territories or any other area in Europe in which occupation forces of any of the Parties were stationed on the date when the Treaty entered into force or the Mediterranean Sea or the North Atlantic area north of the Tropic of Cancer.

ARTICLE 7: This Treaty does not affect, and shall not be interpreted as affecting in any way the rights and obligations under the Charter of the Parties which are members of the United Nations, or the primary responsibility of the Security Council for the maintenance of international peace and security.

Article 8: Each Party declares that none of the international engagements now in force between it and any other of the Parties or any third State is in conflict with the provisions of this Treaty, and undertakes not to enter into any international engagement in conflict with this Treaty.

ARTICLE 9: The Parties hereby establish a Council, on which each of them shall be represented, to consider matters concerning the implementation of this Treaty. The Council shall be so organised as to be able to meet promptly at any time. The Council shall set up such subsidiary bodies as may be necessary; in particular it shall establish immediately a defence committee which shall recommend measures for the implementation of Articles 3 and 5.

ARTICLE 10: The Parties may, by unanimous agreement, invite any other European State in a position to further the principles of this Treaty and to contribute to the security of the North Atlantic area to accede to this Treaty. Any State so invited may become a Party to the Treaty by depositing its instrument of accession with the Government of the United States of America. The Government of the United States of America will inform each of the Parties of the deposit of each such instrument of accession.

ARTICLE 11: This Treaty shall be ratified and its provisions carried out by the Parties in accordance with their respective constitutional processes. The instruments of ratification shall be deposited as soon as possible with the Government of the United States of America, which will notify all the other signatories of each deposit. The Treaty shall enter into force between the States which have ratified it as soon as the ratifications of the majority of the signatories, including the ratifications of Belgium, Canada, France, Luxembourg, the Netherlands, the United Kingdom and the United States, have been deposited and shall come into effect with respect to other States on the date of the deposit of their ratifications.

ARTICLE 12: After the Treaty has been in force for ten years, or at any time thereafter, the Parties shall, if any of them so requests, consult together for the purpose of reviewing the Treaty, having regard for the factors then affecting peace and security in the North Atlantic area, including the development of universal as well as regional arrangements under the Charter of the United Nations for the maintenance of international peace and security.

ARTICLE 13: After the Treaty has been in force for 20 years, any Party may cease to be a Party one year after its notice of denunciation has been given to the Government of the United States of America, which will inform the Governments of the other Parties of the deposit of each notice of denunciation.

ARTICLE 14: This Treaty, of which the English and French texts are equally authentic, shall be deposited in the archives of the Government of the United States of America. Duly certified copies will be transmitted by that Government to the Governments of other signatories.

Tony Benn born 1925

Long-serving Labour Member of Parliament and thorn in the side of party leaders, Tony Benn has changed during his political career from being regarded as a dangerous socialist firebrand to being seen as an elder statesman of his party. However, it is not because his views have changed; he remains as true to those as ever. This comment was made in an interview in The Observer *newspaper, about the Blair leadership's wrenching of the Labour Party to the right and the abandonment of many long-held policies such as Clause IV, which committed the party to nationalization of industry where appropriate.*

Tony Benn was, and remains, a radical socialist.

NATIONALITY:
British
WHEN:
1995
WHERE:
London, England
YOU SHOULD KNOW:
In order to sit as an MP in the House of Commons, Tony Benn renounced his title – Viscount Stansgate.

❝ The paradox at the moment is that the Labour Party is cheering the leader because they think he'll win. The City and the press are cheering him because they think he's going to destroy socialism. ❞

479

Benjamin Disraeli 1804–1881

NATIONALITY:
British
WHEN:
1878
WHERE:
London, England
YOU SHOULD KNOW:
Benjamin Disraeli is so far the only British Prime Minister of Jewish heritage.

Disraeli helped establish the modern Conservative Party.

The Congress of Berlin was convened in 1878 in order to limit Russian powers in southeastern Europe, close to where both the United Kingdom and France had expansionist aims of their own, also to curtail the burgeoning Pan-Slavic movement in the Balkans. It restored some lands to the Ottoman Empire that Russia had won during the Russo-Turkish War of 1877 and recognized as sovereign states Montenegro, Romania and Serbia. The British delegates were Benjamin Disraeli, Earl Beaconsfield; Lord Russell and Lord Salisbury, who returned in triumph, having succeeded in achieving Britain's aims. On his return to London, Disraeli gave a brief speech from the window of 10 Downing Street.

‘ Lord Salisbury and myself have brought you back peace, but a peace, I hope, with honour which may satisfy our Sovereign, and tend to the welfare of the country. ’

Winston S. Churchill 1874–1965

*Less than a year after the end of World War II, after receiving an
honorary degree at Westminster College on March 5, 1946,
Churchill made a speech detailing his fears for the future of the
eastern half of Europe, but calling for dialogue with the Soviet
leadership rather than risk the horrors of another war. As he
had so many times before, Churchill manged to find the perfect
phrase to describe the situation in his evocative image of an
iron curtain descending across Europe. This speech could be
said to mark the beginning of the Cold War.*

NATIONALITY:
British
WHEN:
1946
WHERE:
Fulton, Missouri, USA
YOU SHOULD KNOW:
During World War I, Churchill served
as the First Lord of the Admiralty but
was forced out after the disastrous
Gallipoli campaign that resulted in
the deaths of 145,000 soldiers for no
military gain.

' . . . I have a strong admiration and regard for the valiant Russian
people and for my wartime comrade, Marshal Stalin. There is
deep sympathy and goodwill in Britain – and I doubt not here
also – toward the peoples of all the Russias and a resolve to
persevere through many differences and rebuffs in establishing
lasting friendships . . .

From Stettin in the Baltic to Trieste in the Adriatic an iron
curtain has descended across the Continent. Behind that line lie all
the capitals of the ancient states of Central and Eastern Europe.
Warsaw, Berlin, Prague, Vienna, Budapest, Belgrade, Bucharest and
Sofia; all these famous cities and the populations around them lie in
what I must call the Soviet sphere, and all are subject, in one form or
another, not only to Soviet influence but to a very high and in some
cases increasing measure of control from Moscow.

The safety of the world, ladies and gentlemen, requires a unity
in Europe, from which no nation should be permanently outcast. It
is from the quarrels of the strong parent races in Europe that the
world wars we have witnessed, or which occurred in former times,
have sprung . . .

. . . I do not believe that Soviet Russia desires war. What they
desire is the fruits of war and the indefinite expansion of their power
and doctrines . . .

From what I have seen of our Russian friends and allies during
the war, I am convinced that there is nothing they admire so much as
strength, and there is nothing for which they have less respect than
for weakness, especially military weakness.

For that reason the old doctrine of a balance of power is
unsound. We cannot afford, if we can help it, to work on narrow
margins, offering temptations to a trial of strength.

We must not let it happen again. This can only be achieved by
reaching now, in 1946, a good understanding on all points with
Russia under the general authority of the United Nations
Organization and by the maintenance of that good understanding
through many peaceful years, by the whole strength of the English-
speaking world and all its connections . . . '

Gamal Abdel Nasser 1918–1970

NATIONALITY:
Egyptian
WHEN:
1956
WHERE:
Alexandria, Egypt
YOU SHOULD KNOW:
The code word 'De Lesseps' was the
signal to take over the canal.

The Suez Canal had been built in the middle of the nineteenth century to join the Red Sea and the Mediterranean via the Gulf of Suez. It was constructed under the direction of the French engineer Ferdinand de Lesseps and was adminstered by the Anglo-French Suez Canal Company. In 1956, in response to the US and British governments and the World Bank refusing to fund the building of the Aswan High Dam – itself a reaction to Egypt approaching eastern bloc countries for weapons and a Soviet offer of funding – General Nasser nationalized the canal in order to use the charges for its use to build the dam. The speech itself lasted more than three hours.

After the past four years, and as we celebrate the fifth year of the revolution . . . At this moment as I talk to you, some of your Egyptian brethren are proceeding to administer the canal company and to run its affairs. They are taking over the canal company at this very moment – the Egyptian canal company, not the foreign canal company . . . They are now carrying out this task . . .

Anthony Eden 1897–1977

NATIONALITY:
British
WHEN:
1956
WHERE:
London, England
YOU SHOULD KNOW:
In addition to the fears that the Suez
Canal would be closed to British and
French ships, Eden was concerned
about General Nasser's ambitions for
a pan-Arab nation.

Two weeks after General Nasser had announced the nationalization of the Suez Canal Company, British Prime Minister Anthony Eden made a television and radio broadcast. Although American support was not forthcoming for a planned invasion of Egypt, British, French and Israeli delegations met at Sèvres in France to plan the re-taking of the canal. Israel invaded the Sinai Peninsula and took control of the canal. France and the UK – as had been planned – demanded both Israeli and Egyptian withdrawal and, when Nasser refused, bombed his airforce. He retaliated by sinking ships in the canal to block it. The US and USSR forced the British, French and Israelis to withdraw. A UN peacekeeping force was sent in and the canal was returned to Egyptian control.

Our quarrel is not with Egypt, still less with the Arab world. It is with Colonel Nasser. He has shown that he is not a man who can be trusted to keep an agreement. Now he has torn up all his country's promises to the Suez Canal Company and has even gone back on his own statements . . .
. . . We cannot agree that an act of plunder which threatens the livelihood of many nations should be allowed to succeed.

Alexander Dubcek 1921–1992

In April 1968, the new President of Czechoslovakia announced at the Presidium of the Communist Party of Czechoslovakia a political programme of 'socialism with a human face'. Restrictions on the press were lifted, victims of Stalinist purges were rehabilitated and conservatives ousted from the Presidium. The speed of reform caused great concern to the Soviet leadership in Moscow in case it weakened their position in the Cold War and – after a meeting with Dubcek in July – Brezhnev ordered the tanks of the Soviet Army into Czechoslovakia in late August. Dubcek was forced to abandon many of his planned reforms and his presidency lasted only until the following spring.

NATIONALITY:
Czech
WHEN:
1968
WHERE:
Prague, Czechoslovakia
YOU SHOULD KNOW:
The brief flowering of liberalism in Czechoslovakia in 1968 is known as the Prague Spring.

' Give socialism back its human face. '

Dubcek tried to reform socialism in Czechoslovakia.

Mikhail Gorbachev born 1931

NATIONALITY:
Russian
WHEN:
1991
WHERE:
Moscow, Russia
YOU SHOULD KNOW:
In 1990 Mikhail Gorbachev was
awarded the Nobel Peace Prize.

*In the aftermath of the foiled coup by Soviet hardliners in August
1991, President Gorbachev found that upon his return to Moscow
he was completely sidelined by Boris Yeltsin. On September 3 he
addressed the Congress of People's Deputies and in a rambling
speech covered the issues. Two days later the Congress dissolved
itself and within weeks Estonia, Latvia, Lithuania, Ukraine,
Belarus, Moldova, Georgia, Armenia, Azerbaijan, Kazakhstan,
Kyrgyzstan, Uzbekistan, Tajikstan and Turkmenistan had
declared independence. In December, Gorbachev and Yeltsin
agreed to dissolve the Soviet Union formally. He resigned on
Christmas Day and the Soviet Union passed into history the
next day.*

❛ . . . If there have been
mistakes, if there have
been miscalculations in
tactics and in measures –
but he [Gorbachev
himself] also did not
notice that it was
necessary to move more
rapidly along the path of
liberating ourselves from
those totalitarian
structures . . . Today you
have a president.
Tomorrow you may have
another president. In any
case, we are all one, side
by side, and we shouldn't
spit on each other. ❜

*Gorbachev presided over the
demise of the Soviet Union.*

Vaclav Havel

born 1936

After the 1989 Velvet Revolution, which ended Soviet dominion of Czechoslovakia, Vaclav Havel was unanimously elected as interim President. In his radio broadcast on January 1, 1990 he laid out the moral and economic issues the country faced after years of mismanagement. It is a clarion call to the people to take responsibility for their own future – hoping for a humane republic that serves its people and hoping the people will, in turn, serve the republic. He finishes with the sentence 'People, your government has returned to you!'

'My dear fellow citizens, for 40 years you have heard from my predecessors on this day different variations of the same theme: how our country flourished, how many million tons of steel we produced, how happy we all were . . .

I assume you did not propose me for this office so that I, too, would lie to you . . . Our country is not flourishing . . .

But all this is still not the main problem. The worst thing is that we live in a contaminated moral environment. We fell morally ill because we became used to saying something different from what we thought. We learned not to believe in anything, to ignore each other, to care only about ourselves . . .

If we realize this, then all the horrors that the new Czechoslovak democracy inherited will cease to appear so terrible. If we realize this, hope will return to our hearts. '

Havel was a writer and civil rights activist before becoming President.

NATIONALITY:
Czech
WHEN:
1990
WHERE:
Prague, Czechoslovakia
YOU SHOULD KNOW:
During the period of dissidence against oppression, Vaclav Havel spent many periods in prison.

Cleaver speaking at the
American University in
Washington, DC, USA.

Eldridge Cleaver 1935–1998

*Eldridge Cleaver in the 1960s appeared to epitomize what
white Americans feared. An early member of the Black
Panthers and their Minister for Information, he had a history
of violent crime and a prison record. A few days after the
assassination of Martin Luther King Jr, he addressed a rally
against the Vietnam War in San Francisco, an event also
attended by Coretta Scott King. Over the next few months he
became a highly visible spokesman for the radical left and stood
on the Peace and Freedom Party's ticket for the presidency but
was eventually ruled inegible because he was too young. He
jumped bail late in the year and fled to Algeria, where he
remained until the mid-1970s. When he returned, he
renounced radical politics and joined the Church of Jesus
Christ of Latter-day Saints.*

NATIONALITY:
American
WHEN:
1968
WHERE:
San Francisco, USA
YOU SHOULD KNOW:
Soul on Ice – Eldridge Cleaver's
collection of essays and letters
on American gender relations,
race and culture – was published
in February 1968.

If you're not part of the solution, you're part of the problem.

Mohandas K. Gandhi 1869–1948

After spending two years of a six-year sentence in prison for sedition between 1922 and 1924, Indian independence campaigner Gandhi steered clear of active politics for a few years, concentrating instead on social and human rights issues, such as those of the untouchables. His seven social sins list is a blueprint for what he perceived was wrong with life in India at the time. It was first published in written form in Young India, *the English-language magazine that he published in order to gain a wider audience for his spoken teachings and philosophy. Each of the sins suggests an ideal opposite based on permanent natural principles rather than transient social or cultural values, such as politics* with *principles and science* with *humanity.*

NATIONALITY:
Indian
WHEN:
before 1925
WHERE:
India
YOU SHOULD KNOW:
Gandhi's list of seven social sins are engraved on the wall of his memorial, modestly ignoring capital lettters.

> politics without principles
> wealth without work
> pleasure without conscience
> knowledge without character
> commerce without morality
> science without humanity
> worship without sacrifice.

Mahatma Gandhi was the leader of the civil-disobedience campaign during the struggle for Indian independence.

Simón Bolívar 1783–1830

NATIONALITY:
Venezuelan
WHEN:
1819
WHERE:
Angostura, Venezuela
YOU SHOULD KNOW:
The former Angostura is now called
Ciudad Bolívar.

*At the time when Bolívar gave this speech – the Angostura
Address – on February 15, 1819 Venezuela had been part of
independent Gran Colombia for almost eight years but was
still two years from sovereignty. He asserted that the peoples of
Latin America were so used to tyranny, ignorance and vice
that they would not know what to do with freedom; that
government had to be appropriate to the people; and that
legislators in fledging countries would have to work to create
conditions in which their fellow citizens could enjoy freedom.*

In absolute systems, the central power is unlimited. The will of the
despot is the supreme law, arbitrarily enforced by subordinates
who take part in the organized oppression in proportion to the
authority that they wield. They are charged with civil, political,
military and religious functions; but, in the final analysis, the
satraps of Persia are Persian, the pashas of the Grand Turk are
Turks, and the sultans of Tartary are Tartars. China does not seek
her mandarins in the homeland of Genghis Khan, her conqueror.
[Latin] America, on the contrary, received everything from Spain,
who, in effect, deprived her of the experience that she would have
gained from the exercise of an active tyranny . . .

Subject to the threefold yoke of ignorance, tyranny and vice,
the American people have been unable to acquire knowledge,
power or [civic] virtue. The lessons we received and the models we
studied, as pupils of such pernicious teachers, were most
destructive. We have been ruled more by deceit than by force, and
we have been degraded more by vice than superstition . . .

If a people, perverted by their training, succeed in achieving
their liberty, they will soon lose it, for it would be of no avail to
endeavour to explain to them that happiness consists in the
practice of virtue; that the rule of law is more powerful than the
rule of tyrants, because, as the laws are more inflexible, everyone
should submit to their beneficent austerity; that proper morals,
and not force, are the bases of law; and that to practise justice is to
practise liberty. Therefore, legislators, your work is so much the
more arduous, inasmuch as you have to re-educate men who have
been corrupted by erroneous illusions and false incentives . . . Our
weak fellow citizens will have to strengthen their spirit greatly
before they can digest the wholesome nutriment of freedom. Their
limbs benumbed by chains, their sight dimmed by the darkness of
dungeons, and their strength sapped by the pestilence of
servitude, are they capable of marching toward the august temple
of Liberty without faltering? Can they come near enough to bask in
its brilliant rays and to breathe freely the pure air which reigns
therein? . . .

Louis de Saint-Just 1767–1794

Louis de Saint-Just was a close ally of Robespierre and was heavily involved in one of the most violent stages of the French Revolution. His first speech to the National Convention was critical of Louis XVI and he quickly made a name for himself. During the trial of Louis, the Girondist faction in the Convention had voted in favour of appealing to the people and so lain themselves open to charges of royalism and federalism for their appeal to organize a movement against Paris from the provinces. On June 2, the Jacobins (who were far more revolutionary), including Saint-Just, inspired the Paris mob to turn on the Girondists and the National Guard threw them out of the Convention. Those Girondist leaders who did not escape were executed on October 31.

NATIONALITY:
French
WHEN:
1792
WHERE:
Paris, France
YOU SHOULD KNOW:
The last person to be guillotined in France was murderer Hamida Djandoubi in 1977.

' Those who make revolutions by halves do but dig themselves a grave. '

Barack Obama born 1961

In comparison to the upbeat nature of his acceptance speech on November 4, 2008, President Obama's Inaugural Address was a sober call to restore responsibility – both political and personal – and a pledge to bring about change while respecting the traditions and values of the American people. On a freezing Washington day, standing behind a bullet-proof shield and looking out over the estimated 1,800,000 people on the National Mall stretching towards the Washington Monument, the new President spoke the following words.

NATIONALITY:
American
WHEN:
2009
WHERE:
Washington, DC, USA
YOU SHOULD KNOW:
President Obama became the seventh President to retake the Oath of Office after inadvertant procedural irregularities the first time round.

' My fellow citizens: I stand here today humbled by the task before us, grateful for the trust you have bestowed, mindful of the sacrifices borne by our ancestors. I thank President Bush for his service to our nation, as well as the generosity and co-operation he has shown throughout this transition.

The words have been spoken during rising tides of prosperity and the still waters of peace. Yet, every so often the oath is taken amidst gathering clouds and raging storms. At these moments, America has carried on not simply because of the skill or vision of those in high office, but because We the People have remained faithful to the ideals of our forbearers, and true to our founding documents.

So it has been. So it must be with this generation of Americans.

That we are in the midst of crisis is now well understood. Our nation is at war, against a far-reaching network of violence and hatred. Our economy is badly weakened, a consequence of greed and irresponsibility on the part of some, but also our collective failure to make hard choices and prepare the nation for a new age. Homes have been lost; jobs shed; businesses shuttered. Our health care is too costly; our schools fail too many; and each day brings further evidence that the ways we use energy strengthen our adversaries and threaten our planet.

These are the indicators of crisis, subject to data and statistics. Less measurable but no less profound is a sapping of confidence across our land – a nagging fear that America's decline is inevitable, and that the next generation must lower its sights.

Today I say to you that the challenges we face are real. They are serious and they are many. They will not be met easily or in a short span of time. But know this, America – they will be met.

On this day, we gather because we have chosen hope over fear, unity of purpose over conflict and discord.

On this day, we come to proclaim an end to the petty grievances and false promises, the recriminations and worn out dogmas, that for far too long have strangled our politics.

We remain a young nation, but in the words of Scripture, the time has come to set aside childish things. The time has come to reaffirm our enduring spirit; to choose our better history; to carry forward that precious gift, that noble idea, passed on from generation to generation: the God-given promise that all are equal, all are free, and all deserve a chance to pursue their full measure of happiness.

In reaffirming the greatness of our nation, we understand that greatness is never a given. It must be earned. Our journey has never been one of short-cuts or settling for less. It has not been the path for the faint-hearted – for those who prefer leisure over work, or seek only the pleasures of riches and fame.

Rather, it has been the risk-takers, the doers, the makers of things – some celebrated but more often men and women obscure in their labour, who have carried us up the long, rugged path towards prosperity and freedom.

For us, they packed up their few worldly possessions and travelled across oceans in search of a new life.

For us, they toiled in sweatshops and settled the West; endured the lash of the whip and ploughed the hard earth.

For us, they fought and died, in places like Concord and Gettysburg; Normandy and Khe Sahn.

Time and again these men and women struggled and sacrificed and worked till their hands were raw so that we might live a better life. They saw America as bigger than the sum of our individual ambitions; greater than all the differences of birth or wealth or faction.

This is the journey we continue today. We remain the most prosperous, powerful nation on Earth. Our workers are no less productive than when this crisis began.

Our minds are no less inventive, our goods and services no less needed than they were last week or last month or last year. Our capacity remains undiminished.

But our time of standing pat, of protecting narrow interests and putting off unpleasant decisions – that time has surely passed. Starting today, we must pick ourselves up, dust ourselves off, and begin again the work of remaking America.

For everywhere we look, there is work to be done. The state of the economy calls for action, bold and swift, and we will act – not only to create new jobs, but to lay a new foundation for growth. We will build the roads and bridges, the electric grids and digital lines that feed our

commerce and bind us together. We will restore science to its rightful place, and wield technology's wonders to raise health care's quality and lower its cost. We will harness the sun and the winds and the soil to fuel our cars and run our factories. And we will transform our schools and colleges and universities to meet the demands of a new age. All this we can do. And all this we will do.

Now, there are some who question the scale of our ambitions – who suggest that our system cannot tolerate too many big plans.

Their memories are short. For they have forgotten what this country has already done; what free men and women can achieve when imagination is joined to common purpose, and necessity to courage.

491

What the cynics fail to understand is that the ground has shifted beneath them – that the stale political arguments that have consumed us for so long no longer apply. The question we ask today is not whether our government is too big or too small, but whether it works – whether it helps families find jobs at a decent wage, care they can afford, a retirement that is dignified. Where the answer is yes, we intend to move forward. Where the answer is no, programs will end. And those of us who manage the public's dollars will be held to account – to spend wisely, reform bad habits, and do our business in the light of day – because only then can we restore the vital trust between a people and their government.

Nor is the question before us whether the market is a force for good or ill.

Its power to generate wealth and expand freedom is unmatched, but this crisis has reminded us that without a watchful eye, the market can spin out of control – and that a nation cannot prosper long when it favours only the prosperous. The success of our economy has always depended not just on the size of our gross domestic product, but on the reach of our prosperity; on our ability to extend opportunity to every willing heart – not out of charity, but because it is the surest route to our common good. As for our common defence, we reject as false the choice between our safety and our ideals. Our Founding Fathers, faced with perils we can scarcely imagine, drafted a charter to assure the rule of law and the rights of man, a charter expanded by the blood of generations. Those ideals still light the world, and we will not give them up for expedience's sake. And so to all other peoples and governments who are watching today, from the grandest capitals to the small village where my father was born: know that America is a friend of each nation and every man, woman, and child who seeks a future of peace and dignity, and that we are ready to lead once more. Recall that earlier generations faced down fascism and communism not just with missiles and tanks, but with sturdy alliances and enduring convictions. They understood that our power alone cannot protect us, nor does it entitle us to do as we please. Instead, they knew that our power grows through its prudent use; our security emanates from the justness of our cause, the force of our example, the tempering qualities of humility and restraint. We are the keepers of this legacy. Guided by these principles once more, we can meet those new threats that demand even greater effort – even greater cooperation and understanding between nations. We will begin to responsibly leave Iraq to its people, and forge a hard-earned peace in Afghanistan. With old friends and former foes, we will work tirelessly to lessen the nuclear threat, and roll back the spectre of a warming planet. We will not apologise for our way of life, nor will we waver in its defense, and for those who seek to advance their aims by inducing terror and slaughtering innocents, we say to you now that our spirit is stronger and cannot be broken; you cannot outlast us, and we will defeat you. For we know that our patchwork heritage is a strength, not a weakness. We are a nation of Christians and Muslims, Jews and Hindus – and non-believers. We are shaped by every language and culture, drawn from every end of this Earth; and because we have tasted the bitter swill of civil war and segregation, and emerged from that dark chapter stronger and more united, we cannot help but believe that the old hatreds shall someday pass; that the lines of tribe shall soon dissolve; that as the world grows smaller, our common humanity shall reveal itself; and that America must play its role in ushering in a new era of peace. To the Muslim world, we seek a new way forward, based on mutual interest and mutual respect. To those leaders around the globe who seek to sow conflict, or blame their society's ills on the West – know that your people will judge you on what you can build, not what you destroy. To those who cling to power through corruption and deceit and the silencing of dissent, know that you are on the wrong side of history; but that we will extend a hand if you are willing to unclench your fist. To the people of poor nations, we pledge to work alongside you to make your farms flourish and let clean waters flow; to nourish starved bodies and feed hungry minds. And to those nations like ours that enjoy relative plenty, we say we can no longer afford indifference to suffering outside our borders; nor can we consume the world's resources without regard to effect. For the world has changed, and we must change with it. As we consider the road that unfolds before us, we remember with humble gratitude those brave Americans who, at this very hour, patrol far-off deserts and distant mountains. They have something to tell us today, just as the fallen heroes who lie in Arlington whisper through the ages. We honor them not only because they are guardians of our liberty, but because they embody the spirit of service; a willingness to find meaning in something greater than themselves. And yet, at this moment – a moment that will define a generation – it is precisely this spirit that must inhabit us all. For as much as government can do and must do, it is ultimately the faith and determination of the American people upon which this nation relies. It is the kindness to take in a stranger when the levees break, the selflessness of workers who would rather cut their hours than see a friend lose their job which sees us through our darkest hours. It is the fire-fighter's courage to storm a stairway filled with smoke, but also a parent's willingness to nurture a child, that finally decides our fate. Our challenges may be new. The instruments with which we meet them may be new. But those values upon which our success depends – hard work and honesty, courage and fair play, tolerance and curiosity, loyalty and patriotism – these things are old. These things are true. They have been the quiet force of progress throughout our history. What is demanded then is a return to these truths. What is required of us now is a new era of responsibility - a recognition, on the part of every American, that we have duties to ourselves, our nation, and the world, duties that we do not grudgingly accept but rather seize gladly, firm in the knowledge that there is nothing so satisfying to the spirit, so defining of our character, than giving our all to a difficult task. This is the price and the promise of citizenship. This is the source of our confidence – the knowledge that God calls on us to shape an uncertain destiny. This is the meaning of our liberty and our creed – why men and women and children of every race and every faith can join in celebration across this magnificent mall, and why a man whose father less than 60 years ago might not have been served at a local restaurant can now stand before you to take a most sacred oath. So let us mark this day with remembrance, of who we are and how far we have travelled. In the year of America's birth, in the coldest of months, a small band of patriots huddled by dying campfires on the shores of an icy river. The capital was abandoned. The enemy was advancing. The snow was stained with blood. At a moment when the outcome of our revolution was most in doubt, the father of our nation ordered these words be read to the people: 'Let it be told to the future world . . . that in the depth of winter, when nothing but hope and virtue could survive . . . that the city and the country, alarmed at one common danger, came forth to meet [it].' America. In the face of our common dangers, in this winter of our hardship, let us remember these timeless words. With hope and virtue, let us brave once more the icy currents, and endure what storms may come. Let it be said by our children's children that when we were tested we refused to let this journey end, that we did not turn back nor did we falter; and with eyes fixed on the horizon and God's grace upon us, we carried forth that great gift of freedom and delivered it safely to future generations. Thank you. God bless you, and God bless the United States of America. "

MISCELLANEOUS

The five members of Captain Scott's ill-fated expedition who reached the South Pole.

Captain Lawrence Oates
1880–1912

NATIONALITY:
British
WHEN:
1912
WHERE:
Antarctica
YOU SHOULD KNOW:
The gallant gesture was in vain as the last three survivors died of cold and hunger anyway.

In the Antarctic summer of 1911–1912, two expeditions were racing to be the first to reach the South Pole – a British one led by Captain Robert Falcon Scott and a Norwegian team with Roald Amundsen. They had chosen different routes and made different provisions for pulling the sledges. On January 17 Scott's team reached the pole to discover that the experienced Norwegians with their dog sleds had beaten the Brits by five weeks. On the heart-breaking journey back to base, Edgar Evans died at the foot of the Beardmore Glacier, then with dwindling supplies and knowing that he was holding Scott, Bowers and Wilson back, Oates went out into the blizzard in the hope that his sacrifice would save the others.

I am just going outside, and I may be some time.

Tom Lehrer born 1928

Singer-songwriter and satirist Tom Lehrer appeared on the US version of 'That Was The Week That Was' in the mid-1960s, where his lyrics were often changed by NBC's censors as too political. In 1959, he gave a concert at Harvard and introduced 'We Will All Go Together When We G'o – his take on Mutually Assured Destruction – with the line below. Other songs of his include 'My Home Town', 'Vatican Rag' and 'National Brotherhood Week' and the extremely risqué (for the time) 'Be Prepared'.

NATIONALITY:
American
WHEN:
1959
WHERE:
Cambridge, Massachusetts
YOU SHOULD KNOW:
Lehrer's most famous songs are *Poisoning Pigeons in the Park* and *The Elements*.

'Life is like a sewer – what you get out of it depends on what you put into it.' It's always seemed to me that this is precisely the sort of dynamic, positive thinking that we so desperately need today in these trying times of crisis and universal brouhaha.

Joseph P. Kennedy 1888–1969

Father of the political giants John F., Robert and Teddy Kennedy, Joe was a force to be reckoned with. He made his money in finance, stock market and commodity speculation, steel, movie studios and – after the end of Prohibition – the legal import of alcoholic drinks. He was briefly US Ambassador to the UK between 1938 and 1940. While many other people in his line of work failed completely during the Depression, he made millions by getting out at the right time and investing in real estate when prices were rock bottom. One rumour has it that he divested his stock market holdings after getting tips from a shoe-shine boy. Whether he said the phrase below or not is disputed, but it certainly fits his attitude.

NATIONALITY:
American
WHEN:
Unknown
WHERE:
Unknown
YOU SHOULD KNOW:
He was rumoured to have made money on the side by investing in bootlegging during Prohibition.

When the going gets tough, the tough get going.

Joseph Kennedy whilst US Ambassador to the UK

William Shakespeare 1564–1616

NATIONALITY:
English
WHEN:
Around 1601
WHERE:
In the play *Hamlet*
YOU SHOULD KNOW:
The play was not staged until after Elizabeth I's death.

Possibly the most eloquent suicide threat ever, this soliloquy is the turning point in Hamlet, *marking the beginning of the play's descent into madness and violence. Hamlet's feigned lunacy later in the scene prefigures Ophelia's real insanity and his rage in a tragedy that soon sees most of the protagonists dead. The play is thought to mirror the political situation in England at the time, towards the end of Queen Elizabeth I's life, but opinions differ as to whether the characters are meant to be counterparts to real people. Could the gloomy legitimate heir Hamlet represent James VI of Scotland or might that be Fortinbras, the king waiting just over the border to invade?*

To be, or not to be: that is the question:
Whether 'tis nobler in the mind to suffer
The slings and arrows of outrageous fortune,
Or to take arms against a sea of troubles,
And by opposing end them? To die: to sleep;
No more; and by a sleep to say we end
The heart-ache and the thousand natural shocks
That flesh is heir to, 'tis a consummation
Devoutly to be wish'd. To die, to sleep;
To sleep: perchance to dream: ay, there's the rub;
For in that sleep of death what dreams may come
When we have shuffled off this mortal coil,
Must give us pause: there's the respect
That makes calamity of so long life;
For who would bear the whips and scorns of time,
The oppressor's wrong, the proud man's contumely,
The pangs of despised love, the law's delay,
The insolence of office and the spurns
That patient merit of the unworthy takes,
When he himself might his quietus make
With a bare bodkin? Who would fardels bear,
To grunt and sweat under a weary life,
But that the dread of something after death,
The undiscover'd country from whose bourn
No traveller returns, puzzles the will
And makes us rather bear those ills we have
Than fly to others that we know not of?
Thus conscience does make cowards of us all;
And thus the native hue of resolution
Is sicklied o'er with the pale cast of thought,
And enterprises of great pitch and moment
With this regard their currents turn awry,
And lose the name of action.

David Tennant in a modern version of Hamlet *in 2009.*

Robert E. Lee 1807–1870

On April 9, 1865 the Battle of Appomattox Court proved the final one for the Army of Northern Virginia, and General Robert E. Lee was compelled to surrender to the Union Army under the command of Ulysses S. Grant and negotiate terms. Under condition of parole and surrender of any weapons apart from personal sidearms, the officers and men would be allowed home, were given rations and those who had horses or mules were allowed to take them to help with the spring planting. The following day General Lee made his farewell address to the soldiers who had spent four long years fighting.

'After four years of arduous services, marked by unsurpassed courage and fortitude, the Army of Northern Virginia has been compelled to yield to overwhelming numbers and resources. I need not tell the brave survivors of so many hard fought battles, who have remained steadfast to the last, that I have consented to this result from no distrust of them. But feeling that valor and devotion could accomplish nothing that would compensate for the loss which would have accompanied a continuance of the contest, I determined to avoid the useless sacrifice of those whose past services have endeared them to their countrymen. By the terms of the agreement, Officers and men can return to their homes and remain until exchanged. You will take with you the satisfaction that proceeds from the consciousness of duty faithfully performed; and I earnestly pray that a merciful God will extend to you his blessing and protection. With an unceasing admiration of your constancy and devotion to your country, and a grateful remembrance of your kind and generous consideration for myself, I bid you an affectionate farewell.'

NATIONALITY:
American
WHEN:
April 10, 1865
WHERE:
Appomattox, Virginia, USA
YOU SHOULD KNOW:
After the Army of Northern Virginia's surrender, other Confederate armies began to do the same and most had done so by the end of June.

George Orwell 1903–1950

Orwell was a writer and journalist, a veteran of the fight against fascism in the Spanish Civil War. He loathed totalitarianism and was passionate about social injustice. His two most famous novels, Animal Farm *and* 1984, *are both critiques of political systems, although in other works he would lampoon middle-class mores. The main slogan used in* 1984 *to keep the oppressed population under control, reproduced below, has passed into such common currency (and television folklore) that many people who use it may not even realize its source.*

'Big Brother is watching you.'

NATIONALITY:
British
WHEN:
1949
WHERE:
As a slogan in *1984*
YOU SHOULD KNOW:
Orwell's given name was actually Eric Arthur Blair.

Thomas Hobbes 1588–1679

NATIONALITY:
British
WHEN:
1651
WHERE:
Paris, France
YOU SHOULD KNOW:
Hobbes had briefly been tutor to
King Charles II in 1647 and 1648.

In Leviathan, The Matter, Forme and Power of a Common Wealth
Ecclesiasticall and Civil *the social philosopher Hobbes crystallizes
ideas that he had been discussing for years with friends and
fellow royalist exiles from Britain, on the state of man, the need
for a social contract and the correct structure for society. The
general theme of the book concerns the lot of man before the
development of the state, and of society – when the natural
condition was 'war of every man against every man'. Hobbes
also expounded the idea – controversial at the time – that no
object was intrinsically good or evil. Instead, things that man
wants or desires are seen as good and things that he hates or
abominates are evil.*

'
No arts; no letters; no society; and which is worst of all, continual
fear and danger of violent death; and the life of man, solitary, poor,
nasty, brutish and short. '

God

WHERE:
Genesis Chapters 6–7
YOU SHOULD KNOW:
The *Koran* also has a *sura* devoted to
the story of Noah and similar tales
occur in the legends of many ancient
civilizations.

*In the Biblical version of the story, Noah, the last of the ten
antediluvian patriarchs, was 600 years old when God told him
to build an ark (large boat) and collect from two to seven
members of each animal species, fill it with food and save
himself and his family – his wife, sons (Ham, Shem and Japeth)
and their wives – from the flood that God was about to unleash
on the Earth in order to destroy everything and everyone else
on it because of the wickedness of the rest of the people. The
waters remained for 150 days before the ark came to rest on
Mount Ararat and Noah sent first a raven and then a dove to see
if the flood was subsiding.*

'
And God said unto Noah, The end of all flesh is come before me; for
the earth is filled with violence through them; and, behold, I will
destroy them with the earth.

Make thee an ark of gopher wood; rooms shalt thou make in the
ark, and shalt pitch it within and without with pitch.

And this is the fashion which thou shalt make it of: The length of
the ark shall be three hundred cubits, the breadth of it fifty cubits,
and the height of it thirty cubits.

A window shalt thou make to the ark, and in a cubit shalt thou
finish it above; and the door of the ark shalt thou set in the side
thereof; with lower, second, and third stories shalt thou make it.

Noah's Ark *by Edward Hicks*

And, behold, I, even I, do bring a flood of waters upon the earth, to destroy all flesh, wherein is the breath of life, from under heaven; and every thing that is in the earth shall die.

But with thee will I establish my covenant; and thou shalt come into the ark, thou, and thy sons, and thy wife, and thy sons' wives with thee.

And of every living thing of all flesh, two of every sort shalt thou bring into the ark, to keep them alive with thee; they shall be male and female.

Of fowls after their kind, and of cattle after their kind, of every creeping thing of the earth after his kind, two of every sort shall come unto thee, to keep them alive.

And take thou unto thee of all food that is eaten, and thou shalt gather it to thee; and it shall be for food for thee, and for them.

[Thus did Noah; according to all that God commanded him, so did he.]

And the Lord said unto Noah, Come thou and all thy house into the ark; for thee have I seen righteous before me in this generation.

Of every clean beast thou shalt take to thee by sevens, the male and his female: and of beasts that are not clean by two, the male and his female.

Of fowls also of the air by sevens, the male and the female; to keep seed alive upon the face of all the earth.

For yet seven days, and I will cause it to rain upon the earth forty days and forty nights; and every living substance that I have made will I destroy from off the face of the earth.

English Parliament

NATIONALITY:
English
WHEN:
1696
WHERE:
London, England
YOU SHOULD KNOW:
The 1696 Act was passed because
the English government believed it
was losing revenue as a result of
widespread fraud.

The English Navigation Acts were a series of acts passed to regulate the conduct of trade between the country and its colonies. They caused great resentment because they were all to the advantage of the mother country and of positive disadvantage to the colonies. They prohibited trade between the colonies and other nations and imposed harsh import and export duties. The 1696 Act imposed conditions such as insisting that ships captured from other nations could be used only for government trade for a given time, restricted colonial property sales and allowed the inspection and seizure of goods, warehouses, houses and ships for any transgression.

‘ As ACT for preventing Frauds and regulating Abuses in the Plantation Trade.

. . . Noe Goods or Merchandises whatsoever shall bee imported into or exported out of any Colony or Plantation to His Majesty in Asia Africa or America belonging or in his Possession or which may hereafter belong unto or bee in the Possession of His Majesty . . . or shall bee laden in or carried from any One Port or Place in the said Colonies or Plantations to any other Port or Place in the same, the Kingdome of England Dominion of Wales or Towne of Berwick upon Tweed in any Shipp or Bottome but what is or shall bee of the Built of England or of the Built of Ireland or the said Colonies or Plantations and wholly owned by the People thereof or any of them and navigated with the Masters and Three Fourths of the Mariners of the said Places onely (except such Shipps onely as are or shall bee taken Prize . . . And alsoe except for the space of Three Yeares such Foreigne built Shipps as shall bee employed by the Commissioners of His Majesties Navy for the tyme being or upon Contract with them in bringing onely Masts Timber and other Navall Stores for the Kings Service from His Majesties Colonies or Plantations to this Kingdome to bee navigated as aforesaid and whereof the Property doth belong to English Men) under paine of Forfeiture of Shipp and Goods . . .

. . . For the more effectuall preventing of Frauds and regulating Abuses in the Plantation Trade in America Bee itt further enacted . . . That all Shipps comeing into or goeing out of any of the said Plantations and ladeing or unladeing any Goods or Commodities whether the same bee His Majesties Shipps of Warr or Merchants Shipps and the Masters and Commanders thereof and their Ladings shall bee subject and lyable to the same Rules Visitations Searches Penalties and Forfeitures as to the entring lading or dischargeing theire respective Shipps and Ladings as Shipps and their Ladings and the Commanders and Masters of Shipps are subject and lyable unto in this Kingdome . . . And that the Officers for collecting and manageing His Majesties Revenue and inspecting the Plantation Trade in any of the said Plantations shall have the same Powers and Authorities for visiting and searching of Shipps and takeing their Entries and for seizing and securing or bringing on Shoare any of the Goods prohibited to bee imported or exported into or out of any the said Plantations or for which any Duties are payable or ought to have beene paid by any of the before mentioned Acts as are provided for the Officers of the Customes in England by the said last mentioned Act . . . and alsoe to enter Houses or Warehouses to search for and seize any such Goods . . .

. . . That all Persons and theire Assignees claymeing any Right or (Property) in any Islands or Tracts of Land upon the Continent of America by Charter or Letters Patents shall not att any tyme hereafter alien sell or dispose of any of the said Islands Tracts of Land or Proprieties other than to the Naturall Borne Subjects of England Ireland Dominion of Virales or . . . Berwick upon Tweed without the License and Consent of His Majesty . . . signifyed by His or Their Order in Councill first had and obteyned . . . **"**

Charles de Gaulle 1890–1970

General de Gaulle was the leader in exile of Free French Forces during World War II and the first post-war President of France. He lost power in 1948 and failed to regain it in 1951. After the election he made this enigmatic and widely disseminated comment. During his later period in the Elysée Palace, relations with both the USA and UK were notoriously difficult. This was partly because of his chauvanistic foreign policy but also because he did not acknowledge the sacrifices France's war-time allies had made on her behalf. The idea of the French as a nation of cheese-eaters re-emerged on The Simpsons *in 1995 and was picked up by politicians during the arguments over the rights and wrongs of the 2003 invasion of Iraq, which France vehemently opposed.*

NATIONALITY:
French
WHEN:
1951
WHERE:
Paris, France
YOU SHOULD KNOW:
He appears to have made this remark on several occasions, and the number of speciality cheeses cited varied.

' One can unite the French only under the threat of danger. One cannot unite a country that has 265 speciality cheeses. **"**

Charles de Gaulle speaking from the Town Hall in Strasbourg after the war.

RMS *Titanic* and various other vessels

WHEN:
April 15, 1912
WHERE:
The North Atlantic, off Newfoundland
YOU SHOULD KNOW:
CQD was the Marconi general distress call to all vessels. It was replaced at about this time by SOS.

During the night of April 14–15, 1912 the supposedly unsinkable ship RMS Titanic *hit an iceberg far south of where any would normally be expected at that time of year. Within little over two-and-a-half hours she had sunk, taking 1517 people with her. Because of the rapid timescale, only 711 of the 2223 people on board actually made it to the lifeboats. The two Marconi wireless operators, Jack Phillips and Harold Bride, worked tirelessly until the power supply to the radios gave out just after 2.00 am. RMS* Carpathia *picked up the first survivors from the lifeboats some time after 6.00 am.*

00.15 *Titanic*
CQD (6 times) DE MGY [6 times] position 41.44 N. 50.24 W . . .
(repeated over and again)

00.18 *Carpathia* (to *Titanic*)
Do you know that Cape Cod is sending a batch of messages for you?

Titanic (to *Carpathia*)
Come at once. We have struck a berg.
It's a CQD OM (it's a distress situation old man)
Position 41.46 N. 50.14 W.

Carpathia (to *Titanic*)
Shall I tell my Captain? Do you require assistance?

Titanic (to *Carpathia*)
Yes, come quick.

00.25 *Titanic* (to *Ypiranga* about 15–20 times)
CQD, Here corrected position 41.46 N. 50.14 W.
Require immediate assistance. We have collision with iceberg. Sinking. Can hear nothing for noise of steam.

00.26 *Prinz Friedrich Wilhelm* (to *Titanic*)
Titanic my position at 12 am 39.47 N. 50.10 W.

Titanic (to *Prinz Friedrich Wilhelm*)
Are you coming to our (. . .) We have collision with iceberg. Sinking. Please tell Captain to come.

Prinz Friedrich Wilhelm (to *Titanic*)
OK will tell.

00.27 *Titanic*
I require assistance immediately. Struck by iceberg in 41.46 N. 50.14 W.

00. 34 *Frankfurt* (to *Titanic*)
My position 39.47 N. 52.10 W.

Titanic (to *Frankfurt*)
Are you coming to our assistance?

Frankfurt (to *Titanic*)
What is the matter with you?

Titanic (to *Frankfurt*)
We have struck an iceberg and sinking. Please tell Captain to come.

Frankfurt (to *Titanic*)
OK. Will tell the bridge right away.

Titanic (to *Frankfurt*)
OK, yes, quick.

00.45 *Titanic* (to *Olympic*)
SOS.

00.50 *Titanic*
CQD I require immediate assistance. Position 41.46 N. 50.14 W.

01.00 *Titanic*
CQD I require immediate assistance. Position 41.46 N. 50.14 W.

Titanic (to *Olympic*)
My position is 41.46 N. 50.14 W. We have struck an iceberg.

01.10 *Titanic* (to *Olympic*)
We are in collision with berg. Sinking head down. 41.46 N. 50.14 W. Come soon as possible.

01.10 *Titanic* (to *Olympic*)
Captain says Get your boats ready. What is your position?

01.15 *Baltic* (to *Caronia*)
Please tell *Titanic* we are making towards her.

01.20 *Cape Race* (to *Titanic*)
We are coming to your assistance. Our position 170 miles N. of you.

01.25 *Caronia* (to *Titanic*)
Baltic coming to your assistance.

Olympic (to *Titanic*)
Position 4.24 am GMT 40.52 N. 61.18 W. Are you steering southerly to meet us?

01.30 *Titanic* (to *Olympic*)
We are putting passengers off in small boats. Women and children in boats, cannot last much longer.

01.35 *Olympic* (to *Titanic*)
What weather do you have?

Titanic (to *Olympic*)
Clear and calm.

Another desperate radio message from RMS Titanic.

505

Titanic
Engine room getting flooded.

Frankfurt (to *Titanic*)
Are there any boats around you already?

01.37 *Baltic* (to *Titanic*)
We are rushing to you.

01.40 *Olympic* (to *Titanic*)
Am lighting up all possible boilers as fast as can.

01.45 *Titanic* (to *Olympic*)
Come as quickly as possible old man: the engine-room is filling up to the boilers.

01.47
Faint unreadable signals from *Titanic*

01.48 *Frankfurt* (to *Titanic*)
What is the matter with u?

01.50 *Titanic* (to *Frankfurt*)
You fool, stdbi and keep out.

02.17 *Titanic*
CQ [stops abruptly]

Virginian (to *Titanic*)
Suggest try emergency set.

02.20 *Virginian* (to *Olympic*)
Have you heard anything about *Titanic*.

Olympic (to *Virginian*)
No. Keeping strict watch, but hear nothing more from *Titanic*. No reply from him. ,,

Jubilee 2000

WHEN:
1999
WHERE:
Tegucigalpa, Honduras
YOU SHOULD KNOW:
Some creditor countries have cancelled debts, but by no means all.

Jubilee 2000 is an international coalition of churches, NGOs, charities and trades unions whose aim is the cancellation of debt owed to the international community by poor countries. It was started in the mid-1990s with the purpose of shaming or at least pushing the world's richer governments and international organizations into cancellation of debts on both moral and humanitarian grounds. It is organized into regional areas and below is an extract from the Latin America/Caribbean Platform Declaration. The three main demands are: the unconditional, immediate and total cancellation of the debt; the immediate termination of the conditions attached to all the internationally designed debt relief mechanisms tying this to further economic adjustment; and the scrapping of the Heavily Indebted Poor Countries Initiative (a mechanism for debt repayment that was not meeting its original aims).

' Debt is a direct expression of the unjust global economic order which is the result of a long history of slavery, exploitation and terms of trade which are detrimental to the poor. ,

Stephen Hawking born 1942

Life in the Universe *is one of Professor Hawking's public lectures that he has given on several occasions and is a departure from his normal field of study of higher math and applied and quantum physics. He speculates on the probability of life elsewhere and the prospects for its future. He questions how 'life' is defined. Many of the definitions used to describe living viruses, for example, can also be applied to their computer equivalent. He also gives a succinct history of the Universe, explaining that if the early emergence of life on Earth is duplicated on other planets – rather than developing to intelligence just before its parent star dies – it increases the chance of life. Also that the key to the evolution of humans to become the current dominant species on the planet was the development of language and he speculates as to the different forms our future evolution might take.*

NATIONALITY:
British
WHEN:
Various times
WHERE:
Various places
YOU SHOULD KNOW:
Professor Hawking's condition is a type of motor-neurone disease called amyotrophic lateral sclerosis.

In this talk I would like to speculate a little on the development of life in the universe, and in particular the development of intelligent life. I shall take this to include the human race, even though much of its behaviour throughout history has been pretty stupid and not calculated to aid the survival of the species. Two questions I shall discuss are: what is the probability of life existing elsewhere in the universe, and how may life develop in the future.

Professor Stephen Hawking addressing a news conference to promote his book.

Charles Darwin in the garden of Downe House, his home in Kent

Charles Darwin

1809–1882

In just over four years on HMS Beagle, during her second survey voyage, Darwin visited many parts of the world. He was there to study geology but his role expanded to observation and collection of plants and wildlife. One of the ship's last major ports of call was the biggest town in the penal colony of New South Wales, where Darwin made this sad remark. In 1770, when Captain Cook had landed at Botany Bay a few miles to the south, there had been a thriving aboriginal population but now there were almost none to be seen, repeating a pattern he had observed elsewhere.

Wherever the European has trod, death seems to pursue the aboriginal. We may look to the wide extent of the Americas, Polynesia, the Cape of Good Hope and Australia, and we find the same result.

NATIONALITY:
British
WHEN:
1836
WHERE:
Port Jackson (Sydney), Australia

YOU SHOULD KNOW:
The captain of the *Beagle* on this voyage was Robert FitzRoy, who founded what would later become the British Meteorological Office.

Lin Baio 1908–1971

At the Ninth National Congress of the Chinese Communist Party Lin Baio, Mao's designated successor, gave a long speech about the progress so far in the Cultural Revolution – the movement to purge the party of Mao's opponents and instil 'correct' revolutionary attitudes in the people. His tirade bore little relation to reality and was instead a prolonged verbal attack on perceived anti-Mao elements. During the previous year Mao's Red Guards, a youth corps, had run riot over the country, killing and torturing 'intellectuals' and 'revisionists' to the extent that China was on the brink of civil war. Intellectuals – more or less anyone with anything but a basic education – were sent to the country to work on farms and millions of Mao's opponents were expelled from the party, which in effect amounted to internal exile. The Cultural Revolution came to an end in 1976, having been a complete disaster for the Chinese economy and therefore its people.

NATIONALITY:
Chinese
WHEN:
1969
WHERE:
Beijing, China
YOU SHOULD KNOW:
Lin Baio died in suspicious circumstances in a plane crash after being implicated in a coup against Mao.

‘ . . . Now we have found this form – it is the Great Proletarian Cultural Revolution. It is only by arousing the masses in their hundreds of millions to air their views freely, write big-character posters and hold great debates that the renegades, enemy agents and capitalist-roaders in power who have wormed their way into the Party can be exposed and their plots to restore capitalism smashed . . .

Long live the great victory of the Great Proletarian Cultural Revolution!
Long live the dictatorship of the proletariat!
Long live the Ninth National Congress of the Party!
Long live the great, glorious and correct Communist Party of China!
Long live great Marxism-Leninism-Mao Tsetung Thought!
Long live our great leader Chairman Mao! A long, long life to Chairman Mao! ’

Lin Baio, left, and Chou En Lai waving their little red books containing the wisdom of Chairman Mao.

NATIONALITY:
American
WHEN:
1928
WHERE:
Houston, Texas, USA
YOU SHOULD KNOW:
FDR contracted poliomyelitis in 1921,
which led to his withdrawal from
politics until 1924, when he made a
dramatic appearance on crutches to
nominate Smith.

*President Roosevelt delivering
one of his cosy 'fireside chats'.*

Franklin D. Roosevelt 1882–1945

*FDR first used the term 'Happy Warrior' to describe Alfred Smith in a
speech during the latter's campaign for the presidential nomination
in 1924 and did so again four years later. Smith did not win the
earlier nomination. His unpopular views on racism and
Prohibition played a part, as they did in the presidential election
when he lost to Republican Herbert Hoover in 1928. Roosevelt
himself would win the Democratic nomination and presidential
election four years later, as the Great Depression gathered pace.*

I COME for the third time to urge upon a convention of my party, the
nomination of the Governor of the State of New York. The faith which I
held I still hold. It has been justified in the achievement. The whole
country now has learned the measure of his greatness.

During another four years his every act has been under the
searchlight of friend and foe, and he has not been found wanting.
Slowly, surely, the proper understanding of this man has spread from
coast to coast, from North to South. Most noteworthy is this fact, that
the understanding of his stature has been spread by no paid
propaganda, by no effort on his part to do other than devote his time,
his head, and his heart to the duties of his high office and the welfare of
the State. His most uncompromising opponent will not deny that he has
achieved an unprecedented popularity among the people of this
country. He is well called 'the Pathfinder to the open road for all true
lovers of Humanity' . . .

What sort of President do we need today? A man, I take it, who has
four great characteristics, every one of them an essential to the office.
First of all, leadership articulate, virile willing to bear responsibility,
needing no official spokesman to interpret the oracle. Next, experience,
that does not guess, but knows from long practice the science of
governing, which is a very different thing from mere technical bureau
organizing. Then honesty, the honesty that hates hypocrisy and cannot
live with concealment and deceit.

Last, and, in this time, most vital, that rare ability to make popular
government function as it was intended to by the Fathers, to reverse
the present trend toward apathy and arouse in the citizenship an active
interest a willingness to reassume its share of responsibility for the
Nation's progress. So only can we have once more a government, not
just for the people, but by the people also.

History gives us confident assurance that a man who has displayed
these qualities as a great Governor of a State, has invariably carried
them with him to become a great President. Look back over our list of
Presidents since the war between the States, when our rapid growth
made our Nation's business an expert's task. Who stand out as our great
Presidents? New York gave to us Grover Cleveland teaching in Albany
that public office is a public trust; Theodore Roosevelt preaching the

doctrine of the square deal for all; Virginia and New Jersey gave to us that pioneer of fellowship between nations, our great leader, Woodrow Wilson . . .

His staunchest political adversaries concede the Governor's unique and unparalleled record of constructive achievement in the total reorganization of the machinery of government, in the business-like management of State finance, in the enactment of a legislative programme for the protection of men, women, and children engaged in industry, in the improvement of the public health, and in the attainment of the finest standard of public service in the interest of humanity. This he has accomplished by a personality of vibrant, many-sided appeal, which has swept along with it a legislature of a different political faith . . .

The second great need is experience. By this I refer not merely to length of time in office I mean that practical understanding which comes from the long and thoughtful study of, and daily dealings with, the basic principles involved in the science of taxation, of social welfare, of industrial legislation, of governmental budgets and administration, of penology, of legislative procedure and practice, of constitutional law.

In all these matters the Governor of New York has developed himself into an expert, recognized and consulted by men and women of all parties. In any conference of scholars on these subjects he takes his place naturally as a trained and efficient specialist. He also possesses that most unusual quality of selecting appointees, not only skilled in the theoretical side of their work, but able to give the highest administrative success to their task. The high standard of the appointees of the Governor, their integrity, their ability, has made strong appeal to the Citizens of his State, urban and rural, regardless of party. I add 'rural' advisedly, for each succeeding gubernatorial election has shown for him even greater proportional gains in the agricultural sections than in the large communities . . .

Now, as to the requisite of honesty. I do not mean an honesty that merely keeps a man out of jail, or an honesty that, while avoiding personal smirch, hides the corruption of others. I speak of that honesty that lets a man sleep well of nights, fearing no Senatorial investigation, that honesty that demands faithfulness to the public trust in every public servant, that honesty which takes immediate action to correct abuse.

The whole story of his constant and persistent efforts to insure the practice of the spirit as well as the letter of official and private probity in public places is so well understood by the voters of his State that more and more Republicans vote for him every time he is attacked. This is a topic which need not be enlarged upon. The voting public of the Nation is fully wise enough to compare the ethical standards of official Albany with those of official Washington.

And now, last of all, and where the Governor excels over all the political leaders of this day, comes the ability to interest the people in the mechanics of their governmental machinery, to take the engine apart and show the function of each wheel . . .

That hope lies in the personality of the new man at the wheel, and especially in his purpose to arouse the spirit of interest and the desire to participate.

The Governor of the State of New York stands out today as having that purpose, as having proved during these same eight years not only his desire, but his power to make the people as interested in their government as he is himself.

I have described, so far, qualities entirely of the mind, the mental and moral equipment without which no President can successfully meet the administrative and material problems of his office. It is possible with only these qualities for a man to be a reasonably efficient President, but there is one thing more needed to make him a great President. It is that quality of soul which makes a man loved by little , children, by dumb animals, that quality of soul which makes him a strong help to all those in sorrow or in trouble, that quality which makes him not merely admired, but loved by all the people the quality of sympathetic understanding of the human heart, of real interest in one's fellow men. Instinctively he senses the popular need because he himself has lived through the hardship, the labor, and the sacrifice which must be endured by every man of heroic mould who struggles up to eminence from obscurity and low estate. Between him and the people is that subtle bond which makes him their champion and makes them enthusiastically trust him with their loyalty and their love. Our two greatest Presidents of modern times possessed this quality to an unusual degree. It was, indeed, what above all made them great. It was Lincoln's human heart, and Woodrow Wilson's passionate desire to bring about the happiness of the whole world which will be the best remembered by the historians of a hundred years from now. It is what is so conspicuously lacking in our present administration, a lack which has been at the bottom of the growing dislike and even hatred of the other nations toward us. For without this love and understanding of his fellow men, no Chief Executive can win for his land that international friendship which is alone the sure foundation of lasting peace.

Because of his power of leadership, because of his unequaled knowledge of the science of government, because of his uncompromising honesty, because of his ability to bring the government home to the people, there is no doubt that our Governor will make an efficient President, but it is because he also possesses, to a superlative degree, this rare faculty of sympathetic understanding, I prophesy that he will also make a great President, and because of this I further prophesy that he will again place us among the nations of the world as a country which values its ideals as much as its material prosperity, a land that has no selfish designs on any weaker power, a land the ideal and inspiration of all those who dream a kinder, happier civilization in the days to come . . .

America needs not only an administrator, but a leader, a pathfinder, a blazer of the trail to the high road that will avoid the bottomless morass of crass materialism that has engulfed so many of the great civilizations of the past. It is the privilege of Democracy not only to offer such a man, but to offer him as the surest leader to victory. To stand upon the ramparts and die for our principles is heroic. To sally forth to battle and win for our principles is something more than heroic. We offer one who has the will to win who not only deserves success, but commands it. Victory is his habit the happy warrior Alfred E. Smith. *"*

Alphonse Capone 1899–1947

NATIONALITY:
American
WHEN:
1920s
WHERE:
Chicago, USA
YOU SHOULD KNOW:
Capone's bullet-proof Cadillac was impounded by the IRS and used as President Roosevelt's limousine.

After growing up in Brooklyn, Al Capone moved to Chicago in 1921 to exploit opportunities in the field of bootlegging. Within a few years he was in control of much of Chicago's underworld and had considerable influence with the city's government and law-enforcement agencies. He was behind the 1929 St Valentine's Day Massacre, in which seven members of Bugs Moran's North Side Gang, who had been eating into his profits, were mown down. Prohibition Bureau agent Elliot Ness gradually closed down his rackets and in 1931 he was indicted for tax evasion and breaches of the Volstead Act.

I make my money by supplying a public demand. If I break the law, my customers, who number hundreds of the best people in Chicago, are as guilty as I am. The only difference between us is that I sell and they buy. Everybody calls me a racketeer. I call myself a business man. When I sell liquor, it's bootlegging. When my patrons serve it on a silver try on Lake Shore Drive, it's hospitality. *"*

C. Northcote Parkinson

1909–1993

*In 1955, after a distinguished career and many years of
encounters with the bureaucratic British Foreign and Colonial
Office, Parkinson expounded upon a humorous theory of how, if
one has a given amount of time to complete a task, it will never
take less – particularly with regard to the Colonial Office, whose
staff numbers increased at the very time when it was running
out of colonies to administer. The highly satirical law can be
applied to almost any situation, such as income and expenditure
or computer-processing capacity, and any number of corollaries
have been penned by other people. Parkinson's Law of Trivia is
about how management can happily spend disproportionate
amounts of time on trivial issues that they think they
understand, while ignoring more important ones that they
don't. He used the widely differing examples of a nuclear power
plant, a bicycle shed and coffee purchasing policy to illustrate
his point in detail. This, then, is Parkinson's Law.*

NATIONALITY:
British
WHEN:
1955
WHERE:
The Economist magazine
YOU SHOULD KNOW:
Parkinson also wrote historical
naval novels under the pen name
Richard Delancey.

' Work expands so as to fill the time available for its completion. '

Thomas W. Lamont Jr 1870–1948

*Thomas Lamont was a banker and financial advisor to the US
Government who had served on the US delegation to the Treaty
of Versailles in 1919. In 1929 he was acting head of J. P. Morgan
and on October 22 he gave President Hoover this rather
over-optimistic view of the economy. Just two days later, on the
day that came to be known as Black Thursday, the Wall Street
Crash began. It was followed by even worse falls on the US Stock
Market on Black Monday and Tuesday the following week and a
continued slide for the following month. Ironically, J. P. Morgan
– which survived the Wall Street Crash – was an early casualty
of the 2008 financial crisis.*

NATIONALITY:
American
WHEN:
1929
WHERE:
New York City, USA
YOU SHOULD KNOW:
His former weekend home in
Pallisades, NY is now the site of the
Lamont-Doherty Earth Observatory.

' The future appears brilliant . . . We have the greatest and soundest
prosperity, and the best material prospects of any country in
the world. '

The signing of the Mayflower Compact

The Pilgrim Fathers

On November 11, 1620 the Mayflower *anchored off what is now Massachusetts. This was not the ship's original destination and several passengers – not members of the religious dissenters who formed the bulk of the colonists – declared themselves independent. This prompted the decision to form a government – in effect a social contract that all agreed to be bound by – for the new settlement, based on the knowledge that everyone would need to co-operate in order to survive, as earlier attempts had failed through factionalism. This declaration – The Mayflower Compact – allowed settlers to set up a government and remained in force in the area until 1691.*

NATIONALITY:
British
WHEN:
1620
WHERE:
On the *Mayflower*
YOU SHOULD KNOW:
Only the adult males among the settlers signed the compact.

IN THE name of God, Amen.
We whose names are underwritten, the loyal subjects of our dread sovereign Lord, King James, by the grace of God, of Great Britain, France and Ireland king, defender of the faith, etc., having undertaken, for the glory of God, and advancement of the Christian faith, and honor of our king and country, a voyage to plant the first colony in the

Northern parts of Virginia, do by these presents solemnly and mutually in the presence of God, and one of another, covenant and combine ourselves together into a civil body politic, for our better ordering and preservation and furtherance of the ends aforesaid; and by virtue hereof to enact, constitute, and frame such just and equal laws, ordinances, acts, constitutions, and offices, from time to time, as shall be thought most meet and convenient for the general good of the colony, unto which we promise all due submission and obedience.

In witness whereof we have hereunder subscribed our names at Cape Cod the 11 of November, in the year of the reign of our sovereign lord, King James, of England, France, and Ireland the eighteenth, and of Scotland the fifty-fourth. Anno Domine 1620.

John Carver	Richard Warren	Francis Eaton	Richard Briterige
William Bradford	John Howland	James Chilton	George Soule
Edward Winslow	Stephen Hopkins	John Crackston	Richard Clarke
William Brewster	Edward Tilly	John Billington	Richard Gardiner
Isaac Allerton	John Tilly	Moses Fletcher	John Allerton
Miles Standish	Francis Cook	John Goodman	Thomas English
John Alden	Thomas Rogers	Degory Priest	Edward Dotey
Samuel Fuller	Thomas Tinker	Thomas Williams	Edward Leister
Christopher Martin	John Ridgdale	Gilbert Winslow	
William Mullins	Edward Fuller	Edmund Margeson	
William White	John Turner	Peter Brown	

John Winthrop 1588–1649

John Winthrop, the second governor of the Massachusetts Bay Colony after John Endecott, who had sailed two years earlier, wrote this lay sermon while the Puritan settlers were on their way to the New World. It set out the aims and principles by which the religious colonists would live. It is a synthesis of puritan ethics, and sets out the belief that the colonists had a holy compact with God and a duty to live by his precepts. Also apparent is his strong belief in the importance of maintaining the existing social order with each in his or her place, as ordained by God.

NATIONALITY:
British
WHEN:
1630
WHERE:
On board the *Arbella*
YOU SHOULD KNOW:
This sermon is the source of Ronald Reagan's March 1978 statement 'We must consider that we shall be as a City upon a hill. The eyes of all people are upon us.'

A Model of Christian Charity
GOD ALMIGHTY in his most holy and wise providence, hath so disposed of the condition of mankind, as in all times some must be rich, some poor, some high and eminent in power and dignity; others mean and in submission.

The Reason hereof.
1 Reas. First to hold conformity with the rest of his world, being delighted to show forth the glory of his wisdom in the variety and difference of the creatures, and the glory of his power in ordering

all these differences for the preservation and good of the whole; and the glory of his greatness, that as it is the glory of princes to have many officers, so this great king will have many stewards, counting himself more honoured in dispensing his gifts to man by man, than if he did it by his own immediate hands.

2 Reas. Secondly that he might have the more occasion to manifest the work of his Spirit: first upon the wicked in moderating and restraining them: so that the riche and mighty should not eat up the poor nor the poor and despised rise up against and shake off their yoke. 2ly In the regenerate, in exercising his graces in them, as in the grate ones, their love, mercy, gentleness, temperance &c., in the poor and inferior sort, their faith, patience, obedience &c.

3 Reas. Thirdly, that every man might have need of others, and from hence they might be all knit more nearly together in the Bonds of brotherly affection. From hence it appears plainly that no man is made more honourable than another or more wealthy &c., out of any particular and singular respect to himself, but for the glory of his creator and the common good of the creature, man. Therefore God still reserves the property of these gifts to himself as Ezek. 16. 17. he there calls wealth, his gold and his silver, and Prov. 3. 9. he claims their service as his due, honor the Lord with thy riches &c. All men being thus (by divine providence) ranked into two sorts, riche and poor; under the first are comprehended all such as are able to live comfortably by their own means duly improved; and all others are poor according to the former distribution. There are two rules whereby we are to walk one towards another: Justice and Mercy. These are always distinguished in their act and in their object, yet may they both concur in the same subject in each respect; as sometimes there may be an occasion of showing mercy to a rich man in some sudden danger or distress, and also doing of mere justice to a poor man in regard of some particular contract &c. There is likewise a double Law by which we are regulated in our conversation towards another; in both the former respects, the law of nature and the law of grace, or the moral law or the law of the gospel, to omit the rule of justice as not properly belonging to this purpose otherwise than it may fall into consideration in some particular cases. By the first of these laws man as he was enabled so withal is commanded to love his neighbour as himself. Upon this ground stands all the precepts of the moral law, which concerns our dealings with men. To apply this to the works of mercy; this law requires two things. First that every man afford his help to another in every want or distress. Secondly, that he perform this out of the same affection which makes him careful of his own goods, according to that of our Savior, (Math.) Whatsoever ye would that men should do to you. This was practised by Abraham and Lot in entertaining the angels and the old man of Gibea. The law of Grace or of the Gospel hath some difference from the former; as in these respects, First the law of nature was given to man in the estate of innocency; this of the gospel in the estate of regeneracy. 2ly, the former propounds one man to another, as the same flesh and image of God; this as a brother in Christ also, and in the communion of the same Spirit, and so teacheth to put a difference between Christians and others. Do good to all, especially to the household of faith; upon this ground the Israelites were to putt a difference between the brethren of such as were strangers though not of the Canaanites.

3ly. The law of nature would give no rules for dealing with enemies, for all are to be considered as friends in the state of innocency, but the gospel commands love to an enemy. Proof. If thine Enemy hunger, feed him; Love your Enemies, do good to them that hate you. Math. 5. 44.

This law of the gospel propounds likewise a difference of seasons and occasions. There is a time when a Christian must sell all and give to the poor, as they did in the Apostles times. There is a time also when Christians (though they give not all yet) must give beyond their ability, as they of Macedonia, Cor. 2, 6. Likewise community of perils calls for extraordinary liberality, and so doth community in some special service for the church. Lastly, when there is no other means whereby our Christian brother may be relieved in his distress, we must help him beyond our ability rather than tempt God in putting him upon help by miraculous or extraordinary means . . .

1. First, This love among Christians is a real thing, not imaginary. 2ly. This love is as absolutely necessary to the being of the body of Christ, as the sinews and other ligaments of a natural body are to the being of that body. 3ly. This love is a divine, spiritual, nature; free, active, strong, courageous, permanent; undervaluing all things beneath its proper object and of all the graces, this makes us nearer to resemble the virtues of our heavenly father. 4thly It rests in the love and welfare of its beloved. For the full certain knowledge of those truths concerning the nature, use, and excellency of this grace, that which the holy ghost hath left recorded, 1 Cor. 13. may give full satisfaction, which is needful for every true member of this lovely body of the Lord Jesus, to work upon their hearts by prayer, meditation continual exercise at least of the special [influence] of this grace, till Christ be formed in them and they in him, all in each other, knit together by this bond of love.

It rests now to make some application of this discourse, by the present design, which gave the occasion of writing of it. Herein are 4 things to be propounded; first the persons, 2ly the work, 3ly the end, 4thly the means. 1. For the persons. We are a company professing ourselves fellow members of Christ, in which respect only though we were absent from each other many miles, and had our employments as far distant, yet we ought to account ourselves knit together by this bond of love, and, live in the exercise of it, if we would have comfort of our being in Christ. This was notorious in the practise of the Christians in former times; as is testified of the Waldenses, from the mouth of one of the adversaries Aeneas Sylvius 'mutuo ament pere antequam norunt', they use to love any of their own religion even before they were acquainted with them. 2nly for the work we have in hand. It is by a mutual consent, through a special overvaluing providence and a more than an ordinary approbation of the Churches of Christ, to seek out a place of cohabitation and Consortship under a due form of Government both civil and ecclesiastical. In such cases as this, the care of the public must oversway all private respects, by which, not only conscience, but mere civil policy, doth bind us. For it is a true rule that particular Estates cannot subsist in the ruin of the public. 3ly The end is to improve our lives to do more service to the Lord; the comfort and increase of the body of Christ, whereof we are members; that ourselves and posterity may be the better preserved from the common corruptions of this evil world, to serve the Lord and work out our Salvation under the power and purity of his holy ordinances. 4thly for the means whereby this must be effected. They are twofold, a conformity with the work and end we aim at. These we see are extraordinary, therefore we must not content ourselves with usual ordinary means. Whatsoever we did, or ought to have, done, when we lived in England, the same must we do, and more also, where we go. That which the most in their churches maintain as truth in profession only, we must bring into familiar and constant practise; as in this duty of love, we must love brotherly without dissimulation, we must love one another with a pure heart fervently. We must bear one another's burdens. We must not look only on our own things, but also on the things of our brethren. Neither must we think that the Lord will bear with such failings at our hands as he doth from those among whom we have lived; and that for these 3 Reasons; 1. In regard of the more near bond of marriage between him and us, wherein he hath taken us to be his, after a most strict and peculiar manner, which will make them the more jealous of our love and obedience. So he tells the people of Israel, you only have I known of all the families of the Earth, therefore will I punish you for your Transgressions. 2ly, because the Lord will be sanctified in them that come near him. We know that there were many that corrupted the service of the Lord; some setting up altars before his own; others offering both strange fire and strange sacrifices also; yet there came no fire from heaven, or other sudden judgement upon them, as did upon Nadab and Abihu, who yet we may think did not sin presumptuously. 3ly When God gives a special commission he looks to have it strictly observed in every article; When he gave Saul a commission to destroy Amaleck, he indented with him upon certain articles, and because he failed in one of the least, and that upon a faire pretence, it lost him the kingdom, which should have been his reward, if he had observed his commission. Thus stands the cause between God and us. We are entered into Covenant with Him for this work. We have taken out a commission. The Lord hath given us leave to draw our own articles. We have professed to enterprise these and those accounts, upon these and those ends. We have hereupon besought Him of favour and blessing. Now if the Lord shall please to hear us, and bring us in peace to the place we desire, then hath he ratified this covenant and sealed our Commission, and will expect a strict performance of the articles contained in it; but if we shall neglect the observation of these articles which are the ends we have propounded, and, dissembling with our God, shall fall to embrace this present world and prosecute our carnal intentions, seeking great things for ourselves and our posterity, the Lord will surely break out in wrath against us; be revenged of such a [sinful] people and make us know the price of the breach of such a covenant.

Now the only way to avoid this shipwreck, and to provide for our posterity, is to follow the counsel of Micah, to do justly, to love mercy, to walk humbly with our God. For this end, we must be knit together, in this work, as one man. We must entertain each other in brotherly affection. We must be willing to abridge ourselves of our superfluities, for the supply of other's necessities. We must uphold a familiar commerce together in all meekness, gentleness, patience and liberality. We must delight in each other; make other's conditions our own; rejoice together, mourn together, labour and suffer together, always having before our eyes our commission and community in the work, as members of the same body. So shall we keep the unity of the spirit in the bond of peace. The Lord will be our God, and delight to dwell among us, as his own people, and will command a blessing upon us in all our ways. So that we shall see much more of his wisdom, power, goodness and truth, than formerly we have been acquainted with. We shall find that the God of Israel is among us, when ten of us shall be able to resist a thousand of our enemies; when he shall make us a praise and glory that men shall say of succeeding plantations, 'the Lord make it likely that of New England'. For we must consider that we shall be as a citty upon a hill. The eyes of all people are upon us. So that if we shall deal falsely with our God in this work we have undertaken, and so cause him to withdraw his present help from us, we shall be made a story and a by-word through the world. We shall open the mouths of enemies to speak evil of the ways of God, and all professors for God's sake. We shall shame the faces of many of God's worthy servants, and cause their prayers to be turned into curses upon us till we be consumed out of the good land whither we are a going.

I shall shut up this discourse with that exhortation of Moses, that faithful servant of the Lord, in his last farewell to Israel, Deut. 30. Beloved there is now set before us life and good, Death and evil, in that we are commanded this day to love the Lord our God, and to love one another, to walk in his ways and to keep his Commandments and his Ordinance and his laws, and the articles of our Covenant with him, that we may live and be multiplied, and that the Lord our God may bless us in the land whither we go to possess it. But if our hearts shall turn away, so that we will not obey, but shall be seduced, and worship and serve other Gods, our pleasure and profits, and serve them; it is propounded unto us this day, we shall surely perish out of the good land whither we pass over this vast sea to possess it;

> Therefore let us choose life
> that we, and our seed
> may live, by obeying His
> voice and cleaving to Him,
> for He is our life and
> our prosperity.

H. L. Mencken 1880–1956

This idea, which made its way into print in the Chicago Tribune *of September 19, 1926, is typical of satirical journalist, editor, essayist and writer Henry Louis Mencken's intellectual elitism. He believed that few in any given group could distinguish themselves through their personal achievement, while the rest remained in mediocrity. As well as culturally, he felt that this applied politically, too, claiming that democracy – the worship of jackals by jackasses as he described it – inevitably meant that people would tend to vote for someone more and more like themselves and that eventually they would elect a 'downright moron' to the White House.*

NATIONALITY:
American
WHEN:
September 19, 1926
WHERE:
Baltimore, Maryland, USA
YOU SHOULD KNOW:
Mencken's favourite book was the *Adventures of Huckleberry Finn*, in which the majority of people are portrayed as gullible yokels.

' No one ever went broke underestimating the intelligence of the American people. '

Samuel Goldwyn 1879–1974

Movie mogul and producer Samuel Goldwyn (formerly Goldfish) is renowned for both his temper and his malapropisms, contradictory statements and other fluffs. He is reputed to have said the one below about fellow-producer Herman Mankiewicz, or possibly his younger brother Joseph. He was producer on some of the best-known films of his era including Wuthering Heights *(1939),* The Secret Life of Walter Mitty *(1947),* Hans Christian Anderson *(1952) and* Guys and Dolls *(1955) and set up two film studios: the Goldwyn Pictures Corporation and the Samuel Goldwyn Studio. His* The Best Years of Our Lives *won the 1946 Academy Award for Best Picture.*

NATIONALITY:
American
WHEN:
Before 1937
WHERE:
Los Angeles, California, USA
YOU SHOULD KNOW:
It's thought that Samuel Goldwyn didn't actually say many of the malapropisms that were subsequently attributed to him.

' A verbal contract isn't worth the paper it's written on. '

Francis Scott Key 1779–1843

Francis Scott Key observing the Union flag flying defiantly over Fort McHenry.

Towards the end of the War of 1812, during skirmishes before the Battle of Baltimore in September 1814, Key had been on one of the British ships arranging a prisoner exchange. Although he was theoretically allowed back to his own ship, the British would not let him leave as he had seen too much, so he and his men were forced to watch the British navy bombard Fort Henry. When the smoke cleared in the morning, he saw the American flag still flying above the fort and was inspired to write a poem, The Defence of Fort McHenry, *better known today as 'The Star-Spangled Banner'.*

NATIONALITY:
American
WHEN:
1814
WHERE:
Chesapeake Bay, USA
YOU SHOULD KNOW:
In 1916, President Wilson issued an Executive Order that made 'The Star-Spangled Banner' the US national anthem.

Oh, say can you see by the dawn's early light
What so proudly we hailed at the twilight's last gleaming?
Whose broad stripes and bright stars thru the perilous fight,
O'er the ramparts we watched were so gallantly streaming?
And the rocket's red glare, the bombs bursting in air,
Gave proof through the night that our flag was still there.
Oh, say does that star-spangled banner yet wave
O'er the land of the free and the home of the brave?

On the shore, dimly seen through the mists of the deep,
Where the foe's haughty host in dread silence reposes,
What is that which the breeze, o'er the towering steep,
As it fitfully blows, half conceals, half discloses?
Now it catches the gleam of the morning's first beam,
In full glory reflected now shines in the stream:

'Tis the star-spangled banner! Oh long may it wave
O'er the land of the free and the home of the brave!

And where is that band who so vauntingly swore
That the havoc of war and the battle's confusion,
A home and a country should leave us no more!
Their blood has washed out their foul footsteps' pollution.
No refuge could save the hireling and slave
From the terror of flight, or the gloom of the grave:
And the star-spangled banner in triumph doth wave
O'er the land of the free and the home of the brave!

Oh! thus be it ever, when freemen shall stand
Between their loved home and the war's desolation!
Blest with victory and peace, may the heav'n rescued land
Praise the Power that hath made and preserved us a nation.
Then conquer we must, when our cause it is just,
And this be our motto: 'In God is our trust'.
And the star-spangled banner in triumph shall wave
O'er the land of the free and the home of the brave!

Louis XIV 1638–1715

Louis XIV spent the first 18 years of his reign as the puppet of his Prime Minister, Jules Mazarin, but after the death of the latter in 1661 was eager to assume control. He supposedly made the pithy remark below in April 1663 when parliament was questioning some of his personal legislation on the grounds that it was not in the interests of the state – thus telling the delegates that they were now forbidden from using such justification. Known as the Sun King and the epitome of an absolute monarch he lived extravagantly, taxing his subjects heavily in order to fund his lavish lifestyle and raise money for the wars he waged.

L'état c'est moi. (I am the state.)

NATIONALITY:
French
WHEN:
1663
WHERE:
Paris, France
YOU SHOULD KNOW:
The Sun King reigned for 72 years,
three months and 18 days.

*Louis XIV with plans for his
great Palace of Versailles*

George W. Bush born 1946

NATIONALITY:
American
WHEN:
2001
WHERE:
Washington, DC, USA
YOU SHOULD KNOW:
Australia ratified the protocol in 2007, after a change in government. In February 2009 Kazakhstan ratified the protocol, leaving only six countries as non-signatories, whilst the USA signed but did not ratify the protocol.

On June 11, 2001 President Bush stood in the Rose Garden of the White House to explain his reasons for not ratifying the 1997 Kyoto Protocol on Climate Change. First, he felt that it would impact unfairly on US industries and therefore the US economy, particularly in relation to China – which had no limits imposed. Secondly, a recent report he had seen raised questions about the validity of the science that linked the increased amounts of man-made gases in the atmosphere with climate change. The protocol did not come into force until 2005, after the Russian Government ratified it, taking the number of ratifying countries above the required limit.

Good morning. I've just met with senior members of my administration who are working to develop an effective and science-based approach to addressing the important issues of global climate change . . .

The issue of climate change respects no border. Its effects cannot be reined in by an army nor advanced by any ideology. Climate change, with its potential to impact every corner of the world, is an issue that must be addressed by the world.

The Kyoto Protocol was fatally flawed in fundamental ways. But the process used to bring nations together to discuss our joint response to climate change is an important one.

That is why I am today committing the United States of America to work within the United Nations framework and elsewhere to develop with our friends and allies and nations throughout the world an effective and science-based response to the issue of global warming . . .

First, we know the surface temperature of the earth is warming. It has risen by .6 degrees Celsius over the past 100 years. There was a warming trend from the 1890s to the 1940s. Cooling from the 1940s to the 1970s. And then sharply rising temperatures from the 1970s to today.

There is a natural greenhouse effect that contributes to warming. Greenhouse gases trap heat, and thus warm the earth because they prevent a significant proportion of infrared radiation from escaping into space. Concentration of greenhouse gases, especially CO_2, have increased substantially since the beginning of the industrial revolution. And the National Academy of Sciences indicate that the increase is due in large part to human activity.

Yet, the Academy's report tells us that we do not know how much effect natural fluctuations in climate may have had on warming. We do not know how much our climate could, or will change in the future. We do not know how fast change will occur, or even how some of our actions could impact it . . .

Our country, the United States, is the world's largest emitter of manmade greenhouse gases. We account for almost 20 per cent of the world's manmade greenhouse emissions. We also account for about one-quarter of the world's economic output. We recognize the responsibility to reduce our emissions. We also recognize the other part of the story – that the rest of the world emits 80 per cent of all greenhouse gases. And many of those emissions come from developing countries.

This is a challenge that requires a 100 per cent effort; ours, and the rest of the world's. The world's second-largest emitter of greenhouse gases is China. Yet, China was entirely exempted from the requirements of the Kyoto Protocol.

India and Germany are among the top emitters. Yet, India was also exempt from Kyoto. These and other developing countries that are experiencing rapid growth face challenges in reducing their emissions without harming their economies. We want to work cooperatively with these countries in their efforts to reduce greenhouse emissions and maintain economic growth.

Kyoto also failed to address two major pollutants that have an impact on warming: black soot and tropospheric ozone. Both are proven health hazards. Reducing both would not only address climate change, but also dramatically improve people's health.

Kyoto is, in many ways, unrealistic. Many countries cannot meet their Kyoto targets. The targets themselves were arbitrary and not based upon science. For America, complying with those mandates would have a negative economic impact, with layoffs of workers and price increases for consumers. And when you evaluate all these flaws, most reasonable people will understand that it's not sound public policy . . .

The UN Framework Convention on Climate Change commences to stabilizing concentrations at a level that will prevent dangerous human interference with the climate; but no one knows what that level is. The United States has spent $18 billion on climate research since 1990 – three times as much as any other country, and more than Japan and all 15 nations of the EU combined.

Today, I make our investment in science even greater. My administration will establish the US Climate Change Research Initiative to study areas of uncertainty and identify priority areas where investments can make a difference.

I'm directing my Secretary of Commerce, working with other agencies, to set priorities for additional investments in climate change research, review such investments, and to improve coordination amongst federal agencies. We will fully fund high-priority areas for climate change science over the next five years. We'll also provide resources to build climate observation systems in developing countries and encourage other developed nations to match our American commitment . . .

So we're creating the National Climate Change Technology Initiative to strengthen research at universities and national labs, to enhance partnerships in applied research, to develop improved technology for measuring and monitoring gross and net greenhouse gas emissions, and to fund demonstration projects for cutting-edge technologies, such as bioreactors and fuel cells.

Even with the best science, even with the best technology, we all know the United States cannot solve this global problem alone. We're building partnerships within the Western Hemisphere and with other like-minded countries. Last week, Secretary Powell signed a new CONCAUSA Declaration with the countries of Central America, calling for cooperative efforts on science research, monitoring and measuring of emissions, technology development, and investment in forest conservation.

We will work with the Inter-American Institute for Global Change Research and other institutions to better understand regional impacts of climate change. We will establish a partnership to monitor and mitigate emissions. And at home, I call on Congress to work with my administration on the initiatives to enhance conservation and energy efficiency outlined in my energy plan, to implement the increased use of renewables, natural gas and hydropower that are outlined in the plan, and to increase the generation of safe and clean nuclear power . . .

Our approach must be flexible to adjust to new information and take advantage of new technology. We must always act to ensure continued economic growth and prosperity for our citizens and for citizens throughout the world. We should pursue market-based incentives and spur technological innovation.

And, finally, our approach must be based on global participation, including that of developing countries whose net greenhouse gas emissions now exceed those in the developed countries.

Our administration will be creative. We're committed to protecting our environment and improving our economy, to acting at home and working in concert with the world. This is an administration that will make commitments we can keep, and keep the commitments that we make.

I look forward to continued discussions with our friends and allies about this important issue. 🟥

BBC Radio

The news that the Princess of Wales had been badly hurt in a car accident in Paris had broken on the British media at about 1.15 am on Sunday August 31, 1997. Rumours started flying round that ranged from Diana had been seen walking away from the accident to her dying at the scene. The confirmation of her death was released first on BBC radio at 5.20 am and on the television just before 6 am. The mass display of public grief took the British establishment by surprise.

NATIONALITY:
British
WHEN:
1997
WHERE:
London, England
YOU SHOULD KNOW:
Princess Diana is buried on an island at her brother's estate.

This is BBC Radio. Buckingham Palace has confirmed the death of Diana, Princess of Wales. In a statement it said that the Queen and Prince Philip were deeply shocked and distressed by this terrible news. Other members of the Royal Family are being informed of the Princess's death. 🟥

The military blocked off an area of 30 miles around Chernobyl.

Moscow Radio

More than two days after Reactor Number Four at the Chernobyl nuclear power plant exploded, and after there were reports in Sweden of increased atmospheric radiation levels, the terse announcement below was broadcast. There was no mention of an explosion and no indication of the scale of the disaster. About five per cent of the radioactive material in the reactor escaped, amounting to about 400 times the amount of radiation released by the atomic bombing of Hiroshima. People in the local town of Pripyat were evacuated, some of them into the fallout zone, and winds in the upper atmosphere spread the radiation cloud with nuclear particles reaching as far as Wales. The reactor is now encased in a concrete structure commonly known as the sarcophagus.

‘ An accident has occurred at Chernobyl nuclear power station. One of the atomic reactors has been damaged. Measures are being taken to eliminate the consequences of the accident. Aid is being given to the victims. A government commission has been set up. ’

NATIONALITY:
Russian
WHEN:
1986
WHERE:
Moscow, USSR
YOU SHOULD KNOW:
Two people died in the initial steam explosion, but the total death toll from radiation is unknown and still rising.

525

George Marshall 1880–1959

NATIONALITY:
American
WHEN:
1947
WHERE:
Harvard, Connecticut, USA
YOU SHOULD KNOW:
Many countires never made their repayments. Germany finished paying back its debt in 1971.

In the wake of World War II the economies of western European countries were devastated. Industries collapsed and people starved in large numbers. In June 1947 US Secretary of State George Marshall announced the European Recovery Program (better known as the Marshall Plan), which would provide funds to both ex-allies and former enemies. The aims were not just humanitarian – the USA needed European markets and feared that without aid Western European countries might choose to rebuild their economies on socialist or communist lines. Over the next four years more than $13,000,000,000 of assistance was given, 70 per cent of which was spent on US goods.

‘ I need not tell you gentlemen that the world situation is very serious. That must be apparent to all intelligent people. I think one difficulty is that the problem is one of such enormous complexity that the very mass of facts presented to the public by press and radio make it exceedingly difficult for the man in the street to reach a clear appraisement of the situation. Furthermore, the people of this country are distant from the troubled areas of the earth and it is hard for them to comprehend the plight and consequent reaction of the long-suffering peoples, and the effect of those reactions on their governments in connection with our efforts to promote peace in the world. In considering the requirements for the rehabilitation of Europe the physical loss of life, the visible destruction of cities, factories, mines, and railroads was correctly estimated, but it has become obvious during recent months that this visible destruction was probably less serious than the dislocation of the entire fabric of European economy. For the past 10 years conditions have been highly abnormal. The feverish maintenance of the war effort engulfed all aspects of national economics. Machinery has fallen into disrepair or is entirely obsolete. Under the arbitrary and destructive Nazi rule, virtually every possible enterprise was geared into the German war machine. Long-standing commercial ties, private institutions, banks, insurance companies and shipping companies disappeared, through the loss of capital, absorption through nationalization or by simple destruction. In many countries, confidence in the local currency has been severely shaken. The breakdown of the business structure of Europe during the war was complete. Recovery has been seriously retarded by the fact that 2 years after the close of hostilities a peace settlement with Germany and Austria has not been agreed upon. But even given a more prompt solution of these difficult problems, the rehabilitation of the economic structure of Europe quite evidently will require a much longer time and greater effort than had been foreseen.

There is a phase of this matter which is both interesting and serious. The farmer has always produced the foodstuffs to exchange with the city dweller for the other necessities of life. This division of labor is the basis of modern civilization. At the present time it is threatened with breakdown. The town and city industries are not producing adequate goods to exchange with the food-producing farmer. Raw materials and fuel are in short supply. Machinery is lacking or worn out. The farmer or the peasant cannot find the goods for sale which he desires to purchase. So the sale of his farm produce for money which he cannot use seems to him unprofitable transaction. He, therefore, has withdrawn many fields from crop cultivation and is using them for grazing. He feeds more grain to stock and finds for himself and his family an ample supply of food, however short he may be on clothing and the other ordinary gadgets of civilization. Meanwhile people in the cities are short of food and fuel. So the governments are forced to use their foreign money and credits to procure these necessities abroad. This process exhausts funds which are urgently needed for reconstruction. Thus a very serious situation is rapidly developing which bodes no good for the world. The modern system of the division of labor upon which the exchange of products is based is in danger of breaking down.

The truth of the matter is that Europe's requirements for the next 3 or 4 years of foreign food and other essential products – principally from America — are so much greater than her present ability to pay that she must have substantial additional help, or face economic, social, and political deterioration of a very grave character. The remedy lies in breaking the vicious circle and restoring the confidence of the European people in the economic future of their own countries and of Europe as a whole. The manufacturer and the farmer throughout wide areas must be able and willing to exchange their products for currencies the continuing value of which is not open to question.

Aside from the demoralizing effect on the world at large and the possibilities of disturbances arising as a result of the desperation of the people concerned, the consequences to the economy of the United States should be apparent to all. It is logical that the United States should do whatever it is able to do to assist in the return of normal economic health in the world, without which there can be no political stability and no assured peace. Our policy is directed not against any country or doctrine but against hunger, poverty, desperation, and chaos. Its purpose should be the revival of working economy in the world so as to permit the emergence of political and social conditions in which free institutions can exist. Such assistance, I am convinced, must not be on a piecemeal basis as various crises develop. Any assistance that this Government may render in the future should provide a cure rather than a mere palliative. Any government that is willing to assist in the task of recovery will find full cooperation, I am sure, on the part of the United States Government. Any government which maneuvers to block the recovery of other countries cannot expect help from us. Furthermore, governments, political parties, or groups which seek to perpetuate human misery in order to profit therefrom politically or otherwise will encounter the opposition of the United States. It is already evident that, before the United States Government can proceed much further in its efforts to alleviate the situation and help start the European world on its way to recovery, there must be some agreement among the countries of Europe as to the requirements of the situation and the part those countries themselves will take in order to give proper effect to whatever action might be undertaken by this Government. It would be neither fitting nor efficacious for this Government to undertake to draw up unilaterally a program designed to place Europe on its feet economically. This is the business of the Europeans. The initiative, I think, must come from Europe. The role of this country should consist of friendly aid in the drafting of a European program so far as it may be practical for us to do so. The program should be a joint one, agreed to by a number, if not all European nations. An essential part of any successful action on the part of the United States is an understanding on the part of the people of America of the character of the problem and the remedies to be applied. Political passion and prejudice should have no part. With foresight, and a willingness on the part of our people to face up to the vast responsibilities which history has clearly placed upon our country, the difficulties I have outlined can and will be overcome.

US Government

NATIONALITY:
American
WHEN:
1919
WHERE:
Washington, DC, USA
YOU SHOULD KNOW:
After he signed the order legalizing its consumption, President Roosevelt remarked, 'I think this would be a good time for a beer'.

During the nineteenth and early twentieth centuries, the Temperance movement had grown in strength and by the time the sixty-fifth Congress convened in 1917, 'dries' outnumbered 'wets' in both houses. The Eighteenth Amendment to the US Constitution was introduced that December, ratified in January 1919 and came into force on January 1, 1920. The effect was dramatic as the production and consumption of alcohol was inevitably driven underground, leading to a meteoric rise in organized crime, especially the Mafia. In 1923, President Roosevelt relaxed the laws for consumption of beer and the Twenty-first Amendment formally repealed the Eighteenth in 1933.

'Amendment 18

1. After one year from the ratification of this article the manufacture, sale, or transportation of intoxicating liquors within, the importation thereof into, or the exportation thereof from the United States and all territory subject to the jurisdiction thereof for beverage purposes is hereby prohibited.

2. The Congress and the several States shall have concurrent power to enforce this article by appropriate legislation.

3. This article shall be inoperative unless it shall have been ratified as an amendment to the Constitution by the legislatures of the several States, as provided in the Constitution, within seven years from the date of the submission hereof to the States by the Congress.

Amendment 21

1. The eighteenth article of amendment to the Constitution of the United States is hereby repealed.

2. The transportation or importation into any State, Territory, or possession of the United States for delivery or use therein of intoxicating liquors, in violation of the laws thereof, is hereby prohibited.

3. The article shall be inoperative unless it shall have been ratified as an amendment to the Constitution by conventions in the several States, as provided in the Constitution, within seven years from the date of the submission hereof to the States by the Congress. '

Nelson Algren 1909–1981

American novelist and short-story writer Nelson Algren wrote chiefly about the seedier side of life – corrupt politicians, poverty, drug addicts, gambling, prize fighters, prostitution and alcoholism that he had observed in the back streets of Chicago, although he also set novels in other cities. One of the places in which Algren's 'Three Rules of Life' appear is Walk on the Wild Side *in which the main character tangles with a speakeasy owner called Doc and has a turbulent relationship with a prostitute he tries to rescue. The list has been added to over the years by many people, including such advice as 'Never eat at a restaurant with a dog asleep outside the front'.*

NATIONALITY:
American
WHEN:
1956 is the first occurrence
WHERE:
Various places
YOU SHOULD KNOW:
Lou Reed's song 'A Walk on the Wild Side' was named after Algren's 1956 novel of the same name.

> Never play cards with a man called Doc. Never eat at a place called Mom's. Never go to bed with a woman whose troubles are greater than yours.

David Irving born 1938

One of the most high-profile Holocaust deniers, David Irving's views that the Holocaust is a myth and simply Jewish propaganda have earned him accusations of antisemitism, racism and sympathy with the Third Reich. In 1996, in a libel trial he brought against American historian Deborah Lipstadt and Penguin Books, the judge upheld all of these allegations, adding that Irving 'for his own ideological reasons persistently and deliberately misrepresented and manipulated historical evidence'. As a result of his Milton, Ontario, speech he was barred from re-entry to Canada. He has also at various times been banned from entering New Zealand, Australia, Austria and Italy and fined on several occasions by German courts.

> I'm forming an association especially dedicated to all those liars, the ones who are trying to kid people that they were in these concentration camps. It's called the 'Auschwitz Survivors, Survivors of the Holocaust, and Other Liars' – 'ASSHOLES' . . . these people deserve all our contempt.

NATIONALITY:
British
WHEN:
1991
WHERE:
Milton, Ontario, Canada

YOU SHOULD KNOW:
David Irving served ten months in prison in Austria in 2006 for glorifying and identifying with the German Nazi Party.

Irving in an Austrian courtroom.

Pacific Tsunami Warning Center

WHEN:
2004
WHERE:
Hawaii, USA
YOU SHOULD KNOW:
The magnitude of the earthquake
was later revised to 9.3.

Eight minutes after almost 1,000 miles of the ocean floor surface sprang up by about 50 feet, the seismic waves reached the Pacific Tsunami Warning Center in Hawaii. Seven minutes later, staff issued the advisory below by telephone, text and other methods to the effect that there was little risk of a tsunami in the Pacific. Another bulletin issued 50 minutes later mentioned the possibility of a tsunami near the earthquake's epicentre. A minute later, the first waves struck Northern Sumatra and the Nicobar Islands. The tsunami killed more than 225,000 people, in countries as far away as Somalia. As a result of the tsunami – and the deaths that resulted from the lack of any method of detection or warning of tsunamis in the region – a network of detectors is now being deployed.

‘ TSUNAMI BULLETIN NUMBER 001
PACIFIC TSUNAMI WARNING
CENTER/NOAA/NWS
ISSUED AT 0114Z 26 DEC 2004

THIS BULLETIN IS FOR ALL AREAS OF THE
PACIFIC BASIN EXCEPT ALASKA – BRITISH
COLUMBIA – WASHINGTON – OREGON –
CALIFORNIA.

. . . TSUNAMI INFORMATION BULLETIN . . .

THIS MESSAGE IS FOR INFORMATION ONLY.
THERE IS NO TSUNAMI WARNING OR
WATCH IN EFFECT.

AN EARTHQUAKE HAS OCCURRED WITH
THESE PRELIMINARY PARAMETERS

ORIGIN TIME – 0059Z 26 DEC 2004

COORDINATES – 3.4 NORTH 95.7 EAST
LOCATION – OFF W COAST OF NORTHERN
SUMATERA
MAGNITUDE – 8.0

EVALUATION

THIS EARTHQUAKE IS LOCATED OUTSIDE
THE PACIFIC. NO DESTRUCTIVE TSUNAMI
THREAT EXISTS BASED ON HISTORICAL
EARTHQUAKE AND TSUNAMI DATA.

THIS WILL BE THE ONLY BULLETIN ISSUED
FOR THIS EVENT UNLESS ADDITIONAL
INFORMATION BECOMES AVAILABLE.

THE WEST COAST/ALASKA TSUNAMI
WARNING CENTER WILL ISSUE BULLETINS
FOR ALASKA – BRITISH COLUMBIA –
WASHINGTON – OREGON – CALIFORNIA. ’

Andy Warhol 1928–1987

A successful commercial artist in the 1950s, Andy Warhol shot to fame in the 1960s as a leader in the field of Pop Art, with works featuring such items as Campbell's soup cans and Brillo pads, plus the series of prints featuring repeated images of Marylin Monroe in an assortment of lurid colours. From 1965 he collaborated with singer-songwriter Lou Reed and managed the Velvet Underground. He surrounded himself with an entourage of bohemian artists and personalities who would appear in his Factory films and used to accompany him in large numbers to the best-known clubs in New York, one of which – Studio 54 – he later described as being the place where his famous prediction actually came true.

NATIONALITY:
American
WHEN:
Several occasions
WHERE:
Various places
YOU SHOULD KNOW:
Warhol was shot and seriously wounded by a member of the 'Factory scene' in 1968.

'In the future, everybody will be world famous for 15 minutes.'

Clarence Darrow 1857–1938

In the trial State v Scopes, Clarence Darrow was the head of the team defending teacher John Scopes against the charge that he had taught evolution in school contrary to the Butler Act, a recently introduced piece of restrictive legislation that prohibited doing so in schools within Tennessee that had any state funding. Arguments produced by the defence included that the law was unconstitutional and that the State was forcing teachers to break the law as it provided the book from which Scopes taught. He uttered the line below while cross-examining the chief prosecution laywer, William Jennings Bryan, on whether he believed that aspects of Genesis – such as if Adam and Eve and their sons were the only people on the Earth, where did Cain's wife come from – were literal truth.

NATIONALITY:
American
WHEN:
1925
WHERE:
Nashville, Tennessee, USA
YOU SHOULD KNOW:
Scopes was found guilty but was acquitted on a legal technicality on appeal.

'We are marching backwards to the glorious age of the sixteenth century when bigots lighted faggots to burn men who dared to bring any intelligence and enlightenment and culture to the human mind.'

Liberace taking a bubble bath, surrounded by typical glitz!

Liberace 1919–1987

The flamboyant – and extremely well-paid – performer made this famous statement on many occasions but is thought to have done so first to a group of New York critics in June 1954. He certainly said it in 1959, when he won libel damages from British tabloid newspaper the Daily Mirror, *in which a journalist had described him as being 'fruit-flavoured', an implication that could then have ruined his career. Many critics loathed him, decrying his ability, style and his reworking of classical pieces to suit himself. His fans did not agree. By the early 1950s his fan clubs counted more than one million members, and he made $50,000 a week for his Las Vegas concerts alone, in addition to which he had revenue from his television and promotional work and record sales.*

NATIONALITY:
American
WHEN:
1954
WHERE:
New York City, USA
YOU SHOULD KNOW:
Many of Liberace's lavish costumes, jewellery and pianos are on display at the Liberace Museum in Las Vegas, Nevada.

What you said hurt me very much. I cried all the way to the bank.

Ronald Reagan 1911–2004

Just 73 seconds after lift-off into mission STS-51-L, the Space Shuttle Challenger *disintegrated in a ball of flame, resulting in the loss of the seven astronauts – including high school teacher Christa McAuliffe. That evening, instead of the State of the Union address he had been scheduled to give, the President paid tribute to them. After fragments of the shuttle and the external boosters and fuel tank were collected, a piece-by-piece investigation concluded that an O-ring seal in one of the boosters had failed, which led to a fireball and the disintegration of the spacecraft. The crew compartment was found in the Gulf of Mexico.*

NATIONALITY:
American
WHEN:
1986
WHERE:
Washington, DC, USA
YOU SHOULD KNOW:
The last line of President Reagan's speech comes from a sonnet written by John Gillespie Magee, a Canadian Spitfire pilot, during World War II.

'Ladies and gentlemen, I'd planned to speak to you tonight to report on the state of the Union, but the events of earlier today have led me to change those plans. Today is a day for mourning and remembering. Nancy and I are pained to the core by the tragedy of the shuttle *Challenger*. We know we share this pain with all of the people of our country. This is truly a national loss.

Nineteen years ago, almost to the day, we lost three astronauts in a terrible accident on the ground. But we've never lost an astronaut in flight; we've never had a tragedy like this. And perhaps we've forgotten the courage it took for the crew of the shuttle. But they, the Challenger Seven, were aware of the dangers, but overcame them and did their jobs brilliantly. We mourn seven heroes: Michael Smith, Dick Scobee, Judith Resnik, Ronald McNair, Ellison Onizuka, Gregory Jarvis, and Christa McAuliffe. We mourn their loss as a nation together . . .

I've always had great faith in and respect for our space program, and what happened today does nothing to diminish it. We don't hide our space program. We don't keep secrets and cover things up. We do it all up front and in public. That's the way freedom is, and we wouldn't change it for a minute. We'll continue our quest in space. There will be more shuttle flights and more shuttle crews and, yes, more volunteers, more civilians, more teachers in space. Nothing ends here; our hopes and our journeys continue. I want to add that I wish I could talk to every man and woman who works for NASA or who worked on this mission and tell them: 'Your dedication and professionalism have moved and impressed us for decades. And we know of your anguish. We share it.' . . .

The crew of the space shuttle Challenger honored us by the manner in which they lived their lives. We will never forget them, nor the last time we saw them, this morning, as they prepared for their journey and waved goodbye and 'slipped the surly bonds of earth' to 'touch the face of God'. '

Ludwig Mies van der Rohe
1886–1969

NATIONALITY:
German
WHEN:
Several occasions
WHERE:
Various places
YOU SHOULD KNOW:
He became a naturalized American in 1944.

Visionary architect and Bauhaus founder Mies van der Rohe was responsible for some of the most iconic buildings of the mid-twentieth century, including the IBM Plaza, 860–880 Lake Shore Drive and S. R. Crown Hall in Chicago. He also designed Farnsworth House outside Chicago and the Seagram Building in New York. His architectural style is characterized by simple, strong lines and minimal framework. The simplicity is to some extent deceptive. Materials were all chosen carefully and everything was designed down to the finest detail because any deviation from the design would be far more obvious than on a more complex structure.

‘ The dear God is in the detail. ’

Phineas T. Barnum 1810–1891

NATIONALITY:
American
WHEN:
From 1872
WHERE:
Many locations
YOU SHOULD KNOW:
The slogan was also used as the title of Cecil B. De Mille's 1952 Oscar-winning film about Barnum and Bailey's circus.

Showman, entrepreneur, museum owner and theatre impressario Phineas T. Barnum set up 'P. T. Barnum's Grand Traveling Museum, Menagerie, Caravan & Hippodrome' in 1871. This was a circus, menagerie and freak show. By the following year Barnum had coined the slogan below. At its greatest extent it covered five acres and could seat 10,000 people at a time. In 1881, it was merged with James Bailey's circus. In order to reach as wide an audience as possible the circus travelled by rail in its own train. What is less well known about Barnum is his political activity – he was a strong pro-Unionist and against slavery – or his philanthropy. He gave very large sums of money to Tufts University, among other institutions.

‘ The Greatest Show on Earth! ’

Anonymous

This remark has been attributed to various people including political activist Jerry Rubin, LSD guru Timothy Leary and one of the members of Jefferson Airplane, the ultimate flower-power band. The first time reference to it appears in print is 1987. For a minority of young people, the late 1960s was a period of hippy freedom, music festivals, drug-fuelled free love and a degree of contempt for the values of the majority. In the same vein of exclusiveness as the earlier 'Be there or be square', this implies that if you weren't stoned into forgetfulness you weren't 'there' – an assertion that others fighting in Vietnam or participating in anti-Vietnam War marches, protesting on the streets of Paris or participating in the Prague Spring might contest.

WHEN:
Before 1987
WHERE:
All over the place
YOU SHOULD KNOW:
After his years as a left-wing political activist, Jerry Rubin became a successful businessman and entrepreneur.

'If you can remember the Sixties you weren't really there.'

Preparing a bus for the Acid Test Graduation celebration, San Francisco.

Tony Blair born 1953

NATIONALITY:
British
WHEN:
1997
WHERE:
Sedgefield, England
YOU SHOULD KNOW:
The People's Princess was the title of a book about Princess Mary, Duchess of Teck, one of the Prince of Wales' great grandmothers.

On the morning of the announcement of the death of the Princess of Wales, Prime Minister Tony Blair addressed the media at his Sedgefield constituency. The description of Diana as the People's Princess had been suggested to him by his press chief, Alistair Campbell. Blair gauged the mood of the media and Diana's fans more accurately than the Royal Family did, leading to disagreement between the two about how the latter should be seen to be mourning more openly, in line with 'the people's expectations', whilst the Downing Street spin doctors tried to dictate to the Royal Family what role Princes William and Harry should play in their mother's funeral.

‘ They liked her, they loved her, they regarded her as one of the people . . . She was the People's Princess, and that is how she will stay . . . ’

Flowers left outside Kensington Palace, Princess Diana's home, after her untimely death.

Mervyn Griffith-Jones 1909–1979

In 1960 the British publisher Penguin published Lady Chatterley's Lover, *the last novel by D. H. Lawrence. It was written in 1928 but had been banned from publication because it contravened obscenity laws. A change in the law in 1959 meant that such a work could be published if it was considered to be of literary merit. The jury's verdict in this test case was that the publishers were not guilty, resulting in a general easing of restrictions on the sort of material that could be published in the UK. Prosecution barrister Mervyn Griffith-Jones revealed a startling lack of awareness that the world had moved on since the Victorian era when he challenged the jury with the infamous question below.*

NATIONALITY:
British
WHEN:
1960
WHERE:
London, England
YOU SHOULD KNOW:
The ban on the novel had been overturned in the USA the previous year.

' Is it a book that you would even wish your wife or your servants to read? '

Timothy Leary 1920–1996

Leary was a psychologist who advocated research into the effects of psychedelic drugs. After hearing from a colleague about the mind-altering effects of psilocybin mushrooms in 1957, he travelled to Mexico in 1960 to try them for himself. He and colleagues experimented over the next few years with other psychedelic drugs, such as LSD and mescalin, both before and after his dismissal from Harvard, and he lectured widely on what he saw as their benefits. After two spells in prison, he discontinued this – although he carried on using drugs for personal purposes – and instead advocated the need for colonization of space in order to preserve the human race.

NATIONALITY:
American
WHEN:
1966
WHERE:
New York City, USA
YOU SHOULD KNOW:
Leary coined the shorter version – 'Turn on, tune in, drop out' – at a hippy event in Golden Gate Park, San Francisco in 1967.

' Like every great religion of the past we seek to find the divinity within and to express this revelation in a life of glorification and the worship of God. These ancient goals we define in the metaphor of the present – turn on, tune in, drop out.

I mean drop out of high school, drop out of college, drop out of graduate school . . . '

Charles Dederich 1913–1997

NATIONALITY:
American
WHEN:
After 1958
WHERE:
Santa Monica, California, USA
YOU SHOULD KNOW:
A German branch of Syanon is still in existence.

Charles Dederich, after many years as an alcoholic, kicked the habit with the help of Alcoholics Anonymous and went on to create Syanon. This was apparently a self-help rehab clinic but was in effect an organization in which brain-washing techniques – called 'the game' – were used. It grew into a closed alternative community in which recovering addicts – some sent by the authorities – were under the complete control of Dederich. Syanon eventually became a pseudo-religious institution with its own armed force and an aggressive attitude towards anyone who tried to leave. Dederich's eventual downfall came when he arranged for members to put a de-rattled rattlesnake in the mailbox of a lawyer who was acting against the group.

❛ Today is the first day of the rest of your life. ❜

William Pitkin 1878–1953

NATIONALITY:
American
WHEN:
Before 1932
WHERE:
New York City, USA
YOU SHOULD KNOW:
A film comedy of the same name was released in 1935, as was a hit record by Sophie Tucker in 1937.

In a series of lectures, Professor Pitkin explored the social and personal implications of the increasing life expectancy of American citizens. While some experts saw this as a possible social problem, Pitkin was decidedly upbeat and positive about it and its effects on the quality of life for individuals whose children had moved away to start their own lives and so had time for themselves and increased choices for leisure. He expanded on the lectures in his 1932 book, Life Begins at Forty, *and the idea rapidly caught on in popular culture.*

❛ Every day brings forth some new thing that adds to the joy of life after forty. Work becomes easy and brief. Play grows richer and longer. Leisure lengthens. Life's afternoon is brighter, warmer, fuller of song; and long before shadows stretch, every fruit grows rife . . . Life begins at forty. ❜

Howard Carter 1874–1939

Howard Carter had been excavating archaeological sites in Egypt for almost 30 years when he made his greatest discovery – the virtually intact burial chamber of the eighteenth-dynasty boy-king Tutankhamun, whose existence he had heard of a few years earlier. According to his diary, when a hole had been made in the door to the outer chamber, he pushed a candle through it and as his eyes adjusted to the flickering light he saw 'strange animals, statues and gold – everywhere the glint of gold'. The expedition's financier, Lord Carnarvon – who would be dead within five months, leading to rumours of Pharaoh's Curse – asked him whether he could see anything, and he replied as follows.

NATIONALITY:
British
WHEN:
1922
WHERE:
The Valley of the Kings, Egypt
YOU SHOULD KNOW:
At least two attempts at robbing the tomb had occurred soon after the burial and a large proportion of the jewellery is thought to have been removed.

> Yes, I see wonderful things.

Carter and A. R. Callender, kneeling, opening Tutankhamun's tomb in the Valley of the Kings, Egypt.

ACKNOWLEDGEMENTS

Menachem Begin - © The State of Israel

Tony Blair – Parliamentary copyright material is reproduced with permission of the Controller of Her Majesty's Station Office on behalf of Parliament

Buddha's Fire Sermon – translated by Nanamoli Thera © Buddhist Publication Society

George H.W. Bush – courtesy George Bush Presidential Library and Museum

George W. Bush – courtesy George W. Bush Presidential Center

Jimmy Carter – courtesy Jimmy Carter Library and Museum

Bill Clinton – courtesy William J. Clinton Presidential Center

Albert Einstein – © Institute for Advanced Studies, Philadelphia

Dwight D. Eisenhower – courtesy Dwight D. Eisenhower Presidential Library

Michael Gorbachev – © The Gorbachev Foundation

Che Guevara – from Venceremos by Che Guevara/John Gerassi, © Weidenfeld and Nicholson Ltd

Vaclav Havel – from Open Letters: Selected Writings 1965-1990 by Vaclav Havel, translated by Paul Wilson, copyright © 1991 by A.G. Brain. Preface/translation copyright © 1985, 1988, 1991 by Paul Wilson. Used by permission of Alfred A. Knopf, a division of Random House, Inc.

Stephen Hawking – © Stephen Hawking

Ho Chi Minh – Selected Works, courtesy of the Foreign Languages Publishing House, Hanoi

Herbert Hoover – courtesy Herbert Hoover Presidential Library and Museum

Geoffrey Howe – Parliamentary copyright material is reproduced with permission of the Controller of Her Majesty's Stationery Office on behalf of Parliament

The Hutton Report - Parliamentary copyright material is reproduced with permission of the Controller of Her Majesty's Station Office on behalf of Parliament

Jesse Jackson – © Rev. Jesse L. Jackson, Snr

Lyndon B. Johnson – courtesy Lyndon Baines Johnson Library and Museum

John F. Kennedy – courtesy John F. Kennedy Presidential Library and Museum

Harold Macmillan – Reproduced from the archive of the late Harold Macmillan by kind permission of the Trustees of the Harold Macmillan Book Trust

Richard M. Nixon – courtesy Richard Nixon Presidential Library and Museum

Northern Ireland Agreement – © Crown Copyright

Pope John Paul II – courtesy of the Catholic Truth Society

Enoch Powell – © Enoch Powell/Elliot Right Way Books

Martin Luther King, Jnr – © Estate of Martin Luther King, Jnr, c/o Writers House, New York

F.W. de Klerk – © F.W. de Klerk Foundation www.fwdklerk.org.za

Nelson Mandela – © Nelson Mandela Foundation www.nelsonmandela.org

Barack Obama – courtesy www.whitehouse.gov

Ronald Reagan – courtesy Ronald Reagan Presidential Library

Franklin D. Roosevelt – courtesy Franklin D. Roosevelt Presidential Library and Museum

Alexander Solzhenitsyn – © The Nobel Foundation

Margaret Thatcher – © The Margaret Thatcher Foundation www.margaretthatcher.org

Harry S. Truman – courtesy Harry S. Truman Presidential Museum and Library

Albert Einstein – © Albert Einstein for the Emergency Committee of Atomic Scientists, Inc.

INDEX